BESTSELLER

AF659887

OSWAAL BOOKS®

LEARNING MADE SIMPLE

NCERT

Chapterwise & Topicwise

EXEMPLAR

PROBLEMS-SOLUTIONS

CLASS 11

MATHEMATICS

Strictly as per the Latest Edition of NCERT Exemplar

An exceptionally useful book for School as well as Engineering Entrance Examinations

Powered by

oswaal.ai

LEARNING MADE SMARTER

Smart guidance that helps you learn, practise and improve.

The Only Book You Need To #Wintheboards

1
100% Updated
with the Latest NCERT Exemplar

2
Crisp Revision
with Quick Review

3
Concept Clarity
with Mind Maps & Conceptwise Videos

4
Latest Typologies
with MCQs, VSA, SA & LA

5
100% Exam Readiness
with Commonly Made Errors & Expert Advice

OSWAAL BOOKS®
LEARNING MADE SIMPLE

© 2026 by Oswaal Books and Learning Private Limited. All rights reserved.

No part of this publication may be reproduced, distributed, transmitted, or stored in any form — electronic, mechanical, photocopying, recording, or otherwise — without the Publisher's prior written permission.

This book may not be resold, lent, hired out, or circulated in any binding or cover other than its published form without the Publisher's consent.

This Edition: 2026

ISBN: 9789359586496

Disclaimer

This publication has been prepared by qualified subject matter experts with rigorous editorial review. Despite our best efforts, errors may exist. Readers are encouraged to report any by scanning the QR code on the Table of Contents page so corrections can reach all users.

This book is a study aid. Examination results depend on multiple factors including individual preparation and the specific examination conducted. No particular outcome is guaranteed.

Links in this book provide access to supplementary content. Accessibility depends on internet connectivity and device compatibility. Third-party content linked herein was verified at the time of printing; however, the Publisher does not guarantee that such content will remain accurate, available, or appropriate over time.

Views expressed by individual contributors are their own and do not represent the Publisher's position. The Publisher does not endorse personal opinions or political statements contained herein.

All maps, boundaries, and diagrams are artistic representations for educational reference only and are not geographically or politically authoritative.

For details on personal data processing, see our Privacy Policy at www.oswaalbooks.com/privacy. This publication is governed by the laws of India. Disputes shall be subject to the exclusive jurisdiction of courts in Agra, Uttar Pradesh.

Published by: Oswaal Books and Learning Private Limited, Oswaal House, 1/11, Sahitya Kunj, M.G. Road, Agra-282002 (U.P.), India

contact@oswaalbooks.com

+91-562-2857671

Printed at: Shyamji Printers, Agra

Contents

- Mind Maps 8 - 24

1. **Sets** **1 – 14**
   Topic 1 : Sets, their Types and Representations
   Topic 2 : Venn Diagrams and Operations on Set
   Topic 3 : Application of Set Theory
2. **Relations and Functions** **15 – 28**
   Topic 1 : Cartesian Product and Relations
   Topic 2 : Functions and their Types
3. **Trigonometric Functions** **29 – 49**
   Topic 1 : Measure of an Angle & Trigonometric Functions
   Topic 2 : Trigonometric Equations and Some Applications of Sine and Cosine
4. **Principle of Mathematical Induction** **50 – 58**
5. **Complex Numbers And Quadratic Equations** **59 – 73**
   Topic 1 : Complex Numbers, their Conjugate and Square Roots
6. **Linear Inequalities** **74 – 84**
   Topic 1 : Solution of Linear Inequalities in One Variable
   Topic 2 : Solution of Linear inequalities in two variable
7. **Permutations and Combinations** **85 – 96**
   Topic 1 : Permutations
   Topic 2 : Combinations
8. **Binomial Theorem** **97 – 105**
9. **Sequence and Series** **106 – 118**
   Topic 1 : Sequence, Series and A.P.
   Topic 2 : G.P. and Sum to n terms of Special Series
10. **Straight Lines** **119 – 140**
   Topic 1 : Recall of Two Dimensional Geometry and Slope of a line
   Topic 2 : Various forms of equations of a straight line
   Topic 3 : General equation of a line and equation of family of lines
11. **Conic Sections** **141 – 160**
   Topic 1 : Sections of a Cone (circle.)
   Topic 2 : Parabola, Ellipse and Hyperbola
12. **Introduction to Three Dimensional Geometry** **161 – 169**
13. **Limits and Derivatives** **170 – 194**
   Topic 1 : Limit and its fundamentals
   Topic 2 : Derivatives
14. **Mathematical Reasoning** **195 – 206**
   Topic 1 : Statements and basic logical connectives
   Topic 2 : Implications and validity of statements
15. **Statistics** **207 – 226**
   Topic 1 : Measure of Dispersion
   Topic 2 : Variance and Standard Deviation
16. **Probability** **227 – 240**
   Topic 1 : Experiments, Events and Sample space
   Topic 2 : Axiomatic Approach to Probability

□□

Stay Informed: Board & Content Updates

Board Updates
Be the first to know about syllabus updates and changes!
Scan the QR Code to get the latest scoop!

Latest Content & Corrections
Stay on top of your studies with updated materials!
Mark important changes in your book.
Share feedback and help improve future editions.
Scan the QR Code for fresh content.

Learning is fun when you're always up to date! Keep scanning!

Order Form

ONE FOR ALL OLYMPIADS (Multicolour)
Classes 1 to 8
Mathematics, English, Reasoning, General Knowledge, Science & Cyber

ONE FOR ALL OLYMPIADS Workbooks
Classes 1 to 8
Mathematics, English, Science

ONE FOR ALL WORKBOOKS (Multicolour)
Classes 1 to 5
Mathematics, English, General Knowledge, EVS, Hindi

NCERT WORKBOOKS (B&W)
Classes 1 to 5
English, Hindi, Mathematics & EVS

NCERT & CBSE One For All Workbooks
Classes 6 to 8
Mathematics, English, Science, Social Science, Hindi & Sanskrit

CBSE Work Books
Classes 9 & 10
English Lang. & Literature, Science, Social Science & Mathematics

CBSE & NCERT Laboratory Manual
Classes 6 to 12
Mathematics, Science, Physics, Chemistry & Biology

CBSE QUESTION BANKS (CHAPTER-WISE & TOPIC-WISE SOLVED PAPERS)
Classes 9 & 10
Hindi-A, Hindi-B, English Lang. & Lit. (With NCERT Workbook), Science, Mathematics, Social Science, Computer Applications, Sanskrit & English Communicative (based on CBSE Textbooks), Information Technology (Class-10th only), Artificial intelligence (Class-10th only)

Classes 11 & 12
Hindi Core (For Class-12 Only), English Core, Mathematics, Chemistry, Applied Mathematics (For Class-12 Only), Biology, Physics, Accountancy, Economics, Business Studies, Geography, History, Political Science, Computer Science, Entrepreneurship (For Class-12 Only), Informatics Practices, Physical Education, Sociology (For Class 12th Only), Psychology (For Class 12th Only)

CBSE Textbook Plus
Classes 10 & 12
English Lang. & Lit., Mathematics, Science, Social Science, English Core, Biology, Physics, Chemistry

CBSE Xcellence 95+
Classes 10 & 12
Sanskrit (शेमुषी), Sanskrit Communicative (मणिका), Physics, Chemistry, English Core

NCERT EXEMPLAR PROBLEMS-SOLUTIONS (Hindi & English Medium)
Classes 9 to 12
Science, Mathematics, Physics, Chemistry, Biology, Mathematics,
गणित, विज्ञान, भौतिक विज्ञान, रसायन विज्ञान, जीव विज्ञान

NCERT Textbook Solutions
Classes 6 to 8
Mathematics, English, Hindi, Science, Social Science & Sanskrit

Classes 9 to 12
Science, Mathematics, Physics, Chemistry, Biology

CBSE 10 PREVIOUS YEARS' SOLVED PAPERS
Class 10
Combined: English Lang. & Lit, Science, Social Science,Mathematics Stan.

Class 12
Science (PCM)-(Chemistry, Physics, Mathematics & English Core), **Science (PCB)**-(Chemistry, Physics, English Core & Biology) **Commerce**-(Economics, Accountancy, Business Studies, English Core), **Humanities**-(Geography, History, Political Science & English Core)

CBSE Previous Years' Solved Papers Stand alone Series
Class 10
Hindi-A, Hindi-B, Mathematics Basic, Sanskrit, Computer Applications

Class 12
Applied Mathematics, Mathematics

CBSE RMT FLASH CARDS
Class 10
Mathematics, English Lang. & Lit., Social Science & Science

CBSE ONE FOR ALL
Classes 6 to 8
English, Hindi, Mathematics, Science, Social Science & Sanskrit

Class 10
English Lang. & Lit., Social Science, Science, Hindi-A, Hindi-B, Mathematics (Stand.) & Mathematics Basic

Class 12
English Core, Physics, Chemistry, Mathematics, Biology, Accountancy, Business Studies & Economics

FINAL HUSTLE FOR CBSE
Class 10
Science, Mathematics Standard & Social Science

Class 12
Science (Physics, Chemistry, Mathematics, Biology & English Core), **Commerce** (Accountancy, Business Studies, Economics, Mathematics & English Core), **Humanities** (History, Geography, Political Science & English Core)

CBSE SAMPLE QUESTION PAPERS
Class 9
Science, Mathematics

Class 10
Hindi-A, Hindi-B, English Lang. & Lit., Computer Applications, English Communicative, Mathematics Standard, Mathematics Basic, Science, Social Science, Sanskrit, Samajik Vigyan, Information- Technology, Artificial intelligence, Sanskrit Communicative

Class 12
Hindi Core, Hindi Elective, English Core, Mathematics, Applied Mathematics, Physics, Chemistry, Biology, Accountancy, Economics, Business Studies, Geography, History, Political Science, Computer Science, Informatics Practices, Physical Education, Entrepreneurship, Psychology & Sociology

CBSE 20 Combined Sample Question Papers
Classes 9 to 12
Class- 9 & 10: **Combined Book**
Class- 11 & 12: Science, Commerce & Humanities

CBSE Competency Focused Questions Chapter-wise
Classes 10 & 12
Class 10 :- (Combined Book) Science, Social Science & Mathematics Standard
Class 12 :- Science PCM, Science PCB & Commerce

Exam Preparation Books for Class 1 to 12 : CBSE, CISCE Boards & Karnataka Board | OLYMPIADS | JEE | NEET | CUET | NTSE | NDA | CDS | CAT | CTET | GATE | UPSC | UPPSC | RRB | BPSC | CLAT & AILET | UGC NET | NRA CET

We are available at all leading e-commerce platforms and in all good bookstores

OswaalBooks.com | amazon.in | Flipkart | amazonkindle | Google Play Books | firstcry.com

17-01-26

Preface

In order to maintain a Uniform Education System across the country, many State Boards are implementing a Single Curriculum System via National Council of Educational Research & Training (NCERT).

To ensure in depth study and concept clarity for Secondary and Senior Secondary Students, The Department of Education in Science & Mathematics (DESM) and NCERT has developed Exemplar Problems in Sciences & Mathematics from class VI to XII. The Exemplar Problems cover various typologies of questions across various difficulty levels that aid in better exam preparations. These books have been developed keeping in mind the learning needs of not only the students preparing for Board Examinations but also for Entrance Exams like IIT JEE, NEET, AIIMS etc.

We at Oswaal Books have developed Solutions for every problem from the Latest Edition of NCERT Exemplar Textbooks. We believe that Oswaal NCERT Exemplar Solutions will help students by providing extremely relevant study material for cracking any examination with ease and confidence.

Some Special Features of Oswaal NCERT Exemplar Solutions are:

- Chapter-wise and Topic-wise presentation
- **Chapter-wise Objectives:** A sneak peek into the chapter
- **Mind Map:** A single page snapshot of the entire chapter
- **Revision Notes:** Concept based study materials
- **Tips & Tricks:** Useful guidelines for attempting each question perfectly
- **Some Commonly Made Errors:** Most common and unidentified errors are focused
- **Expert Advice:** Oswaal Expert Advice on how to score more
- **Oswaal QR – Codes:** For Quick Revision on your Mobile Phones and Tablets

We hope that Oswaal NCERT Exemplar Solutions will help students at every step as they move closer to their educational goal. We wish them all great success ahead!

All the Best!

TEAM OSWAAL

We would love to hear from you !

We believe that this book will make your Learning Simple. There are a lot of ways in which you can share your thoughts and experiences about this book with millions of current and future students. Here is how—

- You can log on to **Amazon.in**, search for this book and write a Review.
- You can also share it on our **Facebook Page**
- You can search for Oswaal Books on **Google** and write a Review there.
- You can email us your suggestions / feedback on **contact@oswaalbooks.com**

Exclusive School Books Suppliers

	KARNATAKA
BENGALURU	Pride Book World, 9448685507, Tanwer Books and Garments, 9916049273, Jipsy, 9620325985
MYSORE	Ragavendra Book Agency, 9591911489
	TELANGANA
HYDERABAD	Shri Sharada store Books & Stationers, 9700768789, Sri Balaji Book Depot, 9676996199, Vishal Book Distributors, 9246333166, Pranavi Publishers, 919948853126, Shri Sharada store Books & Stationers, 9700768789
	TAMIL NADU
CHENNAI	M.K. Stores, 9840030099, Sivaa Book Centre, 9952933315, Kamal Book House, 9841077369
ERODE	Selvam Book Centre, 919843199697
MADURAI	Selvi Book Shoppe, 9345037977, Madurai Book Shop, 9751937519
COIMBATORE CUDDALORE	Indian Book Centre, 9443093053
	MAHARASHTRA
PUNE	Madhusheela Books & Stationers, 7875899892, Pravin Sales, 8888038889
NANDED	Vijay Book Centre, 9822994436
JALNA	Anil Paper Mart, 919422722522
CHHATRAPATI SAMBHAJINAGAR	AARTI BOOK CENTRE, 919422203836
NAGPUR	Sandeep Book Depot, 9371078789
VASAI	Dinvin Books Excellence PVT. LTD. , 9867561128
MUMBAI	New Student Agencies LLP, 8355965098, Ravechi Book Stationery, 9769002371
	ANDHRA PRADESH
VISAKHAPATNAM	VKML Books, 8125168946
NANDYAL	Sathyam Book Store & Fancy, 9052439300
NELLORE	S V S Book Centre, 9347100774
VIJAYAWADA	VKML Books, 9966639957
	HARYANA
ROHTAK	Babu Ram Pradeep Kumar, 9813214692
VIZIANAGARAM	Himamsu Book Distributor, 9493434777
	MADHYA PRADESH
INDORE	Mahesh Book Depot, 9893855543
SHAHDOL	Anjali Book Centre, 917067572992
	JHARKHAND
DEOGHAR	Navyug Sahitya Mandir, 919031917035
BOKARO STEEL CITY	Bokaro Student Friends Pvt. Ltd, 919234628152
	MEGHALAYA
SHILLONG	New Book Centre, 9774088719
	WEST BENGAL
KOLKATA	Oriental Pub. Dist. Pvt. Ltd., 919903879153, United Book House, 9831344622
	UTTAR PRADESH
PRAYAGRAJ	Saraswati book depot, 7706855403
KANPUR	Raj Book, 9235616506
MATHURA	Sapra Traders, 9410076716, Agrawal Book House, 7906527213
GHAZIABAD	Vani Enterprises, 919891276834
	DELHI
DELHI	Mittal Books, 919810133323, Prakash Brothers, 919811179840, R.D. Chawla & Sons, 9810045752, Ameen Global Services, 919716028892, Need Prakashan Pvt Ltd, 9968383261
	GUJARAT
VADODARA	Career Skills Education and Research Foundation, 8469149288
BHARUCH	J.D. Agency, 9099944480
	KERALA
ERNAKULAM	Novel House School Supplies, 8792342807
	ASSAM
GUWAHATI	Central Book Agency, 9954707165
SILCHER	New Book Stall, 919435712617
JORHAT	Bajrang stationery, 9706978968
	RAJASTHAN
ANUPGARH	City Pride Departmental Store, 919414095677
BARMER	Dev Indra Enterprises, 7073282106
	MANIPUR
IMPHAL	Global Agencies, 917641814494
	PUNJAB
TARN TARAN	Sital Di Hatti, 919988206890
KHAMMAM	Sri Nivasa Book Stall, 919948247838
	CHHATTISGARH
RAIPUR	Central Book House, 9406016308

Our Distributors

	ANDHRA PRADESH
VISAKHAPA-THAM	Sri Rajeshwari Book Link, 9848036014,
VIJAYAWADA	Sree Vidya Book Depot, 9491830839
	ANDAMAN & NICOBAR ISLAND
PORTBLAIR	Krishna Book Centre, 9474205570
	ARUNACHAL PRADESH
NAHARLAGUN	New Pothi Ghar, 8731832947
	ASSAM
SILCHAR	Book Emporium, 9675972993, 6000763186, New Book Stall, 9435712617
GUWAHATI	Kayaan Enterprises, (0361) 2630443,
	BIHAR
PATNA	Nova Publisher & Distributors, (0612) 2666404, Gyan Ganga Limited, 9304826651, Rishu Pustak Bhandar, 8294576789, Sri Durga Pustak Mandir, 9334477386, Vikas Book Depot, 919504780402, Bokaro Student Friends Pvt. Ltd, 7277931285
BIHAR SHARIF	Good Books , 8210685462
MUZAFFARPUR	Pustak Bhandar, 7870834225
	CHATTISGARH
AMBIKAPUR	M.P Department Stores, 9425254264
BOKARO	Bokaro Student Friends Pvt. Ltd, Bokaro, 7277931285
DURG	Bhagwati Bhawani Book Depot, 0788-2327620, 9827473100
RAIPUR	Gupta Pustak Mandir, 7974220323,
BILASPUR	Pustak Bhawan, 9300667909
	DELHI
DELHI	Mittal Books, (011) 23288887, 9899037390, A One Books, New Delhi, 8800497047, Batheja Super Store, 9871833924, 9811182352, Zombozone, 9871274082, LDS Marketing, 9811182352/9999353491, R.D. Chawla & Sons, 9810045752, Janta Book Depot, 9313046321, Bokaro Student Friends Pvt. Ltd, 7004074900
	GUJARAT
AHMEDABAD	Patel Book Agencies, 9898184248, 9824386112, 9825900335, Shalibhadra Stationers, 9904477855
VAPI	Goutam Book Sellers, 9081790813
VADODARA	Shree ji Book Depot, 9824649375, Nilesh Book Centre, 9924458748, Umakant Book Sellers & Stationer, 6359396370, Sagar Book Suppliers, 9879402375
AHMEDNAGAR	Hira Stationers, 9970150300
	HARYANA
ROHTAK	Swami Kitab Ghar, 9355611088, Babu Ram Pradeep Kumar, 9813214692
GURGAON	Book Care Centre Venture, 9654564783
REWARI	Repro Books Ltd, 8657315914, Annu book depot, 9053246268
	JHARKHAND
BOKARO	Bokaro Student Friends Pvt. Ltd. (0654) 2233094, 7360021503, Bharati Bhawan Agencies, 06542-265302, 9431740797
HAZARIBAGH	Khandelwal Book Depot, 9708607489
DEOGHAR	Navyug Sahitya Mandir, 9031917035
RANCHI	Pustak Mandir, 9431115138, Agarwal Book Depot, 9334869210, Jayshree Book House, 8434430311, Bokaro Student Friends Pvt. Ltd, 7360021508
DHANBAD	Bokaro Student Friends Pvt. Ltd, 6202834756
	KARNATAKA
HUBLI	Renuka Book Distributor, (0836) 2244124, Vidyamandir Book Distributors, 9980773976
BENGALURU	Krishna book house, 9739847334, Sapna Book House Pvt. Ltd., 9980513242, Sree Sai Ram Book Traders, 9738881088
	MADHYA PRADESH
INDORE	Pustak Bhawan, 8982150100, Bhaiya Store, 9425318103, S.P. & Publication, 7000025933
UJJAIN	Shreenath Book Depot, 9827544045
GWALIOR	Agarwal Book Depot, 9425116210
JABALPUR	Vinay Pustak Sadan, 8962362667,

23/04/26

Our Distributors

	Anand Books and Stationers, 9425323508
	Akash Book Distributor, 8989111444, Bharat Book House, 9826541542
KATNI	Shri Mahavir Agency, 9425363412
	MAHARASHTRA
AMRAVATI	Delta Pen House, 9890350073
PUNE	Vikas Book House, 9921331187, Pravin Sales, 9890683475,
	New Saraswati Granth Bhandar, 9422323859
	Sai Book Collection, 9623224343
	Yash Agencies, 9850956542
MUMBAI	New Student Agencies, 7045065799,
	Shivam Books & Stationery, 8619805332
KOLHAPUR	Jai Book Co. 9404671543
NAGPUR	Laxmi Pustakalay and Stationers, (0712) 2727354, Vijay Book Depot, 9860122094
	Renuka Book Distributor, 9765406133, Novelty Book Depot, 9657690220,
	Shree Mahalaxmi Pustakalaya, 7507099360
DHULE	Navjeevan Book Stall, 7020525561
YAVATMAL	Shri Ganesh Pustkalaya, 9423131275
NASHIK	Vishal Book Centre, Nashik - 8208249434
VASAI	Prime Book Centre, Vasai, 9890293662
	ODISHA
CUTTACK	A. K. Mishra Agencies, 9437025991, 9437081319
BHUBANESHWAR	M/s Pragnya, 8847888616, 9437943777, Padmalaya, 9437026922,
KEONJHAR	Students Corner, 7008435418
KORAPUT	Ambica Book Centre, 7008585008
	PUNJAB
AMBALA	Bharat Book Depot, 7988455354
PATIALA	Goel Sons, 9463619978,
	Adarsh Enterprises, 9814347613
JALANDHAR	Cheap Book Store, 9872223458, 9878258592, City Book Shop, 9417440753,
	Subhash Book Depot, 9876453625,
	Gaurav Book world, 9478821183
LUDHIANA	Amit Book Depot, 9815807871,
	Bhatia Book Centre, 9815277131, Gupta Brothers, 9888200206
CHANDIGARH	Mohindra Book Depot, 9814920226
BATHINDA	Goyal Sons , 9464478362, Bhagwati Book Depot, 9463120564
	RAJASTHAN
AJMER	Laxmi General Store, Ajmer, 0145- 2428942 9460652197
KOTA	Raj Traders, 9309232829
BHILWARA	Nakoda Book Depot, (01482) 243653, 9214983594,
JAIPUR	Saraswati Book House, (0141) 2610823, 9829811155,
	Goyal Book Distt., 9460983939, 9414782130
JODHPUR	Kitab Mahal, 9460957875
	TRIPURA
AGARTALA	Books Corner, 8794894165, 8984657146
	TAMIL NADU
COIMBATORE	Majestic Book House, 9791966665
CHENNAI	M.R. Book Store (044) 25364596,
	Kalaimagal Store, (044) 5544072, 9940619404, Vijaya Stores, 9381037417,

	Bookmark It-Books & Stat. Store, 7305151653,
	M.K. Stores, 9840030099, Tiger Books Pvt. Ltd., 9710447000,
MADURAI	Selvi Book Shoppe, 9843057435
	KERALA
ERNAKULAM	Academic Book House, (0484) 2376613, H & C Store, 9864196344
KOTTAYAM	Asad Book Centre, (0481) 2566992
CALICUT	Aman Book Stall, (0495) 2721282,
KOZHIKODE	T.B.S. Publishers Distributors, 7559822223
	TELANGANA
HYDERABAD	Sri Balaji Book Depot, (040) 27613300, 9866355473
	Vishal Book Distributors, 9246333166
	UTTARAKHAND
DEHRADUN	Inder Book Agencies, 9634045280
	Brothers Pustak Bhandar, 9897833882
	UTTAR PRADESH
AGRA	Sparsh Book Agency, 9412257817,
	Sanjay Publication, 8126699922 Arti book centre, 8630128856,
	Om Pustak Mandir, (0562) 2464014, 9319117771
	Panchsheel Books, 9412257962, 9412257961
	Manav Book World, 9760316933
MATHURA	Sapra Traders, 9410076716
PRAYAGRAJ	Mehrotra Book Agency, (0532) 2266865, 9415636890
AZAMGARH	Sasta Sahitya Bhandar, 9450029674
ALIGARH	K.B.C.L. Agarwal, 9897124960,
NAJIBABAD	Gupta News Agency, 8868932500
KANPUR	Radha News Agency, 8957247427,
	Raj Book Dist., 9235616506,
	H K Book Distributors, 9506033137/9935146730
GORAKHPUR	Vidyarthi Sahitya Bhandar, 6394026706
LUCKNOW	Om Book Depot, 7705871398, Azad Book Depot Pvt. Ltd., 7317000250,
	Ashirwad Book Depot, 9235501197, Book.com, 7458922755, Universal Books,
	9450302161, Sheetla Book Agency, 9235832418, Vidyarthi Kendra Publisher & Distributor Pvt Ltd, 9554967415, Tripathi Book House, 9415425943,
	Navyug Book Agencies, 8073564410, Pustak Vatika, 7905317119
MEERUT	Ideal Book Depot, (0121) 4059252, 9837066307
NOIDA	Goyal Books Overseas Pvt.Ltd., 1204655555, 9873387003
PRAYAGRAJ	Kanhaiya Pustak Bhawan, 9415317109
RENUKOOT	Om Stationers, 7007326732
VARANASI	Bokaro Student Friends Pvt. Ltd , 9798050654
	WEST BENGAL
KOLKATA	Oriental Publishers & Distributor (033) 40628367, Katha 'O' Kahini, (033)
	22196313, 22419071, Saha Book House, (033), 22193671, 9333416484,
	United Book House, 9831344622, Bijay Pustak Bhandar, 8961260603,
NORTH DINAJPUR	Sarkar Book Suppliers, 9830949359
COOCH BEHAR	S.B. Book Distributor, Cooch Behar, 9002670771
KHARAGPUR	Subhani Book Store, 9046891334
SINGRAULI	Ambedkar Book Depot, 9826115292
KANPUR	Lamba Book Stall, 9839024277
KARNAL	Chopra Book Store, 8950322681

23/04/26

CHAPTER : 1 SETS

SETS

Introduction

A set is collection of well-defined distinguished objects. The sets are usually denoted by capital letters A, B, C etc., and the members or elements of the set are denoted by lower case letters a, b, c etc.., If x is a member of the set A, we write $x \in A$ (read as 'x' belongs to A) and if x is not a member of set A, we write $x \notin A$(read as 'x' doesn't belongs to A). If x and y both belong to A, we write $x, y \in A$.

Some examples of sets are: A: odd numbers less than 10
N: the set of all natural numbers
V : the vowels in the English alphabates
R: the set of all rational numbers.

Subset

Let A and B be two sets. If every element of A is an element of B,then A is called a subset of B and written as $A \subset B$ or $B \supset A$(read as 'A' is contained in 'B' or 'B contains A'). B is called superset of A.

Note:
1. Every set is a subset and superset of itself.
2. If A is not a subset of B, we write $A \not\subset B$.
3. The empty set is the subset of every set.
4. If A is a set with n(A) = m, then no. of element A are 2^n and the number of proper subsets of A are 2^n-1

e.g., Let A = {3, 4}, then subsets of A are ϕ, {3}, {4}, {3, 4}. Here, n(A) = 2 and number of subsets of A = 2^2=4.

Cardinal Number

The number of elements in a finite set is represented by n (A), known as cardinal number.
e.g., A = {a, b, c, d, e} Then, n (A) = 5

Representation of Sets

Set builder form or Rule Method

In this form, we write a variable (say x) representing any member of the set followed by property satisfied by each member of the set.
e.g., The set A of all prime number less than 10 in set builder form is written as
A = {x | x is a prime number less than10}
The symbol "|" stands for the word "such that". Sometimes, we use symbol ":" in place of symbol "|"

Roaster or Tabular form

In this form, we first list all the members of the set within braces (curly brackets) and separate these by commas.
e.g., The set of all natural number less than 10 in this form is written as: A = {1, 3, 5, 7, 9}
In roaster form, every element of the set is listed only once.
The order in which the elements are listed is immaterial.
e.g., Each of the following sets denotes the same set
{1, 2, 3}, {3, 2, 1}, {1, 3, 2}

Types of Sets

Empty set or Null set

A set which has no element is called null set. It is denoted by symbol ϕ or {}.
e.g., Set of all real numbers whose square is −1.
In set-builder form: {x:x is a real number whose square is −1}
In roaster form: { } or ϕ

Finite and Infinite set

A set which has finite number of elements is called a finite set. Otherwise, it is called an infinite set.
e.g., The set of all days in a week is a finite set whereas the set of all integers, denoted by
{……−2, −1, 0, 1, 2,……} or {x | x is an integer} is an infinite set.
An empty set ϕ which has no element is a finite set A is called empty or void or null set.

Equal set

Two sets A and B are set to be equal, written as A=B, if every element of A is in B and every element of B is in A.
e.g.: (i) A = {1, 2, 3,4} and B = {3, 1, 4, 2}, then A =B
(ii) A = {x: x−5 =0} and B = {x: x is an integral positive root of the equation $x^2 - 2x - 15 = 0$}
Then A= B

Singleton set

A set having one element is called singleton set.
e.g.: (i) {0} is a singleton set, whose only member is 0.
(ii) A = {x: 1<x <3, x is a natural number} is a singleton set which has only one member which is 2.

Equivalent set

Two finite sets A and B are said to be equivalent, if n(A) = n(B). Clearly, equal set are equivalent but equivalent set need not to be equal.
e.g.: The sets A = {4, 5, 3, 2} and B = {1, 6, 8, 9} are equivalent, but are not equal.

CHAPTER : 1 (A) SETS

SETS

Venn Diagram

A Venn diagram is an illustration of the relationships between and among sets, groups of objects that share something common. These diagrams consist of rectangle and closed curves usually circles

Eg:

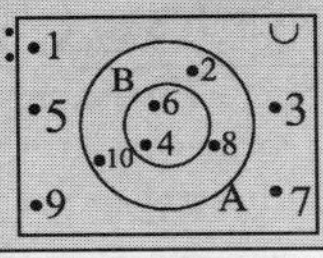

In the given venn diagram U={1,2,3,.......10} universe set of which A={2,4,6,8,10} and B={4,6} are subsets and also B⊂A

Universal Set

The set containing all objects of element and of which all other sets are subsets is known as **universal sets** and denoted by U.

E.g : For the set of all intergers, the universal set can be the set of rational numbers or the set R of real numbers

Power Set

The set of all subset of a given set A is called **power set** of A and denoted by P(A).

E.g : If A ={1,2,3,}, then P (A)={ϕ}, {1},{2}, {3},{1,2},{1,3},{2,3},{1,2,3}.

Clearly, if A has n elements, then its power set P (A) contains exactly 2^n elements.

Algebra of sets

1. For any set A, we have
   (a) A∪A=A, (b) A∩A=A, (c) A∪ϕ=A, (d) A∩ϕ=ϕ, (e) A∪ U=U
   (f) A∩U=A, (g) A– ϕ=A, (h)A–A=ϕ
2. For any two sets A and B we have
   (a) A∪B = B∪A, (b) A∩B= B∩A, (c) A–B⊆ A, (d) B–A⊆B
3. For any three sets A,B and C, we have
   (a) A∪(B∪C)= (A∪B)∪C, (b) A∩(B∩C)= (A∩B)∩C
   (c) A∪(B∩C)=(A∪B)∩(A∪C), (d) A∩(B∪C)=(A∩B) ∪(A∩C)
   (e) A–(B∪C)=(A–B))∩(A–C), (f) A–(B∩C)=(A–B)∪(A–C)

Operations on Sets

Difference of two sets

If A and B are two sets, then their difference A-B is defined as:

A–B = {x : x ∈ A and x ∉B}

Similarly, B – A = {x : x ∈B and x ∉A}

Eg. If A={1,2,3,4,5,} and B={1,3,5,7,9} then

A–B={2,4} and B–A={7,9}

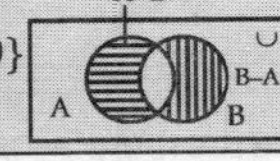

Symmetric Difference

The symmetric difference of two sets A and B, denoted by A Δ B, in defined as (A Δ B)=(A–B) ∪ (B – A)

Eg. If A = {1, 2,3,4,5}
and B = {1,3,5,7,9} then
(A Δ B)= (A–B) ∪ (B – A)
= {2, 4,} ∪ {7, 9}
= {2, 4, 7, 9}

Union

The union of two sets A and B, written as A∪B (read as A union B) is the set of all elements which are either in A or in B in both.

Thus, A∪B = {x: x ∈A or x ∈B}

clearly, x ∈ A∪B ⇒ x ∈A or x ∈ B and x ∉A∪B⇒x ∉A and x ∉B

A∪B

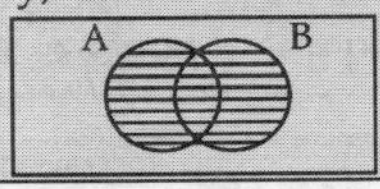

eg: If A = {a, b, c, d} and B ={c, d, e,f } then A∪B = {a, b, c, d, e, f}

Intersection

The intersection of two sets A and B, written as A∩B (read as 'A' intersection 'B') is the set consisting of all the common elements of A and B.

Thus, A∩B = {x : x∈Aand x∈B}

Clearly, x∈A∩B⇒ {x∈A and x∈B} and x∉A∩B ⇒ {x ∉A or x ∉B}.

Eg: If A={a,b,c,d} and B={c,d,e,f}

Then A∩B = {c,d}

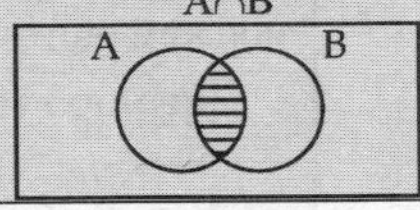

Disjoint sets

Two sets A and B are said to be disjoint, if A∩B =ϕ i.e, A and B have no common element. e.g: if A = {1, 3, 5} and B = {2, 4, 6}

Then, A∩B =ϕ , so A and B are disjoint.

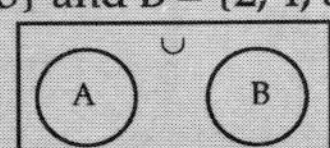

Subsets of a set of real numbers 'R'

- The set of natural numbers
  N={1, 2, 3, 4, 5, – – –}
- The set of integers
  Z={. . . –3, –2, –1, 0, 1, 2, 3,– – –}
- The set of irrational numbers,
  T = {x: x∈R and x∈Q}
- The set of rational number
  Q={x : x = $\frac{p}{q}$, p, q ∈Z and q ≠ 0}

Relation among these subsets are N ⊂ Z ⊂ Q, Q ⊂ R,T ⊂ R, N ⊄T

Interval Notation

Let a and b be real numbers with a < b

Set of Real Numbers	Interval Notation
{x|a< x < b}	(a, b)
{x|a ≤ x < b}	[a, b)
{x|a< x ≤ b}	(a, b]
{x|a ≤ x ≤ b}	[a, b]
{x|x < b}	(–∞, b)
{x|x ≤ b}	(–∞, b]
{x|x >a}	(a, ∞)
{x|x >a}	[a, ∞)
R	(–∞, ∞)

Region on the real number line

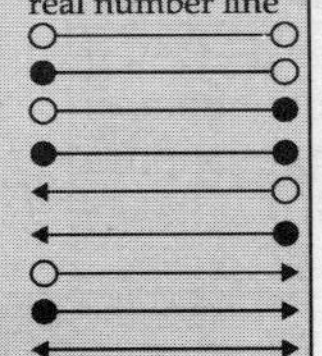

Compliment of Set

If U is a universal set and A is a subset of U, then complement of A is the set which contains those elements of U, which are not present in A and is denoted by A' or A^C. Thus,

A^C = {x: x∈U and x∉A}

e.g.: If U = {1, 2, 3, 4, ...}
and A = {2, 4, 6, 8, ...}
then A^C = {1, 3, 5, 7, ...}

Properties of complement

- <u>Complement law:</u>
  (i) A∪A' = U (ii) A∩A'= ϕ
- <u>De morgan's Law:</u>
  (i) (A∪B)' = A'∩B' (ii) (A∩B)' = A'∪B'
- <u>Double Complement law:</u>
  (A')' =A
- Law of empty set and universal set
  ϕ'=U and U' = ϕ

CHAPTER : 2 RELATIONS & FUNCTIONS

Relations & Functions

Kinds of Functions

One-One Onto function

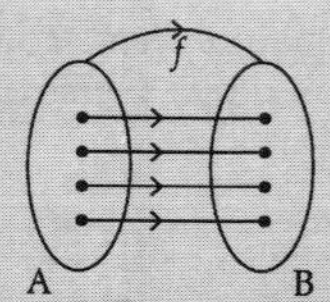

Range=Codomain

One-One Into function

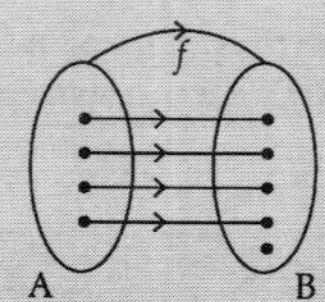

Range ⊂ Codomain

Many-One Onto function

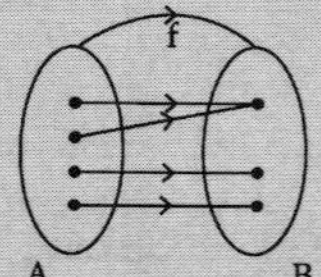

Range=Codomain

Many One Into function

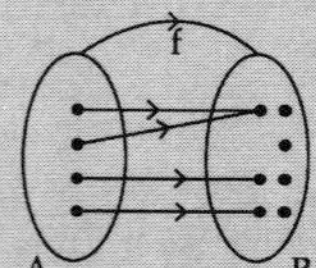

Range⊂Codomain

Functions

Definition: A relation 'f' from a set A to set B is said to be a function if every element of set A has one and only one image in set B.

Notations: Domain(Input) $\xrightarrow{x}$ [f] ⟶ y=f(x) Range(Output)

Domain of 'f'

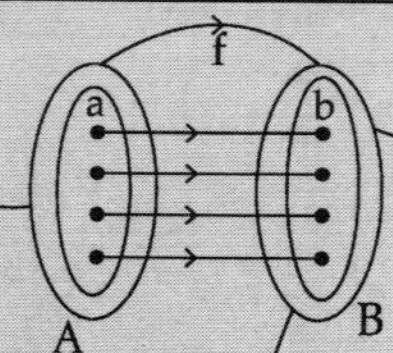

Range of 'f'

Codomain of 'f'

Cartesian product of sets

Given two non empty sets A&B. The cartesian product A×B is the set of all ordered pairs of elements from A&B i.e., A×B={(a,b) : a ∈ A ; b ∈ B}. If n(A)=p and n(B)=q , then n(A×B)=pq

⊂ Relation

Let A&B be two empty sets. Then any subset 'R' of A x B is a relation from A to B.If (a,b) ∈R, then we write a R b , which is read as 'a is related to b' by a relation R, 'b' is also called image of 'a' under R. The total number of relations that can be defined from a set A to a set B is the number of possible subsets of A x B. If n(A)=p and n(B)=q, then n (A x B)=pq and total number relations is 2^{pq}.

Pictorial representation of a relation

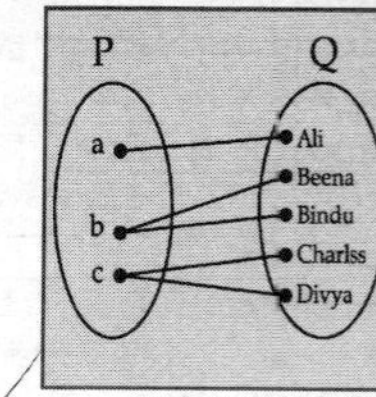

Given, R={(x,y): x is the first letter of the name y, x ∈P, y ∈Q} Then, R={(a,Ali), (b, Beena), (c, charu)}This is a visual or pictorial representation of relation R (called an arrow diagram)is shown in figure.

Domain & range of a Relation

If R is a relation from A to B, then the set of first elements in R is called domain & the set of second elements in R is called range of R. Symbolically, Domain of R={x:(x,y) ∈ R}; Range of R={y:(x,y) ∈ R}
The set B is called co-domain of relation R.
Note: the range ⊆ Codomain.
Eg. Given, R={(1,2),(2,3),(3,4),(4,5),(5,6)}. then Domain of R={1,2,3,4,5}
Range of R={2,3,4,5,6} and
codomain of R={1,2,3,4,5,6}

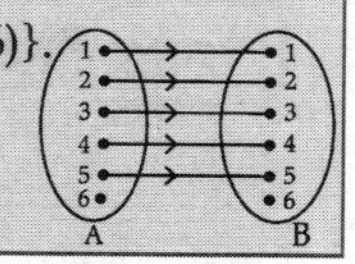

Inverse relation

Let A&B be two sets and R be a relation from set A to set B.Then inverse of R ,denoted by R^{-1}, is a relation from B to Aand is defined by R^{-1}={(b,a) : (a,b) ∈ R}. Clearly, (a,b) ∈ R ⇔ (b,a) ∈ R^{-1}
Also, Dom(R)=Range (R^{-1}) and Range(R)=Dom(R^{-1})

Even and odd function

Even function
f(−x)=f(x), ∀x∈ Domain

Odd function
f(−x)=−f(x), ∀x∈ Domain

Algebra of functions

Let f :x → R and g → R be any two real functions where X⊂R.
Addition: (f+g) x = f(x)+g(x); ∀x∈ R
Subtraction: (f–g) x = f(x)–g(x); ∀ x∈ R
Product: (fg) x = f(x).g(x); ∀ x ∈ R
Quotient: (f/g) (x) = f(x)/g(x); provided g(x) ≠ 0, ∀ x ∈ R

Some standard real functions

Log function: f(x)=$\log_e x$, a>0 , a ≠ 1 Domain=x ∈ (0, ∞) Range=y ∈ R

Identity function: The function f:R → R defined by y=f(x)=x ∀ x ∈R is called identity function. Domain=R and Range=R

Constant function: The function f:R → R defined by y=f(x)=c, ∀ x ∈ R, where c is a constant is called constant function. Domain=R and Range ={c}

Modulus function: The function f:R → R defined by f(x)= $\begin{cases} x; x \geq 0 \\ -x; x < 0 \end{cases}$ is called modulus function.
It is denoted by y=f(x)=|x|. Domain=R and Range =(0, ∞)

Signum function: The function f:R → R defined by f(x)= $\begin{cases} 1, x > 0 \\ 0, x = 0 \\ -1, x < 0 \end{cases}$ is called signum function. It is usually denoted by y=f(x)=sgn(x) Domain=R and Range ={ -1, 0, 1}

Greatest integer function: The function f:R → R defined by as the greatest integer less than or equal to x .It is usually denoted by y=f(x)=[x]. Domain=R and Range=Z(All integers)

Exponential function: f(x)=a^x , a>0 , a ≠ 1,
Domain: x∈R: Range:f(x) ⊂ (0,∞)

CHAPTER : 3 TRIGONOMETRIC FUNCTIONS

Trigonometric Functions

Important Trigonometric Ratios values

- $\sin 15°$ or $\sin\frac{\pi}{12} = \frac{\sqrt{3}-1}{2\sqrt{2}} = \cos 75°$ or $\cos\frac{5\pi}{12}$
- $\cos 15°$ or $\cos\frac{\pi}{12} = \frac{\sqrt{3}+1}{2\sqrt{2}} = \sin 75°$ or $\sin\frac{5\pi}{12}$
- $\tan 15° = \frac{\sqrt{3}-1}{\sqrt{3}+1} = 2-\sqrt{3} = \cot 75°$
- $\tan 75° = \frac{\sqrt{3}+1}{\sqrt{3}-1} = 2+\sqrt{3} = \cot 15°$
- $\sin\frac{\pi}{10}$ or $\sin 18° = \frac{\sqrt{5}-1}{4}$
- $\cos\frac{\pi}{5}$ or $\cos 36° = \frac{\sqrt{5}+1}{4}$

Standard General Solutions of Trigonometrical ratios

General solution: The solution consisting of all possible solutions of a trigonometric equation is called its General Solution.

- $\sin\theta = 0 \Leftrightarrow \theta = n\pi$, $\cos\theta = 0 \Leftrightarrow \theta = (2n+\frac{\pi}{2})$
- $\tan\theta = 0 \Leftrightarrow \theta = n\pi$, $\sin\theta = \sin\alpha \Leftrightarrow \theta = n\pi + (-1)^n\alpha$, where $\alpha \in \left(\frac{-\pi}{2}, \frac{\pi}{2}\right)$
- $\cos\theta = \cos\alpha \Leftrightarrow \theta = 2n\pi \pm \alpha$, where $\alpha \in [0, \pi]$
- $\tan\theta = \tan\alpha \Leftrightarrow \theta = n\pi + \alpha$, where $\alpha \in \left(\frac{-\pi}{2}, \frac{\pi}{2}\right)$
- $\sin^2\theta = \sin^2\alpha \Leftrightarrow \theta = n\pi \pm \alpha$, $\cos^2\theta = \cos^2\alpha \Leftrightarrow n\pi \pm \alpha$
- $\tan^2\theta = \tan^2\alpha \Leftrightarrow \theta = n\pi \pm \alpha$, $\sin\theta = 1 \Leftrightarrow \theta = (4n+1)\frac{\pi}{2}$
- $\cos\theta = 1 \Leftrightarrow \theta = 2n\pi$, $\cos = -1 \Leftrightarrow \theta = (2n+1)\pi$
- $\sin\theta = \sin\alpha$ and $\cos\theta = \cos\alpha \Leftrightarrow \theta = 2n\pi + \alpha$, $\eta \in z$

Factorisation of the Sum or Difference of sine and cosine with two variables

- $\sin C + \sin D = 2\sin\left(\frac{C+D}{2}\right)\cos\left(\frac{C-D}{2}\right)$
- $\sin C - \sin D = 2\cos\left(\frac{C+D}{2}\right)\sin\left(\frac{C-D}{2}\right)$
- $\cos C + \cos D = 2\cos\left(\frac{C+D}{2}\right)\cos\left(\frac{C-D}{2}\right)$
- $\cos C - \cos D = -2\sin\left(\frac{C+D}{2}\right)\sin\left(\frac{C-D}{2}\right)$

Transformation of Product into Sum or Difference of Sines or Cosines

- $2\sin A \sin B = \sin(A+B) + \sin(A-B)$
- $2\cos A \sin B = \sin(A+B) - \sin(A-B)$
- $2\cos A \cos B = \cos(A+B) + \cos(A-B)$
- $2\sin A \sin B = \cos(A-B) - \cos(A+B)$

Trigonometrical Function sum and Difference of Two Angles

- $\sin(A \pm B) = \sin A \cos B \pm \cos A \sin B$
- $\cos(A \pm B) = \cos A \cos B \mp \sin A \sin B$
- $\tan(A \pm B) = \frac{\tan A \pm \tan B}{1 \mp \tan A \tan B}$
- $\cot(A \pm B) = \frac{\cot A \cot B \mp 1}{\cot A \pm \cot B}$
- $\sin^2 A - \sin^2 B = \cos^2 B - \cos^2 A = \sin(A+B)\sin(A-B)$
- $\cos^2 A - \sin^2 B = \cos^2 B - \sin^2 A = \cos(A+B)\cos(A-B)$

Degree & Radian Measures

If in a circle of radius r, an arc of length l subtends an angle of θ radians, then $l = r\theta$.

- Radian Measure $= \frac{\pi}{180} \times$ Degree Measure
- Degree Measure $= \frac{180}{\pi} \times$ Radian Measure

Trigonometric Identities

- $\sin^2\theta + \cos^2\theta = 1$, $-1 \le \sin\theta \le 1$, $-1 \le \cos\theta \le 1$ $\forall\theta \in R$
- $\sec^2\theta - \tan^2\theta = 1$, $|\sec\theta| \ge 1$, $\forall\theta \in R$
- $\operatorname{cosec}^2\theta - \cot^2\theta = 1$, $|\operatorname{cosec}\theta| \ge 1$, $\theta \in R$

Trigonometrical Ratio of allied Angles

- $\sin(-\theta) = -\sin\theta$
- $\cos(-\theta) = \cos\theta$
- $\tan(-\theta) = -\tan\theta$
- $\cot(-\theta) = -\cot\theta$
- $\sec(-\theta) = \sec\theta$
- $\operatorname{cosec}(-\theta) = -\operatorname{cosec}\theta$

- $\sin\theta\left(\frac{\pi}{2} \mp \theta\right) = \cos\theta$
- $\cos\left(\frac{\pi}{2} \mp \theta\right) = \pm\sin\theta$
- $\tan\left(\frac{\pi}{2} \mp \theta\right) = \pm\cot\theta$
- $\cot\left(\frac{\pi}{2} \mp \theta\right) = \pm\tan\theta$
- $\sec\theta\left(\frac{\pi}{2} \mp \theta\right) = \pm\operatorname{cosec}\theta$
- $\operatorname{cosec}\left(\frac{\pi}{2} \mp \theta\right) = \sec\theta$

- $\cos((\pi \mp \theta) = -\cos\theta$
- $\sin(\pi \mp \theta) = \pm\sin\theta$
- $\tan(\pi \mp \theta) = \mp\tan\theta$
- $\cot(\pi \mp \theta) = \mp\cot\theta$
- $\sec(\pi \mp \theta) = -\sec\theta$
- $\operatorname{cosec}(\pi \mp \theta) = \pm\operatorname{cosec}\theta$

- $\sin(2\pi \mp \theta) = \mp\sin\theta$
- $\cos(2\pi \mp \theta) = \cos\theta$
- $\tan(2\pi \mp \theta) = \mp\tan\theta$
- $\cot(2\pi \mp \theta) = \mp\cot\theta$
- $\sec(2\pi \mp \theta) = \sec\theta$
- $\operatorname{cosec}(2\pi \mp \theta) = \mp\operatorname{cosec}\theta$

- $\sin\left(\frac{3\pi}{2} \mp \theta\right) = -\cos\theta$
- $\cos\left(\frac{3\pi}{2} \mp \theta\right) = \mp\sin\theta$
- $\tan\left(\frac{3\pi}{2} \mp \theta\right) = \pm\cot\theta$
- $\cot\left(\frac{3\pi}{2} \mp \theta\right) = \pm\tan\theta$
- $\sec\left(\frac{3\pi}{2} \mp \theta\right) = \mp\operatorname{cosec}\theta$
- $\operatorname{cosec}\left(\frac{3\pi}{2} \mp \theta\right) = \sec\theta$

Multiple and Half Angles

- $\sin 2A = 2\sin A\cos A$
- $\cos 2A = \cos^2 A - \sin^2 A = 2\cos^2 A - 1 = 1 - 2\sin^2 A$
- $\tan 2A = \frac{2\tan A}{1-\tan^2 A}$
- $\sin 2A = \frac{2\tan A}{1+\tan^2 A}$
- $\cos 2A = \frac{1-\tan^2 A}{1+\tan^2 A}$
- $\sin 3A = 3\sin A - 4\sin^3 A$
- $\cos 3A = 4\cos^3 A - 3\cos A$
- $\tan 3A = \frac{3\tan A - \tan^3 A}{1 - 3\tan^2 A}$
- $\sin\theta = 2\sin\frac{\theta}{2}\cos\frac{\theta}{2}$
- $\cos\theta = 2\cos^2\frac{\theta}{2} - 1 = 1 - 2\sin^2\frac{\theta}{2}$
- $\tan\theta = 2\tan\frac{\theta}{2} / \left(1 - \tan^2\frac{\theta}{2}\right)$

Trigonometrical Equations

The equation involving trigonometric functions of unknown angles are known as Trigonometric equations. e.g $\cos\theta = 0$, $\cos^2\theta - 4\cos\theta = 1$

A solution of trigonometric equation is the value of the unknown angle that satisfies the equation.

e.g. $\sin\theta = \frac{1}{\sqrt{2}}$

$\Rightarrow \theta = \frac{\pi}{4}, \frac{3\pi}{4}, \frac{9\pi}{4}, \frac{11\pi}{4}, \ldots$

CHAPTER : 4 PRINCIPLE OF MATHEMATICAL INDUCTION

Principle of Mathematical Induction

Induction

Specific Instances to Generalisation
e.g.: Rohit eats food. Vikas eats food. Rohit and Vikas are men. Then all men eat food. Statement is true for $n=1, n=k$ and $n=k+1$, then, the statement is true for all natural numbers n.

Deduction

Generalisation of Specific Instance
e.g.: Rohit is a man and all men eat food, therefore, Rohit eats food.

Example No.1

Ex: Prove that $2^n > n$ for all positive integer n.
Solution: Step1: Let $P(1): 2^n > n$
Step2: When $n=1$, $2^1 > 1$. Hence P(1) is true
Step3: Assume that P(k) is true for any positive integer k, $2^k > k$
Step4: We shall now prove that P(k+1) is true
Multiplying both sides of step(3) by 2, we get
$2.2^k > 2k$
$\Rightarrow 2^{k+1} > 2k$
$\Rightarrow 2^{k+1} = k+k$
$\Rightarrow 2^{k+1} > k+1$ (since $k>1$)
Therefore, P(k+1) is true when P(k) is true Hence, by P.M.I., P(n) is true for every positive integer n.

Steps for Principle of Mathematical Induction Proof

Step1: Let P(n) be a result or statement formulated in terms of n in a given equation
Step2: Prove that P(1) is true.
Step3: Assume that P(k) is true.
Step4: Using step 3, prove that P(k+1) is true.
Step5: Thus, P(1) is true and P(k+1) is true whenever P(k) is true. Hence, by the principle of mathematical induction, P(n) is true for all natural numbers n.

Example No.2

Ex : Prove the following by using the principle of mathematical induction for all $n \in N$: $10^{2n-1}+1$ is divisible by 11.
Answer:
Let the given statement be $P(n)$, *i.e.,*
$P(n)$: $10^{2n-1}+1$ is divisible by 11.
It can be observed that $P(n)$ is true for $n=1$ since $P(1) = 10^{2.1-1}+1=11$, which is divisible by 11.
Let $P(k)$ be true for some positive integer k, i.e.,
$10^{2k-1}+1$ is divisible by 11.
$\therefore 10^{2k-1}+1=11m$, where $m \in N$.....(1)
we shall now prove that P(K+1) is true whenever P(k) is true.
Consider $10^{2(k+1)-1}+1$
$=10^{2k+2-1}+1$
$=10^{2k+1}+1$
$=10^2(10^{2k-1}+1-1)+1$
$=10^2(10^{2k-1}+1)-10^2+1$
$=10^2.11m-100+1$
$=100\times 11m-99$
$=11(100m-9)$
$=11r$, where $r=(100m-9)$ is some natural number
Therefore, $10^{2(k+1)-1}+1$ is divisible by 11.
Thus, P(k+1) is true whenever P(k) is true.
Hence, by the principle of mathematical induction, statement $P(n)$ is true for all natural numbers i.e., n.

CHAPTER : 5 COMPLEX NUMBER & QUADRATIC EQUATIONS

Complex Number & Quadratic Equations

Polar Representation

Let $a = r\cos\theta$
$b = r\sin\theta$
where,
$r = |z|$
and $\theta = \arg(z)$
$\therefore z = a + ib = r(\cos\theta + i\sin\theta)$

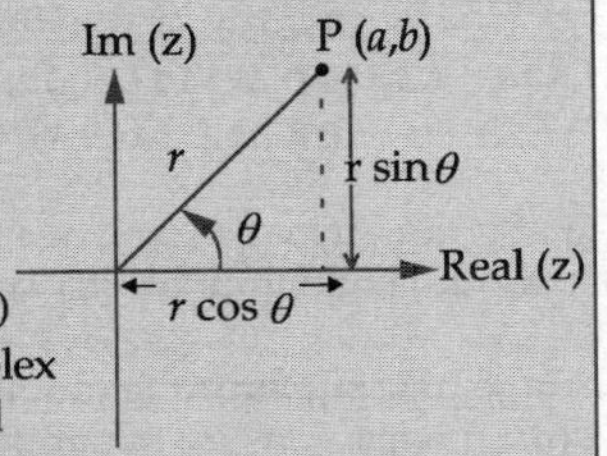

The argument 'θ' of complex number z = a+ib is called principal argument of z if

$-\pi < \theta \le \pi$.

Modulus & Argument of Complex Number

If z= a+ib is a complex number
(i)Distance of z from origin is called as modulus of complex number z.

It is denoted by $r = |z| = \sqrt{a^2 + b^2}$

(ii) Angle θ made by OP with +ve direction of X-axis is called argument of z.

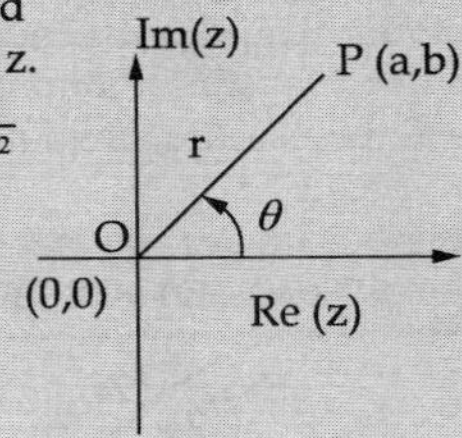

Powers of 'i'

$i = \sqrt{-1}, i^2 = -1$

In general, $i^{4k+r} = \begin{cases} 1; r = 0 \\ i; r = 1 \\ -1; r = 2 \\ -i; r = 3 \end{cases}$

Argand Plane

A complex number z=a+ib can be represented by a unique point P(a,b) in the argand plane

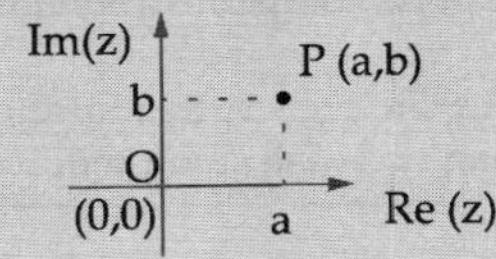

z=a+ib is represented by a point P (a,b)

Algebra of Complex Numbers

Let: $z_1 = a + ib$ and $z_1 = c + id$ be two complex numbers, where a,b,c,d ∈ R and $i = \sqrt{-1}$

1. Addition: $z_1 + z_2 = (a+ib) + (c+id) = (a+c) + i(b+d)$

2. Subtraction: $z_1 - z_2 = (a+ib) - (c+id) = (a-c) + (b-d)i$

3. Multiplication: $z_1 \cdot z_2 = (a+ib)(c+id)$
$= a(c+id) + ib(c+id)$
$= (ac - bd) + (ad + bc)i$
$(\because i^2 = -1)$

4. Division: $\frac{z_1}{z_2} = \frac{a+ib}{c+id} = \frac{a+ib}{c+id} \cdot \frac{c-id}{c-id}$
$= \left(\frac{ac+bd}{c^2+d^2}\right) + \left(\frac{bc-ad}{c^2+d^2}\right)i$

Note: If a+*ib* = c+*id*
⇔ a = c & b = d

Definition of Complex Numbers

A number of the form a+*ib*, where a,b ∈R and $i = \sqrt{-1}$ is called a complex number and denoted by 'z'.

z= a+ib
a → Real part
ib → Imaginary part

Conjugate of a complex number: For a given complex number z=a+*ib*, its conjugate is defined as $\bar{z}$= a – *ib*

Solution of Quadratic Equation

• General form of quadratic equation in *x* is $ax^2+bx+c=0$,
Where a,b,c ∈R & a ≠ 0
The solutions of given quadratic equation are given by $x = \frac{-b \pm \sqrt{b^2 - 4ac}}{2a}$
$\because b^2 - 4ac < 0$

Note: • A monomial equation has one root.
• A polynomial equation of degree n has n roots.

Multiplicative Inverse of complex Number

For a non-zero complex number z=a+ib $(a \ne 0, b \ne 0)$,

there exists a complex number $\frac{a}{a^2+b^2} + \frac{-b}{a^2+b^2}i$

denoted by $\frac{1}{z}$ or z^{-1}, called multiplicative inverse of z

Such that: $(a+ib)\left(\frac{a}{a^2+b^2} + i\frac{-b}{a^2+b^2}\right) = 1 + 0i = 1$

Square root of Complex Number

Let $x + iy = \sqrt{a+ib}$, squaring both sides, we get $(x+iy)^2 = a + ib$ i.e. $x^2 - y^2 = a$, $2xy = b$ solving these equations, we get square root of z.

CHAPTER : 6 LINEAR INEQUALITIES

Linear Inequalities

Notations

- The notation a<b means that 'a is less than b'.
- The notation a>b means that 'a is greater than b'.
- The notation a≥b means that 'a is greater than or equal to b'.
- The notation a≤b means that 'a is less than or equal to b'.
- The notation a≠b means that 'a is not equal to b'.

Solution of Linear Inequality in One Variable

Solution and Solution set

Solution: Values of x , which make inequality a true statement.

e.g.: '3' is the solution for x<7.

Solution Set:

The set of values of x is called its solution set.

e.g.: {1,2,3,4,5,6} is solution set for x<7 , where x is a natural number.

Types of Inequalities

Numerical Inequalities : Relation between numbers e.g.: 3<5, 7>4

Literal or Variable Ineqalities : Relation between two variables or variable and numbers. e.g.:y<8

Double Inequalities: Relationship from two sides e.g.:2<x<5

Strict Inequalities: An inequality that uses the symbol <or> e.g.: x<5, 3<5

Slack Inequality: An inequality that uses the symbols ≤ or ≥. e.g.: y≤5

Linear Inequalities in One Variable: An inequality which involves a linear function in one variable e.g.: x<5

Linear Inequalities in two variables: An inequality which involves a linear function in two variables, e.g.: 3x+2y<5

Quadratic Inequalities: An inequality which involves a quadratic function, eg.: $x^2+2x \leq 5$.

Representation

To represent x<a or x>–a on a number line, put a circle on the number 'a' and dark line to the left (or right) of the number 'a'.

e.g:

x<3

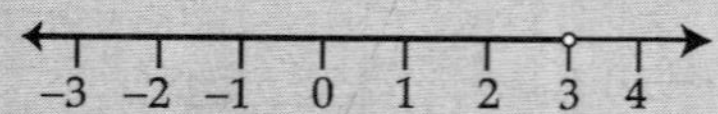

x>-2

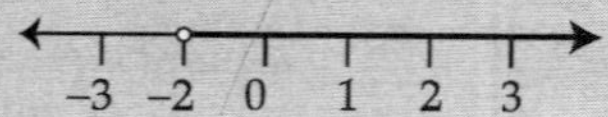

To represent x≤a (or x≥a) on a number line, put a dark circle on the number 'a' and dark the line to the left (or right) of the number 'a'.

e.g:

x≤3

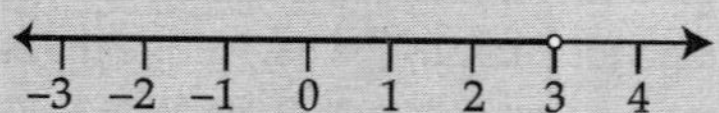

x≥–2

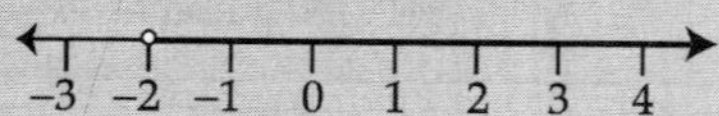

Conditions

- An inequality is a relation that holds between two values, when they are different eg.: x<5, here, there is a relation between x & 5.
- Two real numbers or algebraic expressions related by symbol '<', '>', '≤' or '≥' form inequality. eg,: $y\leq4$, $2x+3y\geq5$, $3>x$.

Rules of Inequality

- Equal numbers may be added to (or subtracted from) both the sides of an inequality without affecting the sign of inequality:
  e.g: x<7 is same as x+2 < 7+2
- Both sides of an inequality can be multiplied (or divided) by the same positive number without affecting the sign of inequality.
  e.g: x+y< 7 is same as (x+y) × 3<7 × 3
- When both sides are multiplied or divided by a – ve number, then sign of inequality is reversed.
  e.g: x+y< 7 is same as (x+7) × (–3) > 7 × (–3)

Graphical Solution of Linear Inequalities in Two Variables

- A line divides the cartesian plane into two equal parts. A point in cartesian plane will either lie on a line or will in either of half planes. The region containing all the solutions of inequality is called the solution region.
- In order to identify the half plane represnted by an inequality, it is just sufficient to take any point (a,b) (not on line) and check whether it satisfies the inequality or not. If it satisifies, then inequality represents the half plane and shade the region which contain the point, otherwise, the inequality represents the half plane which does not contain the point within it.
- If an inequality is of the type $ax+by\geq c$ or $ax+by\leq c$, then the points on the line $ax+by=c$ are also include in the solution region, so draw a dark line in the solution region.
- If an inequality is the form of $ax+by>c$ or $ax+by<c$, then the points on the line $ax+by=c$ are not to be included in the solution region, so draw a broken or dotted line in the solution region.

CHAPTER : 7 PERMUTATIONS & COMBINATIONS

Permutations & Combinations

Combinations

Each of different selections made by taking source or all of a number of distinct objects or item, irrespective of their arrangements or order in which they are placed, is called a combination.

The no. of combinations of n different things taken r at a time, denoted by ${}^nC_r$ is given by

$${}^nC_r = \frac{n!}{r!(n-r)!};\ 0 \le r \le n$$

Fundamental Principle of Counting (F.P.C.)

F.P.C. of Multiplication: If an event can occur in m different ways, following which another event in n different ways, then the total number of occurance of the events in the given order is $m \times n$

F.P.C. of Addition: If there are two events such that they can performed independently in m and n ways respectively, then either of the two events can be performed in $(m+n)$ ways.

Permutation

Each of the different arrangements which can be made by taking some or all of a number of distinct objects is called a **permutation**.

The no. of permutations of n different things taken r at a time, where repetition is not allowed, is denoted by ${}^nP_r$ and is given by

$${}^nP_r = \frac{n!}{(n-r)!}$$

Permutations under given Conditions

The no. of all permutations of 'n' different objects taken r at a time:

(i) When a particular object is to be always included in each arrangement is ${}^{n-1}P_r$

(ii) When a particular object is never taken in each arrangement in ${}^{n-1}P_r$

(iii) The no. of permutation of n different things taken r at a time, where repetition is allowed is $(n)^r$

Permutations of alike Objects

The no. of permutations of n objects taken all at a time, where p_1 objects are of first kind, p_2 objects are of the second kind, ...p_k objects are of the kth kind and rest, if any one are all different is $\frac{n!}{p_1!\,p_2!\,p_3!\ldots p_k!}$

Circular Permutations

1. The no. of circular permutations of 'n' distinct objects is $(n-1)!$
2. If anti-clockwise and clockwise order of arrangements are not distinct then the no. of circular permutations of n distinct items is $\frac{1}{2}(n-1)!$

e.g.: arrangements of beads in a necklace, arrangements of flower in a garland etc.

Some Special Results of ${}^nC_r$

Since,

$${}^nC_r = \frac{n!}{r!(n-r)!}$$

- In particular, $r = n$
- ${}^nC_n = \frac{n!}{n!0!} = 1$
- ${}^nC_{n-r} = {}^nC_r$
- ${}^nC_r + {}^nC_{r-1} = {}^{n+1}C_r$

Relation between ${}^nP_r$ and ${}^nC_r$

${}^nP_r = {}^nC_r \times r!$ $\quad \because 0 < r \le n$

i.e., Corresponding to each combination of ${}^nC_r$, we have r! permutations, because r objects in every combination can be rearranged in $r!$ ways

Combinations under Certain Conditions

- The no. of arrangements of n distinct objects taken r at a time, so that k particular objects are
  (i) Always included: ${}^{n-k}C_{r-k}.r!$
  (ii) Never included: ${}^{n-k}C_r.r!$
- The no. of selections from 'n' different objects, taking at least one $= {}^nC_1 + {}^nC_2 + {}^nC_3 + \ldots\ldots\ldots\ldots {}^nC_n = 2^n - 1$

CHAPTER : 8 BINOMIAL THEOREM

Binomial Theorem

General & Middle Terms in Expansion of $(a+b)^n$

The general term of an expansion $(a+b)^n$ is

$T_{r+1} = {}^nC_r\, a^{n-r} b^r,\ 0 \le r \le n, r \in N$

Middle Terms:

1. In $(a+b)^n$, if n is even, then the no. of terms in the expansion is odd. Therefore, there is only one middle term and it is $\left(\frac{n+2}{2}\right)^{th}$ term.
2. In $(a+b)^n$, if n is odd then the no. of terms in the expansion is even. Therefore, there are two middle terms and those are $\left(\frac{n+1}{2}\right)^{th}$ and $\left(\frac{n+3}{2}\right)^{th}$ terms.

Binomial Theorem for any Index

If n is negative integer, then n! is not defined. We state bionomial theorem in another form

$$(a+b)^n = a^n + \frac{n}{1!}a^{n-1}b + \frac{n(n-1)}{2!}a^{n-2}b^2 + \frac{n(n-1)(n-2)}{3!}a^{n-3}b^3 + --- + \frac{n(n-1)(n-2)\cdots(n-r+1)}{r!}a^{n-r}b^r + \cdots\cdots + b^n$$

Here, $T_{r+1} = \dfrac{n(n-1)(n-2)\cdots\cdots(n-r+1)}{r!}a^{n-r}b^r$

Some Special Cases $(a+b)^n$

In the expansion of $(a+b)^n$,

(i) Taking $a=x$ and $b=-y$, we obtain

$(x-y)^n = {}^nC_0x^n - {}^nC_1x^{n-1}y + {}^nC_2x^{n-2}y^2 + --- + (-1)^n\, {}^nC_ny^n$

(ii) Taking a=1, b=x, we obtain

$(1+x)^n = {}^nC_0 + {}^nC_1x + {}^nC_2x^2 + {}^nC_3x^3 + ------- + {}^nC_nx^n$

(iii) Taking a=1, b=−x, we obtain

$(1-x)^n = {}^nC_0 - {}^nC_1x + {}^nC_2x^2 + ---- + (-1)^n\, {}^nC_nx^n$

Definition

If a, b∈R and n∈N, then

$(a+b)^n = {}^nC_0a^nb^0 + {}^nC_1a^{n-1}b^1 + {}^nC_2a^{n-2}b^2 + ------ + {}^nC_na^0b^n$

- **Remarks:** If the index of the binomial is n then the expansion contains n+1 terms.
- In each term, the sum of indices of a and b is always n.
- Coefficients of the terms in binomial expansion equidistant from both the ends are equal.

$(a-b)^n = {}^nC_0a^nb^0 - {}^nC_1a^{n-1}b^1 + {}^nC_2a^{n-2}b^2 + ------ + (-1)^n\, {}^nC_na^0b^n$

Binomial Coefficients

The coefficient ${}^nC_0, {}^nC_1, {}^nC_2, ------ {}^nC_n$, in the expansion of $(a+b)^n$ are called binomial coefficients and denoted by $C_0, C_1, C_2 ---- C_n$ respectively

Properties of binomial coefficients:

(i) $C_0 + C_1 + C_2 + ------ + C_n = 2^n$

(ii) $C_0 - C_1 + C_2 ------- + (-1)^n C_n = 0$

(iii) $C_0 + C_2 + C_4 + ---- = C_1 + C_3 + C_5 + ---- = 2^{n-1}$

(iv) ${}^nC_{r_1} = {}^nC_{r_2} \Rightarrow r_1 = r_2$ or $r_1 + r_2 = n$

(v) ${}^nC_r + {}^nC_{r-1} = {}^{1+n}C_r$

(vi) ${}^nC_r = \frac{n}{r}\,{}^{n-1}C_{r-1}$

CHAPTER : 9 SEQUENCES AND SERIES

Sequences and Series

Definitions

Sequence is a function whose domain is the set of N natural numbers.

Real sequence: A sequence whose range is a subset of R is called a real sequence

Series: If $a_1, a_2, a_3, \ldots a_n,$ is a sequence, then the expression $a_1+a_2+a_3+\ldots a_n+\ldots$ is a series. A series is finite or infinite according to the no. of terms in the corresponding sequence as finite or infinite.

Progression: Those sequences whose terms follow certain patterns are called progression.

Arithmetic Progression (A.P.)

An A.P. is a sequence in which terms increase or decrease regularly by the fixed number (same constant). This fixed number is called 'common difference' of the A.P. If 'a' is the first term & 'd' is the common difference and 'l' is the last term of A.P., then general term or the nth term of the A.P. is given by $a_n = a + (n-1)d$ from starting and $a_n = l-(n-1)d$ from the end.

The sum S_n of the first n terms of an A.P. is given by

$$S_n = \frac{n}{2}[2a+(n-1)d] = \frac{n}{2}[a+l]$$

Arithmetic Mean (AM)

If three numbers are in A.P., then the middle term is called AM between the other two, so if a, b, c, are in A.P., b is AM of a and c.

AM for any 'n' +ve numbers $a_1, a_2, a_3, \ldots, a_n$ is

$$\text{AM} = \frac{a_1+a_2+a_3+\ldots+a_n}{n}$$

n-Arithmetic Mean between Two Numbers: If a, b are any two given numbers & a, $A_1, A_2, .., A_n$, b are in A.P. then $A_1, A_2, \ldots, A_n$ are n AM's between a & b.

$$A_1 = a+\frac{b-a}{n+1}, A_2 = a+\frac{2(b-a)}{n+1} \ldots A_n = a+\frac{n(b-a)}{n+1}$$

or $A_1 = a+d$, $A_2 = a+2d$, …, $A_n = a+nd$,

where $d = \frac{b-a}{n+1}$

Sum upto terms of some Special Sequences

- Sum of first 'n' natural numbers

$$\sum_{k=1}^{n} k = 1+2+3+\ldots+n = \frac{n(n+1)}{2}$$

- Sum of squares of first n natural numbers

$$\sum_{k=1}^{n} k^2 = 1^2+2^2+3^2+\ldots+n^2 = \frac{n(n+1)(2n+1)}{6}$$

- Sum of cubes of first n natural numbers

$$\sum_{k=1}^{n} k^3 = 1^3+2^3+3^3+\ldots+n^3 = \left(\frac{n(n+1)}{2}\right)^2 = \left(\sum_{k=1}^{n} k\right)^2$$

- Sum of first 'n' odd natural numbers

$$\sum_{k=1}^{n}(2k-1) = 1+3+5+\ldots+(2n-1) = n^2$$

Geometric Progression (G.P.)

A sequence is said to be a geometric progression or G.P., if the ratio of any term to its preceding term is same throughout. This constant factor is called **'Common ratio'**. Usually we denote the first term of a G.P. by 'a' and its common ratio by 'r'. The gereral or n[th] term of G.P. is given by $a_n = ar^{n-1}$

The sum S_n of the first n terms of G.P. is given by

$$S_n = \frac{a(r^n-1)}{r-1} \text{ or } \frac{a(1-r^n)}{1-r} \text{ if } r \neq 1$$

Sum of infinite terms of G.P. is given by

$$S_n = \frac{a}{1-r}; |r|<1$$

Geometric Mean (GM)

- If a, b, c are in G.P., b is the GM between a & c, $b^2 = ac$, therefore $b = \sqrt{ac}$; $a > 0, c > 0$
- If a, b are two given numbers & a, $G_1, G_2, \ldots, G_n$, b are in G.P., then $G_1, G_2, G_3 \ldots G_n$ are n GMs between a & b.

$$G_1 = a\cdot\left(\frac{b}{a}\right)^{1/n+1} G_2 = a\cdot\left(\frac{b}{a}\right)^{2/n+1} \ldots\ldots G_n = a\cdot\left(\frac{b}{a}\right)^{n/n+1}$$

or

$$G_1 = ar,\ G_2 = ar^2,\ \ldots\ G_n = ar^n$$

where $r = \left(\frac{b}{a}\right)^{1/n+1}$

Arithmetico Geometric Series

In a series, where each term is formed by multiplying the corresponding term of an AP & GP is called Arithmetico-Geometric Series.

Eg: $1+3x+5x^2+7x^3+\ldots$

Here, 1, 3, 5, … are in AP and 1, x, x^2, … are in GP.

Properties of AM & GM between two quantities

- If A.M.: G.M. of two positive numbers a and b is m : n, then $a : b = \left(m+\sqrt{m^2-n^2}\right):\left(m-\sqrt{m^2-n^2}\right)$
- If A and G be the AM & GM between two positive numbers, then the numbers are $A \pm \sqrt{A^2-G^2}$

Relationship between AM and GM

Let A and G be the AM and GM of two given positive real numbers a & b, respectively. Then,

$$A = \frac{a+b}{2} \text{ and } G = \sqrt{ab}$$

Thus, we have, $A-G = \frac{a+b}{2} - \sqrt{ab} = \frac{a+b-2\sqrt{ab}}{2}$

$$= \frac{\left(\sqrt{a}-\sqrt{b}\right)^2}{2} \geq 0 \quad \ldots\ldots\ldots\ldots (1)$$

From (1), we obtain the relationship $A \geq G$

CHAPTER : 10 STRAIGHT LINE

Straight Line

Parallel lines

1. When two lines are parallel their slopes are equal. Thus, any line parallel to $y = mx+c$ is of the type $y = mx + d$, where d is any parameter
2. Two lines $ax + by + c = 0$ and $a'x + b'x + c' = 0$ are parallel if $\frac{a}{a'} = \frac{b}{b'} \neq \frac{c}{c'}$
3. The distance between two parallel lines with equations $ax + by + c_1 = 0$ and $ax + by + c_2 = 0$ is $d = \left|\frac{c_1 - c_2}{\sqrt{a^2 + b^2}}\right|$

Angle between two straight lines in terms of their slopes

If m_1 and m_2 are the slopes of two intersecting lines ($m_1 m_2 \neq -1$) and θ be the acute angle between them then $\tan\theta = \left|\frac{m_1 - m_2}{1 + m_1 m_2}\right|$

Slope Formula

- If θ is the angle at which a straight line is inclined to be +ve direction of x-axis and $0° \leq \theta < 180°$, $\theta \neq 90°$, then the slope of the line, denoted by m, is defined by $m = \tan\theta$. If θ is $90°$, m doesn't exist, but the line is parallel to y-axis. If $\theta = 0°$, then $m = 0$ and the line is parallel to x-axis.
- If $A(x_1, y_1)$ and $B(x_2, y_2)$, $x_1 \neq x_2$ are points on straight line, then the slope m of the line is given by $m = \frac{(y_1 - y_2)}{(x_1 - x_2)}$

Area of Triangle

Area of triangle whose vertices are (x_1, y_1), (x_2, y_2) and (x_3, y_3) is $\frac{1}{2}|x_1(y_1 - y_2) + x_2(y_3 - y_1) + x_3(y_1 - y_2)|$

Distance Formula

The distance between the points $A(x_1, y_1)$ and $B(x_2, y_2)$ is $\sqrt{(x_1 - x_2)^2 + (y_1 - y_2)^2}$

Section Formula

The $P(x, y)$ divided the line joining $A(x_1, y_1)$ and $B(x_2, y_2)$ in the ratio m:n, then $x = \frac{mx_2 \pm nx_1}{m \pm n}$; $y_1 = \frac{my_2 \pm ny_1}{m \pm n}$

Note:
- (+ve) sign tells the division is internal, but (–ve) signs tells, the division is external.
- If m = n, then P is the mid-point of the line segment joining A & B.

Equation of Straight Line in various forms

1. **POINT-SLOPE FORM**: $y - y_1 = m(x - x_1)$ is the equation of a straight line whose slope is 'm' and passes through the point (x_1, y_1).
2. **SLOPE INTERCEPT FORM**: $y = mx + c$ is the equation of a straight line whose slope is 'm' and makes an intercept c on the y-axis.
3. **TWO POINT FORM**: $y - y_1 = \frac{y_2 - y_1}{x_2 - x_1}(x - x_1)$ is the equation of a straight line which passes through (x_1, y_1) & (x_2, y_2).
4. **INTERCEPT FORM**: $\frac{x}{a} + \frac{y}{b} = 1$ is the equation of a straight line which makes intercepts a & b on x and y axis respectively.
5. **NORMAL / PERPENDICULAR FORM**: $x\cos\alpha + y\sin\alpha = p$ (where $p > 0, \leq 0\ \alpha < 2\pi$) is the equation of a straight line where the length of the perpendicular from origin O on the line is p and this perpendicular makes an angle α with +ve x-axis.
6. **GENERAL FORM**: $ax + by + c = 0$ is the equation of a straight line in general form. In this case, slope of line $= -\frac{a}{b}$

Length of the perpendicular from a point on a line

The length of the perpendicular from $P(x_1, y_1)$ on $ax + by + c = 0$ is:

$$d = \left|\frac{ax_1 + by_1 + c}{\sqrt{a^2 + b^2}}\right|$$

Reflection & foot of perpendicular a point about a line

1. The image of a point(x_1, y_1) about a line $ax + by + c = 0$ is:

$$\frac{x - x_1}{a} = \frac{y - y_1}{b} = -\frac{ax_1 + by_1 + c}{\sqrt{a^2 + b^2}}$$

2. Similarly, foot of perpendicular from a point on the line is:

$$\frac{x - x_1}{a} = \frac{y - y_1}{b} = \frac{-(ax_1 + by_1 + c)}{\sqrt{a^2 + b^2}}$$

Perpendicular lines

1. When two lines of the slope m_1 & m_2 are at right angles, the Product of their slope is -1, i.e., $m_1 m_2 = -1$. Thus, any line perpendicular to $y = mx + c$ is of the form, $y = \frac{-1}{m}x + d$ where d is any parameter.
2. Two lines $ax + by + c = 0$ and $a'x + b'y + c' = 0$ are perpendicular if $aa' + bb' = 0$. Thus, any line perpendicular to $ax + by + c = 0$ is of the form $bx - ay + k = 0$, where k is any parameter.

CHAPTER : 11 CONIC SECTIONS

Conic Sections

Ellipse

An ellipse is the set of all points in a plane, the sum of whose distances from two fixed points in the plane is constant.
The two fixed points are called the 'foci' of the ellipse.
The midpoint of line segment joining foci is called the 'centre' of the ellipse.
The line segment through the foci of the ellipse is called' major axis'.
The line segment through centre & perpendicular to major axis is called minor axis.

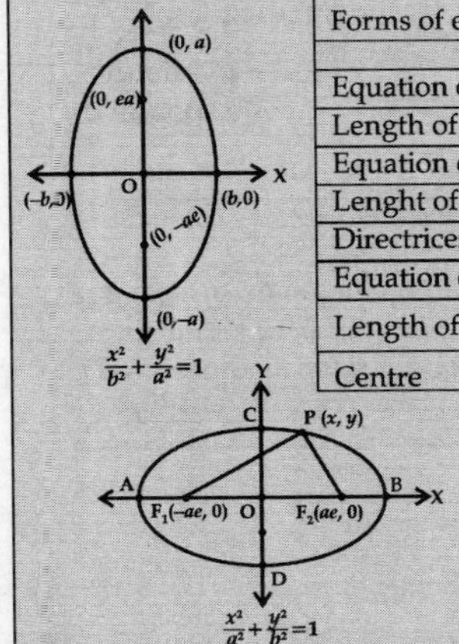

Forms of ellipse	$\frac{x^2}{a^2}+\frac{y^2}{b^2}=1$	$\frac{x^2}{b^2}+\frac{y^2}{a^2}=1$
	$a>b$	$a>b$
Equation of major axis	$y=0$	$x=0$
Length of major axis	$2a$	$2a$
Equation of Minor axis	$x=a$	$y=0$
Lenght of Minor axis	$2b$	$2b$
Directrices	$x=\pm\frac{a}{e}$	$y=\pm\frac{a}{e}$
Equation of latus rectum	$x=\pm ae$	$y=\pm ae$
Length of latus rectum	$\frac{2b^2}{a}$	$\frac{2b^2}{a}$
Centre	(0, 0)	(0, 0)

Here, $a>b$ and $b^2 = a^2(1-e^2)$, $e<1$

Parabola

A parabola is the set of all points in a plane that are equidistant from a fixed line and a fixed point in the plane. Fixed line is called 'directrix' of parabola. Fixed point F is called the 'focus'. A line through focus & perpendicular to directrix is called 'axis'. Point of intersection of parabola with axis is called 'vertex'.

Main facts about the parabola

Forms of Parabolas	$y^2=4ax$	$y^2=-4ax$	$x^2=4ay$	$x^2=-4ay$
Axis	$y=0$	$y=0$	$x=0$	$x=0$
Directix	$x=-a$	$x=a$	$y=-a$	$y=a$
Vertex	(0, 0)	(0, 0)	(0, 0)	(0, 0)
Focus	$(a, 0)$	$(-a, 0)$	$(0, a)$	$(0,-a)$
Lenght of latus rectum	$4a$	$4a$	$4a$	$4a$
Equations of latus rectum	$x=a$	$x=-a$	$y=a$	$y=-a$

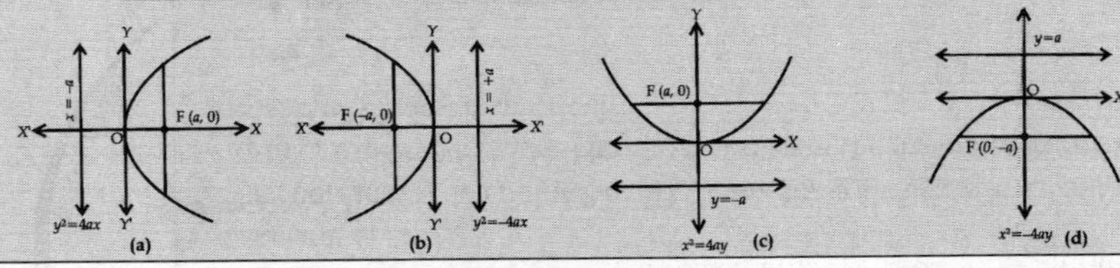

Definition

Circles, ellipses, parabolas and hyperbolas are known as conic sections because they can be obtained as intersections of plane with a double napped right circular cone α. From the given figure.
(i) Section will represent circle, if β =90°
(ii) Section will represent an Ellipse, if $\alpha<\beta<\pi/2$
(iii) Section will represent a parabola if if α=β
(iv) Section will represent a hyperbola if $0 \le \beta<\alpha$

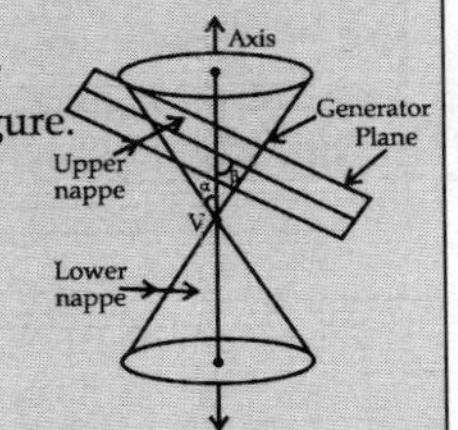

Circle

A circle is a set of all points in a plane that are equidistant from a fixed point in the plane. The fixed point is called the 'centre' of the circle and the distance from the centre to a point on the circle is called the 'radius' of the circle.

The equation of a circle with centre (h, k) and the radius r is $(x-h)^2+(y-k)^2=r^2$
The general equation of circle in $x^2+y^2+2gx+2fy+c=0$
its centre is $(-g, -f)$ and radius $r=\sqrt{g^2+f^2-c}$

Hyperbola

A hyperbola is the set of all points in a plane, the difference of whose distances from two fixed points in the plane is a constant.
The two fixed points are called the 'foci' of the hyperbola.
The mid-point of the line segment joining the foci is called the 'centre' of the hyperbola.
The line through the foci is called 'transverse axis'.
Line through centre and perpendicular to transverse axis is called 'conjugate axis'.
Points at which hyperbola intersects transverse axis are called 'vertices'.

Forms of the hyperbola	$\frac{x^2}{a^2}-\frac{y^2}{b^2}=1$	$\frac{y^2}{a^2}-\frac{x^2}{b^2}=1$
Equation of transverse axis	$y=0$	$x=0$
Equation of conjugate axis	$x=a$	$y=a$
Length of transverse axis	$2a$	$2a$
Foci	$(\pm ae, 0)$	$(\pm ae, 0)$
Equation of latus rectum	$x=\pm ae$	$x=\pm ae$
Length of latus rectum	$\frac{2b^2}{a}$	$\frac{2b^2}{a}$
Centre	(0, 0)	(0, 0)

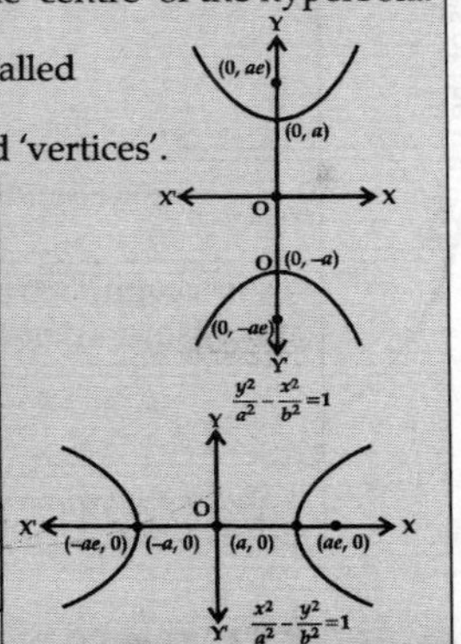

Here, $b^2 = a^2(e^2-1)$, $e>1$

CHAPTER : 12 INTRODUCTION TO THREE DIMENSIONAL GEOMETRY

Introduction to Three Dimensional Geometry

Coordinates of the Centroid of a Triangle

The coordinates of the centroid of the triangle, whose vertices are (x_1, y_1, z_1), (x_2, y_2, z_2) and (x_3, y_3, z_3) are $\left(\frac{x_1+x_2+x_3}{3}, \frac{y_1+y_2+y_3}{3}, \frac{z_1+z_2+z_3}{3}\right)$

Eg: The centroid of a triangle ABC is at the point (1, 1, 1). If the coordinates of A and B are (3, –5, 7) and (–1, 7, –6), respectively, find the coordinates of the point C.

Sol: Let the coordinates of C be (x, y, z) and the coordinates of the centroid G be (1, 1, 1). Then $\frac{x+3-1}{3}=1$, i.e., $x=1$;

$\frac{y-5+7}{3} = 1$, i.e., $y=1$;

$\frac{z+7-6}{3}=1$, i.e., $z=2$. So, C (x,y,z) = (1,1,2)

Coordinates of a Midpoint

The coordinates of the midpoint of the line segment joining two points $P(x_1, y_1, z_1)$ and $Q(x_2, y_2, z_2)$ are $\left(\frac{x_1+x_2}{2}, \frac{y_1+y_2}{2}, \frac{z_1+z_2}{2}\right)$.

Eg: Find the midpoint of the line joining two points P(1, –3, 4) and Q(–4, 1, 2).

Sol: Coordinates of the midpoint of the line joining the points P & Q are

$$\left(\frac{1-4}{2}, \frac{-3+1}{2}, \frac{4+2}{2}\right) \text{ i.e. } \left(\frac{-3}{2}, -1, 3\right)$$

Introduction

- In three dimensions, the coordinate axes of a rectangular cartesian coordinate system are three mutually perpendicular lines. The axes are called x, y and z axes.
- The three planes determined by the pair of axes are the coordinate planes, called xy, yz and zx-planes.
- The three coordinate planes divide the space into eight parts known as octants.
- The coordinates of a point P in 3D Geometry is always written in the form of triplet like (x,y,z). Here, x, y and z are the distances from yz, zx and *yx* planes, respectively.

Eg:

- Any point on x-axis is : (x, 0, 0)
- Any point on y-axis is : (0, y, 0)
- Any point on z-axis is : (0, 0, z)

Section Formula

The coordinates of the point R which divides the line segment joining two points $P(x_1, y_1, z_1)$ and $Q(x_2, y_2, z_2)$ internally and externally in the ratio m : n are given by

$$\left(\frac{mx_2+nx_1}{m+n}, \frac{my_2+ny_1}{m+n}, \frac{mz_2+nz_1}{m+n}\right) \;\&\; \left(\frac{mx_2-nx_1}{m-n}, \frac{my_2-ny_1}{m-n}, \frac{mz_2-nz_1}{m-n}\right)$$

respectively.

Eg: Find the coordinates of the point which divides the line segment joining the points (1,–2, 3)and (3, 4, –5) in the ratio 2:3 internally.

Sol : Let P(x, y, z) be the point which divides line segment joining A (1,–2, 3) and B (3, 4, –5) internally in the ratio 2:3. Therefore,

$$x=\frac{2(3)+3(1)}{2+3}=\frac{9}{5} \quad y=\frac{2(4)+3(-2)}{2+3}=\frac{2}{5} \quad z=\frac{2(-5)+3(3)}{2+3}=\frac{-1}{5}$$

Thus, the required point is $\left(\frac{9}{5}, \frac{2}{5}, \frac{-1}{5}\right)$.

Distance between Two Points

Distance between two points $P(x_1, y_1, z_1)$ and $Q(x_2, y_2, z_2)$ is given by

$$PQ=\sqrt{(x_2-x_1)^2+(y_2-y_1)^2+(z_2-z_1)^2}$$

Eg: Find the distance between the points P(1, –3, 4) and (–4, 1, 2).

Sol: The distance PQ between the points P & Q is given by

$$PQ=\sqrt{(-4-1)^2+(1+3)^2+(2-4)^2}$$

$$=\sqrt{25+16+4} = \sqrt{45} = 3\sqrt{5} \text{ units}$$

CHAPTER : 13 LIMITS AND DERIVATIVES

Limits and Derivatives

Derivative of polynomial function

Let $f(x) = a_nx^n + a_{n-1}x^{n-1} + -- + a_1x + a_0$ be a polynomial function, where a_i s are all real numbers and $a_n \neq 0$. Then the derivative function is given by

$$\frac{d f(x)}{dx} = na_nx^{n-1} + (n-1)a_{n-1}x^{n-2} + -- + 2a_2x + a_1$$

Derivative of a function at 'a'

The derivative of a function f at a is defined by

$$f'(a) = \lim_{h\to 0}\frac{f(a+h)-f(a)}{h}$$

Eg: Find derivative of $f(x) = \frac{1}{x}$.

Sol: We have $f'(x) = \lim_{h\to 0}\frac{f(x+h)-f(x)}{h}$

$$= \lim_{h\to 0}\frac{\frac{1}{x+h}-\frac{1}{x}}{h} = \lim_{h\to 0}\frac{1}{h}\left[\frac{-h}{x(x+h)}\right] = \frac{-1}{x^2}$$

Limit

- We say $\lim_{x\to a^-} f(x)$ is the expected value of f at $x=a$ given that the values of f near x to the left of a. This value is called the left hand limit of f at 'a'
- We say $\lim_{x\to a^+} f(x)$ is the expected value of f at $x=a$ given that the values of f near x to the right of a. This value is called the right hand limit of f 'at a'.
- If the right and left hand limits coincide, we call that common value as the limit of $f(x)$ at $x=a$ and denoted it by $\lim_{x\to a} f(x)$.

Eg: Find limit of function $f(x)=(x-1)^2$ at $x=1$.

Sol: For $f(x)=(x-1)^2$

Left hand limit (LHL) (at x=1) $= \lim_{x\to 1^-}(x-1)^2 = 0$

and Right hand limit (RHL) (at x=1) $= \lim_{x\to 1^+}(x-1)^2 = 0$

$\therefore$ LHL = RHL

$\lim_{x\to 1}(x-1)^2 = 0$

Algebra of derivatives of functions

For functions u and v the following holds:

- $(u \pm v)' = u' \pm v'$
- $(uv)' = u'v + v'u$
- $\left(\frac{u}{v}\right)' = \frac{u'v - uv'}{v^2}$ provided all are defined and $v \neq 0$

Here, $u' = \frac{du}{dx}$ and $v' = \frac{dv}{dx}$

Some Standard Derivatives

- $\frac{d}{dx}(x^n) = nx^{n-1}$
- $\frac{d}{dx}(\sin x) = \cos x$
- $\frac{d}{dx}(\cos x) = -\sin x$

Some Standard Limits

- $\lim_{x\to a}\frac{x^n - a^n}{x - a} = na^{n-1}$
- $\lim_{x\to 0}\frac{\sin x}{x} = 1$
- $\lim_{x\to 0}\frac{1-\cos x}{x} = 0$

Algebra of Limits

For functions f and g the following holds:

- $\lim_{x\to a}[f(x) \pm g(x)] = \lim_{x\to a} f(x) \pm \lim_{x\to a} g(x)$
- $\lim_{x\to a}[f(x).g(x)] = \lim_{x\to a} f(x).\lim_{x\to a} g(x)$
- $\lim_{x\to a}\left[\frac{f(x)}{g(x)}\right] = \frac{\lim_{x\to a} f(x)}{\lim_{x\to a} g(x)}$, $\therefore \lim_{x\to a} g(x) \neq 0$

CHAPTER : 14 MATHEMATICAL REASONING

Mathematical Reasoning

Contrapositive and Converse Statements

- The contrapositive of a statement $p \Rightarrow q$ is the statement $\sim q \Rightarrow \sim p$
- The converse of a statement $p \Rightarrow q$ is the statement $q \Rightarrow p$

e.g. If the physical environment changes, then biological environmental changes.

- **Contrapositive :** If the biological environment does not change then the physical environment does not change.
- **Converse:** If the biological environment changes then physical environment changes.

Validity of Statements

The following methods are used to check the validity of statements
(i) Direct Method
(ii) Contrapositive Method
(iii) Method of Contradiction
(iv) Using a Counter example

Implications

- These are statements with word "if then", "only if" and "if and only if".

e.g.

- r: if a number is a multiple of 9, then it is multiple of 3.
- p: a number is a multiple of 9.
- q: a number is a multiple of 3.
- Then, if p then q is the same as following:

→ p implies q is denoted by $p \Rightarrow q$, then symbol $\Rightarrow$ stands for implies,
→ p is a sufficient condition for q. then symbol $\Rightarrow$
→ p only if q
→ q is a necessary condition for p
→ $\sim q$ implies $\sim p$

Quantifiers

In this statement, the two important symbols are used.

- The symbol '$\forall$' stand for "all values of";
- The symbol '$\exists$' stand for "there exists"

e.g. For every prime number P, P is an irrational number.

- This means that if S denotes the set of all prime numbers, then for all the members of P of the set S, P is an irrational number.

Compound Statement

Many mathematical statements are obtained by combining one or more statements using some connecting words like "and", "or" etc. Each statement is called a "Compound Statement."

e.g.

'The sky is blue' and 'the grass is green' is a compound statement where connecting word is "and"; the components of Compound Statement are

p : The sky is blue
q : The grass is green

Sentence

A sentence is called a mathematically acceptable statement if it is either true or false but not both.

e.g.

- The sum of two positive numbers is positive.
- All prime numbers are odd numbers.
- In above statements, first is 'true' and second is 'false'.

Negation

A statement which is formed by changing the true value of a given statement by using the word like 'no', 'not' is called negation of given statement.

- If P is a statement, then negation is denoted by $\sim p$

e.g. New Delhi is a city.

The negation of this statement:

→ It is not the case that New Delhi is a city.
→ It is false that New Delhi is a city.
→ New Delhi is not a city.

CHAPTER : 15 STATISTICS

Statistics

Variance & Standard Deviation of a discrete frequency distribution

Variance of a discrete frequency distribution

$$\text{Var}\left(\sigma^2\right)=\frac{1}{N}\sum f_i\left(x_i-\bar{x}\right)^2$$

Standard Deviation (S.D.) of a discrete frequency distribution

$$\text{S.D}\ (\sigma)=\sqrt{\frac{1}{N}\sum f_i\left(x_i-\bar{x}\right)^2}$$

where $N=\sum_{i=1}^{n} f_i$ and $\bar{x}$ = mean

Variance and Standard Deviation for ungrouped data

Variance of ungrouped data

$$\text{Var}\ \left(\sigma^2\right)=\frac{1}{n}\sum\left(x_i-\bar{x}\right)^2$$

Standard Deviation (S.D.) for un grouped data:

$$\text{S.D.}\left(\sigma\right)=\sqrt{\frac{1}{n}\sum\left(x_i-\bar{x}\right)^2}$$

Coefficient of Variation

Coefficient of variation (C.V.)

$$=\frac{\sigma}{\bar{x}}\times 100\ ;\ \bar{x}\neq 0$$

where $\bar{x}$ is mean

Measures of Dispersion

The degree to which numerical data tend to spread about an average value is called the dispersion of the data. The four dispersions are: Range, Mean deviation, Standard deviation and Variance.

Range

The difference between the highest and the lowest element of a data called its range.

$$range\ = x_{\max}-x_{\min}$$

Eg: Find the range of the given data:

4, 7, 8, 9, 10, 12, 13, 17

Here, $x_{\max}=17$ and $x_{\min}=4$

Range = 17–4 = 13

Mean Deviation

Mean Deviation (M.D.) for ungrouped data

- M.D. about mean i.e., $M.D.(\bar{x})=\dfrac{\sum|x_i-\bar{x}|}{n}$, where $\bar{x}$ is mean and n = no. of terms
- M.D. about median i.e., $M.D.(M)=\dfrac{\sum|x_i-M|}{n}$, where M is median and n = no. of terms

Mean Deviation (M.D.) for grouped data

M.D. about mean i.e., $M.D.(\bar{x})=\dfrac{\sum f_i|x_i-\bar{x}|}{N}$

M.D. about median i.e., $M.D.(M)=\dfrac{1}{N}\sum f_i|x_i-M|$

where $N=\sum f_i$

Median class

Median class is the class interval whose C.F. is just greater than or equal to $\frac{N}{2}$, f, h and C are respectively the lower limit, the frequency, width of the median class and C the cumulative frequency (C.F.) of class just preceding to median class.

Variance & Standard Deviation of a Continuous frequency distribution

Variance of a continuous frequency distribution

$$\text{Var}\ (\sigma^2)=\frac{1}{N}\Sigma f_i\,(x_i-\bar{x})^2$$

Standard deviation of a continuous frequency distribution

$$\text{S.D}\ (\sigma)=\frac{1}{N}\sqrt{N\Sigma f_i x_i^2-(\Sigma f_i x_i)^2}$$

Step Deviation or Shortcut Method

- $M.D.(\bar{x})=\dfrac{1}{N}\sum f_i|x_i-\bar{x}|$

where $\bar{x}=a+\dfrac{\sum_{i=1}^{n} f_i d_i}{N}\times h$

and $d_i=\dfrac{x_i-a}{h}$

Here, a = assumed mean

h = common factor

N = sum of frequencies

- $M.D.(M)=\dfrac{1}{N}\sum f_i|x_i-M|$

where, M(median) $=l+\dfrac{\frac{N}{2}-C}{f}\times h$

Shortcut method to find variance and standard deviation

Variance

$$\left(\sigma^2\right)=\frac{h^2}{N^2}\left[N\sum f_i y_i^2-\left(\sum f_i y_i\right)^2\right]$$

Standard Deviation

$$\sigma=\frac{h}{N}\sqrt{N\sum f_i y_i^2-\left(\sum f_i y_i\right)^2}$$

where $y_i=\dfrac{x_i-A}{h}$

$N=\sum_{i=1}^{n} f_i$

A = assumed mean

h = width of class interval

CHAPTER : 16 PROBABILITY

Probability

Mutually Exclusive Events

Events A & B are called mutually exclusive events if occurance of any one of them excludes occurrance of other event, i.e. they cannot occur simultaneously.

Eg: A die is thrown. Event A= All even outcomes & event B = All odd outcomes. Then A & B are mutually exclusive events, they cannot occur simultaneously.

Note: Simple events of a sample space are always mutually exclusive.

Probability of A∪B, A∩B and P(notA)

If A and B are any two events, then

- $P(A \cup B) = P(A) + P(B) - P(A \cap B)$
- $P(A \cap B) = P(A) + P(B) - P(A \cup B)$

If A and B are mutually exclusive, then $P(A \cup B) = P(A) + P(B)$

(As) $P(A \cap B) = \phi$

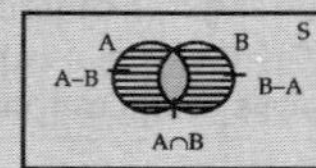

- Probability of the event 'not A'

$P(A') = P(\text{not } A) = 1 - P(A)$

Random Experiment

An Experiment is called random experiment if it satisfies the following two conditions:

- It has more than one possible outcome.
- It is not possible to predict the outcome in advance.

Outcome: A possible result of a random experiment is called its outcome.

Sample Space: Set of all possible outcomes of a random experiment is called sample space. It is denoted by symbol 'S'.

Eg: In a toss of a coin, sample space is Head & Tail. i.e., S= {H,T}

Sample Point: Each element of the Sample Space is called a sample point.

Eg: In a toss of a coin, head is a sample point

Equally Likely Outcomes: All outcome with equal probability.

Exhaustive Events

Many events that together form sample space are called exhaustive events.

Eg: A die is thrown. Event A = All even outcomes and event B = All odd outcomes. Event A & B together forms exhaustive events as it forms sample space.

Algebra of Events

- Event A or B or $(A \cup B)$

$A \cup B = \{w: w \in A \text{ or } w \in B\}$

- Event A and B or $(A \cap B)$

$A \cap B = \{w: w \in A \text{ and } w \in B\}$

- Event A but not B or (A–B)

$A - B = A \cap B'$

Definition

Probability is the measure of uncertainty of various phenomenon, numerically. It can have positive value from 0 to 1.

$$\text{Probability} = \frac{\text{No. of favourable outcomes}}{\text{Total no. of outcomes}}$$

Eg: Probability of getting an even no. in a throw of a die.

Sol. Here, favourable outcomes = {2, 4, 6}

Total no. of outcomes = {1, 2, 3, 4, 5, 6}

$$\text{Probability} = \frac{3}{6} = \frac{1}{2}$$

Types of Events

- **Impossible and Sure Event:** The empty set ϕ is called an Impossible event, where as the whole sample space 'S' is called 'Sure event'.
  Eg: In a rolling of a die, impossible event is that number more than 6 and event of getting number less than or equal to 6 is sure event.
- **Simple Event:** If an event has only one sample point of a sample space, it is called a 'simple event'.
  Eg: In rolling of a die, simple event could be the event of getting number 4.
- **Compound Event:** If an event has more than one sample point, it is called a 'compound event'.
  Eg: In rolling of a die, compound event could be event of getting an even number.
- **Complementary Event:** Complement event to A = 'not A'
  Eg: If an event A= Event of getting odd number in a throw of a die i.e., {1, 3, 5} then, complementary event to A = Event of getting an even number in a throw of a die , i.e. {2, 4, 6}
  $A' = \{W: W \in S \text{ and } W \notin A\} = S - A$ (where S is the sample space)

Event

It is the set of favourable outcomes. Any subset E of a sample space S is called an event.

Eg: Event of getting an even number (outcome) in a throw of a die.

Occurance of event: The event E of a sample space 'S' is said to have occurred if the outcome w of the experiment is such that $w \in E$. If the outcome w is such that $w \notin E$, we say that event E has not occurred.

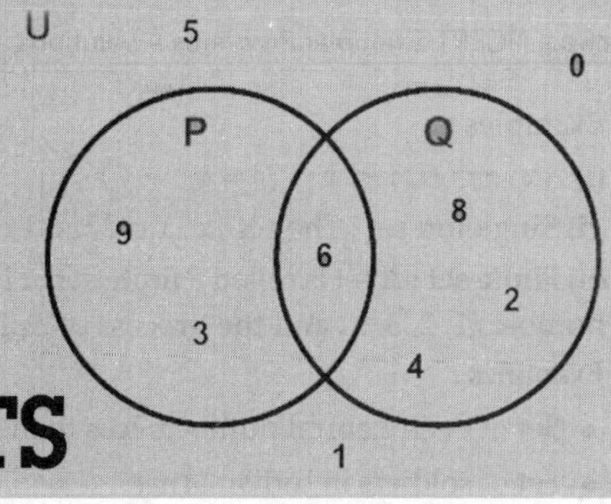

CHAPTER 1 SETS

Chapter Objectives

> *Sets and their representation; Empty set; Singleton set; Finite and Infinite sets; Equal sets; Equivalent sets; Power set; Subset of a set of real number especially intervals (with notation); Proper subset; Super set; Universal set; Venn diagrams; Union and Intersection of sets; Difference of sets, Symmetric difference; Properties of complement of sets; Application of set theory.*

TOPIC - 1
Sets, their Types and Representations P. 01

TOPIC - 2
Venn Diagrams and Operations on Set P. 05

TOPIC - 3
Application of Set Theory P. 11

TOPIC-1
Sets, their Types and Representations

Quick Review

- **Set:** A set is a well defined collection of distinct objects.
- **Elements:** The objects which belong to a set are called members or elements of a set.
- **Representation of a Set:** There are two ways by which the sets can be described:

  (i) Tabular form or Roaster form: Here the elements of a set are actually written down, separated by commas and enclosed within braces (*i.e.,* curly bracket). Eg:
  - *V*, the set of vowels of the English alphabet $= \{a, e, i, o, u\}$,
  - A, the set of odd natural numbers $< 10 = \{1, 3, 5, 7, 9\}$,
  - *N*, the set of natural numbers $= \{1, 2, 3, \ldots\}$,

  (ii) The set builder form or Rule method: A set is described by a characterizing property P(*x*) of its element *x*. In such a case, the set is described by $\{x : P(x) \text{ holds}\}$ or $\{x \mid P(x) \text{ holds}\}$ *e.g.*
  - $M = \{2, 3, 5, 7, 11, 13, 17, 19\} = \{x : x$ is a prime number $< 20\}$,
  - $A = \{6, 7, 8, 9, 10, 11\} = \{x \in N, 5 < x < 12\}$ where $\in$ stands for 'belongs to'.

- **Types of Sets**

  (i) Empty set or Null set or Void set : A set consisting of no element at all, is called an **empty set** or a **null set** or a **void set.** It is denoted by ϕ. In roaster form, it is written as { }.

TIPS...

- *Students should take precaution, while drawing the shaded area of Venn diagram.*
- *Understand different types of sets and learn all the properties of complements of set.*
- *In word problems, students should choose the symbol of objects/items accordingly as given in the question, to avoid mistakes; eg. C for coffee and T for tea.*
- *Practice to solve words problem using Venn diagram method.*

TRICKS...

- *For the two given sets A and B, A-B, B-A and $A \cap B$ are disjoint sets.*
- *Equal sets are equivalent but equivalent sets need not be equal.*
- *Every set is a subset and super set of itself.*
- *Infinite set cannot be expressed in roaster form.*
- *In roaster form, the order in which elements are listed is immaterial.*
- *If x is a subset of universal set U, then its complement x is also a subset of U.*

Examples :

(i) $\{x : x \in N, 1 < x < 2\} = \phi$, **(ii)** $\{x : x \in R, x^2 = -1\} = \phi$

(ii) Singleton set : The set $\{x : x \in N \text{ and } x^2 = 9\}$ is a singleton set equal to $\{3\}$. A set consisting of a single element.

(iii) Finite set : A set is called a finite set, if it is either void or its elements can be listed (counted, labelled) by natural numbers 1, 2, 3, ... and the process of listing terminates at a certain natural number n (say).

Examples :

- Set of even natural numbers less than 100.
- Set of soldiers in Indian army.
- Set of all persons on the earth.

(iv) Infinite set : A set whose elements cannot be listed by the natural numbers 1, 2, 3, ..., n for any natural number n is called an infinite set.

Examples :

- Set of all points in a plane.
- Set of all lines in a plane.
- $\{x \in R, 0 < x < 1\}$.

➢ **Cardinal number of a finite set :** The number n in the above definition is called the cardinal number or order of a finite set A and is denoted by $n(A)$.

➢ **Equal sets :** Two sets A and B are said to be equal, if every element of set A is in set B and every element of set B is in set A.

It is written as $A = B$.

Examples :

- $\{1, 2, 5\} = \{2, 1, 5\} = \{5, 1, 2\}$
- $\{1, 2, 3, 1\} = \{1, 2, 3\} = \{1, 1, 2, 2, 3\}$ etc.

➢ **Equivalent sets :** Two finite sets A and B are said to be equivalent, if $n(A) = n(B)$, where $n(A)$ or $n(B)$ is the number of elements of set A or B. It is written as $A \leftrightarrow B$.

Example : If $A = \{1, 2, 3\}$ and $B = \{a, b, c\}$. Then $A \leftrightarrow B$ since $n(A) = n(B) = 3$.

Whenever $A = B$, then $n(A) = n(B)$. Thus, equal sets are always equivalent. But, equivalent sets need not be equal.

➢ **Subset :** If A and B are two sets given in such a way that every element of A is in B, then A is a subset of set B and it is written as $A \subseteq B$ (read as 'A is contained in B').

➢ If at least one element of A does not belong to B, then A is not a subset of B. It is written as $A \not\subset B$.

➢ **Power set:** The collection of all subsets of a set A is called power set of A, denoted by $P(A)$ i.e. $P(A) = \{B : B \subset A\}$

If A is a set with $n(A) = m$, then $n[P(A)] = 2^m$.

➢ **Proper subset and super set:** If $A \subset B$, then A is called the proper subset of B and B is called the super set of A.

➢ **Universal set:** If there are some sets under consideration, then a set can be chosen arbitrarily which is a super set of each one of the given sets. Such a set is known as the universal set and it is denoted by U.

Example : Let $A = \{2, 4, 6\}$, $B = \{1, 3, 5\}$ and $C = \{0, 7\}$ are only three subsets

Then, $U = \{0, 1, 2, 3, 4, 5, 6, 7\}$ is an universal set.

➢ **Types of Intervals**

(i) Open interval $(a, b) = \{x \in R : a < x < b\}$

i.e. All the points between ***a*** and ***b*** belong to open interval.

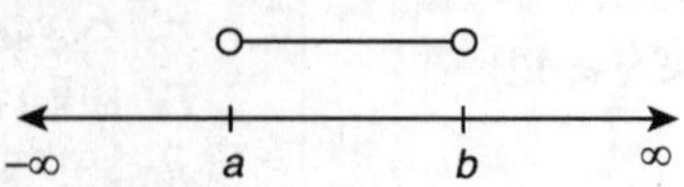

(ii) Closed interval: $[a, b] = \{x \in R : a \leq x \leq b\}$

i.e. The interval which contains the end points also, is called closed interval.

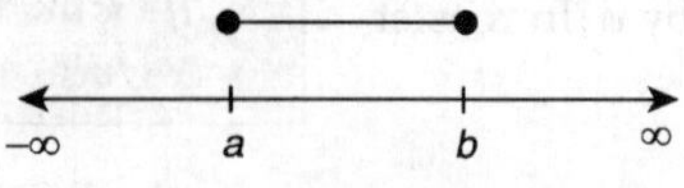

(iii) Semi open or semi closed interval,

$(a, b] = \{ x \in R: a < x \leq b\}$

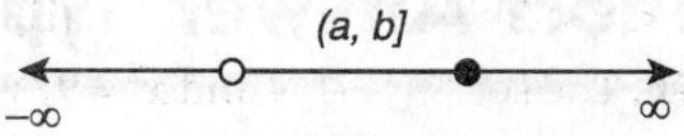

$[a, b) = \{ x \in R: a \leq x < b\}$

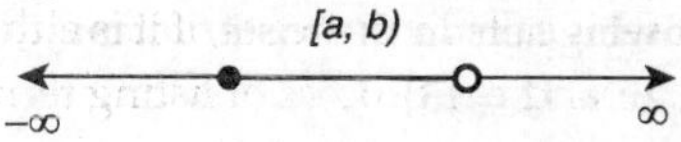

Note: (i) The set $(0, \infty)$ defines the set of non-negative real numbers.

(ii) The set $(-\infty, 0)$ defines the set of negative real numbers.

(iii) The set $(-\infty, \infty)$ defines the set of all real numbers.

- **Length of an interval:** The number $(b - a)$ is called the length of any of the intervals (a, b), $[a, b]$, $[a, b)$ or $(a, b]$.

Know the Terms

We shall denote several sets of numbers by the following symbols :

(i) N : The set of natural numbers
(ii) W : The set of whole numbers
(iii) Z : The set of integers
(iv) Q : The set of rational numbers
(v) R : The set of real numbers
(vi) Z^+ : The set of positive integers
(vii) Q^+ : The set of positive rational numbers
(viii) R^+ : The set of positive real numbers.
(ix) C : The set of all complex numbers.

Multiple Choice Questions

(1 mark each)

[A] Objective Type Questions

Q. 1. Two finite sets have *m* and *n* elements. The number of subsets of the first set is 112 more than that of the second set. The values of *m* and *n* are, respectively,

(A) 4, 7 (B) 7, 4
(C) 4, 4 (D) 7, 7

[NCERT Exemplar Q. 30, Page 15]

Ans. Correct option : (B)

According to the question, $2^m - 2^n = 112$

$$2^n(2^{m-n} - 1) = 2^4.7$$
$$2^n = 2^4 \text{ and } 2^{m-n} - 1 = 7$$
$$n = 4 \text{ and } m = 7$$

Q. 2. Let *R* be set of points inside a rectangle of sides *a* and *b* (*a, b* > 1) with two sides along the positive direction of *x* – axis and *y* – axis. Then

(A) $R = \{(x, y) : 0 \leq x \leq a, 0 \leq y \leq b\}$
(B) $R = \{(x, y): 0 \leq x < a, 0 \leq y \leq b\}$
(C) $R = \{(x, y) : 0 \leq x \leq a, 0 < y < b\}$
(D) $R = \{(x, y) : 0 < x < a, 0 < y < b\}$

[NCERT Exemplar Q. 34, Page 16]

Ans. Correct option : (D)

Since, R be the set of points inside the rectangle.

$\therefore \quad R = \{(x, y) : 0 < x < a \text{ and } 0 < y < b\}$

Q. 3. Let $S = \{x \mid x$ is a positive multiple of 3 less than 100$\}$, $P = \{x \mid x$ is a prime number less than 20$\}$. Then $n(S) + n(P)$ is

(A) 41 (B) 31
(C) 33 (D) 30

[NCERT Exemplar Q. 42, Page 17]

Ans. Correct option : (D)

there, $S = \{3, 6, 9, 12, ..., 99\}$ and $T = \{2, 3, 5, 7, 11, 13, 17, 19\}$

Therefore $\quad n(S) = 33$ and $n(T) = 8$

$\therefore \quad n(S) + n(T) = 33 + 8 = 41$

[B] Fill in the blanks

Q. 1. The set $\{x \in R : 1 \leq x < 2\}$ can be written as ______ [NCERT Exemplar Q. 44, Page 17]

Q. 2. When $A = \phi$, then number of elements in $P(A)$ is ______ [NCERT Exemplar Q. 45, Page 17]

Q. 3. Power set of the set A= {1, 2} is ______ [NCERT Exemplar Q. 48, Page 17]

Q. 4. Given the sets $A = \{1, 3, 5\}$ $B = \{2, 4, 6\}$ and $C = \{0, 2, 4, 6, 8\}$. Then the universal set of all the three sets *A*, *B* and *C* can be ______. [NCERT Exemplar Q. 49, Page 17]

Answer:

1. [1, 2)
2. 1
3. $\{\{1\}, \{2\}, \{1, 2\}, \phi\}$
4. $\{0, 1, 2, 3, 4, 5, 6, 8\}$

[C] True and False

Q. 1. If A is any set, then $A \subset A$ [NCERT Exemplar Q. 53, Page 18]

Q. 2. Given that $M = \{1, 2, 3, 4, 5, 6, 7, 8, 9\}$ and if $B = \{1, 2, 3, 4, 5, 6, 7, 8, 9\}$, then $B \not\subset M$ [NCERT Exemplar Q. 54, Page 18]

Q. 3. The sets { 1, 2, 3, 4} and {3, 4, 5, 6} are equal. [NCERT Exemplar Q. 55, Page 18]

Q. 4. Given $A = \{0, 1, 2\}$, $B = \{x \in R \mid 0 \leq x \leq 2\}$. Then $A = B$. [NCERT Exemplar Q. 58, Page 18]

Answer:

1. True
2. False
3. False
4. False

Very Short Answer Type Questions (1 marks each)

Q. 1. Write the following sets in the roster form:
(i) $A = \{x : x \in R, 2x + 11 = 15\}$
(ii) $B = \{x \mid x^2 = x, x \in R\}$
(iii) $C = \{x \mid x$ is a positive factor of a prime number $p\}$
[NCERT Exemplar Q. 1, Page 12]

Sol. (i) Given, $A = \{x : x \in R, 2x + 11 = 15\}$

$\therefore 2x + 11 = 15$
$2x = 15 - 11$
$2x = 4$
$x = 2$
$\therefore A = \{2\}$

(ii) Given, $B = \{x \mid x^2 = x, x \in R\}$

$\therefore x^2 = x$
$x^2 - x = 0$
$x(x-1) = 0$
$x = 0, 1$
$\therefore B = \{0, 1\}$

(iii) Given, $C = \{x \mid x$ is a positive factor of prime number $p\}$

Since, positive factor of a prime number are 1 and number itself.

$\therefore C = \{1, p\}$

Short Answer Type Questions (2 marks each)

Q. 1. Write the following sets in the roaster form:
(i) $D = \{t \mid t^3 = t, t \in R\}$
(ii) $E \{w \mid \therefore \frac{w-2}{w+3} = 3, w \in R\}$
(iii) $F = \{x \mid x^4 - 5x^2 + 6 = 0, x \in R\}$
[NCERT Exemplar Q. 2, Page 13]

Sol. (i) Given, $D = \{t \mid t^3 = t, t \in R\}$

$\therefore t^3 = t$
$t^3 - t = 0$
$t(t^2 - 1) = 0$
$t(t-1)(t+1) = 0$
$t = 0, 1, -1$
$\therefore D = \{0, 1, -1\}$

(ii) Given, $E = \{w \mid \frac{w-2}{w+3} = 3, w \in R\}$

$\therefore \frac{w-2}{w+3} = 3$
$w - 2 = 3(w+3)$
$w - 2 = 3w + 9$
$w - 3w = 9 + 2$
$-2w = 11$
$w = -11/2$
$\therefore E = \{-11/2\}$

(iii) Given, $F = \{x \mid x^4 - 5x^2 + 6 = 0, x \in R\}$

$\therefore x^4 - 5x^2 + 6 = 0$
$x^4 - 3x^2 - 2x^2 + 6 = 0$
$x^2(x^2 - 3) - 2(x^2 - 3) = 0$
$(x^2 - 3)(x^2 - 2) = 0$
$\therefore x = \pm\sqrt{3}, \pm\sqrt{2}$,
$\therefore F = \{-\sqrt{3}, -\sqrt{2}, \sqrt{2}, \sqrt{3}\}$

Q. 2. If $Y = \{x \mid x$ is a positive factor of the number $2^{P-1}(2^P - 1)$, where $2^P - 1$ is a prime number$\}$. Write Y in the roaster form.
[NCERT Exemplar Q. 3, Page 13]

Sol. Given,

$y = \{x \mid x$ is a positive factor of the number $2^{P-1}(2^P - 1)$, where $2^{r-1} - 1$ is a prime number$\}$

So, the factor of 2^{P-1} are $1, 2, 2^2, 2^3, \ldots, 2^{P-1}$.

$\therefore y = \{1, 2, 2^2, 2^3, \ldots, 2^{P-1}, 2^{P-1}\}$

Q. 3. State which of the following statements are true and which are false. Justify your answer.
(i) $35 \in \{x \mid x$ has exactly four positive factors$\}$.
(ii) $128 \in \{y \mid$ the sum of all the positive factors of y is $2y\}$
(iii) $3 \notin \{x \mid x^4 - 5x^3 + 2x^2 - 112x + 6 = 0\}$
(iv) $496 \notin \{y \mid$ the sum of all the positive factors of y is $2y\}$. **[NCERT Exemplar Q. 4, Page 13]**

Sol. (i) True, since the factors of 35 are 1, 5, 7 and 35.

(ii) False, since the factors of 128 are 1, 2, 4, 8, 16, 32, 64 and 128.

$\therefore$ Sum of factors $= 1 + 2 + 4 + 8 + 16 + 32 + 64 + 128$
$= 255$
$2y = 2 \times 128$
$= 256$

(iii) True

Given, $x^4 - 5x^3 + 2x^2 - 112x + 6 = 0$

For $x = 3$,

$(3)^4 - 5(3)^3 + 2(3)^2 - 112(3) + 6$
$81 - 135 + 18 - 336 + 6$
$-366 \neq 0$

(iv) False

$\therefore 496 = 2^4 \times 31$

So, the factors of 496 are 1, 2, 4, 8, 16, 31, 62, 124, 248 and 496.

$\therefore$ Sum of factors $= 1 + 2 + 4 + 8 + 16 + 31 + 62 + 124 + 248 + 496$
$= 992$
$= 2(496)$

Q. 4. Given $L = \{1, 2, 3, 4\}$, $M = \{3, 4, 5, 6\}$ and $N = \{1, 3, 5\}$.
Verify that $L - (M \cup N) = (L - M) \cap (L - N)$
[NCERT Exemplar Q. 5, Page 13]

Sol. Given,
$L = \{1, 2, 3, 4\}, M = \{3, 4, 5, 6\}$ and $N = \{1, 3, 5\}$
$\therefore M \cup N = \{1, 3, 4, 5, 6\}$
$L - (M \cup N) = \{2\}$
Now, $L - M = \{1, 2\}, L - N = \{2, 4\}$
$\therefore (L - M) \cap (L - N) = \{2\}$
Hence, $L - (M \cup N) = (L - M) \cap (L - N)$

Q. 5. Given that $N = \{1, 2, 3, \ldots, 100\}$. Then write
(i) the subset of N whose elements are even numbers.
(ii) the subset of N whose elements are perfect square numbers
[NCERT Exemplar Q. 7, Page 13]

Sol. We have $N = \{1, 2, 3, \ldots, 100\}$
(i) Required subset $= \{2, 4, 6, 8, \ldots, 100\}$
(ii) Required subset $= \{1, 4, 9, 16, 25, 36, 49, 64, 81, 100\}$

Q. 6. If $X = \{1, 2, 3\}$, if n represents any member of X, Write the following sets containing all numbers represented by
(i) $4n$
(ii) $n + 6$
(iii) $\frac{n}{2}$
(iv) $n - 1$ **[NCERT Exemplar Q. 8, Page 13]**

Sol. Given, $X = \{1, 2, 3\}$
(i) $\{4n \mid n \in X\} = \{4, 8, 12\}$
(ii) $\{n + 6 \mid n \in X\} = \{7, 8, 9\}$
(iii) $\left\{\frac{n}{2} \mid n \in X\right\} = \left\{\frac{1}{2}, 1, \frac{3}{2}\right\}$
(iv) $\{n - 1 \mid n \in X\} = \{0, 1, 2\}$

Q. 7. If $Y = \{1, 2, 3, \ldots 10\}$, and a represents any element of Y, write the following sets, containing all the elements satisfying the given conditions.
(i) $a \in Y$ but $a^2 \notin Y$
(ii) $a + 1 = 6, a \in Y$
(iii) a is less than 6 and $a \in Y$
[NCERT Exemplar Q. 9, Page 13]

Sol. Given,
$Y = \{1, 2, 3, \ldots, 10\}$
(i) $\{a : a \in Y \text{ and } a^2 \notin Y\} = \{4, 5, 6, 7, 8, 9, 10\}$
(ii) $\{a : a + 1 = 6, a \in Y\} = \{5\}$
(iii) $\{a \text{ is less than 6 and } a \in Y\} = \{1, 2, 3, 4, 5\}$

Q. 8. Let $T = \left\{x \mid = \frac{x+5}{x-7} - 5 = \frac{4x-40}{13-x}\right\}$. Is T an empty set? Justify your answer.
[NCERT Exemplar Q. 22, Page 14]

Sol. Given $T = \left\{x \mid = \frac{x+5}{x-7} - 5 = \frac{4x-40}{13-x}\right\}$

$$\therefore \frac{x+5}{x-7} - 5 = \frac{4x-40}{13-x}$$

$$\Rightarrow \frac{-4x+40}{x-7} = \frac{4x-40}{13-x}$$

$$\Rightarrow -(4x-40)(13-x) = (4x-40)(x-7)$$
$$\Rightarrow (4x-40)(x-7) + (4x-40)(13-x) = 0$$
$$\Rightarrow (4x-40)(x-7+13-x) = 0$$
$$\Rightarrow x = 10$$
$$\therefore T = \{10\}$$

From eq (i) and (ii), we get $A = B$

TOPIC-2
Venn Diagrams and Operations on Set

Quick Review

➤ **Venn Diagram:** In a Venn diagram, the universal set is represented by a rectangular region and a set is represented by circle of a closed geometrical figure inside the universal set.

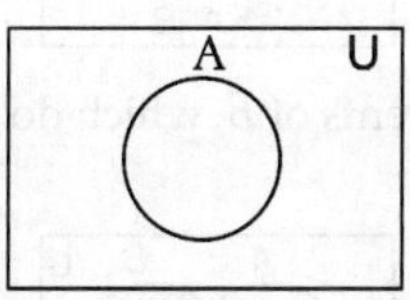

➤ **Operations on Sets :**

(i) Union of Sets: The union of two sets A and B, denoted by $A \cup B$ is the set of all elements, which is either in A or in B or both in A and B

i.e., $A \cup B = \{x : x \in A \text{ or } x \in B\}$

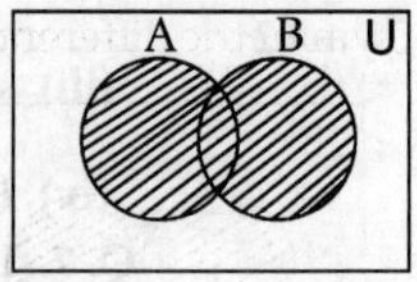

(ii) Intersection of Sets: The intersection of two sets A and B, denoted by $A \cap B$, is the set of all elements, which are common to both A and B.

i.e., $A \cap B = \{x : x \in A \text{ and } x \in B\}$

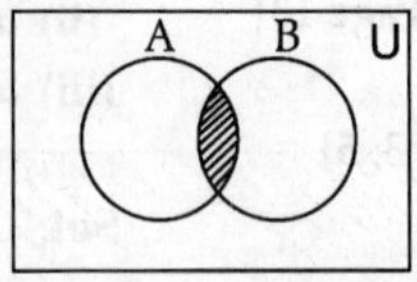

If $A_1, A_2 \ldots, A_n$ is a finite family of sets, then their intersection is denoted by

$$\bigcap_{i=1}^{n} A_i \text{ or } A_1 \cap A_2 \cap \ldots \cap A_n$$

(iii) Disjoint sets:

Two sets A and B are said to be disjoint if $A \cap B = \phi$

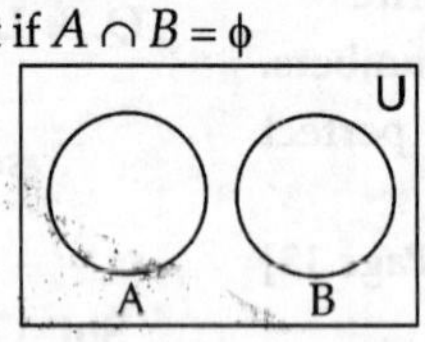

- **Laws of Algebra of Sets**

(i) $A \cup \phi = A$

(ii) $A \cap \phi = \phi$

- **Commutative Law:**

(i) $A \cup B = B \cup A$

(ii) $A \cap B = B \cap A$

- **Associative Law:**

(i) $(A \cup B) \cup C = A \cup (B \cup C)$

(ii) $(A \cap B) \cap C = A \cap (B \cap C)$

- **Distributive Law:**

(i) $A \cap (B \cup C) = (A \cap B) \cup (A \cap C)$

(ii) $A \cup (B \cap C) = (A \cup B) \cap (A \cup C)$

- If $A \subset B$, then $A \cap B = A$ and $A \cup B = B$

(iv) Difference of Sets:

For two sets A and B

- The difference $A - B$ is the set of all elements of A, which do not belong to B.

i.e., $x \in (A - B) \Rightarrow \{x : x \in A \text{ and } x \notin B\}$

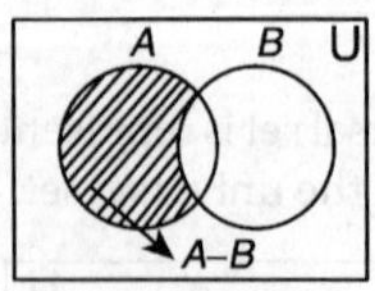

- The difference $B - A$ is the set of all elements of B, which do not belong to A.

i.e., $x \in (B - A) \Rightarrow \{x : x \in B \text{ and } x \notin A\}$

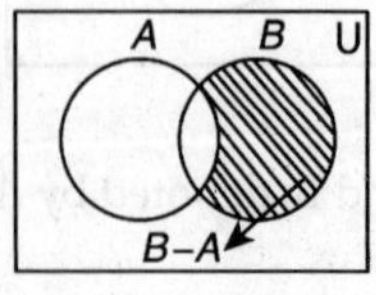

(v) Symmetric Difference: For two sets A and B, symmetric difference is the set $(A-B) \cup (B-A)$ denoted by $A \Delta B$.

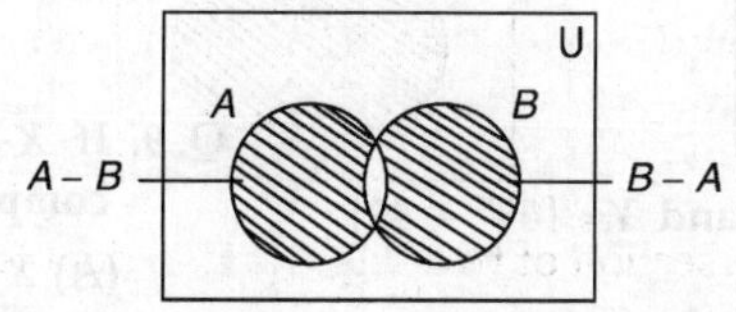

(vi) Complement of set : If A is a set with U as universal set, then complement of a set, denoted by A^c or A' is the set $U-A$.

i.e., $A' = A^c = U - A = \{x : x \in U \text{ and } x \notin A\}$

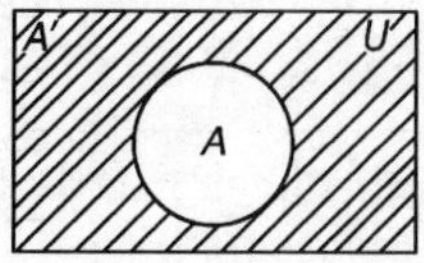

➤ **Properties of Complements:**

(i) Complement Laws:

(a) $A \cup A' = U$ **(b)** $A \cap A' = \phi$

(ii) De-Morgan's Laws:

(a) $(A \cup B)' = A' \cap B'$ **(b)** $(A \cap B)' = A' \cup B'$

(iii) Law of Double Complementation

(a) $(A')' = A$

iv) Complement of ϕ and U:

(a) $\phi' = U$ **(b)** $U' = \phi$

Note: If $A \subset B$, then $B' \subset A'$

Multiple Choice Questions

(1 mark each)

Q. 1. Suppose $A_1, A_2, ..., A_{30}$ are thirty sets each having 5 elements and $B_1, B_2, ..., B_n$ are n sets each with 3 elements, let $\bigcup_{i=1}^{30} A_i = \bigcup_{j=1}^{n} B_j = S$ and each element of S belongs to exactly 10 of the A_i's and exactly 9 of the B_i'S. then n is equal to

(A) 15 **(B) 3**

(C) 45 **(D) 35**

[NCERT Exemplar Q. 29, Page 15]

Ans. Correct option : (C)

Since elements are not repeated, then no. of elements in $A_1 \cup A_2 \cup A_3 .... \cup A_{30}$ is 30×5, but each elements is used 10 times.

$$S = \frac{30 \times 5}{10} = 15$$

Now, total no. of elements in $B1 \cup B_2 \cup B_3 ..... \cup B_n$ is $3n$ *i.e.* $S = \frac{3n}{9} \Rightarrow 15 = \frac{3n}{9} \Rightarrow n = 45$

Q. 2. The set $(A \cap B)' \cup (B \cap C)$ is equal to

(A) $A' \cup B \cup C$ **(B) $A' \cap B$**

(C) $A' \cup C'$ **(D) $A' \cap B$**

[NCERT Exemplar Q. 31, Page 16]

Ans. Correct option : (B)

We know that, $(A \cap B) = A' \cup B'$ (by De Morgan's law)

$$(A \cap B)' \cup (B \cap C) = [A' \cup (B)'] \cup (B \cap C)$$
$$= (A' \cup B')' \cup (B \cap C) = A' \cup B$$

Q. 3. Let F_1 be the set of parallelograms, F_2 the set of rectangles, F_3 the set of rhombuses, F_4 the set of squares and F_5 the set of trapeziums in a plane. Then F_1 may be equal to

(A) $F_2 \cap F_3$

(B) $F_3 \cap F_4$

(C) $F_2 \cap F_5$

(D) $F_2 \cup F_3 \cup F_4 \cap F_1$

[NCERT Exemplar Q. 32, Page 16]

Ans. Correct option : (D)

Every rectangle, rhombus, square in a plane is a parallelogram but every trapezium is not a parallelogram.

Q. 4. Let S = set of points inside the square, T = the set of points inside the triangle and C = the set of points inside the circle. If the triangle and circle intersect each other and are contained in a square. Then

(A) $S \cap T \cap C = \phi$ **(B) $S \cup T \cup C = C$**

(C) $S \cup T \cup C = S$ **(D) $S \cup T = S \cap C$**

[NCERT Exemplar Q. 33, Page 16]

Ans. Correct option : (C)

The given sets are represented in Venn diagram as shown below.

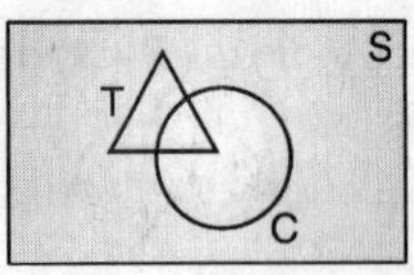

Q. 5. If $X = \{8^n - 7^n - 1 \mid n \in N\}$ and $Y = \{49^n - 49 \mid n \in N\}$. Then

(A) $X \subset Y$ (B) $Y \subset X$

(C) $X = Y$ (D) $X \cap Y = \phi$

[NCERT Exemplar Q. 37, Page 16]

Ans. Correct option : (A)

Here, $X = \{0, 49, 490, ...\}$ and

$Y = \{0, 49, 98, ...\}$

$\therefore$ $X \subset Y$

Q. 6. If sets A and B are defined as

$$A = \left\{(x, y) \mid y = \frac{1}{x}, 0 \neq x \in R\right\} \quad B = \{(x, y) \mid y = -x, x \in R\}, \text{ then}$$

(A) $A \cap B = A$ (B) $A \cap B = B$

(C) $A \cap B = \phi$ (D) $A \cup B = A$

[NCERT Exemplar Q. 39, Page 16]

Ans. Correct option : (C)

It is clear that $y = \frac{1}{x}$ and $y = -x$

$$\frac{1}{x} \neq -x$$

$\therefore$ $A \cap B = \phi$

Q. 7. If A and B are two sets, then $A \cap (A \cup B)$ equals.

(A) A (B) B

(C) ϕ (D) $A \cap B$

[NCERT Exemplar Q. 40, Page 17]

Ans. Correct option : (A)

Let $x \in A \cap (A \cup B)$

$\Rightarrow$ $x \in A$ and $x \in A \cup B$

$\Rightarrow$ $x \in A$ and $(x \in A$ or $x \cup B)$

$\Rightarrow$ $(x \in A$ and $x \in A)$ or $(x \in A$ and $x \in B)$

$\Rightarrow$ $x \in A$ or $x \in (A \cap B)$

$\Rightarrow$ $x \in A$

Q. 8. If $A = \{1, 3, 5, 7, 9, 11, 13, 15, 17\}$ $B = \{2, 4, ..., 18\}$ and N the set of natural numbers is the universal set, then $A' \cup (A \cup B) \cap B')$ is

(A) ϕ (B) N

(C) A (D) B

[NCERT Exemplar Q. 41, Page 17]

Ans. Correct option : (B)

$$A' \cup (A \cup B) \cap B' = A' [(A \cap B') \cup (B \cap B')]$$
$$= A' \cup (A \cap B') \cup \phi$$
$$= (A' \cup A) \cap (A' \cup B')$$
$$= U \cap (A' \cup B')$$
$$= A' \cup B'$$
$$= (A \cap B)' = \phi' = U = N$$

Q. 9. If X and Y are two sets and X' denotes the complement of X, then $X \cap (X \cup Y)'$ is equal to

(A) X (B) Y

(C) ϕ (D) $X \cap Y$

[NCERT Exemplar Q. 40, Page 17]

Ans. Correct option : (C)

Let $x \in X \cap (X \cup Y)'$

$\Rightarrow$ $x \in X \cap (X' \cap Y')$

$\Rightarrow$ $x \in (X \cap X') \cap (X \cap Y')$

$\Rightarrow$ $x \in \phi \cap (X \cap Y')$

$\Rightarrow$ $x \in \phi$

[B] Fill in the blanks

Q. 1. If A and B are finite sets such that $A \subset B$, then $n(A \cup B) =$ ....

[NCERT Exemplar Q. 46, Page 17]

Q. 2. If A and B are any two sets, then $A - B$ is equal to ....

[NCERT Exemplar Q. 47, Page 17]

Q. 3. If U = {1, 2, 3, 4, 5, 6, 7, 8, 9, 10}, A = {1, 2, 3, 5}, B = {2, 4, 6, 7} and C = {2, 3, 4, 8}. Then

(i) $(B \cup C)'$ is .... (ii) $(C - A)'$ is ....

[NCERT Exemplar Q. 50, Page 17]

Q. 4. For all sets A and B, $A - (A \cap B)$ is equal to ....

[NCERT Exemplar Q. 7, Page 17]

Answer:

1. $n(B)$

2. $A \cap B'$

3. (i) {1, 5, 9, 10}, (ii) {1, 2, 3, 5, 6, 7, 9, 10}

4. $A \cap B'$

[C] Match the following :

Q. 1. Match the following sets for all sets A, B and C

(i) $(A' \cup B') - A)'$	(a) $A - B$
(ii) $[B' \cup (B' - A)]'$	(b) A
(iii) $(A - B) - (B - C)$	(c) B
(iv) $(A - B) \cap (C - B)$	(d) $(A \times B) \cap (A \times C)$
(v) $A \times (B \cap C)$	(e) $(A \times B) \cup (A \times C)$
(vi) $A \times (B \cup C)$	(f) $(A \cap C) - B$

[NCERT Exemplar Q. 52, Page 17]

Answer :

(i) $\leftrightarrow$ (b)

(ii) $\leftrightarrow$ (c)

(iii) $\leftrightarrow$ (a)

(iv) $\leftrightarrow$ (f)

(v) $\leftrightarrow$ (d)

(vi) $\leftrightarrow$ (e)

Very Short Answer Type Questions (1 marks each)

Q. 1. If A and B are subsets of the universal set U, then show that
(i) $A \subset (A \cup B)$ (ii) $(A \cap B) \subset A$
[NCERT Exemplar Q. 6, Page 13]

Sol. (i) Let $x \in A$

Let $x \in A$ or $x \in B \Rightarrow x \in (A \cup B)$

Hence, $A \subset (A \cup B)$

(ii) Let $x \in (A \cap B)$

$\Rightarrow x \in A$ and $x \in B \Rightarrow x \in A$

Hence, $(A \cap B) \subset A$

Q. 2. For all sets A and B, $(A - B) \cup (A \cap B) = A$, determined whether the statement is true or false. Justify your answer.
[NCERT Exemplar Q. 13, Page 14]

Sol. True

$$\begin{aligned} \text{L.H.S} &= (A - B) \cup (A \cap B) \\ &= [(A - B) \cup A] \cap [(A - B) \cup B] \\ &= A \cap (A \cup B) \\ &= A \\ &= \text{R. H. S} \end{aligned}$$

Short Answer Type Questions (2 marks each)

Q. 1. A, B and C are subsets of Universal set U. If $A = \{2, 4, 6, 8, 12, 20\}$ $B = \{3, 6, 9, 12, 15\}$, $C = \{5, 10, 15, 20\}$ and U is the set of all whole numbers, draw a Venn diagram showing the relation of U, A, B and C.
[NCERT Exemplar Q. 10, Page 13]

Sol. Relationship among sets A, B, C and U.

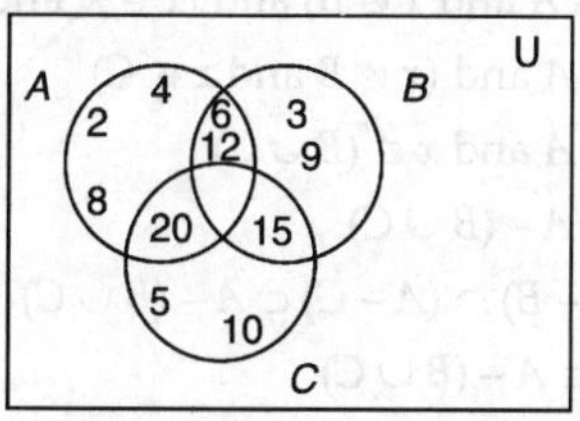

Q. 2. Let U be the set of all boys and girls in a school, G be the set of all girls in the school, B be the set of all boys in the school, and S be the set of all students in the school who take swimming. Some, but not all, students in the school take swimming. Draw a Venn diagram showing one of the possible inter relationship among sets U, G, B and S.
[NCERT Exemplar Q. 11, Page 14]

Sol. Relationship among sets U, G, B and S.

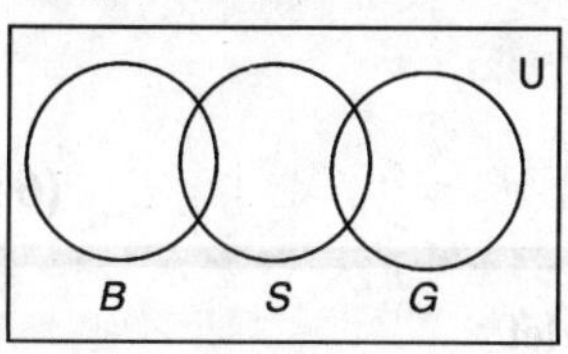

Determine whether each of the statement in Q.9-Q.13 is true or false. Justify your answer.

Q. 3. For all sets A and B, $(A - B) \cup (A \cap B) = A$
[NCERT Exemplar Q. 13, Page 14]

Sol. L.H.S. = $(A - B) \cup (A \cap B) = [(A - B) \cup A] \cap [(A - B) \cup B]$

$= A \cap (A \cup B) = A =$ R.H.S.

Q. 4. For all sets A, B and C, $A - (B - C) = C$
[NCERT Exemplar Q. 14, Page 14]

Sol. False

Let Is solve the given statement by the following Venn diagram.

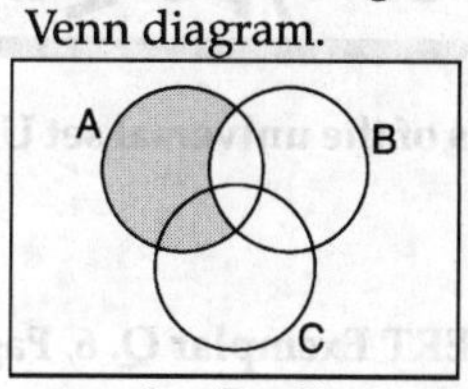

A – (B – C)

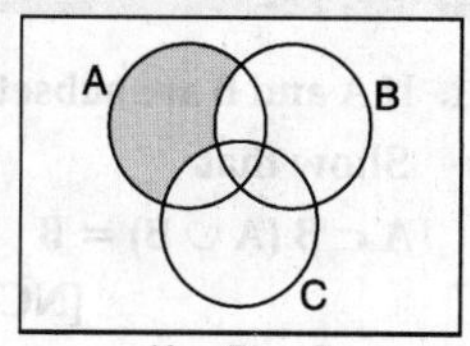

(A – B) – C

Clearly from the abouve diagrams, we calculate that $A - (B - C) \neq (A - B) - C$

Q. 5. For all sets A, B and C, if $A \subset B$, then $A \cap C \subset B \cup C$
[NCERT Exemplar Q. 15, Page 14]

Sol. True.

Let $x \in A \cap C$

$x \in A$ and $x \in C$

$x \in B$ and $x \in C$ $[\because A \subset B$, given$]$

$x \in (B \cap C) \Rightarrow (A \cap C) \subset (B \cap C)$

Q. 6. For all sets A, B and C, if $A \subset B$, then $A \cup C \subset B \cup C$
[NCERT Exemplar Q. 16, Page 14]

Sol. True.

Let $x \in A \cup C$

$x \in A$ or $x \in C$

$x \in B$ or $x \in C$ $[\because A \subset B]$

$x \in (B \cup C)$

$(A \cup C) \subset (B \cup C)$

Q. 7. For all sets A, B and C, if $A \subset C$ and $B \subset C$, then $A \cup B \subset C$.
[NCERT Exemplar Q. 17, Page 14]

Sol. True.

Let $x \in A \cup B$

$x \in A$ or $x \in B$

$x \in C$ or $x \in C$ $[\because A \subset C$ and $B \subset C]$

$x \in C \Rightarrow A \cup B \subset C$

Using properties of sets prove the statements given in Q.8-Q.11.

Q. 8. For all sets A and B, $A \cup (B - A) = A \cup B$
[NCERT Exemplar Q. 18, Page 14]

Sol. L.H.S $= A \cup (B - A)$

$= A \cup (B \cap A')$ $[\because A - B = A \cap B']$

$= (A \cup B) \cap (A \cup A')$
$= (A \cup B) \cap U [\because A \cup A' = U]$
$= A \cup B \quad [\because A \cap U = A]$
= R.H.S.

Q. 9. For all sets A and B, $A - (A - B) = A \cap B$
[NCERT Exemplar Q. 19, Page 14]

Sol. L.H.S. $= A - (A - B)$
$= A - (A \cap B') \quad [\because A - B = A \cap B']$
$= A \cap (A \cap B')'$
$= A \cap [A' \cup (B')'] \quad [\because (A \cap B)' = A' \cup B']$
$= A \cap [A' \cup B] \quad [\because (A')' = A]$
$= (A \cap A') \cup (A \cap B)$
$= \phi \cup (A \cap B)$
$= A \cap B$
= R.H.S.

Q. 10. For all sets A and B, $A - (A \cap B) = A - B$
[NCERT Exemplar Q. 20, Page 14]

Sol. L.H.S $= A - (A \cap B)$
$= A \cap (A \cap B)' \quad [\because A - B = A \cap B']$
$= A \cap (A' \cup B') \quad [\because (A \cap B)' = A' \cup B']$
$= (A \cap A') \cup (A \cap B')$
$= \phi \cup (A \cap B')$
$= A \cap B' \quad [\because \phi \cup A = A]$
$= A - B$ = R.H.S.

Q. 11. For all sets A and B, $(A \cup B) - B = A - B$
[NCERT Exemplar Q. 21, Page 14]

Sol. L.H.S. $= (A \cup B) - B$
$= (A \cup B) \cap B' \quad [\because A - B = A \cap B']$
$= (A \cap B') \cup (B \cap B')$
$= (A \cap B') \cup \phi \quad [\because B \cap B' = \phi]$
$= A - B \quad [\because A \cup \phi = A]$
= R.H.S.

Long Answer Type Question-I (4 marks each)

Q. 1. If A and B are subsets of the universal set U, then Show that
$A \subset B$ $(A \cup B) = B$
[NCERT Exemplar Q. 6, Page 13]

Sol. If $A \subset B$
Let $x \in A \cup B$
$x \in A$ or $x \in B \Rightarrow x \in B \quad [\because A \subset B]$
$(A \cup B) \subset B$ ...(i)
$B \subset (A \cup B)$ ...(ii)
From eqs. (i) and (ii)
$(A \cup B) = B$
If $(A \cup B) = B$
Let $y \in A$
$\Rightarrow y \in (A \cup B) \Rightarrow y \in B$
$\Rightarrow A \subset B$
Hence, $A \subset B \Leftrightarrow (A \cup B) = B$

Q. 2. For all sets A, B and C, show that $(A - B) \cap (A - C) = A - (B \cup C)$
[NCERT Exemplar Q. 12, Page 14]

Sol. To prove $(A - B) \cap (A - C) = A - (B \cup C)$
Let $x \in (A - B) \cap (A - B)$
$\Rightarrow x \in (A - B)$ and $x \in (A - C)$
$\Rightarrow (x \in A$ and $x \notin B)$ and $(x \in A$ and $x \notin C)$
$\Rightarrow x \in A$ and $(x \notin B$ and $x \notin C)$
$\Rightarrow x \in A$ and $x \notin (B \cup C)$
$\Rightarrow x \in A - (B \cup C)$
So, $(A - B) \cap (A - C) \subset A - (B \cup C)$ ... (i)
Let $y \in A - (B \cup C)$
$\Rightarrow y \in A$ and $y \notin (B \cup C)$
$\Rightarrow y \in A$ and $(y \notin B$ and $y \notin C)$
$\Rightarrow (y \in A$ and $y \notin B)$ and $(y \in A$ and $y \notin C)$
$\Rightarrow y \in (A - B)$ and $y \in (A - C)$
$\Rightarrow y \in (A - B) \cap (A - C)$
So, $A - (B \cup C) \subset (A - B) \cap (A - C)$ ... (ii)
From eq. (i) and (ii), we get
$A - (B \cup C) = (A - B) \cap (A - C)$

Long Answer Type Question-II (6 marks each)

Q. 1. Let A, B and C be sets. Then show that
[NCERT Exemplar Q. 23, Page 14]
$A \cap (B \cup C) = (A \cap B) \cup (A \cap C)$

Sol. Let $x \in A \cap (B \cup C)$
$x \in A$ and $x \in (B \cup C)$
$x \in A$ and $(x \in B$ or $x \in C)$
$(x \in A$ and $x \in B)$ or $(x \in A$ and $x \in C)$
$x \in A \cap B$ or $x \in A \cap C$
$x \in (A \cap B) \cup (A \cap C)$
$A \cap (B \cup C) \subset (A \cap B) \cup (A \cap C)$ ...(i)

Again, let
$y \in (A \cap B) \cup (A \cap C)$
$y \in (A \cap B)$ or $y \in (A \cap C)$
$(y \in A$ and $y \in B)$ or $(y \in A$ and $y \in C)$
$y \in A$ and $(y \in B$ or $y \in C)$
$y \in A$ and $y \in (B \cup C)$
$y \in A \cap (B \cup C)$
$(A \cap B) \cup (A \cap C) \subset A \cap (B \cup C)$ ...(ii)
from eqs (i) and (ii)
$A \cap (B \cup C) = (A \cap B) \cup (A \cap C)$

TOPIC-3
Application of Set Theory

Quick Review

➢ In this topic, we will discuss some word problems related to our daily life, which are based on union and intersection of two sets. Before solving these types of problems, we should know the following formulae.

- If A and B are two finite sets, then

  (a) $A \cap B = \phi$ *i.e.,* A and B are disjoint sets

  $\Rightarrow n(A \cup B) = n(A) + n(B)$

  (b) $(A \cap B) \neq \phi \Rightarrow n(A \cup B) = n(A) + n(B) - n(A \cap B)$

- If A and B are any two finite sets, then

  (a) number of elements in A only =

  $n(A - B) = n(A) - n(A \cap B)$

  (b) number of elements in B only =

  $n(B - A) = n(B) - n(A \cap B)$

- If A, B and C are three finite sets, then

  $n(A \cup B \cup C) = n(A) + n(B) + n(C) - n(A \cap B) - n(B \cap C) - n(A \cap C) + n(A \cap B \cap C)$

  If A, B and C are mutually disjoint sets, then

  $n(A \cup B \cup C) = n(A) + n(B) + n(C)$

- If A, B and C are three finite sets, then number of elements in A only $= n(A) - n(A \cap B) - n(A \cap C) + n(A \cap B \cap C)$

- If A, B and C are three finite sets, then number of elements in

  $(A \text{ and } B \text{ only}) = n(A \cap B) - n(A \cap B \cap C)$

- If A and B are two finite sets, then

  $n(A \Delta B) = n[(A - B) \cup (B - A)]$

  $= n(A - B) + n(B - A)$

  [since, $(A - B)$ and $(B - A)$ are disjoint sets]

  $= n(A) + n(B) - 2n(A \cap B)$

Multiple Choice Questions (1 mark each)

Q. 1. In a class of 60 students, 25 students play cricket and 20 students play tennis and 10 students play both the games.

Then, the number of students who play neither is

(A) 0 **(B)** 25

(C) 35 **(D)** 45

[NCERT Exemplar Q. 35, Page 16]

Ans. Correct option : (B)

$$n(C \cup T) = n(C) + n(T) - n(C \cap T)$$
$$= 25 + 20 - 10 = 35$$
$$\therefore \quad n(C' \cap T') = n(u) - n(C \cup T)$$
$$= 60 - 35 = 25$$

Q. 2. In a town of 840 persons, 450 persons read Hindi, 300 read English and 200 read both. Then the number of persons who read neither Hindi nor English newspaper are.

(A) 210 **(B)** 290

(C) 180 **(D)** 260

[NCERT Exemplar Q. 36, Page 16]

Ans. Correct option : (B)

$$n(H \cup E) = n(H) + n(E) - n(H \cap E)$$
$$= 450 + 300 - 200 = 550$$
$$\therefore \quad n(H' \cap E') = n(u) - n(H \cup E)$$
$$= 840 - 550 = 290$$

Q. 3. A survey shows that 63% of the people watch a news channel whereas 76% watch another channel. If x% of the people watch both channel, then

(A) $x = 35$ (B) $x = 63$
(C) $39 \le x \le 63$ (D) $x = 39$

[NCERT Exemplar Q. 38, Page 17]

Ans. Correct option : (C)

Here, $n(p \cup q) \ge n(p) + n(q) - n(p \cap q)$

$100 \ge 63 + 76 - x \Rightarrow x \ge 39$

Now, $n(p) = 63\ n(p \cap q) \le n(p) \Rightarrow x \le 63$

Hence, $39 \le x \le 63$

Long Answer Type Questions-II (6 marks each)

Q. 1. Out of 100 students; 15 passed in English, 12 passed Mathematics, 8 in Science, 6 in English and Mathematics, 7 in Mathematics and Science; 4 in English and Science; 4 in all the three. Find how many passed

(i) in English and Mathematics but not in Science

(ii) in Mathematics and Science but not in English

(iii) in Mathematics only

(iv) in more than one subject only

[NCERT Exemplar, Q. 24, Page 14]

Sol. Let the number of students passed in Mathematics M, E be in English and S be in science. Then, $n(U) = 100$, $n(M) = 12$, $n(E) = 15$, $n(S) = 8$, $n(E \cap M) = 6$, $n(M \cap S) = 7$, $n(E \cap S) = 4$ and $n(E \cap M \cap S) = 4$

Let us draw a Venn diagram.

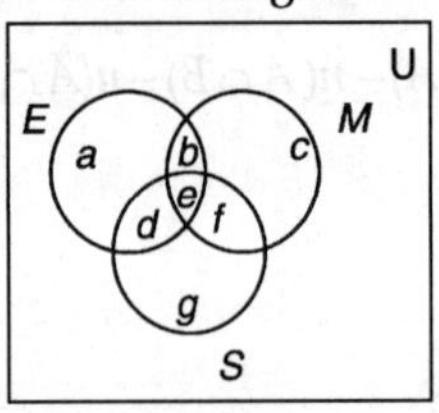

According to Venn diagram, we get

$a + b + d + e = 15$ ...(i)

$b + c + e + f = 12$ ...(ii)

$d + e + f + g = 8$ ...(iii)

$n(E \cap M) = 6 \therefore b + e = 6$ ...(iv)

$n(M \cap S) = 4 \therefore e + f = 7$ ...(v)

$n(E \cap S) = 4 \therefore d + e = 4$ ...(vi)

$n(M \cap E \cap S) = 4 \therefore e = 4$ ...(vii)

From eqs. (iv) and (vii), we get $b + 4 = 6 \therefore b = 2$

From eqs. (v) and (vii), we get $4 + f = 7 \therefore f = 3$

From eqs. (vi) and (vii), we get $d + 4 = 4 \therefore d = 0$

From eqs. (i), we get

$a + b + d + e = 15 \Rightarrow a + 2 + 0 + 4 = 15 \Rightarrow a = 9$

From eqs. (iii), we get

$d + e + f + g = 8 \Rightarrow 0 + 4 + 3 + g = 8 \Rightarrow g = 1$

$\therefore$ (i) No. of students who passed in English and Mathematics but not in science, $b = 2$

(ii) No. of students who passed in Mathematics and science but not in English, $f = 3$

(iii) No. of students who passed in Mathematics only, $c = 3$

(iv) No. of students who passed in more than one subject $= b + e + d + f = 9$.

Q. 2. In a class of 60 students, 25 students play cricket and 20 students play tennis, and 10 students play both the games. Find the number of students who play neither?

[NCERT Exemplar, Q. 25, Page 14]

Sol. Let C and T denote the students who play cricket and tennis, respectively.

Given, $n(C) = 25$, $n(T) = 20$, $n(C \cap T) = 10$ and $n(U) = 60$

Using identity,

$$n(C \cup T) = n(C) + n(T) - n(C \cap T)$$
$$= 25 + 20 - 10$$
$$= 35$$

$\therefore$ Number of students who play neither

$$= n(U) - n(C \cup T)$$
$$= 60 - 35$$
$$= 25$$

Q. 3. In a survey of 200 students of a school, it was found that 120 study Mathematics, 90 study physics and 70 study Chemistry 40 study Mathematics and physics, 30 study Physics and Chemistry, 50 study Chemistry and Mathematics and 20 none of these subject. Find the number of students who study all the three subjects

[NCERT Exemplar, Q. 26, Page 15]

Sol. Let M, P and C denote the students studying Mathematics, Physics and Chemistry.

Also, $n(U) = 200$, $n(M) = 120$, $n(P) = 90$, $n(C) = 70$, $n(M \cap P) = 40$,

$n(P \cap C) = 30$, $n(M \cap C) = 50$, $n(M \cup P \cup C)' = 20$

Now, the number of students who study all the three subjects *i.e.*, $n(P \cap C \cap M)$

Now, we have

$n(M \cup P \cup C)' = 20$

$n(M \cup P \cup C)' = n(U) - n(M \cup P \cup C)$

$20 = 200 - n(M \cup P \cup C)$

$n(M \cup P \cup C) = 200 - 20 = 180$

$n(M \cup P \cup C) = n(M) + n(P) + n(C) - n(M \cap P) - n(P \cap C) - n(C \cap M) + n(C \cap M \cap P)$

$180 = 120 + 90 + 70 - 40 - 30 - 50 + n(C \cap M \cap P)$

$180 = 280 - 120 + n(C \cap M \cap P)$

$180 + 120 - 280 = n(P \cap C \cap M)$

$n(P \cap C \cap M) = 300 - 280 = 20$

Q. 4. In a town of 10,000 families it was found that 40% families buy newspaper *A*,10% families buy newspaper *C*, 5% families buy *A* and *B*, 3% buy *B* and *C* and 4% buy *A* and *C*. If 2% families buy all the three newspapers. Find

(a) The number of families which buy newspaper A only.

(b) The number of families which buy none of *A*, *B* and *C* [NCERT Exemplar, Q. 27, Page 15]

Sol. Let A be the set of families which buy newspaper A, B be the set of families which buy newspaper B and C be the set of families which buy newspaper C.

Then, n (U) = 10,000, n(A) = 40%, n(B) = 20% and n(C) = 10%, $n(A \cap B) = 5\%$, $n(B \cap C) = 3\%$, $n(A \cap C) = 4\%$ and $n(A \cap B \cap C) = 2\%$

(a) Percentage of families which buy news paper A only

$= n(A) - n(A \cap B) - n(A \cap C) + n(A \cap B \cap C)$

$= (40 - 5 - 4 + 2)\% = 33\%$

$\therefore$ Number of families buy newspaper A only

$= 10{,}000 \times \frac{33}{100} = 3300$

(b) Percentage of families which buy none of A, B and C

$= n(U) - n(A \cup B \cup C)$

$= n(U) - [n(A) + n(B) + n(C) - n(A \cup B) - n(B \cap C) - n(A \cap C) + n(A \cap B \cap C)$

$= 100 - [40 + 20 + 10 - 5 - 3 - 4 + 2]$

$= 100 - 60 = 40\%$

$\therefore$ Number of families which by none of A, B and C

$= 10{,}000 \times \frac{40}{100} = 4000$

Q. 5. In a group of 50 students, the number of students studying French, English, Sanskrit were found to be as follows:

French = 17, English = 13, Sanskrit = 15 French and English = 09, English and Sanskrit = 4 French and Sanskrit = 5, English, French and Sanskrit = 3. Find the number of students who study

(i) French only

(ii) English only

(iii) Sanskrit only

(iv) English and Sanskrit but not French

(v) French and Sanskrit but not English

(vi) French and English but not Sanskrit

(vii) at least one of the three languages

(viii) none of the three languages

[NCERT Exemplar, Q. 28, Page 15]

Sol. Let, total no. of students – 50 $\rightarrow n(U) - 50$

No. of students who study French = 17 $\Rightarrow n(F) = 17$

No. of students who study English = 13 $\Rightarrow n(E) = 13$

No. of students who study Sanskrit = 15 $\Rightarrow n(S) = 15$

No. of students who study French and English = 9 $\Rightarrow n(F \cap E) = 9$

Number of students who study English and Sanskrit = 4 $\Rightarrow n(E \cap S) = 4$

Number of students who study French and Sanskrit = 5 $\Rightarrow n(F \cap S) = 5$

Number of students who study French, English and Sanskrit = 3 $\Rightarrow n(F \cap E \cap S) = 3$

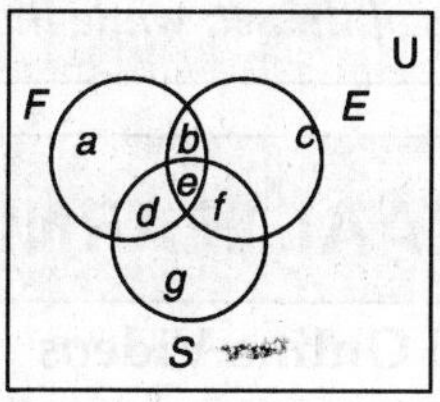

$n(F) = 17$ (i)

$a + b + d + e = 17$

$n(E) = 13$

$b + c + e + f = 13$ (ii)

$n(S) = 15$

$d + e + f + g = 15$ (iii)

$n(F \cap E) = 9 \quad \therefore b + e = 9$ (iv)

$n(E \cap S) = 4 \quad \therefore e + f = 4$ (v)

$n(F \cap S) = 5 \quad \therefore d + e = 5$ (vi)

$n(F \cap E \cap S) = 3 \quad \therefore e = 3$ (vii)

From (iv), $b + 3 = 9 \Rightarrow b = 9 - 3 = 6$

From (v), $3 + f = 4 \Rightarrow f = 4 - 3 = 1$

From (vi), $d + 3 = 5 \Rightarrow d = 5 - 3 = 2$

Now, from eqs. (i), $a + 6 + 2 + 3 = 17 \Rightarrow a = 17 - 11 \Rightarrow a = 6$

Now, from eQ. (ii), $6 + c + 3 + 1 = 13 \Rightarrow c = 13 - 10 \Rightarrow c = 3$

From eQ. (iii), $2 + 3 + 1 + g = 15 \Rightarrow g = 15 \Rightarrow 6 \Rightarrow g = 9$.

(i) No. of students who study French only, $a = 6$

(ii) No. of students who study English only, $c = 6$

(iii) No. of students who study Sanskrit only, $g = 9$

(iv) No. of students who study English and Sanskrit but not French, $f = 1$

(v) No. of students who study French and Sanskrit but not English, $d = 2$

(vi) No. of students who study French and English but not Sanskrit, $b = 6$

(vii) No. of students who study at least one of the three languages $= a + b + c + d + e + f + g$ $= 6 + 6 + 3 + 2 + 3 + 1 + 9 = 30$

(viii) No. of students who study none of the three languages = 50 – 30 = 20.

EXPERT ADVICE

- *Students are advised to understand the definitions and apply these definitions while attempting the paper.*
- *One 4 mark question is sure from the topic "Practice problem on union intersection of two and three sets."*
- *Remember intervals are subsets of R.*
- *In roaster form, all the elements in the sets are listed whereas in set builder form, all the elements of a set posses a single common property which is not possessed by any elements out side the set.*
- *In ABC and A ≠ B, then A is proper subset of B. In such cases B is called super set of set A.*
- *Venn diagrams normally comprise overlapping circles. The interior of the circle symbolically represents the elements of the set, while the exterior represents elements that one not members of the set.*

OSWAAL LEARNING TOOLS

***For* Suggested Online Videos**

Visit : *https://youtu.be/rRk0d6P4oUI* **Or Scan the Code**	**Visit :** *https://youtu.be/vGelH3Jibt4* **Or Scan the Code**

Visit : *https://goo.gl/RQFi3W* **Or Scan the Code**

CHAPTER

2 RELATIONS & FUNCTIONS

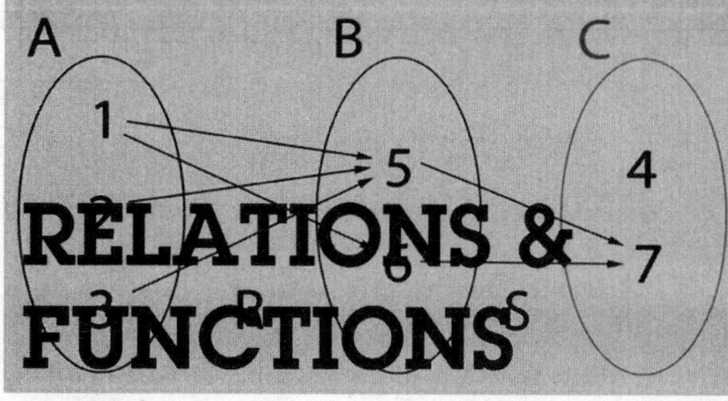

Chapter Objectives

➤ *Ordered pair; Cartesian product of sets; Number of elements in the cartesian product of two finite sets; Cartesian product of the sets of real with itself (upto R×R×R); Definition of relation; Pictorial diagrams; Domain; Co-domain and range of a relation; Void relation; Universal relation; Identify relation; Reflexive relation; Symmetric relation; Anti-symmetric relation; Transitive relation; Equivalence relation; Partial order relation; Functions as a special type of relation; Pictorial representation of a function; Domain, Co-domain and range of a function; Real valued functions: domain and range of these functions; Constant, Identify, Polynomial, Rational, Modulus, Signum, Exponential, Logarithmic and Greatest integer functions with their graphs; Sum, Difference, Product and Quotient of functions.*

TOPIC-1
Cartesian Product and Relations

TOPIC - 1
Cartesian Product and Relations P. 15

TOPIC - 2
Functions and their Types P. 19

Quick Review

➤ For two non–empty sets A and B, the Cartesian Product $A \times B$ is the set of all ordered pairs of elements from sets A and B.

➤ In symbolic form, it is written as,

$$A \times B = \{(a, b) : a \in A, b \in B\}$$

➤ Thus, Cartesian Product of two sets contains the set which represents the coordinates of all the points in two dimensional space.
e.g., If $A = \{a, b, c\}$ and $B = \{p, q\}$ then,
(i) $A \times B = \{(a, p)(a, q)(b, p)(b, q),(c, p)(c, q)\}$
(ii) $B \times A = \{(p, a)(p, b)(p, c), (q, a) (q, b), (q, c)\}$

➤ **Diagrammatic Representation of Cartesian Product of Two Sets**

★ In order to represent A × B, by an arrow diagram, we first draw Venn diagrams representing sets A and B one opposite to the other as shown in given figure and write the elements of sets.
Now, we draw line segments starting from each element of set A and terminating to each element of set B.
e.g., If $A = \{1, 2, 3\}$ and $B = \{f, g\}$,
Then following figure gives the arrow diagram of $A \times B$.

TIPS...

- *Revise the important formulae of this chapter Relations and function and then practice the important questions.*
- *Understand the mapping using diagrams.*
- *Learn all the properties of law's applicable in functions and relation.*
- *Learn the algorithm to find the inverse of the functions.*
- *Remember the graphs of the standard functions.*

TRICKS...

- *To evaluate a function f(x), for a particular value of x, just substitute that value everywhere you see x.*
- *For many functions, you can solve it by plugging the given values in the function.*
- *Plug the values into the functions by replacing the strange symbol and solve it.*
- *The universal relation on non-void set A is reflexive.*
- *The identity relation is always a reflexive relation but the converse may or may not be true.*

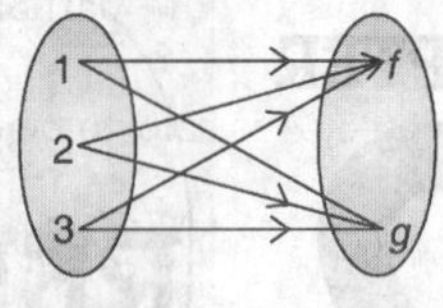

If A, B and C are three sets, then (a, b, c) where $a \in A, b \in B$ and $c \in C$ is called an ordered triplet.

Note :

(i) If $R = \phi$, then R is called an empty or void relation.

(ii) If $R = A \times B$, then R is called the universal relation.

(iii) If R_1 and R_2 are two relations from A to B, then $R_1 \cup R_2$, $R_1 \cap R_2$ and $R_1 - R_2$ are also relations from A to B. In a relation from A to B, such that

$$R = \{(a, b) : a \in A \text{ and } b \in B\}$$

Here, the set of all first elements of ordered pair in a relation R is called the **Domain** and set of all second elements of ordered pairs in a relation R is called the **range.**

The set B is called the **Co-domain** of relation R.

$$\textbf{Range} \subseteq \textbf{Co-domain.}$$

Know the Terms

➤ **Cartesian Product of Sets**

For two sets A and B (non–empty sets), the set of all ordered pairs (a, b) such that $a \in A$ and $b \in B$ is called cartesian product of the sets A and B, denoted by $A \times B$.

$$A \times B = \{(a, b) : a \in A \text{ and } b \in B\}$$

If there are three sets A, B, C and $a \in A$, $b \in B$ and $c \in C$, then we form an ordered triplet (a, b, c). The set of all ordered triplets (a, b, c) is called the cartesian product of these sets A, B and C.

i.e., $A \times B \times C = \{(a, b, c) : a \in A, b \in B, c \in C\}$

➤ **Number of Elements**

If the set A has m elements and the set B has n elements then the number of elements in the cartesian product set is $m \times n$ elements.

i.e., set $A = m$ elements; set $B = n$ elements

Then $n(A \times B) = m \times n$ elements

➤ **Domain and Range of a Relation**

Let R be a relation from a set A to set B. Then, set of all first components or coordinates of the ordered pairs belonging to R is called the domain of R, while the set of all second components or coordinates of the ordered pairs belonging to R is called the range of R.

Thus, domain of $R = \{a : (a, b) \in R\}$ and range of $R = \{b : (a, b) \in R\}$

➤ **Types of Relations**

(i) Void Relation : As $\phi \subset A \times A$, for any set A, so ϕ is a relation on A, called the empty or void relation.

(ii) Universal Relation : Since, $A \times A \subseteq A \times A$, so $A \times A$ is a relation on A, called the universal relation.

(iii) Identity Relation : The relation $I_A = \{(a, a) : a \in A\}$ is called the identity relation on A.

(iv) Reflexive Relation : A relation R is said to be reflexive relation, if every element of A is related to itself.

Thus, $(a, a) \in R, \forall a \in A \Rightarrow R$ is reflexive.

(v) Symmetric Relation : A relation R is said to be symmetric relation, iff

$$(a, b) \in R \Rightarrow (b, a) \in R, \forall a, b \in A$$

i.e., $$a R b \Rightarrow b R a, \forall a, b \in A$$

$$\Rightarrow R \text{ is symmetric.}$$

(vi) Anti–Symmetric Relation : A relation R is said to be anti–symmetric relation, iff

$$(a, b) \in R \text{ and } (b, a) \in R \Rightarrow a = b, \forall a, b \in A$$

(vii) Transitive Relation : A relation R is said to be transitive relation, iff $(a, b) \in R$ and $(b, c) \in R$

$$\Rightarrow (a, c) \in R, \forall a, b, c \in A$$

(viii) Equivalence Relation : A relation R is said to be an equivalence relation, if it is simultaneously reflexive, symmetric and transitive on a set A.

(ix) Partial Order Relation : A relation R is said to be a partial order relation, if it is simultaneously reflexive, symmetric and anti–symmetric on a set A.

(x) Total Order Relation : A relation R on a set A is said to be a total order relation on A, if R is a partial order relation on A.

➤ **Properties of Cartesian Product**

For three sets A, B and C

(i) $n(A \times B) = n(A)\,n(B)$

(ii) $A \times \phi = \phi$ and $\phi \times A = \phi$

(iii) $A \times (B \cup C) = (A \times B) \cup (A \times C)$

(iv) $A \times (B \cap C) = (A \times B) \cap (A \times C)$

(v) $A \times (B - C) = (A \times B) - (A \times C)$

(vi) $(A \times B) \cap (C \times D) = (A \cap C) \times (B \cap D)$

(vii) If $A \subseteq B$ and $C \subseteq D$, then $(A \times C) \subset (B \times D)$

(viii) If $A \subseteq B$, then $A \times A \subseteq (A \times B) \cap (B \times A)$

(ix) $A \times B = B \times A \Leftrightarrow A = B$

(x) If either A or B is an infinite set, then $A \times B$ is an infinite set.

(xi) $A \times (B \cup C) = (A \times B) \cup (A \times C)$

(xii) $A \times (B \cap C) = (A \times B) \cap (A \times C)$

(xiii) If A and B be any two non–empty sets having n elements in common, then $A \times B$ and $B \times A$ have n^2 elements in common.

(xiv) If $A \neq B$, then $A \times B \neq B \times A$

(xvi) If $A \subseteq B$, then $A \times C \subseteq B \times C$ for any set C.

Multiple Choice Questions **(1 mark each)**

[A] Objective Type Questions

Q. 1. Let $n(A) = m$, and $n(B) = n$. Then the total number of non-empty relations that can be defined from A to B is

(A) m^n (B) $n^m - 1$

(C) $mn - 1$ (D) $2^{mn} - 1$

[NCERT Exemplar Q. 24, Page 30]

Ans. Correct option : (D)

Total no. of relation from A to B = No. of subsets of $A \times B = 2^{mn}$

$\therefore$ Total no. of non-empty relations $= 2^{mn} - 1$

Q. 2. If $[x]^2 - 5[x] + 6 = 0$, where [.] denote the greatest integer function, then

(A) $x \in [3, 4]$ (B) $x \in (2, 3]$

(C) $x \in [2, 3]$ (D) $x \in [2, 4)$

[NCERT Exemplar Q. 25, Page 30]

Ans. Correct option : (D)

We have, $[x]^2 - 5[x] + 6 = 0$

$\Rightarrow \quad ([x] - 3)([x] - 2) = 0$

$\Rightarrow \quad [x] = 2, 3$

for $\quad [x] = 2, x \in [2, 3)$

and for $\quad [x] = 3, x \in [3, 4)$ or $x \in [2, 4)$

[B] True and False

Q. 1. The ordered pair (5, 2) belongs to the relation $R = \{(x, y) : y = x - 5, x, y \in Z\}$

[NCERT Exemplar Q. 38, Page 33]

Sol. False $\quad x - 5 = y$

$\Rightarrow \quad y = 0$

when $\quad x = 5$

$\therefore$ (5, 2) does not belong to the relation.

Q. 2. If $P = \{1, 2\}$, then $P \times P \times P = \{(1, 1, 1), (2, 2, 2), (1, 2, 2), (2, 1, 1)\}$

[NCERT Exemplar Q. 39, Page 33]

Sol. False $\quad P = [1, 2]$

$P \times P = \{(1, 1)(1, 2)(2, 11)(2, 2)\}$

$P{\times}P{\times}P = \{(1, 1, 1,), (1, 2, 1), (2, 1, 1), (2, 2, 1), (1, 1, 2), (1, 2, 2)(2, 2, 2)(2, 1, 2)\}$

Q. 3. If $A = \{1, 2, 3\}$, $B = \{3, 4\}$ and $C = \{4, 5, 6\}$, then $(A \times B) \cup (A \times C) = \{(1, 3), (1, 4), (1, 5), (1, 6), (2, 3), (2, 4), (2, 5), (2, 6), (3, 3), (3, 4), (3, 5), (3, 6)\}$.

[NCERT Exemplar Q. 40, Page 33]

Sol. True

Q. 4. If $(x - 2, y + 5) = \left(-2, \frac{1}{3}\right)$ are two equal ordered pairs, then $x = 4, y = \frac{-14}{3}$

[NCERT Exemplar Q. 41, Page 33]

Sol. False $\quad x - 2 = -2$

$x = 0$

$y + 5 = \frac{1}{3}$

$y = -\frac{14}{3}$

Short Answer Type Questions-II (2 marks each)

Q. 1. If $A = \{-1, 2, 3\}$ and $B = \{1, 3\}$, then determine
(i) $A \times B$ (ii) $B \times A$
(iii) $B \times B$ (iv) $A \times A$
[NCERT Exemplar Q. 1, Page 27]

Sol. Given, $A = \{-1,2,3\}$ and $B = \{1,3\}$

(i) $A \times B = \{-1,2,3\} \times \{1,3\}$
$= \{(-1,1),(-1,3),(2,1),(2,3),(3,1),(3,3)\}$

(ii) $B \times A = \{1,3\} \times \{-1,2,3\}$
$= \{(1,-1),(1,2),(1,3),(3,-1),(3,2),(3,3)\}$

(iii) $B \times B = \{1,3\} \times \{1,3\}$
$= \{(1,1),(1,3),(3,1),(3,3)\}$

(iv) $A \times A = \{-1,2,3\} \times \{-1,2,3\}$
$= \{(-1,-1),(-1,2),(-1,3),(2,-1),(2,2),(2,3),(3,-1),(3,2),(3,3)\}$

Q. 2. If $P = \{x : x < 3, x \in N\}$, $Q = \{x : x \leq 2, x \in W\}$, then find $(P \cup Q) \times (P \cap Q)$, where W is the set of whole number. [NCERT Exemplar Q. 2, Page 28]

Sol. We have, $P = \{x : x < 3, x \in N\} = \{1,2\}$
and $Q = \{x : x \leq 2, x \in W\} = \{0,1,2\}$
Now, $P \cup Q = \{1,2\} \cup \{0,1,2\} = \{0,1,2\}$
$P \cap Q = \{1,2\} \cap \{0,1,2\} = \{1,2\}$
$\therefore (P \cup Q) \times (P \cap Q) = \{0,1,2\} \times \{1,2\}$
$= \{(0,1),(0,2),(1,1),(1,2),(2,1),(2,2)\}$

Q. 3. If $R = \{(x, y) : x, y \in W, x^2 + y^2 = 25\}$, then find the domain and range of R.
[NCERT Exemplar Q. 6, Page 28]

Sol. Given, $R = \{(x, y) : x, y \in W, x^2 + y^2 = 25\}$
$= \{(0, 5), (3, 4), (4, 3), (5, 0)\}$.
$\therefore$ Domain of R = Set of first element of ordered pairs in R
$= \{0, 3, 4, 5\}$
and Range of R = Set of second element of ordered pairs in R
$= \{5, 4, 3, 0\}$

Q. 4. If $R_1 = \{(x, y) \mid y = 2x + 7$, where $x \in R$ and $-5 \leq x \leq 5\}$ is a relation. Then, find the domain and range of R_1.
[NCERT Exemplar Q. 7, Page 28]

Sol. Given, $R_1 = \{(x, y) \mid y = 2x + 7$, where $x \in R$ and $-5 \leq x \leq 5\}$
$\therefore$ Domain of $R_1 = \{-5 \leq x \leq 5, x \in R\}$
$= [-5, 5]$
Also, $y = 2x + 7$ (given)
$\Rightarrow$ When $x = -5$, then $y = 2(-5) + 7 = -3$
and when $x = 5$, then $y = 2(5) + 7 = 17$
Hence, range of $R_1 = \{-3 \leq y \leq 17, y \in R\}$
$= [-3, 17]$

Q. 5. If $R_2 = \{(x, y) \mid x$ and y are integers and $x^2 + y^2 = 64\}$ is a relation, then find the value of R_2.
[NCERT Exemplar Q. 8, Page 28]

Sol. Given, $R_2 = \{(x, y) \mid x$ and y are integers and $x^2 + y^2 = 64\}$
$\because$ 64 is the sum of squares of 0 and ± 8.
When $x = 0$, then $y^2 = 64 \Rightarrow y = \pm 8$
$x = 8$, then $y^2 = 64 - 8^2 \Rightarrow 64 - 64 = 0$
$x = -8$, then $y^2 = 64 - (-8)^2 \Rightarrow 64 - 64 = 0$
$\therefore R_2 = \{(0, 8), (0, -8), (8, 0), (-8, 0)\}$

Q. 6. If $R_3 = \{(x, |x|) \mid x$ is a real number$\}$ is a relation, then find domain and range of R_3.
[NCERT Exemplar Q. 9, Page 28]

Sol. Given, $R_3 = \{(x, |x|) \mid x$ is a real number$\}$
$\therefore$ Domain of $R_3 = R$
Since, image of any real number under R_3 is positive real number or zero.
$\therefore$ Range of $R_3 = R^+ \cup \{0\}$ or $[0, \infty)$

Long Answer Type Question-I (4 marks each)

Q. 1. If $A = \{x : x \in W, x < 2\}$, $B = \{x : x \in N, 1 < x < 5\}$ and $C = \{3, 5\}$, then find (i) $A \times (B \cap C)$ (ii) $A \times (B \cup C)$ [NCERT Exemplar Q. 3, Page 28]

Sol. We have, $A = \{x : x \in W, x < 2\} = \{0,1\}$
$B = \{x : x \in N, 1 < x < 5\} = \{2,3,4\}$
and $C = \{3, 5\}$

(i) Now, $B \cap C = \{2, 3, 4\} \cap \{3, 5\}$
$= \{3\}$
$\therefore A \times (B \cap C) = \{0, 1\} \times \{3\}$
$= \{(0, 3), (1, 3)\}$

(ii) Now, $B \cup C = \{2, 3, 4\} \cup \{3, 5\}$
$= \{2, 3, 4, 5\}$
$\therefore A \times (B \cup C) = \{0,1\} \times \{2, 3, 4, 5\}$
$= \{(0, 2), (0, 3), (0, 4), (0, 5), (1, 2), (1, 3), (1, 4), (1, 5)\}$

Q. 2. In each of the following cases, find a and b.
(i) $(2a + b, a - b) = (8, 3)$
(ii) $\left(\frac{a}{4}, a - 2b\right) = (0, 6 + b)$
[NCERT Exemplar Q. 4, Page 28]

Sol. We know that, two ordered pairs are equal, if their corresponding first and second elements are equal.

(i) We have, $(2a + b, a - b) = (8,3)$
$\therefore 2a + b = 8$ (i)

and $a-b=3$ ...(ii)

From eq. (ii), we get

$$b=a-3 \quad ...(iii)$$

On substituting, $b=a-3$, in eq. (i), we get

$\Rightarrow 2a+(a-3)=8$

$\Rightarrow 2a+a-3=8$

$\Rightarrow 3a=11$

$\Rightarrow a=\frac{11}{3}$

Again, on substituting $a=\frac{11}{3}$ in eq. (iii), we get

$$b=\frac{11}{3}-3$$

$$\Rightarrow \quad b=\frac{2}{3}$$

$\therefore \quad a=\frac{11}{3}$ and $b=\frac{2}{3}$

(ii) $\left(\frac{a}{4}, a-2b\right) = (0, 6+b)$

$\therefore \quad \frac{a}{4} = 0, a = 0$

$a - 2b = 6 + b$ ...(i)

Put value of $a = 0$ in eq. (i)

$0 - 2b = 6 + b$

$-3b = 6$

$b = -\frac{6}{3} = -2$

$a = 0$ and $b = -2$

Q. 3. $A = \{1, 2, 3, 4, 5\}$, $S = \{(x, y) : x \in A, y \in A\}$, then find the ordered which satisfy the conditions given below.

(i) $x + y = 5$

(ii) $x + y < 5$

(iii) $x + y > 8$ [NCERT Exemplar Q. 5, Page 28]

Sol. Given, $A = \{1, 2, 3, 4, 5\}$ and $S = \{(x, y) : x \in A, y \in A\}$

(i) The set of ordered pairs satisfying $x + y = 5$ is $\{(1, 4), (2, 3), (3, 2), (4, 1)\}$.

(ii) The set of ordered pairs satisfying $x + y < 5$ is $\{(1, 1), (1, 2), (1, 3), (2, 1), (2, 2), (3, 1)\}$.

(iii) The set of ordered pairs satisfying $x + y > 8$ is $\{(4, 5), (5, 4), (5, 5)\}$

TOPIC-2
Functions and their Types

Quick Review

- If f is a function from a set A to Set B, then we write,

$$f: A \rightarrow B \text{ or } A \xrightarrow{f} B$$

and it is read as f is a function from A to B.

If $(a, b) \in f \Rightarrow f(a) = b$.

Here, b is the **image** of a under f and a is called the **pre–image** of b under f.

- **Few properties to be known :**

(i) For any real number x, we have

$$\sqrt{x^2}=|x|$$

(ii) If n is an integer and x is a real number between n and $n + 1$, then

(a) $[-n] = -[n]$ (b) $[x + k] = [x] + k$ for any integer

(c) $[-x] = -[x] - 1$ (d) $[-x] = -[x] + 1$, where $x \in R - Z$

(iii) For any real function,

$f: D \rightarrow R$ and $n \in N$, we define

$$\underbrace{(f f f....f)(X)}_{n \text{ times}} = \underbrace{f(x) f(x)....f(x)}_{n \text{ times}} = \{f(x)\}^n, \forall x \in D$$

Know the Terms

- **Domain, Co-domain and Range of a Function**

If f is a function from A to B and each element of A corresponds to one and only one element of B, whereas every element in B need not be the image of some x in A. Then the set A is called the **domain** of function f and the set B is called the **co-domain** of f.

The subset of B containing the images of elements of A is called the **range** of the function.

Thus, if a function f is expressed as the set of ordered pairs, then the domain of f is the **set of all first elements** of ordered pairs and the range of f is **the set of second elements** of ordered pairs of f. *i.e.*,

D_f = Domain of $f = \{a : (a, b) \in f\}$

R_f = Range of $f = \{b : (a, b) \in f\}$

➤ **Graphs of some Standard functions**

(a) Identity function: Let R be the set of real numbers. A real valued function f is defined as $f : R \to R$ by $y = f(x) = x$ for each value of $x \in R$. Such a function is called the identity function.

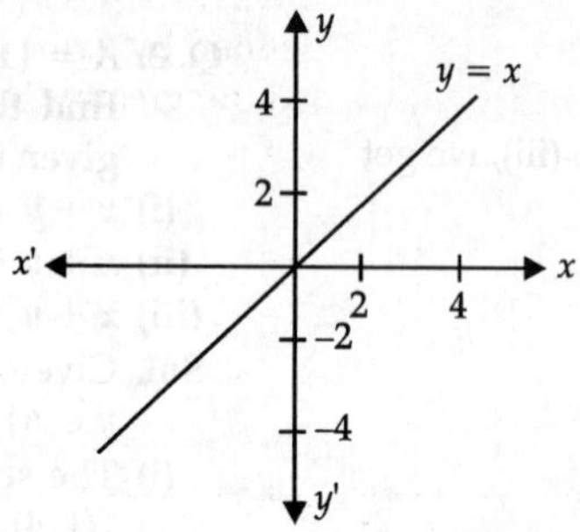

Domain = R and Range = R

(b) Constant function:

The function $f : R \to R$ defined by $f(x) = c$ for each $x \in R$ is called constant function. (where c is a constant)

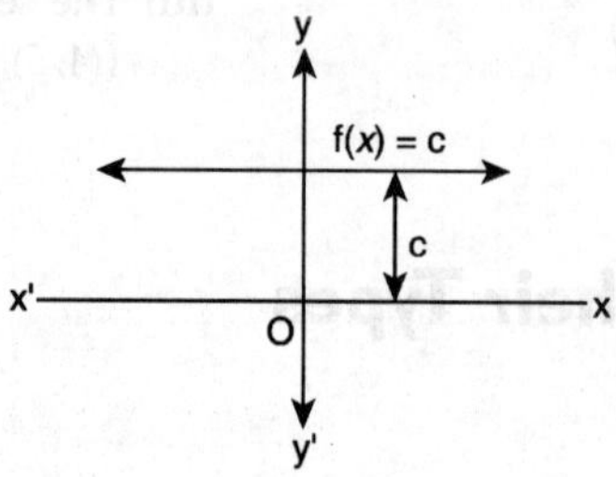

Domain = R and Range = $\{c\}$

(c) Modulus function: The function $f : R \to R$ defined by $f(x) = |x|$ for each $x \in R$ is called modulus function or absolute valued function.

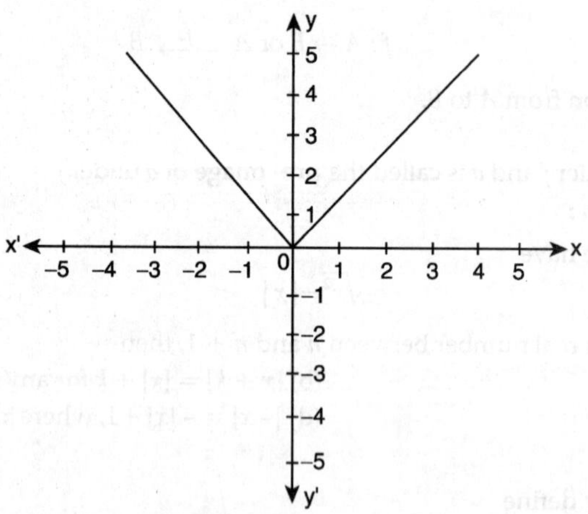

i. e., $f(x) = \begin{cases} x, & x \geq 0 \\ -x, & x < 0 \end{cases}$

Domain = R and Range = $R^+ \cup \{0\} = \{x : x \in R; x \geq 0\}$

(d) Signum function : Let R be the set of real numbers, then the function $f : R \to R$ defined by

$$f(x) = \frac{|x|}{x} = \begin{cases} 1, & x > 0 \\ 0, & x = 0 \\ -1, & x < 0 \end{cases}$$

is known as signum function.

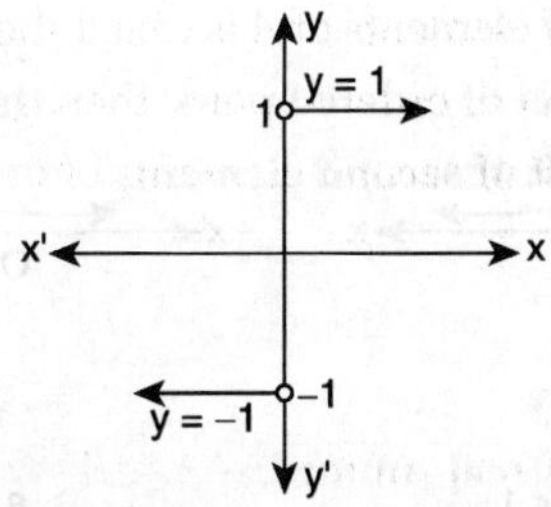

Domain = R and Range = $\{-1, 0, 1\}$

(e) Greatest Integer function : The function $f : R \to R$ defined by $f(x) = [x]$, $x \in R$ assumes the value of the greatest integer, less than or equal to x, such a function is called the greatest integer function.

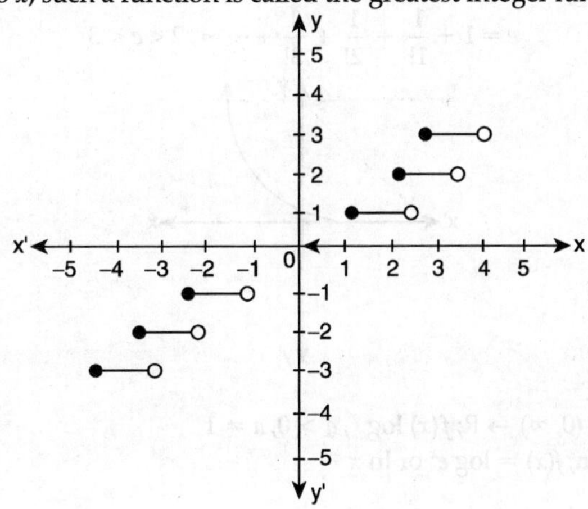

From the definition of $[x]$, we have

$$\begin{aligned}[x] &= -1, \text{ for } -1 < x < 0\\ &= 0, \text{ for } 0 \le x < 1\\ &= 1, \text{ for } 1 \le x < 2\\ &= 2, \text{ for } 2 \le x < 3\\ \text{Domain } &= R \text{ and Range} = Z\end{aligned}$$

➤ **Graphs of some other important functions**

- ***f*: *R* → *R*, *f*(*x*) = x^2**

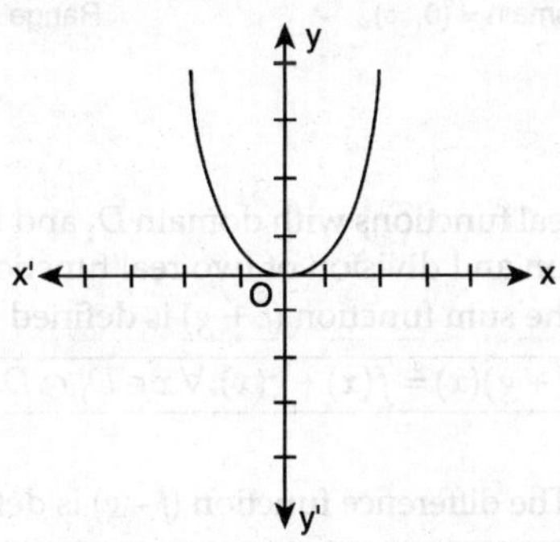

Domain = R and Range = $[0, \infty)$

- ***f* : *R* → *R*, *f*(*x*) = x^3**

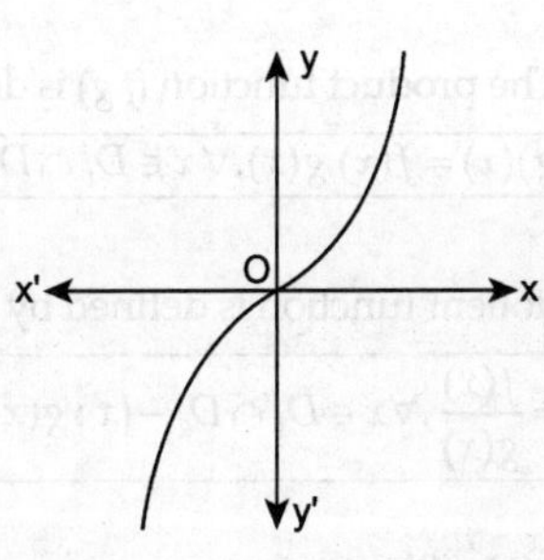

Domain = R and Range = R

- **Exponential function,** $f : R \to R, f(x) = a^x, a > 0, a \ne 1$

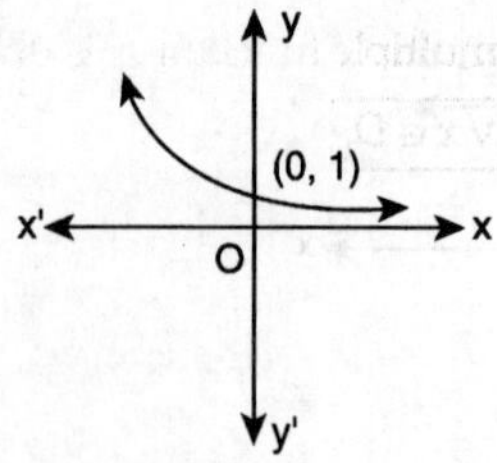

$0 < a < 1$

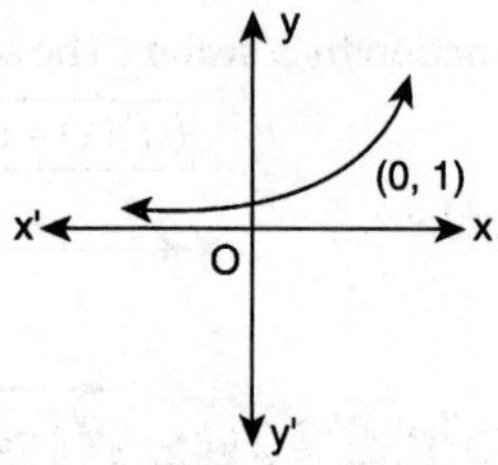

$a > 1$

Domain = R and Range = $(0, \infty)$

- **Natural exponential function,** $f(x) = e^x$

$$e = 1 + \frac{1}{1!} + \frac{1}{2!} + \frac{1}{3!} + \cdots \infty, 2 < e < 3$$

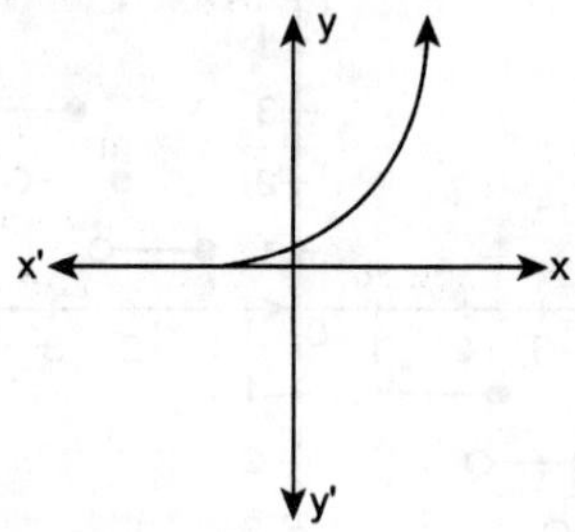

Domain = R and Range = R^+

- **Logarithmic function,** $f : (0, \infty) \to R; f(x) \log_a^x, a > 0, a \neq 1$
- **Natural logarithmic function,** $f(x) = \log e^x$ or $\ln x$

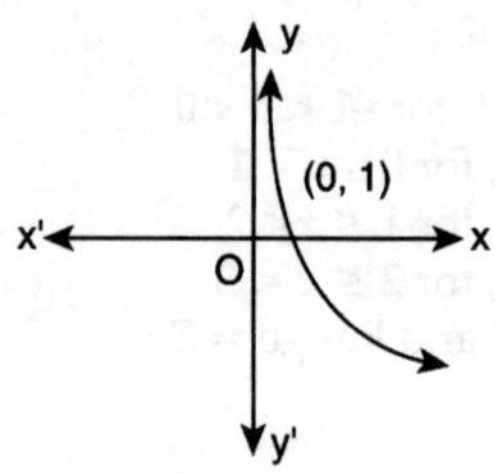

Domain = $(0, \infty)$

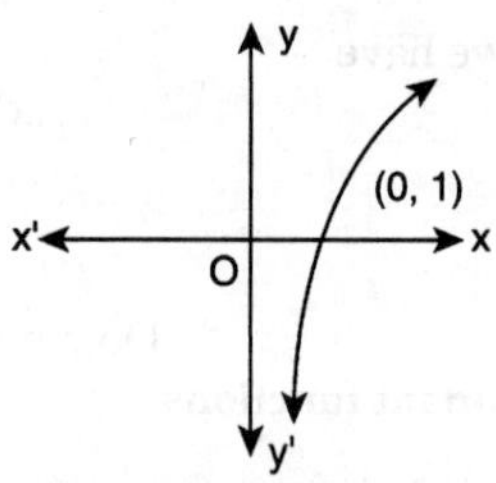

Range = R

Domain = $(0, \infty)$ and Range = R

➤ **Algebra of Real Functions**

Let $f : D_1 \to R$ and $g : D_2 \to R$ be two real functions with domain D_1 and D_2 respectively. Then, algebraic operations as addition, subtraction, multiplication and division of two real functions are given below.

(i) Addition of two real functions : The sum function $(f + g)$ is defined by

$$\boxed{(f+g)(x) = f(x) + g(x), \forall x \in D_1 \cap D_2}$$

The domain of $(f + g)$ is $D_1 \cap D_2$.

(ii) Subtraction of two real functions : The difference function $(f - g)$ is defined by

$$\boxed{(f-g)(x) = f(x) - g(x), \forall x \in D_1 \cap D_2}$$

The domain of $(f - g)$ is $D_1 \cap D_2$.

(iii) Multiplication of two real functions : The product function $(f g)$ is defined by

$$\boxed{(fg)(x) = f(x).g(x), \forall x \in D_1 \cap D_2}$$

The domain of (fg) is $D_1 \cap D_2$.

(iv) Quotient of two real functions : The quotient function is defined by

$$\boxed{\frac{f}{g}(x) = \frac{f(x)}{g(x)}, \forall x \in D_1 \cap D_2 - [x : g(x) \neq 0]}$$

The domain of $\left(\frac{f}{g}\right)$ is $D_1 \cap D_2 - [x : g(x) \neq 0]$

(v) Multiplication of a real function by a scalar : The scalar multiple function cf is defined by

$$(cf)(x) = cf(x), \forall x \in D_1$$

where, c is scalar (real number).

The domain of cf is D_1.

Multiple Choice Questions (1 mark each)

Q. 1. Range of $f(x) = \dfrac{1}{1-2\cos x}$ is

(A) $\left[\frac{1}{3}, 1\right]$ (B) $\left[-1, \frac{1}{3}\right]$

(C) $(-\infty, -1] \cup \left[\frac{1}{3}, \infty\right)$ (D) $\left[-\frac{1}{3}, 1\right]$

[NCERT Exemplar Q. 26, Page 30]

Ans. Correct option : (C)

Since, $-1 \le \cos x \le 1 \Rightarrow -1 \le -\cos x \le 1$

$\Rightarrow -2 \le -2\cos x \le 2$

$\Rightarrow -1 \le 1 - 2\cos x \le 3$

Now, $f(x) = \dfrac{1}{1-2\cos x}$ = is defined if

$$(-1) \ge \frac{1}{1-2\cos x} > -\infty \text{ or } \infty > \frac{1}{1-2\cos x} \ge \frac{1}{3}$$

$$\Rightarrow \frac{1}{1-2\cos x} \in (-\infty, -1) \cup \left[\frac{1}{3}, \infty\right)$$

Q. 2. Let $f(x) = \sqrt{1+x^2}$, then

(A) $f(xy) = f(x).f(y)$ (B) $f(xy) \ge f(x).f(y)$

(C) $f(xy) \le f(x).f(y)$ (D) None of these

[NCERT Exemplar Q. 27, Page 31]

Ans. Correct option : (C)

Here, $f(xy) = \sqrt{1+x^2y^2}$ and

$f(x).f(y) = \sqrt{1+x^2}, \sqrt{1+y^2}$

$= \sqrt{1+x^2+y^2+x^2y^2}$

Now, $\sqrt{1+x^2y^2} \le \sqrt{1+x^2+y^2+x^2y^2}$

$\Rightarrow f(xy) \le f(x).f(y)$

Q. 3. Domain of $\sqrt{a^2-x^2}$ $(a > 0)$ is

(A) $(-a, a)$ (B) $[-a, a]$

(C) $[0, a]$ (D) $(-a, 0]$

[NCERT Exemplar Q. 28, Page 31]

Ans. Correct option : (B)

Clearly $f(x)$ is defined, if $a^2 - x^2 \ge 0$

$\Rightarrow x^2 \le a^2 \Rightarrow -a \le x \le a$

$\therefore$ Do-main of f is $[-a, a]$

Q. 4. If $f(x) = ax + b$, where a and b are integers, $f(-1) = -5$ and $f(3) = 3$, then a and b are equal to

(A) $a = -3, b = -1$ (B) $a = 2, b = -3$

(C) $a = 0, b = 2$ (D) $a = 2, b = 3$

[NCERT Exemplar Q. 29, Page 31]

Ans. Correct option : (B)

Here, $f(-1) = a(-1) + b \Rightarrow -5 = -a + b$ ...(i)

and $f(3) = a(3) + b \Rightarrow 3 = 3a + b$ ...(ii)

On solving eqs (i) & (ii), we get $a = 2$ and $b = -3$

Q. 5. The domain of the function f defined by $f(x) = \sqrt{4-x} + \dfrac{1}{\sqrt{x^2-1}}$ is equal to

(A) $(-\infty, -1) \cup (1, 4]$ (B) $(-\infty, -1] \cup (1, 4]$

(C) $(-\infty, -1) \cup [1, 4]$ (D) $(-\infty, -1] \cup [1, 4)$

[NCERT Exemplar Q. 30, Page 31]

Ans. Correct option : (A)

Since, $f(x)$ is defined when $4 - x \ge 0$ and $x^2 - 1 \ge 0$

$\Rightarrow x - 4 \le 0$ and $(x + 1)(x - 1) \ge 0$

$\Rightarrow x \le 4$ and $(x < -1$ or $x > 1)$

$\therefore$ Domain of $f = (-\infty, -1] \cup [1, 4]$

Q. 6. The domain and range of the real function f defined by $f(x) = \dfrac{4-x}{x-4}$ is given by

(A) Domain = R, Range = $\{-1, 1\}$

(B) Domain = $R - \{1\}$, Range = R

(C) Domain = $R - \{4\}$, Range = $R - \{-1\}$

(D) Domain = $R - \{-4\}$, Range = $\{-1, 1\}$

[NCERT Exemplar Q. 31, Page 31]

Ans. Correct option : (C)

Given, $f(x) = \dfrac{4-x}{x-4}$

We know that f(x) is defined if

$x - 4 \ne 0$

$\Rightarrow x \ne 4$

So, the domain of $f(x)$ is $= R - \{4\}$

Let $f(x) = y = \dfrac{4-x}{x-4}$

$\Rightarrow yx - 4y = 4 - x$

$\Rightarrow yx + x = 4y + 4$

$\Rightarrow x(y + 1) = 4y + 4$

$\Rightarrow x = \dfrac{4y+4}{y+1}$

$\Rightarrow x = \dfrac{4(y+1)}{y+1}$

If x is a real number, then $1 + y \neq 0$

$\Rightarrow \quad y = -1$

$\therefore$ Range of $f(x) = R - \{-1\}$

Q. 7. The domain and range of real function f defined by $f(x) = \sqrt{x-1}$ is given by

(A) Domain = $(1, \infty)$, Range = $(0, \infty)$
(B) Domain = $[1, \infty)$, Range = $(0, \infty)$
(C) Domain = $[1, \infty)$, Range = $[0, \infty)$
(D) Domain = $[1, \infty)$, Range = $[0, \infty)$

[NCERT Exemplar Q. 32, Page 31]

Ans. Correct option : (C)

Clearly $f(x)$ is defined of $x - 1 \geq 0 \Rightarrow x \geq 1$

$\therefore$ Domain of $f = [1, \infty)$

Now for $x \geq 1$; $x - 1 \geq 0$ $\sqrt{x-1} \geq 0 \Rightarrow$ Range of $f = [0, \infty)$

Q. 8. The domain of the function f given by $f(x) = \dfrac{x^2+2x+1}{x^2-x-6}$

(A) R – {3, –2} **(B) R – {–3, 2}**
(C) R – [3, –2] **(D) R – (3, –2)**

[NCERT Exemplar Q. 33, Page 32]

Ans. Correct option : (A)

Clearly $f(x)$ is defined, if $x^2 - x - 6 = 0$

$\Rightarrow \quad (x-3)(x+2) = 0$

$\therefore \quad x = -2, 3$

$\therefore$ Domain of $f = R - \{-2, 3\}$

Q. 9. The domain and range of the function f given by $f(x) = 2 - |x - 5|$ is

(A) Domain = R^+, Range = $(-\infty, 1]$
(B) Domain = R, Range = $(-\infty, 2)$
(C) Domain = R, Range = $(-\infty, 2)$
(D) Domain = R^+, Range = $(-\infty, 2]$

[NCERT Exemplar Q. 34, Page 32]

Ans. Correct option : (B)

Clearly, $f(x)$ is defined for all $x \in R$

$\therefore$ Domain of $f = R$

Now, $|x-5| \geq 0, x \in R \Rightarrow -|x-5| \leq 0$

$\Rightarrow 2 - |x-5| \leq 2$

$\therefore f(x) \leq 2$

$\therefore$ Range of $f = (-\infty, 2]$

Q. 10. The domain for which the function defined by $f(x) = 3x^2 - 1$ and $g(x) = 3 + x$ are equal is

(A) $\left\{-1, \dfrac{4}{3}\right\}$ **(B) $\left[-1, \dfrac{4}{3}\right]$**
(C) $\left(-1, \dfrac{4}{3}\right)$ **(D) $\left[-1, \dfrac{4}{3}\right)$**

[NCERT Exemplar Q. 35, Page 32]

Ans. Correct option : (A)

Put $f(x) = g(x)$ i.e. $3x^2 - 1 = 3 + x \Rightarrow 3x^2 - x - 4 = 0$

$\Rightarrow \quad (3x-4)(x+1) = 0$

$\therefore \quad x = -1, \dfrac{4}{3}$

$\therefore$ Domain $n = \left\{-1, \dfrac{4}{3}\right\}$

[B] Fill in the blanks

Q. 1. Let f and g be two real functions given by
$f = \{(0, 1), (2, 0), (3, -4), (4, 2), (5, 1)\}$
$g = \{(1, 0), (2, 2), (3, -1), (4, 4), (5, 3)\}$
then the domain of $f \times g$ is given by ———.

[NCERT Exemplar Q. 36, Page 32]

Answer :

Domain of $f \times g$ =
Domain of $f \cap$ Domain of $g = \{2, 3, 4, 5\}$

[C] Match the following :

Q. 1. Let $f = \{(2, 4), (5, 6), (8, -1), (10, -3)\}$
$g = \{(2, 5), (7, 1), (8, 4), (10, 13), (11, 5)\}$
be two real functions. Then match the following:

(a) $f - g$	(i) $\left\{\left(2, \dfrac{4}{5}\right), \left(8, \dfrac{-1}{4}\right), \left(10, \dfrac{-3}{13}\right)\right\}$
(b) $f + g$	(ii) $\{(2, 20), (8, -4), (10, -39)\}$
(c) $f \times g$	(iii) $\{(2, -1), (8, -5), (10, -16)\}$
(d) $\dfrac{f}{g}$	(iv) $\{(2, 9), (8, 3), (10, 10)\}$

[NCERT Exemplar Q. 37, Page 33]

Answer :

(a) → (iii) (b) → (iv)
(c) → (ii) (d) → (i)

Very Short Answer Type Questions (1 marks each)

Q. 1. Is the given relation a function? Give reasons for your answer.

(i) $h = \{(4, 6), (3, 9), (-11, 6), (3, 11)\}$
(ii) $f = \{(x, x) \mid x$ is a real number$\}$
(iii) $g = \left\{\left(n, \dfrac{1}{n}\right) \mid n\right.$ is a positive integer$\}$
(iv) $s = \{(n, n^2) \mid n$ is a positive integer$\}$
(v) $t = \{(x, 3) \mid x$ is a real number$\}$.

[NCERT Exemplar Q. 10, Page 28]

Sol. (i) Given, $h = \{(4, 6), (3, 9), (-11, 6), (3, 11)\}$
The given relation is not a function because 3 has two images 9 and 11.

(ii) Given, $f = \{(x, x) \mid x$ is a real number$\}$
The given relation f is a function because every element in domain has unique image.

(iii) Given, $\left\{\left(n, \dfrac{1}{n}\right) \mid n\right.$ is a positive integer$\}$
The given relation is a function because every element in domain has unique image.

(iv) Given, $S = \{(n, n^2) \mid n \text{ is a positive integer}\}$
The given relation is a function, because the square of any positive integer is unique *i.e.* every element in the domain has unique image.

(v) Given, $t = \{(x, 3) \mid x \text{ is a real number}\}$
The given relation is a function (constant function) because every element in the domain has the image 3.

Q. 2. If f and g are two real valued functions defined as $f(x) = 2x + 1$, $g(x) = x^2 + 1$, then find.

(i) $f+g$ **(ii)** $f-g$

(iii) fg **(iv)** $\dfrac{f}{g}$

[NCERT Exemplar Q. 13, Page 29]

Sol. Given, $f(x) = 2x+1$ and $g(x) = x^2+1$

(i) $(f+g)(x) = f(x) + g(x)$
$= 2x+1+x^2+1$
$= x^2+2x+2$

(ii) $(f-g)(x) = f(x) - g(x)$
$= 2x+1-(x^2+1)$
$= 2x+1-x^2-1$
$= 2x-x^2 = x(2-x)$

(iii) $(fg)(x) = f(x) \cdot g(x)$
$= (2x+1)\cdot(x^2+1)$
$= 2x^3+2x+x^2+1$
$= 2x^3+x^2+2x+1$

(iv) $\dfrac{f}{g}(x) = \dfrac{f(x)}{f(x)} = \dfrac{2x+1}{x^2+1}$

Short Answer Type Questions (2 marks each)

Q. 1. Let $A = \{9, 10, 11, 12, 13\}$ and let $f: A \rightarrow N$ defined by $f(n)$ = the highest prime factor of n. Find the range of f.

[NCERT Exemplar Q. 12, Page 47]

Sol. Given, $A = \{9, 10, 11, 12, 13\}$ and $f: A \rightarrow N$ and $f(n)$ = the highest prime factor of 'n'

For $n = 9$, $9 = 1\times 3 \times 3$
$\Rightarrow$ Highest prime factor of 9 = 3

For $n = 10$, $10 = 1 \times 2 \times 5$
$\Rightarrow$ Highest prime factor of 10 = 5

For $n = 11$, $11 = 1 \times 11$
$\Rightarrow$ Highest prime factor of 11 = 11

For $n = 12$, $12 = 1 \times 2 \times 2 \times 3$
$\Rightarrow$ Highest prime factor of 12 = 3

For $n = 13$, $13 = 1 \times 13$
$\Rightarrow$ Highest prime factor of 13 = 13

$\therefore f(n) = \{(9, 3), (10, 5), (11, 11), (12, 3), (13, 13)\}$

$\Rightarrow$ Range = $\{3, 5, 11, 13\}$

Q. 2. If f and g are real functions defined by $f(x) = x^2 + 7$ and $g(x) = 3x + 5$, find each of the following:

(a) $f(3) + g(-5)$ **(b)** $f\left(\frac{1}{2}\right) \times g(14)$

(c) $f(-2) + g(-1)$ **(d)** $f(t) - f(-2)$

(e) $\dfrac{f(t)-f(5)}{t-5}$, if $t \neq 5$

[NCERT Exemplar Q. 11, Page 28]

Sol. Given, f and g are real functions defined by $f(x) = x^2+7$ and $g(x) = 3x+5$

(a) $f(3) = (3)^2+7 = 9+7 = 16$
and $g(-5) = 3(-5)+5 = -15+5 = -10$
$\therefore f(3)+g(-5) = 16-10 = 6$

(b) $f\left(\frac{1}{2}\right) = \left(\frac{1}{2}\right)^2 + 7 = \frac{1}{4} + 7 = \frac{29}{4}$
and $g(14) = 3(14)+5 - 42+5 = 47$

$\therefore f\left(\frac{1}{2}\right) \times g(14) = \frac{29}{4} \times 47 = \frac{1363}{4}$

(c) $f(-2) = (-2)^2+7 = 4+7 = 11$
and $g(-1) = 3(-1)+5 = -3+5 = 2$
$\therefore f(-2)+g(-1) = 11+2 = 13$

(d) $f(t) = (t)^2+7 = t^2+7$
and $f(-2) = (-2)^2+7 = 4+7 = 11$
$\therefore f(t) - f(-2) = t^2+7-11 = t^2-4$

(e) $f(t) = t^2+7$
and $f(5) = (5)^2+7 = 25+7 = 32$
$\therefore \dfrac{f(t)-f(5)}{t-5} = \dfrac{t^2+7-25-7}{t-5} = \dfrac{t^2-25}{t-5} = t+5$

Q. 3. Let f and g be real functions defined by $f(x) = 2x + 1$ and $g(x) = 4x - 7$.

(a) For what real numbers x, $f(x) = g(x)$?

(b) For what real numbers x, $f(x) < g(x)$?

[NCERT Exemplar Q. 12, Page 29]

Sol. Given, $f(x) = 2x+1$ and $g(x) = 4x-7$

(a) $\because f(x) = g(x)$
$\therefore 2x+1 = 4x-7$
$2x = 8$
$x = 4$

(b) $\because f(x) < g(x)$
$\therefore 2x+1 < 4x-7$
$2x-4x+1 < 4x-7-4x$
$-2x+1 < -7$
$-2x < -7-1$
$-2x < -8$
$\dfrac{-2x}{-2} > \dfrac{-8}{-2}$
$x > 4$

Q. 4. Express the following functions as set of ordered pairs and determine their range

$f : x \to R$, $f(x) = x^3 + 1$, where $x = \{-1, 0, 3, 9, 7\}$

[NCERT Exemplar Q. 14, Page 29]

Sol. Given, $f : x \to R$, $f(x) = x^3 + 1$, where $x = \{-1, 0, 3, 9, 7\}$

when $x = -1$, then $f(-1) = (-1)^3 + 1 = -1 + 1 = 0$

when $x = 0$, then $f(0) = (0)^3 + 1 = 0 + 1 = 1$

when $x = 3$, then $f(3) = (3)^3 + 1 = 27 + 1 = 28$

when $x = 9$, then $f(9) = (9)^3 + 1 = 729 + 1 = 730$

when $x = 7$, then $f(7) = (7)^3 + 1 = 343 + 1 = 344$

$\therefore f = \{(-1, 0), (0, 1), (3, 28), (9, 730), (7, 344)\}$

Hence, range of $f = \{0, 1, 28, 730, 344\}$

Q. 5. Find the values of x for which the functions $f(x) = 3x^2 - 1$ and $g(x) = 3 + x$ are equal.

[NCERT Exemplar Q. 15, Page 29]

Sol. Given, $f(x) = g(x)$

$\therefore 3x^2 - 1 = 3 + x$

$\Rightarrow 3x^2 - x - 4 = 0$

or $(3x - 4)(x + 1) = 0$

either $x = -1$ or, $x = \frac{4}{3}$

$x = -1, \frac{4}{3}$

Hence, the values of x are -1 and $\frac{4}{3}$ for which given function are equal.

Long Answer Type Question-II

(6 marks each)

Q. 1. Is $g = \{(1, 1), (2, 3), (3, 5), (4, 7)\}$ a function? Justify. If this is described by the relation, $g(x) = \alpha x + \beta$, then what values should be assigned to α and β?

[NCERT Exemplar Q. 16, Page 29]

Sol. Given, $g = \{(1, 1), (2, 3), (3, 5), (4, 7)\}$

Since, every element of domain has unique image under g. Hence, g is a function.

Let $g(x) = \alpha x + \beta$

when $x = 1$, then $g(1) = \alpha(1) + \beta$

$\Rightarrow 1 = \alpha + \beta$ ... (i)

when $x = 2$, then $g(2) = \alpha(2) + \beta$

$\Rightarrow 3 = 2\alpha + \beta$ ... (ii)

On solving eqs. (i) and (ii), we get

$\alpha = 2$ and $\beta = -1$

Q. 2. Find the domain of each of the following functions given by

(i) $f(x) = \frac{1}{\sqrt{1 - \cos x}}$ **(ii)** $f(x) = \frac{1}{\sqrt{x + |x|}}$

(iii) $f(x) = x|x|$ **(iv)** $f(x) = \frac{x^3 - x + 3}{x^2 - 1}$

(v) $f(x) = \frac{3x}{2x - 8}$

[NCERT Exemplar Q. 17, Page 29]

Sol. (i) Given, $f(x) = \frac{1}{\sqrt{1 - \cos x}}$

We know that, $-1 \le \cos x \le 1$

$\Rightarrow -1 \le -\cos x \le 1$

$\Rightarrow 0 \le 1 - \cos x \le 2$

Hence, $f(x)$ is defined, if $1 - \cos x \ne 0$

or $\cos x \ne 1$

or $x \ne 2n\pi \ \forall\ n \in z$

$\therefore$ Domain of $f = R - \{2n\pi : n \in z\}$

(ii) Given, $f(x) = \frac{1}{\sqrt{x + |x|}}$

$\because x + |x| = x - x = 0, \quad x < 0$

and $x + |x| = x + x = 2x, \ x \ge 0$

Hence, $f(x)$ is defined, if $x > 0$

$\therefore$ Domain of $f = R^+$

(iii) Given, $f(x) = x|x|$

Here, $f(x)$ is defined for any $x \in R$

$\therefore$ Domain of $f = R$.

(iv) Given, $f(x) = \frac{x^3 - x + 3}{x^2 - 1}$

Since, $f(x)$ is defined when

$x^2 - 1 \ne 0$

$\Rightarrow (x + 1)(x - 1) \ne 0$

$\Rightarrow x \ne -1, 1$

$\therefore$ Domain of $f = R - \{-1, 1\}$

(v) Given, $f(x) = \frac{3x}{2x - 8}$

Clearly, $f(x)$ is defined, if $2x - 8 \ne 0$

$\therefore \quad x \ne 4$

$\therefore$ Domain of $f(x) = R - \{4\}$

Q. 3. Find the range of the following functions given by

(i) $f(x) = \frac{3}{2 - x^2}$ **(ii)** $f(x) = 1 - |x - 2|$

(iii) $f(x) = |x - 3|$ **(iv)** $f(x) = 1 + 3\cos 2x$

[NCERT Exemplar Q. 18, Page 29]

Sol. (i) Given, $f(x) = \frac{3}{2 - x^2}$

Let $y = f(x)$

Then, $y = \frac{3}{2-x^2} \Rightarrow 2-x^2 = \frac{3}{y}$

$\Rightarrow x^2 = 2 - \frac{3}{y}$

$\Rightarrow x = \sqrt{\frac{2y-3}{y}}$

x assumes real values, if $2y-3 \geq 0$ and $y \geq 0 \Rightarrow y \geq \frac{3}{2}$

$\therefore$ Range of $f = \left[\frac{3}{2}, \infty\right)$

(ii) Given, $f(x) = 1 - |x-2|$

We know that, $|x-2| \geq 0 \Rightarrow -|x-2| \leq 0$

$\Rightarrow -1 \leq |x-2| \leq 1$

$\Rightarrow f(x) \leq 1$

$\therefore$ Range of $f(x) = (-\infty, 1]$

(iii) Given, $f(x) = |x-3|$

We know that, $|x-3| \geq 0 \Rightarrow f(x) \geq 0$

$\therefore$ Range of $f(x) = [0, \infty)$

(iv) Given, $f(x) = 1 + 3\cos 2x$

We know that, $-1 \leq \cos 2x \leq 1$

$\Rightarrow -3 \leq 3\cos 2x \leq 3$

$\Rightarrow 1-3 \leq 1+3\cos 2x \leq 1+3$

$\Rightarrow -2 \leq 1+3\cos 2x \leq 4$

$\therefore$ Range of $f(x) = [-2, 4]$

Q. 4. Redefine the function

$$f(x) = |x-2| + |2+x|, -3 \leq x \leq 3$$

[NCERT Exemplar Q. 19, Page 29]

Sol. $\therefore$ $|x-2| = -(x-2)$, $x < 2$

and $x-2$, $x \geq 2$

Similarly, $|2+x| = -(2+x)$, $x < -2$

and $2+x$, $x \geq -2$

$f(x) = |x-2| + |2+x|, -3 \leq x \leq -3$

$$= \begin{cases} -(x-2)-(2+x), & -3 \leq x < -2 \\ -(x-2)+2+x, & -2 \leq x < 2 \\ x-2+2+x, & 2 \leq x \leq 3 \end{cases}$$

$$= \begin{cases} -2x, & -3 \leq x < -2 \\ 4, & -2 \leq x < 2 \\ 2x & 2 \leq x \leq 3 \end{cases}$$

Q. 5. If $f(x) = \frac{x-1}{x+1}$ then show that

(i) $f\left(\frac{1}{x}\right) = -f(x)$ **(ii)** $f\left(-\frac{1}{x}\right) = -\frac{1}{f(x)}$

[NCERT Exemplar Q. 19, Page 30]

Sol. Given, $f(x) = \frac{x-1}{x+1}$

(i) $f\left(\frac{1}{x}\right) = \frac{\frac{1}{x}-1}{\frac{1}{x}+1} = \frac{(1-x)/x}{(1+x)/x} = \frac{1-x}{1+x} = \frac{-(x-1)}{x+1} = -f(x)$

(ii) $f\left(-\frac{1}{x}\right) = \frac{-\frac{1}{x}-1}{-\frac{1}{x}+1} = \frac{(-1-x)/x}{(-1+x)/x} = \frac{-(x+1)}{x-1}$

$= \frac{-1}{f(x)}$

Hence, $f\left(-\frac{1}{x}\right) = -\frac{1}{f(x)}$

Q. 6. If $f(x) = \sqrt{x}$, $g(x) = x$ be two functions defined in the domain $R^+ \cup \{0\}$. Find

(i) $(f+g)(x)$ **(ii)** $(f-g)(x)$

(iii) $(fg)(x)$ **(iv)** $\left(\frac{f}{g}\right)(x)$

[NCERT Exemplar Q. 21, Page 30]

Sol. Given, $f(x) = \sqrt{x}$ and $g(x) = x$ be two function defined in the domain $R^+ \cup \{0\}$.

(i) $(f+g)(x) = f(x) + g(x) = \sqrt{x} + x$

(ii) $(f-g)(x) = f(x) - g(x) = \sqrt{x} - x$

(iii) $(fg)(x) = f(x) \cdot g(x) = \sqrt{x} \cdot x = x^{\frac{3}{2}}$

(iv) $\left(\frac{f}{g}\right)(x) = \frac{f(x)}{g(x)} = \frac{\sqrt{x}}{x} = \frac{1}{\sqrt{x}}$

Q. 7. Find the domain and range of function $f(x) = \frac{1}{\sqrt{x-5}}$.

[NCERT Exemplar Q. 22, Page 30]

Sol. Given, $f(x) = \frac{1}{\sqrt{x-5}}$

$f(x)$ is defined, if $x-5 > 0 \Rightarrow x > 5$

$\therefore$ Domain of $f = (5, \infty)$

Let $f(x) = y$

$\therefore y = \frac{1}{\sqrt{x-5}}$

or, $\sqrt{x-5} = \frac{1}{y}$

or, $x-5 = \frac{1}{y^2}$

or, $x = \frac{1}{y^2} + 5$

$\therefore x \in (5, \infty) \Rightarrow y \in R^+$

Hence, range of $f = R^+$

Q. 8. If $f(x) = y = \dfrac{ax-b}{cx-a}$, then prove that $f(y) = x$

[NCERT Exemplar Q. 23, Page 30]

Sol. Given,

$$f(x) = y = \frac{ax-b}{cx-a}$$

$$\therefore \quad f(y) = \frac{ay-b}{cy-a} = \frac{a\left(\dfrac{ax-b}{cx-a}\right)-b}{c\left(\dfrac{ax-b}{cx-a}\right)-a}$$

$$= \frac{a(ax-b)-b(cx-a)}{c(ax-b)-a(cx-a)}$$

$$= \frac{a^2x-ab-bcx+ab}{acx-bc-acx+a^2}$$

$$= \frac{a^2x-bcx}{a^2-bc}$$

$$= \frac{x(a^2-bc)}{(a^2-bc)} = x$$

$$\therefore \quad f(y) = x$$

Hence Proved

EXPERT ADVICE

- *The domain of a function is the set of numbers that can go into a given function.*
- *The domain is the full set of x-values that can be plugged into a function to produce a y-value.*
- *The set of possible y-values is called range.*
- *The type of function will determined the best method for finding a domain.*
- *The proper notation for the domain is easy to learn.*
- *The format for expressing the domain is an open bracket/parenthesis, followed by the two end points of the domain separated by a comma, followed by a closed bracket/par an thesis.*
- *The relation R = ϕ and R = A × A are two extreme relations.*

OSWAAL LEARNING TOOLS

***For* Suggested Online Videos**

Visit : *https://youtu.be/OxZ0JL4Bjzk*

Or Scan the Code

Visit : *https://youtu.be/NlhQqmLN51M*

Or Scan the Code

Visit : *https://youtu.be/M6J9gitUP8I*

Or Scan the Code

Visit : *https://goo.gl/DHS1x2*

Or Scan the Code

Visit : *https://goo.gl/fNM5A9*

Or Scan the Code

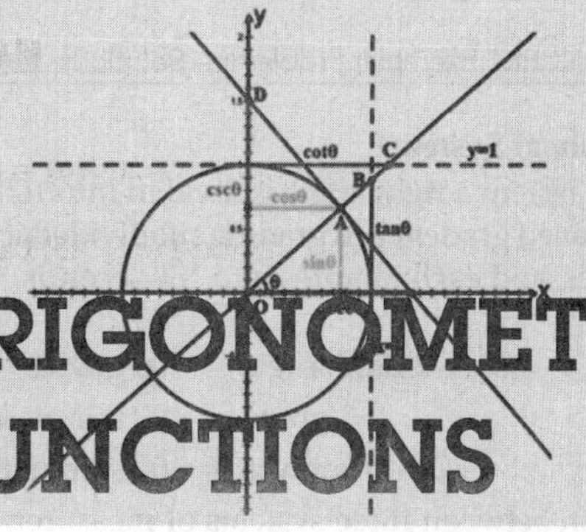

CHAPTER 3

TRIGONOMETRIC FUNCTIONS

Chapter Objectives

> *Positive and negative angles; Measuring angles in radians and in degrees and conversion from one measure to another; Definition of trigonometric functions with the help of unit circle; Truth of the identity $\sin^2 x + \cos^2 x = 1$, for all x; Signs of trigonometric functions; Domain and range of trigonometric functions and their graphs; Expressing sin (x ± y) and cos (x ± y) in terms of sin x, sin y, cos x and cos y and their simple applications; Deducing the identities like the following :*

> $\tan(x \pm y) = \dfrac{\tan x \pm \tan y}{1 \mp \tan x \tan y}$, $\cot(x \pm y) = \dfrac{\cot x \cot y \mp 1}{\cot y \pm \cot x}$

> $\sin\alpha \pm \sin\beta = 2\sin\frac{1}{2}(\alpha \pm \beta)\cos\frac{1}{2}(\alpha \mp \beta)$

> $\cos\alpha + \cos\beta = 2\cos\frac{1}{2}(\alpha \pm \beta)\cos\frac{1}{2}(\alpha \pm \beta)$

> $\cos\alpha - \cos\beta = -2\sin\frac{1}{2}(\alpha + \beta)\sin\frac{1}{2}(\alpha - \beta)$

> *Identities related to sin 2x, cos 2x, tan 2x, sin 3x, cos 3x and tan 3x; General solution of trigonometric equations of the type sin y = sin a, cos y = cos a and tan y = tan a.*

> *Applications of sine and cosine formulae.*

TOPIC - 1
Measure of an Angle & Trigonometric Functions P. 29

TOPIC - 2
Trigonometric Equations and Some Applications of Sine and Cosine P. 45

TOPIC-1 Measure of an Angle & Trigonometric Functions

Quick Review

There are three measures for measuring an angle.

(i) Degree measure : A right angle is divided into 90 equal parts called degree.

One degree is divided into 60 equal parts, called minutes and 1 minute is denoted by 1′. One minute is divided into 60 equal parts called second.

Thus, 1° = 60′, 1′ = 60″

(ii) Radian Measure :

In a circle of radius *r*, an arc of length *l* subtend an angle ′*θ* radian at the centre, then

$$l = r\theta = \frac{l}{r}$$

TIPS...

- *Revise all the formulae of the chapter and practice the important questions.*
- *Learn domain and range of trigonometric function.*
- *Learn trigonometric ratios of standard angles to make the calculation fast.*
- *Student should carefully understand the difference between general solution and principal solution of trigonometric equations.*

(iii) Centesimal System :

In this system a right angle is divided into 100 equal parts called grades each grade is subdivided into 100 minutes, and each minutes into 100 seconds.

Thus,

$$\begin{aligned} 1 \text{ right angle} &= 100 \text{ grades} \\ 1 \text{ grade} &= 100 \text{ minutes} \\ 1 \text{ minute} &= 100 \text{ seconds} \end{aligned}$$

Relation between three systems of measurement of an angle :

$$\frac{D}{90} = \frac{G}{100} = \frac{2R}{\pi}$$

where,

D = Degree measure
G = Grade measure
R = Radian measure

TRICKS...

- *While finding the principal solution, students should remember that the solution of a trigonometric equation for which $0 \le x < 2\pi$ is principal solution.*
- *To remember the signs of different trigonometric functions in different quadrant, remember rule "Add Sugar To Coffee" i.e., in I quadrant all are positive, in II quadrant sine (cosec) is positive, in III quadrant tangent (cot) is positive and in IV quadrant cosine (sec) is positive.*
- *To prove the questions of multiple angles first reduce the multiple angles, using appropriate formulae.*
- *Remember that values of sin, cos, tan repeats after 2π.*

A circle subtends at the centre an angle, whose radian measure is 2π and its degree measure is 360°. It follows that,

$$2\pi \text{ radian} = 360°$$

(or) $$\pi \text{ radian} = 180°$$

$\therefore$ $$1 \text{ rad} = \frac{180°}{\pi} = 57°16'22'' \text{ (approx)} \qquad \text{where } \pi = \frac{22}{7} = 3.14159$$

Thus,

$$\text{Radian} = \frac{\pi}{180°} \times \text{degree measure}$$

$$\text{Degree} = \frac{180°}{\pi} \times \text{radian measure}$$

Note :

(i) The angle between two consecutive digits in a clock is $30° \left(= \frac{\pi}{6} \text{ radians}\right)$

(ii) The minute hand rotates through an angle of 6° in one minute.

(iii) The hour hand rotate though an angle of 30° in one hour.

(iv) $1° = \left(\frac{\pi}{180}\right) \text{rad} = 0.0176 \text{ rad}$

Sign of Trigonometric Function in Different Quadrants

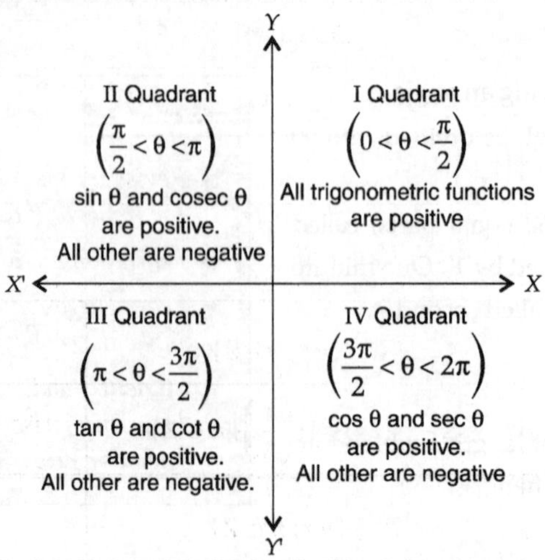

Trigonometric Identities (θ Measured in radian)

An equation involving trigonometric functions, which is true for all those angles for which the functions are defined is called trigonometrical identity. Some identities are

(i) $\sin\theta = \dfrac{1}{\text{cosec}\,\theta}$ or $\text{cosec}\,\theta = \dfrac{1}{\sin\theta}$

(ii) $\cos\theta = \dfrac{1}{\sec\theta}$ or $\sec\theta = \dfrac{1}{\cos\theta}$

(iii) $\cot\theta = \dfrac{1}{\tan\theta} = \dfrac{\cos\theta}{\sin\theta}$ or $\tan\theta = \dfrac{1}{\cot\theta} = \dfrac{\sin\theta}{\cos\theta}$

(iv) $\cos^2\theta + \sin^2\theta = 1$ or $1 - \cos^2\theta = \sin^2\theta$ or $1 - \sin^2\theta = \cos^2\theta$

(v) $1 + \tan^2\theta = \sec^2\theta$ or $\sec^2\theta - \tan^2\theta = 1$

(vi) $1 + \cot^2\theta = \text{cosec}^2\theta$ or $\text{cosec}^2\theta - \cot^2\theta = 1$

Trigonometric Ratios of Some Standard Angles

Angle	0°	30°	45°	60°	90°	120°	135°	150°	180°
sin	0	$\frac{1}{2}$	$\frac{1}{\sqrt{2}}$	$\frac{\sqrt{3}}{2}$	1	$\frac{\sqrt{3}}{2}$	$\frac{1}{\sqrt{2}}$	$\frac{1}{2}$	0
cos	1	$\frac{\sqrt{3}}{2}$	$\frac{1}{\sqrt{2}}$	$\frac{1}{2}$	0	$-\frac{1}{2}$	$-\frac{1}{\sqrt{2}}$	$-\frac{\sqrt{3}}{2}$	-1
tan	0	$\frac{1}{\sqrt{3}}$	1	$\sqrt{3}$	∞	$-\sqrt{3}$	-1	$-\frac{1}{\sqrt{3}}$	0
cot	∞	$\sqrt{3}$	1	$\frac{1}{\sqrt{3}}$	0	$-\frac{1}{\sqrt{3}}$	-1	$-\sqrt{3}$	$-\infty$
sec	1	$\frac{2}{\sqrt{3}}$	$\sqrt{2}$	2	∞	-2	$-\sqrt{2}$	$-\frac{2}{\sqrt{3}}$	-1
cosec	∞	2	$\sqrt{2}$	$\frac{2}{\sqrt{3}}$	1	$\frac{2}{\sqrt{3}}$	$\sqrt{2}$	2	∞

Domain and Range of Trigonometric Functions

Function	Domain	Range
$\sin x$	R	$[-1, 1]$
$\cos x$	R	$[-1, 1]$
$\tan x$	$R - \{(2n+1)\left(\frac{\pi}{2}\right); n \in Z\}$	R
$\text{cosec}\, x$	$R - \{n\pi; n \in Z\}$	$R-(-1, 1)$
$\sec x$	$R - \{(2n+1)\left(\frac{\pi}{2}\right); n \in Z\}$	$R-(-1, 1)$
$\cot x$	$R - \{n\pi; n \in Z\}$	R

(i) Compound Angle Formulae

- $\sin(x+y) = \sin x \cos y + \cos x \sin y$
- $\cos(x+y) = \cos x \cos y - \sin x \sin y$
- $\tan(x+y) = \dfrac{\tan x + \tan y}{1 - \tan x \cdot \tan y}$
- $\cot(x+y) = \dfrac{\cot x \cdot \cot y - 1}{\cot y + \cot x}$
- $\sin(x-y) = \sin x \cos y - \cos x \sin y$
- $\cos(x-y) = \cos x \cos y + \sin x \sin y$

Note: $\sin(x+y)\sin(x-y) = \sin^2 x - \sin^2 y = \cos^2 y - \cos^2 x$

$\cos(x+y)\cos(x-y) = \cos^2 x - \sin^2 y = \cos^2 y - \sin^2 x$

- $\tan(x-y) = \dfrac{\tan x - \tan y}{1 + \tan x \cdot \tan y}$
- $\cot(x-y) = \dfrac{\cot x \cdot \cot y + 1}{\cot y - \cot x}$
- $\tan(x+y+z) = \dfrac{\tan x + \tan y + \tan z - \tan x \tan y \tan z}{1 - \tan x \tan y - \tan y \tan z - \tan z \tan x}$

(ii) Transformation Formulae

- $2\sin x \cos y = \sin(x+y) + \sin(x-y)$
- $2\cos x \sin y = \sin(x+y) - \sin(x-y)$
- $2\cos x \cos y = \cos(x+y) + \cos(x-y)$ $[x > y]$
- $-2\sin x \sin y = \cos(x+y) - \cos(x-y)$
- $\sin x + \sin y = 2\sin\dfrac{x+y}{2}\cos\dfrac{x-y}{2}$
- $\sin x - \sin y = 2\cos\dfrac{x+y}{2}\sin\dfrac{x-y}{2}$
- $\cos x + \cos y = 2\cos\dfrac{x+y}{2}\cos\dfrac{x-y}{2}$
- $\cos x - \cos y = -2\sin\dfrac{x+y}{2}\sin\dfrac{x-y}{2} = 2\sin\left(\dfrac{x+y}{2}\right)\sin\left(\dfrac{y-x}{2}\right)$

(iii) Trigonometric Functions of Multiple and Sub Multiple Angles

- $\sin 2x = 2\sin x \cos x = \dfrac{2\tan x}{1+\tan^2 x}$
- $\cos 2x = \cos^2 x - \sin^2 x = 2\cos^2 x - 1 = 1 - 2\sin^2 x = \dfrac{1-\tan^2 x}{1+\tan^2 x}$
- $\tan 2x = \dfrac{2\tan x}{1-\tan^2 x}$
- $\sin 3x = 3\sin x - 4\sin^3 x$
- $\cos 3x = 4\cos^3 x - 3\cos x$
- $\tan 3x = \dfrac{3\tan x - \tan^3 x}{1 - 3\tan^2 x}$
- $\sin\dfrac{A}{2} = \pm\sqrt{\dfrac{1-\cos A}{2}}\left[\begin{array}{l} + \text{ if } \dfrac{A}{2} \text{ lies in quadrants I or II} \\ - \text{ if } \dfrac{A}{2} \text{ lies in III or IV quadrants}\end{array}\right.$

- $\cos\frac{A}{2} = \pm\sqrt{\frac{1+\cos A}{2}}\begin{cases} + \text{ if } \frac{A}{2} \text{ lies in I or IV quadrants} \\ - \text{ if } \frac{A}{2} \text{ lies in II or III quadrants} \end{cases}$

- $\tan\frac{A}{2} = \pm\sqrt{\frac{1-\cos A}{1+\cos A}}\begin{cases} + \text{if } \frac{A}{2} \text{ lies in I or III quadrants} \\ - \text{if } \frac{A}{2} \text{ lies in II or IV quadrants} \end{cases}$

Trigonometric functions of an angle of 18°

Let $\theta = 18°$. Then $5\theta = 90°$

$$2\theta = 90° - 3\theta$$

Therefore,

$$\sin 2\theta = \sin(90° - 3\theta) = \cos 3\theta$$

or

$$2\sin\theta\cos\theta = 4\cos^3\theta - 3\cos\theta$$

Since, $\cos\theta \neq 0$, we get

$$2\sin\theta = 4\cos^2\theta - 3 = 1 - 4\sin^2\theta$$

or

$$4\sin^2\theta + 2\sin\theta - 1 = 0$$

Hence,

$$\sin\theta = \frac{-2 \pm\sqrt{4+16}}{8} = \frac{-1\pm\sqrt{5}}{4}$$

Since, $\theta = 18°$, $\sin\theta > 0$, $\therefore$ $\sin 18° = \frac{\sqrt{5}-1}{4}$

Also,

$$\cos 18° = \sqrt{1-\sin^2 18°} = \sqrt{1-\frac{6-2\sqrt{5}}{16}} = \sqrt{\frac{10+2\sqrt{5}}{4}}$$

Now, we can easily find cos 36° and sin 36° as follows:

$$\cos 36° = 1 - 2\sin^2 18° = 1 - \frac{6-2\sqrt{5}}{8} = \frac{2+2\sqrt{5}}{8} = \frac{\sqrt{5}+1}{4}$$

Hence,

$$\cos 36° = \frac{\sqrt{5}+1}{4}$$

Also,

$$\sin 36° = \sqrt{1-\cos^2 36°} = \sqrt{1-\frac{6+2\sqrt{5}}{16}} = \frac{\sqrt{10-2\sqrt{5}}}{4}$$

Multiple Choice Questions

(1 mark each)

[A] Objective Type Questions

Q. 1. If $\sin\theta + \csc\theta = 2$, then $\sin^2\theta + \csc^2\theta$ is equal to

(A) 1 **(B)** 4

(C) 2 **(D)** None of these

[NCERT Exemplar Q. 30, Page 53]

Ans. Correct option : (C)

On squaring both sides, we get

$(\sin\theta + \csc\theta)^2 = 2^2$

$\Rightarrow \sin^2\theta + \csc^2\theta + 2\sin\theta.\csc\theta = 4$

$\Rightarrow \sin^2\theta + \csc^2\theta = 2$

Q. 2. If $f(x) = \cos^2 x + \sec^2 x$, then

(A) $f(x) < 1$ **(B)** $f(x) = 1$

(C) $2 < f(x) < 1$ **(D)** $f(x) \geq 2$

[NCERT Exemplar Q. 31, Page 55]

Ans. Correct option : (D)

Since, AM ≥ G.M. $\therefore$ $\frac{\cos^2 x + \sec^2 x}{2} \geq \sqrt{\cos^2 x.\sec^2 x}$

or $\cos^2 x + \sec^2 x \geq 2$

or $f(x) \geq 2$

Q. 3. If $\tan\theta = \frac{1}{2}$ and $\tan\phi = \frac{1}{3}$, then the value of $(\theta + \phi)$ is

(A) $\frac{\pi}{6}$ **(B)** π

(C) 0 **(D)** $\frac{\pi}{4}$

[NCERT Exemplar Q. 32, Page 55]

Ans. Correct option : (D)

We know that,

$$\tan(\theta+\phi) = \frac{\tan\theta+\tan\phi}{1-\tan\theta.\tan\phi} = \frac{\frac{1}{2}+\frac{1}{3}}{1-\frac{1}{2}\times\frac{1}{3}} = \frac{\frac{5}{6}}{\frac{5}{6}} = 1$$

$$\therefore \quad \tan(\theta+\phi) = \tan\frac{\pi}{4} \text{ or } \theta+\phi = \frac{\pi}{4}$$

Q. 4. Which of the following is not correct?

(A) $\sin\theta = -\frac{1}{5}$ **(B)** $\cos\theta = 1$

(C) $\sec\theta = \frac{1}{2}$ **(D)** $\tan\theta = 20$

[NCERT Exemplar Q. 33, Page 55]

Ans. Correct option : (C)

Since, $-1 \le \cos\theta \le 1$

Given, $\sec\theta = \frac{1}{2} \Rightarrow \cos\theta = 2$

Q. 5. The value of tan 1° tan 2° tan 3° ... tan 89° is

(A) 0 **(B)** 1

(C) $\frac{1}{2}$ **(D)** Not defined

[NCERT Exemplar Q. 34, Page 55]

Ans. Correct option : (B)

$\tan1° \tan2° \tan3° .... \tan 89°$

$= \tan1° \tan2° \tan3° .... \tan(45°) \tan(90° - 44°) ....$ $\tan(90° - 1°)$

$= \tan1° \cot1° \tan2° \cot2° \tan3° \cot3° ..... \tan89° \cot89°$

$[\because \tan(90° - \theta) = \cot\theta]$

$= 1$

Q. 6. The value of $\frac{1-\tan^2 15°}{1+\tan^2 15°}$ is

(A) 1 **(B)** $\sqrt{3}$

(C) $\frac{\sqrt{3}}{2}$ **(D)** 2

[NCERT Exemplar Q. 35, Page 56]

Ans. Correct option : (C)

Let $\theta = 15° \therefore 2\theta = 30°$

$$\cos 2\theta = \frac{1-\tan^2\theta}{1+\tan^2\theta} \Rightarrow \cos 30° = \frac{1-\tan^2 15°}{1+\tan^2 15}$$

$$\Rightarrow \quad \frac{\sqrt{3}}{2} = \frac{1-\tan^2 15°}{1+\tan^2 15°}$$

Q. 7. The value of cos 1° cos 2° cos 3° ... cos 179° is

(A) $\frac{1}{\sqrt{2}}$ **(B)** 0

(C) 1 **(D)** –1

[NCERT Exemplar Q. 36, Page 56]

Ans. Correct option : (B)

Given expression in $\cos1° \cos2° \cos3° ...... \cos 179°$

$\Rightarrow \cos1°.\cos2°.\cos3° ...... \cos90° ..... \cos179° \Rightarrow 0$

$[\cos90° = 0]$

Q. 8. If tan θ = 3 and θ lies in third quadrant, then the value of sin θ is

(A) $\frac{1}{\sqrt{10}}$ **(B)** $-\frac{1}{\sqrt{10}}$

(C) $\frac{-3}{\sqrt{10}}$ **(D)** $\frac{3}{\sqrt{10}}$

[NCERT Exemplar Q. 37, Page 56]

Ans. Correct option : (C)

Since, $\tan\theta = 3$, lies in III quadrant

$\therefore \tan\theta = \frac{P}{B} = \frac{P}{B}$, then hypotenuse $= \sqrt{3^2+1^2}$

$= \sqrt{10}$

$\therefore \sin\theta = \frac{3}{\sqrt{10}}$, where θ lies in III quadrant

Q. 9. The value of tan 75° – cot 75° is equal to

(A) $2\sqrt{3}$ **(B)** $2+\sqrt{3}$

(C) $2-\sqrt{3}$ **(D)** 1

[NCERT Exemplar Q. 38, Page 56]

Ans. Correct option : (A)

$\tan75° - \cot75° = \tan75° - \cot(90 - 15°)$

$= \tan75° - \tan15°$

$$= \frac{\sin 75° \cos 15° - \cos 75° \sin 15°}{\cos 75° \cos 15°}$$

$$= \frac{\sin(75° - 15°)}{2\times\frac{1}{2}\cos 75° \cos 15°}$$

$$= \frac{\sin(75° - 15°)}{2\times\frac{1}{2}\cos 75° \cos 15°} = \frac{2\sin 60°}{\cos 90° + \cos 60°}$$

$$= \frac{\sqrt{3}}{0+\frac{1}{2}} = 2\sqrt{3}$$

Q. 10. Which of the following is correct?

(A) $\sin 1° > \sin 1$ **(B)** $\sin 1° < \sin 1$

(C) $\sin 1° = \sin 1$ **(D)** $\sin 1° = \frac{\pi}{18°}\sin 1$

[NCERT Exemplar Q. 39, Page 56]

Ans. Correct option : (B)

If θ increases, then the value of sin θ also increases

$\therefore \sin 1° < \sin 1$ $\left[\because 1 \text{ radian} = \frac{180°}{\pi}\right]$

Q. 11. If $\tan\alpha = \frac{m}{m+1}$, $\tan\beta = \frac{1}{2m+1}$, then $\alpha+\beta$ is equal to

(A) $\frac{\pi}{2}$ **(B)** $\frac{\pi}{3}$

(C) $\frac{\pi}{6}$ **(D)** $\frac{\pi}{4}$

[NCERT Exemplar Q. 40, Page 56]

Ans. Correct option : (D)

$$\tan(\alpha+\beta) = \frac{\tan\alpha+\tan\beta}{1-\tan\alpha\tan\beta} = \frac{\frac{m}{m+1}+\frac{1}{2m+1}}{1-\frac{m}{m+1}\cdot\frac{1}{2m+1}}$$

$$\Rightarrow \tan(\alpha+\beta) = \frac{2m^2+m+m+1}{2m^2+2m+1}$$

$$\Rightarrow \tan(\alpha+\beta) = \tan\frac{\pi}{4} \Rightarrow \alpha+\beta = \frac{\pi}{4}$$

Q. 12. The minimum value of $3\cos x+4\sin x+8$ is

(A) 5 **(B) 9**

(C) 7 **(D) 3**

[NCERT Exemplar Q. 41, Page 56]

Ans. Correct option : (D)

Let $y = 3\cos x + 4\sin x + 8$

$\Rightarrow y - 8 = 3\cos x + 4\sin x$

Minimum value of $y - 8 = -\sqrt{3^2+4^2}$

$\Rightarrow y - 8 = -\sqrt{25}$

$\Rightarrow y - 8 = -5$

$\Rightarrow y = 3$

Q. 13. The value of tan 3A − tan 2A − tan A is equal to

(A) tan 3A tan 2A tan A

(B) −tan 3A tan 2A tan A

(C) tan A tan 2A − tan 2A tan 3A − tan 3A tan A

(D) None of these

[NCERT Exemplar Q. 42, Page 56]

Ans. Correct option : (A)

$$\tan 3A = \tan(2A+A) = \frac{\tan 2A+\tan A}{1-\tan 2A.\tan A}$$

$\Rightarrow \tan 3A(1-\tan 2A.\tan A) = \tan 2A + \tan A$

$\Rightarrow \tan 3A - \tan 2A - \tan A = \tan 3A.\tan 2A.\tan A$

Q. 14. The value of $\sin(45°+\theta)-\cos(45°-\theta)$ is

(A) 2 cos θ **(B) 2 sin θ**

(C) 1 **(D) 0**

[NCERT Exemplar Q. 43, Page 57]

Ans. Correct option : (D)

$$\sin(45°+\theta) = \sin 45°\cos\theta + \cos 45°\sin\theta = \frac{1}{\sqrt{2}}\cos\theta + \frac{1}{\sqrt{2}}\sin\theta$$

$$\cos(45°-\theta) = \cos 45°\cos\theta + \sin 45°\sin\theta = \frac{1}{\sqrt{2}}\cos\theta + \frac{1}{\sqrt{2}}\sin\theta$$

$$\therefore \sin(45°+\theta)-\cos(45°-\theta) = \frac{1}{\sqrt{2}}\cos\theta + \frac{1}{\sqrt{2}}\sin\theta - \left(\frac{1}{\sqrt{2}}\cos\theta+\frac{1}{\sqrt{2}}\sin\theta\right) = 0$$

Q. 15. The value of $\cot\left(\frac{\pi}{4}+\theta\right)\cot\left(\frac{\pi}{4}-\theta\right)$ is

(A) −1 **(B) 0**

(C) 1 **(D) Not defined**

[NCERT Exemplar Q. 44, Page 57]

Ans. Correct option : (C)

$$\cot\left(\frac{\pi}{4}+\theta\right).\cot\left(\frac{\pi}{4}-\theta\right)$$

$$= \frac{\cot\frac{\pi}{4}\cot\theta-1}{\cot\theta+\cot\frac{\pi}{4}} \times \frac{\cot\frac{\pi}{4}\cot\theta+1}{\cot\theta-\cot\frac{\pi}{4}}$$

$$= \frac{\cot\theta-1}{\cot\theta+1} \times \frac{\cot\theta+1}{\cot\theta-1} = 1$$

Q. 16. $\cos 2\theta\cos 2\phi+\sin^2(\theta-\phi)-\sin^2(\theta+\phi)$ is equal to

(A) sin 2(θ + ϕ) **(B) cos 2(θ + ϕ)**

(C) sin 2(θ − ϕ) **(D) cos 2(θ − ϕ)**

[NCERT Exemplar Q. 45, Page 57]

Ans. Correct option : (B)

$\cos 2\theta\cos\phi + \sin^2(\theta-\phi) - \sin^2(\theta-\phi)$

$= \cos 2\theta\cos 2\phi + \sin(\theta-\phi+\theta+\phi)\sin(\theta-\phi-\theta-\phi)$

$[\sin^2 A - \sin^2 B = \sin(A+B)\sin(A-B)]$

$= \cos 2\theta\cos 2\phi + \sin 2\theta\sin(-2\phi)$

$= \cos 2\theta\cos 2\phi - \sin 2\theta\sin 2\phi$ $[\sin(-x) = -\sin x]$

$= \cos(2\theta+2\phi)$ $[\cos A\cos B - \sin A\sin B = \cos(A+B)]$

$= \cos 2(\theta+\phi)$

Q. 17. The value of cos 12° + cos 84° + cos 156° + cos 132° is

(A) $\frac{1}{2}$ **(B) 1**

(C) $-\frac{1}{2}$ **(D) $\frac{1}{8}$**

[NCERT Exemplar Q. 46, Page 57]

Ans. Correct option : (C)

Cos12° + cos84° + cos156° + cos132° = (cos132° + cos12°) + (cos156° + cos84°)

= 2cos72° cos60° + 2 cos120° cos36°

= cos72° − cos36°

= cos(90° − 18°) − cos36° = sin18° − cos36°

$$= \frac{\sqrt{5}-1}{4} - \frac{\sqrt{5}+1}{4} = -\frac{1}{2}$$

Q. 18. If $\tan A = \frac{1}{2}$, $\tan B = \frac{1}{3}$, then tan (2A + B) is equal to

(A) 1 **(B) 2**

(C) 3 **(D) 4**

[NCERT Exemplar Q. 47, Page 56]

Ans. Correct option : (C)

$$\tan 2A = \frac{2\tan A}{1-\tan^2 A} = \frac{2\times\frac{1}{2}}{1-\left(\frac{1}{2}\right)^2} = \frac{1}{\frac{3}{4}} = \frac{4}{3}$$

$$\therefore \tan(2A+B) = \frac{\tan 2A+\tan B}{1-\tan 2A.\tan B} = \frac{\frac{4}{3}+\frac{1}{3}}{1-\frac{4}{3}.\frac{1}{3}}$$

$$= \frac{5\times 3}{5} = 3$$

Q. 19. The value of $\sin\frac{\pi}{10}\sin\frac{13\pi}{10}$ is

(A) $\frac{1}{2}$ (B) $-\frac{1}{2}$

(C) $-\frac{1}{4}$ (D) 1

[NCERT Exemplar Q. 48, Page 57]

Ans. Correct option : (C)

$\sin\frac{\pi}{10}\sin\frac{13\pi}{10} = \sin\frac{\pi}{10}\sin\left(\pi+\frac{3\pi}{10}\right) = \sin\frac{\pi}{10}$

$\left(-\sin\frac{3\pi}{10}\right) = -\sin 18° \sin 54° = -\sin 18° \cos 36°$

$= -\left(\frac{\sqrt{5}-1}{4}\right)\left(\frac{\sqrt{5}+1}{4}\right) = -\frac{1}{4}$

Q. 20. The value of sin 50° – sin 70° + sin 10° is equal to

(A) 1 (B) 0

(C) $\frac{1}{2}$ (D) 2

[NCERT Exemplar Q. 49, Page 57]

Ans. Correct option : (B)

$(\sin 50° - \sin 70°) + \sin 10° = 2\cos\frac{50°+70°}{2}\sin\frac{50°-70°}{2} + \sin 10°$

$= 2\cos 60° (-\sin 10°) + \sin 10°$

$= -2 \times \frac{1}{2}\sin 10° + \sin 10°$

$= -\sin 10° + \sin 10° = 0$

Q. 21. If sin θ + cos θ = 1, then the value of sin 2θ is equal to

(A) 1 (B) $\frac{1}{2}$

(C) 0 (D) –1

[NCERT Exemplar Q. 50, Page 57]

Ans. Correct option : (C)

On squaring both side, we get $(\sin\theta + \cos\theta)^2 = 1^2$

$\Rightarrow \sin^2\theta + \cos^2\theta + 2\sin\theta\cos\theta = 1$

$\Rightarrow 1 + \sin 2\theta = 1$

$\Rightarrow \sin 2\theta = 0$

Q. 22. If $\alpha+\beta=\frac{\pi}{4}$, then the value of $(1+\tan\alpha)(1+\tan\beta)$ is

(A) 1 (B) 2

(C) –2 (D) Not defined

[NCERT Exemplar Q. 51, Page 58]

Ans. Correct option : (B)

$\because \alpha+\beta = \frac{\pi}{4}$ $\because \tan(\alpha+\beta) = \tan\frac{\pi}{4}$

$\Rightarrow \frac{\tan\alpha+\tan\beta}{1-\tan\alpha\tan\beta} = 1$

$\Rightarrow \tan\alpha + \tan\beta = 1 - \tan\alpha\tan\beta$

$\Rightarrow \tan\alpha + \tan\beta + \tan\alpha\tan\beta = 1$

$\Rightarrow 1 + \tan\alpha + \tan\beta + \tan\alpha\tan\beta = 2$

$\Rightarrow (1+\tan\alpha)(1+\tan\beta) = 2$

Q. 23. If $\sin\theta = \frac{-4}{5}$ and θ lies in third quadrant then the value of $\cos\frac{\theta}{2}$ is

(A) $\frac{1}{5}$ (B) $-\frac{1}{\sqrt{10}}$

(C) $-\frac{1}{\sqrt{5}}$ (D) $\frac{1}{\sqrt{10}}$

[NCERT Exemplar Q. 52, Page 58]

Ans. Correct option : (C)

$\because \sin\theta = \frac{-4}{5}$ $\therefore \cos\theta = \sqrt{1-\sin^2\theta} = \pm\frac{3}{5}$

We take $\cos\theta = \frac{-3}{5}$, θ lies in III quadrant

$\cos\theta = 2\cos^2\frac{\theta}{2} - 1 \Rightarrow \frac{-3}{5} = 2\cos^2\frac{\theta}{2} - 1$

$\Rightarrow \cos^2\frac{\theta}{2} = \frac{1}{5} \Rightarrow \cos\frac{\theta}{2} = \pm\frac{1}{\sqrt{5}}$

$\therefore \cos\frac{\theta}{2} = -\frac{1}{\sqrt{5}}$ (θ lies in III quadrant)

Q. 24. Number of solutions of the equation tan x + sec x = 2 cos x lying in the interval [0, 2π] is

(A) 0 (B) 1

(C) 2 (D) 3

[NCERT Exemplar Q. 55, Page 58]

Ans. Correct option : (C)

$\tan x + \sec x = 2\cos x$

$\Rightarrow \frac{\sin x}{\cos x} + \frac{1}{\cos x} = 2\cos x \Rightarrow 1 + \sin x = 2\cos^2 x$

$\Rightarrow 2\cos^2 x - \sin x - 1 = 0$

$\Rightarrow 2\sin^2 x + \sin x - 1 = 0$

Since, the equation is quadratic in sin$x$, therefore it will have 2 solutions.

Q. 25. The value of $\sin\frac{\pi}{18}+\sin\frac{\pi}{9}+\sin\frac{2\pi}{9}+\sin\frac{5\pi}{18}$ is given by

(A) $\sin\frac{7\pi}{18}+\sin\frac{4\pi}{9}$ (B) 1

(C) $\cos\frac{\pi}{6}+\cos\frac{3\pi}{7}$ (D) $\cos\frac{\pi}{6}+\sin\frac{\pi}{9}$

[NCERT Exemplar Q. 54, Page 58]

Ans. Correct option : (A)

$\left(\sin\frac{5\pi}{18}+\sin\frac{\pi}{18}\right) + \left(\sin\frac{2\pi}{9}+\sin\frac{\pi}{9}\right)$

$= 2\sin\frac{\pi}{6}\cos\frac{\pi}{9} + 2\sin\frac{\pi}{6}\cos\frac{\pi}{18}$

$= \cos\frac{\pi}{9} + \cos\frac{\pi}{18}$

$= \sin\left(\frac{\pi}{2}-\frac{\pi}{9}\right) + \sin\left(\frac{\pi}{2}-\frac{\pi}{18}\right)$

$= \sin\frac{7\pi}{18} + \sin\frac{4\pi}{9}$

Q. 26. If A lies in the second quadrant and $3 \tan A + 4 = 0$, then the value of $2 \cot A - 5 \cos A + \sin A$ is equal to

(A) $\frac{-53}{10}$ (B) $\frac{23}{10}$

(C) $\frac{37}{10}$ (D) $\frac{7}{10}$

[NCERT Exemplar Q. 55, Page 58]

Ans. Correct option : (B)

Given, $3\tan A + 4 = 0$, A lies in II quadrant.

$\therefore \tan A = \frac{-4}{3}$ and $\cos A = \frac{-3}{5}$

[A lies is II quadrant]

Similarly, $\sin A = \frac{4}{5}$ and $\cot A = \frac{-3}{4}$

$\therefore 2\cot A - 5\cos A + \sin A = 2\left(\frac{-3}{4}\right) - 5\left(\frac{-3}{5}\right) + \frac{4}{5}$

$= \frac{-15+30+8}{10} = \frac{23}{10}$

Q. 27. The value of $\cos^2 48° - \sin^2 12°$ is

(A) $\frac{23}{10}$ (B) $\frac{\sqrt{5}-1}{8}$

(C) $\frac{\sqrt{5}+1}{5}$ (D) $\frac{\sqrt{5}+1}{2\sqrt{2}}$

[NCERT Exemplar Q. 56, Page 58]

Ans. Correct option : (B)

$\cos^2 48° - \sin^2 12° = \cos(48° + 12°).\cos(48° - 12°)$

$[\because \cos^2 A - \sin^2 B = \cos(A + B)\cos(A - B)]$

$= \cos 60°.\cos 36°$

$= \frac{1}{2} \times \frac{\sqrt{5}+1}{4} = \frac{\sqrt{5}+1}{8}$

Q. 28. If $\tan\alpha = \frac{1}{7}$, $\tan\beta = \frac{1}{3}$, then $\cos 2\alpha$ is equal to

(A) $\sin 2\beta$ (B) $\sin 4\beta$

(C) $\sin 3\beta$ (D) $\cos 2\beta$

[NCERT Exemplar Q. 57, Page 59]

Ans. Correct option : (B)

$$\cos 2\alpha = \frac{1-\tan^2\alpha}{1+\tan^2\alpha} = \frac{1-\left(\frac{1}{7}\right)^2}{1+\left(\frac{1}{7}\right)^2} = \frac{24}{25}$$

$$\text{Now, } \tan 2\beta = \frac{2\tan\beta}{1-\tan^2\beta} = \frac{2\times\frac{1}{3}}{1-\frac{1}{9}} = \frac{3}{4}$$

$$\sin 4\beta = \frac{2\tan 2\beta}{1+\tan^2 2\beta} = \frac{2\times\frac{3}{4}}{1+\left(\frac{3}{4}\right)^2} = \frac{24}{25}$$

$$\cos 2\alpha = \sin 4\beta = \frac{24}{25}$$

Q. 29. If $\tan\theta = \frac{a}{b}$, then $b\cos 2\theta + a\sin 2\theta$ is equal to

(A) a (B) b

(C) $\frac{a}{b}$ (D) None

[NCERT Exemplar Q. 58, Page 59]

Ans. Correct option : (B)

$$b\cos 2\theta + a\sin 2\theta = b\left[\frac{1-\tan^2\theta}{1+\tan^2\theta}\right] + a\left[\frac{2\tan\theta}{1+\tan^2\theta}\right]$$

$$= b\left[\frac{1-\frac{a^2}{b^2}}{1+\frac{a^2}{b^2}}\right] + a\left[\frac{2\frac{a}{b}}{1+\frac{a^2}{b^2}}\right]$$

$$= \frac{b^3-a^2b}{b^2+a^2} + \frac{2a^2b}{b^2+a^2} = \frac{b^3-a^2b+2a^2b}{b^2+a^2}$$

$$= \frac{b(b^2+a^2)}{b^2+a^2} = b$$

Q. 30. If for real values x, $\cos\theta = x + \frac{1}{x}$, then

(A) θ is an acute angle

(B) θ is right angle

(C) θ is an obtuse angle

(D) No value of θ is possible

[NCERT Exemplar Q. 59, Page 59]

Ans. Correct option : (D)

$\cos\theta = x + \frac{1}{x} \Rightarrow \cos\theta = \frac{x^2+1}{x}$

$\Rightarrow x^2 + 1 = x\cos\theta \Rightarrow x^2 - x(\cos\theta + 1) = 0$

For real value of x, $b^2 - 4ac \geq 0$

$\Rightarrow (-\cos\theta)^2 - 4 \times 1 \times 1 \geq 0$

$\Rightarrow \cos^2\theta - 4 \geq 0$

$\Rightarrow \cos\theta \geq \pm 2$,

So, the value of θ is not possible.

[B] Fill in the blanks

Q. 1. The value of is $\frac{\sin 50°}{\sin 130°}$ ____.

[NCERT Exemplar Q. 60, Page 59]

Sol. $\frac{\sin 50°}{\sin 130°} = \frac{\sin 50°}{\sin(182-50)°} = \frac{\sin 50°}{\sin 50°} = 1$

Q. 2. If $k = \sin\left(\frac{\pi}{18}\right)\sin\left(\frac{5\pi}{18}\right)\sin\left(\frac{7\pi}{18}\right)$, then the numerical value of k is ____

[NCERT Exemplar Q. 61, Page 59]

Sol. $k = \sin\frac{\pi}{18}\sin\frac{5\pi}{18}\sin\frac{7\pi}{18}$

$k = \sin 10° \sin 50° \sin 70°$

$k = \sin(90° - 80°)\sin(90° - 40°)\sin(90° - 70°)$

$k = \cos 80° \cos 40° \cos 20°$

$\left[\sin\left(\frac{\pi}{2} - \theta\right) = \cos\theta\right]$

$k = \cos 20° \cos 40° \cos 80°$

$$k = \frac{2\sin 20°\cos 20°\cos 40°\cos 80°}{2\sin 20°}$$

$$k = \frac{\sin 40°\cos 40°\cos 80°}{2\sin 20°}$$

[sin 2A = 2sin A cosA]

$$k = \frac{2\sin 40°\cos 40°\cos 80°}{4\sin 20°}$$

$$= \frac{\sin 80°\cos 80°}{4\sin 20°}$$

$$k = \frac{2\sin 80°\cos 80°}{8\sin 2\theta} = \frac{\sin 160°}{8\sin 20°}$$

$$k = \frac{\sin(180° - 20°)}{8\sin 20°} = \frac{\sin 20°}{8\sin 20°} = \frac{1}{8}$$

$$\therefore \quad k = \frac{1}{8}$$

Q. 3. If $\tan A = \dfrac{1-\cos B}{\sin B}$, then tan 2$A$ = ______

[NCERT Exemplar Q. 62, Page 59]

Sol. $$\tan A = \left(\frac{1-\cos B}{\sin B}\right)$$

$$\tan A = \frac{2\sin^2\frac{B}{2}}{2\sin\frac{B}{2}\cos\frac{B}{2}}$$

$$\tan A = \frac{\sin\frac{B}{2}}{\cos\frac{B}{2}}$$

$$\tan A = \tan\frac{B}{2}$$

$$A = \frac{B}{2}$$

2A = B

∴ tan 2A = tan B

Q. 4. If sin x + cos x = a, then

(i) $\sin^6 x + \cos^6 x$ = ______

(ii) $|\sin x - \cos x|$ = ______

[NCERT Exemplar Q. 63, Page 59]

Sol. (i) $\sin^6 x + \cos^6 x$

$= (\sin^2 x + \cos^2 x)^3 - 3\sin^2 x\cos^2 x(\sin^2 x + \cos^2 x)$

$= 1 - 3\sin^2 x\cos^2 x$

$\sin^6 x + \cos^6 x = 1 - 3\,[\sin^2 x\cos^2 x]$ ...(i)

$\sin x + \cos x = a$

$(\sin x + \cos x)^2 = a^2$

$\sin^2 x + \cos^2 x + 2\sin x\cos x = a^2$

$1 + 2\sin x\cos x = a^2$

$$\sin x\cos x = \frac{a^2-1}{2}$$

$$\sin^2 x\cos^2 x = \frac{3(a^2-1)^2}{4}$$

$$= \frac{1}{4}\left[4 - 3(a^2-1)^2\right]$$

(ii) $|\sin x - \cos x| = x$

$|(\sin x - \cos x)|^2 = x^2$

$\sin^2 + \cos^2 x - 2\sin x\cos x = x^2$

$1 - a^2 + 1 = x^2$

$\sqrt{2-a^2} = x$

$\therefore \quad |\sin x - \cos x| = \sqrt{2-a^2}$

Q. 5. In a triangle ABC with $\angle C = 90°$ the equation whose roots are tan A and tan B is ______

[NCERT Exemplar Q. 64, Page 59]

Sol. The equation whose roots are tan A and tan B

x^2 – (sum of roots)x + Product of roots = 0

x^2 – (tan A + tan B)x + tan A tan B = 0

x^2 – (tan A + tan B(90 – A)x + tan A tan(90 – A) = 0

$$x^2 - \left(\frac{\sin A}{\cos A} + \frac{\cos A}{\sin A}\right)x + \tan A\cot A = 0$$

[A + B = 90°]

$$x^2 - \left(\frac{\sin^2 A + \cos^2 A}{\sin A\cos A}\right)x + \tan A.\frac{1}{\tan A} = 0$$

$$x^2 - \left(\frac{1}{\sin A\cos A}\right)x + 1 = 0$$

$$x^2 - \left(\frac{2}{2\sin A\cos A}\right)x + 1 = 0$$

[sin 2A = 2sinA cos A]

$$x^2 - \frac{2x}{\sin 2A} + 1 = 0$$

Q. 6. $3(\sin x - \cos x)^4 + 6(\sin x + \cos x)^2 + 4(\sin^6 x + \cos^6 x)$ = ______

[NCERT Exemplar Q. 65, Page 59]

Sol. $3(\sin x - \cos x)^4 + 6(\sin x + \cos x)^2 + 4(\sin^4 x + \cos^6 x)$

$3[(\sin x - \cos x)^2]^2 + 6(\sin^2 x + \cos^2 x + 2\sin x\cos x) + 4(\sin^6 x + \cos^6 x)$

$3[\sin^2 x + \cos^2 x - 2\sin x\cos x]^2 + 6(1 + 2\sin x\cos x) + 4(\sin^6 x + \cos^6 x)$

$3(1 - 2\sin x\cos x)^2 + 6 + 12\sin x\cos x + 4[(\sin^2 x + \cos^2 x)^2 - 3\sin^2 x\cos^2 x(\sin^2 x + \cos^2 x)]$

$3(1 + 4\sin^2 x\cos^2 x - 4\sin x\cos x) + 6 + 12\sin x\cos x + 4[1 - 3\sin^2 x\cos^2 x(1)]$

$3 + 12\sin^2 x\cos^2 x - 12\sin x\cos x + 6 + 12\sin x\cos x + 4 - 12\sin^2 x\cos^2 x$

3 + 6 + 4 = 13

Q. 7. Given $x > 0$, the values of $f(x) = -3\cos\sqrt{3+x+x^2}$ lie in the interval ______

[NCERT Exemplar Q. 66, Page 60]

Sol. $-1 \le \cos\theta \le 1$

$-3 \le 3\cos\theta \le 3$ [Let $\theta = \sqrt{3+x+x^2}$]

$-1 \le 3\cos\theta$ or $3\cos\theta \le 3$

$3 \ge -3\cos\theta$ $\quad -3\cos\theta \le -3$

$\therefore -3 \le -3\cos\theta \le 3$

Interval [– 3, 3]

Q. 8. The maximum distance of a point on the graph of the function $y=\sqrt{3}\sin x+\cos x$ from x-axis is ______ [NCERT Exemplar Q. 67, Page 59]

Sol. Maximum distance of a point of the $f(x)$ from x axis is y maximum value of y

Maximum value of $y = \sqrt{3}\sin x+\cos x$

$$= \sqrt{(\sqrt{3})^2+(1)^2}$$

$$= \sqrt{3+1}$$

$$= 2 \text{ unit}$$

[C] True and False

Q. 1. The equality sin A + sin $2A$ + sin $3A$ = 3 holds for some real value of A.

[NCERT Exemplar Q. 69, Page 60]

Sol. False

$$\sin A + \sin 2A + \sin 3A = 3$$

$$\sin 3A + \sin A + \sin 2A = 3$$

$$2 \sin 2A \cos A + \sin 2A = 3$$

$$\sin 2A(2 \cos A + 1) = 3$$

$$2 \sin A \cos A (2 \cos A + 1) = 3$$

$$-1 \le \cos A \le 1$$

$$-2 \le 2 \cos A \le 2$$

$$-1 \le 1 + 2 \cos A \le 3$$

$$\sin 10° < \cos 10°$$

Q. 2. sin 10° is greater than cos 10°.

[NCERT Exemplar Q. 70, Page 60]

Sol. False

$$\sin 10° < \cos 10°$$

Q. 3. $\cos\frac{2\pi}{15}\cos\frac{4\pi}{15}\cos\frac{8\pi}{15}\cos\frac{16\pi}{15}=\frac{1}{16}$

[NCERT Exemplar Q. 71, Page 18]

Sol. True

$$\cos\frac{2\pi}{15}\cos\frac{4\pi}{15}\cos\frac{8\pi}{15}\cos\frac{16\pi}{15}$$

$$\frac{2\sin\frac{2\pi}{15}\cos\frac{2\pi}{15}\cos\frac{4\pi}{15}\cos\frac{8\pi}{15}\cos\frac{16\pi}{15}}{2\sin\frac{2\pi}{15}}$$

$$\frac{1\sin\frac{4\pi}{15}}{2\sin\frac{2\pi}{15}}\cos\frac{4\pi}{15}\cos\frac{8\pi}{15}\cos\frac{16\pi}{15}$$

$$\frac{2\sin\frac{4\pi}{15}}{4\sin\frac{2\pi}{15}}\cos\frac{4\pi}{15}\cos\frac{8\pi}{15}\cos\frac{16\pi}{15}$$

$$\frac{1\sin\frac{4\pi}{15}}{4\sin\frac{2\pi}{15}}\cos\frac{8\pi}{15}\cos\frac{16\pi}{15}$$

$$\frac{1\sin}{8\sin\frac{2\pi}{15}}8\pi\cos\frac{8\pi}{15}\cos\frac{16\pi}{15}$$

$$\frac{1\sin\frac{16\pi}{15}}{8\sin\frac{2\pi}{15}}\cos\frac{16\pi}{15} \quad [\sin 2A = 2 \sin A \cos A]$$

$$\frac{1}{16\sin\frac{2\pi}{15}}\sin\frac{32\pi}{15}$$

$$\frac{1}{16\sin\frac{2\pi}{15}}\sin\left(2\pi+\frac{2\pi}{15}\right)$$

$$\frac{\sin\left(\frac{2\pi}{15}\right)}{16\sin\left(\frac{2\pi}{15}\right)}=\frac{1}{16}$$

Q. 4. One value of θ which satisfies the equation $\sin^4\theta - 2\sin^2\theta - 1$ lies between 0 and 2π.

[NCERT Exemplar Q. 72, Page 60]

Sol. False

$$\sin^4\theta - 2\sin^2\theta - 1 = 0$$

$$(\sin^2\theta - 2)(\sin^2\theta - 11) = 0$$

$$\sin^2\theta = 2 \text{ or } \sin^2\theta = -1$$

$$\sin\theta = \pm\sqrt{2}$$

$$-1 < \sin\theta < 1$$

$\therefore$ sin θ is not lying between 0 and 25.

Q. 5. If $\tan(\pi\cos\theta)=\cot(\pi\sin\theta)$, then $\cos\left(\theta-\frac{\pi}{4}\right)=\pm\frac{1}{2\sqrt{2}}$

[NCERT Exemplar Q. 75, Page 60]

Sol. True

$$\tan(\pi\cos\theta) = \cos(\pi\sin\theta)$$

$$\tan(\pi\cos\theta) = \tan\left(\frac{\pi}{2}-\pi\sin\theta\right)$$

$$\pi\cos\theta = \frac{\pi}{2}-\pi\sin\theta$$

$$\cos\theta = \frac{1}{2}-\sin\theta$$

$$\cos\theta+\sin\theta = \frac{1}{2}$$

$$\cos\theta+\sin\theta = \frac{1}{2}$$

$$\frac{1}{\sqrt{2}}\cos\theta+\frac{1}{\sqrt{2}}\sin\theta = \frac{1}{2\sqrt{2}}$$

$$\cos\theta\cos\frac{\pi}{4}+\sin\frac{\pi}{4}\sin\theta = \frac{1}{2\sqrt{2}}$$

$$\cos\left(\theta-\frac{\pi}{1}\right) = \frac{1}{2\sqrt{2}}$$

[D] Match the following :

In the following match each item given under the column C_1 to its correct answer given under the column C_2. [NCERT Exemplar Q. 76, Page 60]

C_1	C_2
(a) $\sin(x+y)\sin(x-y)$	(i) $\cos^2 x - \sin^2 y$
(b) $\cos(x+y)\cos(x-y)$	(ii) $\theta = \frac{1-\tan\theta}{1+\tan\theta}$
(c) $\cot\left(\frac{\pi}{4}+\theta\right)$	(iii) $\frac{1+\tan\theta}{1-\tan\theta}$
(d) $\tan\left(\frac{\pi}{4}+\theta\right)$	(iv) $\sin^2 x - \sin^2 y$

Sol. (a) ↔ (iv) (b) ↔ (i)
(c) ↔ (ii) (d) ↔ (iii)

Short Answer Type Questions (2 marks each)

Q. 1. If $a\cos\theta + b\sin\theta = m$ and $a\sin\theta - b\cos\theta = n$, then show that $a^2+b^2 = m^2+n^2$
[NCERT Exemplar Q. 7, Page 53]

Sol. Given, $a\cos\theta + b\sin\theta = m$ ...(i)

and $a\sin\theta - b\cos\theta = n$ ...(ii)

On squaring and adding of eqs (i) and (ii), we get

$$m^2+n^2 = (a\cos\theta + b\sin\theta)^2 + (a\sin\theta - b\cos\theta)^2$$

$$\Rightarrow m^2+n^2 = a^2\cos^2\theta + b^2\sin^2\theta + 2ab\cos\theta\sin\theta$$
$$+a^2\sin^2\theta + b^2\cos^2\theta - 2ab\sin\theta\cos\theta$$

$$\Rightarrow m^2+n^2 = a^2(\cos^2\theta+\sin^2\theta) + b^2(\sin^2\theta+\cos^2\theta)$$

$$\Rightarrow m^2+n^2 = a^2+b^2$$ **Hence Proved.**

Q. 2. Prove that :

$\sin 4A = 4\sin A\cos^3 A - 4\cos A\sin^3 A$

[NCERT Exemplar Q. 9, Page 53]

Sol. LHS $= \sin 4A$

$= \sin(A+3A)$

$= \sin A\cos 3A + \cos A\sin 3A$

$\left[\because \cos 3x = 4\cos^3 x - 3\cos x \text{ and } \sin 3x = 3\sin x - 4\sin^3 x\right]$

$= \sin A(4\cos^3 A - 3\cos A) + \cos A(3\sin A - 4\sin^3 A)$

$= 4\sin A\cos^3 A - 3\cos A\sin A + 3\cos A\sin A - 4\sin^3 A\cos A$

$= 4\sin A\cos^3 A - 4\cos A\sin^3 A$

$=$ RHS

$\therefore$ LHS = RHS **Hence proved.**

Q. 3. If $\tan\theta + \sin\theta = m$ and $\tan\theta - \sin\theta = n$, then prove that $m^2 - n^2 = 4\sin\theta\tan\theta$

[NCERT Exemplar Q. 10, Page 53]

Sol. Given, $\tan\theta + \sin\theta = m$ and $\tan\theta - \sin\theta = n$,

LHS $= m^2 - n^2$

$= (m+n)(m-n)$

$= [(\tan\theta+\sin\theta)+(\tan\theta-\sin\theta)]\cdot[(\tan\theta+\sin\theta)-(\tan\theta-\sin\theta)]$

$= (\tan\theta+\sin\theta+\tan\theta-\sin\theta)\cdot(\tan\theta+\sin\theta-\tan\theta-\sin\theta)$

$= (2\tan\theta)(2\sin\theta)$

$= 4\sin\theta\tan\theta =$ RHS

$\therefore$ LHS = RHS **Hence Proved.**

Q. 4. If $\tan(A+B) = p$, $\tan(A-B) = q$, then show that $\tan 2A = \frac{p+q}{1-pq}$

[NCERT Exemplar Q. 11, Page 53]

Sol. Given, $\tan(A+B) = p$, and $\tan(A-B) = q$,

LHS $= \tan 2A = \tan(A+B+A-B)$

$= \tan[(A+B)+(A-B)]$

$= \frac{\tan(A+B)+\tan(A-B)}{1-\tan(A+B)\cdot\tan(A-B)}$

$= \frac{p+q}{1-pq}$

$=$ RHS

$\therefore$ LHS = RHS **Hence Proved.**

Long Answer Type Question-I (4 marks each)

Q. 1. Prove that $\frac{\tan A + \sec A - 1}{\tan A - \sec A + 1} = \frac{1+\sin A}{\cos A}$

[NCERT Exemplar Q. 1, Page 52]

Sol.

$$\text{LHS} = \frac{\tan A + \sec A - 1}{\tan A - \sec A + 1}$$

$$= \frac{\tan A + \sec A - (\sec^2 A - \tan^2 A)}{(\tan A - \sec A + 1)}$$

$[\because \sec^2 A - \tan^2 A = 1]$

$$= \frac{\tan A + \sec A - \{(\sec A - \tan A)(\sec A + \tan A)\}}{(\tan A - \sec A + 1)}$$

$[\because a^2 - b^2 = (a-b)(a+b)]$

$$= \frac{(\sec A + \tan A)(1 - \sec A + \tan A)}{1 - \sec A + \tan A}$$

$= \sec A + \tan A$

$$= \frac{1}{\cos A} + \frac{\sin A}{\cos A}$$

$$= \frac{1 + \sin A}{\cos A} = \text{RHS}$$

Hence Proved.

Q. 2. If $\frac{2\sin a}{1 + \cos a + \sin a} = y$, **then prove that** $\frac{1 - \cos a + \sin a}{1 + \sin a}$ **is also equal to** y.

[NCERT Exemplar Q. 2, Page 52]

Sol. Given, $\frac{2\sin a}{1 + \cos a + \sin a} = y$

Now,

$$\frac{1 - \cos a + \sin a}{1 + \sin a} = \frac{(1 - \cos a + \sin a)}{1 + \sin a} \cdot \frac{(1 + \cos a + \sin a)}{(1 + \cos a + \sin a)}$$

$$= \frac{\{(1 + \sin a) - \cos a\}}{1 + \sin a} \cdot \frac{\{(1 + \sin a) + \cos a\}}{1 + \cos a + \sin a}$$

$$= \frac{(1 + \sin a)^2 - \cos^2 a}{(1 + \sin a)(1 + \cos a + \sin a)}$$

$$= \frac{(1 + \sin^2 a + 2\sin a) - \cos^2 a}{(1 + \sin a)(1 + \cos a + \sin a)}$$

$$= \frac{(1 + \sin^2 a + a\sin a) - \cos^2 a}{(1 + \sin a)(1 + \cos a + \sin a)}$$

$$= \frac{(1 + \sin^2 a + 2\sin a) - (1 - \sin^2 a)}{(1 + \sin a)(1 + \cos a + \sin a)}$$

$$= \frac{2\sin^2 a + 2\sin a}{(1 + \sin a)(1 + \cos a + \sin a)}$$

$$= \frac{2\sin a(\sin a + 1)}{(1 + \sin a)(1 + \cos a + \sin a)}$$

$$= \frac{2\sin a}{1 + \cos a + \sin a} = y$$

Hence Proved.

Q. 3. If $m\sin\theta = n\sin(\theta + 2\alpha)$ **then prove that** $\tan(\theta + \alpha)\cot\alpha = \frac{m+n}{m-n}$

[NCERT Exemplar Q. 3, Page 52]

Sol. Given, $m\sin\theta = n\sin(\theta + 2\alpha)$

$$\therefore \frac{\sin(\theta + 2\alpha)}{\sin\theta} = \frac{m}{n}$$

Applying componendo and dividendo, we get

$$\frac{\sin(\theta + 2\alpha) + \sin\theta}{\sin(\theta + 2\alpha) - \sin\theta} = \frac{m+n}{m-n}$$

$$\Rightarrow \frac{2\sin\left(\frac{\theta + 2\alpha + \theta}{2}\right)\cdot\cos\left(\frac{\theta + 2\alpha - \theta}{2}\right)}{2\cos\left(\frac{\theta + 2\alpha + \theta}{2}\right)\cdot\sin\left(\frac{\theta + 2\alpha - \theta}{2}\right)} = \frac{m+n}{m-n}$$

$$\left[\because \sin C + \sin D = 2\sin\frac{C+D}{2}\cos\frac{C-D}{2} \text{ and } \sin C - \sin D = 2\cos\frac{C+D}{2}\sin\frac{C-D}{2}\right]$$

$$\Rightarrow \frac{\sin(\theta + \alpha)\cdot\cos\alpha}{\cos(\theta + \alpha)\cdot\sin\alpha} = \frac{m+n}{m-n}$$

$$\Rightarrow \tan(\theta + \alpha)\cdot\cot\alpha = \frac{m+n}{m-n}$$

Hence Proved.

Q. 4. If $\cos(\alpha + \beta) = \frac{4}{5}$ **and** $\sin(\alpha - \beta) = \frac{5}{13}$, **where** α, β **lie between 0 and** $\frac{\pi}{4}$, **then find that value of** $\tan 2\alpha$.

[NCERT Exemplar Q. 4, Page 52]

Sol. Given, $\cos(\alpha + \beta) = \frac{4}{5}$ and $\sin(\alpha - \beta) = \frac{5}{13}$

$$\Rightarrow \sin(\alpha + \beta) = \sqrt{1 - \frac{16}{25}} = \sqrt{\frac{9}{25}} = \pm\frac{3}{5}$$

$$\therefore \sin(\alpha + \beta) = \frac{3}{5}$$

$$\text{and } \cos(\alpha - \beta) = \sqrt{1 - \frac{25}{169}} = \sqrt{\frac{144}{169}} = \pm\frac{12}{13}$$

$$\therefore \cos(\alpha - \beta) = \frac{12}{13}$$

$$\text{Now, } \tan(\alpha + \beta) = \frac{\sin(\alpha + \beta)}{\cos(\alpha + \beta)} \quad \left[\because 0 < \alpha < \frac{\pi}{4}\right]$$

$$= \frac{\frac{3}{5}}{\frac{4}{5}} = \frac{3}{4}$$

$$\text{and } \tan(\alpha - \beta) = \frac{\sin(\alpha - \beta)}{\cos(\alpha - \beta)} = \frac{\frac{5}{13}}{\frac{12}{13}} = \frac{5}{12}$$

$$\therefore \tan 2\alpha = \tan(\alpha + \beta + \alpha - \beta)$$

$$= \frac{\tan(\alpha + \beta) + \tan(\alpha - \beta)}{1 - \tan(\alpha + \beta)\tan(\alpha - \beta)}$$

$$= \frac{\frac{3}{4} + \frac{5}{12}}{1 - \frac{3}{4}\cdot\frac{5}{12}} = \frac{\frac{(9+5)}{12}}{\frac{(16-5)}{16}}$$

$$= \frac{14 \times 16}{12 \times 11} = \frac{56}{33}$$

Q. 5. If $\tan x = \frac{b}{a}$, then find the value of $\sqrt{\frac{a+b}{a-b}}+\sqrt{\frac{a-b}{a+b}}$. [NCERT Exemplar Q. 5, Page 53]

Sol. Given, $\tan x = \frac{b}{a}$

$$\sqrt{\frac{a+b}{a-b}}+\sqrt{\frac{a-b}{a+b}} = \frac{\sqrt{(a+b)^2}+\sqrt{(a-b)^2}}{\sqrt{(a-b)(a+b)}}$$

$$= \frac{(a+b)+(a-b)}{\sqrt{a^2-b^2}}$$

$$= \frac{2a}{\sqrt{a^2-b^2}}$$

$$= \frac{2a}{a\sqrt{1-\left(\frac{b}{a}\right)^2}}$$

$$= \frac{2}{\sqrt{1-\tan^2 x}} \qquad \left[\because \frac{b}{a} = \tan x\right]$$

$$= \frac{2\cos x}{\sqrt{\cos^2 x-\sin^2 x}}$$

$$= \frac{2\cos x}{\sqrt{\cos 2x}}$$

$$[\because \cos 2x = \cos^2 x - \sin^2 x]$$

Q. 6. Prove that

$$\cos\theta\cos\frac{\theta}{2}-\cos 3\theta\cos\frac{9\theta}{2} = \sin 7\theta\sin 8\theta$$

[NCERT Exemplar Q. 6, Page 53]

Sol. $\text{LHS} = \cos\theta\cos\frac{\theta}{2}-\cos 3\theta\cos\frac{9\theta}{2}$

$$= \frac{1}{2}\left[2\cos\theta\cos\frac{\theta}{2}-2\cos 3\theta\cos\frac{9\theta}{2}\right]$$

$$= \frac{1}{2}\left[\begin{array}{l}\cos\left(\theta+\frac{\theta}{2}\right)+\cos\left(\theta-\frac{\theta}{2}\right)- \\ \left\{\cos\left(3\theta+\frac{9\theta}{2}\right)+\cos\left(3\theta-\frac{9\theta}{2}\right)\right\}\end{array}\right]$$

$$[\because 2\cos A\cos B = \cos(A+B)+\cos(A-B)]$$

$$= \frac{1}{2}\left(\cos\frac{3\theta}{2}+\cos\frac{\theta}{2}-\cos\frac{15\theta}{2}-\cos\frac{3\theta}{2}\right)$$

$$= \frac{1}{2}\left(\cos\frac{\theta}{2}-\cos\frac{15\theta}{2}\right)$$

$$= -\frac{1}{2}\left[2\sin\left(\frac{\theta+15\theta}{2}\right)\sin\left(\frac{\theta-15\theta}{2}\right)\right]$$

$$\left[\because \cos C-\cos D = -2\sin\frac{C+D}{2}\sin\frac{C-D}{2}\right]$$

$$= -\{\sin 8\theta\sin(-7\theta)\}$$

$$= \sin 8\theta\sin 7\theta \qquad (\because \sin(-\theta) = -\sin\theta)$$

$$= \text{RHS}$$

$\therefore$ LHS = RHS **Hence Proved.**

Q. 7. If $\cos\alpha+\cos\beta = 0 = \sin\alpha+\sin\beta$, then prove that $\cos 2\alpha+\cos 2\beta = -2\cos(\alpha+\beta)$

[NCERT Exemplar Q. 12, Page 53]

Sol. Given, $\cos\alpha+\cos\beta = 0$ and $\sin\alpha+\sin\beta = 0$

$$\therefore\ (\cos\alpha+\cos\beta)^2-(\sin\alpha+\sin\beta)^2 = 0$$

or $\left(\cos^2\alpha+\cos^2\beta+2\cos\alpha\cos\beta\right)-\left(\sin^2\alpha+\sin^2\beta+2\sin\alpha\sin\beta\right) = 0$

or $(\cos^2\alpha-\sin^2\alpha)+(\cos^2\beta-\sin^2\beta)+2(\cos\alpha\cos\beta-\sin\alpha\sin\beta) = 0$

or $\cos 2\alpha+\cos 2\beta+2\cos(\alpha+\beta) = 0$

or $\cos 2\alpha+\cos 2\beta = -2\cos(\alpha+\beta)$

Hence Proved.

Q. 8. If $\frac{\sin(x+y)}{\sin(x-y)} = \frac{a+b}{a-b}$, than show that $\frac{\tan x}{\tan y} = \frac{a}{b}$.

[NCERT Exemplar Q. 13, Page 53]

Sol. Given, $\frac{\sin(x+y)}{\sin(x-y)} = \frac{a+b}{a-b}$

Applying componendo and dividendo rule,

$$\frac{\sin(x+y)+\sin(x-y)}{\sin(x+y)-\sin(x-y)} = \frac{a+b+a-b}{a+b-a+b}$$

$$\frac{2\sin\left(\frac{x+y+x-y}{2}\right)\cos\left(\frac{x+y-x+y}{2}\right)}{2\cos\left(\frac{x+y+x-y}{2}\right)\sin\left(\frac{x+y-x+y}{2}\right)} = \frac{2a}{2b}$$

$$\left[\begin{array}{ll}\because & \sin C+\sin D = 2\sin\frac{C+D}{2}\cos\frac{C-D}{2} \\ & \sin C-\sin D = 2\cos\frac{C+D}{2}\sin\frac{C-D}{2}\end{array}\right]$$

$$\frac{\sin x\cos y}{\cos x\sin y} = \frac{a}{b}$$

$$\frac{\tan x}{\tan y} = \frac{a}{b}$$

Hence Proved.

Q. 9. If $\tan\theta = \frac{\sin\alpha-\cos\alpha}{\sin\alpha+\cos\alpha}$, then show that $\sin\alpha+\cos\alpha = \sqrt{2}\cos\theta$.

[NCERT Exemplar Q. 14, Page 53]

Sol. Given, $\tan\theta = \frac{\sin\alpha-\cos\alpha}{\sin\alpha+\cos\alpha}$

Divide by $\cos\alpha$

$$\Rightarrow \tan\theta = \frac{\tan\alpha - 1}{\tan\alpha + 1}$$

$$\Rightarrow \tan\theta = \frac{\tan\alpha - \tan\frac{\pi}{4}}{1+\tan\frac{\pi}{4}\tan\alpha} \quad \left[\because \tan\frac{\pi}{4}=1\right]$$

$$\Rightarrow \tan\theta = \tan\left(\alpha - \frac{\pi}{4}\right)$$

$$\Rightarrow \theta = \alpha - \frac{\pi}{4}$$

$$\Rightarrow \alpha = \theta + \frac{\pi}{4}$$

$$\therefore \text{LHS} = \sin\alpha + \cos\alpha$$

$$= \sin\left(\theta+\frac{\pi}{4}\right) + \cos\left(\theta+\frac{\pi}{4}\right)$$

$$= \left(\sin\theta\cos\frac{\pi}{4} + \cos\theta\sin\frac{\pi}{4}\right) + \left(\cos\theta\cos\frac{\pi}{4} - \sin\theta\sin\frac{\pi}{4}\right)$$

$$= \left(\sin\theta\cdot\frac{1}{\sqrt{2}} + \cos\theta\cdot\frac{1}{\sqrt{2}}\right) + \left(\cos\theta\frac{1}{\sqrt{2}} - \sin\theta\frac{1}{\sqrt{2}}\right)$$

$$\left[\because \sin\frac{\pi}{4} = \frac{1}{\sqrt{2}} = \cos\frac{\pi}{4}\right]$$

$$= \frac{1}{\sqrt{2}}\left[(\sin\theta+\cos\theta)+(\cos\theta-\sin\theta)\right]$$

$$= \frac{2\cos\theta}{\sqrt{2}}$$

$$= \sqrt{2}\cos\theta$$

$$= \text{RHS}$$

$\therefore$ LHS = RHS **Hence Proved.**

Long Answer Type Question-II (5 marks each)

Q. 1. If $\cos(\theta+\phi) = m\cos(\theta-\phi)$, then prove that $\tan\theta = \frac{1-m}{1+m}\cot\phi$.

[NCERT Exemplar Q. 21, Page 54]

Sol. Given, $\cos(\theta+\phi) = m\cos(\theta-\phi)$

$$\Rightarrow \frac{\cos(\theta+\phi)}{\cos(\theta-\phi)} = \frac{m}{1}$$

Using componendo and dividendo rule, we get

$$\frac{\cos(\theta+\phi)+\cos(\theta-\phi)}{\cos(\theta+\phi)-\cos(\theta-\phi)} = \frac{m+1}{m-1}$$

$$\frac{2\cos\left(\frac{\theta+\phi+\theta-\phi}{2}\right)\cdot\cos\left(\frac{\theta+\phi-\theta+\phi}{2}\right)}{-2\sin\left(\frac{\theta+\phi+\theta-\phi}{2}\right)\cdot\sin\left(\frac{\theta+\phi-\theta+\phi}{2}\right)} = \frac{m+1}{m-1}$$

$$\left[\because \cos C+\cos D = 2\cos\left(\frac{C+D}{2}\right)\cos\left(\frac{C-D}{2}\right) \text{ and } \cos C - \cos D = -2\sin\left(\frac{C+D}{2}\right)\sin\left(\frac{C-D}{2}\right)\right]$$

$$\Rightarrow \frac{\cos\theta\cos\phi}{-\sin\theta\sin\phi} = \frac{m+1}{m-1}$$

$$\Rightarrow -\cot\theta\cot\phi = \frac{m+1}{m-1}$$

$$\Rightarrow \frac{-\cot\phi}{\tan\theta} = \frac{m+1}{m-1} = -\frac{1+m}{1-m}$$

$$\Rightarrow \tan\theta = \frac{1-m}{1+m}\cot\phi$$

Hence Proved.

Q. 2. Find the value of the expression

$$3\left[\sin^4\left(\frac{3\pi}{2}-\alpha\right)+\sin^4(3\pi+\alpha)\right] - 2\left[\sin^6\left(\frac{\pi}{2}+\alpha\right)+\sin^6(5\pi-\alpha)\right]$$

[NCERT Exemplar Q. 22, Page 54]

Sol. Given, $3\left[\sin^4\left(\frac{3\pi}{2}-\alpha\right)+\sin^4(3\pi+\alpha)\right] - 2\left[\sin^6\left(\frac{\pi}{2}+\alpha\right)+\sin^6(5\pi-\alpha)\right]$

$$=3\left[\cos^4\alpha+\sin^4(\pi+\alpha)\right] - 2\left[\cos^6\alpha+\sin^6(\pi-\alpha)\right]$$

$$=3\left[\cos^4\alpha+\sin^4\alpha\right]-2\left[\cos^6\alpha+\sin^6\alpha\right]$$

$$=3\left[\cos^4\alpha+\sin^4\alpha)+2\sin^2\alpha\cos^2\alpha-2\sin^2\alpha\cos^2\alpha\right] - 2\left[(\cos^2\alpha+\sin^2\alpha)^3-3\cos^2\alpha\sin^2\alpha(\cos^2\alpha+\sin^2\alpha)\right]$$

$$=3\left[(\cos^2\alpha+\sin^2\alpha)^2-2\sin^2\alpha\cos^2\alpha\right] - 2\left[1-3\cos^2\alpha\sin^2\alpha\right]$$

$$=3\left[1-2\sin^2\alpha\cos^2\alpha\right]-2+6\cos^2\alpha\sin^2\alpha$$

$$=3-6\sin^2\alpha\cos^2\alpha-2+6\sin^2\alpha\cos^2\alpha$$

$$=1$$

Q. 3. If $a\cos2\theta+b\sin2\theta=c$ has α and β as its roots, then prove that $\tan\alpha+\tan\beta=\frac{2b}{a+c}$

[NCERT Exemplar Q. 23, Page 54]

Sol. Given, $a\cos 2\theta + b\sin 2\theta = c$

$$\Rightarrow a\left[\frac{1-\tan^2\theta}{1+\tan^2\theta}\right] + b\left[\frac{2\tan\theta}{1+\tan^2\theta}\right] = c$$

$$\left[\because \cos 2\theta = \frac{1-\tan^2\theta}{1+\tan^2\theta} \text{ and } \sin 2\theta = \frac{2\tan\theta}{1+\tan^2\theta}\right]$$

$$\Rightarrow a(1-\tan^2\theta) + b(2\tan\theta) = (1+\tan^2\theta)c$$

$$\Rightarrow a - a\tan^2\theta + 2b\tan\theta - c\tan^2\theta - c = 0$$

$$\Rightarrow -(a+c)\tan^2\theta + 2b\tan\theta + (a-c) = 0$$

$$\Rightarrow (a+c)\tan^2\theta - 2b\tan\theta + (c-a) = 0$$

Since, α and β are the roots of this equation

$$\Rightarrow \tan\alpha + \tan\beta = \frac{-(-2b)}{a+c}$$

$$\Rightarrow \tan\alpha + \tan\beta = \frac{2b}{a+c}$$

Hence Proved.

Q. 4. If $x = \sec\phi - \tan\phi$ and $y = \operatorname{cosec}\phi + \cot\phi$, then show that $xy + x - y + 1 = 0$

[NCERT Exemplar Q. 24, Page 54]

Sol. Given, $x = \sec\phi - \tan\phi$ and $y = \operatorname{cosec}\phi + \cot\phi$

$$\text{LHS} = xy + x - y + 1$$

$$= (\sec\phi - \tan\phi)(\operatorname{cosec}\phi + \cot\phi) + (\sec\phi - \tan\phi) - (\operatorname{cosec}\phi + \cot\phi) + 1$$

$$= \left(\frac{1-\sin\phi}{\cos\phi}\right)\left(\frac{1+\cos\phi}{\sin\phi}\right) + \left(\frac{1-\sin\phi}{\cos\phi}\right) - \left(\frac{1+\cos\phi}{\sin\phi}\right) + 1$$

$$= \frac{1-\sin\phi+\cos\phi-\sin\phi\cos\phi}{\cos\phi\sin\phi} + \frac{\sin\phi-\sin^2\phi-\cos\phi-\cos^2\phi}{\cos\phi\sin\phi} + 1$$

$$= \frac{(1-\sin\phi+\cos\phi-\sin\phi\cos\phi+\sin\phi-\sin^2\phi-\cos\phi-\cos^2\phi+\cos\phi\sin\phi)}{\cos\phi\sin\phi}$$

$$= \frac{1-\sin^2\phi+\cos^2\phi}{\cos\phi\sin\phi}$$

$$= \frac{1-1}{\cos\phi\sin\phi}$$

$$= 0$$

$$= \text{RHS}$$

$\therefore$ LHS = RHS **Hence Proved.**

Q. 5 If θ lies in first quadrant and $\cos\theta = \frac{8}{17}$, then find the value of $\cos(30° + p) + \cos(45° - p) + \cos(120° - p)$.

[NCERT Exemplar Q. 25, Page 54]

Sol. Given, $\cos\theta = \frac{8}{17}$

$$\therefore \sin\theta = \sqrt{1-\cos^2\theta} = \sqrt{1-\left(\frac{8}{17}\right)^2}$$

$$= \sqrt{1-\left(\frac{64}{289}\right)} = \sqrt{\frac{225}{289}} = \pm\frac{15}{17}$$

But given θ lies in I quadrant

$$\therefore \sin\theta = \frac{15}{17}$$

Now, $\cos(30° + \theta) + \cos(45° - \theta) + \cos(120° - \theta)$

$$= (\cos 30°\cos\theta - \sin 30°\sin\theta) + (\cos 45°\cos\theta + \sin 45°\sin\theta) + (\cos 120°\cos\theta + \sin 120°\sin\theta)$$

$$\left[\because \cos(A+B) = \cos A\cos B - \sin A\sin B \text{ and } \cos(A-B) = \cos A\cos B + \sin A\sin B\right]$$

$$= \left(\frac{\sqrt{3}}{2}\cos\theta - \frac{1}{2}\sin\theta\right) + \left(\frac{1}{\sqrt{2}}\cos\theta + \frac{1}{\sqrt{2}}\sin\theta\right) + \left(\frac{-1}{2}\cos\theta + \frac{\sqrt{3}}{2}\sin\theta\right)$$

$$= \left(\frac{\sqrt{3}}{2}\cos\theta + \frac{\sqrt{3}}{2}\sin\theta\right) - \frac{1}{2}(\sin\theta + \cos\theta) + \frac{1}{\sqrt{2}}(\cos\theta + \sin\theta)$$

$$= (\cos\theta + \sin\theta)\left(\frac{\sqrt{3}}{2} - \frac{1}{2} + \frac{1}{\sqrt{2}}\right)$$

$$= \left(\frac{8}{17} + \frac{15}{17}\right)\left(\frac{\sqrt{3}-1}{2} + \frac{1}{\sqrt{2}}\right)$$

$$= \frac{23}{17}\left(\frac{\sqrt{3}-1}{2} + \frac{1}{\sqrt{2}}\right)$$

$$= \frac{23}{17}\left(\frac{\sqrt{3}-1+\sqrt{2}}{2}\right)$$

Q. 6. Find the value of the expression :

$$\cos^4\frac{\pi}{8} + \cos^4\frac{3\pi}{8} + \cos^4\frac{5\pi}{8} + \cos^4\frac{7\pi}{8}$$

[NCERT Exemplar Q. 26, Page 54]

Sol. Given, $\cos^4\frac{\pi}{8} + \cos^4\frac{3\pi}{8} + \cos^4\frac{5\pi}{8} + \cos^4\frac{7\pi}{8}$

$$= \cos^4\frac{\pi}{8} + \cos^4\frac{3\pi}{8} + \cos^4\left(\pi - \frac{3\pi}{8}\right) + \cos^4\left(\pi - \frac{\pi}{8}\right)$$

$$= \cos^4\frac{\pi}{8} + \cos^4\frac{3\pi}{8} + \cos^4\frac{3\pi}{8} + \cos^4\frac{\pi}{8}$$

$$= 2\cos^4\frac{\pi}{8} + 2\cos^4\frac{3\pi}{8}$$

$$= 2\left[\cos^4\frac{\pi}{8} + \cos^4\frac{3\pi}{8}\right]$$

$$= 2\left[\cos^4\frac{\pi}{8} + \cos^4\left(\frac{\pi}{2} - \frac{\pi}{8}\right)\right]$$

$$=2\left[\cos^4\frac{\pi}{8}+\sin^4\frac{\pi}{8}\right]$$

$$=2\left[\cos^4\frac{\pi}{8}+\sin^4\frac{\pi}{8}+2\sin^2\frac{\pi}{8}\cos^2\frac{\pi}{8}-2\sin^2\frac{\pi}{8}\cos^2\frac{\pi}{8}\right]$$

$$=2\left[\left(\cos^2\frac{\pi}{8}+\sin^2\frac{\pi}{8}\right)^2-2\sin^2\frac{\pi}{8}\cos^2\frac{\pi}{8}\right]$$

$$=2\left[1-2\sin^2\frac{\pi}{8}\cos^2\frac{\pi}{8}\right]$$

$$=2-4\sin^2\frac{\pi}{8}\cos^2\frac{\pi}{8}$$

$$=2-\left(2\sin\frac{\pi}{8}\cos\frac{\pi}{8}\right)^2$$

$$=2-\left(\sin\frac{\pi}{4}\right)^2$$

$$=2-\left(\frac{1}{\sqrt{2}}\right)^2=2-\frac{1}{2}$$

$$=\frac{3}{2}$$

TOPIC-2
Trigonometric Equations and Some Applications of the Sine and Cosine

Quick Review

Trigonometric Equations

Equations involving trigonometric functions of a variables are called **trigonometric equations**. Equations are called identities, if they are satisfied by all values of the unknown angles for which the functions are defined. The solutions of a trigonometric equations for which $0 \le \theta < 2\pi$ are called **principal solutions**. The expression involving integer n which gives all solutions of a trigonometric equation is called the **general solution.**

General Solution of Trigonometric Equations

(i) If $\sin\theta = \sin\alpha$ for some angle θ, then

$\theta = n\pi + (-1)^n\alpha$ for $n \in Z$, gives general solution of the given equation.

(ii) If $\cos\theta = \cos\alpha$ for some angle θ, then

$\theta = 2n\pi \pm \alpha,\ n \in Z$, gives general solution of the given equation.

(iii) If $\tan\theta = \tan\alpha$ or $\cot\theta = \cot\alpha$, then

$\theta = n\pi + \alpha,\ n \in Z$, gives general solution for both equations.

(iv) The general value of θ satisfying any of the equations $\sin^2\theta = \sin^2\alpha$, $\cos^2\theta = \cos^2\alpha$ and $\tan^2\theta = \tan^2\alpha$ is given by $\theta = n\pi \pm \alpha, n \in Z$.

(v) The general value of θ satisfying equations $\sin\theta = \sin\alpha$ and $\cos\theta = \cos\alpha$ simultaneously is given by $\theta = 2n\pi + \alpha$, $n \in Z$.

(vi) To find the solution of an equation of the form $a\cos\theta + b\sin\theta = c$, we put $a = r\cos\alpha$ and $b = r\sin\alpha$, so that

$r^2 = a^2 + b^2$ and $\tan\alpha = \dfrac{b}{a}$

Thus, we find

$a\cos\theta + b\sin\theta = c$ changed into the form $r(\cos\theta\cos\alpha + \sin\theta\sin\alpha) = c$

or $r\cos(\theta - \alpha) = c$ and hence $\cos(\theta - \alpha) = \dfrac{c}{r}$. This gives the solution of the given equation.

Maximum and Minimum values of the expression $A\cos\theta + B\sin\theta$ are $\sqrt{A^2+B^2}$ and $-\sqrt{A^2-B^2}$ respectively, where A and B are constants.

Some Applications of sine and cosine formulae

We know that a closed figure formed by three intersecting lines forms a triangle. In triangle *ABC*, angles are denoted by *A*, *B* and *C* and the length of corresponding sides opposite to the angles (*i.e.,*) *BC*, *CA* and *AB* are denoted by *a*, *b* and *c* respectively. Also, area and perimeter of a triangle are denoted by Δ and $2s$ respectively.

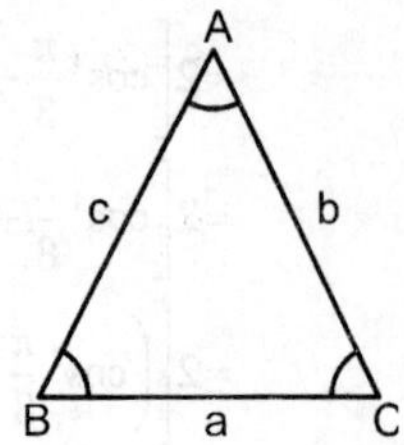

Few Important Results :

(i) Semi-perimeter of the triangle is $s = \dfrac{a+b+c}{2}$

(ii) The sum of all the angles of a triangle is 180° (*i.e.,*)
$\angle A + \angle B + \angle C = 180°$

(iii) The longest side of a triangle have corresponding largest angle and vice-versa.

(iv) The smallest side of a triangle have corresponding smallest angle and vice-versa.

Sine Formula or Sine Rule

In any triangle, the sides are proportional to the sines of the opposite angles *i.e.,* in ΔABC,

$$\frac{a}{\sin A} = \frac{b}{\sin B} = \frac{c}{\sin C} \quad \text{or} \quad \frac{\sin A}{a} = \frac{\sin B}{b} = \frac{\sin C}{c}$$

Cosine Formula or Cosine Rule

Let a, b and c be the lengths or sides of ΔABC, opposite to $\angle A$, $\angle B$ and $\angle C$, respectively. Then,

(i) $a^2 = b^2 + c^2 - 2\,bc \cos A$

(ii) $b^2 = c^2 + a^2 - 2\,ca \cos B$

(iii) $c^2 = a^2 + b^2 - 2\,ab \cos C$

Multiple Choice Questions **(1 mark each)**

[A] True and False

Q. 1. If cosec $x = 1 + \cot x$ then $x = 2n\pi,\ 2n\pi + \dfrac{\pi}{2}$

[NCERT Exemplar Q. 73, Page 60]

Sol.

$$\text{cosec } A = 1 + \cot A$$

$$\text{cosec } A - \cot A = 1$$

$$\frac{1}{\sin A} - \frac{\cos A}{\sin A} = 1$$

$$\frac{1-\cos A}{\sin A} = 1$$

$$\frac{2\sin^2\frac{A}{2}}{2\sin\frac{A}{2}\cos\frac{A}{2}} = 1$$

$$\tan\frac{A}{2} = \tan\frac{\pi}{4}$$

$$\therefore \quad \frac{A}{2} = n\pi + \frac{\pi}{4}$$

$$A = 2n\pi + \frac{\pi}{2}$$

Q. 2. If $\tan\theta + \tan 2\theta + \sqrt{3}\tan\theta\tan 2\theta = \sqrt{3}$, then $\theta = \dfrac{n\pi}{9} + \dfrac{\pi}{9}$

[NCERT Exemplar Q. 74, Page 60]

Sol.

$$\tan\theta + \tan 2\theta + \sqrt{3}\tan\theta\tan 2\theta = \sqrt{3}$$

$$\tan\theta + \tan 2\theta = \sqrt{3} - \sqrt{3}\tan\theta\tan 2\theta$$

$$\tan\theta + \tan 2\theta = \sqrt{3}(1 - \tan\theta\tan 2\theta)$$

$$\frac{\tan\theta + \tan 2\theta}{1 - \tan\theta\tan 2\theta} = \sqrt{3}$$

$$\tan(\theta + 2\theta) = \tan\frac{\pi}{3}$$

$$3\theta = n\pi + \frac{\pi}{3}$$

$$\theta = \frac{n\pi}{3} + \frac{\pi}{9}$$

Answer:

1. True
2. True

Long Answer Type Questions-I **(4 marks each)**

Q. 1. If $\sin\theta + \cos\theta = 1$, then find the general value of θ. **[NCERT Exemplar Q. 15, Page 53]**

Sol. Given, $\sin\theta + \cos\theta = 1$

Dividing both sides by $\sqrt{(1)^2 + (1)^2} = \sqrt{2}$, we get

$$\frac{1}{\sqrt{2}}\sin\theta + \frac{1}{\sqrt{2}}\cos\theta = \frac{1}{\sqrt{2}} \quad \text{(i)}$$

$$\sin\frac{\pi}{4}\sin\theta + \cos\frac{\pi}{4}\cos\theta = \frac{1}{\sqrt{2}}$$

$$\cos\left(\theta - \frac{\pi}{4}\right) = \cos\frac{\pi}{4}$$

$$\theta - \frac{\pi}{4} = 2n\pi \pm \frac{\pi}{4}, \quad n \in Z$$

[if $\cos\theta = \cos\alpha$, then $\theta = 2n\pi \pm \alpha$; $n \in Z$]

$\theta = 2n\pi \pm \frac{\pi}{4} + \frac{\pi}{4}, \quad n \in Z$

$\theta = 2n\pi + \frac{\pi}{4} + \frac{\pi}{4}$ or $2n\pi - \frac{\pi}{4} - \frac{\pi}{4}, n \in Z$

$\theta = 2n\pi + \frac{\pi}{2}$ or $\theta = 2n\pi, \; n \in z$

Hence, the general values of θ are $2n\pi + \frac{\pi}{2}$ and $2n\pi$.

Alternate method:

From eq (i), we get

$\cos\frac{\pi}{4}\sin\theta + \sin\frac{\pi}{4}\cos\theta = \sin\frac{\pi}{4}$

$\sin\left(\theta + \frac{\pi}{4}\right) = \sin\frac{\pi}{4}$

$\theta + \frac{\pi}{4} = n\pi + (-1)^n \frac{\pi}{4}, \quad n \in Z$

[If $\sin\theta = \sin\alpha$, then $\theta = n\pi + (-1)^n.\alpha, \;\; n \in z$]

$\theta = n\pi + (-1)^n \frac{\pi}{4} - \frac{\pi}{4}, \quad n \in Z$

Hence, the general values of

$\theta = n\pi + \frac{\pi}{4}\left[(-1)^n - 1\right]$

Alternate method

Given, $\sin\theta + \cos\theta = 1$

On squaring both sides, We get

$\sin^2\theta + \cos^2\theta + 2\sin\theta\cos\theta = 1$

$1 + 2\sin\theta\cos\theta = 1$

$1 + \sin 2\theta = 1$

$\sin 2\theta = 0$

$2\theta = n\pi, \; n \in Z$

[If $\sin\theta = \sin\alpha$, then $\theta = n\pi + (-1)^n.\alpha, \;\; n \in z$]

$2\theta = n\pi, \quad n \in Z$

$\theta = \frac{n\pi}{2}, \quad n \in Z$

Hence, the general value of θ is $\frac{n\pi}{2}, \; n \in Z$.

Q. 2. Find the most general value of θ satisfying the equation $\tan\theta = -1$ and $\cos\theta = \frac{1}{\sqrt{2}}$.

[NCERT Exemplar Q. 16, Page 53]

Sol. Given, $\tan\theta = -1$ and $\cos\theta = \frac{1}{\sqrt{2}}$

$\therefore \; \tan\theta = -1$

$\tan\theta = -\tan\left(\frac{\pi}{4}\right)$

$\tan\theta = \tan\left(2\pi - \frac{\pi}{4}\right)$

$\tan\theta = \tan\frac{7\pi}{4}$

$\theta = \frac{7\pi}{4}$

Now, $\cos\theta = \frac{1}{\sqrt{2}}$

$\cos\theta = \cos\frac{\pi}{4}$

$\cos\theta = \cos\left(2\pi - \frac{\pi}{4}\right)$

$\cos\theta = \cos\frac{7\pi}{4}$

$\therefore \quad \theta = \frac{7\pi}{4}$

[$\cos\theta$ is +ve in 4th quadrant]

Hence, the most general value of $\theta = 2n\pi + \frac{7\pi}{4}$

Q. 3. If $\cot\theta + \tan\theta = 2\text{cosec}\,\theta$, then find the general value of θ. [NCERT Exemplar Q. 17, Page 54]

Sol. Given, $\cot\theta + \tan\theta = 2\text{cosec}\,\theta$,

$\frac{\cos\theta}{\sin\theta} + \frac{\sin\theta}{\cos\theta} = \frac{2}{\sin\theta}$

$\frac{\cos^2\theta + \sin^2\theta}{\sin\theta\cos\theta} = \frac{2}{\sin\theta}$

$\frac{1}{\sin\theta\cos\theta} = \frac{2}{\sin\theta}$

$2\sin\theta\cos\theta = \sin\theta$

$2\sin\theta\cos\theta - \sin\theta = 0$

$\sin\theta(2\cos\theta - 1) = 0$

$\sin\theta \neq 0$ or $2\cos\theta - 1 = 0$ or $\cos\theta = \frac{1}{2}$

$\cos\theta = \cos\frac{\pi}{3}$

$\therefore \theta = 2n\pi \pm \frac{\pi}{3}$

Hence, the general values of θ is $2n\pi \pm \frac{\pi}{3}$.

Q. 4. If $2\sin^2\theta = 3\cos\theta$, where $0 \le \theta \le 2\pi$, then find the value of θ.

[NCERT Exemplar Q. 18, Page 54]

Sol. Given, $2\sin^2\theta = 3\cos\theta$

$2(1 - \cos^2\theta) = 3\cos\theta$

$2 - 2\cos^2\theta - 3\cos\theta = 0$

$2\cos^2\theta + 3\cos\theta - 2 = 0$

$2\cos^2\theta + 4\cos\theta - \cos\theta - 2 = 0$

$2\cos\theta(\cos\theta + 2) - 1(\cos\theta + 2) = 0$

$(\cos\theta + 2)(2\cos\theta - 1) = 0$

$\cos\theta + 2 = 0$ or $2\cos\theta - 1 = 0$

$\cos\theta \neq -2 \qquad [-1 \le \cos\theta \le 1]$

$2\cos\theta - 1 = 0$

$\cos\theta = \frac{1}{2}$

$\cos\theta = \cos\frac{\pi}{3}, \cos\left(2\pi - \frac{\pi}{3}\right)$

$\cos\theta = \cos\frac{\pi}{3}, \cos\frac{5\pi}{3}$

$\therefore \quad \theta = 2n\pi \pm \frac{\pi}{3} \qquad (n \in Z)$

and $\theta = 2n\pi \pm \frac{5\pi}{3}$

Hence, the principal values of θ are $\frac{\pi}{3}$ and $\frac{5\pi}{3}$.

Q. 5 If $\sec x \cos 5x + 1 = 0$, where $0 < x \le \frac{\pi}{2}$, then find the value of x.

[NCERT Exemplar Q. 19, Page 54]

Sol. Given, $\sec x \cos 5x + 1 = 0$

$\Rightarrow \frac{1}{\cos x} \cdot \cos 5x + 1 = 0$

$\Rightarrow \cos 5x + \cos x = 0$

$\Rightarrow 2\cos\left(\frac{5x + x}{2}\right)\cos\left(\frac{5x - x}{2}\right) = 0$

$[\because \cos C + \cos D = 2\cos\left(\frac{C+D}{2}\right)\cos\left(\frac{C-D}{2}\right)]$

$\Rightarrow \cos 3x \cdot \cos 2x = 0$

$\Rightarrow \cos 3x = 0$ or $\cos 2x = 0$

$3x = (2n \pm 1)\frac{\pi}{2}$

$x = (2n \pm 1)\frac{\pi}{6}$

$2x = (2n + 1)\frac{\pi}{2}$

$\therefore x = (2n + 1)\frac{\pi}{4}$

Q. 6. Find the general solution of the equation $5\cos^2\theta + 7\sin^2\theta - 6 = 0$

[NCERT Exemplar Q. 27, Page 55]

Sol. Given equation : $5\cos^2\theta + 7\sin^2\theta - 6 = 0$

$5\cos^2\theta + 7(1 - \cos^2\theta) - 6 = 0$

$5\cos^2\theta + 7 - 7\cos^2\theta - 6 = 0$

$-2\cos^2\theta + 1 = 0$

$2\cos^2\theta = 1$

$\cos^2\theta = \frac{1}{2}$

$\cos^2\theta = \cos^2\frac{\pi}{4}$

$\therefore \theta = n\pi \pm \frac{\pi}{4}, n \in Z$

[If $\cos^2\theta = \cos^2\alpha$, then $\theta = n\pi \pm \alpha$]

Hence, the general solution of $\theta = n\pi \pm \frac{\pi}{4}, n \in Z$

Long Answer Type Question

(6 marks each)

Q. 1. Find the general solution of the equation: $\sin x - 3\sin 2x + \sin 3x = \cos x - 3\cos 2x + \cos 3x$

[NCERT Exemplar Q. 28, Page 55]

Sol. Given equation:

$\sin x - 3\sin 2x + \sin 3x = \cos x - 3\cos 2x + \cos 3x$

$(\sin 3x + \sin x) - 3\sin 2x = (\cos 3x + \cos x) - 3\cos 2x$

$2\sin\left(\frac{3x + x}{2}\right) \cdot \cos\left(\frac{3x - x}{2}\right) - 3\sin 2x =$

$2\cos\left(\frac{3x + x}{2}\right)\cos\left(\frac{3x - x}{2}\right) - 3\cos 2x$

$$\left[\begin{array}{l}\because \sin C + \sin D = 2\sin\left(\frac{C+D}{2}\right)\cos\left(\frac{C-D}{2}\right) \text{ and} \\ \cos C + \cos D = 2\cos\left(\frac{C+D}{2}\right)\cos\left(\frac{C-D}{2}\right)\end{array}\right]$$

$2\sin 2x \cos x - 3\sin 2x = 2\cos 2x \cos x - 3\cos 2x$

$2\sin 2x \cos x - 2\cos 2x \cos x = 3\sin 2x - 3\cos 2x$

$2\cos x(\sin 2x - \cos 2x) - 3(\sin 2x - \cos 2x) = 0$

$(\sin 2x - \cos 2x)(2\cos x - 3) = 0$

$\sin 2x - \cos 2x = 0$ *and* $2\cos x - 3 \neq 0$

$[\because -1 \le \cos x \le 1]$

$\frac{\sin 2x}{\cos 2x} - 1 = 0$

$\tan 2x = 1$

$\tan 2x = \tan\frac{\pi}{4}$

$2x = n\pi + \frac{\pi}{4}, n \in Z$

[If $\tan\theta = \tan\alpha$, then $\theta = n\pi + \alpha$]

$x = \frac{n\pi}{2} + \frac{\pi}{8}, \quad n \in Z$

Hence, the general solution of the equation is

$x = \frac{n\pi}{2} + \frac{\pi}{8}, \; n \in Z$

Q. 2. Find the general solution of the equation :

$$\left(\sqrt{3}-1\right)\cos\theta+\left(\sqrt{3}+1\right)\sin\theta=2$$

[NCERT Exemplar Q. 29, Page 55]

Sol. Given equation : $\left(\sqrt{3}-1\right)\cos\theta+\left(\sqrt{3}+1\right)\sin\theta=2$

Put $\sqrt{3}-1=r\sin\alpha$, $\sqrt{3}+1=r\cos\alpha$

Squaring and adding, we get

$$r^2=3+1-2\sqrt{3}+3+1+2\sqrt{3}$$

$$\Rightarrow r^2=8$$

$$\Rightarrow r=\pm 2\sqrt{2}$$

Now, the given equation can be written as

$$r\sin\alpha\cos\theta+r\cos\alpha\sin\theta=2$$

$$\Rightarrow r(\sin\alpha\cos\theta+\cos\alpha\sin\theta)=2$$

$$\Rightarrow 2\sqrt{2}\sin(\alpha+\theta)=2$$

$$\Rightarrow \sin(\alpha+\theta)=\frac{2}{2\sqrt{2}}=\frac{1}{\sqrt{2}}$$

$$\Rightarrow \sin(\alpha+\theta)=\sin\frac{\pi}{4}$$

$$\therefore \quad \alpha+\theta=n\pi+(-1)^n\frac{\pi}{4}, \qquad n\in Z \quad \text{(i)}$$

Now, $\dfrac{r\sin\alpha}{r\cos\alpha}=\dfrac{\sqrt{3}-1}{\sqrt{3}+1}$

$$\Rightarrow \quad \tan\alpha=\frac{\tan\frac{\pi}{3}-\tan\frac{\pi}{4}}{1+\tan\frac{\pi}{3}\tan\frac{\pi}{4}}$$

$$\Rightarrow \quad \tan\alpha=\tan\left(\frac{\pi}{3}-\frac{\pi}{4}\right)$$

$$\Rightarrow \quad \tan\alpha=\tan\frac{\pi}{12}\Rightarrow\alpha=\frac{\pi}{12}$$

Putting the value of α in the equation (i), we get

$$\frac{\pi}{12}+\theta=n\pi+(-1)^n\frac{\pi}{4}$$

$$\therefore \theta=n\pi+(-1)^n\frac{\pi}{4}-\frac{\pi}{12}$$

Hence, the general solution of the given equation is $\theta=n\pi+(-1)^n\frac{\pi}{4}-\frac{\pi}{12}$

EXPERT ADVICE

- *Students should have learned all the trigonometric identities to make easy solution in less time.*
- *Students need more practice with the law of sine and cosine, so that they have got enough brain power available to pay attention to all the moving parts while they are trying to solve problems.*
- *To make angle positive, we go anticlockwise i.e. moves in opposite direction of clock.*
- *Trigonometry is full of formula's so learn them all, the easiest way to learn them, is write them on a paper and put it on your room's wall, revise it again and again.*
- *Almost all the topics taught in this chapter hold great importance as this chapter forms a base for trigonometry.*

OSWAAL LEARNING TOOLS

***For* Suggested Online Videos**

Visit : *https://youtu.be/cMqetVG8vRU*	Visit : *https://youtu.be/9uoKutwuCio*
Or Scan the Code	Or Scan the Code

CHAPTER

4 PRINCIPLE OF MATHEMATICAL INDUCTION

Chapter Objectives

> ➤ *Statement; Mathematical statement; Induction; Deduction; Process of the proof by induction; The principal of mathematical induction and simple applications; Motivating the application of the method by looking at natural numbers as the least inductive subset of real numbers.*

Quick Review

➤ **Principle of Mathematical Induction**
In algebra or in other disciplines of Mathematics, there are certain results or statements that are formulated in terms of n (where n is a positive integer). To prove such statements, the well suited principle that used is based on the specific technique of the principle of induction.

➤ **Principle of Mathematical Induction.**
Suppose there is a given statement $P(n)$ involving the natural number n, such that

(i) Statement is true for $n = 1$ (*i.e.,*) $P(1)$ is true and

(ii) If the statement is true for $n = k$, then statement is also true for $n = k + 1$ (*i.e.,*) truth of $P(k)$ implies the truth of $P(k + 1)$.

Then $P(n)$ is true for all natural numbers n.

TIPS...

- *Learn the steps of algorithm of PMI and practice more and more problems.*
- *Take precautions which proving P(k + 1) to avoid mistakes.*

TRICKS...

- *To get P(k)-replace 'n' in P(n) by 'k'*
- *To get LHS of P(k + 1) : Add (k + 1)th term in LHS of P(k)*
- *To get RHS of (k + 1) : Replace 'k' by (k + 1) in P(k).*

Know the Terms

➤ **Statement:** A meaningful sentence which can be judged to be true or false is called a statement.

➤ **Mathematical Statement:** A statement involving mathematical relations is called as mathematical statement.

➤ **Induction** and **Deduction** are two basic processes of reasoning.

Deduction is the application of a general case to particular case.

➤ **Induction** (Mathematical Induction) is a technique for proving general result involving positive integer. The word induction means solving the method of inferring a general statement from the validity of particular cases.

Induction being with observations, from observations we arrive at tentative conclusions called conjectures. The process of induction help in proving the conjectures which may be true.

➤ Principle of Mathematical Induction

- **First Principle :**

Let $P(n)$ be a statement involving the natural number n such that,

(i) $P(1)$ is true *i.e.,* $P(n)$ is true for $n = 1$.

(ii) $P(m + 1)$ is true, whenever $P(m)$ is true *i.e.,* $P(m)$ is true $\Rightarrow P(m + 1)$ is true. $P(n)$ is true for all natural numbers n.

- **Second Principle :**

Let $P(n)$ be a statement involving the natural number n such that,

(i) $P(1)$ is true *i.e.,* $P(n)$ is true for $n = 1$.

(ii) $P(m + 1)$ is true, whenever $P(m)$ is true for all n, where $1 \leq n \geq m$.

Then, $P(n)$ is true for all natural numbers.

For proving that statement $P(n)$ holds for all $n \in N$.

➤ Following steps are applied :

Step 1 : Verify that $P(n)$ holds for $n = 1$ *i.e.*, $P(1)$ is true.

Step 2 : Suppose that $P(n)$ holds for every $k \in N$.

Step 3 : Prove that $P(n)$ holds for $n = k + 1$.

Multiple Choice Questions (1 mark each)

[A] Objective Type Questions

Q. 1. If $10^n + 3.4^{n+2} + k$ is divisible by 9 for all $n \in N$, then the least positive integral value of k is

(A) 5 **(B) 3**
(C) 7 **(D) 1**

[NCERT Exemplar Q. 26, Page 72]

Ans. Correct option : (A)

Let $P(n) = 10^n + 3.4^{n+2} + k$ is divisible by 9, $n \in N$

$P(1) = 10^1 + 3.4^{1+2} + k = 10 + 3 \times 64 + k$

$= 10 + 192 + k = 202 + k$ must be divisible by 9.

If $(202 + k)$ is divisible by 9, then k must be equal to 5.

$= \frac{207}{9} = 23$; so, the least positive integral value of

$k = 5$.

Q. 2. For all $n \in N$, $3.5^{2n+1} + 2^{3n+1}$ is divisible by

(A) 19 **(B) 17**
(C) 23 **(D) 25**

[NCERT Exemplar Q. 27, Page 72]

Ans. Correct option : (B)

Let $P(n)$; $3.5^{2n+1} . 2^{3n+1}$

for $P(1)$; $3.5^{2.1+1} + 2^{3.1+1} = 3.5^3 + 2^4 = 3(125) + 16$

$= 375 + 16 = 391 = 23 \times 17$

So, $P(1)$ is divisible by 17.

Assume $P(k)$ is divisible by $17 \Rightarrow P(k) : 3.5^{2k+1} + 2^{3k+1} = 17\lambda_1, \lambda_1 \in N$

So, $3.2^{2k+1} = 17\lambda_1 - 2^{3k+1}$ ...(i)

Now, we have to prove $P(k + 1)$ is divisible by 17

$P(k + 1) : 3.5^{2k+3} + 2^{3k+4} = 17\lambda_2, \lambda_2 \in N$

$= [17\lambda_1 - 2^{3k+1}].25 + 2^{3k+1} . 2^3 = 17\lambda_1 . 25 - 25.2^{3k+1} + 8.2^{3k+1}$

$= 17\lambda_1 - 25 - 17^{3k+1} = 17 [25\lambda_1 - 2^{3k+1}] = 17\lambda_2$

$, \lambda_2 = 25\lambda_1 - 2^{3k+1}$

So, $P(k+1)$ is divisible by 17, whenever $P(k)$ is divisible by 17.

Q. 3. If $x^n - 1$ is divisible by $x - k$, then the least positive integral value of k is

(A) 1 **(B) 2**
(C) 3 **(D) 4**

[NCERT Exemplar Q. 28, Page 72]

Ans. Correct option : (A)

Let, $P(n) = x^n - 1$ is divisible by $x - k$

$P(1) = x - 1$ is divisible by $x - k$

Since, $x - 1$ is divisible by $x - 1$, the least integral value of k is 1.

[B] Fill in the blanks

Q. 1. If $P(n) : 2n < n!, n \in N$, then $P(n)$ is true for all $n \geq$ ______. [NCERT Exemplar Q. 29, Page 72]

Answer :

1. 4.

[C] True and False

Q. 1. Let $P(n)$ be a statement and let $P(k) \Rightarrow P(k + 1)$, for some natural number k, then $P(n)$ is true for all $n \in N$. [NCERT Exemplar Q. 30, Page 72]

Answer:

1. False

Short Answer Type Questions (2 marks each)

Q. 1. Give an example of a statement $P(n) = 2n < n!$ which is true for all $n \geq 4$ but $P(1)$, $P(2)$ and $P(3)$ are not true. Justify your answer.

[NCERT Exemplar Q. 1, Page 70]

Sol. The required statement is $P(n) = 2n < n!$

Justification: $P(n) : 2n < n!$

$P(1)$: $2.1 < 1! \Rightarrow 2 < 1$ not true

$P(2)$: $2.2 < 2! \Rightarrow 4 < 2.1 \Rightarrow 4 < 2$ not true

$P(3)$: $2.3 < 3! \Rightarrow 6 < 3.2.1 \Rightarrow 6 < 6$ not true

$P(4)$: $2.4 < 4! \Rightarrow 8 < 4.3.2.1 \Rightarrow 8 < 24$ true

$P(5)$: $2.5 < 5! \Rightarrow 10 < 5.4.3.2.1 \Rightarrow 10 < 120$ true

Hence, $P(n) = 2n < n!$ is not true for $P(1)$, $P(2)$ and $P(3)$, but it is true for all values of $n \geq 4$.

Q. 2. Give an example of a statement P(n) : 1 + 2 + 3 + ... + n = $\frac{n(n+1)}{2}$ which is true for all n. Justify your answer. [NCERT Exemplar Q. 2, Page 70]

Sol. The required statement is

$$P(n): 1+2+3+\cdots+n = \frac{n(n+1)}{2}$$

Justification: $P(1): 1 = \frac{1(1+1)}{2}$

Assume that

$P(k): 1+2+3+\cdots+k = \frac{k(k+1)}{2}$ is true.

$$P(k+1): 1+2+3+\cdots+k+(k+1)$$

$$= \frac{k(k+1)}{2} + (k+1)$$

$$= \frac{(k+1)(k+2)}{2}$$

Hence, $P(k + 1)$ is true whenever $P(n)$ is true.

Prove each of the following statement by using principle of mathematical induction (Q. 3 to 12).

Q. 3. $4^n - 1$ is divisible by 3, for each natural number n. [NCERT Exemplar Q. 3, Page 70]

Sol. Let $P(n)$: $4^n - 1$

Step 1: $P(1) = 4 - 1 = 3$, which is divisible by 3, so it is true.

Step 2: $P(k) = 4^k - 1 = 3\lambda$. Let it be true.

Step 3: $P(k + 1) = 4^{k+1} - 1$

$= 4^k \cdot 4 - 1 = 4.4^k - 4 + 3 = 4(4^k - 1) + 3$

$= 4(3\lambda) + 3$ (from Step 2)

$= 3(4\lambda + 1)$, which is true as it is divisible by 3.

Hence, $P(k + 1)$ is true whenever $P(k)$ is true.

Q. 4. $2^{3n} - 1$ is divisible by 7, for all natural numbers n. [NCERT Exemplar Q. 4, Page 70]

Sol. Let $P(n)$: $2^{3n} - 1$

Step 1: $P(1) = 2^{3.1} - 1 = 8 - 1 = 7$, which is divisible by 7.

So, $P(1)$ is true.

Step 2: $P(k) = 2^{3k} - 1 = 7\lambda$. Let it be true.

Step 3: $P(k+1) = 2^{3(k+1)} - 1$

$P(k+1) = 2^{3(k+1)} - 1$

$= 2^{3k+3} - 1 = 2^3 \cdot 2^{3k} - 8 + 7 = 8.2^{3k} - 8 + 7$

$= 8(2^{3k} - 1) + 7$ (from Step 2)

$= 8.7\lambda + 7$

$= 7(8\lambda + 1)$, which is true as it is divisible by 7.

Hence, $P(k + 1)$ is true whenever $P(n)$ is true.

Q. 5. $n^3 - 7n + 3$ is divisible by 3, for all natural numbers n. [NCERT Exemplar Q. 5, Page 70]

Sol. Let $P(n)$: $n^3 - 7n + 3$

Step 1: $P(1) = (1)^3 - 7(1) + 3$

$= 1 - 7 + 3 = -3$, which is divisible by 3.

So, it is true for $P(1)$.

Step 2: $P(k)$: $k^3 - 7k + 3 = 3\lambda$. Let it be true.

$\Rightarrow k^3 = 3\lambda + 7k - 3$

Step 3:

$P(k+1) = (k+1)^3 - 7(k+1) + 3$

$= k^3 + 1 + 3k^2 + 3k - 7k - 7 + 3$

$= k^3 + 3k^2 - 4k - 3$

$= (3\lambda + 7k - 3) + 3k^2 - 4k - 3$ (from Step 2)

$= 3k^2 + 3k + 3\lambda - 6$

$= 3(k^2 + k + \lambda - 2)$, which is divisible by 3.

Hence, $P(k + 1)$ is true whenever it is true for $P(n)$.

Q. 6. $3^{2n} - 1$ is divisible by 8, for all natural numbers n. [NCERT Exemplar Q. 6, Page 70]

Sol. Let $P(n)$: $3^{2n} - 1$

Step 1: $P(1)$: $3^2 - 1 = 9 - 1 = 8$ which is divisible by 8.

So, it is true for $P(1)$.

Step 2: $P(k) = 3^{2k} - 1 = 8\lambda$. Let it be true.

Step 3:

$P(k+1) = 3^{2(k+1)} - 1$

$= 3^{2k+2} - 1 = 3^2 \cdot 3^{2k} - 9 + 8 = 9(3^{2k} - 1) + 8$

$= 9.8\lambda + 8$ (from Step 2)

$= 8(9\lambda + 1)$, which is divisible by 8

Hence, $P(k + 1)$ is true whenever it is true for $P(k)$.

Q. 7. For any natural number n, $7^n - 2^n$ is divisible by 5. [NCERT Exemplar Q. 7, Page 70]

Sol. Let $P(n)$: $7^n - 2^n$

Step 1: $P(1)$: $7^1 - 2^1 = 5$ which is divisible by 5.

So it is true for $P(1)$.

Step 2: $P(k)$: $7^k - 2^k = 5\lambda$. Let it be true for $P(k)$.

Step 3:

$P(k+1) = 7^{k+1} - 2^{k+1}$

$= 7^{k+1} + 7^k \cdot 2 - 7^k \cdot 2 - 2^{k+1}$

$= 7^k(7 - 2) + 2 \cdot (7^k - 2^k)$

$= 5.7^k + 2.5\lambda$ (from Step 2)

$= 5(7^k + 2\lambda)$, which is divisible by 5.

Hence, $P(k + 1)$ is true whenever $P(n)$ is true.

Q. 8. For any natural number $n, x^n - y^n$ is divisible by $x - y$, where x and y are any integers with $x \neq y$ **[NCERT Exemplar Q. 8, Page 71]**

Sol. Let $P(n)$: $x^n - y^n$

Step 1: $P(1)$: $x^1 - y^1 = x - y$, which is divisible by $x - y$.

So, $P(1)$ is true.

Step 2: $P(k)$: $x^k - y^k = (x-y)\lambda$. Let it be true.

Step 3:

$$P(k+1) = x^{k+1} - y^{k+1} = x^{k+1} - x^k y + x^k y - y^{k+1}$$
$$= (x^{k+1} - x^k y) + (x^k y - y^{k+1})$$
$$= x^k(x-y) + y(x^k - y^k)$$
$$= x^k(x-y) + y\cdot(x-y)\lambda \quad \text{(from Step 2)}$$
$$= (x-y)(x^k + y\lambda) \text{ which is divisible by } (x-y).$$

Hence, $P(k+1)$ is true whenever $P(n)$ is true.

Q. 9. $n^3 - n$ is divisible by 6, for each natural number $n \geq 2$. **[NCERT Exemplar Q. 9, Page 71]**

Sol. Let $P(n)$: $n^3 - n$

Step 1: $P(2)$: $2^3 - 2 = 6$ which is divisible by 6. So it is true for $P(2)$.

Step 2: $P(k)$: $k^3 - k = 6\lambda$. Let it be true for $k \geq 2$

$\Rightarrow k^3 = 6\lambda + k$

Step 3: $P(k+1) = (k+1)^3 - (k+1)$

$$= k^3 + 1 + 3k^3 + 3k - k - 1$$
$$= k^3 - k + 3(k^2 + k)$$
$$= 6\lambda + 3(k^2 + k) \quad \text{(from Step 2)}$$

We know that $k(k + 1) = 2$ m, since $k(k + 1)$ is always even for every $k \in N$

So, $P(k + 1)$: $6\lambda + 3.2$ m $= 6(\lambda + \text{m})$, which is divisible by 6.

Hence, $P(k + 1)$ is true whenever $P(k)$ is true.

Q. 10. $2+4+6+\ldots+2n = n^2 + n$, for all natural numbers n. **[NCERT Exemplar Q. 14, Page 71]**

Sol. Let $P(n)$: $2+4+6+\cdots+2n = n^2+n, \quad \forall n \in N$

Step 1: $P(1)$: $2 = 1^2 + 1 = 2$

which is true for $P(1)$

Step 2: $P(k)$: $2+4+6+\cdots+2k = k^2+k$. Let it be true.

Step 3: $P(k + 1)$: $2+4+6+\cdots+2k+2k+2$

$$= k^2 + k + 2k + 2 = k^2 + 3k + 2$$
$$= k^2 + 2k + k + 1 + 1$$
$$= (k+1)^2 + (k+1)$$

which is true for $P(k + 1)$

Hence, $P(k + 1)$ is true whenever $P(n)$ is true.

Q. 11. $1+2+2^2+\ldots..+2^n = 2^{n+1} - 1$ for all natural numbers n. **[NCERT Exemplar Q. 15, Page 71]**

Sol. Let $P(n)$: $1+2+2^2+\cdots+2^n = 2^{n+1} - 1, n \in N$.

$P(n)$: $2^0 + 2^1 + 2^2 + \cdots + 2^n = 2^{n+1} - 1$

Step 1: $P(1) = 2^0 = 2^{0+1} - 1 = 2 - 1 = 1 = 2^0$ which is true.

Step 2: $P(k) = 2^0 + 2^1 + 2^2 + \cdots + 2^k = 2^{k+1} - 1$. Let it be true.

Step 3: $P(k+1) = 2^0 + 2^1 + 2^2 + \cdots + 2^k + 2^{k+1}$

$$= 2^{k+1} - 1 + 2^{k+1} = 2.2^{k+1} - 1 = 2^{k+2} - 1$$
$$= 2^{(k+1)+1} - 1$$

which is true for $P(k+1)$

Hence, $P(k + 1)$ is true whenever $P(n)$ is true.

Q. 12. $1+5+9+\ldots+(4n-3) = n(2n-1)$, for all natural numbers n. **[NCERT Exemplar Q. 16, Page 71]**

Sol. Let P(n):

$1+5+9+\cdots+(4n-3) = n(2n-1), \quad \forall n \in N$

Step 1: $P(1)$: $1 = 1(2.1 - 1) = 1$ which is true for $P(1)$

Step 2: $P(k)$: $1+5+9+\cdots+(4k-3) = k(2k-1)$. Let it be true.

Step 3: $P(k + 1)$: $1+5+9+\cdots+(4k-3)+(4k+1)$

$$= k(2k-1) + (4k+1) = 2k^2 - k + 4k + 1$$
$$= 2k(k+1) + 1(k+1) = (2k+1)(k+1)$$
$$= (k+1)(2k+2-1) = (k+1)[2(k+1)-1]$$

which is true for $P(k + 1)$.

Hence, $P(k + 1)$ is true whenever $P(k)$ is true.

Q. 13. A sequence $a_1, a_2, a_3 \ldots$ is defined by letting $a_1 = 3$ and $a_k = 7a_{k-1}$ for all natural numbers $k \geq 2$. Show that $a_n = 3.7^{n-1}$ for all natural numbers. **[NCERT Exemplar Q. 17, Page 71]**

Sol. Given that: $a_1 = 3$

$a_2 = 7a_{2-1} = 7\cdot a_1 = 7 \times 3 = 21$

$a_3 = 7a_{3-1} = 7\cdot a_2 = 7 \times 21 = 147$

Let $P(n)$: $a_n = 3\cdot 7^{n-1}, \forall n \in$ N

Step 1: $P(2)$: $a_2 = 3\cdot 7^{2-1} = 21 \Rightarrow 21 = 21$, which is true for $P(2)$.

Step 2: $P(k)$: $a_k = 3\cdot 7^{k-1}$. Let it be true.

Step 3: $a_k = 7a_{k-1}$ (given)

Put $k = k + 1$

$$a_{k+1} = 7a_k = 7(3\cdot 7^{k-1}) = 3\cdot 7^{k+1-1} = 3\cdot 7^{(k+1)-1}$$

which is true for $P(k + 1)$

Hence, $P(k + 1)$ is true whenever $P(n)$ is true.

Q. 14. A sequence $b_0, b_1, b_2, \ldots$ is defined by letting $b_0 = 5$ and $b_k = 4 + b_{k-1}$ for all natural numbers k. Show that $b_n = 5 + 4n$ for all natural number n using Mathematical Induction. **[NCERT Exemplar Q. 18, Page 71]**

Sol. We have, $b_0 = 5$ and $b_k = 4 + b_{k-1}$

$\Rightarrow b_0 = 5$, $b_1 = 4 + b_0 = 4 + 5 = 9$ and

$b_2 = 4 + b_1 = 4 + 9 = 13$

Let $P(n) : b_n = 5 + 4n$

Step 1: $P(1)$: $b_1 = 5 + 4 = 9 \Rightarrow 9 = 9$ which is true.

Step 2: $P(k) : b_k = 5 + 4k$. Let it be true $\forall k \in N$

Step 3: Given that: $P(k) = 4 + bk$

$\Rightarrow P(k + 1) : b_{k+1} = 4 + b_{k+1-1}$

$\Rightarrow P(k+1) = 4 + b_k = 4 + 5 + 4k$

$\Rightarrow P(k+1) = 5 + 4(k+1)$, which is true for $P(k + 1)$

Hence, $P(k + 1)$ is true whenever $P(n)$ is true.

Q. 15. A sequence $d_1, d_2, d_3, \ldots$ is defined by letting $d_1 = 2$ and $d_k = \frac{d_{k-1}}{k}$ for all natural numbers $k \geq 2$. Show that $d_n = \frac{2}{n!}$ for all $n \in N$

[NCERT Exemplar Q. 19, Page 71]

Sol. Given that: $d_1 = 2$ and $d_k = \frac{d_{k-1}}{k}$

Let $P(n)$: $d_n = \frac{2}{n!}$

Step 1: $P(1)$: $d_1 = \frac{2}{1!} = 2$ which is true for $P(1)$.

Step 2: $P(k)$: $d_k = \frac{2}{k!}$. Let it be true for $P(k)$.

Step 3: Given that: $d_k = \frac{d_{k-1}}{k}$

$\therefore \; d_{k+1} = \frac{d_{k+1-1}}{k+1} = \frac{d_k}{k+1}$

$\Rightarrow d_{k+1} = \frac{1}{k+1} \cdot d_k = \frac{1}{k+1} \cdot \frac{2}{k!}$

$\Rightarrow d_{k+1} = \frac{2}{(k+1)!}$, which is true for $P(k + 1)$

Hence, $P(k + 1)$ is true whenever $P(k)$ is true.

Q. 16. Prove that number of subsets of a set containing n distinct elements is 2^n, for all $n \in N$.

[NCERT Exemplar Q. 25, Page 72]

Sol. Let $P(n)$: Number of subsets of a set containing n distinct elements is 2^n, $\forall n \in N$

Step 1: It is clear that $P(1)$ is true for $n = 1$. Number of subset $= 2^1 = 2$. which is true.

Step 2: $P(k)$ is assumed to be true for $n = k$. Since the number of subsets $= 2^k$.

Step 3: $P(k + 1) = 2^{k+1}$

We know that if one number (i.e., element) is added to the elements of a given set, the number of subsets become double.

$\therefore$ Number of subsets of set having $(k + 1)$ distinct elements $2 \times 2^k = 2^{k+1}$, which is true for $P(k + 1)$.

Hence, $P(k + 1)$ is true whenever $P(k)$ is true.

Long Answer Type Questions-I (4 marks each)

Prove the following questions by using the principle of mathematical induction for all $n \in N$. (Q. 1 to 3)

Q. 1. $n(n^2 + 5)$ is divisible by 6, for each natural number n. **[NCERT Exemplar Q. 10, Page 71]**

Sol. Let $P(n) : n(n^2 + 5)$

Step 1: $P(1) : 1(1 + 5) = 6$ which is divisible by 6. So, it is true for $P(1)$.

Step 2: $P(k)$:$k(k^2+5) = 6\lambda$. Let it be true.

$\Rightarrow k^3 + 5k = 6\lambda$

$\Rightarrow k^3 = 6\lambda - 5k$

Step 3:

$P(k+1) = (k+1)[(k+1)^2 + 5]$

$= (k+1)[k^2 + 1 + 2k + 5]$

$= (k+1)[k^2 + 2k + 6]$

$= k^3 + 2k^2 + 6k + k^2 + 2k + 6$

$= k^3 + 3k^2 + 8k + 6$

$= k^3 + 5k + 3k^2 + 3k + 6$

$= 6\lambda - 5k + 5k + 3(k^2 + k + 2)$

$= 6\lambda + 3k(k^2 + k + 2)$

$= 6\lambda + 3k(k + 1) + 6$

$\Rightarrow P(k + 1)$ is true whenever $P(k)$ is true.

Hence, by PMI, $p(n)$ is true for all n N.

Q. 2. $n^2 < 2^n$, for all natural numbers $n \geq 5$.

[NCERT Exemplar Q. 11, Page 71]

Sol. Let $P(n)$: $n^2 < 2^2$ for all natural numbers, $n \geq 5$

Step 1: $P(5) : 1^2 < 2^5 \Rightarrow 1 < 32$, which true for P(5).

Step 2: $P(k) : k^2 < 2^k$. Let it be true for $k \in$ N.

Step 3: $P(k + 1) : (k + 1)2 < 2^{k+1}$

From step 2, we get

$k^2 < 2^k$

$\Rightarrow k^2 + 2k + 1 < 2^k + 2k + 1$

$\Rightarrow (k+1)^2 < 2^k + 2k + 1$ (i)

Since, $(2k + 1) < 2^k$

So, $k^2 + 2k + 1 < 2^k + 2^k$

$\Rightarrow k^2 + 2k + 1 < 2.2^k$

$\Rightarrow k^2 + 2k + 1 < 2^{k+1}$ (ii)

From eqn. (i) and (ii), we get $(k+1)^2 < 2^{k+1}$.

Hence, $P(k + 1)$ is true whenever $P(k)$ is true for $k \in N, n \geq 5$. By, PMI, $P(n)$ is true for all $n \in N$.

Q. 3. $2n < (n + 2)!$ for all natural number n.

[NCERT Exemplar Q. 12, Page 71]

Sol. Let $P(n) : 2n < (n + 2)!$ for all $k \in N$.

Step 1: $P(1)$: $2.1 < (1 + 2)!$

$\Rightarrow 2 < 3! \Rightarrow 2 < 6$ which is true for $P(1)$

$(\because 3! = 3 \times 2 \times 1 = 6)$

Step 2: $P(k)$: $2k < (k + 2)!$. Let it be true

Step 3: $P(k + 1)$: $2(k + 1) < (k + 1 + 2)!$

Since $2k < (k + 2)!$ (from Step 2)

$\Rightarrow 2k + 2 < (k + 2)! + 2$

$\Rightarrow 2(k + 1) < (k + 2)! + 2$

Also, $(k + 2)! + 2 < (k + 3)!$

$\therefore 2(k + 1) < (k + 3)!$

$\Rightarrow 2(k + 1) < (k + 2 + 1)!$, which is true for $P(k + 1)$

Hence, $P(k + 1)$ is true whenever $P(k)$ is true.

Q. 4. Prove that:

$$\cos\theta \cdot \cos 2\theta \cdot \cos 2^2\theta \ldots \cos 2^{n-1}\theta = \frac{\sin 2^n\theta}{2^n \sin\theta},$$

for all $n \in N$. [NCERT Exemplar Q. 21, Page 71]

Sol. Let $P(n)$:

$$\cos\theta \cdot \cos 2\theta \cdot \cos 2^2\theta \ldots \cos 2^{n-1}\theta = \frac{\sin 2^n\theta}{2^n \sin\theta}, \forall n \in N.$$

Step 1: $P(1)$:

$$\cos\theta = \frac{\sin 2^1\theta}{2^1 \sin\theta} = \frac{\sin 2\theta}{2\sin\theta} = \frac{2\sin\theta\cos\theta}{2\sin\theta} = \cos\theta$$

$\Rightarrow \cos\theta = \cos\theta$, which is true for $P(1)$.

Step 2:

$$P(k) : \cos\theta \cdot \cos 2\theta \cdot \cos 2^2\theta \ldots \cos 2^{k-1}\theta = \frac{\sin 2^k\theta}{2^k \sin\theta}$$

Let it be true.

Step 3: $P(k + 1)$:

$$\cos\theta \cdot \cos 2\theta \cdot \cos 2^2\theta \ldots \cos 2^{k-1}\theta \cdot \cos 2^{(k+1)-1}\theta$$

$$= \frac{\sin 2^k\theta}{2^k \sin\theta} \cdot \cos 2^{(k+1)-1}\theta = \frac{\sin 2^k\theta}{2^k \sin\theta} \cdot \cos 2^k\theta$$

$$= \frac{2\sin 2^k\theta \cdot \cos 2^k\theta}{2.2^k \sin\theta}$$

$$= \frac{\sin 2.2^k\theta}{2^{k+1}\sin\theta} \quad [\because 2\sin\theta\cos\theta = \sin 2\theta]$$

$$= \frac{\sin 2^{k+1}\theta}{2^{k+1}\sin\theta}$$ which is true for $P(k+1)$.

Hence, $P(k + 1)$ is true whenever $P(k)$ is true.

Q. 5. Show that: $\frac{n^5}{5} + \frac{n^3}{3} + \frac{7n}{15}$ is a natural number for all $n \in N$. [NCERT Exemplar Q. 23, Page 72]

Sol. Let $P(n) : \frac{1^5}{5} + \frac{n^3}{3} + \frac{7n}{15}, n \in N.$

Step 1: $P(1) : \frac{1^5}{5} + \frac{1^3}{3} + \frac{7.1}{15} = \frac{3+5+7}{15} = \frac{15}{15} = 1 \in N$

Which is true for $P(1)$.

Step 2: $P(k)$: $\frac{k^5}{5} + \frac{k^3}{3} + \frac{7 \cdot k}{15}$. Let it be true for $P(k)$

and let $\frac{k^5}{5} + \frac{k^3}{3} + \frac{7k}{15} = \lambda.$

Step 3: $P(k+1) = \frac{(k+1)^5}{5} + \frac{(k+1)^3}{3} + \frac{7(k+1)}{15}$

$$= \frac{1}{5}\left[k^5 + 5k^4 + 10k^3 + 10k^2 + 5k + 1\right] + \frac{1}{3}\left[k^3 + 3k^2 + 3k + 1\right] + \frac{7}{15}k + \frac{7}{15}$$

$$= \left(\frac{k^5}{5} + \frac{k^3}{3} + \frac{7k}{15}\right) + \left(k^4 + 2k^3 + 3k^2 + 2k\right) + \frac{1}{5} + \frac{1}{3} + \frac{7}{15}$$

$= \lambda + k^4 + 2k^3 + 3k^2 + 2k + 1$ [from Step 2]

= positive integers = natural number

which is true for $P(k + 1)$.

Hence, $P(k + 1)$ is true whenever $P(k)$ is true.

Q. 6. Prove that: $\frac{1}{n+1} + \frac{1}{n+2} + \ldots + \frac{1}{2n} > \frac{13}{24}$ for all natural numbers, $n > 1$.

[NCERT Exemplar Q. 24, Page 72]

Sol. Let $P(n) : \frac{1}{n+1} + \frac{1}{n+2} + \cdots + \frac{1}{2n} > \frac{13}{24}, \forall n \in N$

Step 1: $P(2) : \frac{1}{2+1} + \frac{1}{2+2} > \frac{13}{24} \Rightarrow \frac{1}{3} + \frac{1}{4} > \frac{13}{24}$

$\frac{7}{12} > \frac{13}{24} \Rightarrow \frac{14}{24} > \frac{13}{24}$ which is true for $P(2)$.

Step 2: $P(k)$: $\frac{1}{k+1} + \frac{1}{k+2} + \cdots + \frac{1}{2k} > \frac{13}{24}$. Let it be true.

Step 3:

$$P(k+1) : \frac{1}{k+1} + \frac{1}{k+2} + \cdots + \frac{1}{2k} + \frac{1}{2(k+1)} > \frac{13}{24}$$

Since $\frac{1}{k+1} + \frac{1}{k+2} + \cdots + \frac{1}{2k} > \frac{13}{24}$

So $\frac{1}{k+1} + \frac{1}{k+2} + \cdots + \frac{1}{2k} + \frac{1}{2(k+1)} > \frac{13}{24}$

Which is true for $P(k + 1)$.

Hence, $P(k + 1)$ is true whenever $P(k)$ is true.

Long Answer Type Question-II (5 marks each)

Prove the following questions by using the principle of mathematical induction for all $n \in N$ (Q. 1-3)

Q. 1. $\sqrt{n} < \frac{1}{\sqrt{1}} + \frac{1}{\sqrt{2}} + \dots + \frac{1}{\sqrt{n}}$ **for all natural numbers** $n \geq 2$. **[NCERT Exemplar Q. 13, Page 71]**

Sol. Let $P(n): \sqrt{n} < \frac{1}{\sqrt{1}} + \frac{1}{\sqrt{2}} + \dots + \frac{1}{\sqrt{n}} \quad \forall n \geq 2$

Step 1: $P(2): \sqrt{2} < \frac{1}{\sqrt{1}} + \frac{1}{\sqrt{2}}$, which is true.

Step 2: $P(k)$:

$$\sqrt{k} < \frac{1}{\sqrt{1}} + \frac{1}{\sqrt{2}} + \dots + \frac{1}{\sqrt{k}}.$$

Let it be true.

Step 3: $P(k + 1)$: $\sqrt{k+1} < \frac{1}{\sqrt{1}} + \frac{1}{\sqrt{2}} + \dots + \frac{1}{\sqrt{k+1}}$

From Step 2, we have

$$\sqrt{k} < \frac{1}{\sqrt{1}} + \frac{1}{\sqrt{2}} + \dots + \frac{1}{\sqrt{k}}$$

$$\Rightarrow \sqrt{k} + \frac{1}{\sqrt{k+1}} < \frac{1}{\sqrt{1}} + \frac{1}{\sqrt{2}} + \dots + \frac{1}{\sqrt{k}} + \frac{1}{\sqrt{k+1}}$$

$$\Rightarrow \frac{\sqrt{k}\cdot\sqrt{k+1}+1}{\sqrt{k+1}} < \frac{1}{\sqrt{1}} + \frac{1}{\sqrt{2}} + \dots + \frac{1}{\sqrt{k}} + \frac{1}{\sqrt{k+1}} \quad \text{(i)}$$

Now if, $\sqrt{k+1} < \frac{\sqrt{k}\cdot\sqrt{k+1}+1}{\sqrt{k+1}}$

$$\Rightarrow (k+1) < \sqrt{k}\cdot\sqrt{k+1}+1$$

$$\Rightarrow k < \sqrt{k}\cdot\sqrt{k+1} \quad \text{(ii)}$$

From eqn. (i) and (ii) we get

$$\sqrt{k+1} < \frac{1}{\sqrt{1}} + \frac{1}{\sqrt{2}} + \dots + \frac{1}{\sqrt{k+1}}$$

$\Rightarrow P(k + 1)$ is true whenever $P(k)$ is true.

Hence, by PMI, $P(n)$ is true for all $n \in N$.

Q. 2. Prove that for all $n \in N$.

$$\cos\alpha + \cos(\alpha+\beta) + \cos(\alpha+2\beta) + \dots + \cos[\alpha+(n-1)\beta]$$

$$= \frac{\cos\left[\alpha + \left(\frac{n-1}{1}\right)\right]\beta\left[\sin\frac{k\beta}{2}\right]}{\sin\frac{\beta}{2}}$$

[NCERT Exemplar Q. 20, Page 71]

Sol. Step 1: $P(1): \cos\alpha = \frac{(\cos\alpha)\left(\sin\frac{\beta}{2}\right)}{\sin\frac{\beta}{2}} = \cos\alpha$

which is true for P (i)

Step 2: $P(k)$:

$$\cos\alpha + \cos(\alpha+\beta) + \cos(\alpha+2\beta) + \dots + \cos[\alpha+(k-1)\beta]$$

$$= \frac{\cos\left[\alpha + \left(\frac{k-1}{2}\right)\beta\right]\sin\left(\frac{k\beta}{2}\right)}{\sin\frac{\beta}{2}}.$$ Let it be true.

Step 3: $P(k + 1)$:

$$\cos\alpha + \cos(\alpha+\beta) + \cos(\alpha+2\beta) + \dots + \cos[\alpha+(k-1)\beta] + \cos[\alpha+(k+1-1)\beta]$$

$$= \frac{\cos\left[\alpha + \left(\frac{k-1}{2}\right)\beta\right]\sin\left(\frac{k\beta}{2}\right)}{\sin\frac{\beta}{2}} + \cos(\alpha+k\beta) \quad \text{(from Step 2)}$$

$$= \frac{2\cos\left[\alpha + \left(\frac{k-1}{2}\right)\beta\right]\sin\left(\frac{k\beta}{2}\right) + 2\cos(\alpha+k\beta)\cdot\sin\frac{\beta}{2}}{2\sin\frac{\beta}{2}}$$

$$= \frac{\sin\left[\alpha+k\beta-\frac{\beta}{2}\right] - \sin\left[\alpha-\frac{\beta}{2}\right] + \sin\left[\alpha+k\beta+\frac{\beta}{2}\right] - \sin\left[\alpha+k\beta-\frac{\beta}{2}\right]}{2\sin\frac{\beta}{2}}$$

$[\because 2\cos A\sin B = \sin(A+B) - \sin(A-B)]$

$$= \frac{\sin\left[\alpha+k\beta+\frac{\beta}{2}\right] - \sin\left(\alpha-\frac{\beta}{2}\right)}{2\sin\frac{\beta}{2}}$$

$$= \frac{2\cos\left(\alpha+\frac{k\beta}{2}\right)\sin(k+1)\frac{\beta}{2}}{2\sin\frac{\beta}{2}}$$

$$\frac{\cos\left(\alpha+\frac{k\beta}{2}\right)\cdot\sin(k+1)\frac{\beta}{2}}{\sin\frac{\beta}{2}}$$

$$\cos\left[\alpha+\left(\frac{k+1-1}{2}\right)\beta\right]$$

$$= \left| \frac{\sin\left(\frac{k+1}{2}\right)\beta}{\sin\frac{\beta}{2}} \right|$$, which is true for $P(k + 1)$

$\Rightarrow P(k + 1)$ is true whenever $P(k)$ is true.

Hence, by PMI, $P(n)$ is true for all $n \in N$.

Q. 3. Prove that $\sin\theta + \sin 2\theta + \sin 3\theta + ... + \sin n\theta$

$$= \frac{\sin\frac{n\theta}{2} . \sin\frac{n+1}{2}\theta}{\sin\frac{\theta}{2}}$$, **for all $n \in N$.**

[NCERT Exemplar Q. 22, Page 71]

Sol. Let $P(n)$: $\sin\theta + \sin 2\theta + \sin 3\theta + \cdots + \sin n\theta$

$$= \frac{\sin\frac{n\theta}{2} \cdot \sin\left(\frac{n+1}{2}\right)\theta}{\sin\frac{\theta}{2}}, n \in \text{N}.$$

Step 1: $P(1)$:

$$\sin\theta = \frac{\sin\frac{1\theta}{2} \cdot \sin\left(\frac{1+1}{2}\right)\theta}{\sin\frac{\theta}{2}} = \frac{\sin\frac{\theta}{2} \cdot \sin\theta}{\sin\frac{\theta}{2}} = \sin\theta$$

$\therefore \sin\theta = \sin\theta$ which is true for $P(1)$.

Step 2: $P(k)$: $\sin\theta + \sin 2\theta + \sin 3\theta + \cdots + \sin k\theta$

$$= \frac{\sin\frac{k\theta}{2} \cdot \sin\left(\frac{k+1}{2}\right)\theta}{\sin\frac{\theta}{2}}$$. Let it be true for $P(k)$.

Step : 3

$P(k + 1)$: $\sin\theta + \sin 2\theta + \sin 3\theta + \cdots + \sin (k+1)\theta$

$$= \frac{\sin\frac{k\theta}{2} \cdot \sin\left(\frac{k+1}{2}\right)\theta}{\sin\frac{\theta}{2}} + \sin(k+1)\theta$$

$$= \frac{\sin\frac{k\theta}{2} \cdot \sin\left(\frac{k+1}{2}\right)\theta + \sin(k+1)\theta \cdot \sin\frac{\theta}{2}}{\sin\frac{\theta}{2}}$$

$$= \frac{\cos\left(\frac{k\theta}{2} - \frac{k+1}{2}\theta\right) - \cos\left(\frac{k\theta}{2} + \frac{k+1}{2}\theta\right) + \cos\left[(k+1)\theta - \frac{\theta}{2}\right] - \cos\left[(k+1)\theta + \frac{\theta}{2}\right]}{2\sin\frac{\theta}{2}}$$

$$= \frac{\cos\left(-\frac{\theta}{2}\right) - \cos\left(k\theta + \frac{\theta}{2}\right) + \cos\left[k\theta + \frac{\theta}{2}\right] - \cos\left[k\theta + \frac{3\theta}{2}\right]}{2\sin\frac{\theta}{2}}$$

$$= \frac{\cos\left(\frac{\theta}{2}\right) - \cos\left(k\theta + \frac{3\theta}{2}\right)}{2\sin\frac{\theta}{2}}$$

$$= \frac{-2\sin\left(\frac{\frac{\theta}{2} + k\theta + \frac{3\theta}{2}}{2}\right) \cdot \sin\left(\frac{\frac{\theta}{2} - k\theta - \frac{3\theta}{2}}{2}\right)}{2\sin\frac{\theta}{2}}$$

$$\left[\because \cos A - \cos A = -2\sin\frac{(A+B)}{2}\sin\frac{(A-B)}{2}\right]$$

$$= \frac{-2\sin\left(\frac{k\theta + 2\theta}{2}\right) \cdot \sin\left(\frac{-k\theta - \theta}{2}\right)}{2\sin\frac{\theta}{2}}$$

$$= \frac{\sin\left(\frac{k\theta + 2\theta}{2}\right) \cdot \sin\left(\frac{k\theta + \theta}{2}\right)}{\sin\frac{\theta}{2}}$$

$$= \frac{\sin\left[\frac{(k+1)+1}{2}\right]\theta \cdot \sin\left[\frac{k+1}{2}\right]\theta}{\sin\frac{\theta}{2}}$$, which is true for $P(k+1)$.

$\Rightarrow P(k + 1)$ is true whenever $P(k)$ is true.

Hence, by PMI, $P(n)$ is true for all $n \in N$.

EXPERT ADVICE

- *This is student's favorite topic, most of the students find this chapter interesting.*
- *You just need to practice questions from this topic.*
- *One question will surely come from this topic.*

OSWAAL LEARNING TOOLS

For Suggested Online Videos

Visit : *https://youtu.be/dMn5w4_ztSw*

Or Scan the Code

Visit : *https://youtu.be/i9h9_-iTrwk*

Or Scan the Code

Visit : *https://youtu.be/B2Qp3efqn0g*

Or Scan the Code

Visit : *https://youtu.be/CU0qbjxgHKs*

Or Scan the Code

Visit : *https://youtu.be/3QXRLlodr6w*

Or Scan the Code

Visit : *https://goo.gl/eDRcCm*

Or Scan the Code

CHAPTER 5

COMPLEX NUMBERS AND QUADRATIC EQUATIONS

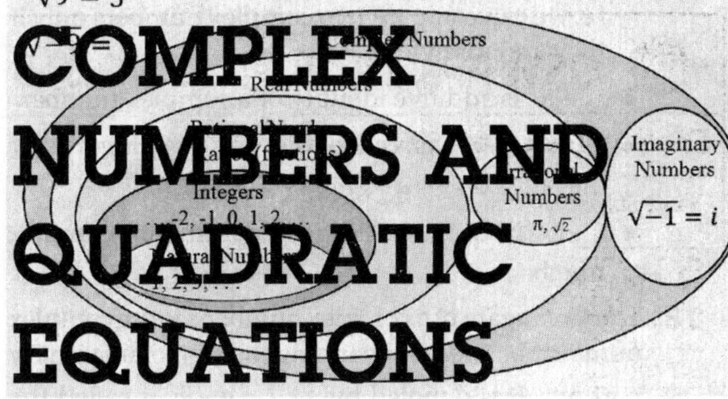

Chapter Objectives

> *Complex number; Integrals powers of 'i'; Real and imaginary parts of a complex numbers; Algebraic properties of complex numbers; Statement of fundamental theorem of Algebra; Solution of quadratic equations (with real coefficients) in the complex number system; Square roots of a complex number.*

TOPIC-1
Complex Numbers, their Conjugate and Square Roots

TOPIC - 1
Complex Numbers, their Conjugate and Square Roots **P. 59**

Quick Review

> A number consisting of real number and imaginary number is called a **Complex number.**

> The coordinate plane that represents the complex numbers is called the Complex plane or Argand plane.

> A complex number can be defined as, "A number of the form $a + ib$, where a and b are real numbers is called a complex number."

> Here, the symbol 'i' is called *iota*. We have $i^2 = -1$ *i.e.*, $\pm i$ is the solution of the equation $x^2 + 1 = 0$.

> **Integral powers of 'i' :**

$$i^{4q} = 1, \quad q \in N$$
$$i^{4q+1} = i, \quad q \in N$$
$$i^{4q+2} = -1, \quad q \in N$$
$$i^{4q+3} = -i, \quad q \in N$$
$$i^{-q} = \frac{1}{i^q}, \quad q \in N$$

TIPS...

- *Student should remember that set R of real numbers is a proper subset of the complex numbers. Hence, the complete number system is $N \subset W \subset I \subset Q \subset R \subset C$.*
- *Zero is purely real as well as purely imaginary but not imaginary.*
- *$\sqrt{a}\sqrt{b} = \sqrt{ab}$ only if one of a or b is non-negative.*
- *Revise all the formulae and practice as many questions as possible.*

> **Real and imaginary parts of a complex numbers:**

- Let $z = a + ib$ be a complex number, then a is **called real part** and b is called the **imaginary part** of z and it may be denoted as Re (z) and Im (z) respectively.

  e.g. : If $z = 2 + 3i$, then

  Re (z) = 2, Im (z) = 3.

- If $a + ib = c + id$ then $a = c$, and $b = d$
- Let $z_1 = a + ib, z_2 = c + id$, In general, we cannot compare and say that $z_1 > z_2$ or but if $b, d = 0$ and $a > c$ then $z_1 > z_2$

i.e. we can compare two complex numbers only if they are purely real.

- $0+i0$ is additive identity of a complex number.
- $-z=-a-ib$ is called the additive inverse or negative of $z=a+ib$
- $1+i0$ is a multiplicative identity of complex number.

➤ The **Conjugate** of a complex number z is the complex number obtained by changing the sign of imaginary part of z. It is denoted by $\bar{z}$. $\bar{Z}=a-ib$ is called the conjugate of $z=a+ib$.

➤ **Modulus** (Absolute value) of *r* complex number, *z* = *a* + *ib* is defined by the non-negative real number $\sqrt{a^2+b^2}$. It is denoted by $|z|$.

- $z^{-1}=\frac{1}{z}=\frac{a-ib}{a^2+b^2}=\frac{\bar{Z}}{|z|^2}$ is called the multiplicative inverse of $z=a+ib$. $(a\neq 0, b\neq 0)$
- $|z_1+z_2|\leq|z_1|+|z_2|$
- $|z_1-z_2|=|z_1|\cdot|z_2|$
- $\left|\frac{z_1}{z_2}\right|=\frac{|z_1|}{|z_2|}$; $|z^n|=|z|^n$; $|z|=|\bar{z}|=|-z|=|-\bar{z}|$; $z\bar{z}=|z|^2$
- $|z_1-z_2|\geq|z_1|-|z_2|$

TRICKS...

For any integer k, $i^{4k}=1$, $i^{4k+1}=i$, $i^{4k+2}=-1$, $i^{4k+3}=-i$

For any non-zero complex number z = a + ib (a ≠ 0, b ≠ 0), there exists complex number $\frac{a}{a^2+b^2}+i\left(\frac{-b}{a^2+b^2}\right)$, denoted by $\frac{1}{z}$ or z^{-1}, called the multiplicative inverse of z s.t. (a + i b) $\left(\frac{a^2}{a^2+b^2}+i\frac{-b}{a^2+b^2}\right)=1+i\,0=1$

A polynomial equation of n degree has n roots. Polynomial equation has at least one root.

The solutions of the quadratic equation $ax^2+bx+c=0$, where a, b, c, ∈ R, a ≠ 0, $b^2-4ac<0$, are given by $x=\frac{-b\pm\sqrt{4ac-b^2}i}{2a}$

➤ Polar form of $z=a+ib$ is,

- $z=r(\cos\theta+i\sin\theta)$, where $r=\sqrt{a^2+b^2}=|z|$ is called the modulus of z, θ is called the argument or amplitude of z.
- The value of θ such that, $-\pi<\theta<\pi$ is called the **principal argument** of z.
- $z=x+iy$, $x>0$ and $y>0$ the argument of z is acute angle given by $\tan\alpha=\frac{y}{x}$.

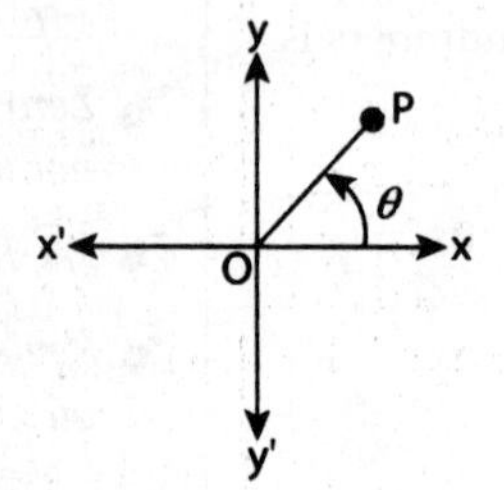

Fig (i)

- $z=x+iy, x<0$ and $y>0$ the argument of z is $\pi-\alpha$, where α is acute angle given by $\tan\alpha=\left|\frac{y}{x}\right|$.

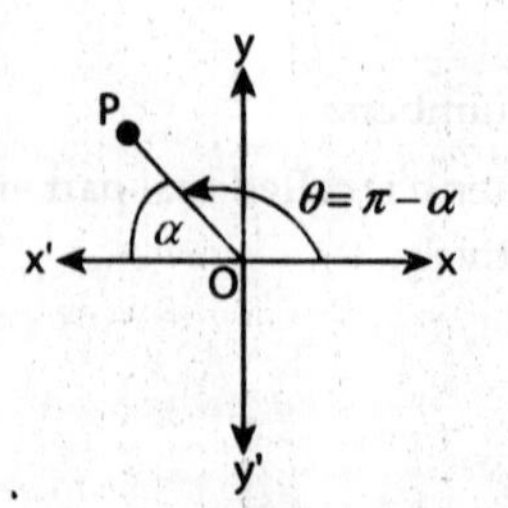

Fig (ii)

- $z=x+iy, x<0$ and $y<0$ the argument of z is $\alpha-\pi$, where π is acute angle given by $\tan\alpha=\left|\frac{y}{x}\right|$.

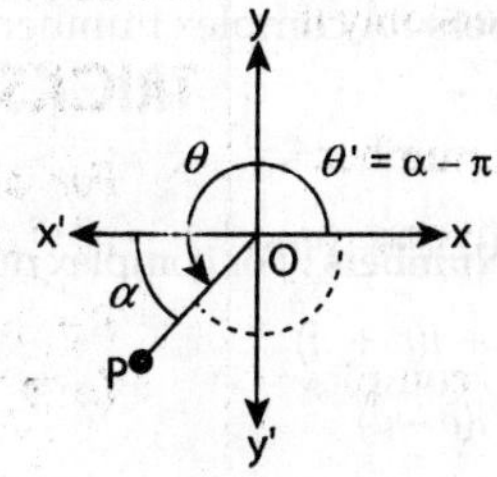

Fig (iii)

- $z = x + iy, x > 0$ and $y < 0$ the argument of z is $-\alpha$, where α is acute angle given by $\tan\alpha = \left|\frac{y}{x}\right|$.

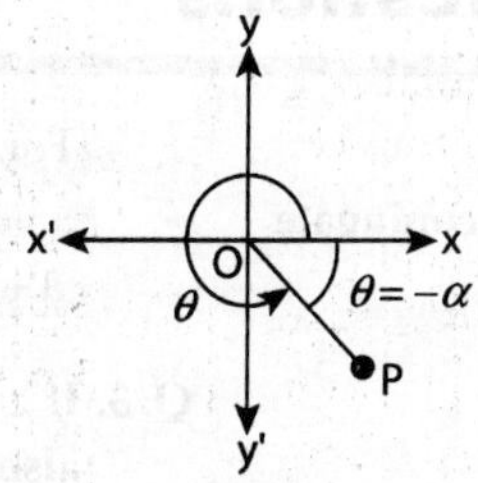

Fig (iv)

- If $z_1 = r_1(\cos\theta_1 + i\sin\theta_1)$
  $z_2 = r_2(\cos\theta_2 + i\sin\theta_2)$
  Then $z_1z_2 = r_1r_2\left[\cos(\theta_1+\theta_2) + i\sin(\theta_1+\theta_2)\right]$
  and $\frac{z_1}{z_2} = \frac{r_1}{r_2}\left[\cos(\theta_1-\theta_2) + i\sin(\theta_1-\theta_2)\right]$

➤ **Properties of Argument of complex numbers :**
If z_1 and z_2 are two complex numbers, then

(i) $\arg(z_1 z_2) = \arg(z_1) + \arg(z_2)$

(ii) $\arg\left(\frac{z_1}{z_2}\right) = \arg(z_1) - \arg(z_2)$

(iii) $\arg\left(\frac{z}{\bar{z}}\right) = 2\arg(z)$

(iv) $\arg(z^n) = n\arg(z)$

(v) If $\arg\left(\frac{z_2}{z_1}\right) = \theta$, then $\arg\left(\frac{z_1}{z_2}\right) = -\theta$

(vi) $\arg(\bar{z}) = -\arg(z)$

(vii) If $\arg(z) = 0 \Rightarrow z$ is real

(ix) $|z_1 + z_2| = |z_1 - z_2| = \arg(z_1) - \arg(z_2)$

(x) $|z_1 + z_2| = |z_1| + |z_2| \Rightarrow \arg(z_1) + \arg(z_2)$

Know the Terms

➤ **Imaginary Number :** A number whose square root is negative is known as an imaginary number, *e.g.*, $\sqrt{-1}, \sqrt{-2}$ etc.

➤ $\sqrt{-1}$ is denoted by the Greek letter i (iota).

➤ **Powers of i :** $i^0 = 1$; $i^2 = -1$; $i^3 = -i$, $i^4 = 1$ etc.

➤ **An Important Result :** For any two real numbers a and b, $\sqrt{a} \times \sqrt{b} = \sqrt{ab}$ is true only when at least one of a and b is either 0 or positive.
In fact, $\sqrt{-a} \times \sqrt{-b} = (i\sqrt{a})(i\sqrt{b}) = i^2\sqrt{ab} = -\sqrt{ab}$, where a and b are positive real numbers.

➤ **Complex Number :** Any number of the form $x + iy$, where x and y are real numbers and $i = \sqrt{-1}$ is called a complex number.
It is denoted by z *i.e.*, $z = x + iy$. The real and imaginary parts of a complex number z are denoted by $Re(z)$ and $Im(z)$ respectively.
Thus, if $z = x + iy$, then $Re(z) = x$ and $Im(z) = y$.
Note : Every real number is a complex number, for if $a \in R$, it can be written as $a = a + i0$.

- **Purely Real and Purely Imaginary Numbers :** A complex number z is said to be
  (i) purely real, if $Im\ (z) = 0$.
  (ii) purely imaginary, if $Re\ (z) = 0$.
- **Sum, Difference and Product of Complex Numbers :** For complex numbers, $z_1 = a + ib$ and $z_2 = c + id$, it is defined as
  (i) $z_1 + z_2 = (a + ib) + (c + id) = (a + c) + i(b + d)$
  (ii) $z_1 - z_2 = (a + ib) - (c + id) = (a - c) + i(b - d)$
  (iii) $z_1 z_2 = (a + ib)(c + id) = (ac - bd) + i(ad + bc)$

Multiple Choice Questions

(1 mark each)

[A] Objective Type Questions

Q. 1. $\sin x + i \cos 2x$ and $\cos x - i \sin 2x$ are conjugate to each other for:

(A) $x = n\pi$

(B) $x = \left(n + \frac{1}{2}\right)\frac{\pi}{2}$

(C) $x = 0$

(D) No value of x

[NCERT Exemplar Q. 35, Page 95]

Ans. Correct option : (C)

Let $z = \sin x + i \cos 2x$ and $\bar{z} = \sin x - i \cos 2x$, but we are given that $\bar{z} = \cos x - i \sin 2x$

$\therefore \sin x - i \cos 2x = \cos x - i \sin 2x$

$\tan x = 1$ and $\tan 2x = 1 \Rightarrow \tan x = \tan \frac{\pi}{4}$ and $\tan 2x$

$= \tan \frac{\pi}{4}$

$\therefore x = n\pi + \frac{\pi}{4}$ and $2x = n\pi + \frac{\pi}{4}$

$\therefore x = 2x \Rightarrow 2x - x = 0 \Rightarrow x = 0$

Q. 2. The real value of α for which the expression $\frac{1 - i\sin\alpha}{1 + 2i\sin\alpha}$ is purely real is :

(A) $(n+1)\frac{\pi}{2}$

(B) $(2n+1)\frac{\pi}{2}$

(C) $n\pi$

(D) None of these, where $n \in N$

[NCERT Exemplar Q. 36, Page 95]

Ans. Correct option : (C)

Let $z = \frac{1 - i\sin\alpha}{1 + 2i\sin\alpha} = \frac{(1 - i\sin\alpha)(1 - 2i\sin\alpha)}{(1 + 2i\sin\alpha)(1 - 2i\sin\alpha)}$

$= \frac{2 - 3i\sin\alpha - 2\sin^2\alpha}{1 - 4i^2\sin^2\alpha}$

$= \frac{1 - 2\sin^2\alpha}{1 + 4\sin^2\alpha} - \frac{3\sin\alpha}{1 + 4\sin^2\alpha}i$

For, z is purely real, then

$\frac{-3\sin\alpha}{1 + 4\sin^2\alpha} = 0 \Rightarrow \sin\alpha = 0$ hence, $\alpha = n\pi,\ n \in N$.

Q. 3. If $z = x + iy$ lies in the third quadrant, then $\frac{\bar{z}}{z}$ also lies in the third quadrant if

(A) $x > y > 0$

(B) $x < y < 0$

(C) $y < x < 0$

(D) $y > x > 0$

[NCERT Exemplar Q. 37, Page 156]

Ans. Correct option : (B)

Given that : $z = x + i\,y$. If z lies in III quadrant. So, $x < 0$ and $y < 0$ $\bar{z} = x = i\,y$.

$\frac{\bar{z}}{z} = \frac{x - iy}{x + iy} = \frac{x - iy}{x + iy} \times \frac{x - iy}{x - iy} = i\frac{x^2 - y^2}{x^2 + y^2} - \frac{2xy}{x^2 + y^2}$

When x lies in III quadrant, then $\frac{\bar{z}}{z}$ will also be lie in III quadrant.

$\therefore x^2 - y^2 < 0$ and $2x\,y > 0 \Rightarrow x^2 < y^2$ and $xy > 0$. So. $x < y < 0$.

Q. 4. The value of $(z+3)(\bar{z}+3)$ is equivalent to

(A) $|z+3|^2$ **(B)** $|z-3|$

(C) $z^2 + 3$ **(D)** None of these

[NCERT Exemplar Q. 38, Page 95]

Ans. Correct option : (A)

Given that $(z + 3)(\bar{z} + 3)$. Let $x = x + i\,y$

$\therefore (z + 3)(\bar{z} + 3) = (x + i\,y + 3)(x - i\,y + 3)$

$= [(x + 3) + i\,y][(x + 3) - i\,y]$

$= (x + 3)^2 - y^2 i^2 = (x + 3)^2 + y^2$

$= |x + 3 + i\,y|^2 = |z + 3|^2$

Q. 5. If $\left(\frac{1+i}{1-i}\right)^x = 1$, then

(A) $x = 2n + 1$ **(B)** $x = 4n$

(C) $x = 2n$ **(D)** $x = 4n + 1$, where $n \in$ N

[NCERT Exemplar Q. 39, Page 95]

Ans. Correct option : (B)

Given : $\left(\frac{1+i}{1-i}\right)^x = 1$

$\Rightarrow \left[\frac{(1+i)(1+i)}{(1-i)(1+i)}\right]^x = 1 \Rightarrow \left(\frac{1+i^2+2i}{1-i^2}\right)^x = 1$

$\Rightarrow \left(\frac{1-1+2i}{1+1}\right)^x = 1 \Rightarrow \left(\frac{2i}{2}\right)^x = 1 \Rightarrow (i)^x = 1$

$\Rightarrow (i)^x = (i)^{4n}, n \in N$

Q. 6. A real value of x satisfies the equation $\left(\frac{3-4ix}{3+4ix}\right) = \alpha - i\beta \,(\alpha, \beta \in R)$ if $\alpha^2 + \beta^2 =$

(A) 1 **(B) −1**

(C) 2 **(D) −2**

[NCERT Exemplar Q. 40, Page 96]

Ans. Correct option : (A)

Given that : $\left(\frac{3-4ix}{3+4ix}\right) = \alpha - i\beta$

$\Rightarrow \left(\frac{3-4ix}{3+4ix} \times \frac{3-4ix}{3-4ix}\right) = \alpha - i\beta$

$\Rightarrow \left(\frac{3-4ix}{3+4ix} \times \frac{3-4ix}{3-4ix}\right) = \alpha - i\beta$

$\Rightarrow \frac{9-16x^2}{9+16x^2} - \frac{24x}{9+16x^2} i = \alpha - i\beta$ ...(i)

$\Rightarrow \frac{9-16x^2}{9+16x^2} + \frac{24x}{9+16x^2} i = \alpha - i\beta$ ...(ii)

Multiplying eq. (i) and (ii), we get

$\left(\frac{9-16x^2}{9+16x^2}\right)^2 + \left(\frac{24x}{9+16x^2}\right)^2 = \alpha^2 + \beta^2$

$\Rightarrow \frac{(9+16x^2)^2}{(9+16x^2)^2} = \alpha^2 + \beta^2 \Rightarrow \alpha^2 + \beta^2 = 1$

Q. 7. Which of the following is correct for any two complex numbers z_1 and z_2?

(A) $|z_1 z_2| = |z_1||z_2|$

(B) $\arg(z_1 z_2) = \arg(z_1) \cdot \arg(z_2)$

(C) $|z_1 + z_2| = |z_1| + |z_2|$

(D) $|z_1 + z_2| \geq |z_1| - |z_2|$

[NCERT Exemplar Q. 41, Page 96]

Ans. Correct option : (A)

Let $z_1 = r_1 (\cos\theta_1 + i \sin\theta_1) \therefore |z_1| = r_1$

and $z_2 = r_2 (\cos\theta_2 + i \sin\theta_2) \therefore |z_2| = r_2$

Now, $z_1 z_2 = r_1 (\cos\theta_1 + i \sin\theta_1) . r_2 (\cos\theta_2 + i \sin\theta_2)$

$= r_1 r_2 [(\cos\theta_1\cos\theta_2 - \sin\theta_1 \sin\theta_2) + i (\sin\theta_1 \cos\theta_2 + \cos\theta_1 \sin\theta_2)]$

$= r_1 r_2 [\cos (\theta_1 + \theta_2) + i \sin (\theta_1 + \theta_2)]$

$\therefore |z_1 z_2| = |z_1| |z_2|$

Q. 8. The point represented by the complex number $2 - i$ is rotated about origin through an angle $\frac{\pi}{2}$ in the clockwise direction, the new position of point is:

(A) $1 + 2i$ **(B) $-1 - 2i$**

(C) $2 + i$ **(D) $-1 + 2i$**

[NCERT Exemplar Q. 42, Page 96]

Ans. Correct option : (B)

Given, $z = 2 - i$

If z rotated through an angle of $\frac{\pi}{2}$ about the origin in clockwise direction.

Then, the new position $= z.e^{-(\pi/2)}$

$= (2 - i)\, e^{-(\pi/2)}$

$= (2 - i) \left[\cos\left(-\frac{\pi}{2}\right) + i \sin\left(-\frac{\pi}{2}\right)\right]$

$= (2 - i)(0 - i) = -1 - 2i$

Q. 9. Let $x, y \in R$, then $x + iy$ is a non real complex number if:

(A) $x = 0$ **(B) $y = 0$**

(C) $x \neq 0$ **(D) $y \neq 0$**

[NCERT Exemplar Q. 43, Page 96]

Ans. Correct option : (D)

$x + iy$ is a non-real complex number

if $y \neq 0$

If $x, y \in R$

Q. 10. If $a + ib = c + id$, then

(A) $a^2 + c^2 = 0$ **(B) $b^2 + c^2 = 0$**

(C) $b^2 + d^2 = 0$ **(D) $a^2 + b^2 = c^2 + d^2$**

[NCERT Exemplar Q. 44, Page 96]

Ans. Correct option : (D)

Given that : $a + ib = c + id$

$\Rightarrow |a + ib| = |c + id| \Rightarrow \sqrt{a^2 + b^2} = \sqrt{c^2 + d^2}$

Squaring both side, we get $a^2 + b^2 = c^2 + d^2$

Q. 11. The complex number z which satisfies the condition $\left|\frac{i+z}{i-z}\right| = 1$ lies on

(A) circle $x^2 + y^2 = 1$

(B) the x-axis

(C) the y-axis

(D) the line $x + y = 1$.

[NCERT Exemplar Q. 45, Page 96]

Ans. Correct option : (B)

Let $x = x + iy$

$\therefore \left|\frac{i + x + yi}{i - x - yi}\right| = 1 \Rightarrow \left|\frac{x + (y+1)i}{-x - (y-1)i}\right| = 1$

$\Rightarrow |x + (y + 1) i| = |-x - (y - 1) i|$

$\Rightarrow \sqrt{x^2 + (y+1)^2} = \sqrt{x^2 + (y-1)^2}$

$\rightarrow x^2 + (y + 1)^2 = x^2 + (y - 1)^2$

$\Rightarrow y^2 + 2y + 1 = y^2 - 2y + 1$

$\Rightarrow 2y = -2y \Rightarrow 4y = 0 \Rightarrow y = 0 \Rightarrow x -$ axis.

Q. 12. If z is a complex number, then

(A) $|z^2|>|z|^2$ (B) $|z^2|=|z|^2$

(C) $|z^2|<|z|^2$ (D) $|z^2|\geq|z|^2$

[NCERT Exemplar Q. 46, Page 96]

Ans. Correct option : (B)

Let $z = x + yi$; $|z| = |x + yi|$ and $|z|^2 = |x + yi|^2$

$\Rightarrow |z|^2 = x^2 + y^2$ ...(i)

Now, $z^2 = x^2 + y^2 i^2 + 2xyi$

$z^2 = x^2 - y^2 + 2xyi$

$|z^2| = \sqrt{(x^2-y^2)^2+(2xy)^2}$

$= \sqrt{x^4+y^4-2x^2y^2+4x^2y^2}$

$= \sqrt{(x^2+y^2)^2}$

So, $|z|^2 = x^2 + y^2 = |z^2| \therefore |z|^2 = |z^2|$

Q. 13. $|z_1+z_2|=|z_1|+|z_2|$ is possible if

(A) $z_2=\bar{z}_1$ (B) $z_2=\dfrac{1}{z_1}$

(C) $\arg(z_1)=\arg(z_2)$ (D) $|z_1|=|z_2|$

[NCERT Exemplar Q. 47, Page 96]

Ans. Correct option : (C)

Let $z_1 = r_1 (\cos\theta_1 + i \sin\theta_1)$ and

$z_2 = r_2 (\cos\theta_2 + i \sin\theta_2)$

Since, $|z_1 + z_2| = |z_1| + |z_2|$

$\therefore (z_1 + z_2) = r_1 \cos\theta_1 + r_1 i \sin\theta_1 + r_2 \cos\theta_2 + i r_2 \sin\theta_2$

Now, $|z_1 + z_2|$

$$= \sqrt{\begin{array}{l} r_1^2\cos^2\theta_1+r_2^2\cos^2\theta_2+2r_1r_2\cos\theta_1\cos\theta_2 \\ +r_1^2\sin^2\theta_1+r_2^2\sin^2\theta_2+2r_1r_2\sin\theta_1\sin\theta_2 \end{array}}$$

$= \sqrt{r_1^2+r_2^2+2r_1r_2\cos(\theta_1-\theta_2)}$

But $|z_1 + z_2| = |z_1| + |z_2|$

So, $\sqrt{r_1^2+r_2^2+2r_1r_2\cos(\theta_1-\theta_2)} = r_1 + r_2$

Squaring both sides, we get

$r_1^2 + r_2^2 + 2r_1r_2 \cos(\theta_1 - \theta_2) = r_1^2 + r_2^2 + 2r_1r_2$

$\Rightarrow 2r_1r_2 - 2r_1r_2 \cos(\theta_1 - \theta_2) = 0 \Rightarrow \cos(\theta_1 + \theta_2) = 1$

$\Rightarrow \theta_1 - \theta_2 = 0 \Rightarrow \theta_1 = \theta_2 \Rightarrow \arg(z_1) = \arg(z_2)$

Q. 14. The real value of θ for which the expression $\dfrac{1+i\cos\theta}{1-2i\cos\theta}$ is a real number is:

(A) $n\pi+\dfrac{\pi}{4}$ (B) $n\pi+(-1)^n\dfrac{\pi}{4}$

(C) $2n\pi\pm\dfrac{\pi}{2}$ (D) none of these.

[NCERT Exemplar Q. 48, Page 97]

Ans. Correct option : (C)

Let $z = \dfrac{1+i\cos\theta}{1-2i\cos\theta} = \dfrac{1+i\cos\theta}{1-2i\cos\theta}\times\dfrac{1+2i\cos\theta}{1+2i\cos\theta}$

$= \dfrac{1+3i\cos\theta+2\cos^2\theta}{1+4\cos^2\theta}$

$= \dfrac{1+2\cos^2\theta}{1+4\cos^2\theta}+\dfrac{3\cos\theta}{1+4\cos^2\theta}i$

If z is a real number, then $\dfrac{3\cos\theta}{1+4\cos^2\theta}=0$

$\Rightarrow 3\cos\theta = 0 \Rightarrow \cos\theta = 0 \therefore \theta = (2n \pm 1)\dfrac{\pi}{2}, n \in N$

Q. 15. The value of arg (x) when $x < 0$ is:

(A) 0 (B) $\dfrac{\pi}{2}$

(C) π (D) none of these

[NCERT Exemplar Q. 49, Page 97]

Ans. Correct option : (C)

Let $z = -x + i\,0$ and $x < 0$

$\therefore |z| = \sqrt{(-1)^2+(0)^2} = 1, x < 0$

Since, the point $(-x, 0)$ lies on the negative side of the real axis ($\because x < 0$)

$\therefore$ Principal argument $(z) = \pi$

Q. 16. If $f(z)=\dfrac{7-z}{1-z^2}$, where $z = 1 + 2i$, then $|f(z)|$ is

(A) $\dfrac{|z|}{2}$ (B) $|z|$

(C) $2|z|$ (D) none of these.

[NCERT Exemplar Q. 50, Page 97]

Ans. Correct option : (A)

Given, $z = 1 + 2i \therefore |z| = \sqrt{1^2+2^2}=\sqrt{5}$

Now, $f(z) = \dfrac{7-z}{1-z^2} = \dfrac{7-(1+2i)}{1-(1+2i)^2} = \dfrac{3-i}{2-2i}\times\dfrac{2+2i}{2+2i}$

$= 1+\dfrac{1}{2}i$

So, $|f(z)| = \sqrt{(1)^2+\left(\dfrac{1}{2}\right)^2} = \dfrac{\sqrt{5}}{2}=\dfrac{|z|}{2}$

[B] Fill in the blanks

[NCERT Exemplar Q. 25, Page 93]

(i) For any two complex numbers z_1, z_2 and any real numbers a, b, $|az_1-bz_2|^2+|bz_1+az_2|^2=$...

(ii) The value of $\sqrt{-25}\times\sqrt{-9}$ is...........

(iii) The number $\dfrac{(1-i)^3}{1-i^3}$ is equal to ....

(iv) The sum of the series $i+i^2+i^3+\ldots$ upto 1000 terms is ....

(v) Multiplicative inverse of $1 + i$ is ....

(vi) If z_1 and z_2 are complex numbers such that $z_1 + z_2$ is a real number, then $z_2 =$ ....

(vii) $\arg(z)+\arg\bar{z}$ ($\bar{z}\neq0$) is ....

(viii) If $|z + 4| \leq 3$, then the greatest and least values of $|z + 1|$ are .... and ....

(ix) If $\left|\frac{z-2}{z+2}\right| = \frac{\pi}{6}$, then the locus of z is ....

(x) If $|z| = 4$ and $\arg(z) = \frac{5\pi}{6}$, then z = ...

Answer:

(i) $(a^2+b^2)(|z_1|^2+|z_2|^2)$ (ii) -15

(iii) -2 (iv) 0

(v) $\frac{1}{2}(1-i)$ (vi) $\bar{z}_1$

(vii) 0 (viii) 6, 0

(ix) a circle (x) $-2\sqrt{3}+2i$

[C] True or False for :

[NCERT Exemplar Q. 26, Page 93]

(i) The order relation is defined on the set of complex numbers.

(ii) Multiplication of a non zero complex number by $-i$ rotates the point about origin through a right angle in the anti-clockwise direction.

(iii) For any complex number z the minimum value of $|z| + |z - 1|$ is 1.

(iv) The locus represented by $|z - 1| = |z - i|$ is a line perpendicular to the join of (1, 0) and (0, 1).

(v) If z is a complex number such that $z \neq 0$ and Re $(z) = 0$, then Im $(z^2) = 0$.

(vi) The inequality $|z - 4| < |z - 2|$ represents the region given by $x > 3$.

(vii) Let z_1 and z_2 be two complex numbers such that $|z_1 + z_2| = |z_1| + |z_2|$, then $\arg(z_1 - z_2) = 0$.

(viii) 2 is not a complex number.

Answer:

(i) False (ii) False (iii) True (iv) False

(v) True (vi) True (vii) False (viii) True

[D] Match the statements of Column A and Column B

Column A	Column B
(a) The polar form of $i+\sqrt{3}$ is	(i) Perpendicular bisector of segment joining (−2, 0) and (2, 0)
(b) The amplitude of $-1+\sqrt{-3}$ is	(ii) On or outside the circle having centre at (0, −4) and radius 3.
(c) If $\|z + 2\| = \|z - 2\|$, then locus of z is	(iii) $\frac{2\pi}{3}$
(d) If $\|z + 2i\| = \|z - 2i\|$, then locus of z is	(iv) Perpendicular bisector of segment joining (0, −2) and (0, 2).
(e) Region represented by $\|z + 4i\| \geq 3$ is	(v) $2\left(\cos\frac{\pi}{6}+i\sin\frac{\pi}{6}\right)$
(f) Region represented by $\|z + 4\| \leq 3$ is	(vi) On or inside the circle having centre (−4, 0) and radius 3 units.
(g) Conjugate of $\frac{1+2i}{1-i}$ lies in	(vii) First quadrant
(h) Reciprocal of 1 − i lies in	(viii) Third quadrant

Answer:

a. (v), b. (iii), c. (i), d. (iv),

e. (ii), f. (vi), g. (viii), h. (vii)

Very Short Answer Type Questions (1 marks each)

Q. 1. For a positive integer n, find the value of $(1-i)^n\left(1-\frac{1}{i}\right)^n$. [NCERT Exemplar Q. 1, Page 91]

Sol. $(1-i)^n\left(1-\frac{1}{i}\right)^n$

$= (1-i)^n(1+i)^n \qquad \left[-\frac{1}{i}=i\right]$

$= [(1-i)(1+i)]^n$

$= [1-i^2]^n$

$= [1+1]^n$

$= 2^n$.

Short Answer Type Questions (2 marks each)

Q. 1. If $(1+i)z=(1-i)\bar{z}$, then show that $z=-i\bar{z}$.

[NCERT Exemplar Q. 7, Page 91]

Sol. Given that: $(1+i)z=(1-i)\bar{z}$

$$\Rightarrow \frac{z}{\bar{z}}=\frac{1-i}{1+i}=\frac{1-i}{1+i}\times\frac{1-i}{1-i}=\frac{1+i^2-2i}{1-i^2}$$

$$=\frac{1-1-2i}{1+1}=\frac{-2i}{2}=-i$$

$$\Rightarrow \frac{z}{\bar{z}}=-i$$

$\therefore\ z=-i\bar{z}$ **Hence Proved.**

Q. 2. If $z = x + iy$, then show that $z\bar{z} - 2(z + \bar{z}) + b = 0$, where $b \in R$ represents a circle.
[NCERT Exemplar Q. 8, Page 91]

Sol. $z = x + iy \Rightarrow \bar{z} = x - iy$

Given, $z\bar{z} - 2(z + \bar{z}) + b = 0$

$(x + iy)(x - iy) - 2(x + iy + x - iy) + b = 0$

$(x^2 - i^2y^2) - 2x + b = 0$

$x^2 + y^2 - 2x + b = 0$

It represents a circle, where $b \in R$.

Q. 3. What is the conjugate of $\frac{2-i}{(1-2i)^2}$?
[NCERT Exemplar Q. 28, Page 94]

Sol. Given,

$$z = \frac{2-i}{(1-2i)^2} = \frac{2-i}{1+4i^2-4i}$$

$$= \frac{2-i}{1-4-4i} = \frac{2-i}{-3-4i}$$

$$= \frac{(2-i)}{-(3+4i)} = -\left[\frac{(2-i)(3-4i)}{(3+4i)(3-4i)}\right]$$

$$= -\left(\frac{6-8i-3i+4i^2}{9+16}\right) = -\left(\frac{-11i+2}{25}\right)$$

$$= -\frac{1}{25}(2-11i)$$

$$= \frac{1}{25}(-2+11i)$$

$\therefore \quad z = \frac{1}{25}(-2+11i)$

and $\quad \bar{z} = \frac{1}{25}(-2-11i)$

Q. 4. If $|z_1| = |z_2|$, is it necessary that $z_1 = z_2$.
[NCERT Exemplar Q. 29, Page 94]

Sol. Given $|z_1| = |z_2|$

Let $z_1 = x_1 + iy_1$, and $z_2 = x_2 + iy_2$

$$|x_1 + iy_1| = |x_2 + iy_2|$$

$$x_1^2 + y_1^2 = x_2^2 + y_2^2$$

$$x_1^2 = x_2^2 \ ; \quad y_1^2 = y_2^2$$

$$x_1 = \pm x_2 \ ; \quad y_1 = \pm y_2$$

$\Rightarrow \quad z_1 = x_1 + iy_1$ or $z_1 = \pm x_2 \pm iy_2$

Hence, it is not necessary that $z_1 = z_2$.

Long Answer Type Question-I (4 marks each)

Q. 1. If $x - iy = \sqrt{\frac{a-ib}{c-id}}$, then prove that

$$(x^2 + y^2)^2 = \frac{a^2+b^2}{c^2+d^2}$$

[NCERT Exemplar Q. 4, Page 112]

Sol. Given, $x - iy = \sqrt{\frac{a-ib}{c-id}} \Rightarrow x + i(-y) = \left(\frac{a-ib}{c-id}\right)^{1/2}$

Taking modulus both side, we get

$$|x + i(-y)| = \left|\left(\frac{a-ib}{c-id}\right)^{1/2}\right|$$

$$\Rightarrow \sqrt{x^2 + (-y)^2} = \left|\frac{a-ib}{c-id}\right|^{1/2} \quad \left(\because |x+iy| = \sqrt{x^2+y^2} \text{ and } |z^n| = |z|^n\right)$$

$$\Rightarrow \sqrt{x^2+y^2} = \left|\frac{a-ib}{c-id}\right|^{1/2}$$

Squaring on both sides, we get

$$x^2 + y^2 = \left|\frac{a-ib}{c-id}\right|$$

$$\Rightarrow x^2 + y^2 = \frac{|a-ib|}{|c-id|} \quad \left(\because \left|\frac{z_1}{z_2}\right| = \frac{|z_1|}{|z_2|}\right)$$

$$\Rightarrow (x^2+y^2) = \frac{\sqrt{a^2+b^2}}{\sqrt{c^2+d^2}} \quad \left(\because |x - iy| = \sqrt{x^2+y^2}\right)$$

Squaring on both sides, we get

$$(x^2+y^2)^2 = \frac{a^2+b^2}{c^2+d^2}$$

Q. 2. Convert the following in the polar form :

(i) $\frac{1+7i}{(2-i)^2}$ (ii) $\frac{1+3i}{1-2i}$

[NCERT Exemplar Q. 5, Page 112]

Sol. (i) Let

$$z = \frac{1+7i}{(2-i)^2} = \frac{1+7i}{4+i^2-4i} \quad [\text{use } (a-b)^2 = a^2+b^2-2ab]$$

$$= \frac{1+7i}{4-1-4i} \quad (\because i^2 = -1)$$

$$= \frac{1+7i}{3-4i} \times \frac{3+4i}{3+4i} = \frac{3+4i+21i+28i^2}{(3)^2-(4i)^2}$$

$$(\because (a-b)(a+b) = a^2-b^2)$$

$$= \frac{3+i(4+21)-28}{9-16i^2} = \frac{-25+25i}{9+16} \quad (\because i^2 = -1)$$

$$z = \frac{-25+25i}{25} = -1+i$$

Now, let $\quad -1 + i = r(\cos\theta + i\sin\theta)$

Comparing the real and imaginary parts of both sides

$$r\cos\theta = 1 \quad \text{(i)}$$

and $\quad r\sin\theta = 1 \quad$ (ii)

Squaring and adding of Eqs (i) and (ii) we get

$$r^2\cos^2\theta + r^2\sin^2\theta = (-1)^2 + (1)^2$$
$$r^2(\cos^2\theta + \sin^2\theta) = 1+1$$
$$\Rightarrow \quad r^2 = 2 \quad (\because \cos^2\theta + \sin^2\theta = 1)$$
$$\Rightarrow \quad r = \sqrt{2}$$

Dividing Eq (ii) by set (i),

$$\frac{r\sin\theta}{r\cos\theta} = \left|\frac{1}{-1}\right| \Rightarrow \tan\theta = 1 = \tan\frac{\pi}{4} \Rightarrow \theta = \frac{\pi}{4}$$

Since, the real part of z is negative and imaginary part of z is positive so the point lies in II quadrant.

$$\therefore \quad \arg(z) = \pi - \theta = \pi - \frac{\pi}{4} = \frac{3\pi}{4}$$

$$\therefore \quad z = -1 + i = \sqrt{2}\left[\cos\frac{3\pi}{4} + i\sin\frac{3\pi}{4}\right],$$

which is the required polar form of $\frac{1+7i}{(2-i)^2}$.

(ii) Let $\frac{1+3i}{1-2i} = z$

$$z = \frac{1+3i}{1-2i} \times \frac{1+2i}{1+2i} = \frac{1+2i+3i+3i\times 2i}{1^2-(2i)^2}$$
$$[\therefore (a+b)(a-b) = a^2 - b^2]$$
$$= \frac{1+5i+6i^2}{1-4i^2} \quad (\therefore i^2 = -1)$$
$$= \frac{1+5i-6}{1+4} = \frac{-5+5i}{5} = -1+i$$

Now, it is same as above question, hence remaining solution is same as given above.

Q. 3. Let $z_1 = 2 - i$, $z_2 = -2 + i$ find

(i) Re $\left[\frac{z_1 z_2}{\bar{z}_1}\right]$ $\quad$ **(ii) Im** $\left[\frac{1}{z_1\bar{z}_2}\right]$

[NCERT Exemplar Q. 12, Page 113]

Sol. Given $z_1 = 2 - i$, $z_2 = -2 + i$

(i) $\text{Re}\left[\frac{z_1 z_2}{\bar{z}_1}\right] = \frac{(2-i)(-2+i)}{(\overline{2-i})}$

$$= \frac{-4+2i+2i-i^2}{2+i}$$
$$= \left(\frac{-4+1+4i}{2+i}\right)\left(\frac{2-i}{2+i}\right)$$
$$= \frac{(-3+4i)(2-i)}{4-i^2} \quad (\therefore i^2 = -1)$$
$$= \frac{-(6-11i-4)}{4-i^2}$$
$$= \frac{-(2-11i)}{4+1}$$
$$= \left(\frac{2}{5} - \frac{11i}{5}\right) = -\frac{2}{5} + \frac{11}{5}i$$
$$\therefore \text{Re}\left(\frac{z_1 z_2}{\bar{z}_1}\right) = -\frac{2}{5}$$

(ii) $\text{Im}\left(\frac{1}{z_1\bar{z}_2}\right)$

$$\because \quad z\bar{z} = |z|^2 \Rightarrow z_1\bar{z}_1 = |z_1|^2$$
$$\Rightarrow \quad z_1\bar{z}_1 = |-2+i|^2 = (\sqrt{4+1})^2 = 5+0i$$
$$\therefore \quad \frac{1}{z_1\bar{z}_1} = \frac{1}{5} + 0i$$
$$\Rightarrow \quad \text{Im}\left(\frac{1}{z_1 z_2}\right) = 0$$

Q. 4. Find the modulus and argument of the complex number $\frac{1+2i}{1-3i}$.

[NCERT Exemplar Q. 13, Page 113]

Sol. Let $z = \frac{1+2i}{1-3i}$

$$\therefore z = \frac{1+2i}{1-3i} \times \frac{1+3i}{1+3i} = \frac{1+3i+2i+6i^2}{1^2-(3i)^2}$$
$$[\therefore (a+b)(a-b) = a^2 - b^2]$$
$$= \frac{1+5i+6(-1)}{1-9i^2} \quad (\because i^2 = -1)$$
$$= \frac{1+5i-6}{1+9} = \frac{-5+5i}{10}$$
$$= \frac{-1+i}{2} \Rightarrow z = \frac{-1}{2} + \frac{1}{2}i$$
$$\therefore \quad |z| = \sqrt{\left(-\frac{1}{2}\right)^2 + \left(\frac{1}{2}\right)^2} \quad (\because |a+ib| = \sqrt{a^2+b^2}).$$
$$= \sqrt{\frac{1}{4} + \frac{1}{4}} = \sqrt{\frac{2}{4}} = \sqrt{\frac{1}{2}} = \frac{1}{\sqrt{2}}$$
$$\therefore \text{ Now, } \tan\theta = \left|\frac{\frac{1}{2}}{-\frac{1}{2}}\right| \quad \left(\because \theta = \tan^{-1}\left|\left(\frac{\text{Im}(z)}{\text{Re}(z)}\right)\right|\right)$$
$$\Rightarrow \tan\theta = 1 = \tan\frac{\pi}{4} \Rightarrow \theta = \frac{\pi}{4}$$

Since, the real part of z is negative and imaginary part of z is positive, so the point lies in II quadrant.

$$\therefore \quad \arg(z) = \pi - \theta = \pi - \frac{\pi}{4} = \frac{3\pi}{4}$$

Hence, modulus $= \frac{1}{\sqrt{2}}$ and $\arg(z) = \frac{3\pi}{4}$

Q. 5. Find the real number of x and y if $(x - iy)(3 + 5i)$ is the conjugate of $(-6-24i)$.

[NCERT Exemplar Q. 14, Page 113]

Sol. $(x-iy)(3+5i) = 3x + 5xi - 3yi - 5yi^2$

$$= 3x + (5x-3y)i + 5y \quad \because (i^2 = -1)$$
$$= (3x+5y) + (5x-3y)i \quad \text{(i)}$$

Given, $(x-iy)(3+5i) = \overline{(-6-24i)}$

$$\Rightarrow (3x+5y) + i(5x-3y) = -6 + 24i$$

[Using Eq.(i) and $z = (a+ib) \Rightarrow \bar{z} = (a-ib)$]

Comparing the real and imaginary parts of both sides, we get

$3x + 5y = -6$ and $5x - 3y = 24$

Solving the above equations by substitution or elimination method, we get $x = 3$, $y = -3$.

Q. 6. If $(x+iy)^3 = u + iv$, then show that $\frac{u}{x} + \frac{v}{y} = 4(x^2 - y^2)$.

[NCERT Exemplar Q. 16, Page 113]

Sol. $(x+iy)^3 = u + iv$

$x^3 + (iy)^3 + 3xiy(x+iy) = u + iv$

$x^3 + i^3y^3 + 3ix^2y + 3xy^2i^2 = u + iv$

$x^3 - iy^3 + 3ix^2y - 3xy^2 = u + iv \quad (\because i^3 = -i, i^2 = -1)$

$(x^3 - 3xy^2) + i(3x^2y - y^3) = u + iv$

Comparing real and imaginary parts,

$x^3 - 3xy^2 = u$ and $3x^2y - y^3 = v$

$\therefore \frac{u}{x} + \frac{v}{y} = \frac{x^3 - 3xy^2}{x} + \frac{3x^2y - y^3}{y}$

$= x^2 - 3y^2 + 3x^2 - y^2 = 4x^2 - 4y^2 = 4(x^2 - y^2)$

Hence Proved.

Q. 7. If α and β are different complex numbers with $|\beta| = 1$, then find $\left|\frac{\beta - \alpha}{1 - \bar{\alpha}\beta}\right|$

[NCERT Exemplar Q. 17, Page 113]

Sol. $\left|\frac{\beta - \alpha}{1 - \bar{\alpha}\beta}\right|^2 = \left(\frac{\beta - \alpha}{1 - \bar{\alpha}\beta}\right)\overline{\left(\frac{\beta - \alpha}{1 - \bar{\alpha}\beta}\right)}$

$= \left(\frac{\beta - \alpha}{1 - \bar{\alpha}\beta}\right)\left(\frac{\bar{\beta} - \bar{\alpha}}{1 - \alpha\bar{\beta}}\right)$

$= \frac{\beta\bar{\beta} - \alpha\bar{\beta} - \bar{\alpha}\beta + \alpha\bar{\alpha}}{1 - \alpha\bar{\beta} - \bar{\alpha}\beta + \alpha\bar{\alpha}\,\beta\bar{\beta}}$

$= \frac{|\beta|^2 - \alpha\bar{\beta} - \bar{\alpha}\beta - |\alpha|^2}{1 + \alpha\bar{\beta} - \bar{\alpha}\beta + |\alpha|^2|\beta|^2}$

$= \frac{1 - \alpha\bar{\beta} - \bar{\alpha}\beta + |\alpha|^2}{1 - \alpha\bar{\beta} - \bar{\alpha}\beta + |\alpha|^2} = 1$

$\therefore \left|\frac{\beta - \alpha}{1 - \bar{\alpha}\beta}\right| = 1$

Q. 8. If $(a+ib)(c+id)(e+if)(g+ih) = A + iB$, then show that $(a^2+b^2)(c^2+d^2)(e^2+f^2)(g^2+h^2) = A^2 + B^2$.

[NCERT Exemplar Q. 19, Page 113]

Sol. $(a+ib)(c+id)(e+if)(g+ih) = A + iB$

Taking modulus on both sides, we get

$|(a+ib)(c+id)(e+if)(g+ih)| = |A + iB|$

$|a+ib||c+id||e+if||g+ih| = |A+iB|$

$(\because |z_1z_2\ldots z_n| = |z_1||z_2||z_3|\ldots|z_n|)$

$\sqrt{a^2+b^2}\sqrt{c^2+d^2}\sqrt{e^2+f^2}\sqrt{g^2+h^2} = \sqrt{A^2+B^2}$

$(\because$ if $z = a + ib$, then $|z| = \sqrt{a^2+b^2})$

Squaring on both sides, we get

$(a^2+b^2)(c^2+d^2)(e^2+f^2)(g^2+h^2) = (A^2+B^2)$

Q. 9. If $\left(\frac{1+i}{1-i}\right)^m = 1$, then find the least positive integral value of m.

[NCERT Exemplar Q. 20, Page 113]

OR

If $\left(\frac{2+2i}{2-2i}\right)^n = 1$, find the least positive integral value of n.

Sol. $\left(\frac{1+i}{1-i}\right)^m = 1$

$\Rightarrow \left[\frac{1+i}{1-i} \times \frac{1+i}{1+i}\right]^m = 1$

$\Rightarrow \left[\frac{(1+i)^2}{1-i^2}\right]^m = 1$

$\Rightarrow \left[\frac{1+i^2+2i}{1+1}\right]^m = 1$

$(\because (a+b)^2 = a^2 + b^2 + 2ab$ and $i^2 = -1)$

$\Rightarrow \left[\frac{1-1+2i}{2}\right]^m = 1$

$\Rightarrow i^m = 1$

$\Rightarrow (\sqrt{-1})^m = 1 \quad (\because i^2 = -1 \Rightarrow i = \sqrt{-1})$

$\Rightarrow (-1)^{\frac{m}{2}} = (-1)^2$

Comparing the power on both sides, we get

$\frac{m}{2} = 2 \quad \Rightarrow \quad m = 4$

Hence, the least positive integral value of m is 4.

Q. 10. Evaluate $\sum_{n=1}^{13}(i^n + i^{n+1})$, where $n \in N$.

[NCERT Exemplar Q. 2, Page 91]

Sol. $\sum_{n=1}^{13}(i^n + i^{n+1}) = \sum_{n=1}^{13} i^n + \sum_{n=1}^{13} i^{n+1}$

$= \sum_{n=1}^{13} i^n + \sum_{n=1}^{13} i^n \times i$

$= (1+i)\sum_{n=1}^{13} i^n = (1+i)(i + i^2 + i^3 + \cdots + i^{13})$

$[i^2 = i^6 = i^{10} = -1$
$i^4 = i^8 = i^{12} = 1$
$i^3 = i^7 = i^9 = -1$
$i = i^5 = i^9 = 1]$

$= (1+i)\frac{i[1-(i)^{13}]}{1-i} = \frac{(1+i)i[1 - i^{12}i]}{1-i}$

$= \frac{(1+i)i(1-i)}{1-i} \quad [\because i^{12} = 1]$

$= i + i^2 = i - 1 = -1 + i$

Q. 11. If $\left(\frac{1+i}{1-i}\right)^3 - \left(\frac{1-i}{1+i}\right)^3 = x+iy$, then find (x, y)

[NCERT Exemplar Q. 3, Page 91]

Sol. We have, $\left(\frac{1+i}{1-i}\right)^3 - \left(\frac{1-i}{1+i}\right)^3 = x+iy$

$$\Rightarrow \left[\frac{1+i}{1-i}\times\frac{1+i}{1+i}\right]^3 - \left[\frac{(1-i)(1-i)}{(1+i)(1-i)}\right]^3 = x+iy$$

$$\Rightarrow \left[\frac{1+i^2+2i}{1-i^2}\right]^3 - \left[\frac{1+i^2-2i}{1-i^2}\right]^3 = x+iy$$

$$\Rightarrow \left[\frac{1-1+2i}{1+1}\right]^3 - \left[\frac{1-1-2i}{1+1}\right]^3 = x+iy$$

$$\Rightarrow \left(\frac{2i}{2}\right)^3 - \left(\frac{-2i}{2}\right)^3 = x+iy$$

$$\Rightarrow (i)^3 - (-i)^3 = x+iy \Rightarrow i^2\cdot i + i^2\cdot i = x+iy$$

$$\Rightarrow -i-i = x+iy \Rightarrow 0-2i = x+iy$$

Comparing the real and imaginary parts, we get $x = 0, y = -2$. Hence, $(x, y) = (0, -2)$.

Q. 12. If $\left(\frac{1-i}{1+i}\right)^{100} = a+ib$, then find (a, b).

[NCERT Exemplar Q. 5, Page 91]

Sol. We have, $\left(\frac{1-i}{1+i}\right)^{100} = a+ib$

$$\Rightarrow \left(\frac{1-i}{1+i}\times\frac{1-i}{1-i}\right)^{100} = a+ib \Rightarrow \left(\frac{1+i^2-2i}{1-i^2}\right)^{100} = a+ib$$

$$\Rightarrow \left(\frac{1-1-2i}{1+1}\right)^{100} = a+ib \Rightarrow \left(\frac{-2i}{2}\right)^{100} = a+ib$$

$$\Rightarrow (-i)^{100} = a+ib \Rightarrow i^{100} = a+ib$$

$$\Rightarrow (i^4)^{25} = a+ib \Rightarrow (1)^{25} = a+ib \Rightarrow 1 = a+ib$$

$$\Rightarrow 1+0i = a+ib$$

Comparing the real and imaginary parts, we get

$a = 1, b = 0$

Hence, $(a, b) = (1, 0)$.

Q. 13. If $a = \cos\theta + i\sin\theta$, then find the value of $\frac{1+a}{1-a}$.

[NCERT Exemplar Q. 6, Page 91]

Sol. Given, $a = \cos\theta + i\sin\theta$

$$\therefore \frac{1+a}{1-a} = \frac{1+\cos\theta+i\sin\theta}{1-(\cos\theta+i\sin\theta)}$$

$$= \frac{\left(2\cos^2\frac{\theta}{2}\right)+i\left(2\sin\frac{\theta}{2}\cos\frac{\theta}{2}\right)}{(1-\cos\theta)-i\sin\theta}\quad\left(\because 1+\cos\theta = 2\cos^2\frac{\theta}{2}\right)$$

$$= \frac{2\cos^2\frac{\theta}{2}+2i\sin\frac{\theta}{2}\cos\frac{\theta}{2}}{2\sin^2\frac{\theta}{2}-2i\sin\frac{\theta}{2}\cos\frac{\theta}{2}}\quad\left(\because 1-\cos\theta = 2\sin^2\frac{\theta}{2}\right)$$

Multiplying by i in numerator and denominator,

$$= \frac{2\cos\frac{\theta}{2}\left[\cos\frac{\theta}{2}+i\sin\frac{\theta}{2}\right]}{2\sin\frac{\theta}{2}\left[\sin\frac{\theta}{2}-i\cos\frac{\theta}{2}\right]} = \frac{i\cot\frac{\theta}{2}\left(\cos\frac{\theta}{2}+i\sin\frac{\theta}{2}\right)}{\left(i\sin\frac{\theta}{2}-i^2\cos\frac{\theta}{2}\right)}$$

$$= \frac{i\cot\frac{\theta}{2}\left(\cos\frac{\theta}{2}+i\sin\frac{\theta}{2}\right)}{\left(\cos\frac{\theta}{2}+i\sin\frac{\theta}{2}\right)} = i\cot\frac{\theta}{2}$$

Q. 14. Show that the complex number z, satisfying the condition $\arg\left(\frac{z-1}{z+1}\right) = \frac{\pi}{4}$ lies on a circle.

[NCERT Exemplar Q. 10, Page 91]

Sol. Let $z = x + iy$

$$\frac{z-1}{z+1} = \frac{x+iy-1}{x+iy+1} = \frac{(x-1)+iy}{(x+1)+iy}\times\frac{(x+1)-iy}{(x+1)-iy}$$

$$= \frac{(x-1)(x+1)-iy(x-1)+iy(x+1)-i^2y^2}{(x+1)^2-i^2y^2}$$

$$= \frac{x^2-1+iy(x+1-x+1)+y^2}{(x+1)^2+y^2}$$

$$= \frac{(x^2+y^2-1)+2iy}{(x+1)^2+y^2}$$

$$\frac{z-1}{z-1} = \frac{x^2+y^2-1}{(x+1)^2+y^2}+\frac{i\times 2y}{(x+1)^2+y^2}$$

$$\arg\left(\frac{z-1}{z+1}\right) = \tan^{-1}\left(\frac{\frac{2y}{(x+1)^2+y^2}}{\frac{x^2+y^2-1}{(x+1)^2+y^2}}\right)$$

Now, $\frac{\pi}{4} = \tan^{-1}\left(\frac{2y}{x^2+y^2-1}\right)$

$$\tan\frac{\pi}{4} = \frac{2y}{x^2+y^2-1} \Rightarrow 1 = \frac{2y}{x^2+y^2-1}$$

$$x^2+y^2-1 = 2y \Rightarrow x^2+y^2-2y-1 = 0$$

Clearly, this equation represents a circle.

Q. 15. Solve the equation $|z| = z+1+2i$

[NCERT Exemplar Q. 11, Page 91]

Sol. Given that: $|z| = z+1+2i$

Let $z = x+iy$

$|z| = (z+1)+2i$

Squaring both sides

$$|z|^2 = |z+1|^2 + 4i^2 + 4(z+1)i$$

$$|z|^2 = |z|^2 + 1 + 2z - 4 + 4(z+1)i$$

$$0 = -3 + 2z + 4(z+1)i$$

$$3-2z-4(z+1)i=0$$
$$3-2(x+iy)-4[x+iy+1]i=0$$
$$3-2x-2iy-4ix-4i^2y-4i=0$$
$$3-2x+4y-2iy-4i-4ix=0$$
$$(3-2x+4y)-i(2y+4x+4)=0$$
$$3-2x+4y=0 \Rightarrow 2x-4y=3 \quad \text{(i)}$$
and $4x+2y+4=0 \Rightarrow 2x+y=-2$ (ii)

Solving eqn. (i) and (ii), we get

$$y=-1 \text{ and } x=-\frac{1}{2}$$

Hence, the value of $z=x+yi=\left(-\frac{1}{2}-i\right)$.

Q. 16. If $\arg(z-1)=\arg(z+3i)$, then find $x-1:y$, where $z=x+iy$. [NCERT Exemplar Q. 13, Page 92]

Sol. We have, $\arg(z-1)=\arg(z+3i)$ Putting $z=x+iy$,

$$\arg(x+iy-1)=\arg(x+iy+3i)$$
$$\Rightarrow \arg[(x-1)+iy]=\arg[x+i(y+3)]$$
$$\Rightarrow \tan^{-1}\frac{y}{x-1}=\tan^{-1}\frac{y+3}{x}$$
$$\Rightarrow \frac{y}{x-1}=\frac{y+3}{x} \Rightarrow xy=(x-1)(y+3)$$
$$\Rightarrow xy=xy+3x-y-3$$
$$\Rightarrow 0=3(x-1)-y$$
$$\Rightarrow y=3(x-1) \Rightarrow \frac{x-1}{y}=\frac{1}{3}$$
$$\Rightarrow (x-1):y=1:3$$

Q. 17. If $\frac{z-1}{z+1}$ is a purely imaginary number $(z \neq -1)$, then find the vale of $|z|$.
[NCERT Exemplar Q. 15, Page 92]

Sol. Let $z = x + iy$

$$\frac{z-1}{z+1}=\frac{x+iy-1}{x+iy+1}=\frac{(x-1)+iy}{(x+1)+iy}\times\frac{(x+1)-iy}{(x+1)-iy}$$
$$=\frac{(x-1)(x+1)-iy(x-1)+iy(x+1)-i^2y^2}{(x+1)^2-i^2y^2}$$
$$=\frac{x^2-1+iy(x+1-x+1)+y^2}{(x+1)^2+y^2}$$
$$\frac{z-1}{z+1}=\frac{(x^2+y^2-1)}{(x+1)^2+y^2}+\frac{i(2y)}{(x+1)^2+y^2}$$

$\therefore \frac{z-1}{z+1}$ is purely imaginary.

$$\therefore \text{Re}\left(\frac{z-1}{z+1}\right)=0 \Rightarrow \frac{x^2+y^2-1}{(x+1)^2+y^2}=0$$
$$x^2+y^2-1=0$$
$$x^2+y^2=1$$
$$|z|^2=1 \Rightarrow |z|=1$$

Q. 18. z_1 and z_2 are two complex numbers such that $|z_1|=|z_2|$ and $\arg(z_1)+\arg(z_2)=\pi$, then show that $z_1=-\bar{z}_2$. [NCERT Exemplar Q. 16, Page 92]

Sol. Let $z_1=r_1(\cos\theta_1+i\sin\theta_1)$ and $z_2=r_2(\cos\theta_2+i\sin\theta_2)$ are polar form of two complex numbers z_1 and z_2.

Given that: $|z_1|=|z_2| \Rightarrow r_1=r_2$ (i)

and $\arg(z_1)+\arg(z_2)=\pi$

$$\theta_1+\theta_2=\pi$$
$$\theta_1=\pi-\theta_2$$

Now, $z_1=r_1[\cos(\pi-\theta_2)+i\sin(\pi-\theta_2)]$

$$z_1=r_1[-\cos\theta_2+i\sin\theta_2]$$
$$z_1=-r_1(\cos\theta_2-i\sin\theta_2) \quad \text{(i)}$$
$$z_2=r_2[\cos\theta_2+i\sin\theta_2]$$
$$\bar{z}_2=r_1[\cos\theta_2-i\sin\theta_2] \quad [\because r_1=r_2] \text{ (ii)}$$

From eqn. (i) and (ii) we get,

$z_1=-\bar{z}_2$. **Hence Proved.**

Q. 19. If $|z_1|=1, (z_1 \neq -1)$ and $z_2=\frac{z_1-1}{z_1+1}$, then show that the real part of z_2 is 0.
[NCERT Exemplar Q. 17, Page 92]

Sol. Let $z_1=x+yi$

$$|z_1|=\sqrt{x^2+y^2}=1 \quad \text{[given that } |z|=1]$$
$$\Rightarrow x^2+y^2=1 \quad \text{(i)}$$

Now,

$$z_2=\frac{z_1-1}{z_1+1}=\frac{x+yi-1}{x+yi+1}$$
$$=\frac{(x-1)+yi}{(x+1)+yi}=\frac{(x-1)+yi}{(x+1)+yi}\times\frac{x+1-yi}{x+1-yi}$$
$$=\frac{(x-1)(x+1)-y(x-1)i+y(x+1)i-y^2i^2}{(x+1)^2-y^2i^2}$$
$$=\frac{x^2-1+yi(x+1-x+1)+y^2}{x^2+1+2x+y^2}$$
$$=\frac{(x^2+y^2-1)+2yi}{x^2+y^2+2x+1}$$
$$=\frac{(1-1)}{x^2+y^2+2x+1}+\frac{2y}{x^2+y^2+2x+1}i$$
$$=0+\frac{2y}{x^2+y^2+2x+1}i$$

Hence, the real part of z_2 is 0.

Q. 20. If z_1, z_2 and z_3, z_4 are two pairs of conjugate complex numbers then find $\arg\left(\frac{z_1}{z_4}\right)+\arg\left(\frac{z_2}{z_3}\right)$.
[NCERT Exemplar Q. 18, Page 92]

Sol. Let the polar form of $z_1=r_1(\cos\theta_1+i\sin\theta_1)$

$$\therefore z_2=\bar{z}_1=r_1(\cos\theta_1-i\sin\theta_1)=r_1[\cos(-\theta_1)+i\sin(-\theta_1)]$$

Similarly, $z_3=r_2(\cos\theta_2+i\sin\theta_2)$

$\therefore z_4 = \bar{z}_3 = r_2(\cos\theta_2 - i\sin\theta_2) = r_2[\cos(-\theta_2) + i\sin(-\theta_2)]$

$$\arg\left(\frac{z_1}{z_4}\right) + \arg\left(\frac{z_2}{z_3}\right) = \arg(z_1) - \arg(z_4) + \arg(z_2) - \arg(z_2)$$

$= \theta_1 - (-\theta_2) + (-\theta_1) - \theta_2$
$= \theta_1 + \theta_1 - \theta_1 - \theta_2 = 0$

Hence, $\arg\left(\frac{z_1}{z_4}\right) + \arg\left(\frac{z_2}{z_3}\right) = 0$.

Long Answer Type Question-II

(6 marks each)

Q. 1. If $|z+1| = z + 2(1+i)$ then find z.

[NCERT Exemplar Q. 12, Page 92]

Sol. Given that: $|z+1| = z + 2(1+i)$

Let $z = x + iy$

So, $|x + iy + 1| = (x+iy) + 2(1+i)$

$|(x+1) + iy| = x + iy + 2 + 2i$

$|(x+1) + iy| = (x+2) + (y+2)i$

$\sqrt{(x+1)^2 + y^2} = (x+2) + (y+2)i$

$\left[\because |x+iy| = \sqrt{x^2+y^2}\right]$

Squaring both sides, we get

$(x+1)^2 + y^2 = (x+2)^2 + (y+2)^2 \cdot i^2 + 2(x+2)(y+2)i$

$\Rightarrow x^2 + 1 + 2x + y^2 = x^2 + 4 + 4x - y^2 - 4y - 4$
$+2(x+2)(y+2)i$

Comparing the real and imaginary parts, we get

$x^2 + 1 + 2x + y^2 = x^2 + 4x - y^2 - 4y$ and

$2(x+2)(y+2) = 0$

$\Rightarrow 2y^2 - 2x + 4y + 1 = 0$ ... (i)

and $(x+2)(y+2) = 0$ ... (ii)

$x + 2 = 0$ or $y + 2 = 0$

$\therefore x = -2$ or $y = -2$

Now, put $x = -2$ in eqn. (i), we get

$2y^2 - 2\times(-2) + 4y + 1 = 0$

$\Rightarrow 2y^2 + 4 + 4y + 1 = 0$

$\Rightarrow 2y^2 + 4y + 5 = 0$

$b^2 - 4ac = (4)^2 - 4\times 2\times 5$
$= 16 - 40 = -24 < 0$, no real roots.

Put $y = -2$ in eqn. (i)

$2(-2)^2 - 2x + 4(-2) + 1 = 0$

$8 - 2x - 8 + 1 = 0 \Rightarrow x = \frac{1}{2}$ and $y = -2$

Hence, $z = x + iy = \left(\frac{1}{2} - 2i\right)$.

Q. 2. Show that $\left|\frac{z-2}{z-3}\right| = 2$ represents a circle. Find its centre and radius.

[NCERT Exemplar Q. 14, Page 92]

Sol. Given that : $\left|\frac{z-2}{z-3}\right| = 2$

Let $z = x + iy$

$\therefore \left|\frac{x+iy-2}{x+iy-3}\right| = 2 \Rightarrow \left|\frac{(x-2)+iy}{(x-3)+iy}\right| = 2$

$\frac{|(x-2)+iy|}{|(x-3)+iy|} = 2$ $\left[\because \left|\frac{a}{b}\right| = \frac{|a|}{|b|}\right]$

$|(x-2)+iy| = 2|(x-3)+iy|$

$\sqrt{(x-2)^2 + y^2} = 2\sqrt{(x-3)^2 + y^2}$

Squaring both sides, we get

$(x-2)^2 + y^2 = 4[(x-3)^2 + y^2]$

$x^2 + 4 - 4x + y^2 = 4[x^2 + 9 - 6x + y^2]$

$x^2 + y^2 - 4x + 4 = 4x^2 + 4y^2 - 24x + 36$

$3x^2 + 3y^2 - 20x + 32 = 0$

$x^2 + y^2 - \frac{20}{3}x + \frac{32}{3} = 0$

Here, $g = \frac{-10}{3}, f = 0, c = \frac{32}{3}$

$r = \sqrt{g^2 + f^2 - c} = \sqrt{\frac{100}{9} + 0 - \frac{32}{3}} = \sqrt{\frac{4}{9}} = \frac{2}{3}$

Hence, the required equation of the circle is

$x^2 + y^2 - \frac{20}{3}x + \frac{32}{3} = 0$

Centre $= (-g, -f) = \left(\frac{10}{3}, 0\right)$ and $r = \frac{2}{3}$.

Q. 3. If $|z_1| = |z_2| = \ldots = |z_n| = 1$, then show that

$$|z_1 + z_2 + z_3 + \ldots + z_n| = \left|\frac{1}{z_1} + \frac{1}{z_2} + \frac{1}{z_3} + \ldots + \frac{1}{z_n}\right|.$$

[NCERT Exemplar Q. 19, Page 92]

Sol. We have $|z_1| = |z_2| = \ldots = |z_n| = 1$

$\Rightarrow |z_1|^2 = |z_2|^2 = \ldots = |z_n|^2 = 1$ ... (i)

$\Rightarrow z_1\bar{z}_1 = z_2\bar{z}_2 = \ldots = z_n\bar{z}_n = 1$ $[\because z\bar{z} = |z|^2]$

$\Rightarrow \quad z_1 = \frac{1}{\bar{z}_1}, z_2 = \frac{1}{\bar{z}_2} = \ldots z_n = \frac{1}{\bar{z}_n}$

L.H.S. $= |z_1 + z_2 + z_3 + \ldots + z_n|$

$$= \left|\frac{z_1\bar{z}_1}{\bar{z}_1} + \frac{z_2\bar{z}_2}{\bar{z}_2} + \frac{z_3\bar{z}_3}{\bar{z}_3} + \cdots + \frac{z_n\bar{z}_n}{\bar{z}_n}\right|$$

$$= \left|\frac{|z_1|^2}{\bar{z}_1} + \frac{|z_2|^2}{\bar{z}_2} + \frac{|z_3|^2}{\bar{z}_3} + \cdots + \frac{|z_n|^2}{\bar{z}_n}\right|$$

$[z\bar{z} = |z|^2]$

$$= \left|\frac{1}{\bar{z}_1} + \frac{1}{\bar{z}_2} + \frac{1}{\bar{z}_3} + \cdots + \frac{1}{\bar{z}_n}\right| \quad \text{[using (i)]}$$

$$= \left|\overline{\frac{1}{z_1} + \frac{1}{z_2} + \frac{1}{z_3} + \cdots + \frac{1}{z_n}}\right|$$

$[\because \bar{z}_1 + \bar{z}_2 = \overline{z_1 + z_2}]$

$$= \left|\frac{1}{z_1} + \frac{1}{z_2} + \frac{1}{z_3} + \cdots + \frac{1}{z_n}\right| \quad [\because |z| = |\bar{z}|]$$

L.H.S. = R.H.S. **Hence Proved.**

Q. 4. If for complex numbers z_1 and z_2, $\arg(z_1) - \arg(z_2) = 0$, then show that $|z_1 - z_2| = |z_1| - |z_2|$.

[NCERT Exemplar Q. 20, Page 92]

Sol. Given that for, z_1 and z_2, $\arg(z_1) - \arg(z_2) = 0$

Let us represent z_1 and z_2 in polar form

$z_1 = r_1(\cos\theta_1 + i\sin\theta_1)$

and $\quad z_2 = r_2(\cos\theta_2 + i\sin\theta_2)$

$\arg(z_1) = \theta_1$ and $\arg(z_2) = \theta_2$

Since, $\arg(z_1) - \arg(z_2) = 0$

$\Rightarrow \quad \theta_1 - \theta_2 = 0 \Rightarrow \theta_1 = \theta_2$

Now,

$z_1 - z_2 = r_1(\cos\theta_1 + i\sin\theta_1) - r_2(\cos\theta_2 + i\sin\theta_2)$

$= r_1\cos\theta_1 + ir_1\sin\theta_1 - r_2\cos\theta_1 - ir_2\sin\theta_1$

$[\because \theta_1 = \theta_2]$

$= (r_1\cos\theta_1 - r_2\cos\theta_1) + i(r_1\sin\theta_1 - r_2\sin\theta_1)$

$\therefore |z_1 - z_2| = \sqrt{(r_1\cos\theta_1 - r_2\cos\theta_1)^2 + (r_1\sin\theta_1 - r_2\sin\theta_1)^2}$

$$= \sqrt{\begin{aligned}&(r_1^2\cos^2\theta_1 + r_2^2\cos^2\theta_1 - 2r_1r_2\cos^2\theta_1\\&+r_1^2\sin^2\theta_1 + r_2^2\sin^2\theta_1 - 2r_1r_2\sin^2\theta_1)\end{aligned}}$$

$$= \sqrt{\begin{aligned}&r_1^2(\cos^2\theta_1 + \sin^2\theta_1) + r_2^2(\cos^2\theta_1 + \sin^2\theta_1)\\&-2r_1r_2(\cos^2\theta_1 + \sin^2\theta_1)\end{aligned}}$$

$= \sqrt{r_1^2 + r_2^2 - 2r_1r_2} = \sqrt{(r_1 - r_2)^2} = r_1 - r_2$

$= |z_1| - |z_2|$

Hence, $|z_1 - z_2| = |z_1| - |z_2|$

Q. 5. Find the complex number satisfying the equation $z + \sqrt{2}\,|(z+1)| + i = 0$.

[NCERT Exemplar Q. 22, Page 92]

Sol. Given that: $z + \sqrt{2}\,|(z+1)| + i = 0$

Let $\quad z = x + iy$

$\therefore \quad (x+yi) + \sqrt{2}|(x+yi+1)| + i = 0$

$x + (y+1)i + \sqrt{2}|(x+1) + yi| = 0$

$x + (y+1)i + \sqrt{2}\sqrt{(x+1)^2 + y^2} = 0$

$x + (y+1)i + \sqrt{2}\sqrt{x^2 + 2x + 1 + y^2} = 0 + 0i$

On comparing real and imaginary parts both sides, we get

$x + \sqrt{2}\sqrt{x^2 + 2x + 1 + y^2} = 0, y + 1 = 0$

$x = -\sqrt{2}\sqrt{x^2 + 2x + 1 + y^2}$ and $y = -1$

Now,

$x^2 = 2(x^2 + 2x + 1 + y^2)$

$x^2 = 2x^2 + 4x + 2 + 2y^2$

$x^2 + 4x + 2 + 2y^2 = 0$

$x^2 + 4x + 2 + 2(-1)^2 = 0 \quad [\because y = -1]$

$x^2 + 4x + 4 = 0$

$(x+2)^2 = 0$

$x + 2 = 0 \Rightarrow x = -2$

Hence, $\quad z = x + yi = -2 - i$.

Q. 6. Write the complex number $z = \dfrac{1-i}{\cos\frac{\pi}{3} + i\sin\frac{\pi}{3}}$ in polar form.

[NCERT Exemplar Q. 23, Page 92]

Sol. Given that:

$$z = \frac{1-i}{\frac{1}{2} + i\frac{\sqrt{3}}{2}} = \frac{2-2i}{1+i\sqrt{3}} = \frac{2-2i}{1+i\sqrt{3}} \times \frac{1-i\sqrt{3}}{1-i\sqrt{3}}$$

$$\Rightarrow \quad z = \frac{2 - 2\sqrt{3}i - 2i + 2\sqrt{3}i^2}{(1)^2 - (i\sqrt{3})^2} = \frac{2 - 2\sqrt{3}i - 2i - 2\sqrt{3}}{1 - 3i^2}$$

$$= \frac{(2-2\sqrt{3}) - (2+2\sqrt{3})i}{4} = \frac{1-\sqrt{3}}{2} - \frac{1+\sqrt{3}}{2}i$$

$$r = \sqrt{\left(\frac{1-\sqrt{3}}{2}\right)^2 + \left(-\frac{1+\sqrt{3}}{2}\right)^2}$$

$$= \sqrt{\frac{4 - 2\sqrt{3} + 4 + 2\sqrt{3}}{4}} = \sqrt{\frac{8}{4}} = \sqrt{2}$$

So, $\quad r = \sqrt{2}$

Now, $\arg(z) = \tan^{-1}\dfrac{y}{x} - \pi$

$$\theta = \tan^{-1}\frac{-\left(\dfrac{1+\sqrt{3}}{2}\right)}{\left(\dfrac{1-\sqrt{3}}{2}\right)} = \tan^{-1}\left[-\left(\frac{1+\sqrt{3}}{1-\sqrt{3}}\right)\right] = \tan^{-1}\frac{\sqrt{3}+1}{\sqrt{3}-1}$$

$$\Rightarrow \theta = \tan^{-1}\left[\tan\left(\frac{\pi}{4}+\frac{\pi}{6}\right)\right] - \pi$$

$$\left[\because \tan\left(\frac{\pi}{4}+\frac{\pi}{6}\right) = \frac{\tan\dfrac{\pi}{4}+\tan\dfrac{\pi}{6}}{1-\tan\dfrac{\pi}{4}\tan\dfrac{\pi}{6}}\right]$$

$$\theta = \frac{5\pi}{12} - \pi = \frac{-7\pi}{12}$$

Hence, the polar is

$$z = \sqrt{2}\left[\cos\frac{-7\pi}{12} + i\sin\frac{-7\pi}{12}\right].$$

Q. 7. If z and w are two complex numbers such that $|zw| = 1$ and $\arg(z) - \arg(w) = \dfrac{\pi}{2}$, then show that $\bar{z}w = -i$. **[NCERT Exemplar Q. 24, Page 92]**

Sol. Let $z = r_1(\cos\theta_1 + i\sin\theta_1)$ and $w = r_2(\cos\theta_2 + i\sin\theta_2)$

Also, $|zw| = |z||w| = r_1 r_2 = 1$

$\therefore \quad r_1 r_2 = 1$

Further, $\arg(z) = \theta_1$ and $\arg(w) = \theta_2$

But $\arg(z) - \arg(w) = \dfrac{\pi}{2} \Rightarrow \theta_1 - \theta_2 = \dfrac{\pi}{2} \Rightarrow \arg\left(\dfrac{z}{w}\right) = \dfrac{\pi}{2}$

Now, to prove $\bar{z}w = -i$

LHS $= \bar{z}w$

$= r_1(\cos\theta_1 - i\sin\theta_1)r_2(\cos\theta_2 + i\sin\theta_2)$

$= r_1 r_2[\cos(\theta_2 - \theta_1) + i\sin(\theta_2 - \theta_1)]$

$= r_1 r_2\left[\cos\left(-\dfrac{\pi}{2}\right) + i\sin\left(-\dfrac{\pi}{2}\right)\right]$

$= 1(0 - i) = -i =$ R.H.S. **Hence Proved.**

EXPERT ADVICE

- *Most of the questions are asked from " Polar representation" and "Quadratic Equations with complex roots".*
- *You can prepare this chapter in less time, so do not keep chapter away from your final exam preparation.*

OSWAAL LEARNING TOOLS

For Suggested Online Videos

Visit : *https://youtu.be/9Fm8aUyf1Yo* **Or Scan the Code**	**Visit :** *https://goo.gl/Jak15x* **Or Scan the Code**
Visit : *https://youtu.be/MDDZG-Y_AfY* **Or Scan the Code**	**Visit :** *https://youtu.be/T647CGsuOVU* **Or Scan the Code**
Visit : *https://goo.gl/D7sWei* **Or Scan the Code**	**Visit :** *https://goo.gl/yuigq9* **Or Scan the Code**

CHAPTER

6 LINEAR INEQUALITIES

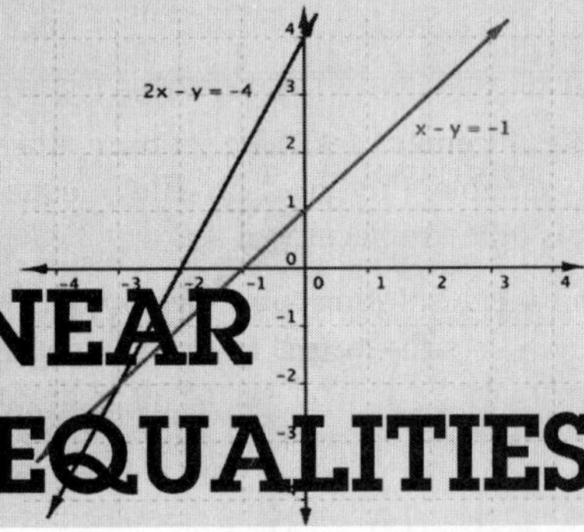

Chapter Objectives

➢ Inequality; Linear inequality; Algebraic solutions of linear inequalities in one variable and their representation on the number line; Graphical solutions of linear inequalities in two variables, Graphical method of finding a solution of system of linear inequalities in two variables.

TOPIC-1
Solution of Linear Inequalities in One Variable

TOPIC - 1
Solution of Linear Inequalities in One Variable ... P. 74

TOPIC - 2
Solution of Linear inequalities in two variable ... P. 80

Quick Review

➢ **Inequality** : Two real numbers or two algebraic expression related by the symbol '<', '>', '≤' or '≥' form an inequality.

➢ **Linear Inequality**
An inequality is said to be linear, if each variable occurs in first degree only and there is no term involving the product of the variables.
e.g., $ax + b \leq 0, ax + by + c > 0, ax \leq 4$.

An inequality in one variable in which degree of variable is 2, is called quadratic inequality in one variables.

e.g., $ax^2 + bx + c \geq 0, 3x^2 + 2x + 4 \leq 0$.

➢ **Linear Inequality in One Variable**
A linear inequality which has only one variable, is called linear inequality in one variable.

e.g., $ax + b < 0$, where $a \neq 0, 4c + 7 \geq 0$.

(i) Rules for solving inequalities:

- If $a \geq b$ then $a \pm k \geq b \pm k$, where k is any real number.
- If $k > 0$ (i.e. positive), then $a \geq b \quad \Rightarrow ka \geq kb$
- If $k < 0$ (i.e. negative), then $a \geq b \quad \Rightarrow ka \leq kb$

Thus, always reverse the sign of inequality while multiplying or dividing both sides of an inequality by a negative number.

(ii) Procedure to solve a linear inequality in one variables :

- Simplify both sides by removing graph symbols and collecting like terms.
- Remove fractions (or decimals) by multiplying both sides by appropriate factor (L.C.M. of denomination or a power of 10 in case of decimals.)
- Isolate the variable on one side and all constants on the other side. Collect like terms whenever possible.
- Make the coefficient of the variable.
- Choose the solution set from the replacement set.

TIPS...

- *Any solution of an inequality in one variable is a value of the variable, which makes it a true statement.*
- *The solution region of a system of inequalities is the region which satisfies all the given inequalities in the system simultaneously.*
- *Equal numbers may be added to (or subtracted from) both sides of an inequality.*
- *Both sides of an inequality can be multiplied (or divide) by the same positive number. But when both sides are multiplied (or divided) by a negative number, then the inequality is reversed.*

Note : Replacement set : The set from which values of the variable (involved in the inequality) are chosen is called replacement set.

Solution set : A solution to an inequality is a number which when substituted for the variable, makes the inequality true. The set of all solutions of an inequality is called the solution set of the inequality.

Know the Terms

Types of Inequality

- **Numerical inequality :** An inequality which does not involve any variable is called a numerical inequality.
e.g., $4 > 2, 8 < 21$
- **Literal inequality :** An inequality which have variables is called literal inequality.
e.g., $x < 7, y \geq 11, x - y \leq 4$
- **Strict inequality :** An inequality which have only < or > is called strict inequality.
e.g., $3x + y < 0, x > 7$
- **Slack inequality :** An inequality which have only ≥ or ≤ is called slack inequality.
e.g., $3x + 2y \leq 0, y \geq 4$

TRICKS...

- *To represent $x < a$ ($x > a$) on number line, put a circle (o) on the number 'a' and dark line to the left (or right) of the number 'a'.*
- *To represent $c \leq a$ ($c \geq a$) on the number line, put a dark circle (•) on the number 'a' and dark line to the left (or right) of the number x.*
- *In order to identify the half plane represented by an inequality, it is just sufficient to take any point (a, b) (not on line) and check whether it satisfies the inequality or not. If it is satisfies, then the inequality represents the half plane and shade the region which contain the point, otherwise inequality represents that half plane which does not contain the point with in it. For convenience, the point (0, 0) is preferred.*

Multiple Choice Questions **(1 mark each)**

[A] Objective Type Questions

Q. 1. If $x < 5$, then

(A) $-x < -5$ **(B)** $-x \leq -5$
(C) $-x > -5$ **(D)** $-x \geq -5$

[NCERT Exemplar Q. 19, Page 109]

Ans. Correct option : (C)

Since $x < 5$, therefore $-x < -5$

Q. 2. If $-3x + 17 < -13$, then

(A) $x \in (10, \infty)$ **(B)** $x \in [10, \infty)$
(C) $x \in (-\infty, 10]$ **(D)** $x \in [-10, 10)$

[NCERT Exemplar Q. 21, Page 109]

Ans. Correct option : (A)

Given, that $-3x + 17 < -13$

$\Rightarrow -3x < -7 - 13 \Rightarrow -3x < -30$

$\Rightarrow 3x > 30 \Rightarrow x > 10$

$\Rightarrow x \in (10, \infty)$

Q. 3. If x is a real number and $|x| < 3$, then

(A) $x \geq 3$ **(B)** $-3 < x < 3$
(C) $x \leq -3$ **(D)** $-3 \leq x \leq 3$

[NCERT Exemplar Q. 22, Page 109]

Ans. Correct option : (B)

Given, $|x| < 3 \Rightarrow -3 < x < 3$

[Since, $|x| < a \Rightarrow -a < x < a$]

Q. 4. x and b are real numbers. If $b > 0$ and $|x| > b$, then

(A) $x \in (-b, \infty)$ **(B)** $x \in [-\infty, b)$
(C) $x \in (-b, b)$ **(D)** $x \in (-\infty, -b) \cup (b, \infty)$

[NCERT Exemplar Q. 23, Page 109]

Ans. Correct option : (D)

Given, $|x| > b, b > 0$

$\Rightarrow x < -b$ or $x > b$

$\Rightarrow x \in (-\infty, -b) \cup (b, \infty)$

Q. 5. If $|x - 1| > 5$, then

(A) $x \in (-4, 6)$
(B) $x \in [-4, 6)$
(C) $x \in (-\infty, -4) \cup (6, \infty)$
(D) $x \in [-\infty, -b) \cup (b, \infty)$

[NCERT Exemplar Q. 24, Page 109]

Ans. Correct option : (C)

Given, $|x - 1| > 5$

$\Rightarrow (x - 1) > 5$ or $(x - 1) < -5$

$\Rightarrow x > 5 + 1$ or $x < -5 + 1$

$\Rightarrow x > 6$ or $x < -4$

$\Rightarrow x \in (-\infty, -4) \cup (6, \infty)$

Q. 6. If $|x + 2| \leq 9$, then

(A) $x \in (-7, 11)$
(B) $x \in [-11, 7]$
(C) $x \in (-\infty, -7) \cup (11, \infty)$
(D) $x \in (-\infty, -7) \cup [11, \infty)$

[NCERT Exemplar Q. 25, Page 109]

Ans. Correct option : (B)

Given, $|x + 2| \leq 9$

$\Rightarrow -9 \leq x + 2 \leq 9$

$\Rightarrow -9 - 2 \leq x \leq 9 - 2$

$\Rightarrow -11 \leq x \leq 7$

$\Rightarrow x \in [-11, 7]$

Q. 7. The inequality representing the following graph is:

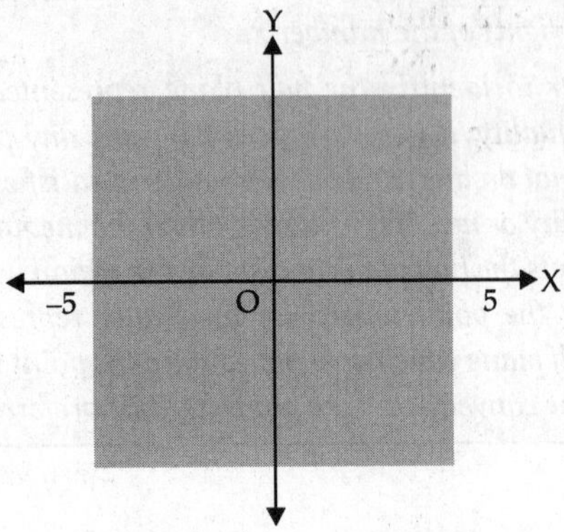

(A) $|x| < 5$ (B) $|x| \leq 5$

(C) $|x| > 5$ (D) $|x| \geq 5$

[NCERT Exemplar Q. 26, Page 110]

Ans. Correct option : (A)

The given graph represents $x < -5$ and $x < 5$ combining the two inequalities $|x| < 5$.

Solution of a linear inequality in variable x is represented on number line in Q. 8 to 11. Choose the correct answer from the given four options in each of the exercises.

[NCERT Exemplar Q. 27-30, Page 110]

Q. 8. (A) $x \in (-\infty, 5)$ **(B)** $x \in (-\infty, 5]$

(C) $x \in [5, \infty)$ **(D)** $x \in (5, \infty)$

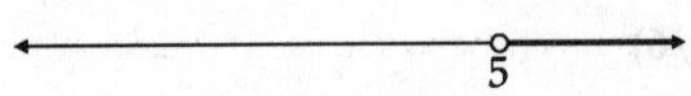

[NCERT Exemplar Q. 27, Page 110]

Ans. Correct option : (D)

The given figure represents all value of x greater than 5 excluding 5 on the real number line.

So, $x \in (5, \infty)$

Q. 9. (A) $x \in (\frac{9}{2}, \infty)$ **(B)** $x \in [\frac{9}{2}, \infty)$

(C) $x \in (-\infty, \frac{9}{2})$ **(D)** $x \in (-\infty, \frac{9}{2}]$

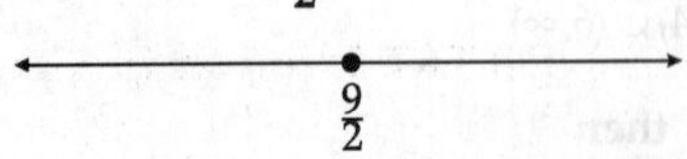

[NCERT Exemplar Q. 28, Page 10]

Ans. Correct option : (B)

The given figure has all real values of x greater than and equal to $\frac{9}{2}$.

So, $x \geq \frac{9}{2} \Rightarrow x \in \left[\frac{9}{2}, \infty\right)$

Q. 10. (A) $x \in (-\infty, \frac{7}{2})$ **(B)** $x \in (-\infty, \frac{7}{2}]$

(C) $x \in [\frac{7}{2}, -\infty)$ **(D)** $x \in (\frac{7}{2}, \infty)$

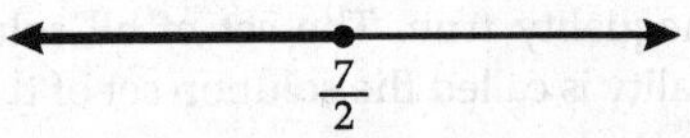

[NCERT Exemplar Q. 29, Page 110]

Ans. Correct option : (A)

The given figure represents all the value of x less than $\frac{7}{2}$ on real number line.

So, $x \left(-\infty, \frac{7}{2}\right)$

Q. 11. (A) $x \in (-\infty, -2)$ **(B)** $x \in (-\infty, -2]$

(C) $x \in (-2, \infty]$ **(D)** $x \in [-2, \infty)$

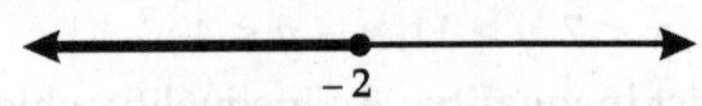

[NCERT Exemplar Q. 30, Page 110]

Ans. Correct option : (B)

The given graph represent all real values of x less than and equal to –2.

So, $x (-\infty, -2)$.

[B] True and False

Q. 1. If $x < -5$ and $x > -2$, then $x \in (-\infty, -5)$

[NCERT Exemplar Q. 31(v), Page 111]

Q. 2. If $x < -5$ and $x > 2$, then $x \in (-5, 2)$

[NCERT Exemplar Q. 31(vi), Page 111]

Q. 3. If $x > -2$ and $x > 9$, then $x \in (-2, 9)$

[NCERT Exemplar Q. 31(vii), Page 111]

Q. 4. If $|x| > 5$, then $x \in (-\infty, -5) \cup [5, \infty)$

[NCERT Exemplar Q. 31(viii), Page 111]

Q. 5. If $|x| \leq 4$, then $x \in [-4, 4]$

[NCERT Exemplar Q. 31(ix), Page 111]

Q. 6. Graph of $x < 3$ is

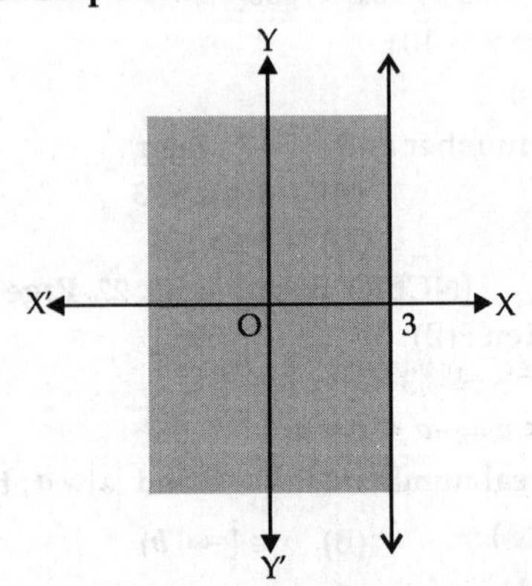

[NCERT Exemplar Q. 31(x), Page 111]

Q. 7. Graph of $x \geq 0$ is

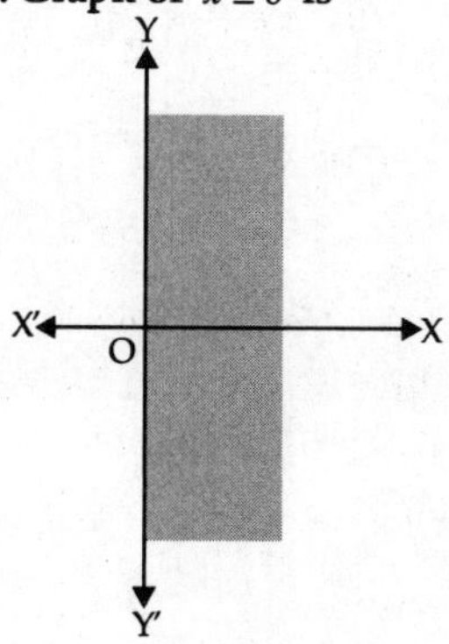

[NCERT Exemplar Q. 31(xi), Page 111]

Q. 8. Graph of $y \leq 0$ is

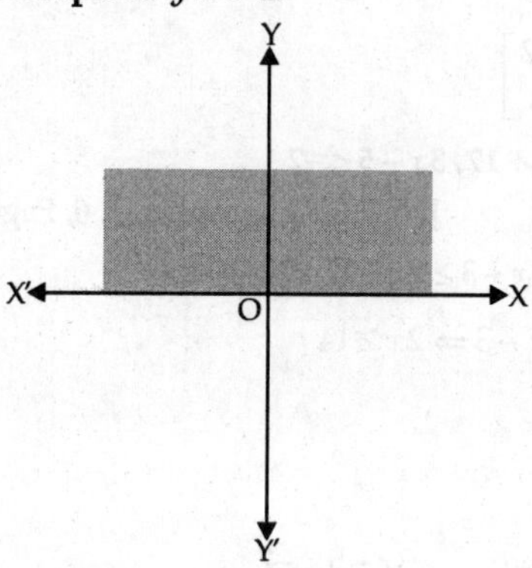

[NCERT Exemplar Q. 31(xii), Page 111]

Answer:

1. True
2. False
3. True
4. False
5. True
6. True
7. True
8. False

[C] Fill in the blanks

Q. 1. If $-4x \geq 12$, then $x \ldots -3$.

[NCERT Exemplar Q. 32(i), Page 113]

Q. 2. If $\frac{-3}{4}x \leq -3$, then $x \ldots 4$.

[NCERT Exemplar Q. 32(ii), Page 113]

Q. 3. If $\frac{2}{x+2} > 0$, then $x \ldots -2$.

[NCERT Exemplar Q. 32(iii), Page 113]

Q. 4. If $x > -5$, then $4x \ldots -20$.

[NCERT Exemplar Q. 32(iv), Page 113]

Q. 5. If $|x+2| > 5$, then $x \ldots -7$ or $x \ldots 3$.

[NCERT Exemplar Q. 32(vii), Page 113]

Q. 6. If $-2x+1 \geq 9$, then $x \ldots -4$.

[NCERT Exemplar Q. 32(viii), Page 113]

Answer:

1. $x \leq -3$
2. $x \geq 4$
3. $x > -2$
4. $4x > -20$
5. $x < -7, x > 3$
6. $x \leq -4$

Short Answer Type Questions (2 marks each)

Solve for x, the inequalities in the following questions (1-6)

Q. 1. $\frac{4}{x+1} \leq 3 \leq \frac{6}{x+1} (x > 0)$

[NCERT Exemplar Q. 1, Page 107]

Sol. Consider first two inequalities, $\frac{4}{x+1} \leq 3$

$\Rightarrow 4 \leq 3(x+1)$

$\Rightarrow 4 \leq 3x+3$

$\Rightarrow 4-3 \leq 3x$ [subtracting 3 on both sides]

$\Rightarrow 1 \leq 3x$

$\therefore x \geq \frac{1}{3}$ (i)

and consider last two inequalities,

$3 \leq \frac{6}{x+1}$

$\Rightarrow 3(x+1) \leq 6$

$\Rightarrow 3x+3 \leq 6$

$\Rightarrow 3x \leq 6-3$ [subtracting 3 on both sides]

$\Rightarrow 3x \leq 3$ [dividing by 3]

$\therefore x \leq 1$ (ii)

From Eqs. (i) and (ii),

$x \in \left[\frac{1}{3}, 1\right]$

$\frac{1}{3} \leq x \leq 1$

Q. 2. $\frac{|x-2|-1}{|x-2|-2} \leq 0$

[NCERT Exemplar Q. 2, Page 107]

Sol. Let $|x-2| = y$

$\frac{y-1}{y-2} \leq 0$ Multiply by $(y-2)$ both sides

$y-1=0$ and $y-2=0$

$y=1$ and $y=2$

$\Rightarrow 1 \leq y < 2$

$\Rightarrow 1 \leq |x-2| < 2$

$\Rightarrow 1 \le |x-2|$ and $|x-2| < 2$

$\Rightarrow x-2 \le -1$

$\Rightarrow x-2 \ge 1$

and $-2 < x-2 < 2$

$\Rightarrow x \le 1$ or $x \ge 3$ and $0 < x < 4$

$\Rightarrow x \in (0,1] \cup [3,4)$

Q. 3. $\dfrac{1}{|x|-3} \le \dfrac{1}{2}$ **[NCERT Exemplar Q. 3, Page 107]**

Sol. Given, $\dfrac{1}{|x|-3} \le \dfrac{1}{2}$

$\Rightarrow |x|-3 \ge 2$ $\left[\because \dfrac{1}{a} < \dfrac{1}{b} \Rightarrow a > b\right]$

$\Rightarrow |x| \ge 5$ [adding 3 to both sides]

$\Rightarrow x \le -5$ or $x \ge 5$ $[\because |x| \ge a \Rightarrow |x| \le -a \Rightarrow |x| \ge a]$

$\Rightarrow x \in (-\infty,-5] \cup [5,\infty)$ **(i)**

But $|x|-3 \ne 0$

Either $|x|-3 < 0$ or $|x|-3 > 0$

$\Rightarrow |x| < 3$ or $|x| > 3$

$\Rightarrow -3 < x < 3$ or $x < -3$ or $x > 3$ **(ii)**

$[\because |x| < a \Rightarrow -a < x < a$

and

$|x| > a \Rightarrow x < -a$ and $x > a]$

From Eqs. (i) and (ii), we get

$x \in (-\infty,-5) \cup (-3,3) \cup [5,\infty)$

Q. 4. $|x-1| \le 5, |x| \ge 2$

[NCERT Exemplar Q. 4, Page 107]

Sol. We have, $|x-1| \le 5$

$-5 \le x-1 \le 5$

$\Rightarrow -4 \le x \le 6$

$\Rightarrow x \in [-4,6]$ (i)

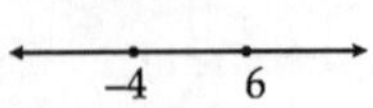

and $|x| \ge 2$

$\Rightarrow x \le -2$ or $x \ge 2$

$\Rightarrow x \in (-\infty,-2] \cup [2,\infty)$ (ii)

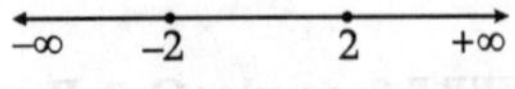

On combining Eqs. (i) and (ii), we get

$x \in (-4,-2] \cup [2,6]$

Q. 5. $-5 \le \dfrac{2-3x}{4} \le 9$

[NCERT Exemplar Q. 5, Page 107]

Sol. We have $-5 \le \dfrac{2-3x}{4} \le 9$

$\Rightarrow -20 \le 2-3x$ [multiplying by 4 on both sides]

$\Rightarrow 3x \le 2+20$

$\Rightarrow 3x \le 22$

$\Rightarrow x \le \dfrac{22}{3}$

and $\dfrac{2-3x}{4} \le 9$

$\Rightarrow 2-3x \le 36$

$\Rightarrow -3x \le 36-2$

$\Rightarrow -3x \le 34$

$\Rightarrow 3x \ge -34$

$\Rightarrow x \ge -\dfrac{34}{3}$

$\Rightarrow -\dfrac{34}{3} \le x \le \dfrac{22}{3}$

$\Rightarrow x \in \left[\dfrac{-34}{3}, \dfrac{22}{3}\right]$

Q. 6. $4x+3 \ge 2x+17, 3x-5 < -2$

[NCERT Exemplar Q. 6, Page 107]

Sol. We have, $4x+3 \ge 2x+17$

$\Rightarrow 4x-2x \ge 17-3 \Rightarrow 2x \ge 14$

$\Rightarrow x \ge \dfrac{14}{2}$

$\Rightarrow x \ge 7$ (i)

Also, we have $3x-5 < -2$

$\Rightarrow 3x < -2+5 \Rightarrow 3x < 3$

$\Rightarrow x < 1$ (ii)

On combining Eqs. (i) and (ii), we see that solution is not possible because nothing is common between these two solutions, (*i.e.*, $x < 1, x \ge 7$).

Q. 7. A company manufactures cassettes. Its cost and revenue functions are $C(x) = 26000 + 30x$ and $R(x) = 43x$, respectively, where x is the number of cassettes produced and sold in a week. How many cassettes must be sold by the company to realise some profit? [NCERT Exemplar Q. 7, Page 107]

Sol. Cost function, $C(x) = 26000 + 30x$

and revenue function, $R(x) = 43x$

For profit, $R(x) > C(x)$

$\Rightarrow 26000 + 30x < 43x$

$\Rightarrow 30x - 43x < -26000$

$\Rightarrow -13x < -26000$

$\Rightarrow 13x > 26000$

$\Rightarrow x > \dfrac{26000}{13}$

$\therefore x > 2000$

Hence, more than 2000 cassettes must be produced to get profit.

Q. 8. The water acidity in a pool is considered normal when the average pH reading of three daily measurements is between 8.2 and 8.5. If the first two pH readings are 8.48 and 8.35, then find the range of pH value for the third reading that will result in the acidity level being normal.

[NCERT Exemplar Q. 8, Page 107]

Sol. Given, first pH value = 8.48

and second pH value = 8.35

Let third pH value be x.

Since, it is given that average pH value lies between 8.2 and 8.5.

$\therefore\ 8.2 < \dfrac{8.48 + 8.35 + x}{3} < 8.5$

$\Rightarrow 8.2 < \dfrac{16.83 + x}{3} < 8.5$

$\Rightarrow 3 \times 8.2 < 16.83 + x < 8.5 \times 3$

$\Rightarrow 24.6 < 16.83 + x < 25.5$

$\Rightarrow 24.6 - 16.83 < x < 25.5 - 16.83$

$\Rightarrow 7.77 < x < 8.67$

Thus, third pH value lies between 7.77 and 8.67.

Q. 9. The longest side of a triangle is twice the shortest side and the third side is 2 cm longer than the shortest side. If the perimeter of the triangle is more than 166 cm, then find the minimum length of the shortest side.

[NCERT Exemplar Q. 11, Page 107]

Sol. Let the length of shortest side be x cm.

According to the given information,

Longest side = 2 x Shortest side

= $2x$ cm

and third side = 2 + Shortest side

= 2 (2 + x) cm

Perimeter of triangle = $x + 2x + (x + 2) = 4x + 2$

According to the question,

Perimeter >166 cm

$\Rightarrow 4x + 2 > 166$

$\Rightarrow 4x > 166 - 2$

$\Rightarrow 4x > 164$

$\therefore\ x > \dfrac{164}{4} = 41$ cm

Hence, the minimum length of shortest side be 41 cm.

Q. 10. In drilling world's deepest hole it was found that the temperature T in degree Celsius, x km below the earth's surface was given by $T = 30 + 25\,(x - 3)$, $3 \le x \le 15$. At what depth will the temperature be between 155°C and 205°C?

[NCERT Exemplar Q. 12, Page 107]

Sol. Given that, $T = 30 + 25(x - 3), 3 \le x \le 15$

According to the question,

$155 < T < 205$

$\Rightarrow 155 < 30 + 25\,(x - 3) < 205$

$\Rightarrow 155 - 30 < 25\,(x - 3) < 205 - 30$ [subtracting 30 in whole]

$\Rightarrow 125 < 25\,(x - 3) < 175$

$\Rightarrow \dfrac{125}{25} < x - 3 < \dfrac{175}{25}$ [dividing by 25 in whole]

$\Rightarrow 5 < x - 3 < 7$

$\Rightarrow 5 + 3 < x < 7 + 3$ [adding 3 in whole]

$\Rightarrow 8 < x < 10$

Hence, at the depth 8 to 10 km temperature lies between 155° to 205°C.

Long Answer Type Question-I

(4 marks each)

Q. 1. IQ of a person is given by the formula $IQ = \dfrac{MA}{CA} \times 100$ where, MA is the mental age and CA is chronological age. If $80 \le$ IQ ≤ 140 for a group of 12 yr old children, find the range of their mental age. [NCERT Exemplar Q. 14, Page 132]

Sol. Given that $80 \le IQ \le 140$ **(i)**

Putting $IQ = \dfrac{MA}{CA} \times 100$ in Eq. (i)

$\Rightarrow 80 \le \dfrac{MA}{CA} \times 100 \le 140$

$\Rightarrow 80 \le \dfrac{MA}{12} \times 100 \le 140$ ($\because$ Given that CA = 12 yr)

Multiplying by 12 in each term,

$\Rightarrow 80 \times 12 \le \dfrac{MA}{12} \times 100 \times 12 \le 140 \times 12$ (Using rule 2)

$\Rightarrow 960 \le MA \times 100 \le 1680$

Dividing by 100 in each term,

$\Rightarrow \dfrac{960}{100} \le \dfrac{MA \times 100}{100} \le \dfrac{1680}{100}$ (Using rule 2)

$\Rightarrow 9.6 \le MA \le 16.8 \rightarrow MA \in [9.6, 16.8]$

Hence, mental age should be greater than equal to 9.6 but less than equal to 16.8.

Q. 2. A solution of 9% acid is to be diluted by adding 3% acid solution to it. The resulting mixture is to be more than 5% but less than 7% acid. If there is 460 L of the 9% solution, how many litres of 3% solution will have to be added?

[NCERT Exemplar Q. 9, Page 107]

Sol. Let x L of 3% solution be added to 460 L of 9% solution of acid.

Then, total quantity of mixture = (460 + x) L

Total acid content in the (460 + x) L of mixture

$= \left(460 \times \dfrac{9}{100} + x \times \dfrac{3}{100}\right)$

It is given that acid content in the resulting mixture must be more than 5% but less than 7% acid.

Therefore,

5% of $(460 + x) < 460 \times \dfrac{9}{100} + \dfrac{3x}{100} < 7\%$ of $(460 + x)$

$\Rightarrow \dfrac{5}{100} \times (460 + x) < 460 \times \dfrac{9}{100} + \dfrac{3}{100}x < \dfrac{7}{100} \times (460 + x)$

$\Rightarrow 5 \times (460 + x) < 460 \times 9 + 3x < 7 \times (460 + x)$

[multiplying by 100]

$\Rightarrow 2300 + 5x < 4140 + 3x < 3220 + 7x$

Taking first two inequalities, $2300+5x<4140+3x$

$\Rightarrow 5x-3x<4140-2300$

$\Rightarrow 2x<1840$

$\Rightarrow x<\frac{1840}{2}$

$\Rightarrow x<920$ **(i)**

Taking last two inequalities, $4140+3x<3220+7x$

$\Rightarrow 3x-7x<3220-4140$

$\Rightarrow -4x<-920$

$\Rightarrow 4x>920$

$\Rightarrow x>\frac{920}{4}$

$\Rightarrow x>230$ **(ii)**

Hence, the number of litres of the 3% solution of acid must be more than 230 L and less than 920 L.

Q. 3. A solution is to be kept between 40°C and 45°C. What is the range of temperature in degree Fahrenheit, if the conversion formula is $F=\frac{9}{5}C+32$?

[NCERT Exemplar Q. 10, Page 107]

Sol. Let the required temperature be $x°$ F.

Given that, $F=\frac{9}{5}C+32$

$\Rightarrow 5F=9C+32\times5$

$\Rightarrow 9C=5F-32\times5$

$\therefore C=\frac{5F-160}{9}$

Since, temperature in degree celsius lies between 40°C to 45°C.

Therefore, $40<\frac{5F-160}{9}<45$

$\Rightarrow 40<\frac{5F-160}{9}<45$

$\Rightarrow 40\times9<5f-160<45\times9$ [multiplying throughout by 9]

$\Rightarrow 360<5f-160<405$ [adding 160 throughout]

$\Rightarrow 360+160<5f<405+160$

$\Rightarrow 520<5f<565$

$\Rightarrow \frac{520}{5}<f<\frac{565}{5}$ [divide throughout by 5]

$\Rightarrow 104<f<113$

Hence, the range of temperature in degree Fahrenheit is 104 °F to 113°F.

Q. 4. Solve the following system of inequalities $\frac{2x+1}{7x-1}>5,\ \frac{x+7}{x-8}>2$.

[NCERT Exemplar Q. 13, Page 108]

Sol. The given system of inequations is

$\frac{2x+1}{7x-1}>5$ **(i)**

and $\frac{x+7}{x-8}>2$ **(ii)**

Now, $\frac{2x+1}{7x-1}-5>0$

$\Rightarrow \frac{(2x+1)-5(7x-1)}{7x-1}>0$

$\Rightarrow \frac{2x+1-35x+5}{7x-1}>0$

$\Rightarrow \frac{-33x+6}{7x-1}>0 \Rightarrow \frac{33x-6}{7x-1}<0$

$\Rightarrow x\in\left(\frac{1}{7},\frac{6}{33}\right)$ **(iii)**

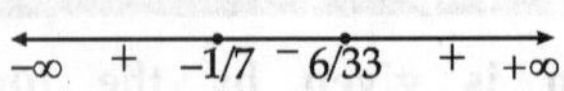

and $\frac{x+7}{x-8}>2 \Rightarrow \frac{x+7}{x-8}-2>0$

$\Rightarrow \frac{x+7-2(x-8)}{x-8}>0 \Rightarrow \frac{x+7-2x+16}{x-8}>0$

$\Rightarrow \frac{-x+23}{x-8}>0 \Rightarrow \frac{x-23}{x-8}<0$

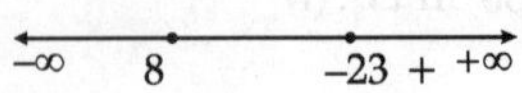

$\Rightarrow x\in(8, 23)$ **(iv)**

Since, the intersection of Eqs. (iii) and (iv) is the null set. Hence, the given system of equation has no solution.

TOPIC-2

Solution of Linear Inequalities in Two Variable

Quick Review

➤ The inequality of form $ax+by+c>0$, $ax+by+c=0$, or $ax+by+c<0$ etc, where $a\neq0$, $b\neq0$ is called a linear in equality in two variables x and y.

➤ **Graphical Solution of Linear Inequalities in Two Variables**

- The graph of the inequality $ax + by > c$ is one of the half planes and is called the solution region.
- When the inequality involves the sign ≤ or ≥ then the points on the line are included in the solution region but if it has the sign < or > then the points on the line are not included in the solution region and it has to be drawn as a dotted line.
- The common values of the variable form the required solution of the given system of linear inequalities in one variable.
- The common part of coordinate plane is the required solution of the system of linear inequations in two variables when solved by graphical method.

Multiple Choice Questions

(1 mark each)

[A] Objective Type Questions

Q. 1. Given that x, y and b are real numbers and $x < y, b < 0$, then

(A) $\frac{x}{b} < \frac{y}{b}$ (B) $\frac{x}{b} \le \frac{y}{b}$

(C) $\frac{x}{b} > \frac{y}{b}$ (D) $\frac{x}{b} \ge \frac{y}{b}$

[NCERT Exemplar Q. 20, Page 109]

Ans. Correct option : (C)

Given that, $x < y, b < 0$

$\Rightarrow \frac{x}{b} > \frac{y}{b}, b < 0$

[B] True and False

Q. 1. If $x < y$ and $b < 0$, then $\frac{x}{b} < \frac{y}{b}$.

[NCERT Exemplar Q. 31(i), Page 111]

Q. 2. If $xy > 0$, then $x > 0$ and $y < 0$.

[NCERT Exemplar Q. 31(ii), Page 111]

Q. 3. If $xy > 0$, then $x < 0$ and $y < 0$.

[NCERT Exemplar Q. 31(iii), Page 111]

Q. 4. If $xy \ge 0$, then $x < 0$ and $y < 0$.

[NCERT Exemplar Q. 31(iv), Page 111]

Q. 5. Solution set of $x \ge 0$ and $y \le 0$ is

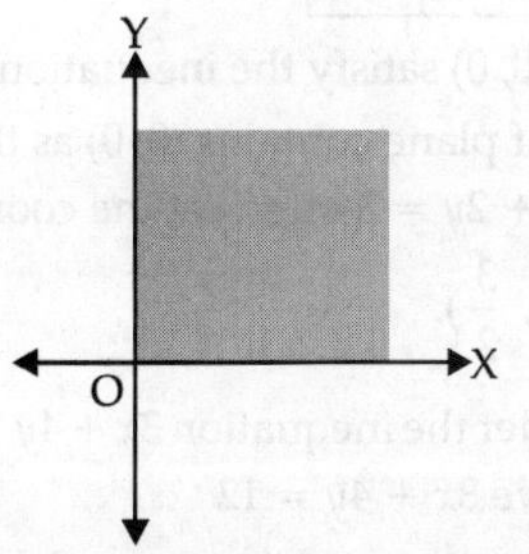

[NCERT Exemplar Q. 31(xiii), Page 112]

Q. 6. Solution set of $x \ge 0$ and $y \le 1$ is

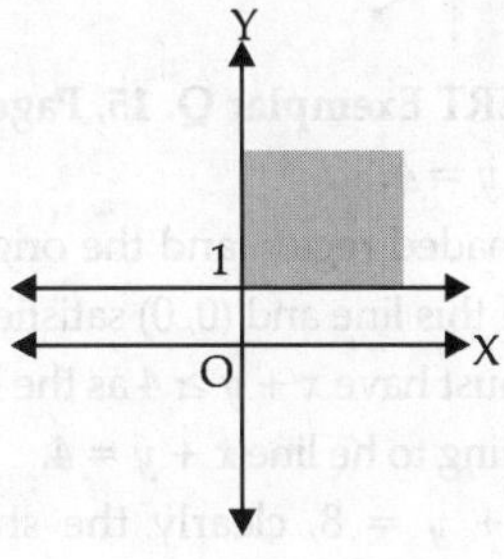

[NCERT Exemplar Q. 32(xiv), Page 112]

Q. 7. Solution set of $x + y \ge 0$ is

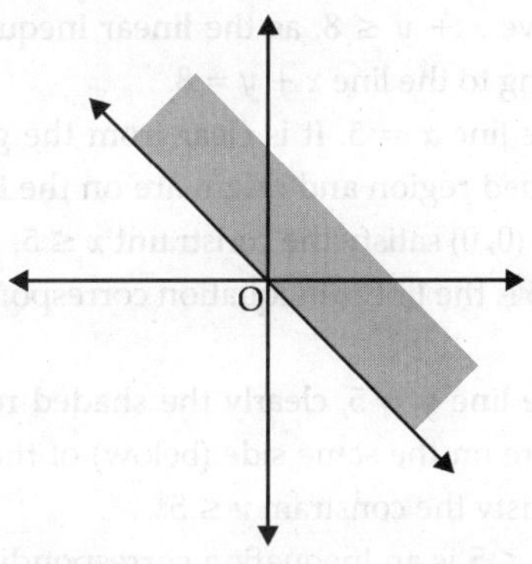

[NCERT Exemplar Q. 32(xv), Page 113]

Answer:

1. False
2. False
3. True
4. False
5. False
6. False
7. True

[B] Fill in the blanks

Q. 1. If $x > y$ and $z < 0$, then $-xz$ ... $-yz$.

[NCERT Exemplar Q. 32(v), Page 113]

Q. 2. If $p < 0$ and $q < 0$, then $p - q$ .... p.

[NCERT Exemplar Q. 32(v), Page 113]

Answer:

1. $-xz > -yz$
2. $p - q > p$

Long Answer Type Questions **(4 marks each)**

Q. 1. Find the linear inequalities for which the shaded region in the given figure is the solution set.

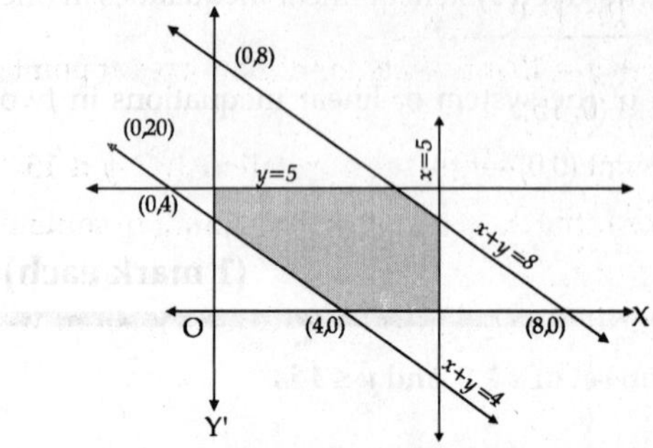

[NCERT Exemplar Q. 15, Page 108]

Sol. Consider the line $x + y = 4$.

We observe that the shaded region and the origin lie on the opposite side of this line and (0, 0) satisfies $x + y \leq 4$. Therefore, we must have $x + y \geq 4$ as the linear inequation corresponding to he line $x + y = 4$.

Consider the line $x + y = 8$, clearly the shaded region and origin lie on the same side of this line and (0, 0) satisfies the constraints $x + y \leq 8$. Therefore, we must have $x + y \leq 8$, as the linear inequation corresponding to the line $x + y = 8$.

Consider the line $x = 5$. It is clear from the graph that the shaded region and origin are on the left of this line and (0, 0) satisfy the constraint $x \leq 5$.

Hence, $x \leq 5$ is the linear inequation corresponding to $x = 5$.

Consider the line $y = 5$, clearly the shaded region and origin are on the same side (below) of the line and (0, 0) satisfy the constrain $y \leq 5$.

Therefore, $y \leq 5$ is an inequation corresponding to the line $y = 5$.

We also notice that the shaded region is above the X-axis and on the right of the Y-axis i.e., shaded region is in first quadrant. So, we must have $x \geq 0, y \geq 0$.

Thus, the linear inequations comprising the given solution set are $x + y \geq 4$; $x + y \leq 8$; $x \leq 5$; $y \leq 5$; $x \geq 0$ and $y \geq 0$.

Q. 2. Find the linear inequalities for which the shaded region in the given figure is the solution set.

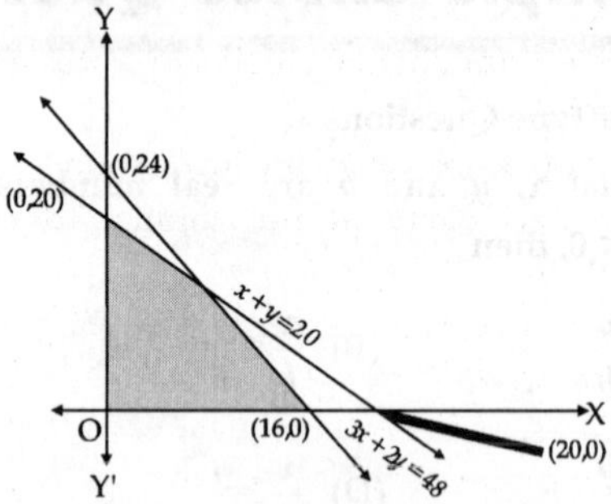

[NCERT Exemplar Q. 14, Page 108]

Sol. Consider the line $3x + 2y = 48$, we observe that the shaded region and the origin are on the same side of the line $3x + 2y = 48$ and (0, 0) satisfy the linear constraint $3x + 2y < 48$. So, we must have one inequation as $3x + 2y < 48$.

Now, consider the line $x + y = 20$. We find that the shaded region and the origin are on the same side of the line $x + y = 20$ and (0, 0) satisfy the constraints $x + y < 20$. So, the second inequation is $x + y \leq 20$.

We also notice that the shaded region is above X-axis and is on the right side of Y-axis, so we must have $x \geq 0, y \geq 0$.

Thus, the linear inequations corresponding to the given solution set are $3x + 2y \leq 48$, $x + y \leq 20$ and $x \geq 0, y \geq 0$.

Long Answer Type Question-II **(6 marks each)**

Q. 1. Show that the following system of linear inequalities has no solution.

$x+2y \leq 3, 3x+4y \geq 12, x \geq 0, y \geq 1.$

[NCERT Exemplar Q. 16, Page 108]

Sol. Consider the inequation $x + 2y \leq 3$ as an equation, we have

$x+2y=3$

$\Rightarrow x=3-2y$

$\Rightarrow 2y=3-x$

x	3	1	0
y	0	1	1.5

Now (0, 0) satisfy the inequation $x + 2y \leq 3$.

So, half plane contains (0, 0) as the solution and the line $x + 2y = 3$ intersect the coordinate axis at (3, 0) and $(0, \frac{3}{2})$.

Consider the inequation $3x + 4y \geq 12$ as an equation, we have $3x + 4y = 12$

$\Rightarrow 4y = 12 - 3x$

x	0	4	2
y	3	0	$\frac{3}{2}$

Thus, coordinate axis intersected by the line $3x + 4y = 12$ at points (4, 0) and (0, 3).

Now, (0, 0) does not satisfy the inequation $3x + 4y = 12$.

Therefore, half plane of the solution does not contained (0, 0).

Consider the inequation $y \geq 1$ as an equation, we have $y = 1$.

It represents a straight line parallel to X-axis passing through point (0, 1).

Now, (0, 0) does not satisfy the inequation $y \geq 1$.

Therefore, half plane of the solution does not contains (0, 0).

Clearly, $x \geq 0$ represents the region lying on the right side of Y-axis.

The solution set of the given linear constraints will be the intersection of the above region.

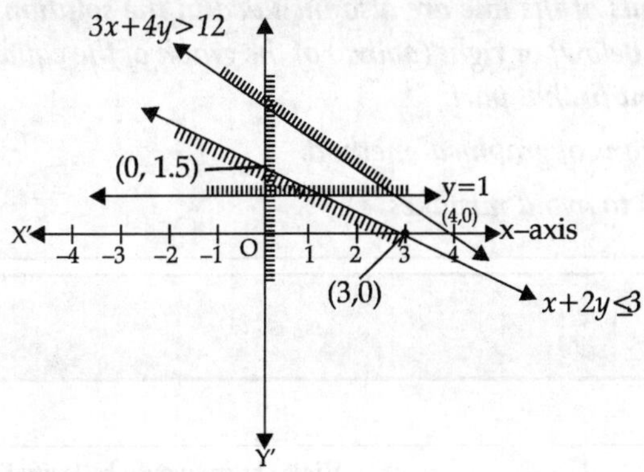

It is clear from the graph the shaded portions do not have common region.

So, solution set is null set.

Q. 2. Solve the following system of linear inequalities $3x + 2y \geq 24$, $3x + y \leq 15$, $x \geq 4$.

[NCERT Exemplar Q. 17, Page 109]

Sol. Consider the inequation $3x + 2y \geq 24$ as an equation, we have $3x + 2y = 24$

$\Rightarrow 2y = 24 - 3x$

x	0	8	4
y	12	0	6

Hence, line $3x + y = 24$ intersect coordinate axes at points (8, 0) and (0, 12).

Now, (0, 0) does not satisfy the inequation $3x + 2y \geq 24$.

Therefore, half plane of the solution set does not contains (0, 0).

Consider the inequation $3x + y \leq 15$ as an equation, we have

$\Rightarrow 3x + y = 15$

$y = 15 - 3x$

x	0	5	3
y	15	0	6

Line $3x + y = 15$ intersects coordinate axes at points (5, 0) and (0, 15).

Now, point (0,0) satisfy the inequation $3x + y \leq 15$.

Therefore, the half plane of the solution contain origin.

Consider the inequality $x \geq 4$ as an equation, we have

$x = 4$

It represents a straight line parallel to Y-axis passing through (4, 0). Now, point (0, 0) does not satisfy the inequation $x \geq 4$.

Therefore, half plane does not contains (0, 0),

The graph of the above inequations is given below.

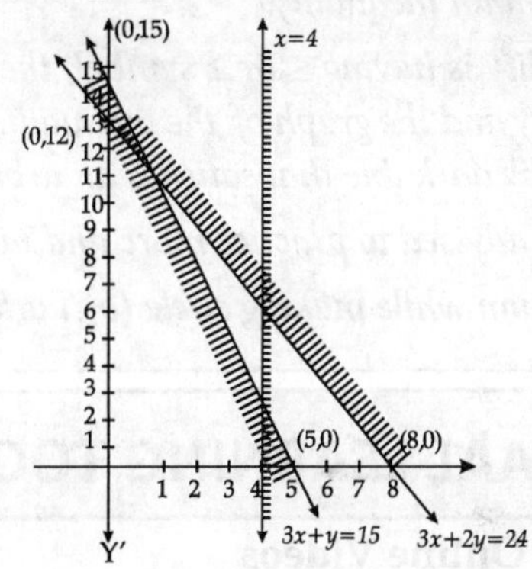

It is clear from the graph that there is no common region corresponding to these inequality.

Hence, the given system of inequalities have no solution.

Q. 3. Show that the solution set of the following system of linear inequalities is an unbounded region $2x + y \geq 8, x + 2y \geq 10, x \geq 0, y \geq 0$.

[NCERT Exemplar Q. 18, Page 109]

Sol. Consider the inequation $2x + y \geq 8$ as an equation, we have

$2x + y = 8$

$\Rightarrow y = 8 - 2x$

x	0	4	3
y	8	0	2

The line $2x + y = 8$ intersects coordinate axes at (4, 0) and (0, 8).

Now, point (0, 0) does not satisfy the inequation $2x + y \geq 8$.

Therefore, half plane does not contain origin.

Consider the inequation $x + 2y \geq 10$, as an equation, we have

$$x + 2y = 10$$

$$\Rightarrow \quad 2y = 10 - x$$

x	10	0	8
y	0	5	1

The line $2x + y = 8$ intersects the coordinate axes at (10, 0) and (0, 5).

Now, point (0, 0) does not satisfy the inequation $x + 2y \geq 10$.

Therefore, half plane does not contain (0, 0).

Consider the inequation $x \geq 0$ and $y \geq 0$ clearly, it represents the region in first quadrant.

The graph of the above inequations is given below

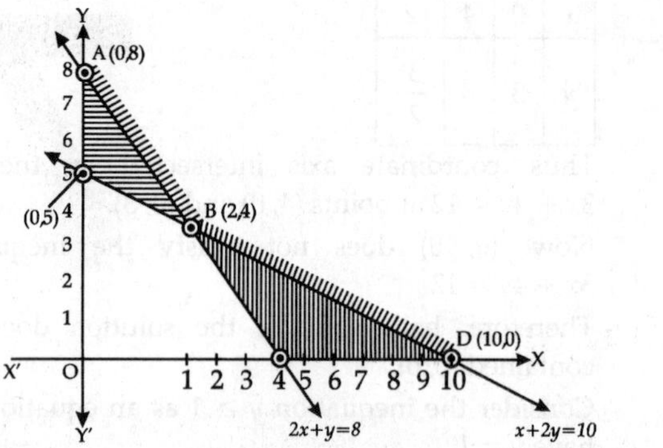

It is clear from the graph that common shaded portion is unbounded.

EXPERT ADVICE

- *Students always remember that two real number or two algebraic expressions related by the symbols <, >, ≤ or ≥ form an inequality.*
- *If an inequality is having ≤ or ≥ symbol, then the points of the line are also included in the solutions of the inequality and the graph of the inequality lies left (below) or right (above) of the graph of the equality represented by dark line that satisfies an arbitrary point in that part.*
- *Students are advised to practice more and more questions of graphical method.*
- *Take precaution while making circle (o)/dark circle (•) to avoid mistakes.*

OSWAAL LEARNING TOOLS

***For* Suggested Online Videos**

Visit : *https://youtu.be/0X-bMeIN53I* **Or Scan the Code**	**Visit :** *https://youtu.be/1raifwKcl5A* **Or Scan the Code**
Visit : *https://youtu.be/P_-c9D6mjGA* **Or Scan the Code**	**Visit :** *https://youtu.be/G8JnAOTdrYw* **Or Scan the Code**
Visit : *https://goo.gl/FYimb6* **Or Scan the Code**	**Visit :** *https://goo.gl/bUv2Fh* **Or Scan the Code**

CHAPTER 7

PERMUTATIONS AND COMBINATIONS

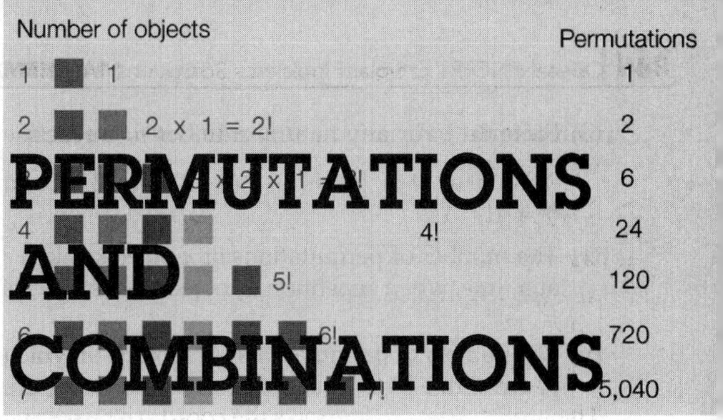

Chapter Objectives

> *Fundamental principles of counting; Multiplication principle, Addition principle; Factorial n (n!); Permutation and Combination; Properties of permutation and combination; Derivation of formulae for ^nP_r and ^nC_r their connections; Simple applications.*

TOPIC-1
Permutations

TOPIC - 1
Permutations P. 85

TOPIC - 2
Combinations P. 90

Quick Review

- If an event can occur in m different ways, following which another event can occur in n different ways, then the total number of occurrence of the events in the given order is $m \times n$.
- A permutation is an arrangement in a definite order of a number of objects taken some or all at a time.
- *e.g.*, If there are three objects say A, B and C, then the permutations of these objects taking two at a time are AB, BC, AC, BA, CB and CA. So, number of permutations is 3! = 1,2,3, = 6.
- If n and r are positive integers such that $0 \leq r \leq n$, then the number of permutations of n distinct things taken r at a time is denoted by ^nP_r or P(n, r).

  We have,

  $$P(n,r) = {}^nP_r = \frac{n!}{(n-r)!}, 0 \leq r \leq n.$$

  Note :

  (i) When $r = 0$, then $^nP_0 = \frac{n!}{(n-0)!} = \frac{n!}{n!} = 1$ [$\because$ 0! = 1]

  (ii) When $r = n$, then $^nP_n = \frac{n!}{(n-n)!} = \frac{n!}{0!} = n!$

  (iii) Number of permutations of different things taken all at a time = n!

TIPS...

- *It is very important topic from exam point of view, most of the students find this chapter interesting. Learn all the concepts and formulae and practice as many questions as possible.*
- *A combination is an arrangement of items in which ORDER DOES NOT MATTER.*
- *A permutation is an arrangement of items in a PARTICULAR ORDER.*
- *The factorial function (symbol: !) just means to multiply a series of descending natural numbers. Remember 0! = 1.*
- *Deeply understand the fundamental principles of counting.*

Know the Terms

- **Fundamental Principles of Counting**

  (i) Multiplication Principle : If first operation can performed in m ways and a second operation can be performed in n ways. Then, the two operations taken together can be performed in mn ways. This can be extended to any finite number of operations.

  (ii) Additional Principle : If first operation can performed in m ways and another operation, which is independent of the first, can be performed in n ways. Then, either of the two operations can be performed in $m + n$ ways. This can be extended to any finite number of exclusive events.

(iii) Factorial : For any natural number n, we define factorial as $n!$ or $\lfloor n = n(n-1)(n-2) ... 3 \times 2 \times 1$ and $0! = 1! = 1$.

(iv) The number of permutations of n objects, taken r at a time, when repetition of objects is allowed is n^r.

(v) The number of permutations of n objects of which p_1 are of one kind, p_2 are of second kind, ... p_k are of kth kind and the rest if any, are of different kinds, is $\frac{n!}{p_1!p_2!...p_k!}$

➤ **Properties of Permutation**

(i) $^nP_n = n(n-1)(n-2)....1 = n!$

(ii) $^nP_0 = \frac{n!}{n!} = 1$

(iii) $^nP_1 = n$

(iv) $^nP_{n-1} = n!$

(v) $^nP_r = n \cdot {}^{n-1}P_{r-1} = n(n-1) \cdot {}^{n-2}P_{r-2}$
$= n(n-1)(n-2) \cdot {}^{n-3}P_{r-3}$

(vi) $^{n-1}P_r + r \cdot {}^{n-1}P_{r-1} = {}^nP_r$

(vii) $\frac{^nP_r}{^nP_{r-1}} = n - r + 1$

TRICKS...

- *No. of permutations of n different things taken r at a time (i) when a particular thing is to be included in each arrangement is* $r.^{n-1}P_{r-1}$ *(ii) when a particular thing is always excluded, then no. of arrangements* $= {}^{n-1}P_r$
- *No. of permutations of n different things taken all at a time when 'm' specified things always come together is m ! (n – m + 1) !.*
- *No. of permutation of n different things taken all at a time when 'm' specified things never come together is n! – m! × (n – m + 1)!*
- *The no. of combinations of n different things taken r at a time (allowing repetitions) is* $^{n+r-1}C_r$
- *The total no. of combinations of n different objects taken r at a time in which*
  - *(i) m particular objects are excluded =* $^{n-m}C_r$
  - *(ii) m particular objects are included =* $^{n-m}C_{r-1}$
- *The no. of selections of n objects out of n identical objects is 1.*
- *Total no. of selections of zero or more objects from n identical objects is n + 1.*

Multiple Choice Questions

(1 mark each)

[A] Objective Type Questions

Q. 1. The number of possible outcomes when a coin is tossed 6 times is

(A) 36 **(B) 64**
(C) 12 **(D) 32**

[NCERT Exemplar Q. 27, Page 124]

Ans. Correct option : (B)

We know that a coin has head and tail (H, T)

∴ when a coin is tossed 6 times, then the possible outcome $= 2^6 = 64$.

Q. 2. The number of different four digit numbers that can be formed with the digits 2, 3, 4, 7 and using each digit only once is

(A) 120 **(B) 96**
(C) 24 **(D) 100**

[NCERT Exemplar Q. 28, Page 124]

Ans. Correct option : (C)

Four digit no.s are to be formed from the digits 2, 3, 4, 7 without repetition.

So, the required 4-digit number $= {}^4P_4$
$= 4!$
$= 24.$

Q. 3. The sum of the digits in unit place of all the numbers formed with the help of 3, 4, 5 and 6 taken all at a time is

(A) 432 **(B) 108**
(C) 36 **(D) 18**

[NCERT Exemplar Q. 29, Page 124]

Ans. Correct option : (B)

If we fix 3 at unit place, then the total possible no.'s = 3!.

If we fix 4, 5 and 6 at unit place, this is each case, total possible number are 3!

Required sum of units digits of all such numbers is
$= 3 \times 3! + 4 \times 3! + 5 \times 3! + 6 \times 3!$
$= (3 + 4 + 5 + 6) \times 3! = 18 \times 3! = 108.$

Q. 4. A five digit number divisible by 3 is to be formed using the numbers 0, 1, 2, 3, 4 and 5 without repetitions. The total number of ways this can be done is

(A) 216 **(B) 600**
(C) 240 **(D) 3125**

[NCERT Exemplar Q. 31, Page 124]

Ans. Correct option : (A)

We know that a no. is divisible by 3 when the sum of its digits is divisible by 3.

If we take the digits 0, 1, 2, 4, 5 then the sum of digits = 0 + 1 + 2 + 4 + 5 = 12, which is divisible by 3.

So, the 5 digits numbers using the digits 0, 1, 2, 4 and 5.

TTh Th H T O

4 4 3 2 1

$= 4 \times 4 \times 3 \times 2 \times 1 = 96$ and if we take the digits 1, 2, 3, 4, 5 then their sum = 1 + 2 + 3 + 4 + 5 = 15 divisible by 3.

So, five digit numbers can be formed using the digits 1, 2, 3, 4, 5 is 5!, ways = 120 ways.

$\therefore$ Total no. of ways = 96 + 120 = 216.

Q. 5. The number of 5-digits telephone numbers having atleast one of their digits repeated is

(A) 90,000 **(B) 10,000**

(C) 30,240 **(D) 69,760**

[NCERT Exemplar Q. 36, Page 125]

Ans. Correct option : (D)

Total no. of 5-digit telephone no, if all the digits are repeated = $(10)^5$ [$\because$ digits are from 0 to 9]

If digit are not repeated, then 5-digits telephone, numbers can be formed in $^{10}P_5$ ways.

$\therefore$ Required ways = $(10)^5 - {}^{10}P_5 = 100000 - 30240$
$= 69760.$

Q. 6. The total number of 9 digit numbers which have all different digits is

(A) 10! **(B) 9!**

(C) 9×9! **(D) 10×10!**

[NCERT Exemplar Q. 38, Page 125]

Ans. Correct option : (C)

We have to form a digit numbers from 0, 1, 2, 3, 4, 5, 6, 7, 8, 9 and we know that 0 cannot be put on extremely left place.

So, first place from the left can be filled in 9 ways.

Now, repetition is not allowed.

So, the remaining 8 places can be filled in 9!.

$\therefore$ The required no. of ways = $9 \times 9!$

Q. 7. The number of words which can be formed out of the letters of the word ARTICLE, so that vowels occupy the even place is

(A) 1440 **(B) 144**

(C) 7! **(D) $^4C_4 \times C_3$**

[NCERT Exemplar Q. 39, Page 125]

Ans. Correct option : (B)

Total no. of letters in the 'ARTICLE' is 7 out of which A, E, I are vowels and R, T, C, L are consonants.

Given that vowels occupy even place.

$\therefore$ Possible arrangement can be shown as below c, v, c, v, c, v, c *i.e.* on 2nd, 4th and 6th places.

Therefore, no. of arrangement = $^3P_3 = 3! = 6$ ways.

Now, consonants can be placed at 1, 3, 5 and 7th place.

$\therefore$ No. of arrangement = $^4P_4 = 4! = 24$.

So, the total no. of arrangements = $6 \times 24 = 144$.

Q. 8. Given 5 different green dyes, four different blue dyes and three different red dyes, the number of combinations of dyes which can be chosen taking at least one green and one blue dye is

(A) 3600 **(B) 3720**

(C) 3800 **(D) 3600**

[NCERT Exemplar Q. 40, Page 125]

Ans. Correct option : (B)

Possible no. of choosing 5 different green dyes = 2^5

Possible no. of choosing 4 different blue dyes = 2^4

Possible no. of choosing 3 different red dyes = 2^3

If at least one blue and one green dyes are selected, then total no. of selection = $(2^5 - 1) \times (2^4 - 1) \times 2^3$
$= 31 \times 15 \times 8 = 3720.$

[B] Fill in the blanks

Q. 1. The number of permutations of *n* different objects, taken *r* at a line, when repetitions are allowed, is ____.

[NCERT Exemplar Q. 43, Page 125]

Q. 2. The number of different words that can be formed from the letters of the word INTERMEDIATE such that two vowels never come together is ____. **[NCERT Exemplar Q. 44, Page 126]**

Q. 3. The number of six-digit numbers, all digits of which are odd is ____.

[NCERT Exemplar Q. 46, Page 126]

Answer:

1. n^r
2. 151200
3. 5^6

[C] True and False

Q. 1. Three letters can be posted in five letter boxes in 3^5 ways. **[NCERT Exemplar Q. 52, Page 126]**

Q. 2. In the permutations of *n* things, *r* taken together, the number of permutations in which *m* particular things occur together is $^{n-m}P_{r-m} \times {}^rP_m$.

[NCERT Exemplar Q. 53, Page 126]

Q. 3. In a steamer there are stalls for 12 animals, and there are horses, cows and calves (not less than 12 each) ready to be shipped. They can be loaded in 3^{12} ways. **[NCERT Exemplar Q. 54, Page 126]**

Q. 4. There will be only 24 selections containing at least one red ball out of a bag containing 4 red and 5 black balls. It is being given that the balls of the same colour are identical.

[NCERT Exemplar Q. 56, Page 127]

Answer:

1. False
2. False
3. True
4. False

[D] Match the following :

Q. 1. Five boys and five girls form a line. Find the number of ways of making the seating arrangement under the following condition:

C_1	C_2
(a) Boys and girls alternate:	(i) 5!×6!
(b) No two girls sit together :	(ii) 10! – 5!6!
(c) All the girls sit together	(iii) $(5!)^2 + (5!)^2$
(d) All the girls are never together :	(iv) 2! 5! 5!

[NCERT Exemplar Q. 61, Page 127]

Q. 2. Using the digits 1, 2, 3, 4, 5, 6, 7, a number of 4 different digits is formed. Find C_1 C_2

C_1	C_2
(a) How many numbers are formed?	(i) 840
(b) How many numbers are exactly divisible by 2?	(ii) 200
(c) How many numbers are exactly divisible by 25?	(iii) 360
(d) How many of these are exactly divisible by 4?	(iv) 40

[NCERT Exemplar Q. 63, Page 128]

Q. 3. How many words (with or without dictionary meaning) can be made from the letters of the word MONDAY, assuming that no letter is repeated, if C_1 C_2

C_1	C_2
(a) 4 letters are used at a time	(i) 720
(b) All letters are used at a time	(ii) 240
(c) All letters are used but the first is a vowel	(iii) 360

[NCERT Exemplar Q. 64, Page 128]

Answers:

1. (a) ↔ (iii), (b) ↔ (i), (c) ↔ (iv), (d) ↔ (ii)
2. (a) ↔ (i), (b) ↔ (iii), (c) ↔ (iv), (d) ↔ (ii)
3. (a) ↔ (iii), (b) ↔ (i), (c) ↔ (ii)

Long Answer Type Question-I

(4 marks each)

Q. 1. Eight chairs are numbered 1 to 8. Two women and 3 men wish to occupy one chair each. First the women choose the chairs from amongst the chairs 1 to 4 and then men select from the remaining chairs. Find the total number of possible arrangements.

[NCERT Exemplar, Q. 1, Page 122]

Sol. First women choose the chairs from among 1 to 4 chairs, *i.e.*, total number of chairs is 4.

Since, there are two women, so number of arrangements = ${}^4P_2$ ways.

Now, men have to choose chairs from remaining 6 chairs.

Since, there are 3 men, so number can be arranged in ${}^6P_3$ ways.

∴ Total number of possible arrangements = ${}^4P_2 \times {}^6P_3$

$$= \frac{4!}{4-2!} \times \frac{6!}{6-3!}$$

$$= \frac{4!}{2!} \times \frac{6!}{3!}$$

$$= \frac{4\times3\times2!}{2!} \times \frac{6\times5\times4\times3!}{3!}$$

$$= 4\times3\times6\times5\times4 = 1440$$

Q. 2. If the letters of the word 'RACHIT' are arranged in all possible ways as listed in dictionary. Then, what is the rank of the word 'RACHIT'?

[NCERT Exemplar, Q. 2, Page 122]

Sol. The letters of the word 'RACHIT' in alphabetical order are A, C, H, I, R and T.

Now, words beginning with A = 5!

words beginning with C = 5!

words beginning with H = 5!

words beginning with I = 5!

Word beginning with R *i.e.*, RACHIT = 1

∴ Rank of the word 'RACHIT' in dictionary = $4\times5!+1 = 4\times120+1$

= 480 + 1 = 481

Q. 3. How many automobile license plates can be made, if each plate contains two different letters followed by three different digits?

[NCERT Exemplar, Q. 7, Page 122]

Sol. There are 26 English alphabets and 10 digits (0 to 9).

Since, it is given that each plate contains two different letters followed by three different digits.

∴ Arrangement of 26 letters, taken 2 at a time =

$${}^{26}P_2 = \frac{26!}{24!} = 26\times25 = 650$$

and three-digit number can be formed out of the 10 digits = ${}^{10}P_3 = 10\times9\times8 = 720$ ways

∴ Total number of license plates = 650 × 720 = 468000

Q. 4. Find the number of different words that can be formed from the letters of the word 'TRIANGLE', so that no vowels are together.

[NCERT Exemplar, Q. 10, Page 122]

Sol. Number of letters in the word 'TRIANGLE' = 8, out of which 5 are consonants and 3 are vowels.

If vowels are not together, then we have following arrangement.

V	C	V	C	V	C	V	C	V	C	V

Consonants can be arranged in = 5! = 120 ways and vowels can occupy at 6 places.

The 3 vowels can be arranged at 6 place in $^6P_3$

$$\text{ways} = \frac{6!}{6-3!} = \frac{6!}{3!}$$

$$= \frac{6\times5\times4\times3!}{3!} = 120$$

Total number of arrangement = 120 × 120
= 14400

Q. 5. Find the number of positive integers greater than 6000 and less than 7000 which are divisible by 5, provided that no digit is to be repeated.

[NCERT Exemplar, Q. 11, Page 122]

Sol. We know that a number is divisible by 5, if at the units place of the number is 0 or 5.

We have to form 4 -digit number which is greater than 6000 and less than 7000. So, unit digit can be filled in 2 ways.

●			●
6 fixed			0 or 5

Since, repetition is not allowed. Therefore, tens place can be filled in 7 ways, similarly, hundreds place can be filled in 8 ways.

But we have to form a number greater than 6000 and less than 7000.

Hence, thousand place can be filled in only 1 ways.

1	8	7	2

Total number of integers = 1 × 8 × 7 × 2

= 14 × 8 = 112

Q. 6. There are 10 persons named P_1, P_2, P_3, ... P_{10}. Out of 10 persons, 5 persons are to be arranged in a line such that in each arrangement P1 must occur whereas P4 and P5 do not occur. Find the number of such possible arrangements.

[NCERT Exemplar, Q. 12, Page 123]

Sol. Given that, P_1, P_2, P_3, ... P_{10} are 10 persons, out of which 5 persons are to be arranged but P_1, must occur whereas P_4 and P_5 never occur.

∴ Selection depends on only 10 – 3 = 7 persons

As, we have already occur P_1 Therefore, we have to select only 4 persons out of 7.

Number of selection =

$$^7C_4 = \frac{7!}{4!(7-4)!} = \frac{7!}{4!3!} = \frac{5040}{24\times6} = 35$$

∴ Required number of arrangement of 5 persons
= 35 × 5! = 35 × 120 = 4200

Q. 7. Find the number of integers greater than 7000 that can be formed with the digits 3, 5, 7, 8 and 9 where no digits are repeated.

[NCERT Exemplar, Q. 16, Page 122]

Sol. Here, we have to find the number of integers greater than 7000 with the digits 3, 5, 7, 8 and 9. So, with these digits we can make maximum five-digit number because repetition is not allowed.

Now, all the five-digit numbers are greater than 7000.

Number of ways of forming 5-digits number = 5 × 4 × 3 × 2 × 1 = 120 and all the four-digit numbers greater than 7000 can be formed in following manner.

Thousand place can be filled in 3 ways. Hundred place can be filled in 4 ways. Tenth place can be filled in 3 ways. Units place can be filled in 2 ways.

Thus, we have total number of 4-digit number = 3 × 4 × 3 × 2 = 72

∴ Total number of integers = 120 + 72 = 192

Q. 8. In a certain city, all telephone numbers have six digits, the first two digits always being 41 or 42 or 46 or 62 or 64. How many telephone numbers have all six digits distinct?

[NCERT Exemplar, Q. 18, Page 123]

Sol. If first two digit is 41, the remaining 4 digits can be arranged in

$$= {}^8P_4 = \frac{8!}{(8-4)!} = \frac{8!}{4!}$$

$$= \frac{8\times7\times6\times5\times4!}{4!}$$

= 8 × 7 × 6 × 5 = 1680

Similarly, if first two digit is 42, 46, 62, or 64, the remaining 4 digits can be arranged in $^8P_4$ ways *i.e.*, 1680 ways.

∴ Total number of telephone numbers have all six digits distinct = 5 × 1680 = 8400

Q. 9. 18 mice were placed in two experimental groups and one control group with all groups equally large. In how many ways can the mice be placed into three groups?

[NCERT Exemplar, Q. 21, Page 123]

Sol. It is given that 18 mice were placed equally in two experimental groups and one control group *i.e.*, three groups.

∴ Required arrangements =

$$\frac{\text{Total arrangement}}{\text{Equally likely arrangement}} = \frac{18!}{6!6!6!}$$

TOPIC-2
Combinations

Quick Review

➤ Each of the different groups or selection which can be made by taking some or all of a number of things or objects at a time irrespective of their arrangement is called a **combination**.

➤ The number of combinations of n distinct objects taken r at a time is given by,

$$^nC_r = \frac{n!}{r!(n-r)!}, \ 0 \le r \le n$$

It is also denoted by $C(n, r)$ or $\binom{n}{r}$.

➤ **Difference between permutations and combinations :**

★ The process of selecting objects is called **combination**, and that of arranging objects is called **permutation**.

➤ **Properties of Combination :**

(i) $^nC_0 = {}^nC_n = 1$

(ii) $^nC_1 = n$

(iii) If $^nC_r = {}^nC_p$, then either $r = p$ or $r + p = n$

(iv) $^nC_r = \frac{^nP_r}{r!}$

(v) $^nC_r + {}^nC_{r-1} = {}^{n+1}C_r$

(vi) $^nC_0 + {}^nC_1 + {}^nC_2 + ... + {}^nC_n = 2^n$

(vii) $^nC_0 + {}^nC_2 + {}^nC_4 + ... = {}^nC_1 + {}^nC_3 + ... = 2^{n-1}$

(viii) $^nC_r = \frac{n}{r}\,{}^{n-1}C_{r-1} = \frac{n(n-1)}{r(r-1)}\,{}^{n-2}C_{r-2}$

(ix) $^{2n+1}C_0 + {}^{2n+1}C_1 + {}^{2n+1}C_2 + ... \ {}^{2n+1}C_n = 2^{2n}$

(x) $^nC_n + {}^{n+1}C_n + {}^{n+2}C_n + ... + {}^{2n-1}C_n = {}^{2n}C_{n+1}$

Multiple Choice Questions **(1 mark each)**

Q. 1. If $^nC_{12} = {}^nC_8$, then n is equal to

(A) 20 **(B) 12**

(C) 6 **(D) 30**

[NCERT Exemplar Q. 26, Page 124]

Ans. Correct option : (A)

Given, $^nC_{12} = {}^nC_8$

$\Rightarrow {}^nC_{12} = {}^nC_{n-8}$ $[\because {}^nC_r = {}^nC_{n-r}]$

$\therefore n - 8 = 12 \Rightarrow n = 20.$

Q. 2. Total number of words formed by 2 vowels and 3 consonants taken from 4 vowels and 5 consonants is equal to

(A) 60 **(B) 120**

(C) 7200 **(D) 720**

[NCERT Exemplar Q. 30, Page 124]

Ans. Correct option : (C)

Given, total no. of vowels = 4

and total no. of consonants = 5

The total no. of words formed by 2 vowels and 3 consonants = $^4C_2 \times {}^5C_3 = 60$

Now, permutation of 2 vowels and 3 consonants = 5! = 120

So, the total no. of words = 60 × 120 = 7200

Q. 3. Every body in a room shakes hands with everybody else. The total number of hand shakes is 66. The total number of persons in the room is

(A) 11 **(B) 12**
(C) 13 **(D) 14**

[NCERT Exemplar Q. 32, Page 125]

Ans. Correct option : (B)

Let the total no. of persons in a room be n. Since, two persons make 1 handshake, therefore no. of handshakes = $^nc_2$

So, $^nc_2 = 66 \Rightarrow \dfrac{n!}{2!(n-2)!} = 66 \Rightarrow n^2 - n = 132$

$\Rightarrow (n-12)(n+11) = 0$

$\Rightarrow n = 12$ and $n = -11$

$\therefore n = 12\ (\because\ n \neq -11)$

Q. 4. The number of triangles that are formed by choosing the vertices from a set of 12 points, seven of which lie on the same line is

(A) 105 **(B) 15**
(C) 175 **(D) 185**

[NCERT Exemplar Q. 33, Page 125]

Ans. Correct option : (D)

Total no. of triangles formed from 12 points taking 3 at a time = $^{12}C_3$

But given that out of 12 point 7 are collinear.

So, these seven points will form no. triangles.

$\therefore$ The required no. of triangles = $^{12}C_3 - {^7C_3}$
$= 220 - 35 = 185.$

Q. 5. The number of parallelograms that can be formed from a set of four parallel lines intersecting another set of three parallel lines is

(A) 6 **(B) 18**
(C) 12 **(D) 9**

[NCERT Exemplar Q. 34, Page 125]

Ans. Correct option : (B)

We know that to form a parallelogram, we require a pair of lines from a set of 4 lines and another pair of lines from another set of 3 lines.

$\therefore$ Required no. of parallelograms
$= {^4c_2} \times {^3c_2} = 6 \times 3 = 18.$

Q. 6. The number of ways in which a team of eleven players can be selected from 22 players always including 2 of them and excluding 4 of them is

(A) $^{16}C_{11}$ **(B) $^{16}C_5$**
(C) $^{16}C_9$ **(D) $^{20}C_9$**

[NCERT Exemplar Q. 35, Page 125]

Ans. Correct option : (C)

Total no. of player = 22

2 players are always included and 4 are always excluding or never included = 22 – 2 – 4 = 16

$\therefore$ Required no. of selections = $^{16}C_9$

Q. 7. The number of ways in which we can choose a committee from four men and six women so that the committee includes at least two men and exactly twice as many women as men is

(A) 94 **(B) 126**
(C) 128 **(D) None**

[NCERT Exemplar Q. 37, Page 125]

Ans. Correct option : (A)

We are given that the committee includes 2 men and exactly twice as many women as men.

Thus, the possible selection can be 2 men and 4 women & 3 men and 6 women.

So, the no. of committee = $^4c_2 \times {^6c_4} + {^4c_3} \times {^6c_6}$
$= 6 \times 15 + 4$
$= 90 + 4 = 94$

[B] Fill in the blanks

Q. 1. If $^nP_r = 840, {^nC_r} = 35$, then r = —.

[NCERT Exemplar Q. 41, Page 125]

Q. 2. $^{15}C_8 + {^{15}C_9} - {^{15}C_6} - {^{15}C_7}$ = ____.

[NCERT Exemplar Q. 42, Page 125]

Q. 3. Three balls are drawn from a bag containing 5 red, 4 white and 3 black balls. The number of ways in which this can be done if at least 2 are red is ___. [NCERT Exemplar Q. 45, Page 126]

Q. 4. In a football championship, 153 matches were played. Every two teams played one match with each other. The number of teams, participating in the championship is __.

[NCERT Exemplar Q. 47, Page 126]

Q. 5. The total number of ways in which six '+' and four signs '−' can be arranged in a line such that no two signs '−' occur together is ___.

[NCERT Exemplar Q. 48, Page 126]

Q. 6. A committee of 6 is to be chosen from 10 men and 7 women so as to contain atleast 3 men and 2 women. In how many different ways can this be done if two particular women refuse to serve on the same committee.

[NCERT Exemplar Q. 49, Page 126]

Q. 7. A box contains 2 white balls, 3 black balls and 4 red balls. The number of ways three balls be drawn from the box if at least one black ball is to be included in the draw is ___.

[NCERT Exemplar Q. 50, Page 126]

Answer:

1. 4
2. 0
3. 80
4. 18
5. 35
6. 7800
7. 64

[C] True and False

Q. 1. There are 12 points in a plane of which 5 points are collinear, then the number of lines obtained by joining these points in pairs is $^{12}C_2 - {}^5C_2$. **[NCERT Exemplar Q. 51, Page 126]**

Q. 2. If some or all of n objects are taken at a time, the number of combinations is $2^n - 1$. **[NCERT Exemplar Q. 55, Page 126]**

Q. 3. Eighteen guests are to be seated, half on each side of a long table. Four particular guests desire to sit on one particular side and three others on other side of the table. The number of ways in which the seating arrangements can be made is $\frac{11!}{5!6!}(9!)(9!)$ **[NCERT Exemplar Q. 57, Page 127]**

Q. 4. A candidate is required to answer 7 questions out of 12 questions which are divided into two groups, each containing 6 questions. He is not permitted to attempt more than 5 questions from either group. He can choose the seven questions in 650 ways. **[NCERT Exemplar Q. 58, Page 127]**

Q. 5. To fill 12 vacancies there are 25 candidates of which 5 are from scheduled castes. If 3 of the vacancies are reserved for scheduled caste candidates while the rest are open to all, the number of ways in which the selection can be made is $^5C_3 \times {}^{20}C_9$. **[NCERT Exemplar Q. 59, Page 127]**

Answer:

1. False
2. True
3. True
4. False
5. False

[D] Match the following :

Q. 1. There are 3 books on Mathematics, 4 on Physics and 5 on English. How many different collections can be made such that each collection consists of:

C_1	C_2
(a) One book of each subject;	(i) 3968
(b) At least one book of each subject:	(ii) 60
(c) At least one book of English:	(iii) 3255

[NCERT Exemplar Q. 60, Page 127]

Q. 2. There are 10 professors and 20 lecturers out of whom a committee of 2 professors and 3 lecturer is to be formed. Find : C_1 C_2.

C_1	C_2
(a) In how many ways committee can be formed :	(i) $^{10}C_2 \times {}^{19}C_3$
(b) In how many ways a particular professor is included :	(ii) $^{10}C_2 \times {}^{19}C_2$
(c) In how many ways a particular lecturer is included :	(iii) $^9C_1 \times {}^{20}C_3$
(d) In how many ways a particular lecturer is excluded :	(iv) $^{10}C_2 \times {}^{20}C_3$

[NCERT Exemplar Q. 62, Page 128]

Answer

1. (a) ↔ (ii), (b) ↔ (iii), (c) ↔ (i)
2. (a) ↔ (iv), (b) ↔ (iii), (c) ↔ (ii), (d) ↔ (i)

Short Answer Type Questions (2 marks each)

Q. 1. If 20 lines are drawn in a plane such that no two of them are parallel and no three are concurrent, in how many points will they intersect each other? **[NCERT Exemplar, Q. 17, Page 123]**

Sol. It is given that no two lines are parallel means all line are intersecting and no three lines are concurrent means three lines not intersect at a point.

Since, we know that for one point of intersection, we required two lines.

∴ Number of point of intersection =

$$^{20}C_2 = \frac{20!}{2!18!} = \frac{20 \times 19 \times 18!}{2 \times 1 \times 18!}$$

$$= \frac{20 \times 19}{2} = 19 \times 10 = 190$$

Long Answer Type Question-II (4 marks each)

Q. 1. A candidate is required to answer 7 questions out of 12 questions, which are divided into two groups, each containing 6 questions. He is not permitted to attempt more than 5 questions from either group. Find the number of different ways of doing questions **[NCERT Exemplar, Q. 3, Page 122]**

Sol. Since, candidate cannot attempt more than 5 questions from either group.

Thus, he is able to attempt minimum two questions from either group.

The number of questions attempted from each group is given in following table :

Group I	5	4	3	2
Group II	2	3	4	5

Since, each group have 6 questions and total attempted 7 questions.

$\therefore$ Total number of possible ways

$= {}^6C_5 \times {}^6C_2 + {}^6C_4 \times {}^6C_3 + {}^6C_3 \times {}^6C_4 + {}^6C_2 \times {}^6C_5$

$= 2[{}^6C_5 \times {}^6C_2 + {}^6C_4 \times {}^6C_3]$

$= 2[6 \times 15 + 15 \times 20]$

$= 2[90 + 300]$

$= 2 \times 390 = 780$

Q. 2. Out of 18 points in a plane, no three are in the same line except five points which are collinear. Find the number of lines that can be formed joining the point.

[NCERT Exemplar, Q. 4, Page 122]

Sol. Total number of points = 18

Out of which 5 points are collinear, we get a straight line by joining any two points.

$\therefore$ Number of straight line formed by joining the 18 points taking 2 at a time = ${}^{18}C_2$

and number of straight line formed by joining 5 points taking 2 at a time = ${}^5C_2$

But 5 collinear points, when joined pairwise give only one line.

$\therefore$ Required number of straight line = ${}^{18}C_2 - {}^5C_2 + 1$

$= 153 - 10 + 1 = 144$

Q. 3. We wish to select 6 person from 8 but, if the person *A* is chosen, then *B* must be chosen. In how many ways can selections be made?

[NCERT Exemplar, Q. 5, Page 122]

Sol. Total number of person = 8

Number of person to be selected = 6

It is given that, if *A* is chosen then, *B* must be chosen.

Therefore, following cases arise.

Case I When *A* is chosen, *B* must be chosen.

Number of ways = ${}^{8-2}C_{6-2} = {}^6C_4$

Case II When *A* is not chosen.

Then, *B* may be chosen.

$\therefore$ Number of ways = ${}^{8-1}C_6 = {}^7C_6$

Hence, required number of ways $= {}^6C_4 + {}^7C_6$

$= 15 + 7 = 22$

Q. 4. How many committee of five person with a chairperson can be selected from 12 persons?

[NCERT Exemplar, Q. 6, Page 122]

Sol. $\because$ Total number of persons = 12

and number of persons to be selected = 5

Out of 12 persons a chairperson is selected = ${}^{12}C_1$ = 12 ways

Now, remaining 4 persons are selected out of 11 persons.

$\therefore$ Number of ways = ${}^{11}C_4 = 330$

$\therefore$ Total number of ways to form a committee of 5 persons = 12 × 330 = 3960

Q. 5. A bag contains 5 black and 6 red balls, determine the number of ways in which 2 black and 3 red balls can be selected from the lot.

[NCERT Exemplar, Q. 8, Page 122]

Sol. It is given that bag contains 5 black and 6 red balls.

So, 2 black balls is selected from 5 black balls in ${}^5C_2$ ways.

and 3 red balls are selected from 6 red balls in ${}^6C_3$ ways.

$\therefore$ Total number of ways in which 2 black and 3 red balls are selected = ${}^5C_2 \times {}^6C_3$

= 10 × 20=200 ways

Q. 6. Find the number of permutations of n distinct things taken *r* together, in which 3 particular things must occur together.

[NCERT Exemplar, Q. 9, Page 122]

Sol. Total number of things = *n*

We have to arrange *r* things out of *n* in which three things must occur together.

Therefore, combination of *n* things taken *r* at a time in which 3 things always occurs

$= {}^{n-3}C_{r-3}$

If three things taken together, then it is considered as 1 group.

Arrangement of these three things = 3!

Now, we have to arrange = $r - 3 + 1 = (r - 2)$ objects

$\therefore$ No. of arrangement of (*r* – 2) objects = *r* – 2!

$\therefore$ Total number of arrangements =

$= {}^{n-3}C_{r-3} \times (r-2)! \times 3!$

Q. 7. There are 10 lamps in a hall. Each one of them can be switched on independently. Find the number of ways in which the hall can be illuminated.

[NCERT Exemplar, Q. 13, Page 123]

Sol. Total number of ways =

${}^{10}C_1 + {}^{10}C_2 + {}^{10}C_3 + {}^{10}C_4 + {}^{10}C_5 + {}^{10}C_6 + \ldots + {}^{10}C_{10}$

$= 2^{10} - 1 \quad [\because {}^nC_0 + {}^nC_1 + {}^nC_2 + \ldots = 2^n] \; \& \; {}^nC_0 = 1$

$= 1024 - 1 = 1023$

Q. 8. A box contains two white, three black and four red balls. In how many ways can three balls be drawn from the box, if atleast one black ball is to be included in the draw?

[NCERT Exemplar, Q. 14, Page 123]

Sol. There are 2 white, three black and four red balls.

We have to draw 3 balls, out of these 9 balls in which atleast one black ball is included.

Hence, we can select the balls in the following ways.

Black balls	1	2	3
Other than black	2	1	0

∴ Required number of selections =
$^3C_1 \times ^6C_2 + ^3C_2 \times ^6C_1 + ^3C_3 \times ^6C_0$

$= 3 \times 15 + 3 \times 6 + 1$

$= 45 + 18 + 1 = 64$

Q. 9. In an examination, a student has to answer 4 questions out of 5 questions, questions 1 and 2 are however compulsory. Determine the number of ways in which the student can make the choice. [NCERT Exemplar, Q. 19, Page 123]

Sol. It is given that 2 questions are compulsory out of 5 questions.

So, these two questions are always included in the selection.

We know that, the selection of n distinct objects taken r at a time in which p objects are always included in $^{n-p}C_{r-p}$ ways.

∴ Total number of ways $= {}^{5-2}C_{4-2} = {}^3C_2$

$= \dfrac{3!}{2!1!} = \dfrac{3 \times 2!}{2!} = 3$

Q. 10. If a convex polygon has 44 diagonals, then find the number of its sides. [NCERT Exemplar, Q. 20, Page 123]

Sol. Let the convex polygon has n sides.

∴ Number of diagonals $= {}^nC_2 - n$

According to the question,

$^nC_2 - n = 44$

$\dfrac{n!}{2!(n-2)!} - n = 44$

$\Rightarrow \dfrac{n(n-1)}{2} - n = 44$

$\Rightarrow n\left[\dfrac{(n-1)}{2} - 1\right] = 44$

$\Rightarrow n\left(\dfrac{n-1-2}{2}\right) = 44$

$\Rightarrow n(n-3) = 44 \times 2$

$\Rightarrow n(n-3) = 88$

$\Rightarrow n^2 - 3n - 88 = 0$

$\Rightarrow (n-11)(n+8) = 0$

$\Rightarrow n = 11, -8$ $[\because n \neq -8]$

$\therefore n = 11$

Q. 11. In how many ways can a football team of 11 players be selected from 16 players? How many of them will

(i) include 2 particular players?

(ii) exclude 2 particular players?

[NCERT Exemplar, Q. 23, Page 124]

Sol. Total number of players = 16

We have to select a team of 11 players

(i) Include 2 particular players $= {}^{16-2}C_{11-2} = {}^{14}C_9$

$= 2002$

[since, selection of n objects taken r at a time in which p objects are always included is $^{n-p}C_{r-p}$]

(ii) Exclude 2 particular players $= {}^{16-2}C_{11} = {}^{14}C_{11} = 364$

[since, selection of n objects taken r at a time in which p objects are never included is $^{n-p}C_r$

Q. 12. A sports team of 11 students is to be constituted, choosing atleast 5 from class XI and atleast 5 from class XII. If there are 20 students in each of these classes, in how many ways can the team be constituted? [NCERT Exemplar, Q. 24, Page 124]

Sol. Total students in each class = 20

We have to selects atleast 5 students from each class.

Hence, selection of sport team of 11 students from each class is given in following table

Class XI	5	6
Class XII	6	5

∴ Total number of ways of selecting a team of 11 players $= {}^{20}C_5 \times {}^{20}C_6 + {}^{20}C_6 \times {}^{20}C_5$

$= 2 \times {}^{20}C_5 \times {}^{20}C_6$

Long Answer Type Question-II (6 marks each)

Q. 1. If $^nC_{r-1} = 36, {}^nC_r = 84$ and $^nC_{r+1} = 126$, then find the value of $^rC_2$. [NCERT Exemplar Q. 15, Page 123]

Sol. Given, $^nC_{r-1} = 36$ (i)

$\Rightarrow {}^nC_r = 84$ (ii)

$\Rightarrow {}^nC_{r+1} = 126$ (iii)

On dividing Eq. (i) by (ii), we get

$\dfrac{^nC_{r-1}}{^nC_r} = \dfrac{36}{84}$ $\left[\because {}^nC_r = \dfrac{n!}{(n-r)!r!} \text{ and } n! = n(n-1)!\right]$

$\Rightarrow \dfrac{n!}{(r-1)!\{n-(r-1)\}!} \cdot \dfrac{r!(n-r)!}{n!} = \dfrac{3}{7}$

$\Rightarrow \dfrac{1}{(r-1)!(n-r+1)!} \cdot \dfrac{r(r-1)!(n-r)!}{1} = \dfrac{3}{7}$

$\Rightarrow \dfrac{1 \cdot r}{(n-r+1)} \cdot (n-r)! = \dfrac{3}{7} \Rightarrow \dfrac{r}{n-r+1} = \dfrac{3}{7}$

$\Rightarrow 7r = 3n - 3r + 3$

$\Rightarrow 10r - 3n = 3$ (iv)

On dividing Eq. (ii) by Eq. (iii), we get

$$\frac{^nC_r}{^nC_{r+1}} = \frac{84}{126}$$

$$\Rightarrow \frac{n!}{r!(n-r)!} \cdot \frac{(r+1)!(n-r-1)!}{n!} = \frac{14}{21}$$

$$\Rightarrow \frac{1}{r!(n-r)(n-r-1)!} \cdot \frac{(r+1)r!(n-r-1)!}{r} = \frac{2}{3}$$

$$\Rightarrow \frac{r+1}{n-r} = \frac{2}{3}$$

$\Rightarrow 3r + 3 = 2n - 2r \Rightarrow 2n - 5r = 3$ (v)

On multiplying Eq. (iv) by 2 and Eq. (v) by 3, we get

$20r - 6n = 6$ (vi)

$6n - 15r = 9$ (vii)

On adding Eqs. (vi) and (vii),

$5r = 15 \Rightarrow r = 3$

From Eq. (v), $2n = 3+15$

$\Rightarrow 2n = 18 \Rightarrow n = 9$

$$\therefore {^rC_2} = {^3C_2} = \frac{3!}{2!1!} = \frac{3\times 2!}{2!} = 3$$

Q. 2. A bag contains six white marbles and five red marbles. Find the number of ways in which four marbles can be drawn from the bag, if (i) they can be of any colour. (ii) two must be white and two red. (iii) they must all be of the same colour.

[NCERT Exemplar Q. 22, Page 123]

Sol. Total number of marbles = 6 white + 5 red = 11 marbles

(i) If they can be of any colour means we have to select 4 marbles out of 11.

$$\therefore \text{Required number of ways} = {^{11}C_4} = \frac{11!}{7!4!} = 330$$

(ii) If two must be white, then selection will be $^6C_2$ and two must be red, then selection will be $^5C_2$

$\therefore$ Required number of ways = ${^6C_2} \times {^5C_2} = 15\times 10$

(iii) If they all must be of same colour, then 150 selection of 4 white marbles out of 6 = $^6C_4$ and selection of 4 red marble out of 5 = $^5C_4$

$\therefore$ Requirednumberofways $= {^6C_2} + {^5C_4} = 5 + 15 = 20$

Q. 3. A group consists of 4 girls and 7 boys. In how many ways can a team of 5 members be selected, if the team has

(i) no girls.

(ii) atleast one boy and one girl.

(iii) atleast three girls.

[NCERT Exemplar Q. 25, Page 123]

Sol. Number of girls = 4 and Number of boys = 7

We have to select a team of 5 members provided that

(i) team having no girls.

$$\therefore \text{Required selection} = {^7C_5} = \frac{7!}{5!2!} = \frac{7\times 6}{2} = 21$$

(ii) atleast one boy and one girl

$\therefore$ Required selection =

$${^7C_1}\times{^4C_4} + {^7C_2}\times{^4C_3} + {^7C_3}\times{^4C_2} + {^7C_4}\times{^4C_1}$$

$$= 7\times 1 + 21\times 4 + 35\times 6 + 35\times 4$$

$$= 7 + 84 + 210 + 140 = 441$$

(iii) when atleast three girls are included =

$${^4C_3}\times{^7C_2} + {^4C_4}\times{^7C_1}$$

$$= 4\times 21 + 7 = 84 + 7 = 91$$

EXPERT ADVICE

- *These two words permutation and combination at the initial level are very confusing and are generally interchangeable, so students are advised to first understand the problem while attempting the paper.*
- *In ^nP_r, always remember $n \rightarrow$ total; $r \rightarrow$ want.*
- *Always aid to memory that factorial is defined only for non-negative integer number.*
- *Permutation gives the answer to the number of arrangements while the combination explains the possible no. of selection.*

OSWAAL LEARNING TOOLS

***For* Suggested Online Videos**

Visit : *https://youtu.be/hJRXKq2GEo8* **Or Scan the Code**	**Visit :** *https://goo.gl/jsoUYY* **Or Scan the Code**
Visit : *https://goo.gl/RJXnqC* **Or Scan the Code**	**Visit :** *https://goo.gl/IZpCNR* **Or Scan the Code**
Visit : *https://goo.gl/7bJeLV* **Or Scan the Code**	**Visit :** *https://goo.gl/wcSfpf* **Or Scan the Code**

CHAPTER 8

BINOMIAL THEOREM

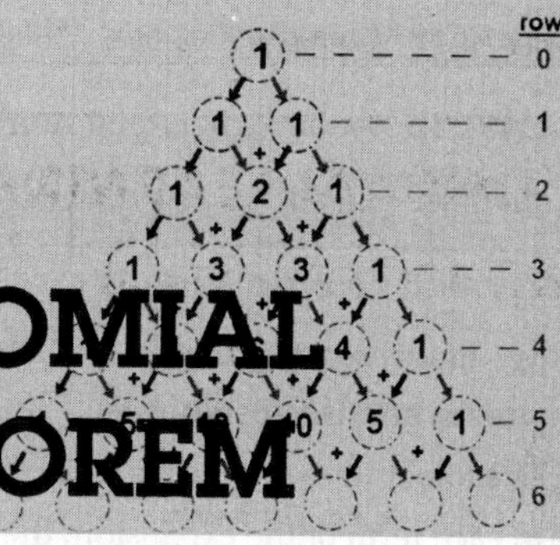

Chapter Objectives

➤ *History; Statement and proof of the Binomial theorem for positive integral indices; Pascal's triangle; General and middle term in Binomial expansion; Simple applications.*

Quick Review

➤ An algebraic expression consisting of two terms with positive or negative sign between them, is called binomial expression. If a and b are two real numbers, then for any positive integer n, we have,

$$(a+b)^n = {}^nC_0a^n + {}^nC_1a^{n-1}b + {}^nC_2a^{n-2}b^2 + \dots {}^nC_nb^n$$

$$\Rightarrow (a+b)^n = \sum_{r=0}^{n} {}^nC_ra^{n-r}b^r$$

where, ${}^nC_0, {}^nC_1, \dots\dots {}^nC_n$ are called binomial coefficients.

➤ **General Term in a Binomial Expansion:** We have the binomial expansion of $(a+b)^n$

i.e., $(a+b)^n = {}^nC_0a^n + {}^nC_1a^{n-1}b + {}^nC_2a^{n-2}b^2 + \dots {}^nC_nb^n$

Here, we observed that

First term $= {}^nC_0a^n$

Second term $= {}^nC_1a^{n-1}b^1$

Third term $= {}^nC_2a^{n-2}b^2$

Fourth term $= {}^nC_3a^{n-3}b^3$

………….. ……….

$(r+1)^{th}$ term $= {}^nC_ra^{n-r}b^r$

Here, $(r+1)^{th}$ term is also called the **general term of the expansion** $(a+b)^n$

i.e., $\boxed{T_{r+1} = {}^nC_ra^{n-r}b^r}$

Thus, $(n+1)^{th}$ term, $T_{n+1} = {}^nC_na^{n-n}b^n = {}^nC_nb^n = b^n$

➤ **Middle Terms in Binomial Expansion:** We know that, the binomial expansion of $(a+b)^n$ has $(n+1)$ terms, So for middle terms, there are two cases.

- **CASE I:** If n is even, then total number of terms *i.e.,* $n+1$ is odd and the middle term is $\left(\frac{n}{2}+1\right)^{th}$ term.

  e.g., In the expansion of $(a+b)^6$, the middle term is $\left(\frac{6}{2}+1\right)^{th}$ term *i.e.,* 4th term.

TIPS...

- *If n is positive integer, then $(1+x)^n$ contains $(n+1)$ terms i.e., finite no. of terms. When n is general exponent, then the expansion of $(1+x)^n$ contains infinitely many terms.*
- *When n is a positive integer, the expansion of $(1+x)^n$ is valid for all values of x. If n is general exponent, the expansion of $(1+x)^n$ is valid for the values of x satisfying the condition $|x| < 1$.*
- *If the coefficient of pth and q^{th} term in the expansion of $(1+x)^n$ are equal, then $p+q = n+2$.*
- *The no. of terms in the expansion of $(x_1 + x_2 + x_3 + \dots\dots + x_r)^n$ is ${}^{n+r-1}C_{r-1}$.*
- *The values of the binomial coefficients steadily increase to maximum and then steadily decrease.*

TRICKS...

- ***Greatest Coefficient :***

  (i) If n is even, then in $(x+a)^n$, the greatest coefficient is $\frac{{}^nC_n}{2}$

  (ii) If n is odd, then in $(x+a)^n$, the greatest coefficient is $\frac{{}^nC_{n-1}}{2}$ or $\frac{{}^nC_{n+1}}{2}$ both being equal.

- ***Greatest Term :** In the expansion of $(x+a)^n$*

  (i) If $n + 1/x/a + 1$ is an integer = P (say), then greatest term is $T_p = T_{p+1}$

  (ii) If $n + 1/x/a + 1$ is not an integer with m as integral part of $n + 1/x/a + 1$, then T_{m+1} is the greatest term.

- *The coefficients of terms equidistant from beginning and end are equal i.e. ${}^nc_r = {}^nc_{n-r}$, $r = 0, 1, 2 \dots\dots n$.*

- **CASE II:** If n odd, then total number of terms *i.e.,* $n + 1$ is even and there are two middle terms which are $\left(\frac{n+1}{2}\right)^{th}$ and $\left(\frac{n+1}{2}+1\right)^{th}$ or $\left(\frac{n+3}{2}\right)^{th}$ term.

e.g., In the expansion of $(a + b)^9$, the middle terms are $\left(\frac{9+1}{2}\right)^{th}$ and $\left(\frac{9+1}{2}+1\right)^{th}$ *i.e.,* 5th and 6th terms.

➤ **Important points to be known:**

- The total number of terms in $(a + b)^n$ is $n + 1$.
- In each term of the expansion, the sum of indices of a and b is the same and is equal to the index of $(a + b)$.
- In the successive terms of the expansion, powers of first quantity a goes on decreasing by 1, whereas the powers of the second quantity b increases by 1.
- The binomial coefficients of terms equidistant from the beginning and end are equal.
- In $(a+b)^n, r^{th}$ term from the end is same as $(n-r+2)^{th}$ term from beginning.
- r^{th} term from the end in $(b+a)^n = r^{th}$ term from the beginning in $(a+b)^n$.
- In the expansion $(a+b)^n$, the term which is free from a and b is known as **Independent** term.
- In $(1+x)^n$, coefficient of x^r is ${}^nC_r$.

Know the Terms

➤ Some particular cases:

$$(1+x)^n = \sum_{r=0}^{n} {}^nC_r x^r$$

$$(1-x)^n = \sum_{r=0}^{n} (-1)^r \, {}^nC_r x^r$$

➤ Some properties of Binomial coefficients:

$${}^nC_0 + {}^nC_1 + {}^nC_2 + \cdots + {}^nC_n = 2^n$$

$${}^nC_0 - {}^nC_1 + {}^nC_2 - {}^nC_3 + \cdots + (-1)^n \, {}^nC_n = 0$$

$${}^nC_0 + {}^nC_2 + {}^nC_4 + \cdots = {}^nC_1 + {}^nC_3 + {}^nC_5 + \cdots = 2^{n-1}$$

Multiple Choice Questions

(1 mark each)

[A] Objective Type Questions

Q. 1. The total number of terms in the expansion of $(x+a)^{100} + (x-a)^{100}$ after simplification is

(A) 50 **(B) 202**

(C) 51 **(D) none of these**

[NCERT Exemplar Q. 18, Page 144]

Ans. Correct option : (C)

No. of terms in the expansion of $(x + a)^{100} = 101$

No. of terms in the expansion of $(x - a)^{100} = 101$

Now, 50 terms of expansion will be cancel out with negative 50 terms of $(x - a)^{100}$

So, the remaining 51 terms of first expansion will be added to 51 terms of others.

Therefore, the no. of terms = 51.

Q. 2. Given the integers $r > 1$, $n > 2$, and coefficients of $(3r)^{th}$ and $(r+2)^{nd}$ terms in the binomial expansion of $(1 + x)^{2n}$ are equal, then

(A) $n = 2r$ **(B) $n = 3r$**

(C) $n = 2r + 1$ **(D) none of these**

[NCERT Exemplar Q. 19, Page 144]

Ans. Correct option : (A)

Given that $r > 1$ and $n > 2$

Then, $T_{3r} = T_{3r-1+1} = {}^{2n}C_{3r-1} \, x^{3r-1}$

and $T_{r+2} = T_{r+1+1} = {}^{2n}C_{r+1} \, x^{r+1}$

As per question, we have

${}^{2n}C_{3r-1} = {}^{2n}C_{r+1}$

$\Rightarrow 3r - 1 + r + 1 = 2n$ $\quad [\because {}^nC_p = {}^nC_q \Rightarrow n = p + q]$

$\Rightarrow 4r = 2n$

$\Rightarrow n = 2r$

Q. 3. The two successive terms in the expansion of $(1 + x)^{24}$ whose coefficients are in the ratio 1:4 are

(A) 3rd and 4th **(B) 4th and 5th**

(C) 5th and 6th **(D) 6th and 7th**

[NCERT Exemplar Q. 20, Page 144]

Ans. Correct option : (C)

Let r^{th} and $(r + 1)^{th}$ be two successive terms in the expansion $(1 + x)^{24}$.

$\therefore T_{r+1} = {}^{24}c_r\, x^r$

$T_{r+2} = T_{r+1+1} = {}^{24}c_{r+1}\, x^{r+1}$

As per the question, we have $\frac{{}^{24}c_r}{{}^{24}c_{r+1}} = \frac{1}{4}$

$$\Rightarrow \frac{\frac{24!}{r!(24-r)!}}{\frac{24!}{(r+1)!(24-r-1)}} = \frac{1}{4}$$

$$\Rightarrow \frac{r+1}{24-r} = \frac{1}{4}$$

$\Rightarrow 4r + 4 = 24 - r$

$\Rightarrow r = 4$

$\therefore T_{4+1} = T_5$ and $T_{4+2} = T_6$

Q. 4. The coefficient of x^n in the expansion of $(1 + x)^{2n}$ and $(1 + x)^{2n-1}$ are in the ratio.

(A) 1 : 2 **(B) 1 : 3**

(C) 3 : 1 **(D) 2 : 1**

[NCERT Exemplar Q. 21, Page 144]

Ans. Correct option : (D)

General term, $T_{r+1} = {}^nc_r\, x^{n-r}\, y^r$

In the expansion of $(1 + x)^{2n}$, we get $T_{r+1} = {}^{2n}c_r\, x^r$

To get the coefficient of x^n, put $r = n$

$\therefore$ Coefficient of $x^n = {}^{2n}c_n$

In the expansion of $(1 + x)^{2n-1}$, we get $T_{r+1} = {}^{2n-1}c_r\, x^r$

$\therefore$ Coefficient of x^n is ${}^{2n-1}c_n$

The required ratio is $\frac{{}^{2n}c_{n-1}}{{}^{2n-1}c_n} = \frac{\frac{2n!}{n!\,n!}}{\frac{(2n-1)!}{(n-1)!(n!)}} = 2 : 1$

Q. 5. If the coefficients of 2nd, 3rd and the 4th terms in the expansion of $(1 + x)^n$ are in A.P., then value of n is

(A) 2 **(B) 7**

(C) 11 **(D) 14**

[NCERT Exemplar Q. 22, Page 144]

Ans. Correct option : (B)

$\because (1 + x)^n = {}^nc_o + {}^nc_1 x + {}^nc_2 x^2 + {}^nc_3 x^3 + ... + {}^nc_n x^n$

Here, coefficient of 2nd term $= {}^nc_1$

coefficient of 3rd term $= {}^nc_2$

coefficient of 4th term $= {}^nc_3$

Given that ${}^nc_1, {}^nc_2$ and ${}^nc_3$ are in A.P.

$\therefore 2.\, {}^nc_2 = {}^nc_1 + {}^nc_3$

$$\Rightarrow 2.\frac{n(n-1)}{2} = n + \frac{n(n-1)(n-2)}{3.2.1}$$

$\Rightarrow 6n - 6 = 6 + n^2 - 3n + 2$

$\Rightarrow n^2 - 9n + 14 = 0$

$\Rightarrow (n - 2)(n - 7) = 0$

$\Rightarrow n = 2, 7 \Rightarrow n = 7$ $\quad(\because n = 2$ is not possible)

Q. 6. If the middle term of $\left(\frac{1}{x} + x\sin x\right)^{10}$ is equal to $7\frac{7}{8}$, then value of x is

(A) $2n\pi + \frac{\pi}{6}$ **(B) $n\pi + \frac{\pi}{6}$**

(C) $n\pi + (-1)^n\frac{\pi}{6}$ **(D) $n\pi + (-1)^n\frac{\pi}{3}$**

[NCERT Exemplar Q. 24, Page 145]

Ans. Correct option : (C)

Given expression is $\left(\frac{1}{x} + x\sin x\right)^{10}$

No. of terms = 10 + 1 = 11 odd

$\therefore$ middle term $= \frac{11+1}{2}$ th term $= 6^{th}$ term

$$T_6 = T_{5+1} = {}^{10}c_5 \left(\frac{1}{x}\right)^{10-5} (x\sin x)^5$$

$$\therefore {}^{10}c_5\left(\frac{1}{x}\right)^5 .\, x^5.\sin^5 x = 7\frac{7}{8}$$

$$\Rightarrow {}^{10}c_5 \sin^5 x = \frac{63}{8}$$

$$\Rightarrow \frac{10.9.8.7.6}{5.4.3.2.1}\sin^5 x = \frac{63}{8}$$

$$\Rightarrow \sin^5 x = \frac{1}{32} = \left(\frac{1}{2}\right)^5$$

$$\Rightarrow \sin x = \frac{1}{2} \Rightarrow \sin x = \sin\frac{\pi}{6}$$

$$\Rightarrow x = n\pi + (-1)^n\frac{\pi}{6}$$

[B] Fill in the blanks

[NCERT Exemplar Q. 25-33, Page 145-146]

Q. 1. The largest coefficient in the expansion of $(1 + x)^{30}$ is ___.

Q. 2. The number of terms in the expansion of $(x + y + z)^n$ ___.

[Hint: $(x + y + z)^n = [x + (y + z)]^n$]

Q. 3. In the expansion of $\left(x^2 - \frac{1}{x^2}\right)^{16}$, the value of constant term is ___.

Q. 4. If the seventh terms from the beginning and the end in the expansion of $\left(\sqrt[3]{2} + \frac{1}{\sqrt[3]{3}}\right)^n$ are equal, then n equals ___.

[Hint: $T_7 = T_{n-7+2} \Rightarrow {}^nC_6\left(2^{\frac{1}{3}}\right)^{n-6}\left(\frac{1}{3^{\frac{1}{3}}}\right)^6 = {}^nC_{n-6}\left(2^{\frac{1}{3}}\right)^6\left(\frac{1}{3^{\frac{1}{3}}}\right)^{n-6}$

$\Rightarrow \left(2^{\frac{1}{3}}\right)^{n-12} = \left(\frac{1}{3^{\frac{1}{3}}}\right)^{n-12}$

$\Rightarrow$ only problem when $n-12=0 \Rightarrow n=12$]

Q. 5. The coefficient of $a^{-6}b^4$ in the expansion of $\left(\frac{1}{a}-\frac{2b}{3}\right)^{10}$ is___.

[Hint: $T_5 = {}^{10}C_4\left(\frac{1}{a}\right)^6\left(\frac{-2b}{3}\right)^4 = \frac{1120}{27}a^{-6}b^4$]

Q. 6. Middle term in the expansion of $(a^3+ba)^{28}$ is ____.

Q. 7. The ratio of the coefficients of x^p and x^q in the expansion of $(1+x)^{p+q}$ is _____.

[Hint: ${}^{p+q}C_p = {}^{p+q}C_q$]

Q. 8. The position of the term independent of x in the expansion of $\left(\sqrt{\frac{x}{3}}+\frac{3}{2x^2}\right)^{10}$ is ___.

Q. 9. If 25^{15} is divided by 13, the reminder is ____.

Answer:

1. ${}^{30}C_{15}$ 2. $\frac{(n+1)(n+2)}{2}$ 3. ${}^{16}C_8$ 4. $n=12$

5. $\frac{1120}{27}$ 6. ${}^{28}C_{14}a^{56}b^{14}$

7. 1 : 1 8. 3rd term 9. 12

[C] True and False

[NCERT Exemplar Q. 34-40, Page 146]

Q. 1. The sum of the series $\sum_{r=0}^{10} {}^{20}C_r$ is $2^{19}+\frac{{}^{20}C_{10}}{2}$

Q. 2. The expression 7^9+9^7 is divisible by 64.

[Hint: $7^9 + 9^7 = (1 + 8)^7 - (1 - 8)^9$]

Q. 3. The number of terms in the expansion of $[(2x+y^3)^4]^7$ is 8

Q. 4. The sum of coefficients of the two middle terms in the expansion of $(1-x)^{2n-1}$ is equal to ${}^{2n-1}C_n$.

Q. 5. The last two digits of the numbers 3^{400} are 01.

Q. 6. If the expansion of $\left(x-\frac{1}{x^2}\right)^{2n}$ contains a term independent of x, then n is a multiple of 2.

Q. 7. Number of terms in the expansion of $(a+b)^n$ where $n \in N$ is one less than the power n.

Answer

1. False 2. True 3. False 4. False

5. True 6. False 7. False

Short Answer Type Questions (2 marks each)

Q. 1. Find the coefficient of x in the expansion of $(1-3x+7x^2)(1-x)^{16}$.

[NCERT Exemplar Q. 3, Page 142]

Sol. Given, expansion = $(1-3x+7x^2)(1-x)^{16}$

$= (1-3x+7x^2)({}^{16}C_0 1^{16} - {}^{16}C_1 1^{15}x^1 + {}^{16}C_2 1^{14}x^2 + \ldots + {}^{16}C_{16}x^{16})$

$= (1-3x+7x^2)(1-16x+120x^2+\ldots)$

$\therefore$ Coefficient of $x = -3-16=-19$

Long Answer Type Question-I (4 marks each)

Q.1. Find the expansion of $(3x^2-2ax+3a^2)^3$ using binomial theorem.

[NCERT Exemplar Q. 10, Page 176]

Sol. $(3x^2-2ax+3a^2)^3 = [3(x^2+a^2)-2ax]^3$

$= {}^3C_0\{3(x^2+a^2)\}^3 - {}^3C_1\{3(x^2+a^2)\}^2 2ax + {}^3C_2 3(x^2+a^2)(2ax)^2 - {}^3C_3(2ax)^3$

$= 27(x^2+a^2)^3 - 3\times 9(x^2+a^2)^2 \times 2ax + 3\times 3(x^2+a^2)4a^2x^2 - 8a^3x^3$

Now, open the expansion of $(x^2+a^2)^3$, $(x^2+a^2)^2$, we get

$= 27[{}^3C_0(x^2)^3 + {}^3C_1(x^2)^2a^2 + {}^3C_2x^2(a^2)^2 + {}^3C_3(a^2)^3] - 27[{}^2C_0(x^2)^2 + {}^2C_1x^2a^2 + {}^2C_2(a^2)^2]\times 2ax + 9(x^2+a^2)4a^2x^2 - 8a^3x^3$

$= 27[x^6+3x^4a^2+3x^2a^4+a^6] - 27[x^4+2x^2a^2+a^4]2ax + 36a^2x^2(x^2+a^2) - 8a^3x^3$

$= 27x^6+81x^4a^2+81x^2a^4+27a^6 - 54ax[x^4+2x^2a^2+a^4] + 36a^2x^2+36a^4x^2-8a^3x^3$

$= 27x^6+117x^4a^2+117a^4x^2+27a^6 - 54ax^5 - 54a^5x - 8a^3x^3 - 108a^3x^3$

$= 27x^6 - 54ax^5 + 117a^2x^4 - 116a^3x^3$
$+ 117a^4x^2 - 54a^5x + 27a^6$

Q. 2. Find the term independent of x, where $x \neq 0$, in the expansion of $\left(\frac{3x^2}{2} - \frac{1}{3x}\right)^{15}$.
[NCERT Exemplar Q. 1, Page 142]

Sol. Given expansion is $\left(\frac{3x^2}{2} - \frac{1}{3x}\right)^{15}$

Let T_{r+1} term is the general term,

Then, $T_r = {}^{15}C_r\left(\frac{3}{2}\right)^{15}\left(-\frac{1}{3}\right)$

$= {}^{15}C_r 3^{15-r} x^{30-2r} 2^{r-15} (-1)^r \cdot 3^{-r} \cdot x^{-r}$
$= {}^{15}C_r (-1)^r 3^{15-2r} 2^{r-15} x^{30-3r}$

For independent of x,

$30 - 3r = 0$

$3r = 30 \Rightarrow r = 10$

$\because T_{r+1} = T_{10+1} = 11\text{th term is independent of } x$

$\because T_{10+1} = {}^{15}C_{10}(-1)^{10} 3^{15-20} 2^{10-15}$

$= {}^{15}C_{10} 3^{-5} 2^{-5}$
$= {}^{15}C_{10} (6)^{-5}$
$= {}^{15}C_{10}\left(\frac{1}{6}\right)^5$

Q. 3. If the term free from x in the expansion of $\left(\sqrt{x} - \frac{k}{x^2}\right)^{10}$ is 405, then find the value of k.
[NCERT Exemplar Q. 2, Page 142]

Sol. Given expansion is $\left(\sqrt{x} - \frac{k}{x^2}\right)^{10}$

Let T_{r+1} is the general term.

Then, $T_{r+1} = {}^{10}C_r(\sqrt{x})^{10-r}\left(\frac{-k}{x^2}\right)^r$

$= {}^{10}C_r (x)^{\frac{1}{2}(10-r)} (-k)^r \cdot x^{-2r}$
$= {}^{10}C_r x^{5-\frac{r}{2}} (-k)^r \cdot x^{-2r}$
$= {}^{10}C_r x^{5-\frac{r}{2}-2r} (-k)^r$
$= {}^{10}C_r x^{\frac{10-5r}{2}} (-k)^r$

For the term free from x, $\frac{10-5r}{2} = 0$

$\Rightarrow \quad 10 - 5r = 0 \Rightarrow r = 2$

Since, $T_{2+1} = T_3$ is free from x.

$\therefore T_{2+1} = {}^{10}C_2 (-k)^2 = 405$

$\Rightarrow \quad \frac{10 \times 9 \times 8!}{2! \times 8!}(-k)^2 = 405$

$\Rightarrow \quad 45k^2 = 405 \rightarrow k^2 = \frac{405}{45} = 9$

$\therefore k = \pm 3$

Q. 4. Find the term independent of x in the expansion of $\left(3x - \frac{2}{x^2}\right)^{15}$.
[NCERT Exemplar Q. 4, Page 142]

Sol. Given expansion is $\left(3x - \frac{2}{x^2}\right)^{15}$.

Let T_{r+1} is the general term.

$\therefore \quad T_{r+1} = {}^{15}C_r(3x)^{15-r}\left(\frac{-2}{x^2}\right)^r = {}^{15}C_r(3x)^{15-r}(-2)^r x^{-2r}$
$= {}^{15}C_r 3^{15-r} x^{15-3r} (-2)^r$

For independent of x, $15 - 3r = 0 \Rightarrow r = 5$

Since, $T_{5+1} = T_6$ is independent of x.

$\therefore \quad T_{5+1} = {}^{15}C_5 3^{15-5}(-2)^5$
$= -\frac{15 \times 14 \times 13 \times 12 \times 11 \times 10!}{5 \times 4 \times 3 \times 2 \times 1 \times 10!} \cdot 3^{10} \cdot 2^5$
$= -3003 \cdot 3^{10} \cdot 2^5$

Q. 5. Find the middle term (terms) in the expansion of

(i) $\left(\frac{x}{a} - \frac{a}{x}\right)^{10}$ **(ii)** $\left(3x - \frac{x^3}{6}\right)^9$

[NCERT Exemplar Q. 5, Page 142]

Sol. (i) Given expansion is $\left(\frac{x}{a} - \frac{a}{x}\right)^{10}$

Here, the power of Binomial *i.e.*, $n = 10$ is even.

Since, it has one middle term $\left(\frac{10}{2} + 1\right)$ th term *i.e.*, 6th term.

$\therefore \quad T_6 = T_{5+1} = {}^{10}C_5\left(\frac{x}{a}\right)^{10-5}\left(\frac{-a}{x}\right)^5$

$= -{}^{10}C_5\left(\frac{x}{a}\right)^5\left(\frac{a}{x}\right)^5$

$= -\frac{10 \times 9 \times 8 \times 7 \times 6 \times 5!}{5! \times 5 \times 4 \times 3 \times 2 \times 1}\left(\frac{x}{a}\right)^5\left(\frac{x}{a}\right)^{-5}$

$= -9 \times 4 \times 7 = -252$

(ii) Given expansion is $\left(3x - \frac{x^3}{6}\right)^9$

Here, $n = 9$ [odd]

Since, the Binomial expansion has two middle terms *i.e.*, $\left(\frac{9+1}{2}\right)$ th and $\left(\frac{9+1}{2} + 1\right)$ th *i.e.*, 5th term and 6th term.

$\therefore \quad T_5 = T_{(4+1)} = {}^9C_4(3x)^{9-4}\left(-\frac{x^3}{6}\right)^4$

$= \frac{9 \times 8 \times 7 \times 6 \times 5!}{4 \times 3 \times 2 \times 1 \times 5!} 3^5 x^5 x^{12} 6^{-4}$

$= \frac{7 \times 6 \times 3 \times 3^1}{2^4} x^{17} = \frac{189}{8} x^{17}$

$\therefore \quad T_6 - T_{5+1} = {}^9C_5(3x)^{9-5}\left(-\frac{x^3}{6}\right)^5$

$$= -\frac{9\times 8\times 7\times 6\times 5!}{5!\times 4\times 3\times 2\times 1}\cdot 3^4\cdot x^4\cdot x^{15}6^{-5}$$

$$= \frac{-21\times 6}{3\times 2^5}x^{19} = \frac{-21}{16}x^{19}$$

Q. 6. Find the coefficient of x^{15} in the expansion of $(x-x^2)^{10}$ [NCERT Exemplar Q. 6, Page 142]

Sol. Given expansion is $(x-x^2)^{10}$

Let the term T_{r+1} is the general term

$$\therefore \quad T_{r+1} = {}^{10}C_r x^{10-r}(-x^2)^r$$
$$= (-1)^r\,{}^{10}C_r\cdot x^{10-r}\cdot x^{2r}$$
$$= (-1)^r\,{}^{10}C_r x^{10+r}$$

For the coefficient of x^{15},

$$10+r=15 \Rightarrow r=5$$
$$T_{5+1} = (-1)^5\,{}^{10}C_5 x^{15}$$

$$\therefore \text{ coefficient of } x^{15} = -1\frac{10\times 9\times 8\times 7\times 6\times 5!}{5\times 4\times 3\times 2\times 1\times 5!}$$
$$= -3\times 2\times 7\times 6$$
$$= -252$$

Q. 7. Find the coefficient of $\frac{1}{x^{17}}$ in the expansion of $\left(x^4-\frac{1}{x^3}\right)^{15}$. [NCERT Exemplar Q. 7, Page 143]

Sol. Given expansion is $\left(x^4-\frac{1}{x^3}\right)^{15}$

Let the term T_{r+1} contains the coefficient of $\frac{1}{x^{17}}$ *i.e.,* x^{-17}

$$\therefore \quad T_{r+1} = {}^{15}C_r(x^4)^{15-r}\left(-\frac{1}{x^3}\right)^r$$
$$= {}^{15}C_r x^{60-4r}(-1)^r x^{-3r}$$
$$= {}^{15}C_r x^{60-7r}(-1)^r$$

For the coefficient x^{-17},

$$60-7r=-17$$
$$\Rightarrow 7r=77 \Rightarrow r=11$$
$$\Rightarrow T_{11+1} = {}^{15}C_{11}x^{60-77}(-1)^{11}$$

$$\therefore \text{ coefficient of } x^{-17} = \frac{-15\times 14\times 13\times 12\times 11!}{11!\times 4\times 3\times 2\times 1}$$
$$= -15\times 7\times 13 = -1365$$

Q. 8. Find the value of r, if the coefficients of $(2r+4)$th and $(r-2)$th terms in the expansion of $(1+x)^{18}$ are equal. [NCERT Exemplar Q. 9, Page 143]

Sol. Given expansion is $(1+x)^{18}$.

Now, $(2r+4)$ th term *i.e.,* T_{2r+3+1}

$$\therefore \quad T_{2r+3+1} = {}^{18}C_{2r+3}(1)^{18-2r-3}(x)^{2r+3}$$
$$= {}^{18}C_{2r+3}x^{2r+3}$$

Now, $(r-2)$th term *i.e.,* T_{r-3+1}

$$\therefore \quad T_{r-3+1} = {}^{18}C_{r-3}x^{r-3}$$

As, ${}^{18}C_{2r+3} = {}^{18}C_{r-3}$ $[\because {}^nC_x = {}^nC_y \Rightarrow x+y=n]$

$$\Rightarrow 2r+3+r-3=18$$
$$\Rightarrow \quad 3r=18$$
$$\Rightarrow \quad r=6$$

Q. 9. Find the coefficient of x^4 in the expansion of $(1+x+x^2+x^3)^{11}$ [NCERT Exemplar Q. 11, Page 143]

Sol. Given, expansion =

$$(1+x+x^2+x^3)^{11} = [(1+x)+x^2(1+x)]^{11}$$
$$= [(1+x)+x^2(1+x)]^{11} = (1+x)^{11}\cdot(1+x^2)^{11}$$

Now, above expansion becomes

$$= ({}^{11}C_0+{}^{11}C_1x+{}^{11}C_2x^2+{}^{11}C_3x^3+{}^{11}C_4x^4+\ldots)$$
$$({}^{11}C_0+{}^{11}C_1x^2+{}^{11}C_2x^4+\ldots)$$
$$= (1+11x+55x^2+165x^3+330x^4+\ldots)$$
$$(1+11x^2+55x^4+\ldots)$$

$$\therefore \text{ Coefficient of } x^4 = 55+605+330 = 990$$

Q. 10. If p is a real number and the middle term in the expansion of $\left(\frac{p}{2}+2\right)^8$ is 1120, then find the value of p. [NCERT Exemplar Q. 12, Page 143]

Sol. Given expansion is $\left(\frac{p}{2}+2\right)^8$

Here, $n=8$ **[even]**

Since, this Binomial expansion has only one middle term *i.e.,* $\left(\frac{8}{2}+1\right)$th = 5th term

$$T_5 = T_{4+1} = {}^8C_4\left(\frac{p}{2}\right)^{8-4}\cdot 2^4$$
$$\Rightarrow 1120 = {}^8C_4p^4\cdot 2^{-4}2^4$$
$$\Rightarrow 1120 = \frac{8\times 7\times 6\times 5\times 4!}{4!4\times 3\times 2\times 1}p^4$$
$$\Rightarrow 1120 = 7\times 2\times 5\times p^4$$
$$\Rightarrow \quad p^4 = \frac{1120}{70} = 16 \Rightarrow p^4 = 2^4$$
$$\Rightarrow \quad p^2 = 4$$
$$\Rightarrow \quad p = \pm 2$$

Q. 11. Show that the middle term in the expansion of $\left(x-\frac{1}{x}\right)^{2n}$ is $\frac{1\times 3\times 5\times\ldots\times(2n-1)}{n!}\times(-2)^n$. [NCERT Exemplar Q. 13, Page 143]

Sol. Given, expansion is $\left(x-\frac{1}{x}\right)^{2n}$. This Binomial expansion has even power. So, this has one middle term.

i.e., $\left(\frac{2n}{2}+1\right)$th term = $(n+1)$th term

$$T_{n+1} = {}^{2n}C_n (x)^{2n-n}\left(-\frac{1}{x}\right)^n = {}^{2n}C_n x^n (-1)^n x^{-n}$$

$$= {}^{2n}C_n (-1)^n = (-1)^n \frac{(2n)!}{n!n!}$$

$$= \frac{1\cdot 2\cdot 3\cdot 4\cdot 5 \ldots (2n-1)(2n)}{n!n!}(-1)^n$$

$$= \frac{1\cdot 3\cdot 5 \ldots (2n-1)\cdot 2\cdot 4\cdot 6 \ldots (2n)}{12\cdot 3 \ldots n(n!)}(-1)^n$$

$$= \frac{1\cdot 3\cdot 5 \ldots (2n-1)\cdot 2^n (1\cdot 2\cdot 3 \ldots n)(-1)^n}{(1\cdot 2\cdot 3 \ldots n)(n!)}$$

$$= \frac{[1\cdot 3\cdot 5 \ldots (2n-1)]}{n!}(-2)^n$$

Hence Proved.

Q. 12. Find n in the Binomial $\left(\sqrt[3]{2}+\frac{1}{\sqrt[3]{3}}\right)^n$, if the ratio of 7th term from the beginning to the 7th term from the end is $\frac{1}{6}$.

[NCERT Exemplar Q. 14, Page 143]

Sol. Here, the Binomial expansion is $\left(\sqrt[3]{2}+\frac{1}{\sqrt[3]{3}}\right)^n$

Now, 7th term from beginning

$$T_7 = T_{6+1} = {}^nC_6 (\sqrt[3]{2})^{n-6}\left(\frac{1}{\sqrt[3]{3}}\right)^6 \quad \text{(i)}$$

and 7th term from end *i.e.*, T_7 from the beginning of $\left(\frac{1}{\sqrt[3]{3}}+\sqrt[3]{2}\right)^n$

$$i.e., \; T_7 = {}^nC_6 \left(\frac{1}{\sqrt[3]{3}}\right)^{n-6} (\sqrt[3]{2})^6 \quad \text{(ii)}$$

Given that, $\dfrac{{}^nC_6 (\sqrt[3]{2})^{n-6}\left(\frac{1}{\sqrt[3]{3}}\right)^6}{{}^nC_6 \left(\frac{1}{\sqrt[3]{3}}\right)^{n-6} (\sqrt[3]{2})^6} = \dfrac{1}{6} \Rightarrow \dfrac{2^{\frac{n-6}{3}}\cdot 3^{-6/3}}{3^{-\left(\frac{n-6}{3}\right)}\cdot 2^{6/3}} = \dfrac{1}{6}$

$$\Rightarrow \left(2^{\frac{n-6}{3}}\cdot 2^{\frac{-6}{3}}\right)\left(3^{\frac{-6}{3}}\cdot 3^{\frac{(n-6)}{3}}\right) = 6^{-1}$$

$$\Rightarrow \left(2^{\frac{n-6}{3}-\frac{6}{3}}\right)\left(3^{\frac{n-6}{3}-\frac{6}{3}}\right) = 6^{-1} \Rightarrow (2\cdot 3)^{\frac{n}{3}-4} = 6^{-1}$$

$$\Rightarrow \frac{n}{3}-4 = -1 \Rightarrow \frac{n}{3} = 3$$

$$\therefore n = 9$$

Q. 13. If x^p occurs in the expansion of $\left(x^2+\frac{1}{x}\right)^{2n}$, then prove that its coefficient is $\dfrac{2n!}{\left(\frac{4n-p}{3}\right)!\left(\frac{2n+p}{3}\right)!}$

[NCERT Exemplar Q. 16, Page 144]

Sol. Given expansion is $\left(x^2+\frac{1}{x}\right)^{2n}$

Let x^p occur in the expansion of $\left(x^2+\frac{1}{x}\right)^{2n}$

$$T_{r+1} = {}^{2n}C_r (x^2)^{2n-r}\left(\frac{1}{x}\right)^r$$

$$= {}^{2n}C_r x^{4n-2r} x^{-r} = {}^{2n}C_r x^{4n-3r}$$

Let $4n-3r = p$

$$\Rightarrow 3r = 4n-p \Rightarrow r = \frac{4n-p}{3}$$

$\therefore$ Coefficient of

$$x^p = {}^{2n}C_r = \frac{(2n)!}{r!(2n-r)!} = \frac{(2n)!}{\left(\frac{4n-p}{3}\right)!\left(2n-\frac{4n-p}{3}\right)!}$$

$$= \frac{(2n)!}{\left(\frac{4n-p}{3}\right)!\left(\frac{6n-4n+p}{3}\right)!}$$

$$= \frac{(2n)!}{\left(\frac{4n-p}{3}\right)!\left(\frac{2n+p}{3}\right)!}$$

Long Answer Type Question-II

(6 marks each)

Q. 1. Find the sixth term of the expansion $(y^{1/2}+x^{1/3})^n$, if the Binomial coefficient of the third term from the end is 45. [NCERT Exemplar, Q. 8, Page 143]

Sol. Given expansion is $(y^{\frac{1}{2}}+x^{\frac{1}{3}})^n$.

The sixth term of this expansion is

$$T_6 = T_{5+1} = {}^nC_5 (y^{\frac{1}{2}})^{n-5}(x^{\frac{1}{3}})^5 \quad \text{(i)}$$

Now, given that the Binomial coefficient of the third term from the end is 45.

We know that, Binomial coefficient of third term from the end = Binomial coefficient of third term from the beginning $= {}^nC_2$

$$\because {}^nC_2 = 45$$

$$\Rightarrow \frac{n(n-1)(n-2)!}{2!(n-2)!} = 45$$

$$\Rightarrow n(n-1) = 90$$

$$\Rightarrow n^2-n-90 = 0$$

$$\Rightarrow n^2-10n+9n-90 = 0$$

$$\Rightarrow n(n-10)+9(n-10) = 0$$

$$\Rightarrow (n-10)(n+9) = 0$$

$$\Rightarrow (n+9) = 0 \text{ or } (n-10) = 0$$

$$\therefore n = 10 \quad [\because n \neq -9]$$

From Eq.(i).

$T_6 = {}^{10}C_5 y^{\frac{5}{2}} x^{\frac{5}{3}} = 252 y^{\frac{5}{2}} \cdot x^{\frac{5}{3}}$

Q. 2. If the coefficient of second, third and fourth terms in the expansion of $(1+x)^{2n}$ are in AP, then show that $2n^2 - 9n + 7 = 0$

[NCERT Exemplar Q. 10, Page 143]

Sol. Given expansion is $(1+x)^{2n}$

Now, coefficient of 2nd term = ${}^{2n}C_1$

Coefficient of 3rd term = ${}^{2n}C_2$

Coefficient of 4th term = ${}^{2n}C_3$

Given that, ${}^{2n}C_1, {}^{2n}C_2$ and ${}^{2n}C_3$ are in A.P.

Then, $2.{}^{2n}C_2 = {}^{2n}C_1 + {}^{2n}C_3$

$$\Rightarrow 2\left[\frac{2n(2n-1)(2n-2)!}{2\times1\times(2n-2)!}\right] = \frac{2n(2n-1)!}{(2n-1)!} + \frac{2n(2n-1)(2n-2)(2n-3)}{3!(2n-3)!}$$

$$\Rightarrow n(2n-1) = n + \frac{n(2n-1)(2n-2)}{6}$$

$$\Rightarrow n(12n-6) = n(6+4n^2-4n-2n+2)$$

$$\Rightarrow 12n-6 = (4n^2-6n+8)$$

$$\Rightarrow 6(2n-1) = 2(2n^2-3n+4)$$

$$\Rightarrow 3(2n-1) = 2n^2-3n+4$$

$$\Rightarrow 2n^2-3n+4-6n+3 = 0$$

$$\Rightarrow 2n^2-9n+7 = 0$$

Q. 3. In the expansion of $(x+a)^n$, if the sum of odd terms is denoted by *0* and the sum of even term by *E*. Then, prove that

(i) $0^2 - E^2 = (x^2-a^2)^n$

(ii) $40E = (x+a)^{2n} - (x-a)^{2n}$.

[NCERT Exemplar Q. 15, Page 143-144]

Sol. (i) Given expansion is $(x+a)^n$

$$\therefore (x+a)^n = {}^nC_0x^na^0 + {}^nC_1x^{n-1}a^1 + {}^nC_2x^{n-2}a^2 + {}^nC_3x^{n-3}a^3 + \ldots + {}^nC_na^n$$

Now, sum of odd terms

i.e., $0 = {}^nC_0x^n + {}^nC_2x^{n-2}a^2 + \ldots$

and sum of even terms

i.e., $E = {}^nC_1x^{n-1}a + {}^nC_3x^{n-3}a^3 + \ldots$

$\because (x+a)^n = 0 + E$ ...(i)

Similarly, $\therefore\ (x-a)^n = 0 - E$ ...(ii)

$\therefore (0+E)(0-E) = (x+a)^n(x-a)^n$

[on multiplying Eqs. (i) and (ii)]

$\Rightarrow 0^2 - E^2 = (x^2-a^2)^n$

(ii) $40E = (0+E)^2 - (0-E)^2 = [(x+a)^n]^2 - [(x-a)^n]^2$

[from Eqs (i) and (ii)]

$= (x+a)^{2n} - (x-a)^{2n}$ **Hence Proved**

Q. 4. Find the term independent of x in the expansion of $(1+x+2x^3)\left(\frac{3}{2}x^2 - \frac{1}{3x}\right)^9$

[NCERT Exemplar, Q. 17, Page 144]

Sol. Given expansion is $(1+x+2x^3)\left(\frac{3}{2}x^2 - \frac{1}{3x}\right)^9$

Now, consider $\left(\frac{3}{2}x^2 - \frac{1}{3x}\right)^9$

$$T_{r+1} = {}^9C_r\left(\frac{3}{2}x^2\right)^{9-r}\left(-\frac{1}{3x}\right)^r$$

$$= {}^9C_r\left(\frac{3}{2}\right)^{9-r} x^{18-2r}\left(\frac{1}{3}\right)^r x^{-r}$$

$$= {}^9C_r\left(\frac{3}{2}\right)^{9-r}\left(-\frac{1}{3}\right)^r x^{18-3r}$$

Hence, the general term in the expansion of $(1+x+2x^3)\left(\frac{3}{2}x^2 - \frac{1}{3x}\right)^9$

$$= {}^9C_r\left(\frac{3}{2}\right)^{9-r}\left(-\frac{1}{3}\right)^r x^{18-3r} + {}^9C_r\left(\frac{3}{2}\right)^{9-r}\left(-\frac{1}{3}\right)^r x^{19-3r} + 2\cdot{}^9C_r\left(\frac{3}{2}\right)^{9-r}\left(-\frac{1}{3}\right)^r x^{21-3r}$$

For term independent of x, putting $18-3r=0, 19-3r=0$ and $21-3r=0$, we get

$$r=6, r=\frac{19}{3}, r=7$$

Since, the possible value of r are 6 and 7.

Hence, second term is not independent of x.

$\therefore$ The term independent of x is

$$= {}^9C_6\left(\frac{3}{2}\right)^{9-6}\left(-\frac{1}{3}\right)^6 + 2\cdot{}^9C_7\left(\frac{3}{2}\right)^{9-7}\left(-\frac{1}{3}\right)^7$$

$$= \frac{9\times8\times7\times6!}{6!\times3\times2}\cdot\frac{3^3}{2^3}\cdot\frac{1}{3^6} - 2\cdot\frac{9\times8\times7!}{7!\times2\times1}\cdot\frac{3^2}{2^2}\cdot\frac{1}{3^7}$$

$$= \frac{84}{8}\cdot\frac{1}{3^3} - \frac{36}{4}\cdot\frac{2}{3^5}$$

$$= \frac{7}{18} - \frac{2}{27}$$

$$= \frac{21-4}{54}$$

$$= \frac{17}{54}$$

EXPERT ADVICE

- *Questions are mostly asked from the topic 'General and Middle Term' of Binomial expansion :*
- *Practice more questions on above topics.*
- *Calculation mistakes here are prone to happen, so practice these questions very well before exam. This chapter is scoring.*

OSWAAL LEARNING TOOLS

***For* Suggested Online Videos**

Visit : *https://youtu.be/1pSD8cYyqUo*

Or Scan the Code

Visit : *https://youtu.be/MqOhV9110y0*

Or Scan the Code

Visit : *https://youtu.be/YmuhRczGJFY*

Or Scan the Code

Visit : *https://goo.gl/zk1j6o*

Or Scan the Code

Visit : *https://goo.gl/31MzPn*

Or Scan the Code

CHAPTER

9 SEQUENCE AND SERIES

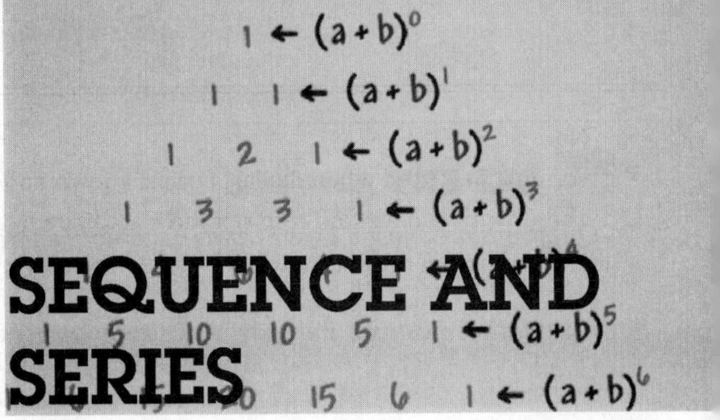

Chapter Objectives

➤ *Sequence; Real sequence; Series; Progression; Finite series; Infinite series; Arithmetic progression (A.P.), Sum of n terms of an A.P.; Arithmetic mean (A.M.), Geometric Progression (G.P.); General term of a G.P.; Sum of first n terms of a G.P., Geometric mean (G.M.); Relation between A.M. and G.M.; Formulae for some special sums :* $\sum_{R=1}^{n} k$, $\sum_{R=1}^{n} k^2$ *and* $\sum_{R=1}^{n} k^3$.

TOPIC-1
Sequence, Series and A.P.

TOPIC - 1
Sequence, Series and A.P. P. 106

TOPIC - 2
G.P. and Sum to n terms of Special Series P. 113

Quick Review

➤ **Sequence :** Sequence is a function whose domain is a subset of natural numbers. It represents the images of 1, 2, 3, ….., n as $f_1, f_2, f_3, \ldots, f_n$, where $f_n = f(n)$.

➤ **Real Sequence :** A sequence whose range is a subset of R is called a real sequence.

➤ **Series :** If $a_1, a_2, a_3, \ldots\ldots, a_n$ is a sequence, then the expression $a_1 + a_2 + a_3 + \ldots.. + a_n$ is a series.

➤ **Progression :** A sequence whose terms follow certain rule is called a progression.

➤ **Finite Series :** A series having finite number of terms is called a finite series.

➤ **Infinite Series :** A series having infinite number of terms is called a infinite series.

➤ **Arithmetic Progression (A.P.) :** A sequence in which the difference of two consecutive terms is constant, is called Arithmetic Progression (A.P.), *i.e.,* $a_{n+1} - a_n =$ constant $(= d)$ $\forall\ n \in N$

General A.P. is $a, a+d, a+2d, a+3d, \ldots\ldots\ldots$

n^{th} term of A.P. $= a_n = a + (n-1)d = l$ (last term)

➤ **Sum of *n* Terms of an *A.P.* :**

(i) $S_n = \frac{n}{2}(a + l)$, where l = last term, a = first term

(ii) $S_n = \frac{n}{2}[2a + (n-1)d]$, where a = first term, d = common difference

TIPS...

- *Student are advised to learn all the formulae and practice as many questions as possible.*
- *Remember A.M. ≥ G.M. i.e., arithmetic mean is always greater than equal to geometric mean.*
- *A sequence is an AP, iff its nth term is of the form $An + B$ i.e., a linear expression in n. The common difference in such a case is A i.e., the coefficient of n.*
- *If $a_1, a_2, a_3 \ldots\ldots, a_n, \ldots\ldots$ is G.P. of non-zero, non-negative terms, then $\log a_1, \log a_2 \ldots\ldots\ldots, \log a_n \ldots\ldots$ is an A.P. and vice versa.*

TRICKS...

- *Sum of first n odd natural numbers = 1 + 3 + 5 ….. + up to n terms = n^2.*
- *Sum of first n even natural number = 2 + 4 + 6 …. + up to n terms = n (n + 1)*
- *With an arithmetic sequence, everything on the values of a and d. Once you have these values you can find anything.*
- *Learn sum of first n terms of some special series, namely Σn, Σn^2, Σn^3, to reduce time while find sum of mixed series up to n terms.*

Note :

Formula (i) is used when the last term is known and formula (ii) is used when the common difference is known. These formula have four terms, if three are known, the fourth can be found out.

(iii) n^{th} term from the end of an A.P. $= a_n + (n-1)(-d)$

$\because$ Taking a_n as the first term and common difference equal to '$-d$'.

➤ **Arithmetic Mean :** When three quantities are in *A.P.*, the middle quantity is said to be Arithmetic Mean *(A.M.)* between the other two.

Thus, if *a, A, b* are in *A.P.*, then *A* is the *A.M.* between *a* and *b*.

So, $A - a = b - A$, [their common difference are equal]

$\Rightarrow$ $2A = a + b$

$\Rightarrow$ $A = \dfrac{a+b}{2}$

$\therefore$ *A.M.* between two numbers = Half of their sum

➤ **An Important Result :** Sum of *n A.M.*'s between two quantities is *n* times the single A.M. between them.

***n* Arithmetic Means :** Let $A_1, A_2, A_3, \ldots, A_n$ be the *n, A.M.*'s between two numbers *a* and *b*.

So we can find the *A.M*'s as

$$A_1 = a + d, d = \frac{b-a}{n+1}, A_2 = a + 2d = a + \frac{2(b-a)}{n+1} \ldots, A_n = a + nd = a + \frac{n(b-a)}{n+1}$$

➤ **Some Important results:**

- If *a, b, c* are in A.P. then $a \pm k, b \pm k, c \pm k$ are in A.P.

  ak, bk, ck are also in A. P., $k \neq 0, \frac{a}{k}, \frac{b}{k}, \frac{c}{k}$ are also in A.P. where $k \neq 0$.
- $S_k - S_{k-1} = a_k$
- $a_m = n, a_n = m \Rightarrow a_r = m + n - r$
- $S_m = S_n \Rightarrow S_{m+n} = 0$
- $S_p = q$ and $S_q = p \Rightarrow S_{p+q} = -p - q$
- In an A.P., the sum of the terms equidistant from the beginning and from the end is always same, and equal to the sum of the first and the last term
- If three terms of A.P. are to be taken then we choose then as $a - d, a, a + d$.
- If four terms of A.P. are to be taken then we choose then as $a - 3d, a - d, a + d, a + 3d$.
- If five terms of A.P. are to be taken, then we choose then as: $a - 2d, a - d, a, a + d, a + 2d$.

Multiple Choice Questions

(1 mark each)

[A] Objective Type Questions

Q. 1. If the sum of *n* terms of an A.P. is given by $S_n = 3n + 2n^2$, then the common difference of the A.P. is

(A) 3 **(B) 2**

(C) 6 **(D) 4**

[NCERT Exemplar Q. 17, Page 162]

Ans. Correct option : (D)

Given that $S_n = 3n + 2n^2$

$S_1 = 3(1) + 2(1)^2 = 5$

$S_2 = 3(2) + 2(4) = 14$

$S_1 = a_1 = 5$

$S_2 - S_1 = a_2 = 14 - 5 = 9$

$\therefore$ Common difference $d = a_2 - a_1$

$= 9 - 5 = 4$

Q. 2. If 9 times the 9th term of an A.P. is equal to 13 times the 13th term, then the 22nd term of the A.P. is

(A) 0 **(B) 22**

(C) 220 **(D) 198**

[NCERT Exemplar Q. 19, Page 163]

Ans. Correct option : (A)

$T_n = a + (n-1)d$

$\therefore T_9 = a + 8d$ and $T_{13} = a + 12d$

According to given condition

$9[a + 18d] = 13[a + 12d]$

$\Rightarrow 13a - 4a = 72d - 156d$

$\Rightarrow 4a = -84d \Rightarrow a = -21d$ ...(i)

Now, $T_{22} = a + 21d = -21d + 21d = 0$ [from (i)]

Q. 3. If in an A.P., $S_n = qn^2$ and $S_m = qm^2$, where S_r denotes the sum of r terms of the A.P.. then S_q equals

(A) $\frac{q^3}{2}$ **(B) mnq**

(C) q^3 **(D) $(m + n)q^2$**

[NCERT Exemplar Q. 21, Page 163]

Ans. Correct option : (C)

$\because S_n = \frac{n}{2}[2a + (n-1)d] = qn^2$

$\Rightarrow 2a + (n-1)d = 2qn$ ...(i)

$S_m = \frac{m}{2}[2a + (m-1)d] = qm^2$

$\Rightarrow 2a + (m-1)d = 2qm$ ...(ii)

On solving eqs (i) & (ii), we get

$d = 2q$ and $a = q$

$\therefore S_q = \frac{q}{2}[2a + (q+1)d] = \frac{q}{2}[2q + (q-1)2q]$

$= \frac{q}{2} \times 2q^2 = q^3$

Q. 4. Let S_n denote the sum of the first n terms of an A.P. If $S_{2n} = 3S_n$ then $S_{3n} : S_n$ is equal to

(A) 4 **(B) 6**

(C) 8 **(D) 10**

[NCERT Exemplar Q. 22, Page 163]

Ans. Correct option : (B)

$\because S_n = \frac{n}{2}[2a + (n-1)d] \therefore S_{2n} = \frac{2n}{2}[2a + (2n-1)d]$

and $S_{3n} = \frac{3n}{2}[2a + (3n-1)d]$

Since, $S_{2n} = 3.S_n$

$\therefore \frac{2n}{2}[2a + (2n-1)d]$

$= \frac{3 \times 3n}{2}[2a + (3n-1)d]$

$\Rightarrow 4a + (4n-2)d = 6a + (3n-3)d$

$\Rightarrow 2a = (n+1)d$ (i)

Now, $S_{3n} : Sn = \frac{3n}{2}[2a + (3n-1)d] : \frac{n}{2}$

$[2a + (n-10)] = \frac{2[2a+(3n-1)d]}{2a+(n-1)d}$

$= \frac{3d(n+1+3n-1)}{d(n+1+n-1)}$

$= \frac{3(4n)}{2n} = 6$

Q. 5. If t_n denotes the nth term of the series 2+3+6+11+18+... then t_{50} is

(A) $49^2 - 1$ **(B) 49^2**

(C) $50^2 + 1$ **(D) $49^2 + 2$**

[NCERT Exemplar Q. 25, Page 163]

Ans. Correct option : (D)

Let $S_n = 2 + 3 + 6 + 11 + 18 + ... + t_{50}$

Suing method of difference, we get

$S_n = 2 + 3 + 6 + 11 + 18 + ... + t_{50}$ (i)

$S_n = 0 + 2 + 3 + 6 + 11 + ... + t_{49} + t_{50}$ (ii)

Subtracting eq (ii) from eq (i), we get

$0 = 2 + 1 + 3 + 5 + 7 + ... t_{50}$ terms

$\Rightarrow t_{50} = 2 + (1 + 3 + 5 + 7 + ...$ up to 49 terms)

$\Rightarrow t_{50} = 2 + \frac{49}{2}[2 \times 1 + (49-1) \times 2]$

$\Rightarrow t_{50} = 49^2 + 2.$

[B] Fill in the blanks

Q. 1. The sum of terms equidistant from the beginning and end in an A.P. is equal to............ .

[NCERT Exemplar Q. 28, Page 164]

Answer:

1. Constant

[C] State True or False

Q. 1. Every progression is a sequence but the converse, i.e., every sequence is also a progression need not necessarily be true.

[NCERT Exemplar Q. 31, Page 164]

Q. 2. Any term of an A.P. (except first) is equal to half the sum of terms which are equidistant from it.

[NCERT Exemplar Q. 32, Page 164]

Q. 3. If the sum of n terms of sequence is quadratic expression then it always represents an A.P.

[NCERT Exemplar Q. 34, Page 164]

Answer:

1. True 2. True 3. False

Short Answer Type Questions (2 marks each)

Q. 1. A carpenter was hired to build 192 window frames. The first day he made five frames and each day, thereafter he made two more frames than he made the day before. How many days did it take him to finish the job?

[NCERT Exemplar, Q. 5, Page 161]

Sol. Here, $a = 5$ and $d = 2$

Let he finished the job in n days.

Then, $S_n = 192$

$S_n = \frac{n}{2}[2a + (n-1)d]$

$\Rightarrow 192 = \frac{n}{2}[2 \times 5 + (n-1)2]$

$\Rightarrow 192 = \frac{n}{2}[10 + 2n - 2]$

$\Rightarrow 192 = \frac{n}{2}[8 + 2n]$

$\Rightarrow 192 = 4n + n^2$

$\Rightarrow n^2 + 4n - 192 = 0$

$\Rightarrow (n-12)(n+16) = 0$

$\Rightarrow n = 12, -16$

$\therefore n = 12$ $\quad [\because n \neq -16]$

Q. 2. Find the rth term of an A.P., sum of whose first n term is $2n+3n^2$.
[Hint $a_n = S_n - S_{n-1}$]
[NCERT Exemplar, Q. 12, Page 162]

Sol. $S_n = 2n + 3n^2$

$S_{n-1} = 2(n-1) + 3(n-1)^2$

$a_n = S_n - S_{n-1}$

$= 2n + 3n^2 - 2(n-1) - 3(n-1)^2$

$= 2n + 3n^2 - 2n + 2 - 3n^2 + 6n - 3$

$a_n = 6n - 1$

$\therefore a_r = 6r - 1$

Long Answer Type Question

(4 marks each)

Q. 1. The first term of an A.P. is a, and the sum of the first p terms is zero, show that the sum of its next q terms is $\frac{-a(p+q)q}{p-1}$.
[NCERT Exemplar Q. 1, Page 161]

Sol. Let the common difference of the A.P. be d.

Given that $S_p = 0$

$\Rightarrow \frac{p}{2}[2a + (p-1)d] = 0$

$\Rightarrow 2a + (p-1)d = 0$

$\Rightarrow d = \frac{-2a}{p-1}$

Now, sum of next q terms $= S_{p+q} - S_p$

$= S_{p+q} - 0$ $\quad$ (given $S_p = 0$)

$= \frac{p+q}{2}[2a + (p+q-1)d]$

$= \frac{p+q}{2}[2a + (p-1)d + qd]$

$= \frac{p+q}{2}\left[0 + \frac{q(-2a)}{p-1}\right]$

$= \frac{-a(p+q)q}{p-1}$ $\quad$ **Hence Proved.**

Q. 2. A man saved ₹66000 in 20 yr. In each succeeding year after the first year, he saved ₹200 more than what he saved in the previous year. How much did he save in the first year?
[NCERT Exemplar Q. 2, Page 161]

Sol. Let saved in first year ₹ a. Since, each succeeding year an increment ₹ 200 has made.

So, it forms an A.P. whose

First term $= a$, common difference $(d) = 200$

and $n = 20$ yr

$\therefore S_{20} = \frac{20}{2}[2a + (20-1)d]$

$\left[\because S_n = \frac{n}{2}\{2a + (n-1)d\}\right]$

$\Rightarrow 66000 = 10[2a + 19d]$

$\Rightarrow 66000 = 20a + 190d$

$\Rightarrow 66000 = 20a + 190 \times 200$

$\Rightarrow 20a = 66000 - 38000$

$\Rightarrow 20a = 28000$

$\therefore a = \frac{28000}{20} = 1400$

Hence, he saved ₹1400 in the first year.

Q. 3. A man accepts a position with an initial salary of ₹5200 per month. It is understood that he will receive an automatic increase of ₹320 in the very next month and each month thereafter.

(i) Find his salary for tenth month.

(ii) What is his total earnings during the first year?
[NCERT Exemplar Q. 3, Page 161]

Sol. Since, the man get a fixed increment of ₹320 each month.

Therefore, this forms an A.P. whose

First term = 5200 and

Common difference $(d) = 320$

(i) Salary for tenth month *i.e.*, for $n = 10$

$a_{10} = a + (n-1)d$

$\Rightarrow a_{10} = 5200 + (10-1) \times 320$

$\Rightarrow a_{10} = 5200 + 9 \times 320$

$\Rightarrow a_{10} = 5200 + 2880$

$\Rightarrow a_{10} = 8080$

(ii) Total earning during the first year.

In a year there are 12 month *i.e.*, $n = 12$,

$S_{12} = \frac{12}{2}[2 \times 5200 + (12-1)320]$

$= 6[10400 + 11 \times 320]$

$= 6[10400 + 3520] = 6 \times 13920 = 83520$

Q. 4. The sum of interior angles of a triangle is 180°. Show that the sum of the interior angles of polygons with 3, 4, 5, 6, ... sides from an arithmetic progression. Find the sum of the interior angles for a 21 sided polygon.
[NCERT Exemplar Q. 6, Page 161]

Sol. We know that, sum of interior angles of a polygon of side $n = (2n-4) \times 90° = (n-2) \times 180°$

Sum of interior angles of a polygon with sides 3 is 180°.

Sum of interior angles of polygon with side $4 = (4-2) \times 180° = 360°$

Similarly, sum of interior angles of polygon with side 5, 6, 7 ... are 540°, 720°, 900°,...

The series will be 180°, 360°, 540°, 720°, 900°,...

Here, $a = 180°$

and $d = 360° - 180° = 180°$

Since, common difference is same between two consecutive terms of the series.

So, it form an A.P.

We have to find the sum of interior angles of a 21 sides polygon.

$S_{21} = (n-2) \times 180 = (21-2) \times 180$
$= 3420°$

Long Answer Type Question-II (6 marks each)

Q. 1. The sums of n terms of two A.P. are in the ratio of $5n+4; 9n+6$. Find the ratio of the their 18th terms.

[NCERT Exemplar Q. 9, Page 185]

Sol. Let the a_1, a_2 be the first terms of two A.P.'s and d_1, d_2 be the common differences of two A.P.'s respectively. Now, according to the question

$$\frac{S_{n_1}}{S_{n_2}} = \frac{5n+4}{9n+6}$$

$$\Rightarrow \frac{\frac{n}{2}[2a_1+(n-1)d_1]}{\frac{n}{2}[2a_2+(n-1)d_2]} = \frac{5n+4}{9n+6}$$

$$\left(\because S_n = \frac{n}{2}[2a+(n-1)d]\right)$$

$$\Rightarrow \frac{2a_1+(n-1)d_1}{2a_2+(n-1)d_2} = \frac{5n+4}{9n+6}$$

(We have to find the ratio of 18th terms, so converted the equation in the form of nth term by taking the 2 as common)

$$\Rightarrow \frac{2\left[a_1+\frac{n-1}{2}d_1\right]}{2\left[a_2+\frac{n-1}{2}d_2\right]} = \frac{5n+4}{9n+6}$$

$$\Rightarrow \frac{a_1+\left(\frac{n-1}{2}\right)d_1}{a_2+\left(\frac{n-1}{2}\right)d_2} = \frac{5n+4}{9n+6} \quad \text{(i)}$$

We have to find $\frac{a_1+17d_1}{a_2+17d_2}$.

$$\Rightarrow \frac{n-1}{2} = 17 \Rightarrow n-1 = 2\times 17$$

$$\Rightarrow n = 34+1 \Rightarrow n = 35$$

Hence, from Eq.(i),

$$\frac{a_1+17d_1}{a_2+17d_2} = \frac{5\times 35+4}{9\times 35+6} = \frac{175+4}{315+6} = \frac{179}{321}.$$

Q. 2. If the sum of first p terms of an A.P. is equal to the sum of the first q terms, then find the sum of the first $(p+q)$ terms.

[NCERT Exemplar Q. 10, Page 185]

Sol. We know that,

$$S_n = \frac{n}{2}[2a+(n-1)d]$$

where, S_n = Sum of n terms of A.P.

n = number of terms

a = first term and d = Common difference

Now, Sum of first p terms $= S_p$

$$= \frac{p}{2}[2a+(p-1)d]$$

Sum of first q terms $= S_q$

$$= \frac{q}{2}[2a+(q-1)d]$$

It is given that,

Sum of first p terms = Sum of first q terms

$$\frac{p}{2}[2a+(p-1)d] = \frac{q}{2}[2a+(q-1)d]$$

$$p[2a+(p-1)d] = q[2a+(q-1)d]$$

$$2ap - 2aq = qd(q-1) - pd(p-1)$$

$$2a(p-q) = d[(q-1)q - (p-1)p]$$

$$2a(p-q) = d[q^2 - p^2 + p - q]$$

$$2a(p-q) = -d[p^2 - q^2 - (p-q)]$$

$$2a(p-q) = -d(p-q)(p+q-1)$$

$$(p-q)[2a + d(p+q-1)] = 0$$

either $p - q = 0$ or $2a + d(p+q-1) = 0$

i.e., $p = q$ (not possible as $p \neq q$)

$\therefore 2a + d(p+q-1) = 0$

Sum of $(p+q)$ terms is $\frac{(p+q)}{2}[2a+(p+q-1)d]$

$$= \frac{(p+q)}{2} \times 0 = 0$$

Hence, Sum of $(p+q)$ terms is zero.

Q. 3. Sum of the first p, q and r terms of an A.P. are a, b and c respectively. Prove that

$$\frac{a}{p}(q-r) + \frac{b}{q}(r-p) + \frac{c}{r}(p-q) = 0$$

[NCERT Exemplar Q. 11, Page 185]

Sol. Let the first term is A and common difference is d.

Given, $S_p = a \Rightarrow \frac{p}{2}[2A+(p-1)d] = a$

$$\left(\because S_n = \frac{n}{2}[2a+(n-1)d]\right) \quad \text{(i)}$$

$$S_q = b \Rightarrow \frac{q}{2}[2A+(q-1)d] = b \quad \text{(ii)}$$

and $S_r = c \Rightarrow \frac{r}{2}[2A+(r-1)d] = c$ (iii)

Now, we are to prove

$$\frac{a}{p}(q-r) + \frac{b}{q}(r-p) + \frac{c}{r}(p-q) = 0$$

$$\text{LHS} = \frac{a}{p}(q-r) + \frac{b}{q}(r-p) + \frac{c}{r}(p-q)$$

Putting the values of a, b and c from Eqs. (i), (ii) and (iii) respectively, we get

$$\therefore \text{ LHS} = \frac{1}{p}\times\frac{p}{2}[2A+(p-1)d](q-r)+\frac{1}{q}\times\frac{q}{2}$$

$$[2A+(q-1)d](r-p)+\frac{1}{r}\times\frac{r}{2}[2A+(r-1)d](p-q)$$

$$=\frac{1}{2}\{\{2A+(p-1)d\}(q-r)+\{2A+(q-1)d\}$$

$$(r-p)+[2A+(r-1)d\}(p-q)]$$

$$=\frac{1}{2}[2A(q-r)+(p-1)d(q-r)+2A(r-p)$$

$$+(q-1)d(r-p)+2A(p-q)+(r-1)d(p-q)]$$

$$=\frac{1}{2}2A(q-r+r-p+p-q)+d$$

$$[(p-1)(q-r)+(q-1)(r-p)+(r-1)(p-q)]$$

$$=\frac{1}{2}\left[\begin{array}{l}2A\times(0)+d(pq-pr-q+r+qr-pq-r\\ \qquad +p+rp-rq-p+q)\end{array}\right]$$

$$=\frac{1}{2}(0+d\times 0)=0$$

$\therefore$ LHS = RHS **Hence Proved.**

Q. 4. In a cricket tournament 16 school teams participated. A sum of ₹8000 is to be awarded among themselves as prize money. If the last placed team is awarded ₹275 in prize money and the award increases by the same amount for successive finishing places, how much amount the first place team receive ?

[NCERT Exemplar Q. 9, Page 161]

Sol. Let the first place team got ₹ a.

Since, award money increases by the same amount for successive finishing places.

Therefore series is an A.P.

Let the constant amount be d.

Here, $l = 275, n = 16$ and $S_{16} = 8000$

$\therefore l = a + (n-1)d$

$\Rightarrow l = a + (16-1)(-d)$

[we take common difference (–ve) because series is decreasing]

$\Rightarrow 275 = a - 15d$ (i)

and $S_{16} = \frac{16}{2}[2a+(n-1).(-d)]$

$\Rightarrow 8000 = 8[2a + (16-1)(-d)]$

$\Rightarrow 8000 = 8[2a - 15d]$

$\Rightarrow 1000 = 2a - 15d$ (ii)

On subtracting Eq. (i) from Eq. (ii), we get

$(2a - 15d) - (a - 15d) = 1000 - 275$

$\Rightarrow 2a - 15d - a + 15d = 725$

$\therefore a = 725$

Hence, first place team receive ₹ 725.

OR

$$S_n = \frac{n}{2}(a+l)$$

$$8000 = \frac{16}{2}(a+275)$$

$$1000 = (a+275)$$

$$a = 1000 - 275 = 725$$

First prize awarded ₹ 725.

Q. 5. If $a_1, a_2, a_3, \ldots, a_n$ are in A.P., where $a_i > 0$ for all i, show that

$$\frac{1}{\sqrt{a_1}+\sqrt{a_2}}+\frac{1}{\sqrt{a_2}+\sqrt{a_3}}+\ldots+\frac{1}{\sqrt{a_{n-1}}+\sqrt{a_n}}=\frac{n-1}{\sqrt{a_1}+\sqrt{a_n}}$$

[NCERT Exemplar Q. 10, Page 162]

Sol. Since $a_1, a_2, a_3, \ldots, a_n$ are in A.P.

$\Rightarrow a_2 - a_1 = a_3 - a_2 = \ldots = a_n - a_{n-1} = d$ [common difference]

If $a_2 - a_1 = d$, then $\left(\sqrt{a_2}\right)^2 - \left(\sqrt{a_1}\right)^2 = d$

$$\Rightarrow \left(\sqrt{a_2}-\sqrt{a_1}\right)\left(\sqrt{a_2}+\sqrt{a_1}\right)=d$$

$$\Rightarrow \frac{1}{\sqrt{a_1}+\sqrt{a_2}}=\frac{\sqrt{a_2}-\sqrt{a_1}}{d}$$

Similarly, $\frac{1}{\sqrt{a_2}+\sqrt{a_3}}=\frac{\sqrt{a_3}-\sqrt{a_2}}{d}$

… … …

… … …

… … …

$$\frac{1}{\sqrt{a_{n-1}}+\sqrt{a_n}}=\frac{\sqrt{a_n}-\sqrt{a_{n-1}}}{d}$$

On adding these terms, we get

$$\frac{1}{\sqrt{a_1}+\sqrt{a_2}}+\frac{1}{\sqrt{a_2}+\sqrt{a_3}}+\ldots+\frac{1}{\sqrt{a_{n-1}}+\sqrt{a_n}}$$

$$=\frac{1}{d}\left[\sqrt{a_2}-\sqrt{a_1}+\sqrt{a_3}-\sqrt{a_2}+\ldots+\sqrt{a_n}-\sqrt{a_{n-1}}\right]$$

[using above relations]

$$=\frac{1}{d}\left[\sqrt{a_n}-\sqrt{a_1}\right] \quad \text{(i)}$$

Again, $a_n = a_1 + (n-1)d$ $[\because T_n = a+(n-1)d]$

$$\Rightarrow a_n - a_1 = (n-1)d$$

$$\Rightarrow (\sqrt{a_n})^2 - (\sqrt{a_1})^2 = (n-1)d$$

$$\Rightarrow (\sqrt{a_n}-\sqrt{a_1})(\sqrt{a_n}+\sqrt{a_1}) = (n-1)d$$

$$\Rightarrow \sqrt{a_n}-\sqrt{a_1} = \frac{(n-1)d}{\sqrt{a_n}+\sqrt{a_1}}$$

On putting this value in Eq. (i), we get

$$\frac{1}{\sqrt{a_1}+\sqrt{a_2}}+\frac{1}{\sqrt{a_2}+\sqrt{a_3}}+\ldots+\frac{1}{\sqrt{a_{n-1}}+\sqrt{a_n}}$$

$$\frac{(n-1)d}{d\sqrt{a_n}+\sqrt{a_1}}=\frac{n-1}{\sqrt{a_n}+\sqrt{a_1}}$$

Hence Proved.

Q. 6. If $\theta_1, \theta_2, \theta_3, \ldots, \theta_n$ are in A.P. whose common difference is d, show that $\sec\theta_1 \sec\theta_2 + \sec\theta_2 \sec\theta_3 + \ldots + \sec\theta_{n-1}\sec\theta_n$

$$= \frac{\tan\theta_n - \tan\theta_1}{\sin d}.$$

[NCERT Exemplar Q. 14, Page 162]

Sol. Since, $\theta_1, \theta_2, \theta_3, \ldots, \theta_n$ are in A.P.

$\Rightarrow \theta_2 - \theta_1 = \theta_3 - \theta_2 = \ldots = \theta_n - \theta_{n-1} = d$ (i)

Now, we have to prove

$$\sec\theta_1\sec\theta_2 + \sec\theta_2\sec\theta_3 + \ldots + \sec\theta_{n-1}\sec\theta_n = \frac{\tan\theta_n - \tan\theta_1}{\sin d}$$

Or it can be written as

$$\sin d\,[\sec\theta_1\sec\theta_2 + \sec\theta_2\sec\theta_3 + \ldots + \sec\theta_{n-1}\sec\theta_n] = \tan\theta_n - \tan\theta_1$$

Now, taking only first term of LHS

$$\sin d \sec\theta_1 \sec\theta_2 = \frac{\sin d}{\cos\theta_1\cos\theta_2} = \frac{\sin(\theta_2-\theta_1)}{\cos\theta_1\cos\theta_2}$$

from Eq. (i)]

$$= \frac{\sin\theta_2\cos\theta_1 - \cos\theta_2\sin\theta_1}{\cos\theta_1\cos\theta_2}$$

$[\because \sin(A-B) = \sin A.\cos B - \cos A.\sin B]$

$$= \frac{\sin\theta_2\cos\theta_1}{\cos\theta_1\cos\theta_2} - \frac{\cos\theta_2\sin\theta_1}{\cos\theta_1\cos\theta_2} = \tan\theta_2 - \tan\theta_1$$

Similarly, we can solve other terms which will be $\tan\theta_3 - \tan\theta_2$, $\tan\theta_4 - \tan\theta_3, \ldots$

$\therefore$ LHS $= \tan\theta_2 - \tan\theta_1 + \tan\theta_3 - \tan\theta_2 + \ldots + \tan\theta_n - \tan\theta_{n-1}$

$= -\tan\theta_1 + \tan\theta_n = \tan\theta_n - \tan\theta_1$

= RHS **Hence Proved.**

Q. 7. If the sum of p terms of an A.P. is q and the sum of q terms is p, then show that the sum of $p+q$ terms is $-(p+q)$, Also, find the sum of first $p-q$ terms (where, $p>q$)

[NCERT Exemplar Q. 15, Page 162]

Sol. Let first term and common difference of the A.P. be a and d, respectively.

Then, $S_p = q$

$$\Rightarrow \frac{p}{2}[2a+(p-1)d] = q$$

$$2a+(p-1)d = \frac{2q}{p} \quad \text{(i)}$$

and $S_q = p$

$$\frac{q}{2}[2a+(q-1)d] = p$$

$$2a+(q-1)d = \frac{2p}{q} \quad \text{(ii)}$$

On subtracting Eq. (ii) from Eq. (i), we get

$$2a+(p-1)d-2a-(q-1)d = \frac{2q}{p} - \frac{2p}{q}$$

$$\Rightarrow [(p-1)-(q-1)]d = \frac{2q^2-2p^2}{pq}$$

$$\Rightarrow [p-1-q+1]d = \frac{2(q^2-p^2)}{pq}$$

$$\Rightarrow (p-q)d = \frac{2(q^2-p^2)}{pq}$$

$$\therefore d = \frac{-2(p+q)}{pq} \quad \text{(iii)}$$

On subtracting the value of d in Eq. (i) we get

$$2a+(p-1)\left(\frac{-2(p+q)}{pq}\right) = \frac{2q}{p}$$

$$\Rightarrow 2a = \frac{2q}{p} + \frac{2(p+q)(p-1)}{pq}$$

$$\Rightarrow a = \left[\frac{q}{p} + \frac{(p+q)(p-1)}{pq}\right] \quad \text{(iv)}$$

Now, $S_{p+q} = \frac{p+q}{2}[2a+(p+q-1)d]$

$$= \frac{p+q}{2}\left[\frac{2q}{p} + \frac{2(p+q)(p-1)}{pq} - \frac{(p+q-1)2(p+q)}{pq}\right]$$

$$= (p+q)\left[\frac{q}{p} + \frac{(p+q)(p-1)-(p+q-1)(p+q)}{pq}\right]$$

$$= (p+q)\left[\frac{q}{p} + \frac{(p+q)(p-1-p-q+1)}{pq}\right]$$

$$= (p+q)\left[\frac{q}{p} - \frac{p+q}{p}\right] = (p+q)\left[\frac{q-p-q}{p}\right]$$

$$S_{p+q} = -(p+q)$$

$$S_{p-q} = \frac{p-q}{2}[2a+(p-q-1)d]$$

$$= \frac{p-q}{2}\left[\frac{2q}{p} + \frac{2(p+q)(p-1)}{pq} - \frac{(p-q-1)2(p+q)}{pq}\right]$$

$$= (p-q)\left[\frac{q}{p} + \frac{(p+q)(p-1-p+q+1)}{pq}\right]$$

$$= (p-q)\left[\frac{q}{p} + \frac{(p+q)q}{pq}\right]$$

$$= (p-q)\left[\frac{q}{p} + \frac{p+q}{p}\right] = (p-q)\frac{(p+2q)}{p}$$

TOPIC-2
G.P. and Sum to *n* terms of Special Series

Quick Review

➤ A sequence of non-zero number is said to be G.P., if the ratio of each term, except the first one, by its preceding term is always the same.

We can say that, a sequence $a_1, a_2, ..., a_n$ is called geometric progression (geometric sequence), if it follows the relation $\frac{a_{k+1}}{a_k} = r$ (constant).

The constant ratio is called **Common ratio** of the *G.P.* and it is denoted by *r*.

In a *G.P.*, we usually denote the first term by *a*, the nth term by T_n or a_n.

Thus, G.P. can be written as, a, ar^2, ar^3 ...... and so on.

➤ **General Term of a G.P.** : If *a* is the first term of a G.P. and its common ratio is *r*, then general term or n^{th} term, $T_n = ar^{n-1}$ or $l = ar^{n-1}$, where *l* is the last term.

m^{th} Term of Finite *G.P.* from the End : Let *a* be the first term and *r* be the common ratio of a *G.P.* having *n* terms. Then, m^{th} term from the end is $(n - m + 1)^{th}$ term from the beginning.

$\therefore$ **m^{th} term from the end** $= ar^{n-m+1-1} = ar^{n-m}$ where, $n > m$

Also, m^{th} term from the end $= l\left(\frac{1}{r}\right)^{n-1}$, where *l* is last term of the finite *G.P.*

➤ **Sum of First *n* Terms of a *G.P.*:** If *a* and *r* are the first term and common ratio of a *G.P.* respectively, then sum of *n* terms of this G.P. is given by

$$S_n = \frac{a(1-r^n)}{1-r}, \text{ where } r < l$$

and $$S_n = \frac{a(r^n - 1)}{r-1}, \text{ where } r > 1$$

➤ **Geometric Mean:** Geometric mean between *a* and *b* is $\sqrt{ab}$ or If *a, b, c* are in G.P., then Geometric mean (G.M.) $b^2 = ac$

Some Important Results:

- Reciprocals of terms in G.P. always form a G.P.
- If $G_1, G_2, G_3, \ldots, G_n$ are *n* numbers inserted between *a* and *b* so that the resulting sequence is G.P., then
$$G_k = a\left(\frac{b}{a}\right)^{k+1}, 1 \le k \le n$$
- If three terms of G.P. are to be taken, then we choose as $\frac{a}{r}$, *a*, *ar*.
- If four terms of G.P. are to be taken, then we choose as $\frac{a}{r^3}, \frac{a}{r}, ar, ar^3$.
- If five terms of G.P. are to be taken, then we choose as $\frac{a}{r^2}, \frac{a}{r}$, *a*, *ar*, ar^2
- If *a, b, c* are in G.P. then *ak, bk, ck* are also in G.P. where $k \neq 0$ and $\frac{a}{k}, \frac{b}{k}, \frac{c}{k}$ also in G.P. where $k \neq 0$.
- In a G.P., the product of the terms equidistant from the beginning and from the end is always same and equal to the product of the first and the last term.
- If each term of a G.P. be raised to some power then the resulting terms are also in G.P.
- $S_\infty = a + ar + ar^2 + ar^3 + \cdots \infty$ term if $-1 < r < 1 \Rightarrow S_\infty = \frac{a}{1-r}$.
such that $-1 < r < 1$ or $|r| < 1$
- $\sum_{r=1}^{n} r = \frac{n(n+1)}{2}$

- $\sum_{r=1}^{n} r^2 = \frac{n(n+1)(2n+1)}{6}$
- $\sum_{r=1}^{n} r^3 = \left[\frac{n(n+1)}{2}\right]^2$
- If a, b, c are A.P. then $2b = a + c$.
- If a, b, c are in G.P. then $b^2 = ac$.
- If A and G be A.M and G.M of two given positive real number 'a' and 'b' respectively then $A = \frac{a+b}{2}$, $G = \sqrt{ab}$ and $A \geq G$.

Multiple Choice Questions (1 mark each)

[A] Objective Type Questions

Q. 1. The third term of G.P.. is 4. The product of its first 5 terms is

(A) 4^3 (B) 4^4

(C) 4^5 (D) None of these

[NCERT Exemplar Q. 18, Page 163]

Ans. Correct option : (C)

Given, $T_3 = 4$

$\Rightarrow ar^{3-1} = 4$ $[\because T_n = ar^{n-1}]$

$\Rightarrow ar^2 = 4$

Product of first 5 terms. $a. ar . ar^2. ar^3. ar^4$

$= a^5 r^{10} = (ar^2)^5 = (4)^5$

Q. 2. If x, $2y$, $3z$ are in A.P. where the distinct numbers x, y, z are in G.P. then the common ratio of the G.P. is

(A) 3 (B) $\frac{1}{3}$

(C) 2 (D) $\frac{1}{2}$

[NCERT Exemplar Q. 20, Page 163]

Ans. Correct option : (B)

Since, x, $2y$, $3z$ are in A.P.

$\therefore 2y - x = 3z - 2y$

$\Rightarrow 4y = x + 3z$ (i)

Now, x, y, z are in G.P.

$\therefore$ Common ratio $r = \frac{y}{x} = \frac{z}{x}$

$\therefore y^2 = xz$ (ii)

Putting the value of x from eq (i), we get

$y^2 = (4y - 3z)\, z \Rightarrow y^2 = 4yz - 3z^2$

$\Rightarrow 3z^2 - 4yz + y^2 = 0 \Rightarrow 3z^2 - 3yz - yz + y^2 = 0$

$\Rightarrow 3z\,(z - y) - y\,(z - y) = 0 \Rightarrow (3z - y)\,(z - y) = 0$

$\Rightarrow 3z - y = 0 \Rightarrow$ and $z - y = 0$ $(z \neq y)$

$\Rightarrow 3z - y$ and $z \neq y$ [$\because$ z and y are distinct numbers]

$\Rightarrow \frac{z}{y} = \frac{1}{3} \Rightarrow r = \frac{1}{3}$ (form eq iii)

Q. 3. The minimum value of $4^x + 4^{1-x}$, $x \in R$, is

(A) 2 (B) 4

(C) 1 (D) 0

[NCERT Exemplar Q. 23, Page 163]

Ans. Correct option : (B)

We know that AM $\geq$ GM

$\therefore \frac{4^x + 4^{1-x}}{2} \geq \sqrt{4^x . 4^{1-x}}$

$\Rightarrow 4^x + 4^{1-x} \geq 2\sqrt{4^{x+1-x}}$

$\Rightarrow 4^x + 4^{1-x} \geq 2\sqrt{4^{x+1-x}}$

$\Rightarrow 4^x + 4^{1-x} \geq 4$

Q. 4. Let S_n denote the sum of the cubes of the first n natural numbers and s_n denote the sum of the first n natural numbers. Then $\sum_{r-1}^{n} \frac{S_r}{S_r}$ equals

(A) $\frac{n(n+1)(n+2)}{6}$ (B) $\frac{n(n+1)}{2}$

(C) $\frac{n^2+3n+2}{2}$ (D) None of these

[NCERT Exemplar Q. 24, Page 163]

Ans. Correct option : (A)

Given that : $\sum_{i=1}^{n} \frac{Sr}{s_n} = \frac{S_1}{s_1} + \frac{S_2}{s_2} + \frac{S_3}{s_3} + ... + \frac{S_n}{s_n}$

Let T_n be the nth term of the above series

$$\therefore T_n = \frac{S_n}{s_n} = \frac{\left[n\frac{(n+1)}{2}\right]^2}{\frac{n(n+1)}{2}} = \frac{n^2 + n}{2}$$

Now, sum of the given series

$$\Sigma T_n = \frac{1}{2}\,\Sigma\,[n^2 + n] = \frac{1}{2}\,[\Sigma n^2 + \Sigma n]$$

$$= \frac{1}{2}\left[\frac{n(n+1)(2x+1)}{6} + \frac{n(n+1)}{2}\right]$$

$$= \frac{n(n+1)(n+2)}{6}$$

Q. 5. The lengths of three unequal edges of a rectangular solid block are in G.P. The volume of the block is 216 cm^3 and the total surface are is 252 cm^2. The length of the longest edge is

(A) 12 cm **(B) 6 cm**

(C) 18 cm **(D) 3 cm**

[NCERT Exemplar Q. 26, Page 163]

Ans. Correct option : (D)

Let the length, breath and height of a rectangular block be $\frac{a}{r}$, a, and ar. [Since they are in G.P.]

Volume = $l \times b \times h$

$216 = \frac{a}{r} \times a \times ar$

$\Rightarrow a = 6$

Now, total surface area = $2[lb + bh + lh]$

$252 = 2\left[\frac{a}{r}.a + a.ar + \frac{a}{r}.ar\right]$

$\Rightarrow 252 = 2a^2\left[\frac{1}{r} + r + 1\right]$

$\Rightarrow 252 = 2(6)^2\left[\frac{1}{r} + r + 1\right]$

$\Rightarrow \frac{252}{72} = \frac{1 + r^2 + r}{r}$

$\Rightarrow 2 + 2r + 2r^2 = 7r$

$\Rightarrow 2r^2 - 5r + 2 = 0$

$\Rightarrow (r - 2)(2r - 1) = 0$

$\Rightarrow r = 2, = \frac{1}{2}$

Therefore, the three edges are :

If $r = 2$, then edges are 3, 6, 12

If $r = \frac{1}{2}$ then edges are 12, 6, 3.

[B] Fill in the blanks

Q. 1. For a, b, c to be in G.P. The value of $\frac{a-b}{b-c}$ is equal to..................

[NCERT Exemplar Q. 27, Page 164]

Q. 2. The sum of terms equidistant from the beginning and end in an A.P. is equal to...........

[NCERT Exemplar Q. 29, Page 164]

Answer:

1. $\frac{a}{b}$ or $\frac{b}{c}$

2. Sum of first and last term

[C] State True or False for the following :

Q. 1. Two sequence cannot be in both A.P. and G.P. together.

[NCERT Exemplar Q. 30, Page 164]

Q. 2. The sum or difference of two G.P.s, is again a G.P.

[NCERT Exemplar Q. 33, Page 164]

Answer:

1. False 2. False

[D] Match the following :

Q. 1.

	Column I		Column II
(a)	$4, 1, \frac{1}{4}, \frac{1}{16}$	(i)	A.P.
(b)	2, 3, 5, 7	(ii)	sequence
(c)	13, 8, 3, –2, –7	(iii)	G.P.

Q. 2.

	Column I		Column II
(a)	$1^2 + 2^2 + 3^2 + \ldots + n^2$	(i)	$\left(\frac{n(n+1)}{2}\right)^2$
(b)	$1^3 + 2^3 + 3^3 + \ldots + n^3$	(ii)	$n(n+1)$
(c)	$2 + 4 + 6 + \ldots + 2n$	(iii)	$\frac{n(n+1)(2n+1)}{6}$
(d)	$1 + 2 + 3 + \ldots + n$	(iv)	$\frac{n(n+1)}{2}$

[NCERT Exemplar Q. 35-36, Page 164]

Answer

Q. 1. (a) ↔ (iii), (b) ↔ (ii), (c) ↔ (i)

Q. 2. (a) ↔ (iii), (b) ↔ (i), (c) ↔ (ii), (d) ↔ (iv)

Long Answer Type Questions

(4 marks each)

Q. 1. If A and G be A.M. and G.M. respectively, between two positive numbers prove that the numbers are $A \pm \sqrt{(A+G)(A-G)}$.

[NCERT Exemplar Q. 29, Page 193]

Sol. Let the numbers are α and β.

Given, $\frac{\alpha+\beta}{2} = A$ (Arithmetic mean)

$\Rightarrow \quad \alpha + \beta = 2A \quad \ldots(i)$

and product of the numbers,

$\sqrt{\alpha\beta} = G$ (Geometric mean) $\Rightarrow \alpha\beta = G^2 \quad \ldots(ii)$

$(\alpha - \beta)^2 = (\alpha + \beta)^2 - 4\alpha\beta$

$= 4A^2 - 4G^2$

$= 4(A^2 - G^2)$

$\alpha - \beta = \pm 2\sqrt{A^2 - G^2}$ ...(iii)

$\alpha + \beta = 2A$ ...(iv)

$2\alpha = 2A \pm 2\sqrt{A^2 - G^2}$ Adding (iv) & (iii)

$\therefore \quad \alpha = A \pm \sqrt{A^2 - G^2}$

$= A \pm \sqrt{(A-G)(A+G)}$

$\therefore$ number are $A \pm \sqrt{(A+G)(A-G)}$ and $A \mp \sqrt{(A+G)(A-G)}$

Hence proved.

Long Answer Type Questions-II

(6 marks each)

Q. 1. A side of an equilateral triangle is 20 cm long. A second equilateral triangle is inscribed in it by joining the mid-points of the sides of the first triangle. The process is continued as shown in the accompanying diagram. Find the perimeter of the sixth inscribed equilateral triangle.

[NCERT Exemplar Q. 7, Page 161]

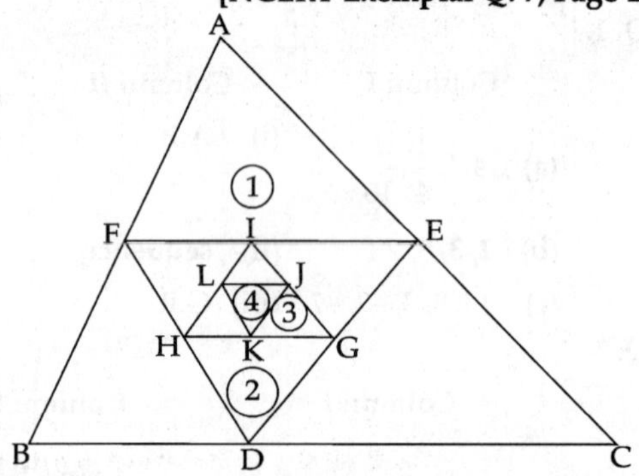

Sol. Side of equilateral ΔABC = 20 cm. By joining the mid-points of this triangle, we get another equilateral triangle of side equal to half of the length of side of ΔABC.

Continuing in this way, we get a set of equilateral triangles with side equal to half of the side of the previous triangle.

$\therefore$ Perimeter of first triangle = $20 \times 3 = 60$ cm

Perimeter of second triangle = $10 \times 3 = 30$ cm

Perimeter of third triangle = $5 \times 3 = 15$ cm

Now, the series will be 60, 30, 15,...

Here, $a = 60$

$\therefore \quad r = \frac{30}{60} = \frac{1}{2}$ $\left[\because \frac{\text{second term}}{\text{first term}} = r\right]$

We have, to find perimeter of sixth inscribed triangle. It is the sixth term of the series.

$\therefore a_6 = ar^{6-1}$ $[\because a_n = ar^{n-1}]$

$= 60 \times \left(\frac{1}{2}\right)^5 = \frac{60}{32} = \frac{15}{8}$ cm.

Q. 2. Find the sum of the series $(3^3 - 2^3) + (5^3 - 4^3) + (7^3 - 6^3) + ...$ to (i) n terms. (ii) 10 terms.

[NCERT Exemplar Q. 11, Page 162]

Sol. Give series, $(3^3 - 2^3) + (5^3 - 4^3) + (7^3 - 6^3) +$ ...(i)

$= (3^3 + 5^3 + 7^3 + ...) - (2^3 + 4^3 + 6^3 + ...)$

Let T_n be the nth term of the series (i),

then T_n = (nth term of $3^3, 5^3, 7^3, ...$) – (nth term of $2^3, 4^3, 6^3, ...$) = $(2n+1)^3 - (2n)^3$

$= (2n+1-2n)[(2n+1)^2 + (2n+1)2n + (2n)^2]$

$[\because a^3 - b^3 = (a-b)(a^2 + ab + b^2)]$

$= [4n^2 + 1 + 4n + 4n^2 + 2n + 4n^2] = [12n^2 + 6n + 1]$

(i) Let S_n denote the sum of n term of series (i).

Then, $S_n = \Sigma T_n = \Sigma(12n^2 + 6n + 1)$

$= 12\Sigma n^2 + 6\Sigma n + \Sigma 1$

$= 12 . \frac{n(n+1)(2n+1)}{6} + \frac{6n(n+1)}{2} + n$

$= 2n(n+1)(2n+1) + 3n(n+1) + n$

$= (2n^2 + 2n)(2n+1) + 3n^2 + 3n + n$

$= 4n^3 + 2n^2 + 4n^2 + 2n + 3n^2 + 3n + n$

$= 4n^3 + 9n^2 + 6n$

(ii) Sum of 10 terms, $S_{10} = 4 \times (10)^3 + 9 \times (10)^2 + 6 \times 10$

$= 4 \times 1000 + 9 \times 100 + 60$

$= 4000 + 900 + 60 = 4960$,

Q. 3. If A is the arithmetic mean and G_1, G_2 be two geometric mean between any two numbers, then prove that $2A = \frac{G_1^2}{G_2} + \frac{G_2^2}{G_1}$.

[NCERT Exemplar Q. 13, Page 162]

Sol. Let the numbers be a and b

Then, $A = \frac{a+b}{2}$

$\Rightarrow \quad 2A = a + b$ ...(i)

and G_1, G_2 be geometric mean between a and b, then a, G_1, G_2, b are in G.P..

Let r be the common ratio.

Then, $b = ar^{4-1}$ $[\because a_n = ar^{n-1}]$

$\Rightarrow b = ar^3 \Rightarrow \frac{b}{a} = r^3 \quad \therefore \quad r = \left(\frac{b}{a}\right)^{1/3}$

Now, $G_1 = ar = a\left(\frac{b}{a}\right)^{1/3}$ $\left[\because r = \left(\frac{b}{a}\right)^{1/3}\right]$

and $G_2 = ar^2 = a\left(\frac{b}{a}\right)^{2/3}$

$\text{RHS} = \frac{G_1^2}{G_2} + \frac{G_2^2}{G_1} = \frac{\left[a\left(\frac{b}{a}\right)^{1/3}\right]^2}{a\left(\frac{b}{a}\right)^{2/3}} + \frac{\left[a\left(\frac{b}{a}\right)^{2/3}\right]^2}{a\left(\frac{b}{a}\right)^{1/3}}$

$$= \frac{a^2\left(\frac{b}{a}\right)^{2/3}}{a\left(\frac{b}{a}\right)^{2/3}} + \frac{a^2\left(\frac{b}{a}\right)^{4/3}}{a\left(\frac{b}{a}\right)^{1/3}}$$

$$= a + a\left(\frac{b}{a}\right) = a + b = 2A$$

[using Eq. (i)]

Hence proved

Q. 4. If *p*th, *q*th and *r*th terms of an A.P. and G.P. are both *a, b* and *c* respectively, then show that $a^{b-c}.b^{c-a}.c^{a-b} = 1$. [NCERT Exemplar Q. 16, Page 162]

Sol. Let *A, d* are the first term and common difference of A.P. and *x, R* are the first term and common ratio of G.P., respectively.

According to the given condition,

$A+(p-1)d = a$ ...(i)

$A+(q-1)d = b$ ...(ii)

$A+(r-1)d = c$ ...(iii)

and

$a = xR^{p-1}$ ...(iv)

$b = xR^{q-1}$ ...(v)

$c = xR^{r-1}$ ...(vi)

On subtracting Eq. (ii) from Eq. (i). we get

$d(p-1-q+1) = a-b$

$\Rightarrow a-b = d(p-q)$ ...(vii)

On subtracting Eq. (iii) from Eq. (ii). we get

$d(q-1-r+1) = b-c$

$b-c = d(q-r)$ ...(viii)

On subtracting Eq. (i) from Eq. (iii). we get

$d(r-1-p+1) = c-a$

$\Rightarrow c-a = d(r-p)$ ...(ix)

Now, we have to prove $a^{b-c}\,b^{c-a}\,c^{a-b} = 1$

Taking LHS$= a^{b-c}\,b^{c-a}\,c^{a-b}$

Using Eqs. (iv), (v), (vi) and (vii), (viii), (ix),

$$\text{LHS} = (xR^{p-1})^{d(q-r)}(xR^{q-1})^{d(r-p)}(xR^{r-1})^{d(p-q)}$$

$$= x^{d(q-r)+d(r-p)+d(p-q)}\,R^{(p-1)d(q-r)+(q-1)d(r-p)+(r-1)d(p-q)}$$

$$= x^{d(q-r+r-p+p-q)}$$

$$\times R^{d(pq-pr-q+r+qr-pq-r+p+rp-rq-p+q)}$$

$$= x^0R^0 = 1$$

= RHS **Hence Proved.**

Q. 5. If *p, q, r* are in G.P. and the equations $px^2+2qx+r=0$ and $dx^2+2ex+f=0$ have a common root, then show that $\frac{d}{p},\frac{e}{q},\frac{f}{r}$ are in A.P.

[NCERT Exemplar Q. 16, Page 162]

Sol. It is given that *p, q, r* are in G.P.

$\therefore\ q^2 = pr$

Now, $px^2+2qx+r=0$

$\Rightarrow px^2+2\sqrt{pr}x+r=0$

$\Rightarrow \left(\sqrt{p}x+\sqrt{r}\right)^2=0$

$\Rightarrow \sqrt{p}x+\sqrt{r}=0$

$\Rightarrow x=-\sqrt{\frac{r}{p}}$

It is given that the equations $px^2+2qx+r=0$ and $dx^2+2ex+f=0$ have a common root and the equation $px^2+2qx+r=0$ has equal roots equal to $-\sqrt{\frac{r}{p}}$

$\therefore\ -\sqrt{\frac{r}{p}}$ is a root of the equation $dx^2+2ex+f=0$

$\Rightarrow d\frac{r}{p}-2e\sqrt{\frac{r}{p}}+f=0$

$\Rightarrow \frac{d}{p}-2e\sqrt{\frac{1}{pr}}+\frac{f}{r}=0$ [Dividing through out by *r*]

$\Rightarrow \frac{d}{p}-\frac{2e}{q}+\frac{f}{r}=0$ $[\because q^2=pr]$

$\Rightarrow 2\frac{e}{q}=\frac{d}{p}+\frac{f}{r}$

$\Rightarrow \frac{d}{p},\frac{e}{q},\frac{f}{r}$ are in A.P.

Hence Proved.

Q. 6. If the *p* th and *q*th terms of G.P. are *q* and *p* respectively, then show that its (*p* + *q*)th terms is $\left(\frac{q^p}{p^q}\right)^{\frac{1}{p-q}}$. [NCERT Exemplar Q. 4, Page 161]

Sol. On substituting the value of *r* in eqn (i) we get

$$a\left(\frac{q}{p}\right)^{\frac{p-1}{p-q}} = q$$

$$a = q\left(\frac{p}{q}\right)^{\frac{p-1}{p-q}}$$

$$T_{p+q} = ar^{p+q-1}$$

$$= q\left(\frac{p}{q}\right)^{\frac{p-1}{p-q}}\left(\frac{q}{p}\right)^{\frac{p+q-1}{p-q}}$$

$$= q\left(\frac{p}{q}\right)^{\frac{p-1}{p-q}}\left(\frac{q}{p}\right)^{\frac{p-q}{p-q}}\cdot\left(\frac{q}{p}\right)^{\frac{d}{p-q}}$$

$$= q\left(\frac{p}{q}\times\frac{q}{p}\right)^{\frac{p-1}{p-q}}\cdot\left(\frac{q}{p}\right)^{\frac{q}{p-q}}$$

$$= \left[q^{p-d}\cdot\frac{q^q}{p^q}\right]^{\frac{1}{p-q}}$$

$$= \left[\frac{q^{p-q+q}}{p^q}\right]^{\frac{1}{p-q}}$$

$$= \left[\frac{q^p}{p^q}\right]^{\frac{1}{p-q}}$$ **Hence Proved.**

EXPERT ADVICE

- *Since this chapter is very fast, the variety of questions can be asked from this topic, so about from NCERT text book, practise from other reference books too.*
- *These questions can take much time, so try a variety of questions, so that you gain confidence for final examination.*
- *Most probably questions asked on sum of series. In this "sum of n terms of special series" is teacher's favorite area. We suggest you to try different questions on this topic from different reference books.*

OSWAAL LEARNING TOOLS

***For* Suggested Online Videos**

Visit : *https://youtu.be/HtTiuaymsBU* Or Scan the Code	**Visit :** *https://youtu.be/j21OCjqEkEo* Or Scan the Code
Visit : *https://youtu.be/VgVJrSJxkDk* Or Scan the Code	**Visit :** *https://youtu.be/V02nV_qR_xQ* Or Scan the Code
Visit : *https://goo.gl/FgbKLq* Or Scan the Code	**Visit :** *https://goo.gl/hQYYL7* Or Scan the Code

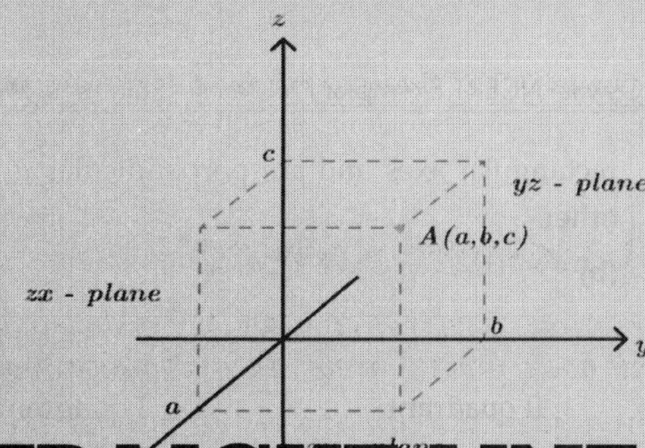

CHAPTER 10 STRAIGHT LINES

Chapter Objectives

> *Brief recall of two dimensional Geometry from earlier classes; Shifting of origin; slope of a line and angle between two lines; Collinearity of three points, various forms of a straight line (parallel to axis, point slope form, slope intercept form two point form intercept form and normal form); General equation of a line; Equation of family of lines passing through the point of intersection of two lines; Distance of a point from line; Condition for two lines to be parallel and perpendicular; Angle between two lines, having general equations, Equations of perpendicular and parallel lines through a given point.*

TOPIC-1
Recall of Two Dimensional Geometry and Slope of a Line

Quick Review

TOPIC - 1
Recall of Two Dimensional Geometry and Slope of a line **P. 119**

TOPIC - 2
Various forms of equations of a straight line. **P. 127**

TOPIC - 3
General equation of a line and equation of family of lines **P. 133**

> **Coordinate axes and plane**

- The Position of a point in a plane is fixed by selecting the axes or reference which are formed by two number lines intersecting each other at right angle. The horizontal number line is called x-axis and vertical number line is called y-axis.

(a)

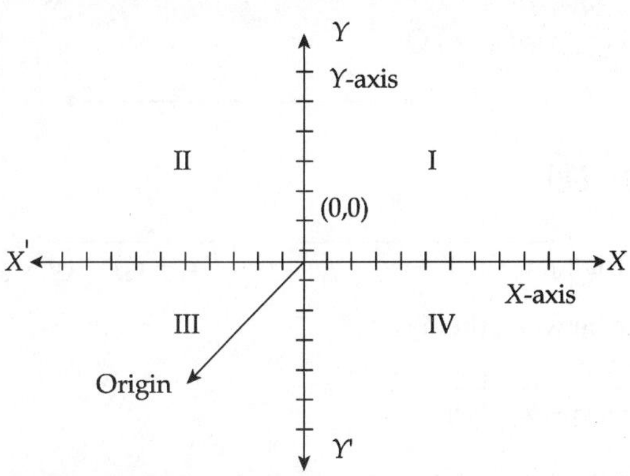

- The point of intersection of these two lines is called the origin. The intersection of x-axis and y-axis divide the plane into four equal parts. These four parts are called quadrants, Each part is (¼th) of the whole portion. These are numbered I, II, III and IV anticlockwise from OX. Thus, the plane consists of the axes and four quadrants is known as XY-plane or equation plane or coordinate plane and the axes are known as co-ordinate axes. These axes are also known as

TIPS...

- *Area of n-sided polygon formed by points $(x_1\ y_1)$, (x_2, y_2), (x_3, y_3) .... (x_n, y_n) is given by :*

$$\frac{1}{2}\begin{vmatrix} x_1 & x_2 \\ y_1 & y_2 \end{vmatrix} + \begin{vmatrix} x_2 & x_3 \\ y_2 & y_3 \end{vmatrix} + ... \begin{vmatrix} x_{n-1} & x_n \\ y_{n-1} & y_n \end{vmatrix}$$

- *If m_1, m_2, m_3 are the slopes of three lines $L_1 = 0$, $L_2 = 0$, $L_3 = 0$, where $m_1 > m_2 > m_3$, then the interior angles of ΔABC formed by these lines are given by*

$$\tan A = \frac{m_1 - m_2}{1 + m_1 m_2};\ \tan B = \frac{m_2 - m_3}{1 + m_2 m_3};$$

$$\tan C = \frac{m_3 - m_1}{1 + m_3 m_1}$$

- *A homogeneous equation of degree n represents a straight lines passing through origin.*
- *Equation of the horizontal line having distance 'a' from x-axis is either $y = a$ or $y = -a$ and equation of the vertical line having distance 'b' from y-axis is either $x = b$ or $x = -b$.*

rectangular axes and are perpendicular to each other.

(b)

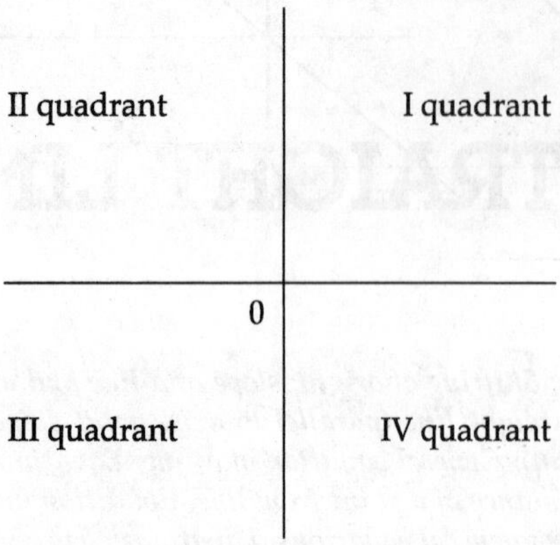

TRICKS...

- *In section formula, if $\frac{m}{n}$ is positive, then division is interval, but if $\frac{m}{n}$ is negative, the division is external.*
- *Slope of horizontal line is zero and slope of vertical line is undefined.*
- *If a line with slope m makes x-intercept 'd'. Then equation of line is $y = m(x - d)$.*
- *In the general equation of the straight line i.e. $Ax + By + C = 0$, the intercept on x-axis can be obtained by putting $y = 0$ (ie x-intercept $= \frac{-C}{A}$). and intercept on y-axis can be obtained by putting $x = 0$ (i.e., y-intercept $= \frac{-C}{B}$)*
- *In the normal form $x \cos \alpha + y \sin \alpha = p$, p is always taken as positive.*

➤ **Section Formulae**

- If a point R divide the segments joining the points $p(x_1, y_1)$ and $Q(x_2, y_2)$ internally in the ratio $m : n$, then its coordinate are

$$\left(\frac{mx_2 + nx_1}{m+n}, \frac{my_2 + ny_1}{m+n}\right)$$

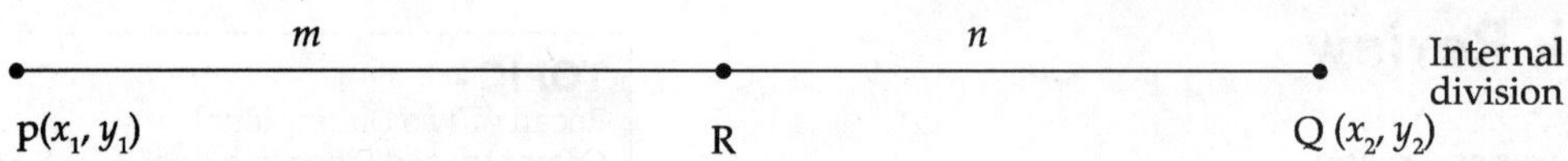

- If the division is external, then the co-ordinate of R are

$$\left(\frac{mx_2 - nx_1}{m-n}, \frac{my_2 - ny_1}{m-n}\right).$$

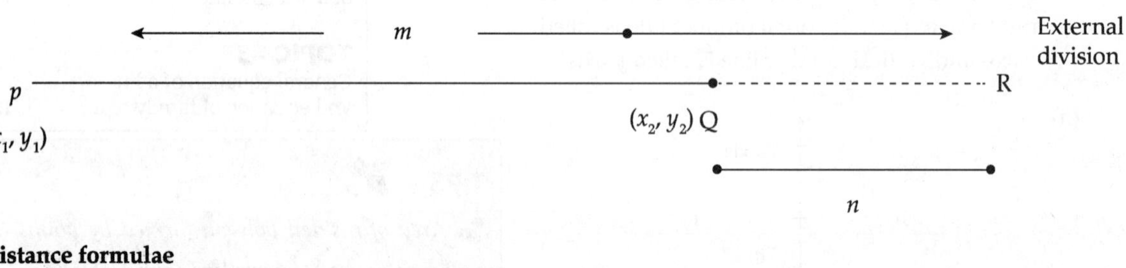

➤ **Distance formulae**

- Distance between two points $P(x_1, y_1)$ and $Q(x_2, y_2)$ is $\left|\sqrt{(x_2 - x_1)^2 + (y_2 - y_1)^2}\right|$ or $\left|\sqrt{(x_1 - x_2)^2 + (y_1 - y_2)^2}\right|$.
- If the points are $P(r_1, \theta_1)$ and $Q(r_2, \theta_2)$, then distance between them is

$$\left|\sqrt{r_1^2 + r_2^2 - 2r_1r_2 \cos(\theta_1 - \theta_2)}\right|.$$

- Distance of a point $P(x_1, y_1)$ from origin is $\sqrt{x_1^2 + y_1^2}$.

➤ **Area Formulae**

- Area of ΔABC with vertices $A(x_1, y_1)$, $B(x_2, y_2)$ and $C(x_3, y_3)$ is given by

$$\Delta = \frac{1}{2}\begin{vmatrix} x_1 & y_1 & 1 \\ x_2 & y_2 & 1 \\ x_3 & y_3 & 1 \end{vmatrix}$$

$$= \frac{1}{2}\left|x_1(y_2 - y_3) + x_2(y_3 - y_1) + x_3(y_1 - y_2)\right|$$

- If $\Delta = 0$, then the points A, B, C are collinear (i.e., they lie in a same straight line).

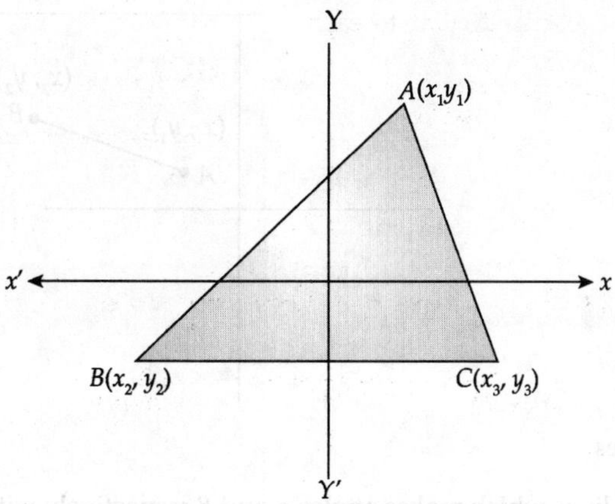

- Area of quadrilateral $ABCD$ with vertices $A(x_1,y_1)$, $B(x_2,y_2)$, $C(x_3,y_3)$ and $D(x_4,y_4)$ is

$$=\frac{1}{2}\begin{vmatrix} x_1-x_3 & x_2-x_4 \\ y_1-y_3 & y_2-y_4 \end{vmatrix}$$

$$=\frac{1}{2}|(x_1-x_3)(y_2-y_4)-(x_2-x_4)(y_1-y_3)|$$

- Area of a trapezium formed by joining the vertices $P(x_1,y_1)$, $Q(x_2,y_2)$, $R(x_3,y_3)$ and $S(x_4,y_4)$ is

$$\left|\frac{1}{2}[(y_1+y_2)(x_1-x_2)+(y_3+y_1)(x_3-x_1)+(y_2+y_3)(x_3-x_2)]\right|$$

➤ **Equation of the locus of a point**

- The equation of the locus of a point is the relation which is satisfied by the co-ordinates of every point on the locus of the point.
- The slope of a line '*l*' is the tangent of the angle made by the line in the anti-clockwise direction with the positive *x*-axis.

  i.e., slope, $m=\tan\theta$,

  where '*m*' represents slope and 'θ' is the angle made by the line with positive *x*-axis.

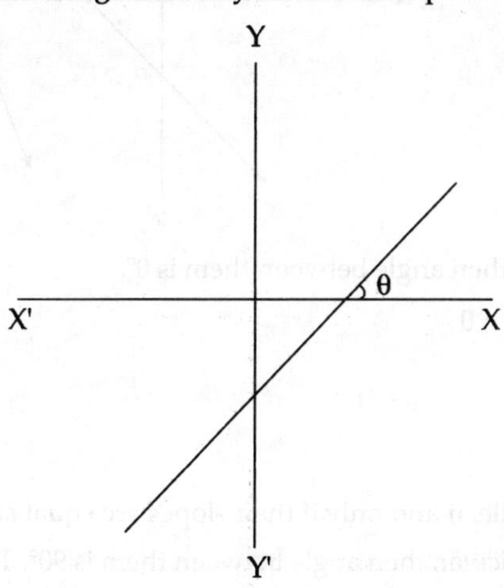

➤ **Slope of a line joining two points**

- The slope '*m*' of a line segment AB joining the points $A(x_1,y_1)$ and $B(x_2,y_2)$, and making angle 'θ' with positive *x*-axis, is given by

$$m=\tan\theta=\frac{y_2-y_1}{x_2-x_1}=\frac{y_1-y_2}{x_1-x_2}.$$

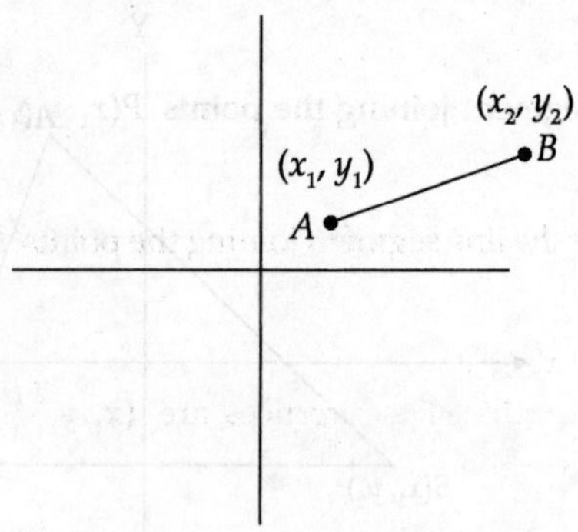

➤ Angle between two lines

- Let l_1 and l_2 be two lines which makes angles α and β respectively with positive x-axis. Then, their slopes are $m_1 = \tan\alpha$ and $m_2 = \tan\beta$.
- Let 'θ' be the angle between l_1 and l_2, then

$$\theta = \tan^{-1}\left|\frac{m_2 - m_1}{1 + m_1m_2}\right|$$

and $\theta' = \pi - \tan^{-1}\left|\frac{m_2 - m_1}{1 + m_1m_2}\right|$

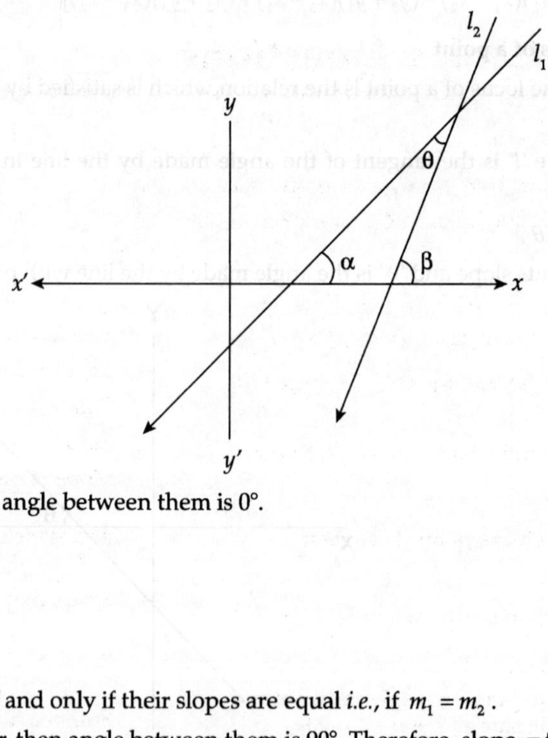

- If two lines are parallel, then angle between them is 0°.

$\therefore$ Slope $= \tan\theta = \tan 0° = 0$

$$\Rightarrow \frac{m_2 - m_1}{1 + m_1m_2} = 0$$

$$\Rightarrow m_1 = m_2$$

Thus, two lines are parallel if and only if their slopes are equal *i.e.*, if $m_1 = m_2$.

- If two lines are perpendicular, then angle between them is 90°. Therefore, slope $= \tan 90° = \infty$

$$\Rightarrow \frac{m_2 - m_1}{1 + m_1m_2} = \infty$$

$$\Rightarrow 1 + m_1m_2 = 0$$

$$\Rightarrow m_1m_2 = -1$$

Thus, two lines are perpendicular, if and only if their slopes m_1 and m_2 satisfy $m_1m_2 = -1$ or $m_1 = -\frac{1}{m_2}$.

➤ Collinearity of three points

- Three points A,B,C is XY-plane are collinear *i.e.*, they lie on the same line if and only if slope of AB = slope of BC.

➤ **Extra Information**

- If a point R trisect the line segment joining the points $P(x_1, y_1)$ and $Q(x_2, y_2)$, then it will divide PQ in the ratio 2 :1 or 1: 2.
- If a point R is the mid-point of the line segment joining the points $P(x_1, y_1)$ and $Q(x_2, y_2)$, then the co-ordinates of R are $\left(\frac{x_1+x_2}{2}, \frac{y_1+y_2}{2}\right)$.
- If G is the centroid of a triangle whose vertices are (x_1, y_1), (x_2, y_2) and (x_3, y_3), then co-ordinates of $G = \left(\frac{x_1+x_2+x_3}{3}, \frac{y_1+y_2+y_3}{3}\right)$.
- The centroid divides each median of the triangle in the ratio 2 :1.
- If the origin $O(0,0)$ is shifted to another point (α, β), then the co-ordinates of point $P(x, y)$ are changed to $P'(x-\alpha, y-\beta)$.
- The angle 'θ', which a line makes with positive direction of x-axis, is called inclination angle of the line.
- The slope of y-axis (or any line parallel to it) is, $m = \tan 90° = \infty$, which is not defined.
- Let 'θ' be the angle between two lines. Then
  - **(i)** If tan θ is positive, then θ will be an acute angle.
  - **(ii)** If tan θ is negative, then θ will be an obtuse angle.

Multiple Choice Questions **(1 mark each)**

[A] Objective Type Questions

Q. 1. The equation of the line passing through the point (1, 2) and perpendicular to the line $x + y + 1 = 0$ is

(A) $y - x + 1 = 0$ **(B) $y - x - 1 = 0$**

(C) $y - x + 2 = 0$ **(D) $y - x - 2 = 0$**

[NCERT Exemplar Q. 25, Page 180]

Ans. Correct option : (B)

Eq. of any line perpendicular to the given line $x + y + 1 = 0$ is $x - y + k = 0$ ...(i)

If eq (i) passes through the point (1, 2), then

$1 - 2 + k = 0 \Rightarrow k = 1$

Putting the value of k in eq. (i),. we get

$x - y + 1 = 0 \Rightarrow y - x - 1 = 0$

Q. 2. One vertex of the equilateral triangle with centroid at the origin and one side as $x + y - 2 = 0$ is

(A) (–1, –1) **(B) (2, 2)**

(C) (–2, –2) **(D) (2, –2)**

[NCERT Exemplar Q. 41, Page 183]

Ans. Correct option : (C)

Let ABC be an equilateral triangle with vertex (x_1, y_1).

$AD \perp BC$ and let (a, b) be the co-ordinates of D

Given that the centroid G lies at the origin *i.e.* (0, 0).

Since, the centroid of a triangle, divides the median in the ratio 1 : 2

So, $0 = \frac{1 \times x_1 + 2 \times a}{1+2}$

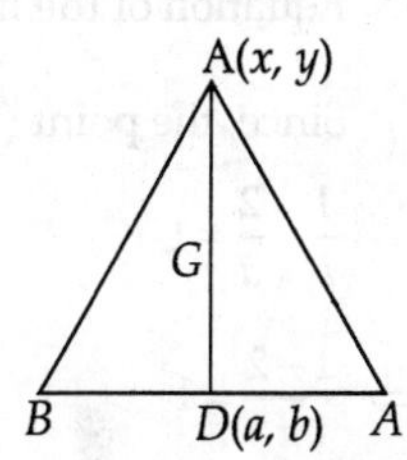

$\Rightarrow x_1 + 2a = 0$ ...(i)

and $0 = \frac{1 \times y_1 + 2 \times b}{1+b}$ ...(ii)

$y_1 + 2b = 0$ ...(i)

Eq. of BC is given by $x + y - 2 = 0$ ...(iii)

Point $D(a, b)$ lies on the line $x + y - 2 = 0$

So, $a + b - 2 = 0$ ...(iv)

Slope of eq.(iii) is = – 1

and slope of $AG = \frac{y_1 - 0}{x_1 - 0} = \frac{y_1}{x_1}$

Since, they are perpendicular to each other

$\therefore -1 \times \frac{y_1}{x_1} = -1 \Rightarrow y_1 = x_1$

From eq.(i) and (ii), we get

$x_1 + 2a = 0 \Rightarrow 2a = -x_1$

$y_1 + 2b = 0 \Rightarrow 2b = -y_1$

$\therefore a = b$

From eq.(iv) we get

$a + b - 2 = 0$

$\Rightarrow a + a - 2 = 0$

$\Rightarrow 2a - 2 = 0$

$\Rightarrow a = 1$ and $b = 1$ $[\because a = b]$

$\therefore x_1 = -2 \times 1 = -2$

and $y_1 = -2 \times 1 = -2$

[B] True/False

Q. 1. If the vertices of a triangle have integral coordinates, then the triangle cannot be equilateral. [NCERT Exemplar Q. 48, Page 183]

Q. 2. The points A (–2, 1), B (0, 5) and C (–1, 2) are collinear. [NCERT Exemplar Q. 49, Page 183]

Q. 3. The lines $ax + 2y + 1 = 0$, $bx + 3y + 1 = 0$ and $cx + 4y + 1 = 0$ are concurrent, if a, b and c are in GP. [NCERT Exemplar Q. 55, Page 184]

Q. 4. Line joining the points (3, –4) and (–2, 6) is perpendicular to the line joining the points (–3, 6) and (9, –18). [NCERT Exemplar Q. 56, Page 184]

Answer:
1. True
2. False
3. False
4. False

[C] Fill in the blanks of the following

Q. 1. If a, b and c are in AP, then the straight lines $ax + by + c = 0$ will always pass through .... [NCERT Exemplar Q. 48, Page 183]

Ans. (1, – 2)

Short Answer Type Questions (2 marks each)

Q. 1. Find the equation of the straight line which passes through the point (1, – 2) and cuts off equal intercepts from axes. [NCERT Exemplar, Q. 1, Page 178]

Sol. Let the intercepts along the X and Y-axes are a and a respectively.

$\therefore$ Equation of the line is $\frac{x}{a}+\frac{y}{a}=1$ ...(i)

Since, the point (1, –2) lies on the line,

$\therefore \quad \frac{1}{a}-\frac{2}{a}=1$

$\Rightarrow \frac{1-2}{a}=1$

$\Rightarrow a = -1$

On putting $a = -1$ in Eq. (i)

$\frac{x}{-1}+\frac{y}{-1}=$

$x + y = -1 \Rightarrow x + y + 1 = 0$ required equation of line.

Q. 2. Find the equation of the line passing through the point (5, 2) and perpendicular to the line joining the points (2, 3) and (3, –1). [NCERT Exemplar, Q. 2, Page 178]

Sol. Consider the given points $A(5, 2)$, $B(2, 3)$ and $C(3, -1)$.

Slope of the line passing through the points B and C, $m=\frac{-1-3}{3-2}=-4$

So, the slope of required line is $\frac{1}{4}$.

Since, the equation of a line passing the point $A(5, 2)$ and slope $\frac{1}{4}$ is $y-2=\frac{1}{4}(x-5)$

$\Rightarrow 4y - 8 = x - 5$

$\Rightarrow x - 4y + 3 = 0.$

Q. 3. If the sum of the distance of a moving point in a plane from the axes is 1, then find the locus of the point. [NCERT Exemplar, Q. 19, Page 179]

Sol. Let the co-ordinates of moving point B be (x, y).

Given that, the sum of distances of this point in a plane from the axes is 1.

$\therefore \quad |x|+|y|=1$

$\Rightarrow \pm x \pm y=1$

$\Rightarrow x+y=1$

$\Rightarrow -x-y=1$

$\Rightarrow -x+y=1$

$\Rightarrow x-y=1$

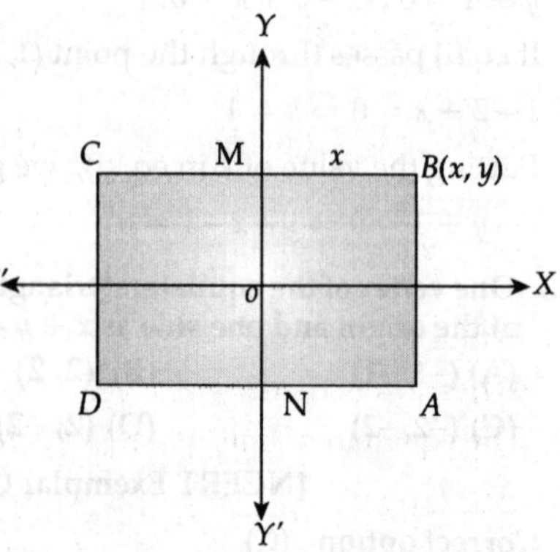

So, these equation give us locus of the point which is a square.

Long Answer Type Questions-I

(4 marks each)

Q. 1. Find the angle between the lines $y = (2-\sqrt{3})(x+5)$ and $y = (2+\sqrt{3})(x-7)$.

[NCERT Exemplar Q. 3, Page 178]

Sol. Given lines, $y = (2-\sqrt{3})(x+5)$ ...(i)

Slope of the line, $m_1 = (2-\sqrt{3})$

and $y = (2+\sqrt{3})(x-7)$ ...(ii)

Slope of the line, $m_2 = (2+\sqrt{3})$

Let θ be the angle between lines (i) and (ii), then

$$\tan\theta = \left|\frac{m_1 - m_2}{1+m_1m_2}\right|$$

$$\Rightarrow \tan\theta = \left|\frac{(2-\sqrt{3})-(2+\sqrt{3})}{1+(2-\sqrt{3})(2+\sqrt{3})}\right| \Rightarrow \tan\theta = \left|\frac{-2\sqrt{3}}{1+4-3}\right|$$

$\Rightarrow \tan\theta = \sqrt{3}$

$\Rightarrow \tan\theta = \tan \pi/3$

$\therefore \theta = \pi/3 = 60°$

For obtuse angle $= \pi - \pi/3 = 2\pi/3 = 120°$

Hence, the angle between the lines are 60° or 120°.

Q. 2. Find the equation of the lines which passes through the point (3, 4) and cuts off intercepts from the co-ordinates axes such that their sum is 14. **[NCERT Exemplar Q. 4, Page 178]**

Sol. Let the intercept along the axes be a and b.

Given, $a + b = 14 \Rightarrow b = 14 - a$

Now, the equation of line is $\frac{x}{a}+\frac{y}{b}=1$.

$$\Rightarrow \frac{x}{a}+\frac{y}{14-a}=1$$

Since, the point (3, 4) lies on the line.

$$\therefore \frac{3}{a}+\frac{4}{14-a}=1$$

$$\Rightarrow \frac{42-3a+4a}{a(14-a)}=1 \Rightarrow 42+a=14a-a^2$$

$\Rightarrow a^2 - 13a + 42 = 0 \Rightarrow a^2 - 7a - 6a + 42 = 0$

$\Rightarrow a(a-7) - 6(a-7) = 0 \Rightarrow (a-7)(a-6) = 0$

$\Rightarrow a - 7 = 0$ or $a - 6 = 0$

$\therefore a = 7$, then $a = 6$

When $a = 7$, then $b = 7$

When $a = 6$, then $b = 8$

$\therefore$ The equation of line, when $a = 7$ and $b = 7$ is

$$\frac{x}{7}+\frac{y}{7}=1 \Rightarrow x+y=7$$

So, the equation of line, when $a = 6$ and $b = 8$ is

$$\frac{x}{6}+\frac{y}{8}=1 \Rightarrow 4x+3y=24.$$

Q. 3. Find the equation of lines passing through (1, 2) and making angle 30° with Y – axis.

[NCERT Exemplar Q. 7, Page 178]

Sol. Given that, angle with Y – axis = 30°

and angle with X – axis = 60°

$\therefore$ Slope of the line, $m = \tan 60° = \sqrt{3}$

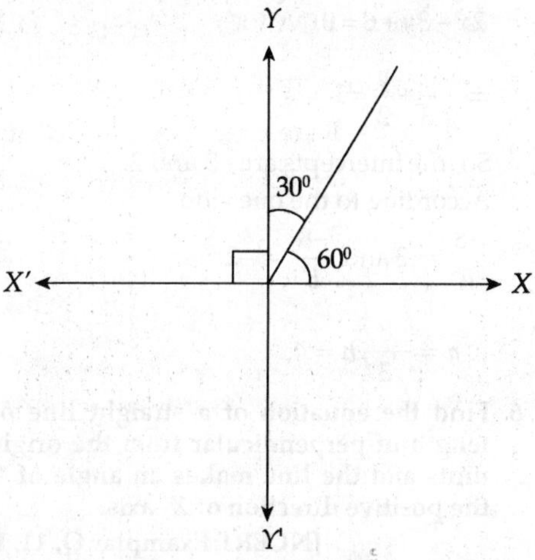

So, the equation of a line passing through (1, 2) and having slope $\sqrt{3}$, is

$y - 2 = \sqrt{3}(x-1)$

$\Rightarrow y - 2 = \sqrt{3}x - \sqrt{3}$

$\Rightarrow y - \sqrt{3}x - 2 + \sqrt{3} = 0.$

Q. 4. Find the equation of the line passing through the point of intersection of $2x + y = 5$ and $x + 3y + 8 = 0$ and parallel to the line $3x + 4y = 7$.

[NCERT Exemplar Q. 8, Page 178]

Sol. Given equation of lines $2x+y=5$ ...(i)

and $x+3y=-8$ ...(ii)

From Eq. (i) $y=5-2x$

Now, put the value of y in Eq. (ii), we get

$x+3(5-2x)=-8$

$\Rightarrow x+15-6x=-8$

$$\Rightarrow -5x=-23 \Rightarrow x=\frac{23}{5}$$

Now, $x = \frac{23}{5}$ put in Eq. (i), we get

$$y=5-\frac{46}{5}=\frac{25-46}{5}=\frac{-21}{5}$$

Since, the required line is parallel to the line $3x+4y=7$. So, slope of the line is $m = \frac{-3}{4}$.

Now equation of line passing $\left(\frac{23}{5},\frac{-21}{5}\right)$ with slope $\frac{-3}{4}$ is $y+\frac{21}{5}=\frac{-3}{4}\left(x-\frac{23}{5}\right)$ required line

$3x + 4y + 3 = 0.$

Q. 5. For what values of a and b the intercepts cut off on the coordinate axes by the line $ax + by + 8 = 0$ are equal in length but opposite in signs to those cut off by line $2x - 3y + 6 = 0$ on the axes?

[NCERT Exemplar Q. 9, Page 178]

Sol. Given equation of line $ax + by + 8 = 0$

$\Rightarrow \dfrac{x}{\frac{-8}{a}}+\dfrac{y}{\frac{-8}{b}}=1$ (in intercept form)

So, the intercepts are $\dfrac{-8}{a}$ and $\dfrac{-8}{b}$.

and another given equation of line is $2x-3y+6=0$.

$\Rightarrow \dfrac{x}{-3}+\dfrac{y}{2}=1$

So, the intercepts are –3 and 2.

According to the question,

$\dfrac{-8}{a} = 3$ and $\dfrac{-8}{b} = -2$.

$\therefore a = -\dfrac{8}{3}, b = 4.$

Q. 6. Find the equation of a straight line on which length of perpendicular from the origin is four units and the line makes an angle of 120° with the positive direction of X–axis.

[NCERT Examplar Q. 11, Page 178]

Sol. Given that, $OC = p = 4$ units

$\angle BAX = 120°$

Let $\angle POA = \alpha, \angle OPA = 90°$

$\because \angle BAX = \angle POA + \angle OPA$ [Exterior Angle Property]

$\Rightarrow 120° = \alpha + 90°$

$= 30°$

Now, the equation of required line is

$x \cos 30° + y \sin 30° = (x \cos\alpha + y \sin \alpha) = p$

$\Rightarrow x.\dfrac{\sqrt{3}}{2}+y.\dfrac{1}{2}=4$

$\Rightarrow \sqrt{3}x+y=8$

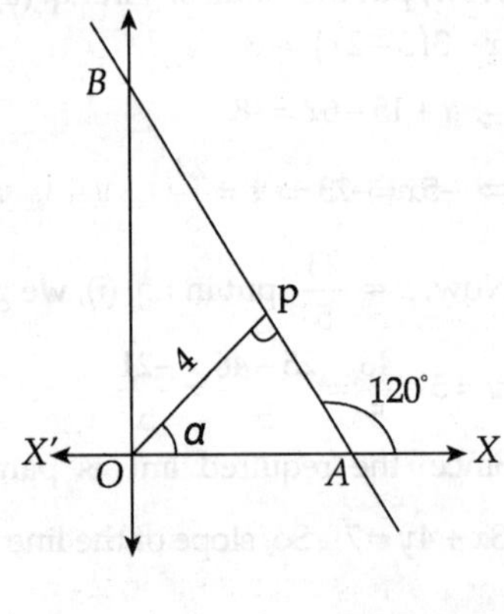

Q. 7. P_1 and P_2 are points on either of the two lines $y-\sqrt{3}|x|=2$ at a distance of 5 units from their point of intersection. Find the co-ordinates of the foot of perpendiculars drawn from P_1, P_2 on the bisector of the angle between the gives lines.

[NCERT Exemplar Q. 20, Page 180]

Sol. Given equation of lines are $y-\sqrt{3}x=2$ when $x>0$

and $y+\sqrt{3}x=2$ when $x<0$

$\because y=\sqrt{3}x+2$ ...(i)

and $y=-\sqrt{3}x+2$ ...(ii)

$\Rightarrow -\sqrt{3}x+2=-\sqrt{3}x+2$

$\Rightarrow 2\sqrt{3}x=0 \Rightarrow x=0$

On putting $x = 0$ in Eq. (i), we get

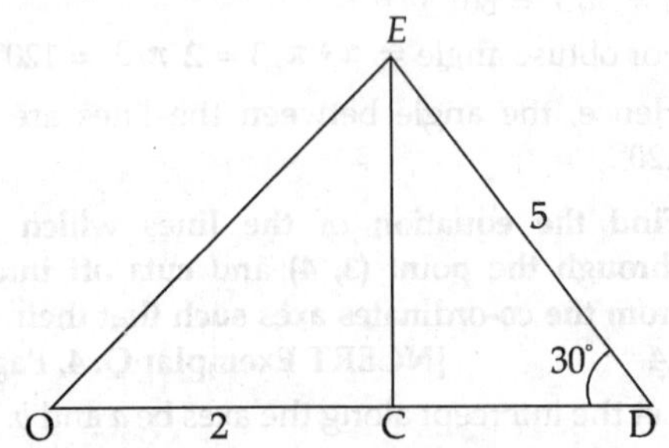

So, the point of intersection of the line (i) and (ii) is (0, 2).

Here, $OC = 2$

$\dfrac{CD}{DE}=\cos 30°$

$\therefore CD = 5\cos 30°$

$=5\cdot\dfrac{\sqrt{3}}{2}$

$\Rightarrow OD = OC + CD = 2+5\dfrac{\sqrt{3}}{2}$

So, the co-ordinates of the foot of perpendiculars are $\left(0, 2+\dfrac{5\sqrt{3}}{2}\right)$.

Long Answer Type Questions-II (6 marks each)

Q. 1. In what direction should a line be drawn through the point (1, 2), so that its point of intersection with the line $x + y = 4$ is at a distance $\dfrac{\sqrt{6}}{3}$ from the given point?

[NCERT Exemplar Q. 15, Page 179]

Sol. Let slope of the line be m. line passes through the point $A(1, 2)$.

$\therefore$ Equation of line is $y - 2 = m(x - 1)$

$mx - y + 2 - m = 0$

and $x + y - 4 = 0$ ...(i)

$$\frac{x}{(4-2+m)}=\frac{y}{2-m+4m}=\frac{1}{1+m}$$

(By Cross Multiplication Method)

$$\Rightarrow \frac{x}{2+m}=\frac{y}{3m+2}=\frac{1}{1+m}$$

$$\Rightarrow x=\frac{2+m}{1+m}$$

$$y=\frac{3m+2}{1+m}$$

So, the point of intersection is $B\left(\frac{m+2}{m+1},\frac{3m+2}{m+1}\right)$.

Now, $AB^2=\left(\frac{m+2}{m+1}-1\right)^2+\left(\frac{3m+2}{m+1}-2\right)^2$

(By Distance Formula)

$\because \; AB=\frac{\sqrt{6}}{3}$ [Given]

$$\therefore \left(\frac{m+2-m-1}{m+1}\right)^2+\left(\frac{3m+2-2m-2}{m+1}\right)^2=\frac{6}{9}$$

$$\Rightarrow \left(\frac{1}{m+1}\right)^2+\left(\frac{m}{m+1}\right)^2=\frac{6}{9}$$

$$\Rightarrow \frac{1+m^2}{(1+m)^2}=\frac{6}{9}$$

$$\Rightarrow \frac{1+m^2}{1+m^2+2m}=\frac{6}{9}$$

$$\Rightarrow 9+9m^2=6+6m^2+12m$$

$$\Rightarrow 3m^2-12m+3=0$$

$$\Rightarrow m^2-4m+1=0$$

$$m=\frac{4\pm\sqrt{16-4}}{2}$$

$$\therefore \quad =2\pm\sqrt{3}$$

$$=2+\sqrt{3} \text{ or } 2-\sqrt{3}$$

$$\therefore \quad \theta=75^\circ \text{ or } 15^\circ$$

TOPIC-2
Various forms of equations of a straight line

Quick Review

- **Horizontal and vertical lines**
  - The equation of a horizontal line (*i.e.*, any line parallel to *x*-axis) is $y = a$ or $y = -a$. If the line lies above *x*-axis, then '*a*' is positive and if the line lie below the *x*-axis, then '*a*' is negative.
  - The equation of a vertical line (*i.e.*, any line parallel to *y*-axis) is $x = b$ or $x = -b$. If line lie to the left of *y*-axis, then '*b*' is negative and if the line lie to the right of *y*-axis, then '*b*' is positive.
- **Slope intercept form**
  - If a line '*L*' has slope '*m*' and make an intercept '*c*' on *y*-axis, then the equation of the line is $y = mx + c$.
  - If the line passes through the origin, then its equation becomes $y = mx$.
- **Point-slope form**
  - The equation of the straight line having slope '*m*' and passing through the point $P_0(x_0, y_0)$ is $y-y_0=m(x-x_0)$
- **Two points form**
  - The equation of a line passing through the points (x_1, y_1) and (x_2, y_2) is given by

    $$y-y_1=\frac{y_2-y_1}{x_2-x_1}(x-x_1)$$
- **Normal (perpendicular) form**
  - The equation of the straight line upon which the length of perpendicular from the origins is *p* and this perpendicular makes an angle 'α' with the positive direction of *x*-axis is $x\cos\alpha+y\sin\alpha=p$
  - Slope of the line $=-\frac{1}{\tan\alpha}$

    $$=-\frac{\cos\alpha}{\sin\alpha}$$
- **Intercept form**
  - The equation of a line which cuts-off intercepts *a* and *b* on the *x*-axis and *y*-axis respectively, is given by

    $$\frac{x}{a}+\frac{y}{b}=1$$

➤ **Note :**

- Equation of x-axis is $y = 0$ and equation of y-axis is $x = 0$.
- If a line 'L' has slope 'm' and x-intercept 'd', then the equation of the line is $y = m(x - d)$.

Multiple Choice Questions (1 mark each)

[A] Objective Type Questions

Q. 1. A line cutting off intercept –3 from the Y-axis and the tangent at angle to the X-axis is $\frac{3}{5}$, its equation is

(A) $5y - 3x + 15 = 0$ **(B) $3y - 5x + 15 = 0$**

(C) $5y - 3x - 15 = 0$ **(D) None of the above**

[NCERT Exemplar Q. 22, Page 180]

Ans. Correct option : (A)

Given, $\tan\theta = \frac{3}{5}$ = slope of line $m = \frac{3}{5}$

$\therefore$ Equation of the line is

$y - y_1 = m(x - x_1)$

$\Rightarrow y + 3 = \frac{3}{5}(x - 0)$

$\Rightarrow 5y - 3x + 15 = 0$

Q. 2. Slope of a line which cuts off intercepts of equal lengths on the axes is

(A) –1 **(B) 0**

(C) 2 **(D) $\sqrt{3}$**

[NCERT Exemplar Q. 23, Page 180]

Ans. Correct option : (A)

Since, intercept form of a line is $\frac{x}{a} + \frac{y}{b} = 1$

$\therefore \frac{x}{a} + \frac{y}{a} = 1$ $(\because a = b)$

$\Rightarrow y = -x + a$

$\therefore$ Slope $= -1$

Q. 3. The equation of straight line passing through the point (3, 2) and perpendicular to the line $y = x$ is

(A) $x - y = 5$ **(B) $x + y = 5$**

(C) $x + y = 1$ **(D) $x - y = 1$**

[NCERT Exemplar Q. 24, Page 180]

Ans. Correct option : (B)

Equation of line 'l' is given by $y - y_1 = m(x - x_1)$

Since 'l' passes through the point $P(2, 3)$

$\therefore y - 2 = m(x - 3)$

$\Rightarrow y = mx + 2 - 3m$ ...(i)

Since it is given that the lines $y = x$ and 'l' are perpendicular to each other,

$\therefore m \times 1 = -1$ $[\because m_1 \times m_2 = -1]$

$\Rightarrow m = -1$

Put $m = -1$ in eq. (i), we get

$y = -x + 2 - 3(-1)$

$\Rightarrow y = -x + 5 \Rightarrow y + x = 5.$

Q. 4. The tangent of angle between the lines whose intercepts on the axes are a, $-b$ and b, $-a$ respectively, is

(A) $\frac{a^2 - b^2}{ab}$ **(B) $\frac{b^2 - a^2}{2}$**

(C) $\frac{b^2 - a^2}{2ab}$ **(D) None of these**

[NCERT Exemplar Q. 26, Page 180]

Ans. Correct option : (C)

First eq. of line having intercepts on the axes $a, -b$ is

$\frac{x}{a} - \frac{y}{b} = 1 \Rightarrow bx - ay = ab$ ...(i)

Second eq. of line having intercepts on the axes b, $-a$ is $\frac{x}{b} - \frac{y}{a} = 1 \Rightarrow bx - ay = ab$ ...(ii)

Slope of eq (i) $m_1 = \frac{b}{a}$

Slope of eq (ii) $m_2 = \frac{a}{b}$

$$\therefore \tan\theta = \left|\frac{m_1 - m_2}{1 + m_1 m_2}\right| = \frac{\frac{b}{a} - \frac{a}{b}}{1 + \frac{b}{a}\cdot\frac{a}{b}} = \frac{b^2 - a^2}{2ab}$$

Q. 5. If the line $\frac{x}{a} + \frac{y}{b} = 1$ passes through the points (2, – 3) and (4, – 5), then (a, b) is

(A) (1, 1) **(B) (– 1, 1)**

(C) (1 – 1) **(D) (– 1, – 1)**

[NCERT Exemplar Q. 27, Page 181]

Ans. Correct option : (D)

Eqn. of line passing through the points (2, – 3) and (4, – 5) is

$$\therefore \quad y + 3 = \frac{-5 + 3}{4 - 2}(x - 2)$$

$$\Rightarrow \quad y + 3 = \frac{-2}{2}(x - 2)$$

$$\Rightarrow \quad y + 3 = -(x - 2)$$

$$\Rightarrow \quad x + y = -1$$

$$\Rightarrow \quad \frac{x}{-1} + \frac{y}{-1} = 1 \quad \text{(intercept form)}$$

$$\therefore \quad a = -1, b = -1$$

Q. 6. The equation of the lines which pass through the point $(3, -2)$ and are inclined at 60° to the line $\sqrt{3}x + y = 1$ is

(A) $y+2=0, \sqrt{3}x-y+2+3\sqrt{3}=0$

(B) $x-2=0, \sqrt{3}x-y+2+3\sqrt{3}=0$

(C) $\sqrt{3}x-y-2-3\sqrt{3}=0$

(D) None of the above

[NCERT Exemplar Q. 29, Page 181]

Ans. Correct option : (A)

Eq. of line is given by

$\sqrt{3}\ x+y+1=0 \Rightarrow y=-\sqrt{3}\ x-1$

$\therefore$ slope of this line, $m_1 = -\sqrt{3}$

Let m_2 be the slope of the required line

$\therefore \tan\theta = \left|\dfrac{m_1-m_2}{1+m_1m_2}\right|$

$\Rightarrow \tan 60^\circ = \left|\dfrac{-\sqrt{3}-m_2}{1+(-\sqrt{3})m_2}\right| = \pm\left(\dfrac{-\sqrt{3}-m_2}{1-\sqrt{3}m_2}\right)$

$\Rightarrow \sqrt{3} = \dfrac{-\sqrt{3}-m_2}{1-\sqrt{3}m_2}$ (taking + ve sign)

$\Rightarrow \sqrt{3} - 3m_2 = -\sqrt{3} - m_2$

$\Rightarrow m_2 = \sqrt{3}$

and $\sqrt{3} = \dfrac{\sqrt{3}+m}{1-\sqrt{3}m_2}$ (Taking – ve sign)

$\Rightarrow \sqrt{3} - 3m_2 = \sqrt{3} + m_2$

$\Rightarrow m_2 = 0$

$\therefore$ Eq. of the line passing through (3, –2) with slope $\sqrt{3}$ is $y+2=\sqrt{3}\ (x-3)$

$\Rightarrow \sqrt{3}\,x-y-2-3\sqrt{3}=0$

and the eq. of the line passing through (3, –2) with slope 0 is

$y+2=0\,(x-3)$

$\Rightarrow y+2=0$

Q. 7. The co-ordinates of the foot of perpendiculars from the point (2, 3) on the line $y = 3x + 4$ is given by

(A) $\left(\dfrac{37}{10}, \dfrac{-1}{10}\right)$ (B) $\left(\dfrac{-1}{10}, \dfrac{37}{10}\right)$

(C) $\left(\dfrac{10}{37}, -10\right)$ (D) $\left(\dfrac{2}{3}, -\dfrac{1}{3}\right)$

[NCERT Exemplar Q. 32, Page 182]

Ans. Correct option : (B)

Given eq. is $y = 3x + 4 \Rightarrow 3x - y + 4 = 0$ ...(i)

$\therefore$ Slope = 3

Eq. of any line passing through the point (2, 3) is

$y-3=m(x-2)$ ...(ii)

If eq. (i) is perpendicular to eq. (ii), we get

$m\times 3=-1$ $[\because m_1\times m_2=-1]$

$\Rightarrow m = -\dfrac{1}{3}$

Putting the value of m in eq (ii), we get

$y-3=-\dfrac{1}{3}(x-2)$

$\Rightarrow x+3y=11$ ...(iii)

Solving eqs. (i) and (iii), we get

$y=3x+4$ ...(iv)

Putting the value of y in eq. (iii), we get

$x+3(3x+4)=11$

$\Rightarrow x=-\dfrac{1}{10}$

From eq. (iv), we get $y=3\left(-\dfrac{1}{10}\right)+4 \Rightarrow y=\dfrac{37}{10}$

So, required coordinates are $\left(\dfrac{-1}{10}, \dfrac{37}{10}\right)$.

Q. 8. If the co-ordinates of the middle point of the portion of a line intercepted between the co-ordinate axes is (3 , 2), then the equation of the line will be

(A) $2x + 3y = 12$ (B) $3x + 2y = 12$

(C) $4x - 3y = 6$ (D) $5x - 2y = 10$

[NCERT Exemplar Q. 33, Page 182]

Ans. Correct option : (A)

Let the given line meets the axes at $A\,(a, 0)$ and $B(0, b)$

Given that C(3, 2) is the mid point of AB.

$\therefore 3=\dfrac{a+0}{2} \Rightarrow a=6$ and $2=\dfrac{0+b}{2} \Rightarrow b=4$

Intercept form of the line AB

$\dfrac{x}{a}+\dfrac{y}{b}=1$

$\Rightarrow \dfrac{x}{6}+\dfrac{y}{4}=1$

$\Rightarrow 2x+3y=12$

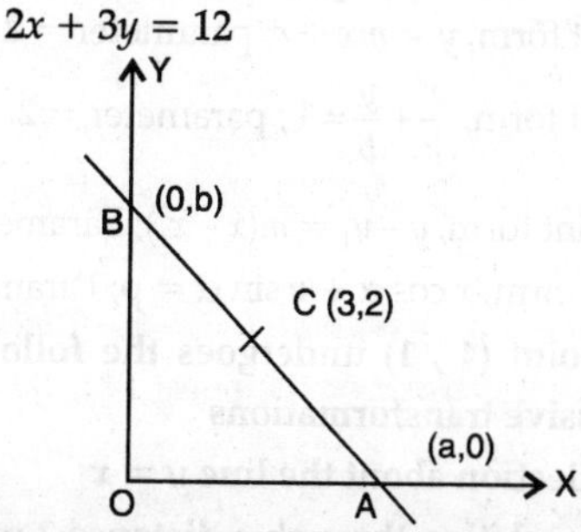

Q. 9. Equation of the line passing through (1 , 2) and parallel to the line $y = 3x - 1$ is

(A) $y + 2 = x + 1$ (B) $(y + 2) = 3(x + 1)$

(C) $y - 2 = 3(x - 1)$ (D) $(y - 2) = (x - 1)$

[NCERT Exemplar Q. 34, Page 182]

Ans. Correct option : (C)

Given eq. is $y = 3x - 1$

$\therefore$ slope = 3

Slope of the line passing through the given point (1, 2) and parallel to the given line having slope 3.

So, the eq. the required line is

$y - 2 = 3(x - 1)$

Q. 10. Equation of diagonals of the square formed by the lines $x = 0, y = 0, x = 1$ and $y = 1$ are

(A) $y = x, y + x = 1$ **(B) $y = x, x + y = 2$**

(C) $2y = x, y + x = \frac{1}{3}$ **(D) $y = 2x, y + 2x = 1$**

[NCERT Exemplar Q. 35, Page 182]

Ans. Correct option : (A)

Given eq. $x = 0, y = 0, x = 1$ and $y = 1$ form a square of side 1 unit.

From figure, we get that OABC is square having corners O(0, 0), A(1, 0), B(1, 1) and C(0, 1).

Eq. of diagonal AC ; $y - 0 = \frac{1-0}{0-1}(x-1)$

$\Rightarrow y + x = 1$

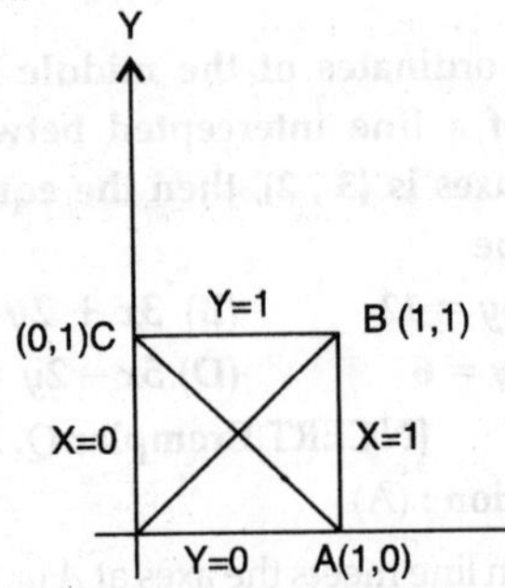

Eq. of diagonal OB is $y - 0 = \frac{1-0}{1-0}(x-0) \Rightarrow y = x$

Q. 11. For specifying a straight line, how many geometrical parameters should be known?

(A) 1 **(B) 2**

(C) 4 **(D) 3**

[NCERT Exemplar Q. 36, Page 182]

Ans. Correct option : (B)

Different form of eq. of straight line are slope intercept form, $y = mx + c$; parameter = 2

Intercept form, $\frac{x}{a} + \frac{y}{b} = 1$; parameter = 2

One-point form, $y - y_1 = m(x - x_1)$; Parameter = 2

Normal form, $x \cos \alpha + y \sin \alpha = p$; Parameter = 2

Q. 12. The point (4 , 1) undergoes the following two successive transformations

(i) Reflection about the line $y = x$

(ii) Translation through a distance 2 units along the positive X-axis.

Then, the final co-ordinates of the point are

(A) (4, 3) **(B) (3, 4)**

(C) (1, 4) **(D) $\left(\frac{7}{2}, \frac{7}{2}\right)$**

[NCERT Exemplar Q. 37, Page 182]

Ans. Correct option : (B)

Let the reflection of $A(4, 1$ in $y = x$ be $B(a, b)$ mid-point of AB.

$= \left(\frac{4+a}{2}, \frac{1+b}{2}\right)$ which lies on $y = x$

$\Rightarrow \frac{4+a}{2} = \frac{1+b}{2}$

$\Rightarrow 4 + a = 1 + b$

$\Rightarrow a - b = 3$ ...(i)

The slope of the line $y = x$ is 1 and

slope of $AB = \frac{b-1}{a-4}$

$\therefore 1\left(\frac{b-1}{a-4}\right) = -1$

$\Rightarrow b - 1 = -a + 4$

$\Rightarrow a + b = 5$ ...(ii)

Solving eq. (i) & (ii), we get

$a = 1$, and $b = 4$

$\therefore$ the point after translation (3, 4)

Q. 13. A line passes through (2, 2) and is perpendicular to the line $3x + y = 3$.

Its y-intercept is

(A) $\frac{1}{3}$ **(B) $\frac{2}{3}$**

(C) 1 **(D) $\frac{4}{3}$**

[NCERT Exemplar Q. 39, Page 182]

Ans. Correct option : (D)

Any line perpendicular to $3x + y = 3$

$x - 3y = \lambda$ (constant)

If it passes through the point (2, 2), then

$2 - 3(2) = \lambda$

$\Rightarrow \lambda = -4$

$\therefore$ Required equation is $x - 3y = -4$

$\Rightarrow y = \frac{1}{3}x + \frac{4}{3}$ $[\because y = m + c]$

So, the y-intercept is $\frac{4}{3}$.

[B] Fill in the blanks

Q. 1. The line which cuts off equal intercept from the axes and pass through the point (1, –2) is ....

[NCERT Exemplar Q. 43, Page 183]

Q. 2. Equation of the line through the point (3, 2) and making an angle of 45° with the line $x - 2y = 3$ are .... **[NCERT Exemplar Q. 44, Page 183]**

Q. 3. Locus of the mid-points of the portion of the line $x\sin\theta + y\cos\theta = p$ intercepted between the axes is .... **[NCERT Exemplar Q. 47, Page 183]**

Answer:

1. $x + y + 1 = 0$.

2. $3x - y - 7 = 0$ and $x + 3y - 9 = 0$.

1. $4x^2 y^2 = p^2(x^2 + y^2)$.

[C] State True or False for the following :

Q. 1. Equation of the line passing through the point ($a\cos^3\theta$, $a\sin^3\theta$) and perpendicular to the line $x\sec\theta + y\,\text{cosec}\,\theta = a$ is $x\cos\theta - y\sin\theta = a\sin 2\theta$. [NCERT Exemplar Q. 50, Page 183]

Q. 2. The straight line $5x + 4y = 0$ passes through the point of intersection of the straight lines $x + 2y - 10 = 0$ and $2x + y + 5 = 0$. [NCERT Exemplar Q. 51, Page 183]

Q. 3. The vertex of an equilateral triangle is (2, 3) and the equation of the opposite side is $x + y = 2$. [NCERT Exemplar Q. 52, Page 183]

Q. 4. The line $\frac{x}{a}+\frac{y}{b}=1$ moves in such a way that $\frac{1}{a^2}+\frac{1}{b^2}=\frac{1}{c^2}$, where c is a constant. The locus of the foot of the perpendicular from the origin on the given line is $x^2+y^2=c^2$. [NCERT Exemplar Q. 54, Page 184]

Answer:

1. False
2. True
3. True
4. True

[D] Match the following :

Q. 1. The value of λ, if the lines $(2x + 3y + 4) + \lambda(6x - y + 12) = 0$ are

	Column I	Column II
(i)	Parallel to Y-axis is	(a) $\lambda = -\frac{3}{4}$
(ii)	Perpendicular to $7x + y - 4 = 0$ is	(b) $\lambda = -\frac{1}{3}$
(iii)	Passes through (1, 2) is	(c) $\lambda = -\frac{17}{41}$
(iv)	Parallel to X-axis is	(d) $\lambda = 3$

[NCERT Exemplar Q. 58, Page 184-185]

Q. 2. The equation of the line through the intersection of the lines $2x - 3y = 0$ and $4x - 5y = 2$ and

	Column I	Column II
(i)	through the point (2, 1) is	(a) $2x - y = 4$
(ii)	perpendicular to the line $x + 2y + 1 = 0$	(b) $x + y - 5 = 0$
(iii)	parallel to the line $3x - 4y + 5 = 0$ is	(c) $x - y - 1 = 0$
(iv)	equally inclined to the axis is	(d) $3x - 4y - 1 = 0$

[NCERT Exemplar Q. 59, Page 185]

Answer:

1. (i) → (d)
   (ii) → (c)
   (iii) → (a)
   (iv) → (b)
2. (i) → (b)
   (ii) → (d)
   (iii) → (a)
   (iv) → (c)

Short Answer Type Questions (2 marks each)

Q. 1. A straight line moves so that the sum of the reciprocals of its intercepts made on axes is constant. Show that the line passes through a fixed point. [NCERT Examplar Q. 16, Page 179]

Sol. Since, the intercept form of a line is $\frac{x}{a}+\frac{y}{b}=1$.

Given that, $\frac{1}{a}+\frac{1}{b}$ = constant

$\because \quad \frac{1}{a}+\frac{1}{b}=\frac{1}{k}$ (where k is constant)

$\Rightarrow \quad \frac{k}{a}+\frac{k}{b}=1$

So, (k, k), lies on $\frac{x}{a}+\frac{y}{b}=1$.

Hence, the line passes through the fixed point.

Long Answer Type Questions-I (4 marks each)

Q. 1. Show that the tangent of an angle between the lines $\frac{x}{a}+\frac{y}{b}=1$ and $\frac{x}{a}-\frac{y}{b}=1$ is $\frac{ab}{a^2\ b^2}$ [NCERT Exemplar Q. 6, Page 178]

Sol. Given equation of lines are

$$\frac{x}{a}+\frac{y}{b}=1 \quad \text{...(i)}$$

$\therefore$ Slope, $m_1 = -\frac{b}{a}$

and $\frac{x}{a}-\frac{y}{b}=1$ ...(ii)

$\therefore$ Slope, $m_2 = \frac{b}{a}$

Let θ be the angle between the given lines, then

$$\tan\theta = \left|\frac{m_1 - m_2}{1+m_1 m_2}\right| \Rightarrow \tan\theta = \left|\frac{-\frac{b}{a}-\frac{b}{a}}{1+\left(\frac{-b}{a}\right)\left(\frac{b}{a}\right)}\right|$$

$$\Rightarrow \tan\theta = \left|\frac{-\frac{2b}{a}}{\frac{a^2-b^2}{a^2}}\right| \Rightarrow \tan\theta = \frac{2ab}{a^2-b^2}$$

Hence proved.

Q.2. Find the equation of the line which passes through the point (–4, 3) and the portion of the line intercepted between the axes is divided internally in the ratio 5 : 3 by this point.

[NCERT Exemplar Q. 17, Page 179]

Sol. Since, the line intersect *X* and *Y*-axes respectively at A(*x*, 0) and B(0, *y*) and passes through (–4, 3)

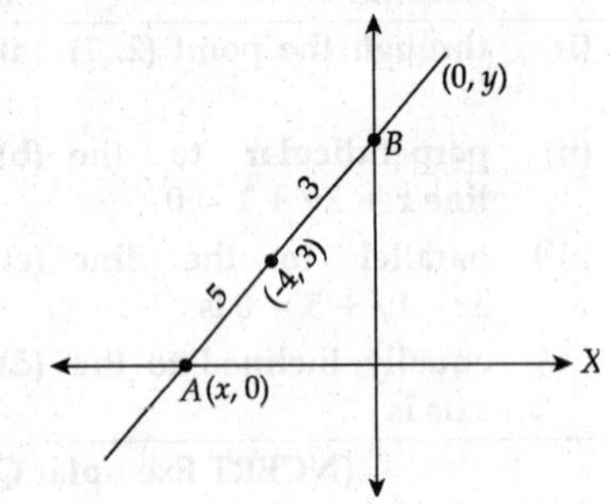

$$-4 = \frac{5\times 0+3x}{5+3} \quad \textbf{(by section formula)}$$

$$\Rightarrow -4 = \frac{3x}{8} \Rightarrow x = \frac{-32}{3}$$

$$\text{and } 3 = \frac{5.y+3.0}{5+3}$$

$$\Rightarrow 3 = \frac{5y}{8} \Rightarrow y = \frac{24}{5}$$

Since, the intercept on the *X* and *Y*-axes respectively are $\frac{-32}{3}$ and $\frac{24}{5}$

$\therefore$ Equation of required line is

$$\frac{x}{-\frac{32}{3}} + \frac{y}{\frac{24}{5}} = 1$$

$$\Rightarrow \frac{-3x}{32} + \frac{5y}{24} = 1$$

$$\Rightarrow -9x + 20y = 96$$

$$\Rightarrow 9x - 20y + 96 = 0.$$

Q. 3. If p is the length of perpendiculars from the origin on the line $\frac{x}{a}+\frac{y}{b}=1$ and a^2, p^2 and b^2 are in A.P, then show that $a^4+b^4=0$.

[NCERT Exemplar Q. 21, Page 180]

Sol. Given equation of line is,

$$\frac{x}{a} + \frac{y}{b} = \quad \text{...(i)}$$

Perpendicular length from the origin on the line (i) is given by p

$$\text{i.e., } p = \left|\frac{1}{\sqrt{\frac{1}{a^2}+\frac{1}{b^2}}}\right| = \left|\frac{ab}{\sqrt{a^2+b^2}}\right|$$

$$\therefore p^2 = \frac{a^2b^2}{a^2+b^2}$$

Given that, a^2, p^2 and b^2 are in A.P.

$$\therefore 2p^2 = a^2 + b^2$$

$$\Rightarrow \frac{2a^2b^2}{a^2+b^2} = a^2 + b^2$$

$$\Rightarrow 2a^2b^2 = \left(a^2+b^2\right)^2$$

$$\Rightarrow 2a^2b^2 = a^4 + b^4 + 2a^2b^2$$

$$\Rightarrow a^4 + b^4 = 0$$

Q. 4. Find the equation of the line parallel to y-axis and draw through the point of intersection of the lines $x - 7y + 5 = 0$ and $3x + y = 0$.

[NCERT Exemplar Q. 6, Page 234]

Sol. The equation of any line parallel to the *y*-axis is of the form

$x = a$ ...(i)

The two given lines are

$x - 7y + 5 = 0$ ...(ii)

$3x + y = 0$ ...(iii)

On solving eq (i) & (ii), we get $x = -\frac{5}{22}$ and $y = \frac{15}{22}$

$\therefore \left(\frac{-15}{22}, \frac{15}{22}\right)$ is the point of intersection of lines (ii) & (iii)

Since, line $x = a$ passes through point $\left(\frac{-15}{22}, \frac{15}{22}\right)$,

$$a = \frac{-5}{22}$$

Thus, the required equation of the line $x = \frac{-5}{22}$

Long Answer Type Questions-II

(6 marks each)

Q. 1. Find the equation of one of the sides of an isosceles right angled triangle whose hypotenuse is given by $3x + 4y = 4$ and the opposite vertex of the hypotenuse is (2, 2).

[NCERT Exemplar Q. 12, Page 179]

Sol. Let slope of line *AC* be *m* and slope of line *BC* is $\frac{-3}{4}$ and let angle between line *AC* and *BC* be θ.

$$\therefore \tan\theta = \left|\frac{m+\frac{3}{4}}{1-\frac{3m}{4}}\right| \Rightarrow \tan 45^\circ = \pm\left[\frac{m+\frac{3}{4}}{1-\frac{3m}{4}}\right]$$

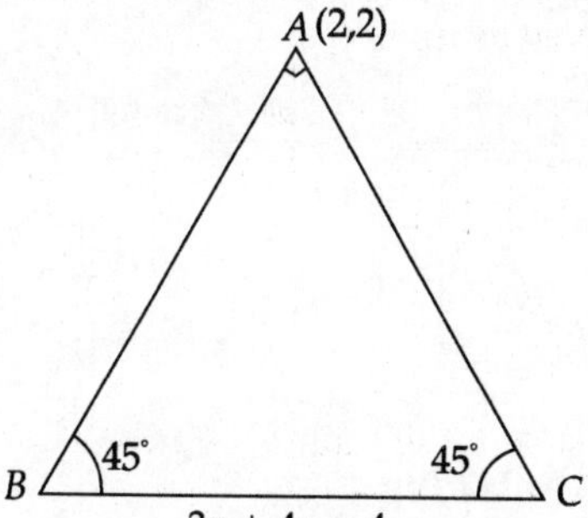

$3x + 4y = 4$

Taking positive sign, $1 = \dfrac{m+\frac{3}{4}}{1-\frac{3m}{4}}$

$$\Rightarrow m + \frac{3}{4} = 1 - \frac{3m}{4}$$

$$\Rightarrow m + \frac{3m}{4} = 1 - \frac{3}{4}$$

$$\Rightarrow \frac{7m}{4} = \frac{1}{4} \Rightarrow m = \frac{1}{7}$$

Taking negative sign,

$$1 = -\left(\frac{m+\frac{3}{4}}{1-\frac{3m}{4}}\right) \Rightarrow 1 - \frac{3m}{4} = -m - \frac{3}{4}$$

$$\Rightarrow m - \frac{3m}{4} = -1 - \frac{3}{4}$$

$$\Rightarrow \frac{m}{4} = \frac{-7}{4} \Rightarrow m = -7$$

$\therefore$ Equation of side AC having slope $\left(\frac{1}{7}\right)$ is

$$y - 2 = \frac{1}{7}(x-2)$$

$$\Rightarrow 7y - 14 = x - 2$$

$$\Rightarrow x - 7y + 12 = 0$$

and equation of side AB having slope (-7) is

$$y - 2 = -7(x-2)$$

$$\Rightarrow y - 2 = -7x + 14$$

$$\Rightarrow 7x + y - 16 = 0$$

TOPIC-3
General Equation of a line and Equation of family of lines

Quick Review

➤ **General Equation of a line**

- An equation of the form $Ax + By + C = 0$, where A, B and C are real constants and at least one of A or B is non-zero, is called general linear equation or general equation of a line.

➤ **Various forms of $Ax + By + C = 0$** The general equation of a line can be reduced into various forms of equations of a line, which are as follows

- **Slope-intercept form** If $B \neq 0$, then $Ax + By + C = 0$ can be written as

  $y = -\frac{A}{B}x - \frac{C}{B}$ or $y = mx + c$, where

  $m = -\frac{A}{B}$ and $c = -\frac{C}{B}$.

- **Intercept form:** If $C \neq 0$, then $Ax + By + C = 0$ can be written as

  $\dfrac{x}{-\frac{C}{A}} + \dfrac{y}{-\frac{C}{B}} = 1$ or $\frac{x}{a} + \frac{y}{b} = 1$, where $a = -\frac{C}{A}$ and $b = -\frac{C}{B}$.

- **Normal form:** The normal form of the equation $Ax + By + C = 0$ can be written as

  $x\cos\alpha + y\sin\alpha = p$, where

  $\cos\alpha = \pm\frac{A}{\sqrt{A^2+B^2}}$, $\sin\alpha = \pm\frac{B}{\sqrt{A^2+B^2}}$ and $\overline{\sqrt{A^2\quad B^2}}$

➤ **Angle between two lines, having general equations**

Let $A_1x + B_1y + C_1 = 0$ and $A_2x + B_2y + C_2 = 0$ be the general equations of two lines.

Then, the slope of the lines are $m_1 = -\frac{A_1}{B_1}$ and $m_2 = -\frac{A_2}{B_2}$

Let 'θ' be the angle between the two lines, then

$$\tan\theta = \pm\left(\frac{m_2 - m_1}{1 + m_1 m_2}\right) = \pm\left(\frac{-\frac{A_2}{B_2} + \frac{A_1}{B_1}}{1 + \frac{A_1}{B_1}\cdot\frac{A_2}{B_2}}\right)$$

For acute angle, we take $\theta = \tan^{-1}\left|\frac{A_1B_2 - A_2B_1}{A_1A_2 + B_1B_2}\right|$

For obtuse angle, we take $\theta = \pi - \tan^{-1}\left|\frac{A_1B_2 - A_2B_1}{A_1A_2 + B_1B_2}\right|$

➤ **Condition for two lines to be parallel and perpendicular**

Let $A_1x + B_1y + C_1 = 0$ and $A_2x + B_2y + C_2 = 0$ be the general equations of two lines.

Then, their slopes are, $m_1 = -\frac{A_1}{B_1}$, $m_2 = -\frac{A_2}{B_2}$

The lines are parallel if $m_1 = m_2$

$\Rightarrow -\frac{A_1}{B_1} = -\frac{A_2}{B_2} \Rightarrow \frac{A_1}{B_1} = \frac{A_2}{B_2} \Rightarrow A_1B_2 = A_2B_1$

and the lines are perpendicular if $m_1m_2 = -1$

$\Rightarrow \left(-\frac{A_1}{B_1}\right)\left(-\frac{A_2}{B_2}\right) = -1$

$\Rightarrow A_1A_2 + B_1B_2 = 0$

➤ **Equations of perpendicular and parallel lines through a given point**

Let the general equation of a line be $Ax + By + C = 0$.

Then, the slope of the line is $m_1 = -\frac{A}{B}$.

Let, m_2 be the slope of perpendicular line, then we have $m_1m_2 = -$

$\Rightarrow -\frac{A}{B}m_2 = -1$

$\Rightarrow m_2 = \frac{B}{A}$

∴ Equation of a line passing through (x_1, x_2) and perpendicular to $Ax + By + C = 0$ is

$y - y_1 = \frac{B}{A}(x - x_1)$

$\Rightarrow Bx - Ay + (Ay_1 - Bx_1) = 0$

Again, let m_2' be the slope of parallel, then we have

$m_1 = m_2'$

$\Rightarrow m_2' = -\frac{A}{B}$

∴ Equation of a line parallel to the line $Ax + By + C = 0$ and passing through (x_1, y_1) is

$y - y_1 = -\frac{A}{B}(x - x_1)$

$\Rightarrow Ax + By - (Ax_1 + By_1) = 0$

➤ **Condition for collinearity of three points**

Three points A, B and C are said to be collinear if $AB + BC = CA$, or $AC + CB = AB$, or $AB + AC = BC$

Condition for concurrency of three lines

Three or more straight lines are said to be concurrent if they pass through a common point (*i.e.,*) they meet at the same point.

To check concurrency of three straight lines, we follow the following two rules

- If the equation of three lines are $A_1x+B_1y+C_1=0$, $A_2x+B_2y+C_2=0$, $A_3x+B_3y+C_3=0$ and if three constants L, M and N can be found such that $L(A_1x+B_1y+C_1), M(A_2x+B_2y+C_2)$ and $N(A_3x+B_3y+C_3)=0$ identically (*i.e.,* $=0\ \forall$ values of x and y), then the three straight lines meet in a point.

or,

- If the point of intersection of two lines satisfies the equation of the third line, then the three lines are concurrent.

Equation of Family of Lines passing through the intersection of Two lines

➢ Let the two intersecting lines L_1 and L_2 be given by

$L_1 \equiv A_1x+B_1y+C_1=0$ ...(i)

and $L_2 \equiv A_2x+B_2y+C_2=0$ ...(ii)

Then, the equation of the family of lines passing through the intersection of lines (i) and (ii) is

$A_1x+B_1y+C_1+\lambda(A_2x+B_2y+C_2)=0$ (iii) ...(iii)

where λ is an arbitrary constant called parameter.

Equation (iii) represents a family of lines and a particular member of this family can be obtained by substituting a value of λ.

➢ **Distance of a point from a line**

The distance of a point from a line is the length of perpendicular drawn from the point to the line. Let $L: A_1x+B_1y+C_1=0$ be a line, whose perpendicular distance from the point $P(x_1, y_1)$ is d. Then

$$d=\left|\frac{A_1x+B_1y+C_1}{\sqrt{A^2+B^2}}\right|$$

Distance between two parallel lines

The distance between two parallel lines

$y=mx+c_1$

$y=mx+c_2$, is given by

$$d=\left|\frac{c_1-c_2}{\sqrt{1+m^2}}\right|$$

If the lines are given in general form *i.e.,* $Ax+By+C_1=0$ and $Ax \Re By\ \ C_2\ \ 0$, then the distance between them is

$$d=\left|\frac{c_1-c_2}{\sqrt{A^2+B^2}}\right|$$

➢ **Note:**

- In general, we consider the equation of a line perpendicular to line $Ax+By+C_1=0$ as $Bx-Ay+K=0$. The value of 'K' can be evaluated by substituting any particular point (a,b) which lies on the line.
- In general, we consider the equation of a line parallel to line $A_1x+B_1y+C_1=0$ as $A_1x+B_1y+K=0$ The value of 'K' can be evaluated by substituting any particular point (a,b) which lies on the line.
- If $A=0, B\neq 0$, then $Ax+By+C=0$, which reduces to $y=-\frac{C}{B}$, which is the equation of horizontal line (*i.e.,* parallel to x,- axis).
- If $A=C=0, B\neq 0$, then $Ax+By+C=0$, reduces to $y=0$, which is the equation of x - axis.
- If $A\neq 0, B=C=0$, then $Ax+By+C=0$ reduces to x = 0, which is the equation of y - axis.
- If $A\neq 0, B\neq 0, C=0$, then $Ax+By+C=0$ reduces to $y=-\frac{A}{B}x$, which is the equation of a straight line passing through the origin.

Multiple Choice Questions (1 mark each)

[A] Objective Type Questions

Q. 1. The distance of the point of intersection of the lines $2x - 3y + 5 = 0$ and $3x + 4y = 0$ from the line $5x - 2y = 0$ is

(A) $\frac{130}{17\sqrt{29}}$ (B) $\frac{13}{7\sqrt{29}}$

(C) $\frac{130}{7}$ (D) None of these

[NCERT Exemplar Q. 28, Page 181]

Ans. Correct option : (A)

Given eq. are :

$2x - 3y + 5 = 0$ ...(i)

$3x + 4y = 0$ ...(ii)

From eq. (ii) we get,

$4y = -3x \Rightarrow y = \frac{-3}{4}x$ ...(iii)

Putting the value of y in eq (i), we get

$$2x - 3\left(\frac{-3}{4}x\right) + 5 = 0$$

$$\Rightarrow 17x + 20 = 0 \Rightarrow x = \frac{-20}{17}$$

Putting the value of x in eq (iii), we get

$$y = \frac{-3}{4}\left(\frac{-20}{17}\right) \Rightarrow y = \frac{15}{17}$$

$\therefore$ Point of intersection is $\left(\frac{-20}{17}, \frac{15}{17}\right)$

Now, perpendicular distance from the point $\left(\frac{-20}{17}, \frac{15}{17}\right)$ to the given line $5x - 2y = 0$ is

$$\left|\frac{5\left(-\frac{20}{17}\right) - 2\left(\frac{15}{17}\right)}{\sqrt{25+4}}\right| = \left|\frac{-\frac{100}{17} - \frac{30}{17}}{\sqrt{29}}\right| = \frac{130}{17\sqrt{29}}$$

Q. 2. The equations of the lines passing through the point (1, 0) and at a distance $\frac{\sqrt{3}}{2}$ from the origin, are

(A) $\sqrt{3}x + y - \sqrt{3} = 0, \sqrt{3}x - y - \sqrt{3} = 0$

(B) $\sqrt{3}x + y + \sqrt{3} = 0, \sqrt{3}x - y + \sqrt{3} = 0$

(C) $x + \sqrt{3}y - \sqrt{3} = 0, x - \sqrt{3}y - \sqrt{3} = 0$

(D) None of the above

[NCERT Exemplar Q. 30, Page 181]

Ans. Correct option : (A)

Eq. of any line passing through (1, 0) is $y - 0 = m(x - 1) \Rightarrow mx - y - m = 0$

Distance of the line from origin is $\frac{\sqrt{3}}{2}$

$$\therefore \frac{\sqrt{3}}{2} = \left|\frac{m \times 0 - 0 - m}{\sqrt{1+m^2}}\right|$$

$$\Rightarrow \frac{\sqrt{3}}{2} = \left|\frac{-m}{\sqrt{1+m^2}}\right|$$

Squaring both sides, we get

$$\frac{3}{4} = \frac{m^2}{1+m^2} \Rightarrow 4m^2 = 3 + 3m^2 \Rightarrow m^2 = 3$$

$\therefore m = \pm\sqrt{3}$

$\therefore$ Required eqs are

$\pm\sqrt{3}x - y \mp \sqrt{3} = 0$

i.e. $\sqrt{3}x - y - \sqrt{3} = 0$ and $-\sqrt{3}x - y + \sqrt{3} = 0$

Q. 3. The distance between the lines $y = mx + c_1$ and $y = mx + c_2$ is

(A) $\frac{c_1 c_2}{\sqrt{m^2+1}}$ (B) $\frac{|c_1 - c_2|}{\sqrt{1+m^2}}$

(C) $\frac{c_2 - c_1}{\sqrt{1+m^2}}$ (D) 0

[NCERT Exemplar Q. 31, Page 181]

Ans. Correct option : (B)

Given eqs. are $y = mx + c_1$ ...(i)

and $y = mx + c_2$ ...(ii)

Slopes of eq (i) and eq (ii) are same *i.e.*, 'm'.

So, they are parallel lines

$\therefore$ Distance between the two lines $= \frac{|c_1 - c_2|}{\sqrt{1+m^2}}$

Q. 4. A point equidistant from the lines $4x + 3y + 10 = 0$, $5x - 12y + 26 = 0$ and $7x + 24y - 50 = 0$ is

(A) (1, –1) (B) (1, 1)

(C) (0, 0) (D) (0, 1)

[NCERT Exemplar Q. 38, Page 182]

Ans. Correct option : (C)

Given eq. are :

$4x + 3y + 10 = 0$ ...(i)

$5x - 12y + 26 = 0$ ...(ii)

and $7x + 24y - 50 = 0$ ...(iii)

Let (x_1, y_1) be any point equidistant from eq. (i), eq. (ii) and eq. (iii).

Distance of (x_1, y_1) from eq. (i)

$$= \left|\frac{4x_1 + 3y_1 + 10}{\sqrt{16+9}}\right| = \left|\frac{4x_1 + 3y_1 + 10}{5}\right|$$

Distance of (x_1, y_1) from eq. (ii)

$$= \left|\frac{5x_1 - 12y_1 + 26}{\sqrt{25+144}}\right| = \left|\frac{5x_1 - 12y_1 + 26}{13}\right|$$

Distance of (x_1, y_1) from eq. (iii)

$$= \left|\frac{7x_1+24y_1-50}{\sqrt{49+576}}\right| = \left|\frac{7x_1+24y_1-50}{25}\right|$$

If the point (x_1, y_1) is equidistant from the given lines, then

$$\left|\frac{4x_1+3y_1+10}{5}\right| = \left|\frac{5x_1-12y_1+26}{13}\right|$$

$$= \left|\frac{7x_1+24y_1-50}{25}\right|$$

We see that putting $x_1 = 0$ and $y_1 = 0$, the above relation is satisfied *i.e.*,

$$\frac{10}{5} = \frac{26}{13} = \frac{50}{25} = 2.$$

Q. 5. The ratio in which the line $3x + 4y + 2 = 0$ divides the distance between the lines $3x + 4y + 5 = 0$ and $3x + 4y - 5 = 0$ is

(A) 1 : 2 (B) 3 : 7

(C) 2 : 3 (D) 2 : 5

[NCERT Exemplar Q. 40, Page 183]

Ans. Correct option : (B)

The given equations are

$3x + 4y + 5 = 0$ ...(i)

$3x + 4y - 5 = 0$ ...(ii)

and $3x + 4y + 2 = 0$ ...(iii)

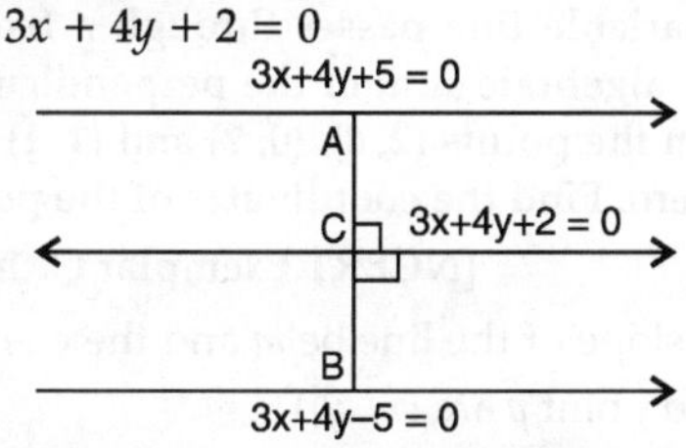

Clearly. eq. (i). & (iii) are parallel to each other as the coefficients of x and y are same.

Distance between parallel lines (i) and (iii), we get

$$\left|\frac{5-2}{\sqrt{3^2+4^2}}\right| = \frac{3}{5}$$

$$\left[\because \text{Distance between two parallel lines} = \left|\frac{c_1-c_2}{\sqrt{a^2+b^2}}\right|\right]$$

Distance between parallel lines (ii) and (iii), we get

$$\left|\frac{-5-2}{\sqrt{3^2+4^2}}\right| = \frac{7}{5}$$

$\therefore$ Ratio between the distance $= \frac{3}{5} : \frac{7}{5} = 3 : 7$

[B] Fill in the blanks

Q. 1. The points (3, 4) and (2, –6) are situated on the …….. of the line $3x - 4y - 8 = 0$.

[NCERT Exemplar Q. 45, Page 183]

Q. 2. A point moves such that square of its distance from the point (3, –2) is numerically equal to its distance from the line $5x - 12y = 3$. The equation of its locus is …….

[NCERT Exemplar Q. 46, Page 183]

Answer:

1. Opposite

2. $13x^2 + 13y^2 - 83x + 64y + 172 = 0$

[C] State True or False for the following :

Q. 1. The equation of the line joining the point (3, 5) to the point of intersection of the lines $4x + y - 1 = 0$ and $7x - 3y - 35 = 0$ is equidistant from the points (0, 0) and (8, 34).

[NCERT Exemplar Q. 53, Page 184]

Answer:

1. True

[D] Match the following :

Q. 1. Match the following.

	Column I	Column II
(i)	The co-ordinates of the points P and Q on the line $x + 5y = 13$ which are at a distance of 2 units from the line $12x - 5y + 26 = 0$ are	(a) (3, 1), (–7, 11)
(ii)	The co-ordinates of the point on the line $x + y = 4$, which are at a unit distance from the line $4x + 3y - 10 = 0$ are	(b) $\left(-\frac{1}{3}, \frac{11}{3}\right), \left(\frac{4}{3}, \frac{7}{3}\right)$
(iii)	The co-ordinates of the point on the line joining $A(-2, 5)$ and $B(3, 1)$ such that $AP = PQ = QB$ are	(c) $\left(1, \frac{12}{5}\right), \left(-3, \frac{16}{5}\right)$

[NCERT Exemplar Q. 57, Page 184]

Answer:

1. (i) → (c)

(ii) → (a)

(iii) → (b)

Long Answer Type Questions-I

(4 marks each)

Q. 1. If 'p' is the length of perpendicular from the origin to the line whose intercepts on the axes are a and b, then show that $\frac{1}{p^2}=\frac{1}{a^2}+\frac{1}{b^2}$.

[NCERT Exemplar Q. 21, Page 234]

Sol. The equation of the given lines are

$x + y - 5 = 0$ ...(i)

$3x - 2y + 7 = 0$ ...(ii)

The perpendicular distance of P(x, y) from lines (i) and (ii) are respectively given by

$$d_1=\frac{|x+y-5|}{\sqrt{(1)^2+(1)^2}} \text{ and } d_2=\frac{|3x-2y+7|}{\sqrt{(3)^2+(-2)^2}}$$

$$\text{i.e., } d_1=\frac{|x+y-5|}{\sqrt{2}} \text{ and } d_2=\frac{|3x-2y+7|}{\sqrt{13}}$$

it is given that $d_1+d_2=10$

$$\therefore \frac{|x+y-5|}{\sqrt{2}}+\frac{|3x-2y+7|}{\sqrt{13}}=10$$

$$\Rightarrow \sqrt{13}|x+y-5|+\sqrt{2}|3x-2y+7|-10\sqrt{26}=0$$

$$\Rightarrow \sqrt{13}(x+y-5)+\sqrt{2}(3x-2y+7)-10\sqrt{26}=0$$

[Assuming $(x+y-5)$ and $(3x-2y+7)$ are positive]

$$\Rightarrow \sqrt{13}x+\sqrt{13}y-5\sqrt{13}+3\sqrt{2}x-2\sqrt{2}y+7\sqrt{2}-10\sqrt{26}=0$$

$$\Rightarrow x\left(\sqrt{13}+3\sqrt{2}\right)+y\left(\sqrt{13}-2\sqrt{2}\right)+\left(7\sqrt{2}-5\sqrt{13}-10\sqrt{26}\right)=0,$$ which is the equation of a line.

Similarly, we can obtain the equation of line for any signs of ($x + y - 5$) and ($3x - 2y + 7$).

Thus, point P must move on a line.

Q. 2. If the equation of the base of an equilateral triangle is $x + y = 2$ and the vertex is (2, –1), then find the length of the side of the triangle.

[NCERT Exemplar Q. 13, Page 179]

Sol. Given that, equilateral ΔABC having equation of base is $x + y = 2$.

In ΔABD, $\sin 60° = \frac{AD}{AB}$

$\Rightarrow AD = AB \sin 60° = AB\,\frac{\sqrt{3}}{2}$

$\because AD = AB\,\frac{\sqrt{3}}{2}$ ...(i)

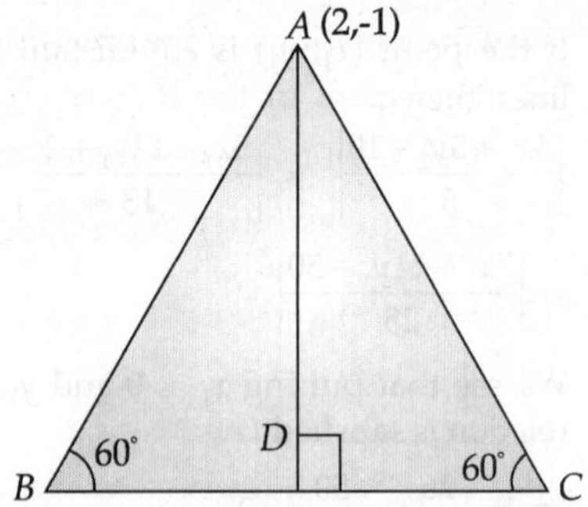

Now, the length of perpendicular from (2, –1) to line $x + y = 2$ is given by

$$AD=\left|\frac{2+(-1)-2}{\sqrt{1^2+1^2}}\right|=\frac{1}{\sqrt{2}}$$

From Eq. (i) $\frac{1}{\sqrt{2}} = AB\,\frac{\sqrt{3}}{2}$

$$AB=\sqrt{\frac{2}{3}}=\frac{\sqrt{6}}{3}$$

Q. 3. A variable line passes through a fixed point P. The algebraic sum of the perpendiculars drawn from the points (2, 0), (0, 2) and (1, 1) on the line is zero. Find the coordinates of the point P.

[NCERT Exemplar Q. 14, Page 179]

Sol. Let slope of the line be m and the co-ordinates of fixed point p are (x_1, y_1)

$\therefore$ Equation of line $y - y_1 = m(x - x_1)$

Since, the given points are $A(2, 0)$, $B(0, 2)$ and $C(1, 1)$.

Now, perpendicular distance from A, is

$$\left|\frac{0-y_1-m(2-x_1)}{\sqrt{1+m^2}}\right|$$

Perpendicular distance from B, is

$$\left|\frac{2-y_1-m(0-x_1)}{\sqrt{1+m^2}}\right|$$

Perpendicular distance from C, is

$$\left|\frac{1-y_1-m(1-x_1)}{\sqrt{1+m^2}}\right|$$

According to problem

$$\left|\frac{-y_1-2m+mx_1+2-y_1+mx_1+1-y_1-m+mx_1}{\sqrt{1+m^2}}\right|=0$$

$\Rightarrow -3y_1 - 3m + 3mx_1 + 3 = 0$

$\Rightarrow -y_1 - m + mx_1 + 1 = 0$

Since, (1, 1) lies on this, So, the point P is (1, 1).

Long Answer Type Questions-II (6 marks each)

Q.1. Find the equations of the lines through the point of intersection of the lines $x - y + 1 = 0$ and $2x - 3y + 5 = 0$ and whose distance from the point (3, 2) is $\frac{7}{5}$. [NCERT Exemplar Q. 18, Page 179]

Sol. Given equation of lines $x - y + 1 = 0$ ...(i)

and $2x - 3y + 5 = 0$ ...(ii)

From Eq. (i), $x = y - 1$

Now, put the value of x in Eq. (ii), we get

$2(y - 1) - 3y + 5 = 0$

$\Rightarrow 2y - 2 - 3y + 5 = 0$

$\Rightarrow 3 - y = 0 \Rightarrow y = 3$

$y = 3$ put in Eq. (i), we get

$x = 2$

Since, the point of intersection is (2, 3).

Let slope of the required line be m.

$\therefore$ Equation of line is $y - 3 = m(x - 2)$

$\Rightarrow mx - y + 3 - 2m = 0$ ...(iii)

Since, the distance from (3, 2) to line (iii) is $\frac{7}{5}$.

$$\therefore \frac{7}{5} = \left|\frac{3m - 2 + 3 - 2m}{\sqrt{1+m^2}}\right|$$

$$\Rightarrow \frac{49}{25} = \frac{(m+1)^2}{1+m^2}$$

$$\Rightarrow 49 + 49m^2 = 25(m^2 + 2m + 1)$$

$$\Rightarrow 49 + 49m^2 = 25m^2 + 50m + 25$$

$$\Rightarrow 24m^2 - 50m + 24 = 0$$

$$\Rightarrow 12m^2 - 25m + 12 = 0$$

$$\therefore m = \frac{25 \pm \sqrt{625 - 4 \cdot 12 \cdot 12}}{24}$$

$$= \frac{25 \pm \sqrt{49}}{24} = \frac{25 \pm 7}{24} = \frac{32}{24} \text{ or } \frac{18}{24} = \frac{4}{3} \text{ or } \frac{3}{4}$$

$\therefore$ First equation $y - 3 = \frac{4}{3}(x - 2)$

$\Rightarrow 3y - 9 = 4x - 8$

$\Rightarrow 4x - 3y + 1 = 0$

and second equation $y - 3 = \frac{3}{4}(x - 2)$

$\Rightarrow 4y - 12 = 3x - 6$

$\Rightarrow 3x - 4y + 6 = 0$

OR

Equation of the line thought the point of Intersection of the lines $x - y + 1 = 0$ and $2x - 3y + 5 = 0$ is $(x - y + 1) + k(2x - 3y + 5) = 0$

$(1 + 2k)x + (-1 - 3k)y + 1 + 5k = 0$ ...(i)

Given: Perpendicular distance from the point (3, 2) and the required line $= \frac{7}{5}$

$$\left|\frac{(1+2k)3 + (-1-3k)2 + 1 + 5k}{\sqrt{(1+2k)^2 + (-1-3k)^2}}\right| = \frac{7}{5}$$

$$\left|\frac{3 + 6k - 2 - 6k + 1 + 5k}{\sqrt{1 + 4k^2 + 4k + 1 + 6k + 9k^2}}\right| = \frac{7}{5}$$

Squaring both side

$$\frac{(5k+2)^2}{13k^2 + 10k + 2} = \frac{49}{25}$$

$$\frac{25k^2 + 20k + 4}{13k^2 + 10k + 2} = \frac{49}{25}$$

$$637k^2 + 490k + 98 = 625k^2 + 500k + 100$$

$$12k^2 - 10k - 2 - 0$$

$$6k^2 - 5k - 1 = 0$$

$$(k - 1)(6k + 1) = 0$$

$$k - 1 = 0 \Rightarrow k = 1$$

$$6k + 1 = 0 \Rightarrow k = -1/6$$

Equation of the line when $k = 1$ from eq. (i)

$(1 + 2)x + (-1 - 3)y + 1 + 5 = 0$

$3x - 4y + 6 = 0$

Equation of the line when $k = -1/6$

$$\left(1 - \frac{2}{6}\right)x\left(-1 + \frac{3}{6}\right)y + 1 - \frac{5}{6} = 0$$

$$\frac{4x}{6} - \frac{3y}{6} + \frac{1}{6} = 0$$

$$4x - 3y + 1 = 0$$

EXPERT ADVICE

- *Figures should be neatly drawn with proper labelling.*
- *Make sure you know all the forms of straight lines and all other formulas given in the chapter.*
- *Write all the formulas used in the chapter on a seminole sheet and do revise then before the exams.*
- *Practice all the examples and problems given is NCERT Text book.*

OSWAAL LEARNING TOOLS

For Suggested Online Videos

Visit : *https://youtu.be/260KIQxRLWI*

Or Scan the Code

Visit : *https://youtu.be/hh6RAEPlza4*

Or Scan the Code

Visit : *https://youtu.be/4bGt5wQf818*

Or Scan the Code

Visit : *https://youtu.be/1LmUDReu1aU*

Or Scan the Code

Visit : *https://youtu.be/v9-wXYX8gEc*

Or Scan the Code

Visit : *https://goo.gl/nycQ2p*

Or Scan the Code

CHAPTER 11 CONIC SECTIONS

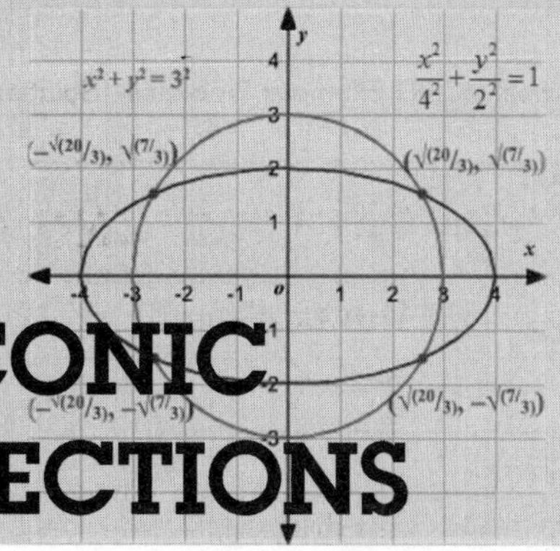

Chapter Objectives

> *Section of cone : Circle, Parabola, Ellipse, Hyperbola, a point, a straight line and a pair of intersecting lines as degenerated case of a conic sections; Standard equations of a circle; Diameter form of equation of a circle; Standard equation and simple properties of parabola, Ellipse and Hyperbola; Types of parabola .*

TOPIC-1
Sections of a Cone (circle)

TOPIC - 1
Sections of a Cone (circle.) **P. 141**

TOPIC - 2
Parabola, Ellipse and Hyperbola **P. 148**

Quick Review

- **Geometrical Definition of conic sections**

  A conic section is the locus of a point which moves in a plane in such a way that the ratio of its distance from a fixed point and a fixed line is a constant. Then

  (i) The fixed point is called focus and is denoted by *S*.

  (ii) The fixed straight line is called directrix.

  (iii) The constant ratio is called eccentricity and is denoted by '*e*'.

  In the adjacent figure,

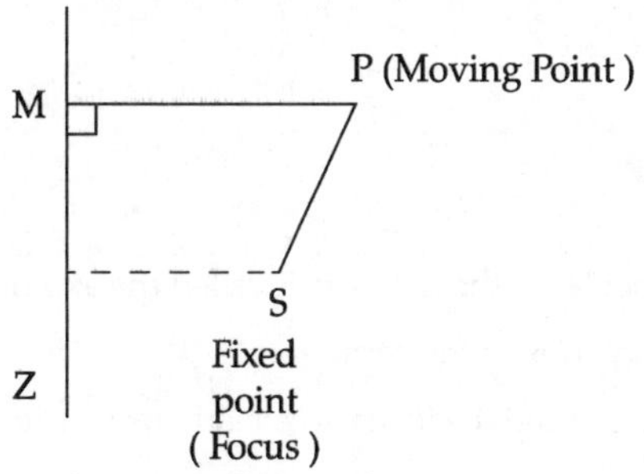

$$\frac{SP}{PM} = e = \text{constant.}$$

$= \text{eccentricity.}$

Depending on the eccentricity '*e*', the different cases are as follows

- Circle : When eccentricity, $e = 0$, then the conic is a circle.

TIPS...

- *Depending upon the eccentricity, the different conics are:*

  when, $e = 0$ conic is circle

  when, $e = 1$ conic is parabola

  when, $e < 1$ conic is ellipse

  when, $e > 1$ conic is hyperbola
- *The centre of a conic section is the point such that all the chords of the conic which passing through it are bisected there.*
- *In an ellipse, if $b > a$, then y-axis will become major axis and x-axis will become minor axis and all other points and lines will change accordingly.*
- *Two parabolas are said to be equal it they have the same latus section.*
- *All the diameters of ellipse passes through its centre.*

(a)

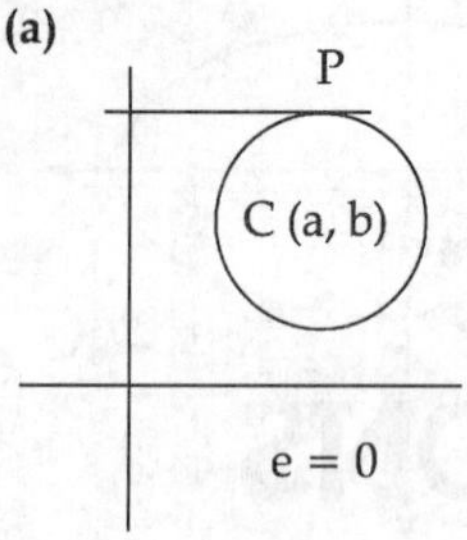

- Parabola : When eccentricity $e = 1$, then the conic is a parabola.

(b)

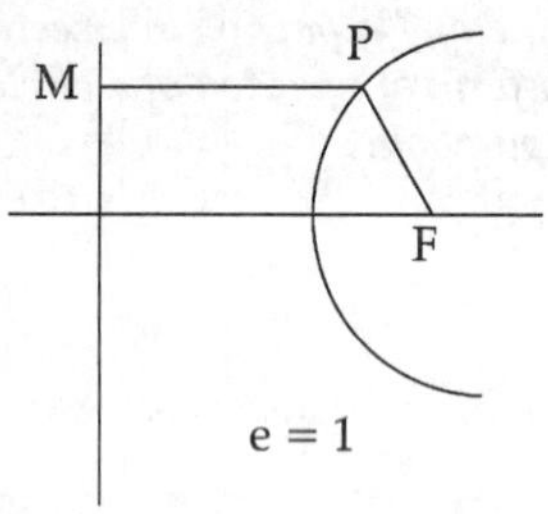

- Ellipse : When eccentricity $e < 1$, then the conic is an ellipse.

(c)

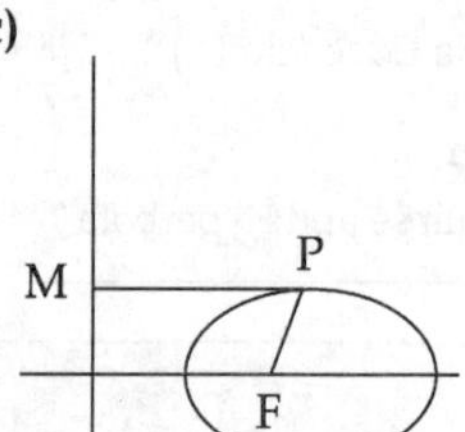

TRICKS...

- *If any straight line touches a circle then the perpendicular distance of the centre from the tangent is equal to the radius of the circle.*
- *In the general equation to a circle the coefficients of x^2 and y^2 be 1, then*

  x-co-ordinate of centre $= -\frac{1}{2}$ (coefficient of x)

  and *y-co-ordinate of centre* $= -\frac{1}{2}$ (coefficient of y)
- *In hyperbola, conjugate axis is equal to transverse axis i.e. $2a = 2b$ ($\Rightarrow a = b$), then such a hyperbola is called rectangular or equilateral hyperbola and its equation is $x^2 - y^2 = a^2$.*
- *In parabola, perpendicular distance from focus on directrix = half the latus rectum.*
- *If e_1 and e_2 are the eccentricities of hyperbola and its conjugate then $e_1^{-2} + e_2^{-2} = 1$.*

- Hyperbola : When eccentricity $e > 1$, then the conic is a hyperbola.

(d)

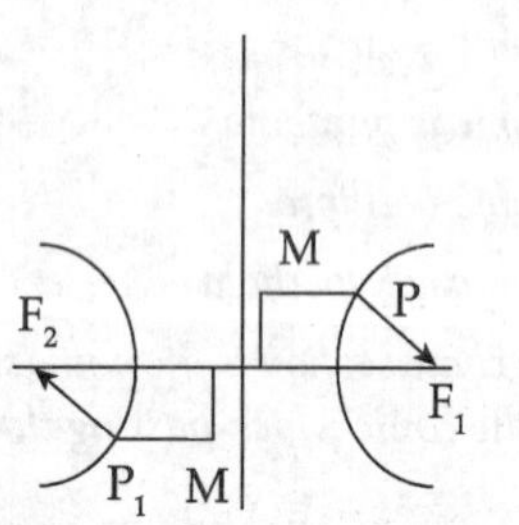

(iv) The straight line passing through the focus and perpendicular to the directrix is called the axis of the conic.

(v) The point of intersection of the conic and its axis, is called vertex of the conic.

(vi) A line perpendicular to the axis of the conic and passing through its focus is called latus rectum.

(vii) The point which bisects every chord of the conic passing through it, is called the centre of the conic.

➤ **CIRCLE**

- A circle is defined as the locus of a point in a plane, which moves in such a way that its distance from a fixed point in that plane is always constant from a fixed point. The fixed point is called the centre of the circle and the constant distance from the centre is called the radius of the circle.

➤ **Standard equation of a Circle**

Equation of a circle having centre (h, k) and radius r is

$$(x-h)^2 + (y-k)^2 = r^2.$$

If centre is at the origin (0, 0), then the equation of the circle with radius 'r' is

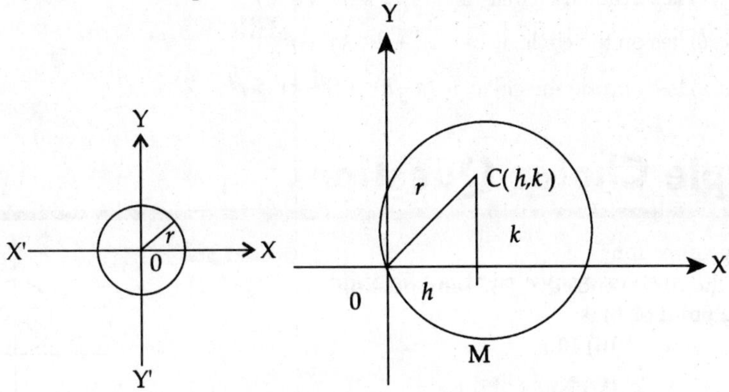

$$x^2 + y^2 = r^2.$$

(i) When the circle passes through the origin, then equation of the circle is

$$x^2 + y^2 - 2hx - 2ky = 0.$$

(ii) When the centre lies on x-axis, then equation of the circle is $(x-h)^2 + y^2 = r^2$, and when the centre lies on y-axis, then equation of the circle is $x^2 + (y-k)^2 = r^2$.

(iii) When the circle touches x-axis, then its equation is

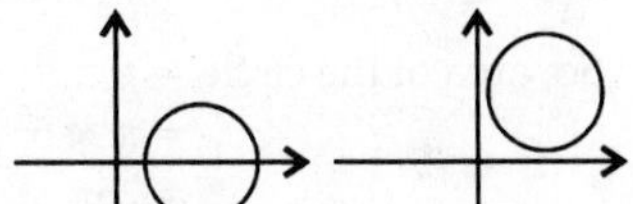

$$(x-h)^2 + (y \mp r)^2 = r^2$$

when the circle touches y-axis, then its equation is

$$(x \mp r)^2 + (y-k)^2 = r^2$$

When the circle touches both the co-ordinate axes, then its equation is

$$(x \mp r)^2 + (y \mp r)^2 = r^2$$

➢ **General Equation of a Circle**

The general equation of a circle having centre (h, k) and radius r is

$x^2 + y^2 + 2gx + 2fy + c = 0$, where

$g = -h$, $f = -k$ and $c = h^2 + k^2 - r^2$

The above equation of a circle is called the general equation of a circle with centre $(-g, -f)$ and radius

$$r = \sqrt{h^2 + k^2 - c} \text{ or } \sqrt{g^2 + f^2 - c}.$$

(i) If $g^2 + f^2 - c > 0$, then the radius of the circle is real and hence the circle is also real.

(ii) If $g^2 + f^2 - c = 0$, then the radius of the circle is 0 and the circle is a point circle.

(iii) If $g^2 + f^2 - c < 0$, then the radius of the circle is imaginary and is not possible to draw.

➢ **Diameter form of Equation of a Circle**

Let (x_1, y_1) and (x_2, y_2) be the end points of the diameter of a circle. Then, equation of circle drawn on the diameter is

$$(x - x_1)\cdot(x - x_2) + (y - y_1)\cdot(y - y_2) = 0$$

➢ **Note :**

- Circle, ellipse, parabola and hyperbola are curves which are obtained by intersection of a plane and cone in different positions.
- A circle is the set of all points in a plane that are equidistant from a fixed point in that plane.
- Two circles having the same centre $c(h, k)$ and different radii r_1 and $r_2 (r_1 \neq r_2)$ are called concentric circles. For e.g., the circles $(x-h)^2 + (y-k)^2 = r_1^2$, and $(x-h)^2 + (y-k)^2 = r_2^2$ $(r_1 \neq r_2)$ are concentric circles.
- Let $(x-h)^2 + (y-k)^2 = r^2$ be the equation of a circle with centre (h, k) and radius r and let (a, b) be any point in the plane. Then,

(i) The point (a, b) lies inside the circle, if $(a-h)^2+(b-k)^2<r^2$.

(ii) The point (a, b) lies on the circle, if $(a-h)^2+(b-k)^2=r^2$.

(iii) The point (a, b) lies outside the circle, if $(a-h)^2+(b-k)^2>r^2$.

Multiple Choice Questions

(1 mark each)

[A] Objective Type questions

Q. 1. The area of the circle centred at (1, 2) and passing through the point (4, 6) is

(A) 5π **(B)** 10π

(C) 25π **(D)** None of these

[NCERT Exemplar Q. 47, Page 205]

Ans. Correct option : (C)

Given that the centre of the circle is (1, 2)

Radius of the circle $= \sqrt{(4-1)^2+(6-2)^2}$

$= \sqrt{9+16} = 5$

So, area of the circle $= \pi r^2$

$= \pi \times 5^2$

$= 25\pi$

Q. 2. Equation of a circle which passes through (3, 6) and touches the axes is

(A) $x^2 + y^2 + 6x + 6y + 3 = 0$

(B) $x^2 + y^2 - 6x - 6y - 9 = 0$

(C) $x^2 + y^2 - 6x - 6y + 9 = 0$

(D) None of these

[NCERT Exemplar Q. 48, Page 205]

Ans. Correct option : (C)

Let the required circle touch the axes at $(a, 0)$ and $(0, a)$

$\therefore$ centre is (a, a) and $r = a$

So, the eq. of the circle is $(x-a)^2 + (y-a)^2 = a^2$

If passes through a point (3, 6), then

$(3-a)^2 + (6-a)^2 = a^2$

$\Rightarrow a^2 - 18a + 45 = 0$

$\Rightarrow (a-3)(a-15)$

$\Rightarrow a = 3$ and $a = 15$

if $a = 3$

So, the required eq. of the circle is

$(x-3)^2 + (y-3)^2 = 9$

$\Rightarrow x^2 + y^2 - 6x - 6y + 9 = 0$

Q. 3. Equation of the circle with centre on the Y-axis and passing through the origin and the point (2, 3) is

(A) $x^2 + y^2 + 13y = 0$

(B) $3x^2 + 3y^2 + 13x + 3 = 0$

(C) $6x^2 + 6y^2 - 13y = 0$

(D) $x^2 + y^2 + 13x + 3 = 0$

[NCERT Exemplar Q. 49, Page 205]

Ans. Correct option : (A)

Let the eq. of circle be $(x-h)^2 + (y-k)^2 = r^2$

Let the centre be $(0, a)$ and radius 'r' $= a$

$\therefore$ The eq. of circle is $(x-0)^2 + (y-a)^2$

$\Rightarrow x^2 + y^2 - 2ay = 0$ ...(i)

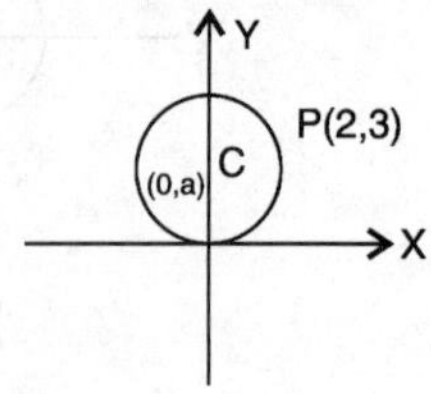

Now, $CP = r$

$\Rightarrow \sqrt{(2-0)^2+(3-a)^2} = a$

$\Rightarrow \sqrt{4+9+a^2-6a} = a$

$\Rightarrow \sqrt{13+a^2-6a} = a \Rightarrow 13 + 6a - a^2 \Rightarrow a = 13/6$

putting the value of a in eq. (i), we get

$x^2 + y^2 - 2\left(\frac{13}{6}\right)y = 0 \Rightarrow 3x^2 + 3y^2 - 13y = 0$

[Note : the correct option is (a) and it should be $3x^2 + 3y^2 - 13y = 0$]

Q. 4. The equation of a circle with origin as centre and passing through the vertices of an equilateral triangle whose median is of length 3*a* is

(A) $x^2+y^2=9a^2$ **(B)** $x^2+y^2=16a^2$

(C) $x^2+y^2=4a^2$ **(D)** $x^2+y^2=a^2$

[NCERT Exemplar Q. 50, Page 206]

Ans. Correct option : (C)

Let ABC be an equilateral triangle in which median $AD = 3a$. Centre of the circle is same as the centroid of the triangle *i.e.* (0, 0).

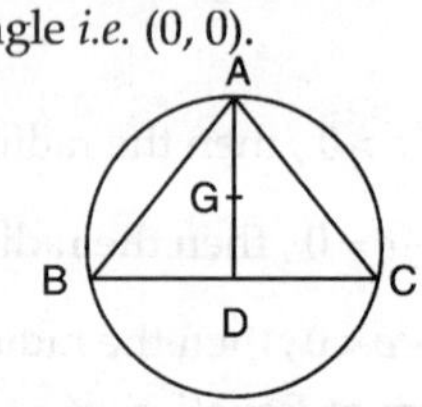

$AG : GD = 2 : 1$

So, $AG = \frac{2}{3}AD = \frac{2}{3} \times 3a = 2a$

$\therefore$ The eq. of the circle is $(x-0)^2 + (y-0)^2 = (2a)^2$

$\Rightarrow x^2 + y^2 = 4a^2$

[B] True or False

Q. 1. The line $x+3y=0$ is a diameter of the circle $x^2+y^2+6x+2y=0$

[NCERT Exemplar Q. 33, Page 204]

Q. 2. The shortest distance from the point (2, –7) to the circle $x + y^2 - 14x - 10y - 151 = 0$ is equal to 5.

[NCERT Exemplar Q. 34, Page 204]

Q. 3. If the line $lx + my = -1$ is a tangent to the circle $x^2 + y^2 = a^2$, then the point (l, m) lies on a circle.

[NCERT Exemplar Q. 35, Page 204]

Q. 4. The point (1, 2) lies inside the circle $x^2 + y^2 - 2x + 6y + 1 = 0$. [NCERT Exemplar Q. 36, Page 204]

Answer

1. False 2. False 3. True 4. True

[C] Fill in the blanks of the following

Q. 1. The equation of the circle having centre at (3, –4) and touching the line $5x + 12y - 12 = 0$ is .... [NCERT Exemplar Q. 41, Page 205]

Q. 2. The equation of the circle circumscribing the triangle whose sides are the lines $y = x + 2$, $3y = 4x$, $2y = 3x$ is .... [NCERT Exemplar Q. 42, Page 205]

Answer:

1. $(x-3)^2 + (y-4)^2 = \left(\frac{45}{13}\right)^2$

2. $x^2 + y^2 - 46x + 22y = 0$

Short Answer Type Questions (2 marks each)

Q. 1. Find the equation of the circle which touches the both axes in first quadrant and whose radius is *a*. [NCERT Exemplar Q. 1, Page 202]

Sol. Given that radius of the circle is *a* *i.e.*, (*h*, *k*)

$(x-h)^2 + (y-x)^2 = r^2$

Put $h = k = r = a$

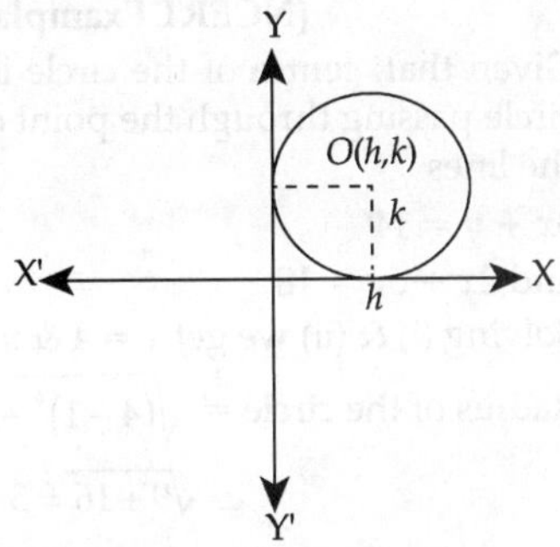

So, the equation of required circle is

$(x-a)^2 + (y-a)^2 = a^2$

$\Rightarrow x^2 - 2ax + a^2 + y^2 - 2ay + a^2 = a^2$

$\Rightarrow x^2 + y^2 - 2ax - 2ay + a^2 = 0$

Q. 2. Find the equation of the circle which touches X-axis and whose centre is (1, 2). [NCERT Exemplar Q. 3, Page 202]

Sol. Given that, centre of the circle is (1, 2).

$(x-h)^2 + (y-k)^2 = r^2$

Put $h = 1, k = 2$

$\because r = 2$

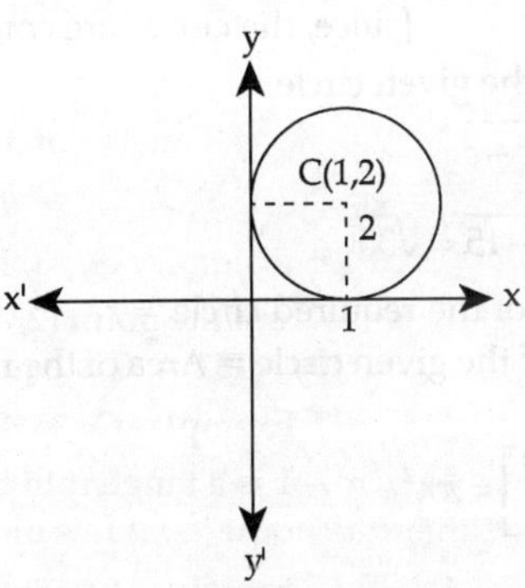

So, the equation of circle is

$(x-1)^2 + (y-2)^2 = 2^2$

$\Rightarrow x^2 - 2x + 1 + y^2 - 4y + 4 = 4$

$\Rightarrow x^2 - 2x + y^2 - 4y + 1 = 0$

$\Rightarrow x^2 + y^2 - 2x - 4y + 1 = 0.$

Q. 3. If the lines $3x - 4y + 4 = 0$ and $6x - 8y - 7 = 0$ are tangents to a circle, then find the radius of the circle. [NCERT Exemplar, Q. 4, Page 202]

Sol. Given lines,

$3x - 4y + 4 = 0$ (i)

$6x - 8y - 7 = 0$

or $3x - 4y - 7/2 = 0$ (ii)

It is clear that lines (i) and (ii) parallel.

Now, distance between them *i.e.*,

$$d = \left|\frac{c_1 - c_2}{\sqrt{a^2 + b^2}}\right|$$

$$d = \left|\frac{4 + 7/2}{\sqrt{9 + 16}}\right| = \left|\frac{\frac{8+7}{2}}{5}\right| = \frac{3}{2}$$

$\therefore$ Distance between these line = Diameter of these circle

$\therefore$ Diameter of the circle $= \frac{3}{2}$ and radius of the circle $= \frac{3}{4}$.

Q. 4. If one end of a diameter of the circle $x^2 + y^2 - 4x - 6y + 11 = 0$ is (3, 4), then find the co-ordinates of the other end of the diameter. [NCERT Exemplar, Q. 6, Page 202]

Sol. Given equation of the circle is

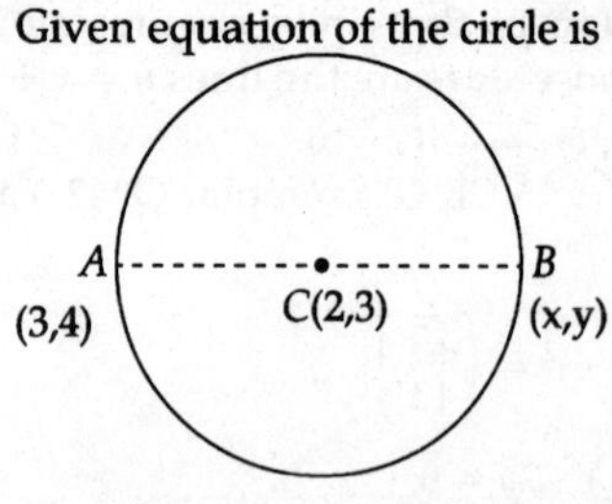

$$x^2+y^2-4x-6y+11=0$$

$\therefore$ $2g = -4$ and $2f = -6$

So, the centre of the circle is $(-g, -f)$ *i.e.*, (2, 3).

Since, the mid-point of AB is (2, 3).

Then, $2=\frac{3+x_1}{2}$

$\Rightarrow$ $4 = 3 + x_1$

$\therefore$ $x_1 = 1$

and $3=\frac{4+y_1}{2}$

$\Rightarrow 6 = 4 + y_1 \Rightarrow y = 2$

So, the coordinates of other end of the diameter will be (1, 2).

Long Answer Type Question-I

(4 marks each)

Q. 1. Find the equation of a circle which touches both the axes and the line $3x - 4y + 8 = 0$ and lies in the third quadrant.

[NCERT Exemplar Q. 5, Page 202]

Sol.

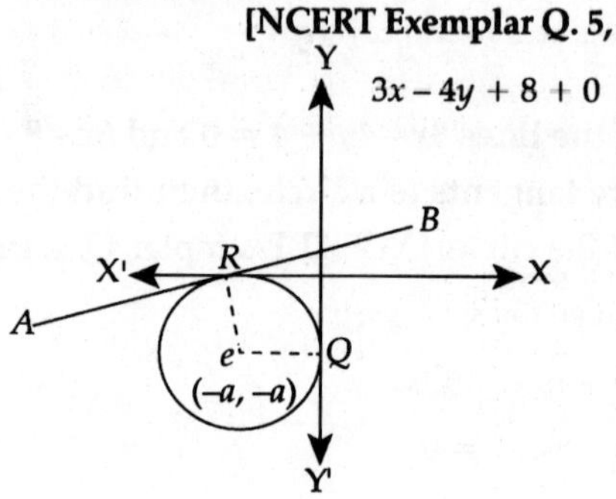

Let a be the radius of the circle. Then, the co-ordinates of the circle are $(-a, -a)$. Now, perpendicular distance from C to the line AB = Radius of the circle

$$d=\left|\frac{-3ü+4\ \ +8}{\sqrt{ü+}}\right|=\left|\frac{+8}{5}\right|$$

$\because$ $a=\left(\frac{a+8}{5}\right)$

$a=\frac{a+8}{5}$

$\Rightarrow$ $5a = a + 8$

$\Rightarrow$ $4a = 8 \Rightarrow a = 2$

or

$a=\frac{-(a+8)}{5}$

$5a=-a-8$

$6a=-8$

$a=-8$

$a \neq -8$

So, the equation of circle is

$$(x+2)^2+(y+2)^2=2^2$$

$\Rightarrow$ $x^2+4x+4+y^2+4y+4=4$

$\Rightarrow$ $x^2+y^2+4x+4y+4=0$.

Q. 2. Find the equation of the circle having (1, –2) as its centre and passing through point of intersection $3x + y = 14$, $2x + 5y = 18$.

[NCERT Examplar Q. 8, Page 202]

Sol. Given that, centre of the circle is (1, –2) and the circle passing through the point of intersection of the lines

$3x + y = 14$ ...(i)

and $2x + 5y = 18$ ...(ii)

Solving (i) & (ii) we get $x = 4$ & $y = 2$

$\therefore$ Radius of the circle = $\sqrt{(4-1)^2+(2+2)^2}$

$= \sqrt{9+16}=5$

Now, equation of the circle is C (1, – 2), radius 5

$$(x-1)^2+(y+2)^2=5^2$$

$\Rightarrow$ $x^2-2x+1+y^2+4y+4=25$

$\Rightarrow$ $x^2+y^2-2x+4y-20=0$.

Q. 3. Find the equation of a circle concentric with the circle $x^2 + y^2 - 6x + 12y + 15 = 0$ and has double of its area. [NCERT Exemplar Q. 10, Page 202]

Sol. Given, equation of the circle is

$x^2 + y^2 - 6x + 12y + 15 = 0$ (i)

$\therefore$ $2g = -6 \Rightarrow g = -3$

$2f = 12 \Rightarrow f = 6$

and $c = 15$

$\therefore$ Centre = $(-g, -f)$ = (3, –6)

So, the centre of the required circle will be (3, –6).

[since, the circles are concentric]

Radius of the given circle

$=\sqrt{g^2+f^2-c}$

$=\sqrt{9+36-15}=\sqrt{30}$

Let radius of the required circle = r_1

$\therefore$ 2 × Area of the given circle = Area of the required circle.

$\Rightarrow$ $2\left[\pi\left(\sqrt{30}\right)^2\right]=\pi r_1^2$

$\Rightarrow$ $60=r_1^2$

$\Rightarrow r_1 = \sqrt{60}$

$\therefore \sqrt{g^2 + f^2 - c} = \sqrt{60}$

$\Rightarrow 9 + 36 - c = 60$

$\Rightarrow c = -15$

So, the required equation of circle is $x^2 + y^2 - 6x + 12y - 15 = 0$.

Q. 4. If the lines $2x - 3y = 5$ and $3x - 4y = 7$ are the diameter of a circle of area 154 square units, then obtain the equation of the circle.

[NCERT Exemplar Q. 23, Page 203]

Sol. Given lines are $2x - 3y = 5$ (i)

and $3x - 4y = 7$ (ii)

From Eqs. (i) and (ii),

$\Rightarrow x = 1,\ y = -1$

Let the radius of the circle is r.

Then $\pi r^2 = 154$

$\Rightarrow \frac{22}{7} \times r^2 = 154$

$\Rightarrow r^2 = \frac{154 \times 7}{22}$

$\Rightarrow r^2 = \frac{14 \times 7}{2} \Rightarrow r^2 = 49$

So, the equation of circle is

$(x-1)^2 + (y+1)^2 = 49$

$\Rightarrow x^2 - 2x + 1 + y^2 + 2y + 1 = 49$

$\Rightarrow x^2 + y^2 - 2x + 2y = 47$

$\Rightarrow x^2 + y^2 - 2x + 2y - 47 = 0$.

Q. 5. Find the Equation of a circle whose centre is (3, –1) and which cuts off a chord length 6 units on the line $2x - 5y + 18 = 0$.

[NCERT Exemplar Q. 24, Page 203]

Sol. Given centre of the circle is (3, – 1),

Now, $OM = \left|\frac{6+5+18}{\sqrt{4+25}}\right| = \frac{29}{\sqrt{29}} = \sqrt{29}$

In ΔOMB, $OB^2 = OM^2 + MB^2$

$\left[\because AB = 6 \Rightarrow AM = MB = \frac{1}{2}, AB = 3\right]$

$\Rightarrow OB^2 = 29 + 9 \Rightarrow OB^2 = 38$

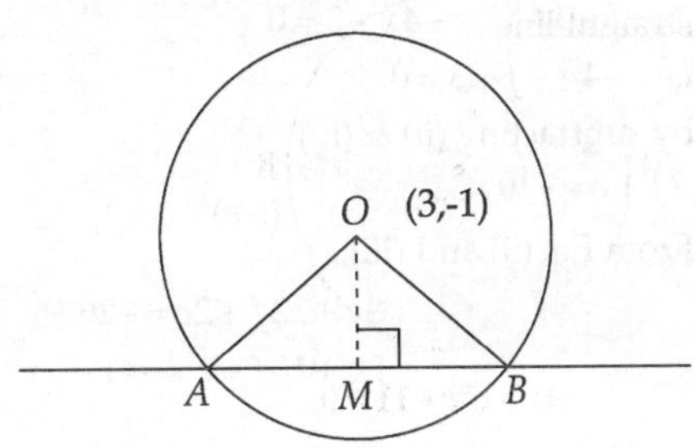

So, the radius of circle is $\sqrt{38}$,

$\therefore$ Equation of the circle with radius $r = \sqrt{38}$ and centre (3, – 1) is

$\Rightarrow (x-3)^2 + (y+1)^2 = 38$

$\Rightarrow x^2 - 6x + 9 + y^2 + 2y + 1 = 38$

$\Rightarrow x^2 + y^2 - 6x + 2y = 28$.

Q. 6. Find the equation of a circle of radius 5 which is touching another circle $x^2 + y^2 - 2x - 4y - 20 = 0$ at (5, 5). [NCERT Exemplar Q. 25, Page 203]

Sol. Let the co-ordinates of centre of the required circle are (h, k), then the centre of another circle is (1, 2).

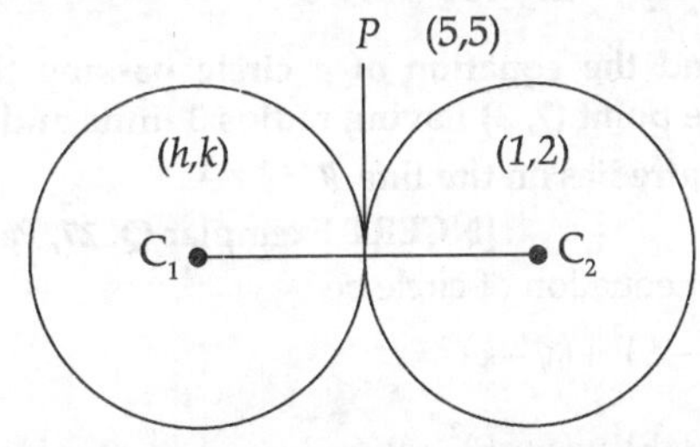

Radius $= \sqrt{1+4+20} = 5$

P is the mid-point of C_1C_2.

$\therefore 5 = \frac{1+h}{2} \Rightarrow h = 9$

and $5 = \frac{2+k}{2} \Rightarrow k = 8$

the equation of required circle is,

$(x-9)^2 + (y-8)^2 = 25$

$\Rightarrow x^2 - 18x + 81 + y^2 - 16y + 64 = 25$

$\Rightarrow x^2 + y^2 - 18x - 16y + 120 = 0$.

Long Answer Type Questions-II

(6 marks each)

Q. 1. Find the equation of the circle which passes through the points (2, 3) and (4, 5) and the centre lies on the straight line $y - 4x + 3 = 0$.

[NCERT Exemplar Q. 23, Page 203]

Sol. Let the general equation of the circle is

$x^2 + y^2 + 2gx + 2fy + c = 0$ ...(i)

Since, this circle passes through the points (2, 3) and (4, 5).

$\therefore 4 + 9 + 4g + 6f + c = 0$

$\Rightarrow 4g + 6f + c = -13$ ...(ii)

and $16 + 25 + 8g + 10f + c = 0$

$\Rightarrow 8g + 10f + c = -41$ ...(iii)

Since, the centre of the circle $(-g,-f)$ lies on the straight line $y-4x+3=0$

i.e., $+4g-f+3=0$ ...(iv)

by subtracting (ii) & (iv)

$\Rightarrow 7f+c=-10$ ...(v)

From Eq. (ii) and (iii),

$$\begin{array}{r} 8g+12f+2c=-26 \\ 8g+10f+c=-41 \\ -\quad -\quad -\quad + \\ \hline 2f+c=15 \end{array}$$ ...(vi)

From Eq. (ii) and (vi),

$$\begin{array}{r} 7f+c=-10 \\ 2f+c=15 \\ -\quad -\quad - \\ \hline 5f=-25 \end{array}$$

$\therefore f=-5$

Now, $c=10+15=25$

From Eq. (iv), $4g+5+3=0$

$\Rightarrow g=-2$

From Eq. (i), equation of the circle is $x^2+y^2-4x-10y+25=0$.

Q. 2. Find the equation of a circle passing through the point (7, 3) having radius 3 units and whose centre lies on the line $y=x-1$.

[NCERT Exemplar Q. 27, Page 203]

Sol. Let equation of circle be

$(x-h)^2+(y-k)^2=r^2$

$\Rightarrow (x-h)^2+(y-k)^2=9$ ...(i)

Now, the circle passes through the point (7, 3)

$\therefore (7-h)^2+(3-k)^2=9$ ...(ii)

$\Rightarrow 49-14h+h^2+9-6k+k^2=9$

$\Rightarrow h^2+k^2-14h-6k+49=0$ ...(iii)

Now, $y=x-1$, $k=h-1$

On putting $k=h-1$ in Eq. (iii), we get

$h^2+(h-1)^2-14h-6(h-1)+49=0$

$\Rightarrow h^2+h^2-2h+1-14h-6h+6+49=0$

$\Rightarrow 2h^2-22h+56=0$

$\Rightarrow h^2-11h+28=0$

$\Rightarrow h^2-7h-4h+28=0$

$\Rightarrow h(h-7)-4(h-7)=0$

$\Rightarrow (h-7)(h-4)=0$

$\therefore h=4,7$

When $h=7$ then $k=7-1=6$

$\therefore$ Centre (7, 6)

When $h=4$ then $k=3$

$\therefore$ Centre (4, 3)

So, the equation of circle when centre (7, 6), is

$(x-7)^2+(y-6)^2=9$

$\Rightarrow x^2-14x+49+y^2-12y+36=9$

$\Rightarrow x^2+y^2-14x-12y+76=0$

when centre (4, 3), then the equation of circle is,

$(x-4)^2+(y-3)^2=9$

$\Rightarrow x^2-8x+16+y^2-6y+9=9$

$\Rightarrow x^2+y^2-8x-6y+16=0$

TOPIC-2
Parabola, Ellipse and Hyperbola

Quick Review

➤ **Parabola :** A parabola is the locus of a point which moves in a place such that its distance from a fixed point is always equal to its distance from a straight line.

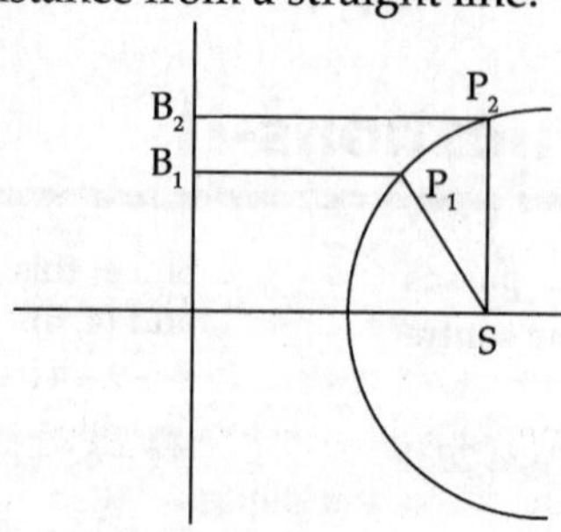

In the figure, $P_1B_1 = P_1S$

$$P_2B_2 = P_2S$$

Here, the fixed line is called the directrix and the fixed point is called the focus of the parabola. A line through the focus and perpendicular to the directrix is called the axis of the parabola and point of intersection of parabola with the axis is called the vertex of the parabola. In case of parabola, eccentricity, $e = 1$.

➢ **Types of Parabola**

- Right handed Parabola
- Left handed Parabola
- Upward Parabola
- Downward Parabola

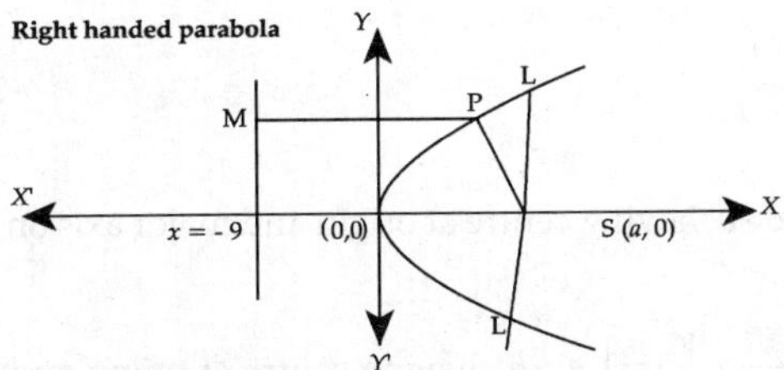

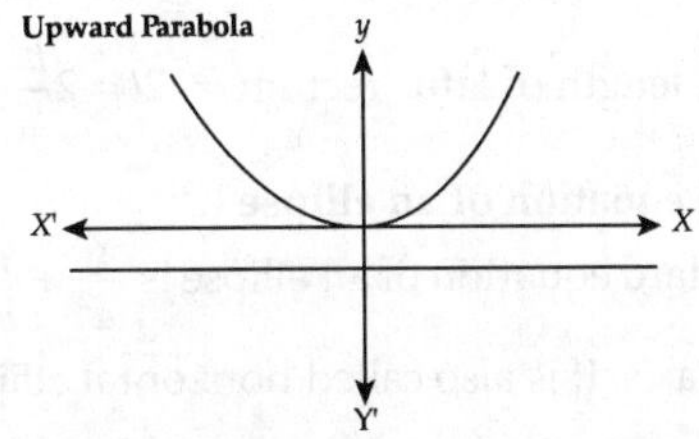

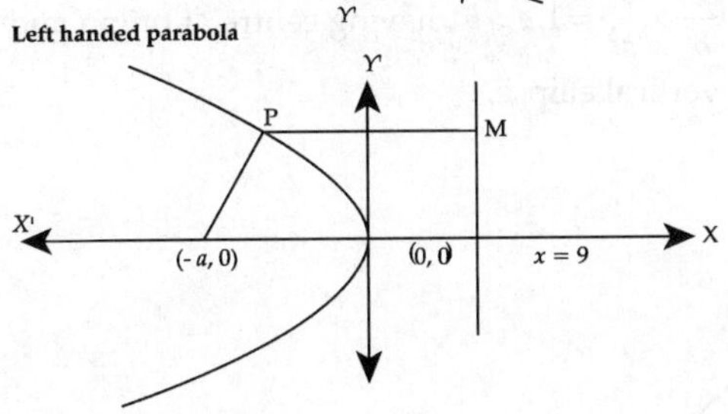

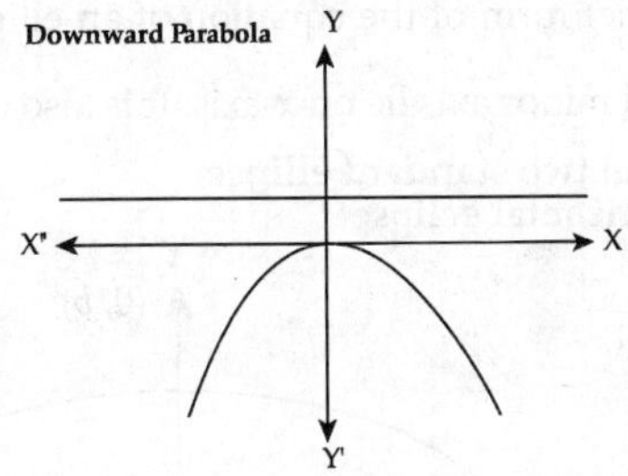

➢ **Main facts about four types of Parabola**

Parabola	Vertex	Focus	Latus Rectum	Co-ordinate of L·R	Axis	Directrix	Symmetry
$y^2 = 4ax$	(0, 0)	(a, 0)	4a	$(a \pm 2a)$	$y = 0$	$x = -a$	X-axis
$y^2 = -4ax$	(0, 0)	(−a, 0)	4a	$(-a \pm 2a)$	$y = 0$	$x = a$	X-axis
$x^2 = 4ay$	(0, 0)	(0, a)	4a	$(\pm 2a, a)$	$x = 0$	$y = -a$	Y-axis
$x^2 = -4ay$	(0, 0)	(0, −a)	4a	$(\pm 2a, -a)$	$x = 0$	$y = a$	Y-axis

Parabola with y^2 term	Parabola with x^2 term
1 Symmetrical about X-axis	1 Symmetrical about Y-axis
2 Axis is along the X-axis	2 Axis is along the Y-axis
3 It open right handed when co-efficient of 'x' is positive and left handed when co-efficient of 'x' is negative.	3 It opens upwards if co-efficient of 'y' is positive and downwards if co-efficient of 'y' is negative.

➢ **Ellipse**

An ellipse is the set of all points in a plane, the sum of whose distance from two fixed points in the plane is a constant.

$\therefore\ P_1S_1 + P_1S_2 = P_2S_1 + P_2S_2 = P_3S_1 + P_3S_2 =$ constant.

➢ **Terms related to an Ellipse**

- **Focus** - Two fixed points are called foci of the ellipse and denoted by S_1 and S_2. The distance between two foci S_1 and S_2 is $2c$.
- **Centre** - The mid-point of the line - segment joining the foci, is called centre of ellipse.
- **Major Axis** - The line segment through the foci of the ellipse is called major axis. The length of major axis is $2a$.
- **Minor axis** - The line segment through the centre and perpendicular to the major axis is called minor axis. The Length of minor axis is denoted by $2b$.

- **Vertices** - The end points of the major axis are called the vertices of the ellipse.
- **Eccentricity** - The eccentricity of ellipse is the ratio of the distance from the centre of the ellipse to one of the foci and to one of the vertices of the ellipse. It is denoted by 'e'.

$$e = \frac{c}{a} \Rightarrow c = ae$$

$$\text{Since } c < a \Rightarrow \frac{c}{a} < a \Rightarrow e < 1.$$

- **Latus Rectum** - Latus rectum of an ellipse is a line segment perpendicular to the major axis through any of the foci and whose end points lie on the ellipse.

Thus, the length of latus rectum $= 2l = 2\frac{b^2}{a}$

➢ **Standard equation of an ellipse**

The standard equation of an ellipse is $\frac{x^2}{a^2}+\frac{y^2}{b^2}=1, a>b$ having centre at origin and major axis on x-axis and minor axis on y-axis. It is also called horizontal ellipse.

The another form of the equation of an ellipse is $\frac{x^2}{b^2}\times\frac{y^2}{a^2}=1, a>b$, having centre at origin and major axis lie on y-axis and minor axis lie on x-axis. It is also called vertical ellipse.

➢ **Facts about two standard ellipse**

(a) Horizontal eclipse

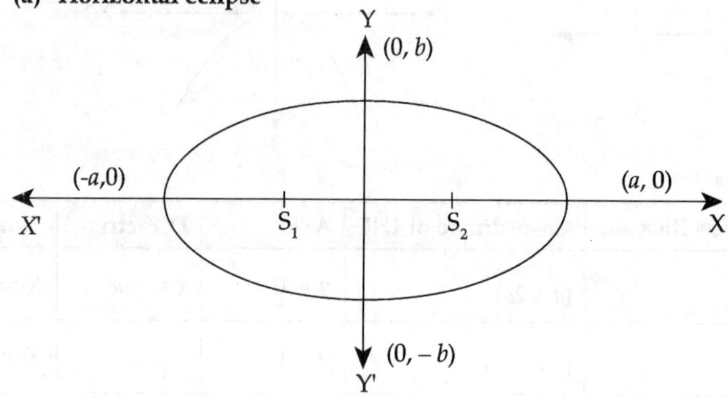

(b) Vertical eclipse

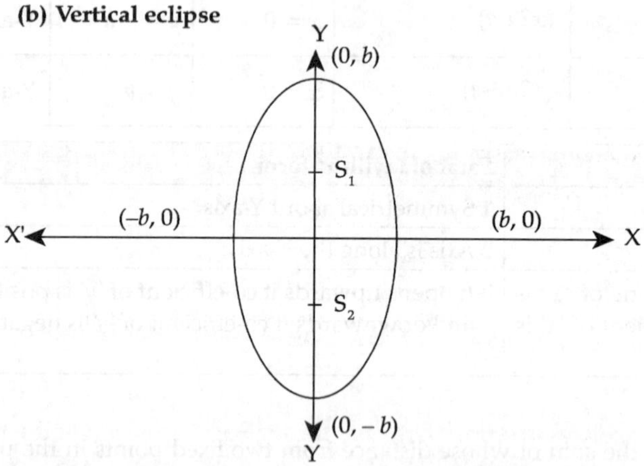

	Horizontal ellipse	Vertical ellipse
	$\frac{x^2}{a^2}+\frac{y^2}{b^2}=1, a>b$	$\frac{x^2}{b^2}+\frac{y^2}{a^2}=1, a>b$
1. Centre	(0, 0)	(0, 0)
2. Vertices	$(\pm a, 0)$	$(0, \pm a)$
3. Major axis	$2a$	$2a$
4. Minor axis	$2b$	$2b$

5. Value of c	$c=\sqrt{a^2-b^2}$	$c=\sqrt{a^2-b^2}$
6. Equation of major axis	$y=0$	$x=0$
7. Equation of minor axis	$x=0$	$y=0$
8. Directrix	$x=\pm\frac{a^2}{c}$ or $\pm\frac{a}{e}$	$y=\pm\frac{b^2}{c}$ or $\pm\frac{b^2}{ae}$
9. Foci	$(\pm c,0)$ or $(ae,0)$	$(0,\pm c)$ or $(0,\pm ae)$
10. Eccentricity	$e=\frac{c}{a}=\sqrt{1-\frac{b^2}{a^2}}$	$e=\frac{c}{a}=\sqrt{1-\frac{b^2}{a^2}}$
11. Length of latus rectum	$\frac{2b^2}{a}$	$\frac{2b^2}{a}$
12. Co-ordinate of latus rectum	$\left(\pm c,\pm\frac{b^2}{a}\right)$	$\left(\pm\frac{b^2}{a},\pm c\right)$
13. Focal distance	$2c$	$2c$

➢ **Hyperbola**

A hyperbola is the set of all points in a plane, the difference of whose distances from two fixed points in the plane is a constant.

$$\therefore\ P_1S_2-P_1S_1=P_2S_2-P_2S_1=P_3S_2-P_3S_1$$

➢ The term difference means the distance to the further point minus the distance to the closer point.

➢ **Terms Related to Hyperbola**

- **Focus** - The two fixed points are called the foci of the hyperbola and denoted by S_1 and S_2. The distance between two foci S_1 and S_2 is $2c$.
- **Centre** - The midpoint of the line segment joining the foci, is called centre of hyperbola.
- **Transverse axis** - The line through the foci is called transverse axis.
- **Conjugate axis** - The line through the centre and perpendicular to the transverse axis is called conjugate axis.
- **Vertices** - The points at which the hyperbola intersects the transverse axis are called the vertices of the hyperbola. The distance between two vertices is $2a$.
- **Eccentricity** - Eccentricity of the hyperbola is the ratio of the distance of any focus from the centre and the distance of any vertex from the centre and it is denoted by e.

$$\therefore\ e=\frac{c}{a} \text{ and } c>a\Rightarrow e>1.$$

- **Directrix** - It is a line perpendicular to the transverse axis and cuts it at a distance of $\frac{a^2}{c}$ from the centre. *i.e.* $x=\pm\frac{a^2}{c}$ or $y=\pm\frac{a^2}{c}$
- **Latus rectum** - It is a line segment perpendicular to the transverse axis through any of the foci and whose end points lie on the hyperbola.

Thus, length of latus rectum $=2l=\frac{2b^2}{a}$.

➢ **Standard Equation of Hyperbola**

Standard equation of hyperbola is of the form $\frac{x^2}{a^2}-\frac{y^2}{b^2}=1$, whose X-axis as transverse and Y-axis as conjugate axis.

The equation of the hyperbola of the form $\frac{y^2}{a^2}-\frac{x^2}{b^2}=1$ is called conjugate hyperbola, whose X-axis as conjugate axis and Y-axis as transverse axis.

➤ Facts about two standard Hyperbolas

(a) Hyperbola

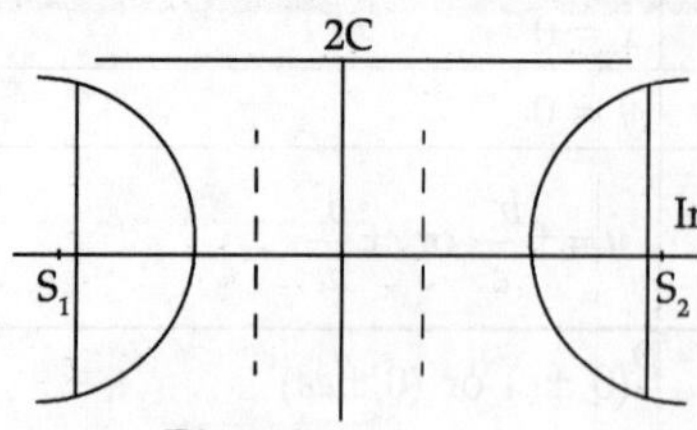

(b) Conjugate Hyperbola

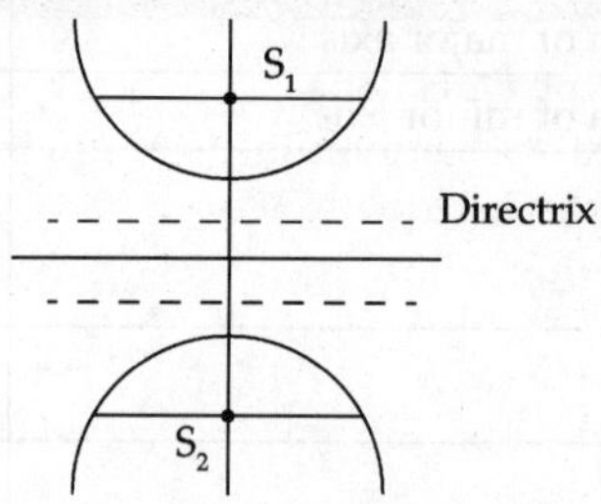

	Hyperbola	Conjugate Hyperbola
Equation	$\frac{x^2}{a^2}-\frac{y^2}{b^2}=1$	$\frac{y^2}{a^2}-\frac{x^2}{b^2}=1$
1. Transverse axis	$2a$	$2a$
2. Conjugate axis	$2b$	$2b$
3. Value of c	$c=\sqrt{a^2+b^2}$	$c=\sqrt{a^2+b^2}$
4. Vertices	$(\pm a,0)$	$(0,\pm a)$
5. Directrices	$x=\pm\frac{a^2}{c}$ or $\pm\frac{a}{e}$	$y=\pm\frac{a^2}{c}$ or $\pm\frac{a}{e}$
6. Foci	$(\pm ae,0)$ or $(\pm c,0)$	$(0,\pm ae)$ or $(0,\pm c)$
7. Eccentricity	$e=\sqrt{1+\frac{b^2}{a^2}}$ or $\frac{c}{a}$	$e=\sqrt{1+\frac{b^2}{a^2}}$ or $\frac{c}{a}$
8. Length of latus rectum	$\frac{2b^2}{a}$	$\frac{2b^2}{a}$

➤ Extra Information

- The standard equation of parabolas have focus on one of the co-ordinate axis, vertex at the origin and the directrix is parallel to the other coordinate axis.
- In case of an ellipse, where $c^2=a^2-b^2$, if $c = 0$, then the ellipse is a circle and if $c = a$, then the ellipse reduces to a line segment.
- Foci of an ellipse always lie on the major axis. If the coefficient of x^2 has the larger denominator, then major axis is along x-axis. If the coefficient of y^2 has the larger denominator, then major axis is along y-axis.
- Ellipse and Hyperbola are symmetrical with respect to both the axes.
- In hyperbola, foci always lie on the transverse axis. If the denominator of x^2 gives the positive term, then transverse axis is along x-axis and if the denominator of y^2 gives the positive term, then transverse axis id along y-axis.
- In a hyperbola, no portion of the curve lies between $x = a$ and $x = -a$.

Multiple Choice Questions (1 mark each)

[A] Objective Type Questions

Q. 1. If the focus of a parabola is (0, –3) and its directrix is $y = 3$, then its equation is

(A) $x^2 = -12y$ **(B) $x^2 = 12y$**

(C) $y^2 = -12x$ **(D) $y^2 = 12x$**

[NCERT Exemplar Q. 51, Page 206]

Ans. Correct option : (A)

According to the definition of parabola

$$\sqrt{(x-0)^2+(y+3)^2} = \left|\frac{y-3}{\sqrt{0^2+1^2}}\right|$$

$$\sqrt{x^2+y^2+9+6y} = |y-3|$$

Squaring both sides, we get

$x^2 + y^2 + 9 + 6y = y^2 + 9 - 6y$

$\Rightarrow x^2 = -12y$

Q. 2. If the parabola $y^2 = 4ax$ passes through the point (3, 2), then the length of its latus rectum is

(A) $\frac{2}{3}$ **(B) $\frac{4}{3}$**

(C) $\frac{1}{3}$ **(D) 4**

[NCERT Exemplar Q. 52, Page 206]

Ans. Correct option : (B)

Given parabola is $y^2 = 4ax$

If the parabola is passing through (3, 2), then

$(2)^2 = 4a \times 3 \Rightarrow a = \frac{1}{3}$

$\therefore$ length of latus rectum $= 4a = 4 \times \frac{1}{3} = \frac{4}{3}$

Q. 3. If the vertex of the parabola is the point (–3, 0) and the directrix is the line $x + 5 = 0$, then its equation is

(A) $y^2 = 8(x+3)$ **(B) $x^2 = 8(y+3)$**

(C) $y^2 = -8(x+3)$ **(D) $y^2 = 8(x+5)$**

[NCERT Exemplar Q. 53, Page 206]

Ans. Correct option : (A)

Given that vertex = (–3, 0)

$\therefore a = -3$ and directrix is $x + 5 = 0$

According to the definition of the parabola, we get

$AF = AD$ i.e. A is the mid point of DF

$\therefore -3 = \frac{x_1 - 5}{2}$

$\Rightarrow x_1 = -1$

and $0 = \frac{0+y_1}{2} \Rightarrow y_1 = 0$

$\therefore$ Focus $f = (-1, 0)$

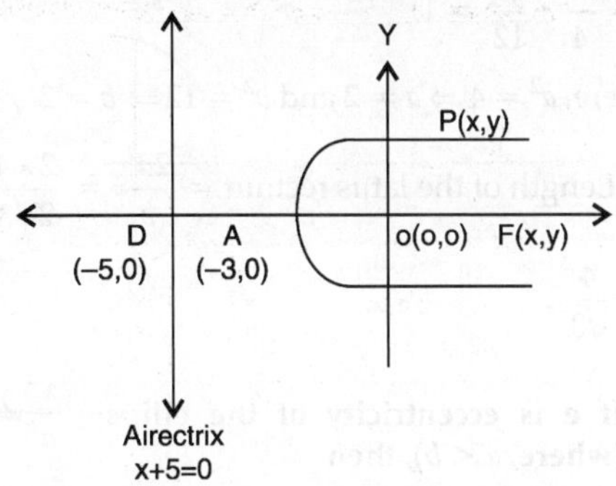

Now, $\sqrt{(x+1)^2-(y-0)^2} = \left|\frac{x+5}{\sqrt{1^2+0^2}}\right|$

Squaring both sides, we get

$(x + 1)^2 + y^2 = (x + 5)^2$

$\Rightarrow x^2 + 2x + 1 + y^2 = x^2 + 10x + 25$

$\Rightarrow y^2 = 8(x + 3)$

Q. 4. If equation of the ellipse whose focus is (1, –1), then directrix the line $x - y - 3 = 0$ and eccentricity $\frac{1}{2}$ is

(A) $7x^2+2xy+7y^2-10x+10y+7=0$

(B) $7x^2+2xy+7y^2+7=0$

(C) $7x^2+2xy+7y^2+10x-10y-7=0$

(D) None of the above

[NCERT Exemplar Q. 54, Page 206]

Ans. Correct option : (A)

Given that focus of the ellipse is (1, –1) and the eq. of the directrix is $x - y - 3 = 0$ and $e = \frac{1}{2}$

Let $P(x, y)$ be any point on the ellipse

$$\therefore \frac{PF}{\text{distance of the point P from the directrix}} = e$$

$$\frac{\sqrt{(x-1)^2+(y+1)^2}}{\left|\frac{x-y-3}{\sqrt{1^2+(-1)^2}}\right|} = \frac{1}{2}$$

$$\Rightarrow 2\sqrt{x^2+1-2x+y^2+1+2y} = \left|\frac{x-y-3}{\sqrt{2}}\right|$$

Squaring both sides, we have

$$4(x^2 + y^2 - 2x + 2y + 2) = \frac{x^2+y^2+9-2xy+6y-6x}{2}$$

$\Rightarrow 7x^2 + 7y^2 + 2xy - 10x + 10y + 7 = 0.$

Q. 5. The length of the latus rectum of ellipse $3x^2 + y^2 = 12$ is

(A) 4 **(B) 3**

(C) 8 **(D) $\frac{4}{\sqrt{3}}$**

[NCERT Exemplar Q. 55, Page 206]

Ans. Correct option : (D)

Eq. of the ellipse is $3x^2 + y^2 = 12$

$\Rightarrow \frac{x^2}{4} + \frac{y^2}{12} = 1$

Here, $a^2 = 4 \Rightarrow a = 2$ and $b^2 = 12 \Rightarrow b = 2\sqrt{3}$

$\therefore$ Length of the latus rectum $= \frac{2a^2}{b} = \frac{2\times4}{2\sqrt{3}}$

$= \frac{4}{\sqrt{3}}$.

Q. 6. If e is eccentricity of the ellipse $\frac{x^2}{a^2} + \frac{y^2}{b^2} = 1$ (where, $a < b$), then

(A) $b^2 = a^2(1-e^2)$ (B) $a^2 = b^2(1-e^2)$

(C) $a^2 = b^2(e^2-1)$ (D) $b^2 = a^2(e^2-1)$

[NCERT Exemplar Q. 56, Page 206]

Ans. Correct option : (B)

Given eq. $\frac{x^2}{a^2} + \frac{y^2}{b^2} = 1\ (a < b)$

$\therefore$ Eccentricity $e = \sqrt{1 - \frac{a^2}{b^2}} \Rightarrow e^2 = 1 - \frac{a^2}{b^2}$

$\Rightarrow \frac{a^2}{b^2} = (1 - e^2) \Rightarrow a^2 = b^2(1 - e^2)$.

Q. 7. The eccentricity of the hyperbola whose latus rectum is 8 and conjugate axis is equal to half of the distance between the foci is

(A) $\frac{4}{3}$ (B) $\frac{4}{\sqrt{3}}$

(C) $\frac{2}{\sqrt{3}}$ (D) None of these

[NCERT Exemplar Q. 57, Page 207]

Ans. Correct option : (C)

Length of latus rectum of the hyperbola $= \frac{2b^2}{a} = 8$

$\Rightarrow b^2 = 4a$ ...(i)

Distance between the foci $= 2ae$

Transverse axis $= 2a$

and conjugate axis $= 2b$

$\therefore \frac{1}{2}(2ae) = 2b \Rightarrow ae = 2b \Rightarrow b = \frac{ae}{2}$ ...(ii)

$\Rightarrow b^2 = \frac{a^2e^2}{4} \Rightarrow 4a = \frac{a^2e^2}{4}$ [from (i)]

$16 = ae^2 \Rightarrow a = \frac{16}{e^2}$ ...(ii)

Now, $b^2 = a^2(e^2 - 1)$

$\Rightarrow 4a = a^2(e^2 - 1)$

$\Rightarrow \frac{4}{a} = e^2 - 1$

$\Rightarrow \frac{4}{\frac{16}{e}} = e^2 - 1$

$\Rightarrow \frac{e^2}{4} = e^2 - 1$

$\Rightarrow \frac{3e^2}{4} = 1 \Rightarrow e^2 = \frac{4}{3} \Rightarrow e = \frac{2}{\sqrt{3}}$.

[B] True or False :

Q. 1. The line $lx + my + n = 0$ will touch the parabola $y^2 = 4ax$, if $ln = am^2$

[NCERT Exemplar Q. 37, Page 204]

Q. 2. If P is a point on the ellipse $\frac{x^2}{16} + \frac{y^2}{25} = 1$ whose foci are S and S^1, then $PS + PS^1 = 8$

[NCERT Exemplar Q. 38, Page 204]

Q. 3. The line $2x + 3y = 12$ touches the ellipse $\frac{x^2}{9} + \frac{y^2}{4} = 2$ at the point (3, 2).

[NCERT Exemplar Q. 39, Page 204]

Q. 4. The Locus of the point of intersection of lines $\sqrt{3}x - y - 4\sqrt{3}k = 0$ and $\sqrt{3}kx + ky - 4\sqrt{3} = 0$ for different value of k is a hyperbola whose eccentricity is 2.

[NCERT Exemplar Q. 40, Page 204]

Answer:

1. True
2. False
3. True
4. True

[C] Fill in the blanks

Q. 1 An ellipse is described by using an endless string which is passed over two pins. If the axes are 6 cm and 4 cm, the length of the string and distance between the pins are ....

[NCERT Exemplar Q. 43, Page 205]

Q. 2. The equation of the ellipse having foci (0, 1), (0, –1) and minor axis of length 1 is ....

[NCERT Exemplar Q. 44, Page 205]

Q. 3. The equation of the parabola having focus at (–1, –2) and directrix is $x - 2y + 3 = 0$, is ....

[NCERT Exemplar Q. 45, Page 205]

Q. 4. The equation of the hyperbola with vertices at (0, ± 6) and eccentricity $\frac{5}{3}$ is .... and its foci are ....

[NCERT Exemplar Q. 46, Page 205]

Answer:

1. $2\sqrt{5}$
2. $\frac{4x^2}{1} + \frac{4y^2}{5} = 1$
3. $4x^2 + y^2 + 4x + 4xy + 32y + 16 = 0$
4. $\frac{y^2}{36} - \frac{x^2}{64} = 1$, (0, ± 10)

Very Short Answer Type Questions (1 mark each)

Find the equation of the parabola (from Questions. 1 – 4) that satisfies the following conditions.
[NCERT Exemplar, Q. 7-10, Page 246-247]

Q. 1. Focus (6, 0); directrix $x = -6$.

Sol. Given focus = (6, 0), so $a = 6$

and directrix $x = -6$, so the parabola is of the form $y^2 = 4ax$

$\Rightarrow y^2 = 24x$.

Q. 2. Focus (0, –3) and directrix $y = 3$.

Sol. Since focus is (0, –3), so it lies on Y-axis.

$\therefore a = 3$

and directrix $y = 3$, so the parabola is of the form

$x^2 = -4ay$

$\Rightarrow x^2 = -12y$.

Q. 3. Vertex (0, 0), Focus (3, 0).

Sol. Since Focus (3, 0) lies on x-axis, I Quadrant so $a = 3$ and the parabola is of the form

$y^2 = 4ax$

$\Rightarrow y^2 = 12x$.

Q. 4. Vertex (0, 0), focus (–2, 0).

Sol. Since focus (–2, 0), lies on X-axis, II Quadrant so $a = 2$ and the parabola is of the from

$y^2 = -4ax$

$\Rightarrow y^2 = -8x$.

Short Answer Type Questions (2 marks each)

Q. 1. If the latus rectum of an ellipse is equal to half of minor axis, then find its eccentricity.
[NCERT Exemplar Q. 11, Page 202]

Sol. Consider the equation of the ellipse is $\frac{x^2}{a^2} + \frac{y^2}{b^2} = 1$.

and length of latus rectum = $\frac{2b^2}{a}$

Now $\frac{2b^2}{a} = b$

$b = \frac{a}{2}$

$\Rightarrow b^2 = a^2(1 - e^2)$

We know that,

$\Rightarrow \left(\frac{a}{2}\right)^2 = a^2(1 - e^2)$

$\Rightarrow \frac{a^2}{4} = a^2(1 - e^2)$

$\Rightarrow 1 - e^2 = \frac{1}{4}$

$\Rightarrow e^2 = 1 - \frac{1}{4}$

$\therefore e = \sqrt{\frac{3}{4}} = \frac{\sqrt{3}}{2}$.

Q. 2. If the ellipse with equation $9x^2 + 25y^2 = 225$, then find the eccentricity and foci.
[NCERT Exemplar Q. 11, Page 362]

Sol. Given equation of ellipse, $9x^2 + 25y^2 = 225$

$\Rightarrow \frac{x^2}{25} + \frac{y^2}{9} = 1$

$\Rightarrow a = 5, b = 3$

We know that, $b^2 = a^2(1 - e^2)$

$\Rightarrow 9 = 25(1 - e^2)$

$\Rightarrow \frac{9}{25} = 1 - e^2$

$\Rightarrow e^2 = 1 - \frac{9}{25}$

$\therefore e = \sqrt{1 - \frac{9}{25}} = \sqrt{\frac{25 - 9}{25}}$

$= \sqrt{\frac{16}{25}} = \frac{4}{5}$

Foci = $(\pm ae, 0)$ $ae = 5 \times \frac{4}{5} = 4$

$(\pm 4, 0)$

Q. 3. Find the equation of ellipse whose eccentricity is $\frac{2}{3}$, latus rectum is 5 and the centre is (0, 0).
[NCERT Exemplar Q. 14, Page 203]

Sol. Given that, $e = \frac{2}{3}$ and latus rectum = 5

i.e., $\frac{2b^2}{a} = 5 \Rightarrow b^2 = \frac{5a}{2}$

We know that, $b^2 = a^2(1 - e^2)$

$\Rightarrow \frac{5a}{2} = a^2\left(1 - \frac{4}{9}\right)$

$\Rightarrow \frac{5}{2} = \frac{5a}{9} \Rightarrow a = \frac{9}{2} \Rightarrow a^2 = \frac{81}{4}$

$\Rightarrow b^2 = \frac{5 \times 9}{2 \times 2} = \frac{45}{4}$

So, the required equation of the ellipse is $\frac{4x^2}{81} + \frac{4y^2}{45} = 1$.

Q. 4. Find the distance between the directrices of ellipse $\frac{x^2}{36}+\frac{y^2}{20}=1$.

[NCERT Exemplar Q. 15, Page 203]

Sol. The equation of ellipse is $\frac{x^2}{36}+\frac{y^2}{20}=1$.

$a=6, b=2\sqrt{5}$

We know that, $b^2=a^2(1-e^2)$

$\Rightarrow\ 20=36(1-e^2)$

$\Rightarrow\ \frac{20}{30}=1-e^2$

$\therefore\ e=\sqrt{1-\frac{20}{36}}=\sqrt{\frac{16}{36}}$

$e=\frac{4}{6}=\frac{2}{3}$

Now, directrices $=\left(+\frac{a}{e},-\frac{a}{e}\right)$

$\therefore\ \frac{a}{e}=\frac{6}{\frac{2}{3}}=\frac{6\times 3}{2}=9$

and $-\frac{a}{e}=-9$

$\therefore$ Distance between the directrices $=|9-(-9)|=18$

Q. 5. Find the co-ordinates of a point on the parabola $y^2=8x$, whose focal distance is 4.

[NCERT Exemplar Q. 16, Page 203]

Sol. Given parabola is $y^2=8x$ (i)

$8x=4ax \Rightarrow a=2$

$\therefore$ Focal distance $=|x+a|=4$

$\Rightarrow |x+2|=4$

$\Rightarrow x+2=\pm 4$

$\Rightarrow x=2,-6$

But $x\neq -6$

For $x=2$, $y^2=8\times 2$

$\therefore\ y^2=16 \Rightarrow y=\pm 4$

So, the points are $(2,4)$ and $(2,-4)$.

Q. 6. Find the eccentricity of the hyperbola $9y^2-4x^2=36$.

[NCERT Exemplar Q. 21, Page 203]

Sol. Given equation of the hyperbola is

$9y^2-4x^2=36$

$\Rightarrow \frac{9y^2}{36}-\frac{4x^2}{36}=\frac{36}{36}$

$\Rightarrow \frac{y^2}{4}-\frac{x^2}{9}=1$

$a=2, b=3$

$\therefore\ e=\sqrt{1+\left(\frac{b}{a}\right)^2}$

$=\sqrt{1+\frac{9}{4}}=\frac{\sqrt{13}}{2}$

Q. 7. Find the equation of the hyperbola with eccentricity $\frac{3}{2}$ and foci at $(\pm 2,0)$.

[NCERT Exemplar Q. 21, Page 203]

Sol. Given that eccentricity $e=\frac{3}{2}$

$\therefore\ ae=2$

$\Rightarrow\ a\cdot\frac{3}{2}=2 \Rightarrow a=\frac{4}{3}$

$\because\ b^2=a^2(e^2-1)$

$\Rightarrow\ b^2=\frac{16}{9}\left(\frac{9}{4}-1\right)$

$\Rightarrow\ b^2=\frac{16}{9}\left(\frac{5}{4}\right)=+\frac{20}{9}$

So, the equation of hyperbola is

$\frac{x^2}{\frac{16}{9}}-\frac{y^2}{\frac{20}{9}}=1$

$\Rightarrow\ \frac{x^2}{4}-\frac{y^2}{5}=\frac{4}{9}$.

Q. 8. If the distance between the foci of a hyperbola is 16 and its eccentricity is $\sqrt{2}$, then obtain the equation of the hyperbola.

[NCERT Exemplar Q. 20, Page 203]

Sol. Distance between the foci *i.e.*, $2ae=16 \Rightarrow ae=8$

and $e=\sqrt{2}$

$\therefore\ a\sqrt{2}=8$

$a=4\sqrt{2}$

We know that, $b^2=a^2(e^2-1)$

$\Rightarrow\ b^2=(4\sqrt{2})^2\left[(\sqrt{2})^2-1\right]$

$=16\times 2(2-1)$

$=32(2-1)$

$=32$

So, the equation of hyperbola is

$\frac{x^2}{32}-\frac{y^2}{32}=1$

$\Rightarrow\ x^2-y^2=32$.

Long Answer Type Questions-I (4 marks each)

Q. 1. A rod of length 12 cm moves with its ends always touching the co-ordinate axes. Determine the equation of the locus of a point P on the rod, which is 3 cm, from the end in contact with the X-axis. [NCERT Exemplar Q. 5, Page 264]

Sol. Let AB be the rod making an angle θ with OX and P (x, y) be the point on it such that AP=3 cm.

Then, PB = $AB - AB$ = (12 – 3) cm = 9 cm [AB = 12 cm]

From P, draw PQ⊥OY and PR⊥OX.

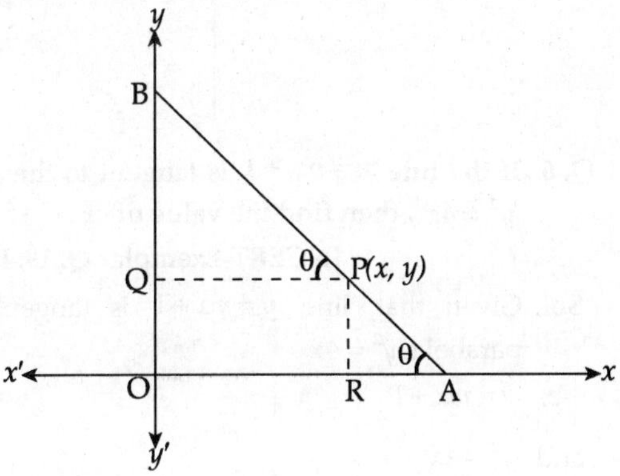

In ΔPBQ, $\cos\theta = \frac{PQ}{PB} = \frac{x}{9}$

In ΔPRA, $\sin\theta = \frac{PR}{PA} = \frac{y}{3}$

Since, $\sin^2\theta + \cos^2\theta = 1$,

$$\left(\frac{y}{3}\right)^2 + \left(\frac{x}{9}\right)^2 = 1$$

or, $\frac{x^2}{81} + \frac{y^2}{9} =$

Thus, the equation of the locus of point P on the rod is $\frac{x^2}{81} + \frac{y^2}{9} = 1$.

Q. 2. Find the area of the triangle formed by the lines joining the vertex of the parabola $x^2 = 12y$ to the ends of its latus rectum. [NCERT Exemplar Q. 6, Page 264]

Sol. The given parabola is $x^2 = 12y$.

On comparing this equation with $x^2 = 4ay$, we obtain $4a = 12 \Rightarrow a = 3$

∴ The co-ordinates of foci are S $(0, a)$ = S (0, 3)

Let AB be the latus rectum of the given parabola.

The given parabola can be roughly drawn as

At $y = 3$, $x^2 = 12(3) \Rightarrow x^2 = 36 \Rightarrow x = \pm 6$

∴ The co-ordinates of A are (–6, 3), while co-ordinates of B are (6, 3).

Therefore, the vertices of ΔOAB are (–6, 3), and B (6, 3).

Area of ΔOAB =

$$\Delta OAB = \frac{1}{2}\left|0(3-3)+(-6)(3-0)+6(0-3)\right| \text{unit}^2$$

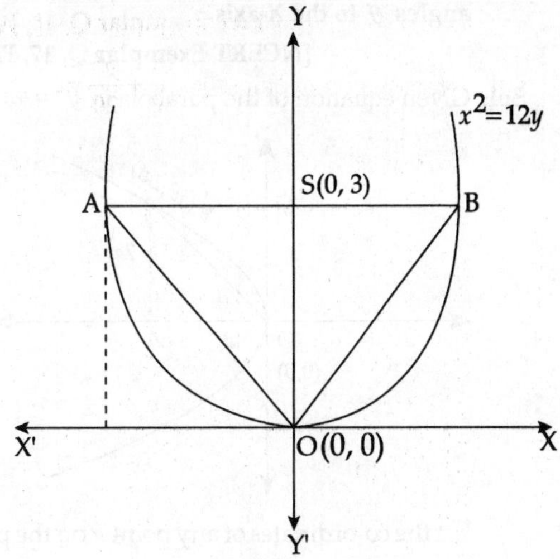

$$= \frac{1}{2}\left|(-6)(3)+6(-3)\right| \text{unit}^2$$

$$= \frac{1}{2}\left|-18-18\right| \text{unit}^2$$

$$= \frac{1}{2}\left|-36\right| \text{unit}^2$$

$$= \frac{1}{2} \times 36 \text{unit}^2$$

$$= 18 \text{ unit}^2$$

The, the required area of the triangle is 18 unit^2.

Q. 3. If the eccentricity of an ellipse is $\frac{5}{8}$ and the distance between its foci is 10, then find latus rectum of the ellipse. [NCERT Exemplar Q. 13, Page 202]

Sol. Given that, eccentricity $e = \frac{5}{8}$

Let equation of the ellipse be $\frac{x^2}{a^2} + \frac{y^2}{b^2} = 1$

Since the foci of this ellipse is $(\pm ae, 0)$

∴ Distance between foci = $2ae = 10$ [Distance between its foci = 10]

$\Rightarrow e = \frac{5}{8}$

∴ $a = 8$

We know that,

$$\Rightarrow b^2 = a^2(1-e^2)$$

$$\Rightarrow b^2 = 64\left(1 - \frac{25}{64}\right)$$

$$\Rightarrow b^2 = 64\left(\frac{64-25}{64}\right)$$

$$b^2 = 39$$

∴ Length of latus rectum of ellipse

$$= \frac{2b^2}{a} = 2\left(\frac{39}{8}\right) = \frac{39}{4}.$$

Q. 4. Find the length of the line segment joining the vertex of the parabola $y^2 = 4ax$ and a point on the parabola, where the line segment makes an angles θ to the X-axis.

[NCERT Exemplar Q. 17, Page 203]

Sol. Given equation of the parabola is $y^2 = 4ax$

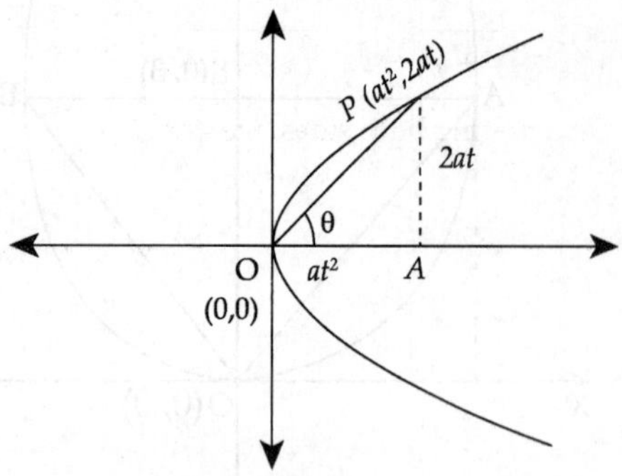

Let the co-ordinates of any point P on the parabola be $(at^2, 2at)$.

In ΔPOA, $\tan\theta = \frac{2at}{at^2} = \frac{2}{t}$

$\Rightarrow \tan\theta = \frac{2}{t} \Rightarrow t = 2\cot\theta$

$\therefore$ Length of $OP = \sqrt{(0-at^2)^2 + (0-2at)^2}$

$= \sqrt{a^2t^4 + 4a^2t^2}$

$= at\sqrt{t^2+4}$

$= 2a\cot\theta\sqrt{4\cot^2\theta + 4}$

$= 4a\cot\theta\sqrt{1+\cot^2\theta}$

$= 4a\cot\theta \cdot \operatorname{cosec}\theta$

$= \frac{4a\cos\theta}{\sin\theta} \cdot \frac{1}{\sin\theta} = \frac{4a\cos\theta}{\sin^2\theta}$.

Q. 5. If the points (0, 4) and (0, 2) are respectively the vertex and focus of a parabola, then find the equation of the parabola.

[NCERT Exemplar Q. 18, Page 203]

Sol. Given that the co-ordinates, vertex of the parabola (0, 4) and focus of the parabola (0,2).

$PM = PS$

$\Rightarrow \left|\frac{0+y-6}{\sqrt{0+1}}\right| = \sqrt{(x-0)^2 + (y-2)^2}$

$\Rightarrow |y-6| = \sqrt{x^2 + y^2 - 4y + 4}$

$\Rightarrow x^2 + y^2 - 4y + 4 = y^2 + 36 - 12y$

$\Rightarrow x^2 + 8y = 32$.

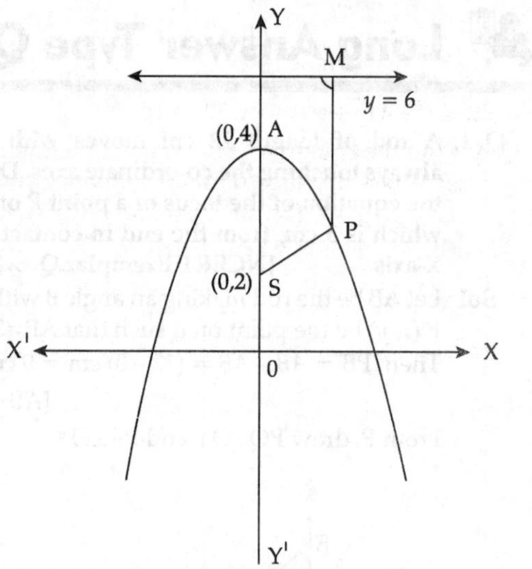

Q. 6. If the line $y = mx + 1$ is tangent to the parabola $y^2 = 4x$, then find the value of m.

[NCERT Exemplar Q. 19, Page 203]

Sol. Given that, line $y = mx + 1$ is tangent to the parabola $y^2 = 4x$.

$\therefore \quad y = mx + 1$ (i)

and $\quad y^2 = 4x$ (ii)

putting the value of y from (i) in to (ii)

$m^2x^2 + 2mx + 1 = 4x$

$\Rightarrow m^2x^2 + 2mx - 4x + 1 = 0$

$\Rightarrow m^2x^2 + x(2m-4) + 1 = 0$ [for tangent $B^2 - 4AC = 0$]

$\Rightarrow (2m-4)^2 - 4m^2 \times 1 = 0$

$\Rightarrow 4m^2 + 16 - 16m - 4m^2 = 0$

$\Rightarrow 16m = 16$

$\therefore m = 1$

[$y = mx + 1$ is the tangent to the parabola]

Q. 7. Find the equation of each of the following parabolas

(i) directrix $x = 0$, focus at (6, 0)

(ii) focus at (–1, –2), directrix $x - 2y + 3 = 0$

[NCERT Exemplar Q. 28, Page 203]

Sol. (i) Given that, directrix $x = 0$ and focus = (6, 0)

So, the equation of the parabola

$(x-6)^2 + y^2 = x^2$

$\Rightarrow x^2 + 36 - 12x + y^2 = x^2$

$\Rightarrow y^2 - 12x + 36 = 0$

(ii) Given that, focus at (–1, –2) and directrix $x - 2y + 3 = 0$

So, the equation of parabola is

$\sqrt{(x+1)^2 + (y+2)^2} = \left|\frac{x-2y+3}{\sqrt{1+4}}\right|$

$$x^2+2x+1+y^2+4y+4=\frac{1}{5}\left[x^2+4y^2+9-4xy-12y+6x\right]$$

$\Rightarrow\ 4x^2+4xy+y^2+4x+32y+16=0$.

Q. 8. Find the equation of the set of all points the sum of whose distances From the points (3, 0), (9, 0) is 12. [NCERT Exemplar Q. 29, Page 204]

Sol. According to the problems

$$\sqrt{(x-3)^2+y^2}+\sqrt{(x-9)^2+y^2}=12$$

$$\sqrt{(x-3)^2+y^2}=12-\sqrt{(x-9)^2+y^2}$$

On squaring both sides, we get

$$x^2-6x+9+y^2$$

$$=144+\left(x^2-18x+81+y^2\right)-24\sqrt{(x-9)^2+y^2}$$

$\Rightarrow\ 12x-216=-24\sqrt{(x-9)^2+y^2}$

$\Rightarrow\ x-18=-2\sqrt{(x-9)^2+y^2}$

$\Rightarrow\ x^2-36x+324=4\left(x^2-18x+81+y^2\right)$

$\Rightarrow\ 3x^2+4y^2-36x=0$.

Q. 9. Find the equation of the set of all points whose distance from (0, 4) are $\frac{2}{3}$ of their distance from the line y = 9.[NCERT Exemplar Q. 30, Page 204]

Sol. Let the point be $P(x, y)$

$\therefore$ Distance from $(0,4)=\sqrt{x^2+(y-4)^2}$

So, the distance from the line y = 9 is $\left|\frac{y-9}{\sqrt{1}}\right|$

$\therefore\ \sqrt{x^2+(y-4)^2}=\frac{2}{3}\left|\frac{y-9}{\sqrt{0+1}}\right|$

$\Rightarrow\ x^2+y^2-8y+16=\frac{4}{9}\left(y^2-18y+81\right)$

$\Rightarrow\ 9x^2+9y^2-72y+144=4y^2-72y+324$

$\Rightarrow\ 9x^2+5y^2=180$.

Q. 10. Show that the set of all points such that the difference of their distance from (4, 0) and (–4, 0) is always equal to 2 represent a hyperbola. [NCERT Exemplar Q. 31, Page 204]

Sol. According to the problems

$$\sqrt{(x+4)^2+y^2}-\sqrt{(x-4)^2+y^2}=2$$

$$\sqrt{(x+4)^2+y^2}=2+\sqrt{(x-4)^2+y^2}$$

On squaring both sides, we get

$$x^2+8x+16+y^2=4+x^2-8x+16+y^2+4\sqrt{(x-4)^2+y^2}$$

$\Rightarrow\ 16x-4=4\sqrt{(x-4)^2+y^2}$

$\Rightarrow\ 4(4x-1)=4\sqrt{(x-4)^2+y^2}$

$\Rightarrow\ 16x^2-8x+1=x^2+16-8x+y^2$

$\Rightarrow\ 15x^2-y^2=15$ which is a hyperbola.

Q. 11. Given the ellipse with equation $9x^2 + 25y^2 = 225$, find the eccentricity and foci. [NCERT Exemplar Q. 12, Page 202]

Sol. Given equation of ellipse is $9x^2 + 25y^2 = 225$

$\Rightarrow\ \frac{9}{225}x^2+\frac{25}{225}y^2=1$

$\Rightarrow\ \frac{x^2}{25}+\frac{y^2}{9}=1$

Hence a = 5 and b = 3

$b^2 = a^2(1 - e^2)$

$\Rightarrow 9 = 25(1 - e^2)$

$\Rightarrow 1 - e^2 = \frac{9}{25} \Rightarrow e^2 = 1 - \frac{9}{25} = \frac{16}{25} \Rightarrow e = \frac{9}{25} = \frac{16}{25}$

Now foci = (± ae, 0) = $\left(\pm 5\times\frac{4}{5},0\right)$ = (± 4, 0)

Hence, eccentricity = $\frac{4}{5}$, foci = (± 4, 0)

Long Answer Type Questions-II

(6 marks each)

Q. 1. Find the equation of the hyperbola with

(i) Vertices $(\pm 5, 0)$, foci $(\pm 7, 0)$

(ii) Vertices $(0, \pm 7)$, e $=\frac{7}{3}$.

(iii) Foci $(0, \pm\sqrt{10})$, passing through $(2, 3)$.

[NCERT Exemplar Q. 32, Page 204]

Sol. (i) Given that, vertices = $(\pm 5, 0)$, foci $(\pm 7, 0)$ and $a=\pm 5$

$\Rightarrow\ (\pm ae, 0)=(\pm 7, 0)$

Now $ae=7\Rightarrow 5e=7$

$\Rightarrow\ e=\frac{7}{5}$

$\Rightarrow\ b^2=a^2\left(e^2-1\right)$

$\Rightarrow\ b^2=25\left(\frac{49}{25}-1\right)$

$\Rightarrow\ b^2=25\left(\frac{49-25}{25}\right)$

$\Rightarrow\ b^2=24$

The equation

$\frac{x^2}{25}-\frac{y^2}{24}=1$ $\qquad [\because\ a^2=25 \text{ and } b^2=24]$

(ii) vertices = $(\pm 7, 0)$, $e=\frac{4}{3}$

$\therefore b = 7, e = \frac{4}{3}$

$\because e^2 = 1 + \frac{a^2}{b^2}$

$\Rightarrow \frac{16}{9} - 1 = \frac{a^2}{49}$

$\Rightarrow \frac{7}{9} = \frac{a^2}{49} \Rightarrow a^2 = \frac{343}{9}$

The equation is

$-\frac{x^2 \times 9}{343} + \frac{y^2}{49} = 1$

$\Rightarrow \frac{y^2}{49} - \frac{9x^2}{343} = 1$

(iii) Given that, foci $= (0, \pm\sqrt{10})$

$\because ae = \sqrt{10}$

$\Rightarrow a^2 + b^2 = 10$

$\therefore$ Equation of the hyperbola be $b^2 = 10 - a^2$

Since, this hyperbola passes through the point (2, 3)

$\Rightarrow \frac{y^2}{a^2} - \frac{x^2}{b^2} = 1$

$\Rightarrow \frac{y^2}{a^2} - \frac{x^2}{10 - a^2} = 1$

passing (2, 3)

$\Rightarrow \frac{9}{a^2} - \frac{4}{10 - a^2} = 1$

$9(10 - a^2) - 4(a^2) = a^2(10 - a^2)$

$\Rightarrow a^4 - 23a^2 + 90 = 0$

$\Rightarrow (a^2 - 18)(a^2 - 5) = 0$

$\Rightarrow a = \sqrt{5}, b = \sqrt{5}$

So, the equation of hyperbola is $\frac{y^2}{5} - \frac{x^2}{5} = 1$.

EXPERT ADVICE

- *Make sure you know all the formulas used in the chapter.*
- *You can write down all the formulas to speed up recollection of the same during the exam.*
- *Make neat figures and label it properly.*
- *Practise the questions and examples given in the NCERT text book.*

OSWAAL LEARNING TOOLS

For **Suggested Online Videos**

Visit : *https://youtu.be/rCfriRsKTcQ* Or Scan the Code	**Visit :** *https://youtu.be/X7B8vbXz9t0* Or Scan the Code
Visit : *https://youtu.be/1-Q_BQ0ypmg* Or Scan the Code	**Visit :** *https://youtu.be/O8xvTF2otoo* Or Scan the Code
Visit : *https://youtu.be/0BvW8Dh1MOU* Or Scan the Code	**Visit :** *https://goo.gl/m71FRb* Or Scan the Code

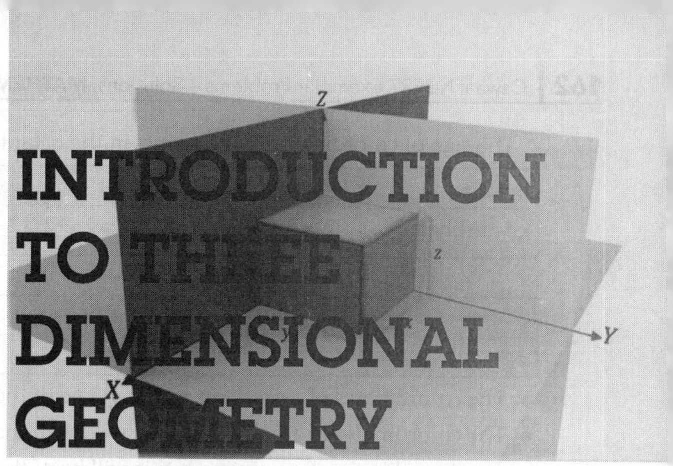

CHAPTER 12 INTRODUCTION TO THREE DIMENSIONAL GEOMETRY

Chapter Objectives

> *Co-ordinates axes and co-ordinate planes in three dimensions; Co-ordinates of a point. Distance between two points and Section Formulae; Co-ordinate of the centroid of a triangle;*

Quick Review

- Coordinate Axes and co-ordinates planes in Three Dimensional space

  Let XOX', YOY' and ZOZ' be three mutually perpendicular lines, intersecting at O. The point O(O, O, O) is called the origin and the lines (XOX', YOY', ZOZ') are called co-ordinate or rectangular axes $(X, Y$ and Z respectively). $X'OX$ is called X-axis, YOY' is called Y-axis and ü ′ is called Z-axis.

  The three co-ordinate axes defines three mutually perpendicular planes XOY, YOZ and $ZOX($ or $XY, YZ, ZX)$ are called coordinate planes which divide space into eight parts called octants.

  XOY-XY plane, YOZ-YZ plane, ZOX-ZX plane, $XOYZ, X'OYZ, XOY'Z, X'OY'Z', XOYZ', X'OYZ', XOY'Z'$ and $X'OY'Z'$ are called octants.

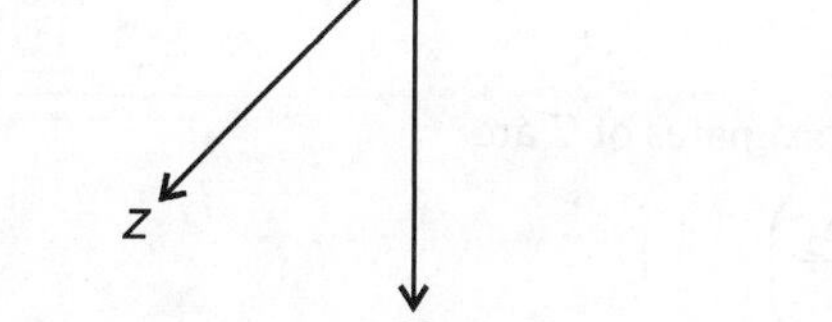

- Co-ordinates of a point in space.

  Let P be a point in space. Then, $P(x, y, z)$ are its co-ordinates where x-co-ordinate of P = length of perpendicular from P to YZ-plane with sign.

  y-co-ordinate of P = length of perpendicular from P to ZX-plane with sign.

TIPS...

- *All the formulae are very much similar to two dimension co-ordinate geometry, so you can learn easily.*
- *To locate the position of a object on a line, you just need the distance of the object from the point of reference.*
- *To locate the position of a point in a plane, we need two interesting mutually perpendicular lines in the plane. These lines are called the co-ordinate axes and the two number are called the co-ordinate of the point w.r.t. the axes.*
- *The three planes determined by the pair of axes are the co-ordinate planes, called XY, YZ and ZX-planes. The three coordinate planes divide the space in eight parts known as octants.*

TRICKS...

- *Planes parallel to the co-ordinate planes*
  - *(i) Equation of yz-plane is $x = 0$*
  - *(ii) Equation of xz-plane is $y = 0$*
  - *(iii) Equation of xy-plane is $z = 0$*
- *The distance of a point $P(x, y, z)$ from the origin $O(0, 0, 0)$ is $\sqrt{x^2+y^2+z^2}$*
- *The co-ordinates of a point P which divides line AB in the ratio K : 1 are*

  $$\left(\frac{kx_2+x_1}{k+1}, \frac{ky_2+y_1}{k+1}, \frac{kz_2+z_1}{k+1}\right)$$

The sign of co-ordinates of the points in the octants in which the space is divided are given as follows

octants	I	II	III	IV	V	VI	VII	VIII
co-ordinates	OXYZ	OX′YZ	OX′Y′Z	OXY′Z	OXYZ′	OX′YZ′	OX′Y′Z′	OXY′Z′
x	+	–	–	+	+	–	–	+
y	+	+	–	–	+	+	–	–
z	+	+	+	+	–	–	–	–

- The co-ordinates of a point on x-axis will be of the form $(x, 0, 0)$.
- The co-ordinates of a point on y-axis will be of the form $(0, y, 0)$.
- The co-ordinates of a point on z-axis will be of the form $(0, 0, z)$.
- The co-ordinates of a point in xy plane is of the form $(x, y, 0)$.
- The co-ordinates of a point in yz plane is of the form $(0, y, z)$.
- The co-ordinates of a point in zx-plane is of the form $(x, 0, z)$.

➤ **Distance formula and its application in Geometry**

The distance between two points $P(x_1, y_1, z_1)$ and $Q(x_2, y_2, z_2)$ is given by

$$PQ = \left|\sqrt{(x_2 - x_1)^2 + (y_2 - y_1)^2 + (z_2 - z_1)^2}\right|$$

$$\text{or } PQ = \left|\sqrt{(x_1 - x_2)^2 + (y_1 - y_2)^2 + (z_1 - z_2)^2}\right|$$

➤ Three points A, B and C are said to be collinear if AB + BC= AC or BC + CA = AB or CA + AB = BC.

➤ **Properties of some Geometrical figures**

- **Properties of Triangles**
  (i) Scalene triangle - All three sides are unequal
  (ii) Right angled triangle - The sum of squares of any two sides is equal to the square of the third side.
  (iii) Isosceles triangle - Any two sides of a triangle are equal
  (iv) Equilateral triangle - All three sides of a triangle are equal.

- **Properties of Quadrilaterals**
  (i) Rectangle - Opposite sides are equal and diagonals are equal.
  (ii) Parallelogram - Opposite sides are equal and diagonals are unequal, OR, diagonals bisect each other.
  (iii) Rhombus - All four sides are equal and diagonals are unequal
  (iv) Square - All four sides are equal and diagonals are equal.

➤ **Section Formulae**

- Let $A(x_1, y_1, z_1)$ and $B(x_2, y_2, z_2)$ be end points of a line segment AB and C be any point on AB which divides AB in the ration $m : n$

  (i) If C divides AB internally, then the co-ordinates of C are

$$\left(\frac{mx_2 + nx_1}{m+n}, \frac{my_2 + ny_1}{m+n}, \frac{mz_2 + nz_1}{m+n}\right)$$

  (ii) If C divides AB externally, then the co-ordinates of C are

$$\left(\frac{mx_2 - nx_1}{m-n}, \frac{my_2 - ny_1}{m-n}, \frac{mz_2 - nz_1}{m-n}\right)$$

  (iii) If 'C' is the midpoint of AB, then $m : n = 1 : 1$, so the co-ordinates of C are

$$\left(\frac{x_1 + x_2}{2}, \frac{y_1 + y_2}{2}, \frac{z_1 + z_2}{2}\right)$$

  (iv) If 'C' trisect the line segment AB, then $m : n = 1 : 2$ or $m : n = 2 : 1$. So, the co-ordinates of C are

$$\left(\frac{2x_1 + x_2}{3}, \frac{2y_1 + y_2}{3}, \frac{2z_1 + z_2}{3}\right) \text{ or } \left(\frac{x_1 + 2x_2}{3}, \frac{y_1 + 2y_2}{3}, \frac{z_1 + 2z_2}{3}\right)$$

➢ **Co-ordinates of centroid of a triangle**

- If $A(x_1, y_1, z_1), B(x_2, y_2, z_2)$ and $C(x_3, y_3, z_3)$ are the vertices of ABC, then the co-ordinates of the centroid G of ΔABC are

$$G\left(\frac{x_1+x_2+x_3}{3}, \frac{y_1+y_2+y_3}{3}, \frac{z_1+z_2+z_3}{3}\right)$$

Multiple Choice Questions

(1 mark each)

[A] Objective Type Questions

Q. 1. The distance of point P(3, 4, 5) from the *YZ-plane* is

(A) 3 units **(B) 4 units**
(C) 5 units **(D) 550**

[NCERT Exemplar Q. 22, Page 222]

Ans. Correct option : (A)

Given point is (3, 4, 5)

$\therefore$ Distance of P from *yz*-plane

$$= \left|\sqrt{(0-3)^2+(4-4)^2+(5-5)^2}\right|$$

$$= \left|\sqrt{9}\right| = 3 \text{ units.}$$

Q. 2. What is the length of foot of perpendicular drawn from the point P(3, 4, 5) on Y-axis?

(A) $\sqrt{41}$ **(B) $\sqrt{34}$**
(C) 5 **(D) None of these**

[NCERT Exemplar Q. 23, Page 222]

Ans. Correct option : (B)

On *y*-axis, $x = 0$ and $z = 0$ and given point $P(3, 4, 5)$

$\therefore$ The point A is (0, 4, 0)

$$\therefore PA = \left|\sqrt{(0-3)^2+(4-4)^2+(0-5)^2}\right|$$

$$= \left|\sqrt{9+0+25}\right| = \sqrt{34}$$

Q. 3. Distance of point(3, 4, 5) from the origin (0,0,0) is

(A) $\sqrt{50}$ **(B) 3**
(C) 4 **(D) 5**

[NCERT Exemplar Q. 24, Page 222]

Ans. Correct option : (A)

Given point A(3, 4, 5) and give O(0, 0, 0)

$$\therefore \left|\sqrt{(3-0)^2+(4-0)^2+(5-0)^2}\right|$$

$$= \left|\sqrt{9+16+25}\right|$$

$$= \sqrt{50}.$$

Q. 4. If the distance between the points (a, 0, 1) and (0, 1, 2) is $\sqrt{27}$, then the value of *a* is

(A) 5 **(B) ±5**
(C) –5 **(D) None of these**

[NCERT Exemplar Q. 25, Page 222]

Ans. Correct option : (B)

Let the given points be $A(a, 0, 1)$ and $B(0, 1, 2)$

$$\therefore \left|\sqrt{(a-0)^2+(0-1)^2+(1-2)^2}\right| = \sqrt{27}$$

$$\left|\sqrt{a^2+1+1}\right| = \sqrt{27}$$

Squaring both sides, we get

$a^2 + 2 = 27 \Rightarrow a^2 = 25 \Rightarrow a = \pm 5.$

Q. 5. X-axis is the intersection of two planes

(A) *XY* and *XZ* **(B) *YZ* and *ZX***
(C) *XY* and *YZ* **(D) None of these**

[NCERT Exemplar Q. 26, Page 222]

Ans. Correct option : (A)

We know that on the *xz* and *xy* planes, the line of intersection is *x*-axis.

Q. 6. Equation of *Y*-axis is considered as

(A) $x = 0, y = 0$ **(B) $y = 0, z = 0$**
(C) $z = 0, x = 0$ **(D) None of these**

[NCERT Exemplar Q. 27, Page 222]

Ans. Correct option : (C)

On *y*-axis, $x = 0$ and $z = 0$

Q. 7. The point (–2, –3, –4) lies in the

(A) first octant **(B) seventh octant**
(C) second octant **(D) eight octant**

[NCERT Exemplar Q. 28, Page 222]

Ans. Correct option : (B)

The point (–2, –3, –4) lies in seventh octant.

Q. 8. A plane is parallel to *YZ*-plane, so it is perpendicular to

(A) *X*-axis **(B) *Y*-axis**
(C) *Z*-axis **(D) None of these**

[NCERT Exemplar Q. 29, Page 222]

Ans. Correct option : (A)

Any plane parallel to *yz* plane, so it is perpendicular to *x*-axis.

Q. 9. The locus of a point for which *Y*=0 and *Z*=0, is

(A) equation of *X*-axis **(B) equation of *Y*-axis**
(C) equation of *Z*-axis **(D) None of these**

[NCERT Exemplar Q. 30, Page 222]

Ans. Correct option : (A)

We know that the equation of *x*-axis; $y = 0, x = 0$

Hence, the locus of the point is equation of *x*-axis.

Q. 10. The locus of a point for which $x = 0$ is

(A) *XY*-plane **(B) *YZ*-plane**
(C) *ZX*-plane **(D) None of these**

[NCERT Exemplar Q. 31, Page 223]

Ans. Correct option : (B)

On the yz-plane, $x = 0$

Hence, the locus of the point is yz-plane.

Q. 11. If a parallelepiped is formed by planes drawn through the points (5, 8, 10) and (3, 6, 8) parallel to the coordinate planes, then the length of diagonal of the parallelepiped is

(A) $2\sqrt{3}$ (B) $3\sqrt{2}$

(C) $\sqrt{2}$ (D) $\sqrt{3}$

[NCERT Exemplar Q. 32, Page 223]

Ans. Correct option : (A)

Given points are $A(5, 8, 10)$ and $B(3, 6, 8)$

$$\therefore AB = \left|\sqrt{(5-3)^2+(8-6)^2+(10-8)^2}\right|$$

$$= \left|\sqrt{4+4+4}\right|$$

$$= 2\sqrt{3}.$$

Q. 12. L is the foot of the perpendicular drawn from a point P (3, 4, 5) on the XY-plane. The coordinates of point L are

(A) (3, 0, 0) (B) (3, 4, 0)

(C) (3, 0, 5) (D) None of these

[NCERT Exemplar Q. 33, Page 223]

Ans. Correct option : (B)

We know that on xy plane, $z = 0$

So, co-ordinates of the point L are (3, 4, 0).

Q. 13. L is the foot of the perpendicular drawn from a point (3, 4, 5) on X-axis. The co-ordinates of L are

(A) (3, 0, 0) (B) (0, 4, 0)

(C) (0, 0, 5) (D) None of these

[NCERT Exemplar Q. 34, Page 223]

Ans. Correct option : (A)

We know that x-axis, $y = 0$ and $z = 0$

So, the required co-ordinates are (3, 0, 0).

[B] Fill in the blanks

Q. 1. The three axes OX, OY and OZ determine ....

[NCERT Exemplar Q. 35, Page 223]

Q. 2. The three planes determine a rectangular parallelepiped which has .... of rectangular faces.

[NCERT Exemplar Q. 36, Page 223]

Q. 3. The co-ordinates of a point are the perpendicular distance from the .... on the respective axes. [NCERT Exemplar Q. 37, Page 223]

Q. 4. The three co-ordinate planes divide the space into................ parts.

[NCERT Exemplar Q. 38, Page 223]

Q. 5. If a point P lies in YZ-plane, then the co-ordinates of a point on YZ-plane is of the form ....

[NCERT Exemplar Q. 39, Page 223]

Q. 6. The equation of YZ-plane is ....

[NCERT Exemplar Q. 40, Page 223]

Q. 7. If the point P lies on Z-axis, then co-ordinates of P are of the form ....

[NCERT Exemplar Q. 41, Page 223]

Q. 8. The equation of Z-axis, are ....

[NCERT Exemplar Q. 42, Page 223]

Q. 9. A line is parallel to XY-plane if all the points on the line have equal ......

[NCERT Exemplar Q. 43, Page 223]

Q. 10. A line is parallel to X-axis, if all the points on the line have equal ....

[NCERT Exemplar Q. 44, Page 223]

Q. 11. $x = a$ represent a plane parallel to ....

[NCERT Exemplar Q. 45, Page 223]

Q. 12. The plane parallel to YZ-plane is perpendicular to .... [NCERT Exemplar Q. 46, Page 223]

Q. 13. The length of the longest piece of a string that can be stretched straight in a rectangular room whose dimensions are 10, 13 and 8 units are ......

[NCERT Exemplar Q. 47, Page 223]

Q. 14. If the distance between the points (a, 2, 1) and (1, –1, 1) is 5, then a ......

[NCERT Exemplar Q. 48, Page 223]

Q. 15. If the mid-points of the sides of a triangle AB, BC and CA are D (1, 2, –3), E (3, 0, 1) and F (–1, 1, –4), then the centroid of the ΔABC is ....

[NCERT Exemplar Q. 49, Page 223]

Answer

1. Three coordinate planes
2. Three pairs
3. Given points
4. Eight parts
5. (0, y, z)
6. X = 0
7. (0, 0, z)
8. X = 0 and Y = 0
9. z-coordinate
10. y and z coordinate
11. YZ plane
12. X – axis
13. $\sqrt{333}$
14. 5 or –3
15. (1, 1, –2)

[C] Match the Column

Q. 1. Match each item given under the Column I to its correct answer given under Column II.

Column I	Column II
(i) In *XY*-plane	(A) 1st octant
(ii) Point (2,3,4) lies in the	(B) *YZ*-plane
(iii) Locus of the points having *X* coordinate O is	(C) *z*-co-ordinate is zero
(iv) A line Is parallel to *X*-axis If and only	(D) *Z*-axis
(v) If $X = 0$, $y = 0$ taken together will represent the	(E) Plane parallel to *XY*-plane
(vi) $z = c$ represent the plane	(F) If all the points on the line have equal *y* and *z*-coordinates
(vii) Planes $X = a$, $Y = b$ represent the line	(H) parallel to *Z*-axis
(viii) Co-ordinates of a point are the distances from the origin to the feet of perpendiculars	(G) from the point on the respective
(ix) A ball is the solid region in the space enclosed by a	(I) disc
(x) Region in the plane enclosed by a circle is known as a	(J) sphere

[NCERT Exemplar Q. 50, Page 224]

Answers :

(i) ↔ (C), (ii) ↔ (A), (iii) ↔ (B) (iv) ↔ (F), (v) ↔ (D), (vi) ↔ (E), (vii) ↔ (H) (viii) ↔ (G), (ix) ↔ (F), (x) ↔ (I)

Very Short Answer Type Questions (1 mark each)

Q. 1. How far apart are the points (2, 0, 0) and (–3, 0, 0)?
[NCERT Exemplar Q. 5, Page 221]

Sol. Given points, A (2, 0, 0) and B (–3, 0, 0)

$$AB = \left|\sqrt{(x_2 - x_1)^2 + (y_2 - y_1)^2 + (z_2 - z_1)^2}\right|$$

$$AB = \left|\sqrt{(2+3)^2 + 0^2 + 0^2}\right| = 5 \text{ unit}$$

Q. 2. Find the distance from the origin to (6, 6, 7).
[NCERT Exemplar Q. 6, Page 221]

Sol. Distance from origin to the point to (6, 6, 7).

$$= \left|\sqrt{(0-6)^2 + (0-6)^2 + (0-7)^2}\right|$$

$$= \left|\sqrt{36+36+49}\right|$$

$$= \left|\sqrt{121}\right| = 11 \text{ unit}$$

$$\left[\because d = \left|\sqrt{(x_1 - x_2)^2 + (y_1 - y_2)^2 + (z_1 - z_2)^2}\right|\right]$$

Short Answer Type Questions (2 marks each)

Q. 1. Locate the following points
(i) (1, –1, 3) (ii) (–1, 2, 4)
(iii) (–2, –4, –7) (iv) (–4, 2, –5)
[NCERT Exemplar, Q. 1, Page 220]

Sol. Given, co-ordinates are
Let A (1, –1, 3) B (–1, 2, 4)
C (–2, –4, –7) D (–4, 2, –5)

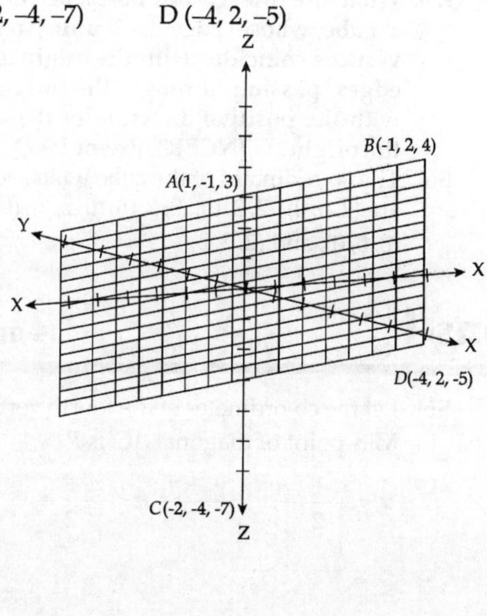

Q. 2. Name the octant in which each of the following points lies.
(i) (1, 2, 3) (ii) (4, –2, 3)
(iii) (4, –2, –5) (iv) (4, 2, –5)
(v) (–4, 2, 5) (iv) (–3, –1, 6)
(vii) (2, –4, –7) (viii) (–4, 2, –5).
[NCERT Exemplar Q. 2, Page 220]

Sol. (i) Point (1, 2, 3) in first quadrant.
(ii) (4, –2, 3) in fourth octant.
(iii) (4, –2, –5) in eight octant.
(iv) (4, 2, –5) in fifth octant.
(v) (–4, 2, 5) in second octant.
(vi) (–3, –1, 6) in third octant.
(vii) (2, –4, –7) in eight octant.
(viii) (–4, 2, –5) in sixth octant.

Q. 3. If *A, B, C* be the feet of perpendiculars from a point *P* on the *X, Y* and *Z*-axes respectively, then find the co-ordinates of *A, B* and *C* in each of the following where the point *P* is
(i) A (3, 4, 2) (ii) B (–5, 3, 7)
(iii) C (4, –3, –5)
[NCERT Exemplar Q. 3, Page 220]

Sol. The co-ordinates of A, B and C are the following

(i) A (3, 0, 0), B (0, 4, 0), C (0, 0, 2)

(ii) A (–5, 0, 0), B (0, 3, 0), C (0, 0, 7)

(iii) A (4, 0, 0), B (0, –3, 0), C (0, 0, –5).

Q. 4. If A, B, and C be the feet of perpendiculars from a point P on the XY, YZ and ZX-planes respectively, then find the co-ordinates of A, B and C in each of the following where the point P is

(i) (3, 4, 5) (ii) (–5, 3, 7)

(iii) (4, –3, –5) [NCERT Exemplar Q. 4, Page 221]

Sol. On XY-plane Z=0, on YZ-plane, $x = 0$ and on ZX-plane, $y = 0$, co-ordinate of A, B, and C *are*

(i) A (3, 4, 0), B (0, 4, 5), C (3, 0, 5)

(ii) A (–5, 3, 0), B (0, 3, 7), C (–5, 0, 7)

(iii) A (4, –3, 0), B (0, –3, –5), C (4, 0, –5)

Q. 5. Show that, if $x^2+y^2=1$, then the point $(x, y, \sqrt{1-x^2-y^2})$ is at a distance 1 unit from the origin. [NCERT Exemplar Q. 7, Page 221]

Sol. Given that, $x^2+y^2=1$.

$\therefore$ Distance of the point $(x, y, \sqrt{1-x^2-y^2})$ from origin is given as

$$d = \left|\sqrt{x^2+y^2+\left(\sqrt{1-x^2-y^2}\right)^2}\right|$$

$$= \left|\sqrt{x^2+y^2+1-x^2-y^2}\right| = 1.$$ **Hence Proved.**

Q. 6. Show that the point A (1, –1, 3), B (2, –4, 5) and C (5, –13, 11) are collinear. [NCERT Exemplar Q. 8, Page 221]

Sol. A (1, –1, 3), B (2, –4, 5) and C (5, –13, 11).

$$AB = \left|\sqrt{(1-2)^2+(-1+4)^2+(3-5)^2}\right|$$

$$= \left|\sqrt{1+9+4}\right| = \sqrt{14} \text{ unit}$$

$$BC = \left|\sqrt{(2-5)^2+(-4+13)^2+(5-11)^2}\right|$$

$$= \left|\sqrt{9+81+36}\right| = \sqrt{126} \text{ unit}$$

$$AC = \left|\sqrt{(1-5)^2+(-1+13)^2+(3-11)^2}\right|$$

$$= \left|\sqrt{16+144+64}\right| = \sqrt{224} \text{ unit}$$

$\because$ $AB + BC = AC$

$\Rightarrow \sqrt{14}+\sqrt{126} = \sqrt{224}$

$\Rightarrow \sqrt{14}+3\sqrt{14} = 4\sqrt{14}$

So, the points A, B and C are collinear.

Q. 7. Show that the ΔABC with vertices A (0, 4, 1), B (2, 3, –1) and C (4,5,0) is right angled. [NCERT Exemplar Q. 10, Page 221]

Sol. Given that, the vertices of the ΔABC are A (0, 4, 1), B (2, 3,–1) and C (4, 5, 0).

Now, $$AB = \left|\sqrt{(0-2)^2+(4-3)^3+(1+1)^2}\right|$$

$$= \left|\sqrt{4+1+4}\right| = 3 \text{ unit}$$

$$BC = \left|\sqrt{(2-4)^2+(3-5)^2+(-1-0)^2}\right|$$

$$= \left|\sqrt{4+4+1}\right| = 3 \text{ unit}$$

$$AC = \left|\sqrt{(0-4)^2+(4-5)^2+(1-0)^2}\right|$$

$$= \left|\sqrt{16+1+1}\right| = \sqrt{18} \text{ unit}$$

$\because$ $AC^2 = AB^2 + BC^2$

$\Rightarrow 18 = 9 + 9$

Hence, vertices ΔABC is a right angled triangle.

Q. 8. Find the third vertex of triangle whose centroid is origin and two vertices are (2, 4, 6) and (0, –2 , 5). [NCERT Exemplar Q. 11, Page 221]

Sol. Let third vertex of ΔABC *i.e.*, A (x, y, z)

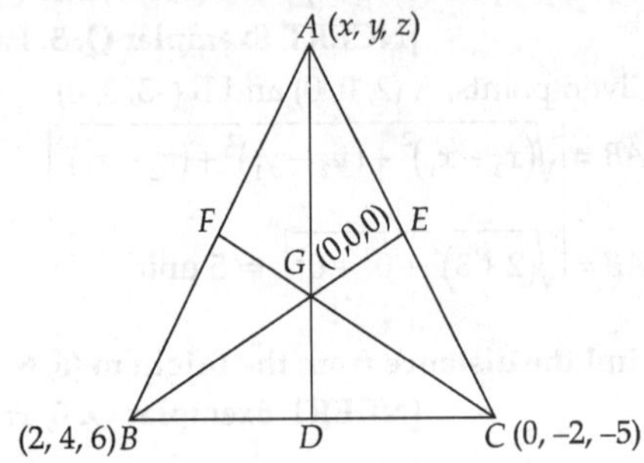

Given that, the co-ordinate of centroid G are (0, 0, 0)

$$\because 0 = \frac{x+2+0}{3} \Rightarrow x = -2$$

$$0 = \frac{y+4-2}{3} \Rightarrow y = -2$$

$$0 = \frac{z+6-5}{2} \Rightarrow z = -1$$

Hence, third vertex of triangle is (–2, –2, –1).

Q. 9. What are the co-ordinates of the vertices of a cube whose edge is 2 units, one of whose vertices coincides with the origin and the three edges passing through the origin, coincides with the positive direction of the axes through the origin? [NCERT Exemplar Q. 21, Page 222]

Sol. The co-ordinates of the cube which edge is 2 units, are (2, 0, 0), (2, 2, 0), (0, 2, 0), (0, 2, 2), (0, 0, 2), (2, 0, 2) (0, 0, 0), and (2, 2, 2).

Long Answer Type Questions-I (4 marks each)

Q. 1. Three consecutive vertices of a parallelogram $ABCD$ are A (6, –2, 4), B (2, 4, –8) and C (–2, 2, 4). Find the co-ordinates of the fourth vertex. [NCERT Exemplar Q. 9, Page 221]

Sol. Let the co-ordinates of the fourth vertices D (x, y, z)

Mid-point of diagonal AC, is P

$$x = \frac{x_1+x_2}{2}, y = \frac{y_1+y_2}{2}, z = \frac{z_1+z_2}{2}$$

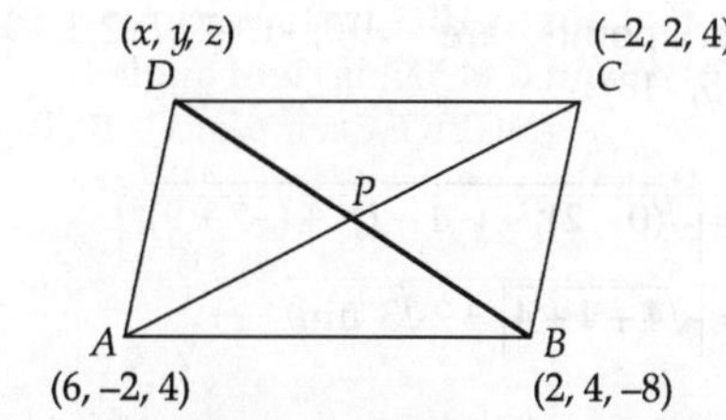

and $x=\dfrac{6-2}{2}=2, y=\dfrac{-2+2}{2}=0, z=\dfrac{4+4}{2}=4$

Since the mid-point of AC are P (2, 0, 4).

Mid-point of BD is also 'P'

[as diagonal bisect each other]

Mid-point of BD, $2=\dfrac{x+2}{2}\Rightarrow x=2$

$$\Rightarrow 0=\frac{y+4}{2}\Rightarrow y=-4$$

$$\Rightarrow 4=\frac{z-8}{2}\Rightarrow z=16$$

Co-ordinates of fourth vertex D is (2, –4, 16).

Q. 2. If the vertices of a parallelogram *ABCD* are *A* (1, 2, 3), *B* (–1, –2, –1) and *C* (2, 3, 2), then find the fourth vertex *D*.

[NCERT Exemplar Q. 14, Page 221]

Sol. Let the fourth vertex of the parallelogram $ABCD$ is $D(x, y, z)$.Then, the mid-point of AC is P.

$$P\left(\frac{1+2}{2},\frac{2+3}{2},\frac{3+2}{2}\right)\ i.e.,\ P\left(\frac{3}{2},\frac{5}{2},\frac{5}{2}\right).$$

Mid-point of BD is also P (as diagonal bisect each other)

$$\frac{3}{2}=\frac{-1+x}{2}\Rightarrow x=4$$

$$\frac{5}{2}=\frac{-2+y}{2}\Rightarrow y=7$$

$$\frac{5}{2}=\frac{-1+z}{2}\Rightarrow z=6$$

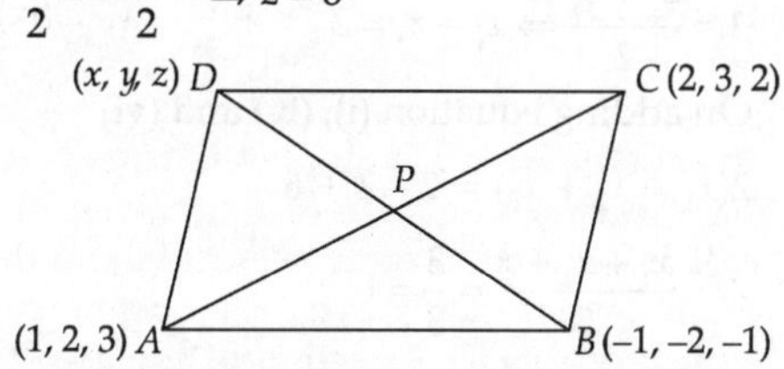

∴ The co-ordinates of fourth vertex is (4, 7, 6).

Q. 3. Find the coordinate of the points which trisect the line segment joining the points *A* (2, 1,–3) and *B* (5, –8, 3).

[NCERT Exemplar Q. 15, Page 221]

Sol. Let the $P(x_1, y_1, z_1)$ and $Q(x_2, y_2, z_2)$ trisect line segment AB

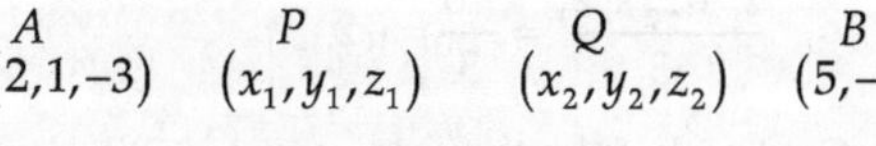

Since, the point P divided line AB in 1:2 internally then

$$x_1=\frac{2\times2+1\times5}{1+2}=\frac{9}{3}=3$$

$$y_1=\frac{2\times1+1\times(-8)}{3}=\frac{-6}{3}=-2$$

$$z_1=\frac{2\times(-3)+1\times3}{3}=\frac{-6+3}{3}=-1$$

Since, the point Q divide the line segment AB in 2 : 1, then

$$x_2=\frac{1\times2+2\times5}{3}=4$$

$$y_2=\frac{1\times1+(-8\times2)}{3}=-5$$

$$z_2=\frac{1\times(-3)+2\times3}{3}=-1$$

So, the co-ordinates of P are (3, –2, –1) and the co-ordinates of Q are (4, –5, 1).

Q. 4. If *A* (2, 2, –3), *B* (5, 6, 9), *C* (2, 7, 9) be the vertices of a triangle. The internal bisector of the angle *A* meets *BC* at the point *D*, then find the co-ordinates of *D*. [NCERT Exemplar Q. 17, Page 221]

Sol. Let the coordinates of D are (x, y, z).

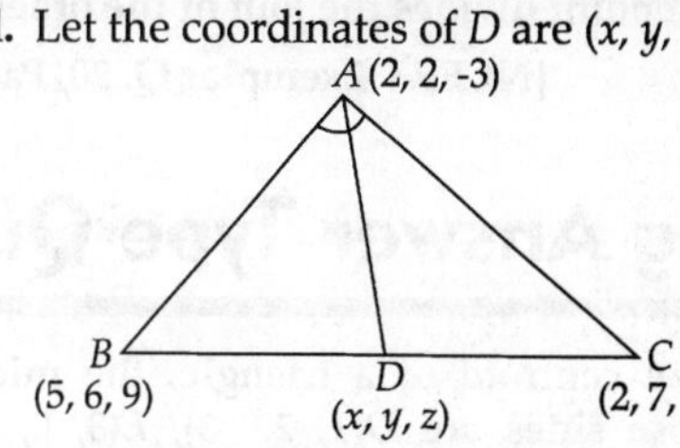

$$AB=\left|\sqrt{9+16+144}\right|=\left|\sqrt{169}\right|=13\text{ unit}$$

$$AC=\left|\sqrt{0+25+144}\right|=\left|\sqrt{169}\right|=13\text{ unit}$$

$$\Rightarrow\quad \frac{AB}{AC}=\frac{13}{13}\Rightarrow AB=AC$$

$$\frac{BD}{DC}=\frac{1}{1}\Rightarrow BD=DC\qquad\left[\frac{AB}{AC}=\frac{BD}{DC}\right]$$

∴D is mid point of BC

$$\therefore\quad x=\frac{5+2}{2}=\frac{7}{2}$$

$$\Rightarrow\quad y=\frac{6+7}{2}=\frac{13}{2}$$

$$\Rightarrow\quad z=\frac{9+9}{2}=9$$

So, the co-ordinates of D are $\left(\dfrac{7}{2},\dfrac{13}{2},9\right)$.

Q. 5. Show that the three points *A* (2, 3, 4), *B* (1, 2, –3) and *C* (–4, 1, –10) are collinear and find the ratio in which *C* divides *AB*.

[NCERT Exemplar Q. 18, Page 221]

Sol. Given points are A (2, 3, 4), B (–1, 2, –3) and C (–4, 1, –10).

$$\therefore \quad AB = \left|\sqrt{(2+1)^2+(3+2)^2+(4+3)^2}\right|$$

$$= \left|\sqrt{9+1+49}\right| = \sqrt{59} \text{ unit}$$

$$BC = \left|\sqrt{(-1+4)^2+(2-1)^2+(-3+10)^2}\right|$$

$$= \left|\sqrt{9+1+49}\right| = \sqrt{59} \text{ unit}$$

$$AC = \left|\sqrt{(2+4)^2+(3-1)^2+(4+10)^2}\right|$$

$$= \left|\sqrt{36+4+196}\right|$$

$$= \left|\sqrt{236}\right| = 2\sqrt{59} \text{ unit}$$

Now, $AB + BC = \sqrt{59} + \sqrt{59} = 2\sqrt{59}$ unit

$\because \quad AB + BC = AC$

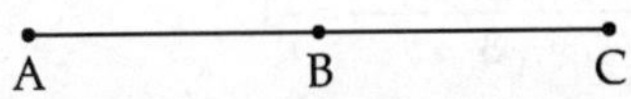

Hence, the points A, B and C are collinear.

Now, $AC : BC = 2\sqrt{59} : \sqrt{59} = 2:1$

So, C divide AB In 2 : 1 externally.

Q. 6. Prove that the points (0, –1, –7), (2, 1, –9) , and (6, 5, –13) are collinear. Find the ratio in which the first point divides the join of the other two.

[NCERT Exemplar Q. 20, Page 221]

Sol. Given points are $A(0,-1,-7), B(2,1,-9)$ and $C(6,5,-13)$

$$AB = \left|\sqrt{(0-2)^2+(-1-1)^2+(-7+9)^2}\right|$$

$$= \left|\sqrt{4+4+4}\right| = 2\sqrt{3} \text{ unit}$$

$$BC = \left|\sqrt{(2-6)^2+(1-5)^2+(-9+13)^2}\right|$$

$$= \left|\sqrt{16+16+16}\right| = 4\sqrt{3} \text{ unit}$$

$$AC = \left|\sqrt{(0-6)^2+(-1-5)^2+(-7+13)^2}\right|$$

$$= \left|\sqrt{36+36+36}\right| = 6\sqrt{3} \text{ unit}$$

$\because AB + BC = 2\sqrt{3} + 4\sqrt{3} = 6\sqrt{3}$

So, $AB + BC = AC$

Hence, the points A, B and C are collinear.

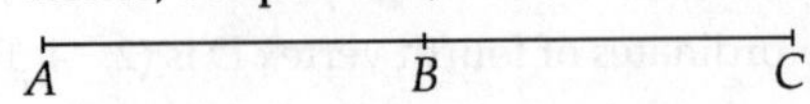

$AB : AC = 2\sqrt{3} : 6\sqrt{3} = 1:3$

So, point A divide B and C in 1 : 3 externally.

Long Answer Type Questions-II

(6 marks each)

Q. 1. Find the centroid of a triangle, the mid-point of whose sides are $D(1, 2, -3)$, $E(3, 0, 1)$ and $F(-1, 1, -4)$. [NCERT Exemplar, Q. 12, Page 221]

Sol. Given that, mid-point of sides are $D(1, 2, -3)$ and $F(-1, 1, -4)$.

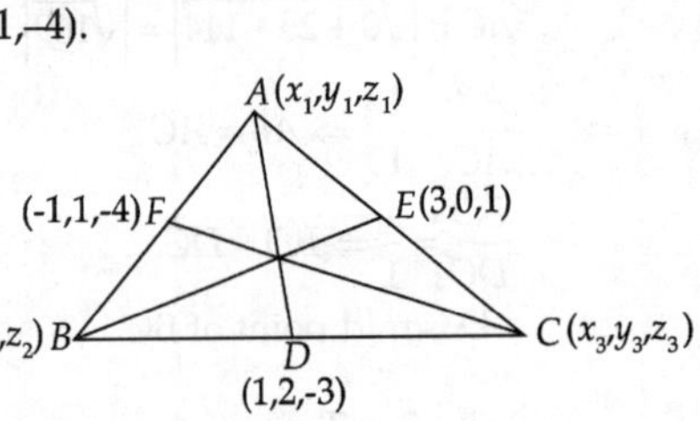

Let the vertices of the ΔABC are $A(x_1, y_1, z_1)$, $B(x_2, y_2, z_3)$ and $C(x_3, y_3, z_3)$

Then, mid-point of BC are (1, 2,–3).

$$\therefore 1 = \frac{x_2 + x_3}{2} \Rightarrow x_2 + x_3 = 2 \quad \text{...(i)}$$

$$2 = \frac{y_2 + y_3}{2} \Rightarrow y_2 + y_3 = 4 \quad \text{...(ii)}$$

$$-3 = \frac{z_2 + z_3}{2} \Rightarrow z_2 + z_3 = -6 \quad \text{...(iii)}$$

Now the mid-points of AC & AB

$$\Rightarrow \quad -1 = \frac{x_1 + x_2}{2} \Rightarrow x_1 + x_2 = -2 \quad \text{...(iv)}$$

$$\Rightarrow \quad 1 = \frac{y_1 + y_2}{2} \Rightarrow y_1 + y_2 = 2 \quad \text{...(v)}$$

$$\Rightarrow \quad -4 = \frac{z_1 + z_2}{2} \Rightarrow z_1 + z_2 = -8 \quad \text{...(vi)}$$

$$\Rightarrow \quad 3 = \frac{x_1 \quad x_3}{2} \Rightarrow x_1 + x_3 = 6 \quad \text{...(vii)}$$

$$\Rightarrow \quad 0 = \frac{y_1 + y_3}{2} \Rightarrow y_1 + y_3 = 0 \quad \text{...(viii)}$$

$$\Rightarrow \quad 1 = \frac{z_1 + z_3}{2} \Rightarrow z_1 + z_3 = 2 \quad \text{...(ix)}$$

On adding equation (i), (iv) and (vi)

$$2(x_1 + x_2 + x_3) = 2 - 2 + 6$$

$$\therefore \quad \frac{x_1 + x_2 + x}{3} = \frac{3}{3} = 1$$

On adding equation (ii), (iv) and (viii)

$$2(y_1 + y_2 + y_3) = 4 + 2 + 0$$

$$\therefore \quad \frac{y_1 + y_2 + y_3}{3} = \frac{3}{3} = 1$$

On adding equation (iii), (vi) and (ix)

$$2(z_1 + z_2 + z_3) = -6 - 8 + 2$$

$$\therefore \quad \frac{z_1 + z_2 + z_3}{3} = \frac{-6}{3} = -2$$

Centroid of the triangle = (1, 1, – 2)

EXPERT ADVICE

- *Learn the formulae for finding the distance between two points and section formula. Revise all the formulae before exam as well.*
- *Focus on solving as many problems as you can, rather than just reading theories, formulae and solutions.*
- *Don't be in such to solve problems dining exams. High speed with low accuracy rain your results. you need to be quick as well as accurate.*

OSWAAL LEARNING TOOLS

For Suggested Online Videos	
Visit : *https://youtu.be/tpIqhNNOM-M*	Visit : *https://youtu.be/WL1DxE-8If8*
Or Scan the Code	Or Scan the Code

CHAPTER

13 LIMITS AND DERIVATIVES

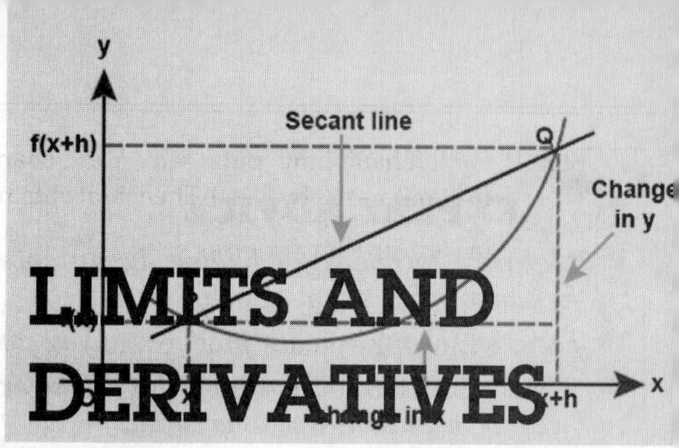

Chapter Objectives

> *Definition of Limits; Limits of polynomials and rational functions, trigonometric, exponential and logarithmic functions; Algebra of limits; Sandwich theorem; some standard limits; Derivative introduced as rate of change both as that of distance function and geometrically; Derivatives of sum, difference, product and quotient of function; Derivatives of polynomials and trigonometric functions.*

TOPIC-1
Limit And Its Fundamentals

TOPIC - 1
Limit and its fundamentals P. 170

TOPIC - 2
Derivatives P. 185

Quick Review

- **Definition of Limit**

Let $y = f(x)$ be a function of x. If at $x = a$, $f(x)$ takes indeterminate form, then we consider the value of the function which is very near to a. If these values tend to a definite unique number as x tends to a then the unique number, so obtained is called the limit of $f(x)$ at $x = a$ and is written as $\lim\limits_{x \to a} f(x)$.

OR

If $f(x)$ approaches to a real number l, when x approaches to a *i.e.*, if $f(x) \longrightarrow l$ when $x \longrightarrow a$, then l is called the limit of the function $f(x)$. In symbolic form, it on be written as—

$$\lim_{x \to a} f(x) = l$$

- **Left hand and right hand limit.**

A real number l, is the left hand limit of function $f(x)$ at $x = a$, if the value of $f(x)$ can be made as close as l, at point closed to a and on the left of a. Symbolically,

$$\text{L.H.L} = \lim_{x \to a^+} f(x) = l_1$$

A real number l_2 is the right hand limit of function $f(x)$ at $x = a$, if the values of $f(x)$ can be made as close as l_2 at points closed to a and on the right of a symbolically,

$$\text{R.H.L.} = \lim_{x \to a^+} f(x) = l_2$$

TIPS...

- *The students must not think that $\frac{dy}{dx}$ is a fraction i.e. dy divides by dx, for dy and dx have no meaning according to ever definition $\frac{dy}{dx}$ is merely a symbol for the derivative of y, which denotes the limiting value of fraction $\frac{\delta y}{\delta x}$.*
- *When the derivative of a function is evaluated directly by using the definition, then this method is called 'differentiation from the first principle'. In evaluating derivatives by definition, standard formulae of derivatives are not be used.*
- *Always remember for $0 < |x| < \frac{\pi}{2}$; $\cos x < \frac{\sin x}{x} < 1$*
- *Learn all the standard derivatives, to make the calculation fast.*
- *Limit is used when we have to find value of a function near to some value.*

- **Method to find left hand and right hand limit**

Step I For left hand limit, write the given function as $\lim\limits_{x \to a-} f(x)$ and for right hand limit, write the given function as $\lim\limits_{x \to a^+} f(x)$.

Step II For left hand limit, put $x = a - h$ and change the limit $x \to a^-$ by $h \to 0$. Then limit obtained in step I in $\lim_{h\to 0} f(a-h)$.

For right hand limit, put $x = a + h$ and change the limit $x \to a^+$ by $h \to 0$. Then, Limit obtained in step I is $\lim_{h\to 0} f(a+h)$

Step III Simplify the result obtained in step II *i.e.*, $\lim_{h\to 0} f(a-h)$ or $\lim_{h\to 0} f(a+h)$.

➤ **Existence of limit**

If the right hand limit and left hand limit coincide, then we say that limit exists and their common value is called the limit of $f(x)$ at $x = a$ and is denoted by $\lim_{x\to a} f(x)$.

➤ **Algebra of limits**

Let 'f' and 'g' be two real function with common domain D, such that $\lim_{x\to a} f(x)$ and $\lim_{x\to a} g(x)$ exists, then,

(i) Limit of sum of two function is sum of the limits of the function *i.e.*,

$$\lim_{x\to a}(f+g)(x) = \lim_{x\to a} f(x) + \lim_{x\to a} g(x)$$

(ii) Limit of difference of two functions is difference of the limits of the function *i.e.*,

$$\lim_{x\to a}(f-g)(x) = \lim_{x\to 0} f(x) - \lim_{x\to a} g(x)$$

(iii) Limit of product of two functions is product of the limits of the function *i.e.*,

$$\lim_{x\to 0}\left[f(x).g(x)\right] = \lim_{x\to a} f(x).\lim_{x\to a} g(x)$$

(iv) Limit of quotient of two functions is quotient of the limits of the function *i.e.*,

$$\lim_{x\to a}\frac{f(x)}{g(x)} = \frac{\lim_{x\to a} f(x)}{\lim_{x\to a} g(x)}, \text{ where } \lim_{x\to a} g(x) \neq 0.$$

TRICKS...

- *Remember some standard limits of following forms.*

  (i) $\lim_{\theta\to 0}\frac{\sin\theta}{\theta} = 1$ *(ii)* $\lim_{\theta\to 0}\frac{\tan\theta}{\theta} = 1$

  (iii) $\lim_{x\to 0}\frac{\sin^{-1} x}{x} = 1$ *(iv)* $\lim_{x\to 0}\frac{\tan^{-1} x}{x} = 1$

- $\lim_{x\to a}\frac{x^n - a^n}{x-a} = na^{n-1}$ *is true, if n is any rational number and a > 0.*

- *To find the differential coefficient of x^n, decrease the index of x by 1 and multiply the result by the original index.*

- *We can generalise the formula of sum or difference for more that two functions, i.e.*

  $$\frac{d}{dx}[f_1(x) \pm f_2(x) \pm f_3(x) \pm \ldots\ldots \pm f_n(x)]$$

  $$= \frac{d}{dx}\{f_1(x)\} \pm \frac{d}{dx}\{f_2(x)\} \pm \frac{d}{dx}\{f_3(x)\} \pm \ldots\ldots \pm \frac{d}{dx}\{f_n(x)\}$$

- *To find the derivative by first principle, revise the following trigonometric identities.*

  $$\sin C + \sin D = 2\sin\left(\frac{C+D}{2}\right)\cos\left(\frac{C-D}{2}\right)$$

  $$\sin C - \sin D = 2\cos\left(\frac{C+D}{2}\right)\sin\left(\frac{C-D}{2}\right)$$

  $$\cos C + \cos D = 2\cos\left(\frac{C+D}{2}\right)\cos\left(\frac{C-D}{2}\right)$$

  $$\cos C - \cos D = -2\sin\left(\frac{C+D}{2}\right)\sin\left(\frac{C-D}{2}\right)$$

(v) Limit of product of a constant and on function is the product of that constant and limit of the function *i.e.*,

$$\lim_{x\to a}\{c\cdot f(x)\} = c\lim_{x\to 0} f(x), \text{ where 'c' is a constant.}$$

➤ **Limit of polynomial function**

Let $f(x) = a_0 + a_1x + a_2x^2 + \ldots\ldots + a_nx_n$ be a polynomial function.

then,

$$\lim_{x\to a} f(x) = \lim_{x\to a}[a_0 + a_1x + a_2x^2 + \ldots.. + a_nx^n]$$

$$= a_0 + a_1\lim_{x\to a} x + a_2\lim_{x\to a} x^2 + \ldots. + a_n\lim_{x\to a} x^n$$

$$= a_0 + a_1a + a_2a_2 + \ldots.. + a_na^n = f(a).$$

➤ **Limit of Rational Function**

A function f is said to be a rational functional if $f(x) = \frac{g(x)}{h(x)}$, where $g(x)$ and $h(x)$ are polynomial functions such that $h(x) \neq 0$. $x \to a$

(a) $$\lim_{x\to a} f(x) = \lim_{x\to a}\frac{g(x)}{h(x)} = \frac{g(a)}{h(a)}$$

If $g(a) = 0$ and $h(a) = 0$ *i.e.*, this is of the form $\frac{0}{0}$, then factor $(x - a)$ of $g(x)$ and $h(x)$ are determined and then $(x - a)$ cancelled out.

Let,
$$g(x) = (x - a)\, p(x)$$
$$h(x) = (x - a)\, q(x)$$

Then,
$$\lim_{x\to a} f(x) = \lim_{x\to a}\frac{g(x)}{h(x)} = \lim_{x\to a}\frac{(x-a)p(x)}{(x-a)q(x)} \quad (x \neq a)$$
$$= \lim_{x\to a}\frac{p(x)}{q(x)}$$
$$= \frac{p(a)}{q(a)}$$

(b) For any positive integer n,
$$\lim_{x\to a}\frac{x^n - a^n}{x - a} = n\,a^{n-1}$$

➤ **Limits of Trigonometric, exponential and logarithmic Functions.**

To find the limits of trigonometric functions, we use the following theorems—

(i) Let f and g be two real valued functions with the same domain, such that $f(x) \leq g(x)$ for all x in domain in definition. For some a, if both limit exist, then $\lim_{x\to a} f(x) \leq \lim_{x\to a} g(x)$.

(ii) Sandwich Theorem—Let f, g and h be real functions, such that $f(x) \leq g(x) \leq h(x)$ for all x in the common domain in definition. For some real number a, if $\lim_{x\to a} f(x) = \lim_{x\to a} h(x) = 1$, then $\lim_{x\to a} g(x) = 1$.

➤ **Some Standard Limits**

(i) $\lim_{x\to 0}\frac{x^n - a^n}{x - a} = na^{n-1}$

(ii) $\lim_{x\to 0}\frac{\sin x}{x} = 1$

(iii) $\lim_{x\to 0}\frac{\tan x}{x} = 1$

(iv) $\lim_{x\to a}\frac{\sin(x-a)}{x-a} = 1$

(v) $\lim_{x\to a}\frac{\tan(x-a)}{x-a} = 1$

(vi) $\lim_{x\to 0}\frac{\log(1+x)}{x} = 1$

(vii) $\lim_{x\to 0}\frac{a^x - 1}{x} = \log_e a \neq 0, a > 1$

(viii) $\lim_{x\to 0}\frac{e^x - 1}{x} = 1$

(ix) $\lim_{x\to 0}\frac{1-\cos x}{x}=0$

➤ **Note :**

- $x \to a^-$ is read as x tends to 'a' from left and it means that x is very close to 'a' but it is always less than a.
- $x \to a^+$ is read as x tends to 'a' from right and it means that x is very close to 'a' but it is always greater than 'a'.
- $x \to a$ is read as x tends to 'a' and it means that x is very close to a but it is not equal to 'a'.
- Left hand limit and right hand limit of a constant function is the constant itself. *e.g.,*

  $\lim_{x\to 1^-} 3=3,\ \lim_{x\to 3^+} 4=4.$

- Some factorization formulae which we use in finding limit of a function are—

  (i) If $f(a) = 0$, then $(x - a)$ is a factor of $f(x)$.

  (ii) $a^2 - b^2 = (a - b)(a + b)$

  (iii) $a^3 + b^3 = (a + b)(a^2 - ab + b^2)$

  (iv) $a^3 - b^3 = (a - b)(a^2 + ab + b^2)$

  (v) $a^4 - b^4 = (a^2 + b^2)(a^2 - b^2) = (a^2 + b^2)(a+b)(a - b)$.

- The result $\lim_{x\to a}\frac{x^n-a^n}{x-a} = na^{n-1}$ is also true for any rational number 'n' and positive 'a'.
- The domain of exponential function $f(x) = e^x$ is $(-\infty, \infty)$ and its range is $(0, \infty)$.
- The domain of logarithmic function $f(x) = \log_e x$ is $(0, \infty)$ and its range is $(-\infty, \infty)$.

Multiple Choice Questions

(1 mark each)

[A] Objective Type Questions

Q. 1. $\lim_{x\to\pi}\frac{\sin x}{x-\pi}$ **is equal to :**

(a) 1 (b) 2

(c) –1 (d) –2

[NCERT Exemplar Q. 54, Page 242]

Ans. Correct option : (C)

Given, $\lim_{x\to\pi}\frac{\sin x}{\pi-x}=\frac{\sin(\pi-x)}{-(\pi-x)}=-1$

$[\because \lim_{x\to 0}\frac{\sin x}{\pi-x}=1 \text{ and } \pi-x\to 0 \Rightarrow x\to\pi]$

Q. 2. $\lim_{x\to 0}\frac{x^2\cos x}{1-\cos x}$ **is equal to :**

(a) 2 (b) $\frac{2}{3}$

(c) $\frac{-3}{2}$ (d) 1

[NCERT Exemplar Q. 55, Page 242]

Ans. Correct option : (A)

Given, $\lim_{x\to 0}\frac{x^2\cos x}{1-\cos x}=\lim_{x\to 0}\frac{x^2\cos x}{2\sin^2 x\frac{x}{2}}$

$[\because 1-\cos x = 2\sin^2\frac{x}{2}]$

$$=\lim_{x\to 0}\frac{\frac{x^2}{4}\times 4\cos x}{2\sin^2\frac{x}{2}}$$

$$=\frac{\lim_{x\to 0\Rightarrow \frac{x}{2}\to 0}\left(\frac{x}{2}\right)^2.2\cos x}{\sin^2\frac{x}{2}}$$

$= 2\cos 0° = 2 \times 1 = 2$ $\left[\because \lim_{x\to 0}\frac{x}{\sin x}=1\right]$

Q. 3. $\lim_{x\to 0}\frac{(1+x)^n-1}{x}$ **is equal to :**

(a) n (b) 1

(c) $-n$ (d) 0

[NCERT Exemplar Q. 56, Page 242]

Ans. Correct option : (A)

Given, $\lim_{x\to 0}\frac{(1+x)^n-1}{x}=\lim_{x\to 0}\frac{(1+x)^n-(1)^n}{(1+x)-1}$

$$=\lim_{1+x\to 1}\frac{(1+x)^n-(1)^n}{(1+x)-(1)} = n(1)^{n-1} = n$$

$\left[\because \lim_{x\to a}\frac{x^n-a^n}{x-a}=na^{n-1}\right]$

Q. 4. $\lim_{x\to1}\frac{x^m-1}{x^n-1}$ **is equal to :**

(a) 1 (b) $\frac{m}{n}$

(c) $-\frac{m}{n}$ (d) $\frac{m^2}{n^2}$

[NCERT Exemplar Q. 57, Page 242]

Ans. Correct option : (B)

Given, $\lim_{x\to1}\frac{x^m-1}{x^n-1} = \lim_{x\to1}\frac{\frac{x^m-1^m}{x-1}}{\frac{x^n-1^n}{x-1}} = \frac{m(1)^{m-1}}{n(1)^{n-1}} = \frac{m}{n}$

$$\left[\because \lim_{x\to a}\frac{x^n-a^n}{x-a} = na^{n-1}\right]$$

Q. 5. $\lim_{\theta\to0}\frac{1-\cos4\theta}{1-\cos6\theta}$ **is equal to :**

(a) $\frac{4}{9}$ (b) $\frac{1}{2}$

(c) $\frac{-1}{2}$ (d) –1

[NCERT Exemplar Q. 58, Page 242]

Ans. Correct option : (A)

Given, $\lim_{\theta\to0}\frac{1-\cos4\theta}{1-\cos6\theta} = \lim_{\theta\to0}\frac{2\sin^2 2\theta}{2\sin^2 3\theta}$

$$[\because 1-\cos\theta = 2\sin^2\frac{\theta}{2}]$$

$$= \lim_{\theta\to0}\frac{\sin^2 2\theta}{\sin^2 3\theta} = \lim_{\theta\to0}\left[\frac{\sin2\theta}{\sin3\theta}\right]^2$$

$$= \lim_{\substack{\theta\to0\\2\theta\to0\\3\theta\to0}}\left[\frac{\frac{\sin2\theta}{2\theta}\times2\theta}{\frac{\sin3\theta}{3\theta}\times3\theta}\right]^2 = \left[\frac{2\theta}{3\theta}\right]^2 = \frac{4}{9}$$

Q. 6. $\lim_{x\to0}\frac{\operatorname{cosec}x-\cot x}{x}$ **is equal to :**

(a) $\frac{-1}{2}$ (b) 1

(c) $\frac{1}{2}$ (d) 1

[NCERT Exemplar Q. 59, Page 243]

Ans. Correct option : (C)

Given, $\lim_{x\to0}\frac{\operatorname{cosec}x-\cos+x}{x} = \lim_{x\to0}\frac{\frac{1}{\sin x}-\frac{\cos x}{\sin x}}{x}$

$$= \lim_{x\to0}\frac{1-\cos x}{x\sin x}$$

$$= \lim_{x\to0}\frac{2\sin^2\frac{x}{2}}{x.2\sin\frac{x}{2}\cos\frac{x}{2}}$$

$$= \lim_{x\to0}\frac{\sin\frac{x}{2}}{x\cos\frac{x}{2}} = \lim_{x\to0}\frac{\tan\frac{x}{2}}{x} = \lim_{x\to0}\frac{\tan\frac{x}{2}}{2\times\frac{x}{2}}$$

$$= \frac{1}{2}\times1 = \frac{1}{2} \qquad \left[\because \lim_{x\to0}\frac{\tan x}{x} = 1\right]$$

Q. 7. $\lim_{x\to0}\frac{\sin x}{\sqrt{x+1}-\sqrt{1-x}}$ **is equal to :**

(a) 2 (b) 0

(c) 1 (d) –1

[NCERT Exemplar Q. 60, Page 243]

Ans. Correct option : (C)

Given, $\lim_{x\to0}\frac{\sin x}{\sqrt{x+1}-\sqrt{1-x}}$

$$= \lim_{x\to0}\frac{\sin x\left[\sqrt{x+1}+\sqrt{1-x}\right]}{\left(\sqrt{x+1}-\sqrt{1-x}\right)\left(\sqrt{x+1}+\sqrt{1-x}\right)}$$

$$= \lim_{x\to0}\frac{\sin x\left[\sqrt{x+1}-\sqrt{1-x}\right]}{x+1-1+x}$$

$$= \lim_{x\to0}\frac{\sin x\left[\sqrt{x+1}+\sqrt{1-x}\right]}{2x}$$

$$= \frac{1}{2}\lim_{x\to0}\frac{\sin x}{x}\left[\sqrt{x+1}+\sqrt{1-x}\right]$$

Taking limit, we get $= \frac{1}{2}\times1\times\left[\sqrt{0+1}-\sqrt{0-1}\right]$

$$= \frac{1}{2}\times1\times2 = 1$$

Q. 8. $\lim_{x\to\pi/4}\frac{\sec^2x-2}{\tan x-1}$ **is :**

(a) 3 (b) 1

(c) 0 (d) 2

[NCERT Exemplar Q. 61, Page 243]

Ans. Correct option : (D)

Given, $\lim_{x\to\frac{\pi}{4}}\frac{\sec^2x-2}{\tan x-1} = \lim_{x\to\frac{\pi}{4}}\frac{1+\tan^2x-2}{\tan x-1}$

$$= \lim_{x\to\frac{\pi}{4}}\frac{\tan^2x-1}{\tan x-1}$$

$$= \lim_{x\to\frac{\pi}{4}}\frac{(\tan x-1)(\tan x+1)}{(\tan x-1)}$$

$$= \lim_{x\to\frac{\pi}{4}}(\tan x+1) = \tan\frac{\pi}{4}+1 = 1+1 = 2.$$

Q. 9. $\lim_{x\to1}\frac{(\sqrt{x}-1)(2x-3)}{2x^2+x-3}$ **is equal to :**

(a) $\frac{1}{10}$ (b) $\frac{-1}{10}$

(c) 1 (d) None of these

[NCERT Exemplar Q. 62, Page 243]

Ans. Correct option : (B)

Given, $\lim_{x\to1}\frac{(\sqrt{x}-1)(2x-3)}{2x^2+3x-2x-3}$

$= \lim_{x\to1}\frac{(\sqrt{x}-1)(2x-3)}{x(2x+3)-1(2x+3)} = \lim_{x\to1}\frac{(\sqrt{x}-1)(2x-3)}{(x-1)(2x+3)}$

$= \lim_{x\to1}\frac{(\sqrt{x}-1)(\sqrt{x}+1)(2x-3)}{(x-1)(\sqrt{x}+1)(2x+3)}$

$= \lim_{x\to1}\frac{(x-1)(2x-3)}{(x-1)(\sqrt{x}+1)(2x+3)} = \lim_{x\to1}\frac{2x-3}{(\sqrt{x}+1)(2x+3)}$

Taking limit, we have,

$= \frac{2(1)-3}{(\sqrt{1}+1)(2\times1+3)} = \frac{-1}{2\times5} = \frac{-1}{10} \quad (x \neq 1)$

Q. 10. If $f(x)$ $\begin{cases}\frac{\sin[x]}{[x]}, & [x]\neq0\\ 0, & [x]=0\end{cases}$, where [.] denotes the greatest integer function, then $\lim_{x\to0}f(x)$ is equal to :

(a) 1 **(b) 0**

(c) –1 **(d) Does not exist**

[NCERT Exemplar Q. 63, Page 243]

Ans. Correct option : (D)

Given, $f(x) = \begin{cases}\frac{\sin[x]}{[x]}, & [x]\neq0\\ & [x]=0\end{cases}$

LHL $= \lim_{x\to0^-}\frac{\sin[x]}{[x]} = \lim_{h\to0}\frac{\sin[0-h]}{[0-h]}$

$= \lim_{h\to0}\frac{-\sin[-h]}{[-h]} = -1$

RHL $= \lim_{h\to0^+}\frac{\sin[x]}{[x]} = \lim_{h\to0}\frac{\sin[0+h]}{[0+h]}$

$= \lim_{h\to0}\frac{\sin[h]}{[h]} = 1$

LHL ≠ RHL; So, limit does not exist.

Q. 11. If $f(x) = \begin{cases}x^2-1, & 0<x<2\\ 2x+3, & 2\leq x<3\end{cases}$, then the quadratic equation whose roots are $\lim_{x\to2^-}f(x)$ and $\lim_{x\to2^+}f(x)$ is :

(a) $x^2 - 6x + 9 = 0$ **(b) $x^2 - 7x + 8 = 0$**

(c) $x^2 - 14x + 49 = 0$ **(d) $x^2 - 10x + 21 = 0$**

[NCERT Exemplar Q. 65, Page 243]

Ans. Correct option : (D)

Given, $f(x) = \begin{cases}x^2-1, 0<x<2\\ 2x+3, 2\leq x<3\end{cases}$

$\therefore \lim_{x\to2^-} = f(x) \lim_{x\to2^-}(x^2-1) = \lim_{h\to0}[(2-h)^2-1]$

$= \lim_{h\to0}(4-h^2-4h-1) = \lim_{h\to0}[h^2-4h+3] = 3$

and $\lim_{x\to2^+}f(x) = \lim_{x\to2^+}(2x+3)$

$= \lim_{h\to0}[2(2+h)+3] = 7$

Therefore, the quadratic equation whose roots are 3 and 7 is $x^2 - (3 + 7)x + 3 \times 7 = 0$

i.e. $x^2 - 10x + 21 = 0$

Q. 12. $\lim_{x\to0}\frac{\tan2x-x}{3x-\sin x}$ is equal to :

(a) 2 **(b) $\frac{1}{2}$**

(c) $\frac{-1}{2}$ **(d) $\frac{1}{4}$**

[NCERT Exemplar Q. 66, Page 244]

Ans. Correct option : (B)

Given, $f(x) = \lim_{x\to0}\frac{\tan2x-x}{3x-\sin x} = \lim_{x\to0}\frac{x\left[\frac{\tan2x}{x}-1\right]}{x\left[3-\frac{\sin x}{x}\right]}$

$= \lim_{\substack{x\to0\\ \therefore 2x\to0}}\frac{\left[\frac{\tan2x}{2x}\times2-1\right]}{\left[3-\frac{\sin x}{x}\right]} = \frac{1.2-1}{3-1} = \frac{2-1}{2} = \frac{1}{2}$

[B] Fill in the Blanks

Q. 1. If $f(x) = \frac{\tan x}{x-\pi}$, then $\lim_{x\to\pi}f(x) = ...$

[NCERT Exemplar Q. 77, Page 245]

Q. 2. $\lim_{x\to0}\left(\sin mx\cot\frac{x}{\sqrt{3}}\right) = 2$, then $m = ...$

[NCERT Exemplar Q. 78, Page 245]

Q. 3. $\lim_{h\to0}\frac{(3+h)}{3} = ...$

[NCERT Exemplar Q. 80, Page 245]

Answers

1. $-\frac{\tan(\pi-x)}{-(\pi-x)}$

2. $\frac{2\sqrt{3}}{3}$

3. $1 + 6y + 1 = 0.$

Very Short Answer Type Questions **(1 mark each)**

Evluate the following limits (Q. 1 to 6)

Q. 1. Evaluate $\lim_{x\to 3}\dfrac{x^2-9}{x-3}$

[NCERT Exemplar, Q. 1, Page 239]

Sol. $\lim_{x\to 3}\dfrac{x^2-9}{x-3} = \lim_{x\to 3}\dfrac{x^2-(3)^2}{x-3}$

$= \lim_{x\to 3}\dfrac{(x+3)(x-3)}{(x-3)}$

$= \lim_{x\to 3}(x+3) \quad [x \neq 3]$

$= 3 + 3 = 6$

Q. 2. Evaluate $\lim_{x\to 1/2}\dfrac{4x^2-1}{2x-1}$

[NCERT Exemplar, Q. 2, Page 239]

Sol. $\lim_{x\to \frac{1}{2}}\dfrac{4x^2-1}{2x-1} = \lim_{x\to \frac{1}{2}}\dfrac{(2x)^2-(1)^2}{2x-1}$

$= \lim_{x\to \frac{1}{2}}\dfrac{(2x+1)(2x-1)}{(2x-1)}$

$= \lim_{x\to \frac{1}{2}}(2x+1) \quad \left[x \neq \frac{1}{2}\right]$

$= 2\times\frac{1}{2}+1 = 1+1 = 2$

Q. 3. Evaluate $\lim_{x\to 0}\dfrac{\sqrt{x+h}-\sqrt{x}}{h}$

[NCERT Exemplar, Q. 3, Page 239]

Sol. $\lim_{x\to 0}\dfrac{\sqrt{x+h}-\sqrt{x}}{h}$

$\lim_{x\to 0}\dfrac{\sqrt{x+h}-\sqrt{x}}{h}\times\dfrac{\sqrt{x+h}+\sqrt{x}}{\sqrt{x+h}+\sqrt{x}}$

$\lim_{x\to 0}\dfrac{x+h-x}{h\left(\sqrt{x+h}+\sqrt{x}\right)}$

$\lim_{x\to 0}\dfrac{h}{h\left(\sqrt{x+h}+\sqrt{x}\right)} \quad [h \neq 0]$

$\lim_{x\to 0}\dfrac{1}{\sqrt{x+h}+\sqrt{x}} = \dfrac{1}{2\sqrt{x}}$

Q. 4. Evaluate $\lim_{x\to 0}\dfrac{(x+2)^{1/3}-2^{1/3}}{x}$

[NCERT Exemplar, Q. 4, Page 239]

Sol. $\lim_{x\to 0}\dfrac{(x+2)^{1/3}-2^{1/3}}{x}$

Let $x + 2 = y$

$\therefore \lim_{x\to 0}\dfrac{y^{1/3}-2^{1/3}}{y-2}$

$= \frac{1}{3}(2)^{\frac{1}{3}-1} \quad \left[\lim_{x\to a}\dfrac{x^n-a^n}{x-a} = na^{n-1}\right]$

$= \frac{1}{3}(2)^{-\frac{2}{3}}$

$= \dfrac{1}{3(2)^{2/3}}$

Q. 5. Evaluate $\lim_{x\to 0}\dfrac{\sin^2 2x}{\sin^2 4x}$

[NCERT Exemplar, Q. 16, Page 240]

Sol. Given, $\lim_{x\to 0}\dfrac{\sin^2 2x}{\sin^2 4x} = \lim_{x\to 0}\dfrac{\sin^2 2x}{(2\sin 2x\cos 2x)^2}$

$= \lim_{x\to 0}\dfrac{\sin^2 2x}{4\sin^2 2x\cos^2 2x}$

$[\because \sin 2\theta = 2\sin\theta\cos\theta]$

$= \lim_{x\to 0}\dfrac{1}{4\cos^2 2x} = \dfrac{1}{4}$

$[\because \cos 0 = 1]$

Q. 6. Evaluate $\lim_{x\to 0}\dfrac{1-\cos 2x}{x^2}$

[NCERT Exemplar, Q. 17, Page 240]

Sol. $\lim_{x\to 0}\dfrac{1-\cos 2x}{x^2} = \lim_{x\to 0}\dfrac{2\sin^2 x}{x^2}$

$(1 - \cos 2x = 2\sin^2 x)$

$= \lim_{x\to 0}\dfrac{2\sin^2 x}{x^2}$

$= 2\lim_{x\to 0}\dfrac{\sin^2 x}{x^2}$

$= 2\lim_{x\to 0}\left(\dfrac{\sin x}{x}\right)^2$

$\left[\because \lim_{\theta\to 0}\dfrac{\sin\theta}{\theta} = 1\right]$

$= 2 \times 1 = 2$

Short Answer Type Questions

(2 marks each)

Q. 1. Evaluate $\lim\limits_{x\to 0}\dfrac{(1+x)^6-1}{(1+x)^2-1}$

[NCERT Exemplar, Q. 5, Page 239]

Sol. $\lim\limits_{x\to 0}\dfrac{(1+x)^6-1}{(1+x)^2-1}$

Let $1+x=y$

$\therefore \lim\limits_{y\to 1}\dfrac{y^6-1}{y^2-1}$

$\Rightarrow = \lim\limits_{y\to 1}\dfrac{(y^2-1)(y^4+y^2+1)}{(y^2-1)}$

$= \lim\limits_{y\to 1}(y^4+y^2+1)$ $[y\neq 1]$

$= 1+1+1=3$

Q. 2. Evaluate $\lim\limits_{x\to 0}\dfrac{(2+x)^{5/2}-(a+2)^{5/2}}{x-a}$

[NCERT Exemplar, Q. 6, Page 239]

Sol. $\lim\limits_{x\to a}\dfrac{(2+x)^{5/2}-(a+2)^{5/2}}{x-a}$

Let $2+x=y$

When $x\to a$ the $y\to(a+2)$

$\therefore \lim\limits_{y\to(a+2)}\dfrac{y^{5/2}-(a+2)^{5/2}}{y-(a+2)}$

$= \dfrac{5}{2}(a+2)^{\frac{5}{2}-1}$ $\left[\lim\limits_{x\to a}\dfrac{x^n-a^n}{x-a}=na^{n-1}\right]$

$= \dfrac{5}{2}(a+2)^{3/2}$

Q. 3. Evaluate $\lim\limits_{x\to 0}\dfrac{x^4-\sqrt{x}}{\sqrt{x}-1}$

[NCERT Exemplar, Q. 1, Page 240]

Ans. $\lim\limits_{x\to 1}\dfrac{x^4-\sqrt{x}}{\sqrt{x}-1}$

$\lim\limits_{x\to 1}\dfrac{\sqrt{x}(x^{7/2}-1)}{\sqrt{x}-1}$

Let $\sqrt{x}=y$

$\therefore \lim\limits_{y\to 1}\dfrac{y(y^7-1)}{y-1}$ $\left[\lim\limits_{x\to a}\dfrac{x^n-a^n}{x-a}=na^{x-1}\right]$

$\therefore \lim\limits_{y\to 1}y\lim\limits_{y\to 1}\dfrac{y^7-1}{y-1}$

$= 1\times 7(1)^6$

$= 7$

Q. 4. Evaluate $\lim\limits_{x\to 0}\dfrac{\sqrt{1+x^3}-\sqrt{1-x^3}}{x^2}$

[NCERT Exemplar, Q. 11, Page 240]

Sol. $\lim\limits_{x\to 0}\dfrac{\sqrt{1+x^3}-\sqrt{1-x^3}}{x^2}$

$= \lim\limits_{x\to 0}\dfrac{\sqrt{1+x^3}-\sqrt{1-x^3}}{x^2}.\dfrac{\sqrt{1+x^3}+\sqrt{1-x^3}}{\sqrt{1+x^3}+\sqrt{1-x^3}}$

$= \lim\limits_{x\to 0}\dfrac{(1+x^3)-(1-x^3)}{x^2(\sqrt{1+x^3}+\sqrt{1-x^3})}$

$= \lim\limits_{x\to 0}\dfrac{1+x^3-1+x^3}{x^2(\sqrt{1+x^3}+\sqrt{1-x^3})}$

$= \lim\limits_{x\to 0}\dfrac{2x^3}{x^2(\sqrt{1+x^3}+\sqrt{1-x^3})}$

$= \lim\limits_{x\to 0}\dfrac{2x}{(\sqrt{1+x^3}+\sqrt{1-x^3})}$

$= 0$

Q. 5. Evaluate $\lim\limits_{x\to -3}\dfrac{x^3+27}{x^5+243}$ **[NCERT Exemplar, Q. 12, Page 240]**

Sol. Given, $\lim\limits_{x\to -3}\dfrac{x^3+27}{x^5+243}$

$= \lim\limits_{x\to -3}\dfrac{\dfrac{x^3+27}{x+3}}{\dfrac{x^5+243}{x+3}}$

$= \lim\limits_{x\to -3}\dfrac{\dfrac{x^3-(-3)^3}{x-(-3)}}{\dfrac{x^5-(-3)^5}{x-(-3)}} = \dfrac{\lim\limits_{x\to -3}\dfrac{x^3-(-3)^3}{x-(-3)}}{\lim\limits_{x\to -3}\dfrac{x^5-(-3)^5}{x-(-3)}}$

$\left[\lim\limits_{x\to a}\dfrac{x^n-a^n}{x-a}=na^{n-1}\right]$

$= \dfrac{3(-3)^2}{5(-3)^4}=\dfrac{1}{15}$

Q. 6. Find the value of n, if $\lim\limits_{x\to 2}\dfrac{x^n-2^n}{x-2}=80$, **$n\in$ N.**

[NCERT Exemplar, Q. 14, Page 240]

Sol. Given, $\lim\limits_{x\to 2}\dfrac{x^n-2^n}{x-2}=80$

$\Rightarrow n(2)^{n-1}=80$ $\left[\because \lim\limits_{x\to a}\dfrac{x^n-a^n}{x-a}=na^{n-1}\right]$

$\Rightarrow n(2)^{n-1}=5\times 16$

$\Rightarrow n\times 2^{n-1}=5\times(2)^4$

$\Rightarrow n\times 2^{n-1}=5\times(2)^{5-1}$

$\therefore n=5$

Q7. Evaluate $\lim_{x\to 0}\frac{\sin 3x}{\sin 7x}$

[NCERT Exemplar, Q. 15, Page 240]

Sol. Given, $\lim_{x\to 0}\frac{\frac{\sin 3x}{3x}.3x}{\frac{\sin 7x}{7x}.7x} = \frac{\lim_{x\to 0}\frac{\sin 3x}{3x}}{\lim_{x\to 0}\frac{\sin 7x}{7x}}\left(\frac{3x}{7x}\right)$

$$= \frac{3}{7}.\frac{\lim_{x\to 0}\frac{\sin 3x}{3x}}{\lim_{x\to 0}\frac{\sin 7x}{7x}} \qquad \left[\because \lim_{\theta\to 0}\frac{\sin\theta}{\theta}=1\right]$$

$$= \frac{3}{7}\times\frac{1}{1} = \frac{3}{7}$$

Q. 8 Evaluate $\lim_{x\to 0}\frac{2\sin x-\sin 2x}{x^3}$ **[NCERT Exemplar, Q. 18, Page 240]**

Sol. Given, $\lim_{x\to 0}\frac{2\sin x-\sin 2x}{x^3} = \lim_{x\to 0}\frac{2\sin x-2\sin x\cos x}{x^3}$ $[\because \sin 2x = 2\sin x\cos x]$

$$= \lim_{x\to 0}\frac{2\sin x(1-\cos x)}{x^3}$$

$$= 2\lim_{x\to 0}\frac{\sin x}{x}.\lim_{x\to 0}\left(\frac{1-\cos x}{x^2}\right)$$

$$= 2.1\lim_{x\to 0}\frac{1-\cos x}{x^2} \qquad \left[\because \lim_{\theta\to 0}\frac{\sin\theta}{\theta}=1\right]$$

$$= 2\lim_{x\to 0}\frac{2\sin^2\frac{x}{2}}{x^2} = 4\lim_{x\to 0}\frac{\sin^2\frac{x}{2}}{4\times\frac{x^2}{4}} \qquad \left[(1-\cos x)=2\sin^2\frac{x}{2}\right]$$

$$= \frac{4}{4}\lim_{x\to 0}\left[\frac{\sin\frac{x}{2}}{\frac{x}{2}}\right]^2 = \lim_{x\to 2}\left(\frac{\sin\frac{x}{2}}{\frac{x}{2}}\right)^2 = 1$$ Apply the limit

Q. 9. Evaluate $\lim_{x\to\frac{\pi}{3}}\frac{\sqrt{1-\cos 6x}}{\sqrt{2}\left(\frac{\pi}{3}-x\right)}$ **[NCERT Exemplar, Q. 20, Page 240]**

Sol. Given, $\lim_{x\to\pi/3}\frac{\sqrt{1-\cos 6x}}{\sqrt{2}\left(\frac{\pi}{3}-x\right)} = \lim_{x\to\pi/3}\frac{\sqrt{2}\sin 3x}{\sqrt{2}\left(\frac{\pi}{3}-x\right)}$

$$= \lim_{x\to\pi/3}\frac{\sin 3x}{\frac{\pi}{3}-x} = \lim_{x\to\pi/3}\frac{\sin(\pi-3x)}{\frac{\pi-3x}{3}} \qquad (y=\pi-3x)\left[\because \lim_{\theta\to 0}\frac{\sin\theta}{\theta}=1\right]$$

$$= \lim_{y\to 0}\frac{3\sin y}{y} = 3\times 1$$

$$= 3$$

Q. 10. Evaluate $\lim_{x\to\frac{\pi}{4}}\frac{\sin x-\cos x}{x-\frac{\pi}{4}}$ **[NCERT Exemplar, Q. 21, Page 240]**

Sol. $\lim_{x\to\frac{\pi}{4}}\frac{\sqrt{2}\left(\sin x\cdot\frac{1}{\sqrt{2}}-\cos x\cdot\frac{1}{\sqrt{2}}\right)}{\left(x-\frac{\pi}{4}\right)} = \lim_{x\to\frac{\pi}{4}}\frac{\sqrt{2}\left(\sin x\cos\frac{\pi}{4}-\cos x\cdot\sin\frac{\pi}{4}\right)}{\left(x-\frac{\pi}{4}\right)}$

$$= \lim_{x\to\frac{\pi}{4}}\frac{\sqrt{2}\left\{\sin\left(x-\frac{\pi}{4}\right)\right\}}{\left(x-\frac{\pi}{4}\right)}$$

$$= \sqrt{2} \lim_{x \to \frac{\pi}{4}} \frac{\sin\left(x - \frac{\pi}{4}\right)}{\left(x - \frac{\pi}{4}\right)} \qquad \left[\because \lim_{\theta \to 0} \frac{\sin\theta}{\theta} = 1\right]$$

$$\therefore \quad = \sqrt{2} \lim_{y \to 0} \frac{\sin y}{y} = \sqrt{2} \qquad \text{Let } x - \frac{\pi}{4} = y$$

Q. 11. Evaluate $\lim_{x \to \frac{\pi}{6}} \dfrac{\sqrt{3}\sin x - \cos x}{x - \frac{\pi}{6}}$ **[NCERT Exemplar, Q. 22, Page 240]**

Sol.
$$\lim_{x \to \frac{\pi}{6}} \frac{\sqrt{3}\sin x - \cos x}{x - \frac{\pi}{6}} = \lim_{x \to \frac{\pi}{6}} \frac{2\left(\frac{\sqrt{3}}{2}\sin x - \frac{1}{2}\cos x\right)}{\left(x - \frac{\pi}{6}\right)}$$

$$= \lim_{x \to \frac{\pi}{6}} \frac{2\left(\sin x \cos\frac{\pi}{6} - \cos x \sin\frac{\pi}{6}\right)}{\left(x - \frac{\pi}{6}\right)} = \frac{2\sin\left(x - \frac{\pi}{6}\right)}{\left(x - \frac{\pi}{6}\right)} \qquad \left[y = x - \frac{\pi}{6}\right]$$

$$= 2\lim_{y \to 0} \frac{\sin y}{y} \qquad \left[\because \lim_{\theta \to 0} \frac{\sin\theta}{\theta} = 1\right] [\because \sin A \cos B - \cos A \sin B = \sin(A - B)]$$

$$= 2$$

Q. 12. Evaluate $\lim_{x \to 0} \dfrac{\sin 2x + 3x}{2x + \tan 3x}$ **[NCERT Exemplar, Q. 23, Page 240]**

Sol.
$$\lim_{x \to 0} \frac{\sin 2x + 3x}{2x + \tan 3x} = \lim_{x \to 0} \frac{\frac{\sin 2x + 3x}{2x} \cdot 2x}{\frac{2x + \tan 3x}{3x} \cdot 3x}$$

$$= \lim_{x \to 0} \frac{\left(\frac{\sin 2x}{2x} + \frac{3x}{2x}\right)2x}{\left(\frac{2x}{3x} + \frac{\tan 3x}{3x}\right)3x} = \lim_{x \to 0} \frac{\frac{\sin 2x}{2x} + \frac{3}{2}}{\frac{2}{3} + \frac{\tan 3x}{3x}} \cdot \frac{2}{3}$$

$$= \frac{2}{3} \frac{\lim_{x \to 0} \frac{\sin 2x}{2x} + \frac{3}{2}}{\frac{2}{3} + \lim_{x \to 0} \frac{\tan 3x}{3x}}$$

$$= \frac{2}{3}\left(\frac{1 + \frac{3}{2}}{\frac{2}{3} + 1}\right) \qquad \left[\because \lim_{\theta \to 0} \frac{\sin\theta}{\theta} = 1 \text{ and } \lim_{\theta \to 0} \frac{\tan\theta}{\theta} = 1\right]$$

$$= \frac{2}{3} \times \frac{\frac{5}{2}}{\frac{5}{3}} = \frac{2}{3} \times \frac{5}{2} \times \frac{3}{5} = 1$$

Q. 13. Evaluate $\lim_{x \to \frac{\pi}{6}} \dfrac{\cot^2 x - 3}{\operatorname{cosec} x - 2}$ **[NCERT Exemplar, Q. 25, Page 240]**

Sol.
$$\lim_{x \to \frac{\pi}{6}} \frac{\cot^2 x - 3}{\operatorname{cosec} x - 2} = \lim_{x \to \frac{\pi}{6}} \frac{\operatorname{cosec}^2 x - 1 - 3}{\operatorname{cosec} x - 2} \qquad [\because \operatorname{cosec}^2 x = 1 + \cot^2 x]$$

$$= \lim_{x \to \frac{\pi}{6}} \frac{\operatorname{cosec}^2 x - 4}{\operatorname{cosec} x - 2} = \lim_{x \to \frac{\pi}{6}} \frac{(\operatorname{cosec} x)^2 - (2)^2}{\operatorname{cosec} x - 2}$$

$$= \lim_{x \to \frac{\pi}{6}} \frac{(\operatorname{cosec} x + 2)(\operatorname{cosec} x - 2)}{(\operatorname{cosec} x - 2)} = \lim_{x \to \frac{\pi}{6}} (\operatorname{cosec} x + 2) \qquad \left[\because \lim_{\theta \to 0} \frac{\sin\theta}{\theta} = 1\right]$$

$$= 2 + 2 = 4$$

(Apply to limit)

Q. 14. Evaluate $\lim_{x \to 0} \frac{\sin x - 2\sin 3x + \sin 5x}{x}$ **[NCERT Exemplar, Q. 27, Page 240]**

Sol.

$$\lim_{x \to 0} \frac{\sin x - 2\sin 3x + \sin 5x}{x} = \lim_{x \to 0} \frac{\sin 5x + \sin x - 2\sin 3x}{x}$$

$$= \lim_{x \to 0} \frac{2\sin 3x \cos 2x - 2\sin 3x}{x}$$

$$= \lim_{x \to 0} \frac{2\sin 3x(\cos 2x - 1)}{x} = \lim_{x \to 0} \frac{2\sin 3x}{\frac{1}{3} \times 3x}(\cos 2x - 1)$$

$$= 6 \lim_{x \to 0} \frac{\sin 3x}{3x}(\cos 2x - 1) = 6 \times 1 \times 0 = 0$$

Q. 15. Evaluate $\lim_{x \to 1} \frac{x^4 - 1}{x - 1} = \lim_{x \to k} \frac{x^3 - k^3}{x^2 - k^2}$**, then find the value of** k**.**

[NCERT Exemplar, Q. 28, Page 240]

Sol.

$$\lim_{x \to 1} \frac{x^4 - 1}{x - 1} = \lim_{x \to k} \frac{x^3 - k^3}{x^2 - k^2}$$

$$4(1)^3 = \lim_{x \to k} \frac{\frac{x^3 - k^3}{x - k}}{\frac{x^2 - k^2}{x - k}}$$

$$\left[\because \lim_{x \to a} \frac{x^n - a^n}{x - a} = na^{n-1}\right]$$

$$\Rightarrow \quad 4 = \frac{\lim_{x \to k} \frac{x^3 - k^3}{x - k}}{\lim_{x \to k} \frac{x^2 - k^2}{x - k}}$$

$$\Rightarrow \quad 4 = \frac{3}{2}(k)$$

$$\left[\lim_{x \to a} \frac{x^m - a^m}{x^n - a^n} = \frac{m}{n} a^{m-n}\right]$$

$$\therefore \quad k = \frac{8}{3}$$

Q. 16. Show that $\lim_{x \to \pi/4} \frac{|x - 4|}{x - 4}$ **does not exist.**

[NCERT Exemplar, Q. 51, Page 241]

Sol. Given, $\lim_{x \to \pi/4} \frac{|x - 4|}{x - 4}$

Let $f(x) = \begin{cases} -(x-4), & x < 4 \\ (x-4), & x > 4 \end{cases}$

$$\text{LHL} = \lim_{x \to \frac{\pi^-}{4}} \frac{-(x-4)}{x - 4}$$

$$= -1$$

$$\text{RHL} = \lim_{x \to \frac{\pi^+}{4}} \frac{(x-4)}{x - 4} = 1$$

$\therefore$ LHL $\neq$ RHL

So, limit does not exist.

Long Answer Type Questions-I

(4 marks each)

Q. 1. Evaluate $\lim_{x \to 2} \frac{x^2 - 4}{\sqrt{3x - 2} - \sqrt{x + 2}}$ **[NCERT Exemplar, Q. 8, Page 240]**

Sol.

$$\lim_{x \to 2} \frac{x^2 - 4}{\sqrt{3x-2} - \sqrt{x+2}} = \lim_{x \to 2} \frac{(x^2 - 4)(\sqrt{3x-2} + \sqrt{x+2})}{(\sqrt{3x-2}) - (\sqrt{x+2})(\sqrt{3x-2} - \sqrt{x+2})}$$

$$= \lim_{x \to 2} \frac{(x^2 - 4)(\sqrt{3x-2} + \sqrt{x+2})}{(\sqrt{3x-2})^2 - (\sqrt{x+2})^2} \qquad [\because (a+b)(a-b) = a^2 - b^2]$$

$$= \lim_{x \to 2} \frac{(x^2 - 4)(\sqrt{3x-2} + \sqrt{x+2})}{(3x-2) - (\sqrt{x+2})}$$

$$= \lim_{x\to 2}\frac{(x^2-4)(\sqrt{3x-2}+\sqrt{x+2})}{3x-2-x-2}$$

$$= \lim_{x\to 2}\frac{(x^2-4)(\sqrt{3x-2}+\sqrt{x+2})}{2x-4}$$

$$= \lim_{x\to 2}\frac{(x+2)(x-2)(\sqrt{3x-2}+\sqrt{x+2})}{2(x-2)}$$

$$= \lim_{x\to 2}\frac{(x+2)(\sqrt{3x-2}+\sqrt{x+2})}{2} \quad [x \neq 2]$$

$$= \frac{(2+2)(\sqrt{6-2}+\sqrt{2+2})}{2}$$

$$= \frac{4(2+2)}{2} = 8$$

Q. 2. Evaluate $\lim_{x\to\sqrt{2}}\frac{x^4-4}{x^2+3\sqrt{2}x-8}$

[NCERT Exemplar, Q. 9, Page 240]

Sol. $\lim_{x\to\sqrt{2}}\frac{x^4-4}{x^2+3\sqrt{2}x-8}$

$$= \lim_{x\to\sqrt{2}}\frac{(x^2)^2-(2)^2}{x^2+3\sqrt{2}x-8}$$

$$= \lim_{x\to\sqrt{2}}\frac{(x^2)^2-(2)^2}{x^2+3\sqrt{2}x-8}$$

$$= \lim_{x\to\sqrt{2}}\frac{(x^2-2)(x^2+2)}{x^2+4\sqrt{2}x-\sqrt{2}x-8}$$

$$= \lim_{x\to\sqrt{2}}\frac{(x-\sqrt{2})(x+\sqrt{2})(x^2+2)}{(x-\sqrt{2})(x+4\sqrt{2})} \quad [x \neq \sqrt{2}\,]$$

$$= \lim_{x\to\sqrt{2}}\frac{(x+\sqrt{2})(x^2+2)}{(x+4\sqrt{2})}$$

$$= \frac{(\sqrt{2}+\sqrt{2})\left[(\sqrt{2})^2+2\right]}{(\sqrt{2}+4\sqrt{2})}$$

$$= \frac{2\sqrt{2}(2+2)}{5\sqrt{2}} = \frac{8}{5}$$

Q. 3. Evaluate $\lim_{x\to 1}\frac{x^7-2x^5+1}{x^3-3x^2+2}$

[NCERT Exemplar, Q. 10, Page 240]

Sol. $\lim_{x\to 1}\frac{x^7-2x^5+1}{x^3-3x^2+2}$

$$= \lim_{x\to 1}\frac{x^7-x^5-x^5+1}{x^3-x^2-2x^2+2}$$

$$= \lim_{x\to 1}\frac{x^5(x^2-1)-1(x^5-1)}{x^2(x-1)-2(x^2-1)}$$

$$= \lim_{x\to 1}\frac{\frac{x^5(x^2-1)}{(x-1)}-\frac{1(x^5-1)}{(x-1)}}{\frac{x^2(x-1)}{(x-1)}-\frac{2(x^2-1)}{(x-1)}}$$

$$= \frac{\lim_{x\to 1}x^5(x+1)-\lim_{x\to 1}\left(\frac{x^5-1}{x-1}\right)}{\lim_{x\to 1}x^2-2\lim_{x\to 1}(x+1)}$$

$$= \frac{1\times 2-5\times(1)^4}{1-2\times 2} = \frac{2-5}{1-4}$$

$$= \frac{-3}{-3} = 1$$

Q. 4. Evaluate $\lim_{x\to\frac{1}{2}}\left(\frac{8x-3}{2x-1}-\frac{4x^2+1}{4x^2-1}\right)$

[NCERT Exemplar, Q. 13, Page 240]

Sol. $\lim_{x\to\frac{1}{2}}\left(\frac{8x-3}{2x-1}-\frac{4x^2+1}{4x^2-1}\right)$

$$= \lim_{x\to\frac{1}{2}}\left[\frac{(8x-3)(2x+1)-(4x^2+1)}{(4x^2-1)}\right]$$

$$= \lim_{x\to\frac{1}{2}}\left[\frac{16x^2+8x-6x-3-4x^2-1}{4x^2-1}\right]$$

$$= \lim_{x\to\frac{1}{2}}\left[\frac{12x^2+2x-4}{4x^2-1}\right]$$

$$= \lim_{x\to\frac{1}{2}}\frac{2\left(6x^2+x-2\right)}{4x^2-1}$$

$$= \lim_{x\to\frac{1}{2}}\frac{2\left(6x^2+4x-3x-2\right)}{4x^2-1}$$

$$= \lim_{x\to\frac{1}{2}}\frac{2\left[(3x+2)(2x-1)\right]}{(2x)^2-(1)^2}$$

$$= \lim_{x\to\frac{1}{2}}\frac{2(3x+2)(2x-1)}{(2x-1)(2x+1)} \quad \left[x \neq \frac{1}{2}\right]$$

$$= \lim_{x\to\frac{1}{2}}\frac{2(3x+2)}{2x+1} = \frac{2\left(3\times\frac{1}{2}+2\right)}{2\times\frac{1}{2}+1}$$

$$= \frac{3}{2}+2 = \frac{7}{2}$$

Q. 5. Evaluate $\lim\limits_{x\to 0}\dfrac{1-\cos mx}{1-\cos nx}$ **[NCERT Exemplar, Q. 19, Page 240]**

Sol. $$\lim_{x\to 0}\frac{1-\cos mx}{1-\cos nx}=\lim_{x\to 0}\frac{2\sin^2\frac{mx}{2}}{2\sin^2\frac{nx}{2}}=\lim_{x\to 0}\frac{\dfrac{\sin^2\frac{mx}{2}}{\left(\frac{mx}{2}\right)^2}\cdot\left(\frac{mx}{2}\right)^2}{\dfrac{\sin^2\frac{nx}{2}}{\left(\frac{nx}{2}\right)^2}\cdot\left(\frac{nx}{2}\right)^2}=\frac{\lim\limits_{x\to 0}\left(\dfrac{\sin\frac{mx}{2}}{\frac{mx}{2}}\right)^2}{\lim\limits_{x\to 0}\left(\dfrac{\sin\frac{nx}{2}}{\frac{nx}{2}}\right)^2}\cdot\frac{m^2\frac{x^2}{4}}{n^2\frac{x^2}{4}}\qquad [x\neq 0]$$

$$=\frac{m^2}{n^2}\cdot\frac{\lim\limits_{x\to 2}\left(\dfrac{\sin\frac{mx}{2}}{\frac{mx}{2}}\right)^2}{\lim\limits_{x\to 2}\left(\dfrac{\sin\frac{nx}{2}}{\frac{nx}{2}}\right)^2}=\frac{m^2}{n^2}\qquad\left[\because \lim_{\theta\to 0}\frac{\sin\theta}{\theta}=1\right]$$

Q. 6. Evaluate $\lim\limits_{x\to a}\dfrac{\sin x-\sin a}{\sqrt{x}-\sqrt{a}}$

[NCERT Exemplar, Q. 24, Page 240]

Sol. $$\lim_{x\to a}\frac{\sin x-\sin a}{\sqrt{x}-\sqrt{a}}$$

$$=\lim_{x\to a}\frac{\sin x-\sin a}{\sqrt{x}-\sqrt{a}}\times\frac{\sqrt{x}+\sqrt{a}}{\sqrt{x}+\sqrt{a}}$$

$$=\lim_{x\to a}\left(\sqrt{x}+\sqrt{a}\right)\lim_{x\to a}\frac{\sin x-\sin a}{x-a}$$

$$=\left(\sqrt{a}+\sqrt{a}\right)\lim_{x\to a}\frac{2\cos\frac{x+a}{2}\sin\frac{x-a}{2}}{x-a}$$

$$=2\sqrt{a}\lim_{x\to a}2\cos\left(\frac{x+a}{2}\right)\lim_{x\to a}\frac{\sin\frac{x-a}{2}}{x-a}$$

$$=2\sqrt{2}\cdot 2\cos a\lim_{x\to a}\frac{\sin\left(\frac{x-a}{2}\right)}{x-a}$$

Let $x-a=y$

$$\therefore\quad =4\sqrt{2}\cos a\lim_{y\to 0}\frac{\sin\frac{y}{2}}{y}$$

$$=4\sqrt{2}\cos a\lim_{y\to 0}\frac{\sin\frac{y}{2}}{2\frac{y}{2}}\qquad\left[\lim_{\theta\to 0}\frac{\sin\theta}{\theta}=1\right]$$

$$=4\sqrt{2}\cos a\times\frac{1}{2}\times 1$$

$$=4\sqrt{2}\cos a$$

Q. 7. Evaluate $\lim\limits_{x\to 0}\dfrac{\sqrt{2}-\sqrt{1+\cos x}}{\sin^2 x}$ **[NCERT Exemplar, Q. 26, Page 240]**

Sol. Given, $$\lim_{x\to 0}\frac{\sqrt{2}-\sqrt{1+\cos x}}{\sin^2 x}=\lim_{x\to 0}\frac{\sqrt{2}-\sqrt{1+2\cos^2\frac{x}{2}-1}}{\sin x^2}\qquad\left[\because \cos x=2\cos^2\frac{x}{2}-1\right]$$

$$=\lim_{x\to 0}\frac{\sqrt{2}-\sqrt{2\cos^2\frac{x}{2}}}{\sin^2 x}\qquad\left[\because \cos x=2\sin\frac{x}{2}\cos\frac{x}{2}\right]$$

$$=\lim_{x\to 0}\frac{\sqrt{2}\left(1-\cos\frac{x}{2}\right)}{\sin^2 x}=\lim_{x\to 0}\frac{\sqrt{2}\left(1-1+2\sin^2\frac{x}{4}\right)}{\sin^2 x}$$

$$=\lim_{x\to 0}\frac{\sqrt{2}\left(2\sin^2\frac{x}{4}\right)}{\sin^2 x}=\lim_{x\to 0}2\sqrt{2}\frac{\sin^2\frac{x}{4}}{\left(\frac{x}{4}\right)^2}\cdot\frac{\left(\frac{x}{4}\right)^2}{\sin^2 x}$$

$$= 2\sqrt{2}\lim_{x\to 0}\left(\frac{\sin\frac{x}{4}}{\frac{x}{4}}\right)^2 \cdot \lim_{x\to 0}\left(\frac{x}{\sin x}\right)^2 \cdot \frac{1}{16} \qquad \left(\lim_{\theta\to 0}\frac{\theta}{\sin\theta}=1\right)$$

$$= 2\sqrt{2}\cdot 1\cdot 1\cdot\frac{1}{16} = \frac{1}{4\sqrt{2}}$$

Q. 8. Evaluate $\lim_{x\to\frac{\pi}{4}}\dfrac{\tan^3 x-\tan x}{\cos\left(x+\frac{\pi}{4}\right)}$

[NCERT Exemplar, Q. 49, Page 241]

Sol. Given, $\lim_{x\to\frac{\pi}{4}}\dfrac{\tan^3 x-\tan x}{\cos\left(x+\frac{\pi}{4}\right)}$ $\quad\left[\frac{0}{0}\text{ form}\right]$

$$= \lim_{x\to\frac{\pi}{4}}\frac{\tan x(\tan^2 x-1)}{\cos\left(x+\frac{\pi}{4}\right)}$$

$$= \lim_{x\to\frac{\pi}{4}}\tan x\cdot\lim_{x\to\pi/4}\left(\frac{-(1-\tan^2 x)}{\cos\left(x+\frac{\pi}{4}\right)}\right)$$

$$= -1\times\lim_{x\to\frac{\pi}{4}}\frac{(1+\tan x)(1-\tan x)}{\cos\left(x+\frac{\pi}{4}\right)}$$

$[\because a^2-b^2=(a+b)(a-b)]$

$$= -\lim_{x\to\frac{\pi}{4}}(1+\tan x)\lim_{x\to\frac{\pi}{4}}\left[\frac{(\cos x-\sin x)}{\cos x\cdot\cos\left(x+\frac{\pi}{4}\right)}\right]$$

$$= -(1+1)\times\lim_{x\to\frac{\pi}{4}}\frac{\sqrt{2}\left[\frac{1}{\sqrt{2}}\cdot\cos x-\frac{1}{\sqrt{2}}\cdot\sin x\right]}{\cos x\cdot\cos\left(x+\frac{\pi}{4}\right)}$$

$$= -2\sqrt{2}\times\lim_{x\to\frac{\pi}{4}}\left[\frac{\cos\frac{\pi}{4}\cdot\cos x-\sin\frac{\pi}{4}\cdot\sin x}{\cos x\cdot\cos\left(x+\frac{\pi}{4}\right)}\right]$$

$[\because \cos A\cdot\cos B-\sin A\sin B=\cos(A+B)]$

$$= -2\sqrt{2}\lim_{x\to\frac{\pi}{4}}\frac{\cos\left(x+\frac{\pi}{4}\right)}{\cos x\cdot\cos\left(x+\frac{\pi}{4}\right)}$$

$$= -2\sqrt{2}\times\frac{1}{\frac{1}{\sqrt{2}}} = -2\sqrt{2}\times\sqrt{2} = -4$$

Q. 9. $\lim_{x\to\pi}\dfrac{1-\sin\frac{x}{2}}{\cos\frac{x}{2}\cos\frac{x}{4}-\sin\frac{x}{4}}$ **[NCERT Exemplar, Q. 50, Page 241]**

Sol. $\lim_{x\to\pi}\dfrac{1-\sin\frac{x}{2}}{\cos\frac{x}{2}}\left(\sin\frac{x}{4}-\sin\frac{x}{4}\right)\left(\cos\frac{x}{4}-\sin\frac{x}{4}\right) = \lim_{x\to\pi}\dfrac{\cos^2\frac{x}{4}+\sin^2\frac{x}{4}-2\sin\frac{x}{4}\cos\frac{x}{4}}{\cos\frac{x}{4}\,(\cos\frac{x}{4}-\sin\frac{x}{4})}$

$[\because \sin^2\theta+\cos^2\theta=1,\ \sin 2\theta=2\sin\theta\cos\theta]$

$$= \lim_{x\to\pi}\frac{\left(\cos\frac{x}{4}-\sin\frac{x}{4}\right)}{\left(\cos\frac{x}{4}+\sin\frac{x}{4}\right)\left(\cos\frac{x}{4}-\sin\frac{x}{4}\right)\left(\cos\frac{x}{4}-\sin\frac{x}{4}\right)}$$ $[\because \cos 2\theta=\cos^2\theta-\sin^2\theta]$

$$= \lim_{x\to\pi}\frac{\left(\cos\frac{x}{4}-\sin\frac{x}{4}\right)}{\left(\cos\frac{x}{4}+\sin\frac{x}{4}\right)\left(\cos\frac{x}{4}-\sin\frac{x}{4}\right)}$$ $[\because a^2-b^2=(a+b)(a-b)]$

$$= \lim_{x\to\pi}\frac{1}{\cos\frac{x}{4}+\sin\frac{x}{4}} = \frac{1}{\frac{1}{\sqrt{2}}+\frac{1}{\sqrt{2}}} = \frac{\sqrt{2}}{2} = \frac{1}{\sqrt{2}}$$

Q. 10. If $f(x)=\begin{cases}x+2, & x\le -1\\ cx^2, & x\ge -1\end{cases}$**, then find** c **when** $\lim_{x\to -1}f(x)$ **exists.**

[NCERT Exemplar, Q. 53, Page 242]

Sol. $f(x)=\begin{cases}x+2, & x\le -1\\ cx^2, & x\ge -1\end{cases}$,

$$\text{LHL} = \lim_{x\to -1^-}f(x) = \lim_{x\to -1^-}(x+2)$$

$= \lim_{h\to 0}(-1-h+2) = \lim_{h\to 0} c(-1+h)^2$

$\text{RHL} = \lim_{x\to -1^+} f(x) = \lim_{x\to -1^+} cx^2$

$= \lim_{x\to 0} c(-1+h)^2$

$\therefore \quad = c$

If $\lim_{x\to -1} f(x)$ exist, then LHL = RHL

$\therefore \quad c = 1$

Long Answer Type Questions-II

(6 marks each)

Q. 1. $\lim_{y\to 0} \frac{(x+y)\sec(x+y) - x\sec x}{y}$

[NCERT Exemplar Q. 47, Page 241]

Sol. Given, $\lim_{y\to 0} \frac{(x+y)\sec(x+y) - x\sec x}{y}$

$$= \lim_{y\to 0} \frac{\frac{x+y}{\cos(x+y)} - \frac{x}{\cos x}}{y}$$

$$= \lim_{y\to 0} \frac{(x+y)\cos x - x\cos(x+y)}{y\cos x\cos(x+y)}$$

$$= \lim_{y\to 0}\left[\frac{x\cos x + y\cos x - x\cos(x+y)}{y\cos x\cos(x+y)}\right]$$

$$= \lim_{y\to 0}\left[\frac{x\cos x - x\cos(x+y) + y\cos x}{y\cos x\cos(x+y)}\right]$$

$$= \lim_{y\to 0} \frac{x(\cos x - \cos(x+y)+y\cos x}{y\cos x\cos(x+y)}$$

$$= \lim_{y\to 0} \frac{x\left[-2\sin\left(x+\frac{y}{2}\right)\sin\left(\frac{-y}{2}\right)\right] + y\cos x}{y\cos x\cos(x+y)}$$

$$\left[\because \cos C - \cos D = -2\sin\frac{C+D}{2}\cdot\sin\frac{C-D}{2}\right]$$

$$= \lim_{y\to 0}\left[\frac{x\left\{2\sin\left(x+\frac{y}{2}\right)\sin\frac{y}{2}\right\} + y\cos x}{y\cos x\cos(x+y)}\right]$$

$$= \lim_{y\to 0} \frac{2x\sin\left(x+\frac{y}{2}\right)}{\cos x\cos(x+y)}\cdot \lim_{y\to 0}\frac{\sin\frac{y}{2}}{\frac{y}{2}}\cdot\frac{1}{2} + \lim_{y\to 0}\sec(x+y)$$

$$= \lim_{x\to 0} \frac{2x\sin\left(x+\frac{y}{2}\right)}{\cos x\cos(x+y)}\cdot\frac{1}{2} + \lim_{y\to 0}\sec(x+y)$$

$$= \lim_{x\to 0} \frac{2x\sin\left(x+\frac{y}{2}\right)}{\cos x\cos(x+y)}\cdot\frac{1}{2} + \lim_{y\to 0}\sec(x+y)$$

$$= \frac{2x\sin x}{\cos x\cos x}\cdot\frac{1}{2} + \sec x$$

$= x \tan x \sec x + \sec x$

$= \sec x\,(x \tan x + 1)$

Q. 2. Evaluate :

$\lim_{x\to 0} \frac{\sin(\alpha+\beta)x + \sin(\alpha-\beta)x + \sin 2\alpha x}{\cos 2\beta x - \cos 2\alpha x}\cdot x$

[NCERT Exemplar Q. 48, Page 241]

Sol. Given, $\lim_{x\to 0} \frac{\sin(\alpha+\beta)x + \sin(\alpha-\beta)x + \sin 2\alpha x}{\cos 2\beta x - \cos 2\alpha x}\cdot x$

$$= \lim_{x\to 0} \frac{[2\sin\alpha x\cdot\cos\beta x + \sin 2\alpha x]}{\cos 2\beta x - \cos 2\alpha x}\cdot x$$

$$\left[\because \sin C + \sin D = 2\sin\frac{C+D}{2}\cos\frac{C-D}{2}\right]$$

$$= \lim_{x\to 0} \frac{[2\sin\alpha x\cos\beta x + \sin 2\alpha x]x}{2\sin(\alpha+\beta)x\sin(\alpha-\beta)x}$$

$$\left[\because \cos C - \cos D = 2\sin\frac{C+D}{2}\cdot\sin\frac{D-C}{2}\right]$$

$$= \lim_{x\to 0} \frac{[2\sin\alpha x\cos\beta x + \sin 2\alpha x]x}{2\sin(\alpha+\beta)x\sin(\alpha-\beta)x}$$

$$= \lim_{x\to 0} \frac{[2\sin\alpha x\cos\beta x + 2\sin\alpha x\cos\alpha x]x}{2\sin(\alpha+\beta)x\sin(\alpha-\beta)x}$$

$$= \lim_{x\to 0} \frac{2\sin\alpha x[\cos\beta x + \cos\alpha x]x}{2\sin(\alpha+\beta)x.\sin(\alpha-\beta)x}$$

$$\left[\because \cos C + \cos D = 2\cos\frac{C+D}{2}\cos\frac{C-D}{2} \text{ and } \sin 2\theta = 2\sin\theta\cos\theta\right]$$

$$= \lim_{x\to 0} \frac{\sin \alpha x . x}{2\sin\left(\frac{\alpha+\beta}{2}\right)\cos\left(\frac{\alpha+\beta}{2}\right)x\cos\left(\frac{\alpha-\beta}{2}\right)x}$$

$$= \lim_{x\to 0} \frac{\frac{\sin \alpha x}{\alpha x}.x.(\alpha x)}{\left[2\sin\frac{\left(\frac{\alpha+\beta}{2}\right)x}{\left(\frac{\alpha+\beta}{2}\right)x}.\sin\frac{\left(\frac{\alpha-\beta}{2}\right)x}{\left(\frac{\alpha-\beta}{2}\right)x}\right]\left(\frac{\alpha+\beta}{2}\right)x\cdot\left(\frac{\alpha-\beta}{2}\right)x}$$

$$= \frac{\frac{1}{2}\lim_{x\to 0}\frac{\sin \alpha x}{\alpha x}.\alpha x^2}{\lim_{x\to 0}\sin\frac{\left(\frac{\alpha+\beta}{2}\right)x}{\left(\frac{\alpha+\beta}{2}\right)x}\lim_{x\to 0}\frac{\left(\frac{\alpha-\beta}{2}\right)x}{\left(\frac{\alpha-\beta}{2}\right)x}.\left(\frac{\alpha^2-\beta^2}{2}\right)x^2} \qquad \left[\because \lim_{\theta\to 0}\frac{\sin\theta}{\theta}=1\right]$$

$$= \frac{1}{2}.\frac{\alpha\cdot 4}{\alpha^2-\beta^2}\left[\frac{\lim_{x\to 0}\frac{\sin \alpha x}{\alpha x}}{\lim_{x\to 0}\sin\frac{\left(\frac{\alpha+\beta}{2}\right)x}{\left(\frac{\alpha+\beta}{2}\right)x}\lim_{x\to 0}\sin\frac{\left(\frac{\alpha-\beta}{2}\right)x}{\left(\frac{\alpha-\beta}{2}\right)x}}\right]$$

$$= \frac{1}{2}.\frac{4\alpha}{\alpha^2-\beta^2} = \frac{2\alpha}{\alpha^2-\beta^2} = \frac{2\alpha}{\alpha^2-\beta^2}$$

TOPIC-2
Derivatives

Quick Review

➤ **Derivative at a point**

Suppose f is a real valued function and 'a' is a point in its domain. Then, Derivative of f at a is defined by $\lim_{h\to 0}\frac{f(a+h)-f(a)}{h}$, provided this limit exists.

The derivative of $f(x)$ at a is denoted by $f'(a)$.

➤ **First Principle of Derivative**

Suppose f is a real valued function, the function defined by $\lim_{h\to 0}\frac{f(x+h)-f(x)}{h}$, wherever the limit exists and is defined to be the derivative of f and is denoted by $f'(x)$. This definition of derivative is called the first principle of derivative. Thus, $f'(x) = \lim_{h\to 0}\frac{f(x+h)-f(x)}{h}$

$f'(x)$ is also denoted by $\frac{d}{dx}[f(x)]$ or if $y = f(x)$, then it is denoted by $\frac{dy}{dx}$ and referred to as derivative of $f(x)$ or y with respect to x.

➤ **Algebra of Derivative of Functions**

Let f and g be two function such that their derivatives are defined in a common domain. Then,

(i) Derivative of sum of two functions is sum of the derivatives of the functions.

$$\frac{d}{dx}[f(x)+g(x)] = \frac{d}{dx}f(x)+\frac{d}{dx}g(x)$$

or $\quad (u + v)' = u' + v'$

(ii) Derivative of difference of two function is difference of the derivative of the functions.

$$\frac{d}{dx}[f(x)-g(x)] = \frac{d}{dx}f(x)-\frac{d}{dx}g(x)$$

or $\qquad (u-v)' = u'-v'$

(iii) Derivative of product of two functions is given by the following product rule.

$$\frac{d}{dx}[f(x)\cdot g(x)] = \left[\frac{d}{dx}f(x)\right]g(x)+f(x)\left[\frac{d}{dx}g(x)\right]$$

or $\qquad (u.v)' = u'.v + v.u'$

(iv) Derivative of quotient of two functions is given by the following quotient rule.

$$\frac{d}{dx}\left[\frac{f(x)}{g(x)}\right] = \frac{g(x)\frac{d}{dx}f(x)-f(x)\frac{d}{dx}g(x)}{[g(x)]^2}, g(x)\neq 0$$

or $\qquad \left(\frac{u}{v}\right)' = \frac{vu'-uv'}{v^2}$

➤ **Some Important derivatives**

➤ **(i)** $\frac{d}{dx}x^n = nx^{n-1} = nx^{n-1}$

(ii) $\frac{d}{dx}[Cf(x)] = C\frac{d}{dx}f(x)$ C is a constant.

(iii) $\frac{d}{dx}(ax+b)^n = na(ax+b)^{n-1}$

(iv) If $f(x) = a_nx^n + a_{n-1}x^{n-1} + a_{n-2}x^{n-2} + ... + a_1x + a_0$,
then $f(x) = na_nx^{n-1} + (n-1)\,a_{n-1}x^{n-2} + (n-2)\,a_{n-2}x^{n-3} + ... + a_1$.

(v) $\frac{d}{dx}(\sin x) = \cos x$

(vi) $\frac{d}{dx}(\cos x) = -\sin x$

(vii) $\frac{d}{dx}(\tan x) = \sec^2 x$

(viii) $\frac{d}{dx}(\text{cosec } x) = -\text{cosec } x \cot x$

(ix) $\frac{d}{dx}(\sec x) = \sec x \tan x$

(x) $\frac{d}{dx}(\cot x) = -\text{cosec}^2 x$

(xi) $\frac{d}{dx}(a^x) = a^x \log_e a$

(xii) $\frac{d}{dx}(\log_a x) = \frac{1}{x\log_e a}$

(xiii) $\frac{d}{dx}(\log_e x) = \frac{1}{x}$

(xiv) $\frac{d}{dx}e^x = e^x$

(xv) $\frac{d}{dx}[C] = 0$, where 'c' is a constant.

➤ **Geometrical meaning of Derivative at a point**

Geometrically, derivative of a function at a point x = the slope of tangent to the curve $y = f(x)$ at the point {C}.

Slope of tangent at P $= \lim_{x \to c} \frac{f(x)-f(c)}{x-c}$

$= \left\{\frac{df(x)}{dx}\right\}_{x=c}$ or $f'(c)$

➤ **Note :**

- Derivative of f at $x = a$ is also given by substituting $x = a$ in $f'(x)$ and it is denoted by $\left.\frac{d}{dx}f(x)\right|_a$ or $\left.\frac{d}{dx}\right|_a$ or $\left(\frac{df}{dx}\right)_{x=a}$.

Multiple Choice Questions (1 mark each)

[A] Objective Type Questions

Q. 1. If $f(x) = x - [x]$, $\in$ R, then $f'\left(\frac{1}{2}\right)$ is equal to :

(a) $\frac{3}{2}$ (b) 1

(c) 0 (d) –1

[NCERT Exemplar Q. 67, Page 244]

Ans. Correct option : (a)

Given, $f(x) = x - [x]$; we to first check for differentiability of $f(x)$ at $x = \frac{1}{2}$

$$\therefore Lf^1\left(\frac{1}{2}\right) = \text{LHD} = \lim_{h \to 0} \frac{f\left[\frac{1}{2}-h\right]-f\left[\frac{1}{2}\right]}{-h}$$

$$= \lim_{h \to 0} \frac{\left(\frac{1}{2}-h\right)-\left(\frac{1}{2}-h\right)-\frac{1}{2}+\frac{1}{2}}{-h}$$

$$= \lim_{h \to 0} \frac{\frac{1}{2}-h-0-\frac{1}{2}+0}{-h} = \frac{-h}{-h} = 1$$

$$Rf^1\left(\frac{1}{2}\right) = \text{RHD} = \lim_{x \to 0} \frac{f\left(\frac{1}{2}+h\right)-f\left(\frac{1}{2}\right)}{h}$$

$$= \lim_{x \to 0} \frac{\frac{1}{2}+h-1-\frac{1}{2}+1}{h} = \frac{h}{h} = 1$$

LHD = RHD

$$\therefore f^1\left(\frac{1}{2}\right) = 1$$

Q. 2. If $y = \sqrt{x} + \frac{1}{\sqrt{x}}$, then $\frac{dy}{dx}$ at $x = 1$ is equal to :

(a) 1 (b) $\frac{1}{2}$

(c) $\frac{1}{\sqrt{2}}$ (d) 0

[NCERT Exemplar Q. 68, Page 244]

Ans. Correct option : (d)

Given that $y = \sqrt{x} + \frac{1}{\sqrt{x}}$

$$\therefore \frac{dy}{dx} = \frac{1}{2\sqrt{x}} - \frac{1}{2x^{3/2}}$$

$$\left(\frac{dy}{dx}\right)_{at x=1} = \frac{1}{2} - \frac{1}{2} = 0$$

Q. 3. If $f(x) = \frac{x-4}{2\sqrt{x}}$, then $f'(1)$ is equal to :

(a) $\frac{5}{4}$ (b) $\frac{4}{5}$

(c) 1 (d) 0

[NCERT Exemplar Q. 69, Page 244]

Ans. Correct option : (a)

Given, that $f(x) = \frac{x-4}{2\sqrt{x}}$

$$\therefore f^1(x) = \frac{1}{2}\left[\frac{\sqrt{x}.1-(x-4).\frac{1}{2\sqrt{x}}}{x}\right]$$

$$= \frac{1}{2}\left[\frac{2x-x+4}{2\sqrt{x}.x}\right] = \frac{1}{2}\left[\frac{x+4}{2(x)^{3/2}}\right]$$

$$\therefore [f^1(x)]_{\text{at } x=1} = \frac{1}{2}\left[\frac{1+4}{2\times1}\right] = \frac{5}{4}$$

Q. 4. If $y = \frac{1+\frac{1}{x^2}}{1-\frac{1}{x^2}}$, then $\frac{dy}{dx}$ is equal to :

(a) $\frac{-4x}{(x^2-1)^2}$ (b) $\frac{-4x}{x^2-1}$

(c) $\frac{1-x^2}{4x}$ (d) $\frac{4x}{x^2-1}$

[NCERT Exemplar Q. 70, Page 244]

Ans. Correct option : (a)

Given, $y = \dfrac{1+\dfrac{1}{x^2}}{1-\dfrac{1}{x^2}} \Rightarrow y = \dfrac{x^2+1}{x^2-1}$

$\therefore \dfrac{dy}{dx} = \dfrac{(x^2-1).2x-(x^2+1).2x}{(x^2-1)^2}$

$= \dfrac{2x(x^2-1-x^2-1)}{(x^2-1)^2}$

$= \dfrac{2x(-2)}{(x^2-1)^2} = \dfrac{-4x}{(x^2-1)^2}$

Q. 5. If $y = \dfrac{\sin x+\cos x}{\sin x-\cos x}$, then $\dfrac{dy}{dx}$ at $x = 0$ is equal to :

(a) –2 (b) 0

(c) $\lim\limits_{x\to\pi} f(x)$ (d) Does not exist

[NCERT Exemplar Q. 71, Page 244]

Ans. Correct option : (a)

Given, $y = \dfrac{\sin x+\cos x}{\sin x-\cos x}$

$\dfrac{dy}{dx} = \dfrac{(\sin x-\cos x)(\cos x-\sin x)-(\sin x+\cos x)(\cos x+\sin x)}{(\sin x-\cos x)^2}$

$= \dfrac{-(\sin x-\cos x)^2-(\sin x+\cos x)^2}{(\sin x-\cos x)^2}$

$= \dfrac{-[\sin^2 x+\cos^2 x-2\sin x\cos x] + [\sin^2 x+\cos^2 x+2\sin x\cos x]}{(\sin x-\cos x)^2}$

$= \dfrac{-2}{(\sin x-\cos x)^2}$

$\therefore \left(\dfrac{dy}{dx}\right)_{at\, x=0} = \dfrac{-2}{(\sin 0-\cos 0)^2}$

$= \dfrac{-2}{(-1)^2} = -2$

Q. 6. If $y = \dfrac{\sin(x+9)}{\cos x}$ then $\dfrac{dy}{dx}$ at $x = 0$ is equal to :

(a) cos 9 (b) sin 9

(c) 0 (d) 1

[NCERT Exemplar Q. 72, Page 245]

Ans. Correct option : (a)

Given, $y = \dfrac{\sin(x+9)}{\cos x}$

$\dfrac{dy}{dx} = \dfrac{\cos x.\cos(x+9)-\sin(x+9)(-\sin x)}{\cos^2 x}$

$= \dfrac{\cos x\cos(x+9)+\sin x\sin(x+9)}{\cos^2 x}$

$= \dfrac{\cos(x+9-x)}{\cos^2 x} = \dfrac{\cos 9}{\cos^2 x}$

$\therefore \left(\dfrac{dy}{dx}\right)_{\text{at } x=0} = \dfrac{\cos 9}{\cos^2 0} = \dfrac{\cos 9}{1} = \cos 9$

Q. 7. If $f(x) = 1+x+\dfrac{x^2}{2}+...+\dfrac{x^{100}}{100}$, then $f'(1)$ is equal to :

(a) $\dfrac{1}{100}$ (b) 100

(c) 0 (d) Does not exist

[NCERT Exemplar Q. 73, Page 245]

Ans. Correct option : (b)

Given, $f(x) = 1 + x + \dfrac{x^2}{2} + ... + \dfrac{x^{100}}{100}$

$f^1(x) = 1 + \dfrac{2x}{2} + ... + \dfrac{100x^{99}}{100}$

$\therefore f^1(x) = 1 + 1 + 1$ .... + 1 (100 times)

= 100

Q. 8. If $f(x) = \dfrac{x^n - a^n}{x - a}$ for some constant a, then $f'(a)$ is equal to :

(a) 1 (b) 0

(c) $\dfrac{1}{2}$ (d) Does not exist

[NCERT Exemplar Q. 74, Page 244]

Ans. Correct option : (c)

Given, $f(x) = \dfrac{x^n-a^n}{x-a}$

$f^1(x) = \dfrac{(x-a)(nx^{n-1})-(x^n-a^n).1}{(x-a)^2}$

$\therefore f^1(a) = \dfrac{(a-a)(na^{n-1})-(a^n-a^n).1}{(a-a)^2}$

So, $f^1(a) = \dfrac{0}{0}$ = does not exist.

Q. 9. If $f(x) = x^{100} + x^{99} + ... + x + 1$, then $f'(1)$ is equal to :

(a) 5050 (b) 5049

(c) 5051 (d) 50051

[NCERT Exemplar Q. 75, Page 244]

Ans. Correct option : (a)

Given, $f(x) = x^{100} + x^{99} + ... + x + 1$

$\therefore f^1(x) = 100x^{99} + 99.x^{98} + ... + 1$

So, $f^1(1) = 100 + 99 + 98 + ... + 1$

$= \dfrac{100}{2}[2\times 100+(100-1)(-1)]$

$= 50\,[200 - 99] = 50 \times 101$

$= 5050$

Q. 10. If $f(x) = 1 - x + x^2 - x^3 + ... + x^{99} + x^{100}$, then $f'(1)$ is equal to :

(a) 150 **(b) –50**

(c) –150 **(d) 50**

[NCERT Exemplar Q. 76, Page 244]

Ans. Correct option : (d)

Given, $f(x) = 1 - x + x^2 - x^3 + ... - x^{99} + x^{100}$

$f^1(x) = -1 + 2x - 3x^2 + ... + 99x^{98} + 100x^{99}$

$\therefore f^1(1) = -1 + 2 - 3 .... - 99 + 100$

$= (-1 - 3 - 5 .... - 99) + (2 + 4 + 6 + ... + 100)$

$= \frac{50}{2}\left[2\times(-1)+(50-1)(-1)\right]+\frac{50}{2}\left[2\times 2+(50-1)^2\right]$

$= 25\,[-2 - 98] + 25\,[4 + 98]$

$= 25 \times (-100) + 25\,(102) = 25[-100 + 102]$

$= 25 \times 2 = 50$

[B] Fill in the blanks of the following

Q. 1. If $y = 1+\frac{x}{1!}+\frac{x^2}{2!}+\frac{x^3}{3!}$, then $\frac{dy}{dx}$ = ...

[NCERT Exemplar Q. 79, Page 245]

Sol. $y = e^x$

$\frac{dy}{dx} = \frac{d}{dx}e^x = e^x$

$\frac{dy}{dx} = y$

Short Answer Type Questions

(2 marks each)

Q. 1. Find the derivative of $x^n + ax^{n-1} + a^2x^{n-2} + ... + a^{n-1}x + a^n$, for some real number a.

[NCERT Exemplar Q. 6, Page 313]

Sol. Let, $f(x) = x^n + ax^{n-1} + a^2x^{n-2} + ... + ax^{n-1} + a^n$

$\Rightarrow \frac{d}{dx}\{f(x)\} = \frac{d}{dx}[x^n + ax^{n-1} + a^2x^{n-2} + ... + a^{n-1}x + a^n]$

$\Rightarrow f'(x) = nx^{n-1} + (n-1)\,ax^{n-2} + (n-2)\,ax^{n-3} + ... + a^{n-1}$

$\left[\because \frac{d}{dx}x^n = nx^{n-1} \text{ and } \frac{d}{dx}a^n = 0\right]$

since a is a real no.

$= \quad f'(x) = nx^{n-1} + (n-1)\,ax^{n-2} + (n-2)\,ax^{n-3} + ... + a^{n-1}.$

Q. 2. For some constants a and b, find the derivative of

(i) $(x - a)(x - b)$

[NCERT Exemplar Q. 7, Page 313]

Sol. Let, $f(x) = (x - a)(x - b)$

$\therefore \frac{d}{dx}f(x) = \frac{d}{dx}\{(x-a)(x-b)\}$

$\Rightarrow f'(x) = (x-a)\frac{d}{dx}(x-b)+(x-b)\frac{d}{dx}(x-a)$

$= (x-a)\left[\frac{d}{dx}x-\frac{d}{dx}b\right]+(x-b)\left[\frac{d}{dx}x-\frac{d}{dx}a\right]$

$= (x - a)\,[1 - 0] + (x - b)\,[1 - 0]$

$= (x - a) + (x - b)$

$= 2x - (a + b)$

(ii) $(ax^2 + b)^2$

Sol. Let $f(x) = (ax^2 + b)^2$

$\Rightarrow \frac{d}{dx}f(x) = \frac{d}{dx}\left(ax^2+b\right)^2$

$= \frac{d}{dx}\left(a^2x^4+2abx^2+b^2\right)$

$= a^2\frac{d}{dx}x^4+2ab\frac{d}{dx}x^2+\frac{d}{dx}b^2$

$= a^2 \cdot 4x^3 + 2ab \cdot 2x + 0$

$\Rightarrow f'(x) = 4a^2x^3 + 4abx$

(iii) $\frac{x-a}{x-b}$

Sol. Let $f(x) = \frac{x-a}{x-b}$

$\Rightarrow \frac{d}{dx}f(x) = \frac{d}{dx}\left(\frac{x-a}{x-b}\right)$

$= \frac{(x-b)\frac{d}{dx}(x-a)-(x-a)\frac{d}{dx}(x-b)}{(x-b)^2}$

$= \frac{(x-b)\left[\frac{d}{dx}x-\frac{d}{dx}a\right]-(x-a)\left[\frac{d}{dx}x-\frac{d}{dx}b\right]}{(x-b)^2}$

$= \frac{(x-b)[1-0]-(x-a)[1-0]}{(x-b)^2}$

$= \frac{(x-b)-(x-a)}{(x-b)^2}$

$= \frac{a-b}{(x-b)^2}$

Q. 3. Find the derivatives of—

(i) $2x-\frac{3}{4}$ **[NCERT Exemplar Q. 8, Page 313]**

Sol. Let $f(x) = 2x - \frac{3}{4}$

$\therefore \quad f'(x) = \frac{d}{dx}\left(2x - \frac{3}{4}\right)$

$= 2\frac{d}{dx}x - \frac{d}{dx}\left(\frac{3}{4}\right)$

$= 2 \cdot 1 - 0$

$= 2$

(ii) $(5x^3 + 3x - 1)(x - 1)$

Sol. Let, $f(x) = (5x^3 + 3x - 1)(x - 1)$

$\therefore \quad f'(x) = \frac{d}{dx}\{(5x^3 + 3x - 1)(x - 1)\}$

$= (5x^3 + 3x - 1)\frac{d}{dx}(x-1) + (x-1)\frac{d}{dx}(5x^3 + 3x - 1)$

$= (5x^3 + 3x - 1) \cdot 1 + (x-1)(15x^2 + 3)$

$= 20x^3 - 15x^2 + 6x - 4$

(iii) $x^{-3}(5 + 3x)$

Sol. Let, $f(x) = x^{-3}(5 + 3x) = 5x^{-3} + 3x^{-2}$

$\therefore \quad \frac{d}{dx}f(x) = \frac{d}{dx}(5x^{-3} + 3x^{-2})$

$= 5\frac{d}{dx}x^{-3} + 3\frac{d}{dx}x^{-2}$

$= 5(-3)x^{-3-1} + 3 \cdot (-2)x^{-2-1}$

$\Rightarrow \quad f'(x) = \frac{-3(2x+5)}{x^4}$

(iv) $x^5(3 - 6x^{-9})$

Sol. Let, $f(x) = x^5(3 - 6x^{-9}) = 3x^5 - 6x^{-4}$

$\therefore \quad \frac{d}{dx}f(x) = \frac{d}{dx}(3x^5 - 6x^{-4})$

$= \frac{3d}{dx}(x^5) - 6\frac{d}{dx}(x^{-4})$

$= 3(5)x^{5-1} - 6(-4)x^{-4-1}$

$= 15x^4 + 24x^{-5}$

$\Rightarrow f'(x) = 15x^4 + 24x^{-5}$

(v) $\frac{2}{x+1} - \frac{x^2}{3x-1}$

Sol. Let, $f(x) = \frac{2}{x+1} - \frac{x^2}{3x-1}$

$\therefore \quad \frac{d}{dx}f(x) = \frac{d}{dx}\left(\frac{2}{x+1} - \frac{x^2}{3x-1}\right)$

$= 2\frac{d}{dx}\left(\frac{1}{x+1}\right) - \frac{d}{dx}\left(\frac{x^2}{3x-1}\right)$

By quotient rule

$f'(x) = \left[\frac{(x+1)\frac{d}{dx}(2) - 2\frac{d}{dx}(x+1)}{(x+1)^2}\right]$

$- \left[\frac{(3x-1)\frac{d}{dx}(x^2) - x^2\frac{d}{dx}(3x-1)}{(3x-1)^2}\right]$

$= \left[\frac{(x+1)(0) - 2(1)}{(x+1)^2}\right] - \left[\frac{(3x-1)(2x) - x^2(3)}{(3x-1)^2}\right]$

$= \frac{-2}{(x+1)^2} - \left[\frac{6x^2 - 2x - 3x^2}{(3x-1)^2}\right]$

$= \frac{-2}{(x+1)^2} - \left[\frac{3x^2 - 2x}{(3x-1)^2}\right]$

$= \frac{-2}{(x+1)^2} - \frac{x(3x-2)}{(3x-1)^2}$

Q. 4. Find the derivatives of the following functions.

(i) $\sin x \cos x$. **[NCERT Exemplar Q. 11, Page 313]**

Sol. Let $f(x) = \sin x \cos x$

$\therefore \quad \frac{d}{dx}f(x) = \sin x \cos x$

$= \frac{d}{dx}\{\sin x \cos x\}$

$= \sin x \frac{d}{dx}\cos x + \cos x \frac{d}{dx}\sin x.$

$= \sin x \cdot (-\sin x) + \cos x \cdot \cos x$

$\Rightarrow f'(x) = \cos 2x$

Alternative method

$f(x) = \frac{2\sin\cos x}{2}$

$f(x) = \frac{1}{2}\sin 2x$

$f(x) = \frac{1}{2}\sin 2x$

$f'(x) = \frac{1}{2}\frac{d}{dx}\sin 2x$

$f'(x) = \cos 2x$

(ii) $\sec x$.

Sol. Let $f(x) = \sec x = \frac{1}{\cos x}$

$\therefore \quad \frac{d}{dx}f(x) = \frac{d}{dx} \cdot \frac{1}{\cos x}$

$$= \frac{\cos x \cdot \frac{d}{dx}1 - 1 \cdot \frac{d}{dx}\cos x}{(\cos x)^2}$$

$$= \frac{\cos x\, 0 - 1 \cdot (-\sin x)}{(\cos x)^2}$$

$$= \frac{\sin x}{\cos^2 x}$$

$$= \frac{\sin x}{\cos^2 x}$$

$$= \frac{\sin x}{\cos^2 x}$$

$\Rightarrow \quad f'(x) = \tan x \cdot \sec x$

(iii) 5 sec x + 4 cos x

Sol. Let $f(x) = 5 \sec x + 4 \cos x$

$\therefore \quad \frac{d}{dx} f(x) = \frac{d}{dx}(5 \sec x + 4 \cos x)$

$$= 5\frac{d}{dx}\sec x + 4\frac{d}{dx}\cos x$$

$$= 5 \cdot \sec x \tan x + 4(-\sin x)$$

$\Rightarrow \quad f'(x) = 5 \sec x \tan x + 4(-\sin x)$

(iv) cosec x

Sol. Let $\quad f(x) = \operatorname{cosec} x = \frac{1}{\sin x}$

$\therefore \quad \frac{d}{dx} f(x) = \frac{d}{dx}\left(\frac{1}{\sin x}\right)$

$$= \frac{\sin x \cdot \frac{d}{dx}1 - 1 \cdot \frac{d}{dx}\sin x}{(\sin x)^2}$$

$$= \frac{\sin x \cdot 0 - 1 \cdot \cos x}{\sin^2 x}$$

$$= -\frac{\cos x}{\sin^2 x}$$

$$= -\frac{\cos x}{\sin x} \cdot \frac{1}{\sin x}$$

$\Rightarrow f'(x) = -\cot x . \operatorname{cosec} x$

(v) 3 cot x + 5 cosec x

Sol. Let, $\quad f(x) = 3 \cot x + \operatorname{cosec} x$

$\therefore \quad \frac{d}{dx} f(x) = \frac{d}{dx}(3 \cot x + 5 \operatorname{cosec} x)$

$$= 3\frac{d}{dx}\cot x + 5\frac{d}{dx}\operatorname{cosec} x$$

$$= 3(-\operatorname{cosec}^2 x) + 5(-\cot x \operatorname{cosec} x)$$

$\Rightarrow \quad f'(x) = -\operatorname{cosec} x (3 \operatorname{cosec} x + 5 \cot x)$

(vi) 5 sin x – 6 cos x + 7

Sol. Let $\quad f(x) = 5 \sin x - 6 \cos x + 7$

$\therefore \quad \frac{d}{dx} f(x) = \frac{d}{dx}(5 \sin x - 6 \cos x + 7)$

$$= 5\frac{d}{dx}\sin x - 6\frac{d}{dx}\cos x + \frac{d}{dx}7$$

$$= 5 \cdot \cos x - 6 \cdot (-\sin x) + 0$$

$$= 5 \cos x + 6 \sin x$$

(vii) 2 tan x – 7 sec x

Sol. Let $\quad f(x) = 2 \tan x - 7 \sec x$

$\therefore \quad \frac{d}{dx} f(x) = \frac{d}{dx}(2 \tan x - 7 \sec x)$

$$= 2\frac{d}{dx}\tan x - 7\frac{d}{dx}\sec x$$

$$= 2 \cdot \sec^2 x - 7 \sec x \cdot \tan x$$

$\Rightarrow \quad f'(x) = \sec x (2 \sec x - 7 \tan x)$

Long Answer Type Questions-I

(4 marks each)

Q. 1. Find the derivative of the following function :

$\frac{\cos x}{1 + \sin x}$ **[NCERT Exemplar Q. 16, Page 317]**

Sol. Lef $f(x) = \frac{\cos x}{1 + \sin x}$

By quotient rule,

$$f'(x) = \frac{(1+\sin x)\frac{d}{dx}(\cos x) - (\cos x)\frac{d}{dx}(1+\sin x)}{(1+\sin x)^2}$$

$$= \frac{(1+\sin x)(-\sin x) - (\cos x)(\cos x)}{(1+\sin x)^2}$$

$$= \frac{-\sin x - \sin^2 x - \cos^2 x}{(1+\sin x)^2}$$

$$= \frac{-\sin x - (\sin^2 x + \cos^2 x)}{(1+\sin x)^2}$$

$$= \frac{-\sin x - 1}{(1+\sin x)^2}$$

$$= \frac{-(1+\sin x)}{(1+\sin x)^2}$$

$$= \frac{-1}{1+\sin x}$$

Q. 2. Find the derivative of the following function : $\dfrac{\sin x+\cos x}{\sin x-\cos x}$ **[NCERT Exemplar Q. 17, Page 318]**

Sol. Let $\quad f(x) = \dfrac{\sin x+\cos x}{\sin x-\cos x}$

By quotient rule,

$$f'(x) = \frac{(\sin x-\cos x)\frac{d}{dx}(\sin x+\cos x)-(\sin x+\cos x)\frac{d}{dx}(\sin x-\cos x)}{(\sin x-\cos x)^2}$$

$$= \frac{(\sin x-\cos x)(\cos x-\sin x)-(\sin x+\cos x)(\cos x+\sin x)}{(\sin x-\cos x)^2}$$

$$= \frac{-(\sin x-\cos x)^2-(\sin x+\cos x)^2}{(\sin x-\cos x)^2}$$

$$= \frac{-[\sin^2 x+\cos^2 x-2\sin x\cos x+\sin^2 x+\cos^2 x+2\sin x\cos x]}{(\sin x-\cos x)^2}$$

$$= \frac{-[1+1]}{(\sin x-\cos x)^2}$$

$$= \frac{-2}{(\sin x-\cos x)^2}$$

Q. 3. Find the derivative of the following function : $\dfrac{\sec x-1}{\sec x+1}$ **[NCERT Exemplar Q. 18, Page 419]**

Sol. Let $f(x) = \dfrac{\sec x-1}{\sec x+1}$

$$f(x) = \frac{\frac{1}{\cos x}-1}{\frac{1}{\cos x}+1} = \frac{1-\cos x}{1+\cos x}$$

By quotient rule,

$$f'(x) = \frac{(1+\cos x)\frac{d}{dx}(1-\cos x)-(1-\cos x)\frac{d}{dx}(1+\cos x)}{(1+\cos x)^2}$$

$$= \frac{(1+\cos x)(\sin x)-(1-\cos x)(-\sin x)}{(1+\cos x)^2}$$

$$= \frac{\sin x+\cos x\sin x+\sin x-\sin x\cos x}{(1+\cos x)^2}$$

$$= \frac{2\sin x}{(1+\cos x)^2}$$

$$= \frac{2\sin x}{\left(1+\frac{1}{\sec x}\right)^2} = \frac{2\sin x}{\frac{(\sec x+1)^2}{\sec^2 x}}$$

$$= \frac{2\sin x\sec^2 x}{(\sec x+1)^2}$$

$$= \frac{\frac{2\sin x}{\cos x}\sec x}{(\sec x+1)^2}$$

$$= \frac{2\sec x\tan x}{(\sec x+1)^2}$$

Q. 4. Find the derivative of the following functions. $\dfrac{4x+5\sin x}{3x+7\cos x}$ **[NCERT Exemplar Q. 26, Page 318]**

Sol. Let $\quad f(x) = \dfrac{4x+5\sin x}{3x+7\cos x}$

By quotient rule,

$$f'(x) = \frac{(3x+7\cos x)\frac{d}{dx}(4x+5\sin x)-(4x+5\sin x)\frac{d}{dx}(3x+7\cos x)}{(3x+7\cos x)^2}$$

$$= \frac{(3x+7\cos x)\left[4\frac{d}{dx}(x)+5\frac{d}{dx}(\sin x)\right]-(4x+5\sin x)\left[3\frac{d}{dx}(x)+7\frac{d}{dx}(\cos x)\right]}{(3x+7\cos x)^2}$$

$$= \frac{(3x+7\cos x)[4+5\cos x]-(4x+5\sin x)[3-7\sin x]}{(3x+7\cos x)^2}$$

$$= \frac{12x+15x\cos x+28\cos x+35\cos^2 x-12x+28x\sin x-15\sin x+35\sin^2 x}{(3x+7\cos x)^2}$$

$$= \frac{15x\cos x + 28\cos x + 28x\sin x - 15\sin x + 35(\cos^2 x + \sin^2 x)}{(3x + 7\cos x)^2}$$

$$= \frac{35 + 15x\cos x + 28\cos x + 28x\sin x - 15\sin x}{(3x + 7\cos x)^2}$$

Differentiate each of the function with respect to x in following question using first principle.

Q. 5. $\cos(x^2 + 1)$ **[NCERT Exemplar Q. 43, Page 241]**

Sol. Let $f(x) = \cos(x^2 + 1)$ and $f(x + h) = \cos\{(x + h)^2 + 1\}$

$$\therefore \frac{d}{dx}f(x) = \lim_{h\to 0}\frac{f(x+h)-f(x)}{h}$$

$$= \lim_{h\to 0}\frac{\cos\left\{(x+h)^2+1\right\}-\cos(x^2+1)}{h}$$

$$= \lim_{h\to 0}\frac{-2\sin\left\{\left[\frac{(x+h)^2+1+x^2+1}{2}\right]\right\}\sin\left\{\left[\frac{(x+h)^2+1-x^2-1}{2}\right]\right\}}{h}$$

$$\left[\because \cos C - \cos D = -2\sin\frac{C+D}{2}\cdot\sin\frac{C-D}{2}\right]$$

$$= \lim_{h\to 0}\frac{1}{h}\left[-2\sin\left\{\left[\frac{(x+h)^2+x^2+2}{2}\right]\right\}\sin\left\{\left[\frac{(x+h)^2-x^2}{2}\right]\right\}\right]$$

$$= \lim_{h\to 0}\frac{1}{h}\left[-2\sin\left\{\left[\frac{(x+h)^2+x^2+2}{2}\right]\right\}\sin\left\{\left[\frac{x^2+h^2+2xh-x^2}{2}\right]\right\}\right]$$

$$= \lim_{h\to 0}\frac{1}{h}\left[-2\sin\left\{\left[\frac{(x+h)^2+x^2+2}{2}\right]\right\}\sin\left\{\left[\frac{h^2+2xh}{2}\right]\right\}\right]$$

$$= -2\lim_{h\to 0}\sin\left\{\left[\frac{(x+h)^2+x^2+2}{2}\right]\right\}\lim_{h\to 0}\left[\frac{\sin h\left(\frac{h+2x}{2}\right)}{h\left(\frac{h+2x}{2}\right)}\right]\times\left(\frac{h+2x}{2}\right) \qquad \left[\because \lim_{\theta\to 0}\frac{\sin\theta}{\theta}=1\right]$$

$$= -2x\sin(x^2 + 1)$$

Q. 6. $\frac{ax+b}{cx+d}$ **[NCERT Exemplar Q. 44, Page 241]**

Sol. Let $f(x) = \frac{ax+b}{cx+d}$

$$f(x+h) = \frac{a(x+h)+b}{c(x+h)+d}$$

$$\therefore \frac{d}{dx}f(x) = \lim_{h\to 0}\frac{1}{h}[f(x+h)-f(x)]$$

$$= \lim_{h\to 0}\frac{1}{h}\left[\frac{a(x+h)+b}{c(x+h)+d}-\frac{ax+b}{cx+d}\right]$$

$$= \lim_{h\to 0}\frac{1}{h}\left[\frac{ax+b+ah}{c(x+h)+d}-\frac{ax+b}{cx+d}\right]$$

$$= \lim_{h\to 0}\frac{1}{h}\left[\frac{(ax+ah+b)(cx+d)-(ax+b)\{c(x+h)+d\}}{\{c(x+h)+d\}(cx+d)}\right]$$

$$= \lim_{h\to 0}\frac{1}{h}\left[\frac{(ax+ah+b)(cx+d)-(ax+b)(cx+ch+d)}{\{c(x+h)+d\}(cx+d)}\right]$$

$$= \lim_{h\to 0}\frac{1}{h}\left[\frac{acx^2+achx+bcx+adx+adh+bd-\{acx^2+achx+adx+bcx+bch+bd\}}{\{c(x+h)+d\}(cx+d)}\right]$$

$$= \lim_{h\to 0}\frac{1}{h}\left[\frac{acx^2+achx+bcx+adx+adh+bd-acx^2-achx-adx-bcx-bch-bd\}}{\{c(x+h)+d\}(cx+d)}\right]$$

$$= \lim_{h\to 0}\frac{1}{h}\left[\frac{adh-bch}{\{c(x+h)+d\}(cx+d)}\right]$$

$$= \lim_{h\to 0}\frac{ac-bd}{\{c(x+h)+d\}(cx+d)} \qquad (h \neq 0)$$

$$= \frac{ac-bd}{(cx+d)^2}$$

Q. 7. $x^{2/3}$ **[NCERT Exemplar Q. 45, Page 438]**

Sol. Let $f(x) = x^{2/3}$

$$f(x+h) = (x+h)^{2/3}$$

Now, $\frac{d}{dx}f(x) = \lim_{h\to 0}\frac{f(x+h)-f(x)}{h}$

$$= \lim_{h\to 0}\frac{1}{h}\left[(x+h)^{2/3}-x^{2/3}\right]$$

$$= \lim_{h\to 0}\frac{1}{h}\left[x^{2/3}\left(1+\frac{h}{x}\right)^{2/3}-x^{2/3}\right]$$

$$= \lim_{h\to 0}\frac{1}{h}\left[x^{2/3}\left(1+\frac{h}{x}\cdot\frac{2}{3}+\frac{\frac{2}{3}\left(\frac{2}{3}-1\right)\frac{h^2}{x^2}}{21}\cdots\right)\cdots 1\right]$$

$$\left[\because (1+x)^n = 1+nx+\frac{n(n-1)}{21}x^2+\cdots\right]$$

$$= \lim_{h\to 0}\frac{1}{h}\left[x^{2/3}\left(\frac{2}{3}\cdot\frac{h}{x}-\frac{1}{9}\cdot\frac{h^2}{x^2}+\cdots\right)\right]$$

$$= \lim_{h\to 0}\frac{x^{2/3}}{h}\cdot\frac{2}{3}\frac{h}{x}\left(1-\frac{1}{6}\cdot\frac{h}{x}+\cdots\right)$$

$$= \frac{2}{3}x^{\frac{2}{3}-1} = \frac{2}{3}x^{-1/3}$$

Q. 8. $x \cos x$ **[NCERT Exemplar Q. 46, Page 438]**

Sol. Let $f(x) = x\cos x$

$\therefore \quad f(x+h) = (x+h)\cos(x+h)$

$$\therefore \quad \frac{d}{dx}f(x) = \lim_{h\to 0}\frac{f(x+h)-f(x)}{h}$$

$$= \lim_{h\to 0}\frac{1}{h}[(x+h)\cos(x+h)-x\cos x]$$

$$= \lim_{h\to 0}\frac{1}{h}[x\cos(x+h)+h\cos(x+h)-x\cos x]$$

$$= \lim_{h\to 0}\frac{1}{h}\left[x\left\{-2\sin\left(\frac{2x+h}{2}\right)\sin\frac{h}{2}\right\}+h\cos(x+h)\right]$$

$$= \lim_{h\to 0}\left[-2x\sin\left(x+\frac{h}{2}\right)\frac{\sin\frac{h}{2}}{h}+\cos(x+h)\right] \qquad \left[\because \cos C-\cos D = -2\sin\frac{C+D}{2}\cdot\sin\frac{C-D}{2}\right]$$

$$= -2\lim_{h\to 0}x\sin\left(x+\frac{h}{2}\right)\lim_{h\to 0}\frac{\sin\frac{h}{2}}{\frac{h}{2}}\cdot\frac{1}{2}+\lim_{h\to 0}\cos(x+h)$$

$$= -2\cdot\frac{1}{2}x\sin x+\cos x$$

$$= \cos x - x\sin x$$

EXPERT ADVICE

- *This chapter requires lot of practice. You should know which formula will be applied in which questions.*
- *Learn the formulas and practice as much questions as possible.*
- *Product and quotient rule are important in derivers.*

OSWAAL LEARNING TOOLS

***For* Suggested Online Videos**

Visit : *https://youtu.be/4pfjLCJncA8*

Or Scan the Code

Visit : *https://youtu.be/3R_wiVYsphI*

Or Scan the Code

CHAPTER

14 MATHEMATICAL REASONING

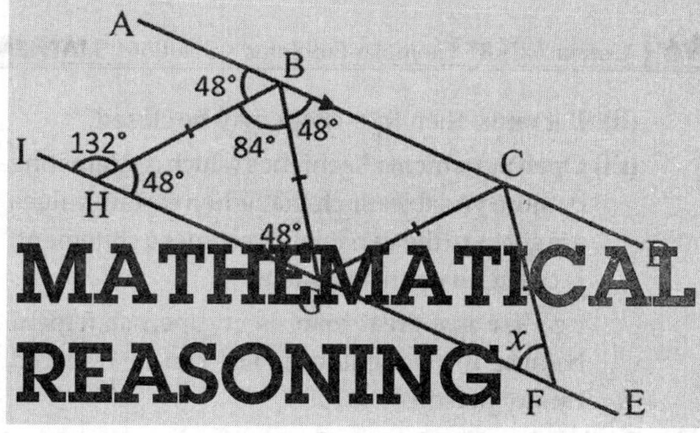

Chapter Objectives

> Mathematically acceptable statements; Types of statements; Connecting words/phrases; Quantifiers; Consolidating the understanding of " if and only if (necessary and sufficient) conditions", "implies', "and/or', implied by', 'there exists' and their uses through variety of examples related to real life and Mathematics; validating the Statements involving the connecting words. Difference between contradiction, converse and contrapositive.

TOPIC-1

Statements and Basic Logical Connectives

TOPIC - 1
Statements and basic logical connectives. P. 195

TOPIC - 2
Implications and validity of statements. P. 200

Quick Review

- **Statements**

  A sentence (or proposition) is called a mathematically acceptable statement, if it is either true or false, but not both. It is represented by the lower case letter like p, q, r, s, ... etc.

  e.g.,

  (i) p : A triangle has three sides.

  (ii) q : Delhi is the capital of India.

  Here, Example (i) is a true statement and example (ii) is a true statement.

  A true statement is a Valid Statement ; a false statement is known as a invalid statement ; imperative, exclamatory, interrogative and optative sentence are not statement.

  The following two sentences are not statements.

  (i) How beautiful !

  (ii) Who are you ?

- **Types of Statements**

  (i) Simple Statement : A statement which cannot be broken into two or more statements is called a simple statement. Generally, simple statement are denoted by small latter. $p,q.$, etc.

  e.g., **(i)** $p : \sqrt{2}$ is a rational number. **False**

  (ii) q : sun sets in the west. **True**

  (ii) Compound Statement : A statement that can be formed by combining two or more simple statements is called a compound statement.

  Each statement is called component statement.

  A compound statement is formed by using the connecting words/phrases like 'and', 'or', 'if then' , 'if and only if' etc.

  e.g., **(i)** Roses are red and Violets are blue.

TIPS...

- *The negation of any statement is obtained by including the word 'not' in the statement but does require a little care since this is offer used very loosely in every day speech.*
- *A sentence is neither imperative nor interrogative nor exclamatory.*
- *In truth table, no. of rows of table is depend on the no. of statements.*
- *In beginning often find phraseology of 'if and only if' or 'a necessary and sufficient condition' difficult, and it is desirable that they should state $p \Rightarrow q$ and $q \Rightarrow p$ in the form of two theorems rather than attempt to join them in 'one' theorem.*
- *The compound statements which are true for every value of their components are called tautology. The compound statements which are false for every value of their components are called contradiction (fallacy).*

(ii) If it rains, then the school may be closed.

(iii) Open Statement: A sentence which contains one or more variables such that when certain values are given to the variable, it becomes a statement, is called an open statement.

e.g., **'He** is a great man' is an open statement because in this sentence, 'He' can be replaced by any person.

➤ **Truth value of a statement**

The truth or falsity of a statement is called its truth value. If *a* statement is true, then its value is 'TRUE' denoted by T. If it is false, then its truth value is 'FALSE' denoted by F.

e.g., **(i)** 'Delhi' is capital of India'. Its true value is T.

(ii) 'Paris' is capital of India. Its truth value is F.

Negation of a Statement :

It p is any statement, then the denial of statement p is called the negation of statement p is formed by writing, 'It is not the case that' or 'or' it is false that ; before p or if possible by inserting the word 'not' in p.

TRICKS...

- *The negation of a statement is true when the original statement is false and it is false when the original statement is true.*
- *The compound statement with 'AND' is 'true' if all the component statements are **true** and 'false' if any of the component statement is **false.***
- *A compound statement with on 'OR' is **true** when on component statement is true or both the are true. If is False statements both the component statements are false.*
- *To prove the statement $p \Rightarrow q$, it is enough to show that $\sim q \Rightarrow \sim p$, which is contrapositive of the statement $p \Rightarrow q$.*

Let us consider the statement

p : I did not go to the temple yesterday.

This can also be written as—

$\sim p$: It is false that I went to the temple yesterday

$\sim p$: It is not the case that I went to the temple yesterday.

➤ **Basic Logical Connectives and Quantifiers.**

Two or more simple statements can be combined to form new statements in many ways. The words which combine to change simple statements to compound statement are called logical connectives. The basic connectives are the word 'and' 'or'.

➤ **The word or connective 'AND'**

If any two simple statement combined by the word 'and', then it form a compound statement. This connective word is also called conjunction and is denoted by the symbol '$\wedge$'. *e.g.*, it is raining today and 2 is an even number. This statement is a compound statement. It is denoted by 'p and q' or '$p \wedge q$', whose component statement are.

p : It is raining today.

q : 2 is an even number.

➤ **Truth table for connective 'AND'**

If p and q are two statement, then the truth, table for 'p and q' is as follows—

p	q	$p \wedge q$
T	T	T
T	F	F
F	T	F
F	F	F

➤ **The word or connective 'OR'**

If any two simple statement are combined by the word 'or', then it form a compound statement. This connective word is called disjunction and is denoted by the symbol '$\vee$'. e.g., Let p represents the statement 'Ravi' teaches Maths' and q represents the statement 'Ravi teaches English'.

Then, p or q represents the statement 'Ravi teaches Maths or English.

There are two types of 'OR' connective - These are—

(i) Exclusive OR—In a statement p or q, if one of the statement either p or q is true, then connecting of word 'OR' is exclusive.

(ii) Inclusive OR—In a statement, if either both p or q are true, then the connective of word 'OR' is inclusive.

➤ **Truth table for connective 'OR'**

If p and q are two statements, then the truth-table for 'p or q' is a s follows—

➤ **Truth table for connective 'OR'**

If p and q are two statement, then the truth-table for 'p and q' is as follows—

p	q	$p \vee q$
T	T	T
T	F	T
F	T	T
F	F	F

➤ **Quantifiers**

In mathematics, we come across many mathematical statements containing phrases "There exists" or "For all" or "For every" Theses phrases are called quantifiers.

For e.g., There exists a triangle, whose all sides are equal.

Consider the statement p : For every prime number q, $\sqrt{q}$ is an irrational number. This means that, if s denotes the set of all prime numbers, then for all the members q of the set s, $\sqrt{q}$ is an irrational number.

Note :

- A sentence which is both true and false simultaneously is not a statement, rather it is a paradox. It may be true or false *e.g.*, I am always right.
- The truth value of a simple statement does not depend on any other statement.
- The truth value of a compound statement is completely depend on the truth values of the component statements together with the way in which they are connected.
- A statement with 'and' is not always a compound statement e.g., A mixture of alcohol and water can be separated by chemical method. Here, the word 'and' is not used as a connective.
- A table that shows the relationship between the truth value of compound statement and the truth value of its sub-statements is called the truth-table. It consists rows and columns with top row representing sub-statements and compound statements.
- Phase 'for every' or 'For all' is denoted by the symbol '$\forall$' called the universal quantifier and the phrase 'There exists' is denoted by the symbol '*', known as existential quantifier.
- A statement is said to be a quantified statement, if it contains quantifiers.

Multiple Choice Questions

(1 mark each)

[A] Objective Type Questions

Q. 1. Which of the following is a statement ?

(a) x is a real number
(b) Switch off the fan
(c) 6 is a natural number
(d) Let me go

[NCERT Exemplar Q. 17, Page 265]

Ans. Correct option : (C)

Since, Statement is a sentence, which is either true or false. So, 6 is a natural number is true.

Q. 2. Which of the following is not a statement.

(a) Smoking is injurious to health
(b) 2 + 2 = 4
(c) 2 is the only even prime number
(d) Come here

[NCERT Exemplar Q. 18, Page 265]

Ans. Correct option : (D)

To given order cannot be statement.

So, 'come' here' is not a statement.

Q. 3. The connective in the statement '2 + 7 > 9 or 2 + 7 < 9' is

(a) and **(b) or**
(c) > **(d) <**

[NCERT Exemplar Q. 19, Page 265]

Ans. Correct option : (B)

In '2 + 7 > 9 or 2 + 7 < 9' the connective is "or".

Q. 4. The connective in the statement "Earth revolves round the Sun and Moon is a satellite of earth" is

(a) or **(b) Earth**
(c) Sun **(d) and**

[NCERT Exemplar Q. 20, Page 266]

Ans. Correct option : (D)

Connective word is "and".

Q. 5. The negation of the statement "A circle is an ellipse" is

(a) An ellipse is a circle

(b) An ellipse is not a circle

(c) A circle is not an ellipse

(d) A circle is an ellipse

[NCERT Exemplar Q. 21, Page 266]

Ans. Correct option : (C)

Let p : A circle is an ellipse

∴ ~p : A circle is not an ellipse.

Q. 6. The negation of the statement "7 is greater than 8" is

(a) 7 is equal to 8

(b) 7 is not greater than 8

(c) 8 is less than 7

(d) None of these

[NCERT Exemplar Q. 22, Page 266]

Ans. Correct option : (B)

Let p : 7 is greater than 8.

∴ ~p : 7 is not greater than 8.

Q. 7. The negation of the statement "72 is divisible by 2 and 3" is

(a) 72 is not divisible by 2 or 72 is not divisible by 3

(b) 72 is not divisible by 2 and 72 is not divisible by 3

(c) 72 is divisible by 2 and 72 is not divisible by 3

(d) 72 is not divisible by 2 and 72 is divisible by 3

[NCERT Exemplar Q. 23, Page 266]

Ans. Correct option : (B)

Let p : 72 is divisible by 2 and 3 and q : 72 is divisible by 2 and r : 72 is divisible by 3

∴ ~q : 72 is not divisible by 2 and ~r : 72 is not divisible by 3

So, $\sim(q \wedge r) : \sim q \vee \sim r$

Q. 8. The negation of the statement "Plants take in CO_2 and give out O_2" is

(a) Plants do not taken in CO_2 and do not given out O_2

(b) Plants do not taken in CO_2 or do not given out O_2

(c) Plants take is CO_2 and do not given out O_2

(d) Plants take in CO_2 or do not give out O_2

[NCERT Exemplar Q. 24, Page 266]

Ans. Correct option : (B)

Let p : plants take CO_2 and give out O_2

q : plants take CO_2 and r : plants give out O_2

$\sim p$: plants do not take in CO_2 and $\sim r$: plants do not give out O_2

$\therefore \sim(q \wedge r) = (\sim q \vee \sim r)$

Q. 9. The negative of the statement "Rajesh or Rajni lived in Bangalore" is

(a) Rajesh did not live in Bangalore or Rajni lives in Bangalore

(b) Rajesh lives in Bangalore and Rajni did not live in Bangalore

(c) Rajesh did not live in Bangalore and Rajni did not live in Bangalore

(d) Rejesh did not live in Bangalore or Rajni did not live in Bangalore

[NCERT Exemplar Q. 25, Page 267]

Ans. Correct option : (C)

Let p : Rajesh or Rajni lives Bangalore.

and q : Rajesh lives in Bangalore and r : Rajni lives in Bangalore.

$\sim q$: Rajesh does not live in Bangalore and $\sim r$: Rajni does not live in Bangalore.

Q. 10. The negation of the statement "101 is not a multiple of 3" is

(a) 101 is a multiple of 3

(b) 101 is a multiple of 2

(c) 101 is an odd number

(d) 101 is an even number

[NCERT Exemplar Q. 26, Page 267]

Ans. Correct option : (A)

Let p : 101 is not multiple of 3

$\sim p$: 101 is multiple of 3.

Q. 11. The negation of the statement "The product of 3 and 4 is 9" is

(a) it is false that the product of 3 and 4 is 9

(b) the product of 3 and 4 is 12

(c) the product of 3 and 4 is not 12

(d) it is false that the product of 3 and 4 is not 9

[NCERT Exemplar Q. 34, Page 268]

Ans. Correct option : (A)

Negation of the statement is " It is false that the product of 3 and 4 is 9.

Q. 12. Which of the following is not a negation of "A natural number is greater than zero".

(a) A natural number is not greater than zero

(b) It is false that a natural number is greater than zero

(c) It is false that a natural number is not greater than zero

(d) None of the above

[NCERT Exemplar Q. 35, Page 269]

Ans. Correct option : (C)

The negation of the given statement is false *i.e.* It is false that a natural number is not greater than zero.

Q. 13. Which of the following statement is a conjunction ?

(a) Ram and Shyam are friends

(b) Both Ram and Shyam are tall

(c) Both Ram and Shyam are enemies

(d) None of the above

[NCERT Exemplar Q. 36, Page 269]

Ans. Correct option : (D)

Let the two statements p and q be simple statements. If they are corrected with and. Then resulting compound statement p and q is called a conjunction of p and q.

Very Short Answer Type Questions (1 mark each)

Q. 1. State whether the following sentences are statement or not

(i) The angles opposite to equal sides of a triangle are equal.

(ii) The moon is a satellites of Earth.

(iii) May God bless you

(iv) Asia is a continent.

(v) How are you ?

[NCERT Exemplar Q. 37, Page 269]

Sol. (i) It is statement.

(ii) It is a statement.

(iii) It is an exclamation. Hence It is not a statement.

(iv) It is a statement.

(v) It is a questions. Hence it is not a statement.

Q. 2. Which of the following sentences are statements? Justify

(i) 0 is a complex number,

(ii) Sky is red.

(iii) Every set is an infinite set.

(iv) $15 + 8 > 23$.

(v) $y + 9 = 7$

(vi) Where is your bag?

(vii) Every square is a rectangle.

(viii) Sum of opposite angles of a cyclic quadrilateral is 180°.

(ix) $\sin^2 x + \cos^2 x = 0$

[NCERT Exemplar Q. 1, Page 261]

Sol. Statement is a sentence which is either true or false but not both simultaneously.

(i) It is true statement.

(ii) It is true statement.

(iii) It is false statement.

(iv) It is false statement.

(v) It is false statement.

The value of y is not given not the statement.

(vi) It is not a statement.

(vii) It is a true statement.

(viii) It is true statement.

(ix) it is false statement,

Q. 3. Find the component statements of the following compound statements.

(i) Number 7 is prime and odd.

(ii) Chennai is in India and is the capital of Tamil Nadu.

(iii) The number 100 is divisible by 3, and 11.

(iv) Chandigarh is the capital of Haryana and UP.

(v) $\sqrt{7}$ is a rational number or an irrational number.

(vi) 0 is less than every positive integer and every negative integer.

(vii) Plants use sunlight, water and carbon dioxide for photosynthesis.

(viii) Two lines in a plane either intersect at one point or they are parallel.

(ix) A rectangle is a quadrilateral or a 5 sided polygon.

[NCERT Exemplar Q. 2, Page 262]

Sol. (i) p : 7 is prime number.

(ii) q : 7 is odd number.

(ii) p : Chennai is in India.

q : Chennai is capital of Tamil Nadu.

(iii) p : 100 is divisible by 3.

q : 100 is divisible by 11.

(iv) p : Chandigarh is capital of Haryana.

q : Chandigarh is capital of UP.

(v) p : $\sqrt{7}$ is a rational number.

q : $\sqrt{7}$ is an irrational number.

(vi) p : 0 is less than every positive integer.

q : 0 is less than every negative integer.

(vii) p : Plants use sunlight for photosynthesis.

q : Plants use water for photosynthesis.

r : Plants use carbon dioxide for photosynthesis.

(viii) p : Two lines in a plane intersect at one point.

q : Two lines in a plane are parallel.

(ix) p : A rectangle is a quadrilateral,

q : A rectangle is a 5-sided polygon.

Q. 4. Write the negation on the following simple statements.

(i) The number 17 is prime.

(ii) $2 + 7 = 6$.

(iii) Violets are blue.

(iv) $\sqrt{5}$ is a rational number.

(v) 2 is not a prime number.

(vi) Every real number is an irrational number.

(vii) Cow has four legs.

(viii) A leap year has 366 days.

(ix) All similar triangles are congruent.

(x) Area of a circle is same as the perimeter of the circle. **[NCERT Exemplar Q. 4, Page 262]**

Sol. (i) The number 17 is not prime.

(ii) $2 + 7 \neq 6$.

(iii) Violets are not blue.

(iv) $\sqrt{5}$ is not a rational number.

(v) 2 is a prime number

(vi) Every real number is not an irrational number.

(vii) Cow has not four legs.

(viii) A leap year has not 366 days.

(ix) There exist similar triangles which are not congruent.

(x) Area of a circle is not same as the perimeter of the circle.

Short Answer Type Questions (2 marks each)

Q. 1. Write the component statements of the following compound statements and check whether the compound statement is true or false.

(i) 57 is divisible by 2 or 3.

(ii) 24 is a multiple of 4 and 6.

(iii) All living things have two eyes and two legs.

(iv) 2 is an even number and a prime number.

[NCERT Exemplar Q. 3, Page 262]

Sol. (i) p : 57 is divisible by 2. [False]

q : 57 is divisible by 3. [True]

(ii) Component statements are

p : 24 is multiple of 4 [True]

q : 24 is multiple of 6. [True]

(iii) Component statements are

p : All living things have two eyes.

q : All living things have two legs.

(iv) It is a true statement.

component statements are

p : 2 is an even number. [True]

q : 2 is a prime number. [True]

Q. 2. Translate the following statements into symbolic form.

(i) Rahul passed in Hindi and English.

(ii) x and y are even integers.

(iii) 2, 3 and 6 are factors of 12.

(iv) Either x or x + I is an odd integer.

(v) A number is either divisible by 2 or 3.

(vi) Either $x = 2$ or $x = 3$ is a root of $3x^2 - x - 10 = 0$.

(vii) Students can take Hindi or English as an optional paper. [NCERT Exemplar Q. 5, Page 262]

Sol. (i) p : Rahul passed in Hindi.

q : Rahul passed in English.

$p \wedge q$: Rahul passed in Hindi and English.

(ii) p : x is even integers.

q : y is even integers.

$p \cap q$: x and y are even integers,

(iii) p : 2 is factor of 12.

q : 3 is factor of 12.

r : 6 is factor of 12.

$p \wedge q \wedge r$: 2, 3 and 6 are factor of 12.

(iv) p : x is an odd integer,

q : $(x + 1)$ is an odd integer.

$p \vee q$: Either x or $(x + 1)$ is an odd integer.

(v) p : A number is divisible by 2.

q : A number is divisible by 3.

$p \vee q$: A number is either divisible by 2 or 3.

(vi) p : $x = 2$ is a root of $3x^2 - x - 10 = 0$.

q : $x = 3$ is a root of $3x^2 - x - 10 = 0$

$p \vee q$: Either $x = 2$ or $x = 3$ is a root of $3x^2 - x - 10 = 0$.

(vii) p : Students can take Hindi as an optional paper.

q : Students can take English as an optional subject.

$p \vee q$: Students can take Hindi or English as an optional paper.

TOPIC-2
Implications and Validity of Statements

Quick Review

➤ **Implications**

If any two simple statements are combined by the phase 'If-then', then it form a compound statement. This compound statement is called an implication or a conditional statement. The conditional statement 'If p then q' can be expressed in the following ways—

(i) p implies q, denoted by $p \Rightarrow q$ or $p \rightarrow q$, The symbol '$\Rightarrow$' or '$\rightarrow$' stands for implies.

(ii) p is sufficient for q.

(iii) p only if q.

(iv) q is necessary condition for p.

(v) $\sim q$ implies $\sim p$ or $\sim q \Rightarrow \sim p$.

e.g., Let p : Bus reaches in time.

and q : I can attend the meeting.

Then $p \rightarrow q \equiv$ If bus reaches in time, then I can attend the meeting. Here 'p' is called the antecedent and q is called the consequent.

➢ **Truth table for implication**

If p and q are two statements, then the truth table for $p \Rightarrow q$ is given as—

p	q	$p \Rightarrow q$
T	T	T
T	F	F
F	T	T
F	F	T

➢ **Contrapositive of Implication**

The statement "$\sim q \Rightarrow \sim p$" is called the contrapositive of the statement $p \Rightarrow q$.

➢ **Converse of Implication**

If p and q are two statements, then the converse of the implication 'if p, then q' is 'if q, then p' *i.e.*, $q \Rightarrow p$.

➢ **Inverse of implication**

If p and q are two statements, then the inverse of 'it p, then q' is 'if $\sim p$, then $\sim q$' *i.e.*, $\sim p \Rightarrow \sim q$.

➢ **If and only if implication (Biconditional or Equivalence Statement)**

If any two simple statements are combined with the phrase 'if and only if', then it form a compound statement, which is called biconditional.

The equivalent forms of biconditional statement 'p if and only if q' are.

(i) $p \Leftrightarrow q$ or $p \leftrightarrow q$, where the symbol $\leftrightarrow$ or $\Leftrightarrow$ stands for if and only if.

(ii) q if and only if p.

(iii) p is necessary and sufficient condition for q and vice-verse.

e.g., Let p : ABC is an isosceles triangle.

and q : Two sides of a triangle are equal.

The $p \Leftrightarrow q \equiv$ ABC is an isosceles triangle, if and only if two sides of the triangle are equal.

➢ **Truth Table for 'If and only If' implication.**

If p and q are two statements then the truth table for $p \Rightarrow q$ is—

p	q	$p \Rightarrow q$
T	T	T
T	F	F
F	T	F
F	F	T

➢ **Negation of a compound statement**

The negation of compound statements according to connectives / Implication are given below—

(i) Negation of p and q (conjunction)—The negative of p and q *i.e.*, conjunction $p \wedge q$ is the disjunction of the negation of the negation of p and the negation of q.

i.e., $\sim (p \wedge q) = \sim p \vee \sim q$.

The negation of the conjunction would mean the negation of at least one of the two component statements.

(ii) Negation of p or q (disjunction)—The negation of p or q *i.e.*, disjunction $p \vee q$ is the conjunction of the negation of p and negation of q.

i.e., $\sim (p \vee q) = \sim p \wedge \sim q$.

The negation of the conjunction would mean the negation of at least one of the two component statements.

(ii) Negation of p or q (disjunction)—The negation of p or q *i.e.*, disjunction $p \vee q$ is the conjunction of the negation of p and negation of q.

i.e., $\sim (p \vee q) = \sim pV \sim q$.

The negation of the disjunction would mean the negation of both p and q simultaneously.

(iii) Negation of negation—Negation of negation of a statement is the statement itself.

$\sim (\sim p) \equiv p$.

(iv) Negation of conditional Statement 'if p, then q'—

The truth table for negation of implication 'if p then q' is given below.

p	q	$p \Rightarrow q$	$\sim (p \Rightarrow q)$	$\sim q$	$p \cap \sim q$
T	T	T	F	F	F
T	F	F	T	T	T
F	T	T	F	F	F
F	F	F	T	T	F

Thus, $\sim (p \Rightarrow q) \equiv p \vee \sim q$.

(v) Negation of a biconditional statement 'p if any only if q'—

The truth for negation of the biconditional 'p if and any it q' is—

p	q	$p \Rightarrow q$	$\sim p$	$\sim q$	$p \wedge \sim q$	$\sim p \wedge q$	$(p \wedge \sim q)$	$\sim (p \Leftrightarrow q)$
T	T	T	F	F	F	F	F	F
T	F	F	F	T	T	F	T	T
F	T	F	T	F	F	T	F	T
F	F	T	T	T	F	F	F	T

$\therefore \quad \sim (p \Leftrightarrow q) \equiv (p \wedge \sim q) \vee (\sim q \wedge q)$

➤ **Validity of Statements**

The process of checking a statement for its truth value (true or false) is called validity of the statement. This depends on which of the connectives and quantifiers used in the statement. The following methods are used to check the validity of the statement.

(i) Direct method

To Show '$p \wedge q$' is true, show that statement p is true and show that statement q is true.

To show '$p \vee q$' is true, assume that p is false and show that q must be true, or , assume that q is false, show that p must be true.

To show '$p \Rightarrow q$' is true, assume that p is true, show that q must be true.

To show '$p \Leftarrow q$' is true, show that if p is true then q is true and if q is true then p is true.

(ii) Contrapositive Method

To check the validity of $p \Rightarrow q$, first assume that q is false, then prove that p is false *i.e.*, $nq \Rightarrow np$.

(iii) Contradiction Method

To check the validity of $p \Rightarrow q$, first assume that p is true and q is false and then obtain a contradiction from the assumption.

(iv) By Giving a counter example

In mathematics, counter examples are used to disprove the statement. However, generating examples in favour of a statement do not provide validity of the statement. To prove that given statement is false, we give a counter example.

Note :

- The conditional statement $p \Rightarrow q$ is false, only if p is true and q is false and it is true in all other cases.
- The biconditional statement $p \Leftarrow q$ is true, if either both the statement are true or both are false. The statement $p \Leftarrow q$ is false, if exactly one of the statement is false.

Multiple Choice Questions **(1 mark each)**

[A] Objective Type Questions

Q. 1. The contrapositive of the statement "If 7 is greater than 5, then 8 is greater than 6" is

(a) If 8 is greater than 6, then 7 is greater than 5

(b) If 8 is not greater than 6, then 7 is greater than 5

(c) If 8 is not greater than 6, then 7 is not greater than 5

(d) If 8 is greater than 6, then 7 is not greater than 5 [NCERT Exemplar Q. 27, Page 267]

Ans. Correct option : (C)

Let p : 7 is grater than 5 & q ; 8 is greater than 6.

$\therefore p \to q$ i.e. $\sim p$: 7 is not greater than 5.
and $\sim q$: 8 is not greater than 6.
So, $\sim p \to \sim q$: If 8 is not greater than 6, then 7 is not greater than 5.

Q. 2. The converse of the statement 'If $x > y$, then $x + a > y + a$" is
(a) If $x < y$, then $x + a < y + a$
(b) If $x < y > y < a$, then $x < y$
(c) If $x < y$, then $x + a < y + a$
(d) If $x < y$, then $x + a < y + a$

[NCERT Exemplar Q. 28, Page 267]

Ans. Correct option : (B)
Let $p : x > y$ and $q; x + a > y + a$
$p \to q$
converse of the above statement is $q \to q$
$\therefore$ If $x + a > y + a$, then $x > a$, then $x > y$

Q. 3. The converse of the statement "If sun is not shining, then sky is filled with clouds" is
(a) If sky is filled with clouds, then the sun is not shining
(b) If sun is shining, then sky is filled with clouds
(c) If sky is clear, then sun is shining
(d) If sun is not shining then sky is not filled with clouds.

[NCERT Exemplar Q. 29, Page 267]

Ans. Correct option : (A)
Let p : sun is not shining
q : sky is filled with clouds.
So, the converse of the statement $p \to q$ is $q \to p$ i.e.
If sky is filled with clouds, then sun is not shining.

Q. 4. The contrapositive of the statement "if p, then q", is
(a) if q, then p
(b) if p, then $\sim q$
(c) if $\sim q$, then $\sim p$
(d) if $\sim p$, then $\sim q$

[NCERT Exemplar Q. 30, Page 268]

Ans. Correct option : (c)
Here, the statement is "If p, then q" i.e. $p \to q$ contrapositive of statement $p \to q$ is $(\sim q) \to (\sim p)$ i.e. If $\sim q$ then $\sim p$.

Q. 5. The statement "If x^2 is not even, then x is not even" is converse of the statement
(a) If x^2 is odd, then x is even
(b) If x is not even, then x^2 is not even
(c) If x is even, then x^2 is even
(d) If x is odd, then x^2 is even

[NCERT Exemplar Q. 30, Page 268]

Ans. Correct option : (B)
Let $p : x^2$ is not even & $q : x$ is not even
So, the converse of the statement $p \to q$ is $q \to p$ i.e.
If x is not even, then x^2 is not even.

Q. 6. The contrapositive of statement 'If Chandigarh is capital of Punjab, then Chandigarh is in India' is
(a) If Chandigarh is not in India, then Chandigarh is not the capital of Punjab
(b) If Chandigarh is in India, then Chandigarh is Capital of Punjab
(c) If Chandigarh is not capital of Punjab, then Chandigarh is not capital of India
(d) If Chandigarh is capital of Punjab, then Chandigarh is not is India.

[NCERT Exemplar Q. 32, Page 268]

Ans. Correct option : (A)
Let p : Chandigarh is a capital of Punjab;
q : Chandigarh is in India.
$\sim p$: Chandigarh is not a capital of Panjab;
$\sim q$: Chandigarh is not in India.
If $(\sim q)$, then $(\sim p)$ i.e. If Chandigarh is not in India, then Chandigarh is not a capital of Punjab.

Q. 7. Which of the following is the conditional $p \to q$?
(a) q is sufficient for p
(b) p is necessary for q
(c) p only if q
(d) if q and p

[NCERT Exemplar Q. 33, Page 268]

Ans. Correct option : (C)
We know that $p \to q$ is same as p only if q.

Very Short Answer Type Questions (1 marks each)

Q. 1. Rewrite each of the following statements in the form of conditional statements.
(i) The square of an odd number is odd.
(ii) You will get a sweet dish after the dinner.
(iii) You will fail, if you will not study.
(iv) The unit digit of an integer is 0 or 5, if it is divisible by 5.
(v) The square of a prime number is not prime.
(vi) $2b = a + c$, if a, b and c are in AP.

[NCERT Exemplar Q. 7, Page 459]

Sol. Conditional statement $p \to q$ are :
(i) If the number is odd number, then its square is odd number.
(ii) If you take the dinner, then you will get sweet dish.
(iii) If you will not study, then you will fail.
(iv) If an integer is divisible by 5, then its unit digits are 0 or 5.
(v) If the number is prime, then its square is not prime.
(vi) If a, b and c are in A. P. then $2b = a + c$.

Q. 2. Write, down the contrapositive of the following statements.

(i) If $x = y$ and $y = 3$, then $x = 3$.

(ii) If n is a natural number, then n is an integer

(iii) If all three sides of a triangle are equal, then the triangle is equilateral.

(iv) If x and y are negative integers, then xy is positive.

(v) If natural number n is divisible by 6, then n is divisible by 2 and 3.

(vi) If it snow then the weather will be cold.

(vii) If x is a real number such that $0 < x < 1$ then $x^2 < 1$. **[NCERT Exemplar, Q. 9, Page 263]**

Sol. (i) If $x \neq 3$. then $x \neq y$ or $y \neq 3$.

(ii) If, n is not an integer, then it is not a natural number.

(iii) If the triangle is not equilateral, then all three sides of the triangle are not equal.

(iv) If xy is not positive integer, then either x or y is not negative integer.

(v) If natural number n is not divisible by 2 or 3, then n is not divisible by 6.

(vi) The weather will not be cold, if it does not snow.

(vii) If $x^2 > 1$, then x is not a real number such that $0 < x < 1$.

Q. 3. Write down the converse of following statements.

(i) If a rectangle 'R' is a square, then R is a rhombus.

(ii) If today is Monday, then tomorrow is Tuesday.

(iii) If you go to Agra, then you must visit Taj Mahal.

(iv) If sum of squares of two sides of a triangle is equal to the square of third side of a triangle, then the triangle is right angled.

(v) If all three angles of a triangle are equal, then the triangle is equilateral.

(vi) If $x : y = 3 : 2$, then $2x - 3y$.

(vii) If S is a cyclic quadrilateral, then the opposite angles of S are supplementary.

(viii) If x is zero, then x is neither positive nor negative.

(ix) If two triangles are similar, then the ratio of their corresponding sides are equal.

[NCERT Exemplar, Q. 10, Page 264]

Sol. (i) If the rectangle 'R' rhombus, then it is square.

(ii) If tomorrow is Tuesday, then today is Monday.

(iii) If you must visit Taj Mahal, you go to Agra.

(iv) If the triangle is right angle, then sum of squares of two sides of a triangle square of third side.

(v) If the triangle is equilateral, then all three angles of triangle are equal.

(vi) If $2x = 3y$, then $x : y = 3 : 2$

(vii) If the opposite angles of a quadrilateral are supplementary, then S is cyclic,

(v) If x is neither positive nor negative, then x is 0.

(ix) If the ratio of corresponding sides of two triangles are equal, then triangles are similar.

Q. 4. Identify the quantifiers in the following statements.

(i) There exists a triangle which is not equilateral.

(ii) For all real numbers x and y, $xy = yx$.

(iii) There exists a real number which is not a rational number.

(iv) For every natural number x, $x + 1$ is also a natural number.

(v) For all real numbers x with $x > 3$, x^2 is greater than 9.

(vi) There exists a triangle which, :is not an isosceles triangle.

(vii) For all negative integers x, x^3 is also a negative integers.

(viii) There exists a statement in above statements which is not true.

(ix) There exists an even prime number other than 2.

(x) There exists a real number x such that $x^2 + 1 = 0$.

[NCERT Exemplar, Q. 11, Page 264]

Sol. Quantifier phrase are 'there exist' and 'For every', 'For all' etc.

(i) There exists (ii) For all

(iii) There exists (iv) For every

(v) For all (vi) There exists

(vii) For all (viii) There exists

(ix) There exists (x) There exists

Short Answer Type Questions (2 marks each)

Q. 1. Write down the negation of following compound statements.

(i) All rational numbers are real and complex.

(ii) All real numbers are rationals or irrationals.

(iii) $x - 2$ and $x - 3$ are roots of the quadratic equation $x^2 - 5x + 6$

(iv) A triangle has either 3–sides or 4–sides.

(v) 35 is a prime number or a composite number.

(vi) All prime integers are either even or odd.

(vii) $|x|$ is equal to either x or $-x$.

(viii) 6 is divisible by 2 and 3.

[NCERT Exemplar Q. 6, Page 263]

Sol. (i) Let p : All rational numbers are real.

q : All rational numbers are complex.

$\sim p$: All rational number are not real.

$\sim q$: All rational numbers are not complex.

$\sim (p \wedge q)$: All rational numbers are not real or not complex. $[\because (p \wedge q) = -p \vee \sim q]$

(ii) Let p : All real numbers are rationals.
q : All real numbers are irrational.
Then, the negation of compound statement is
$\sim (p \vee q)$: All real numbers are not rational and all real numbers are not irrational.
$[\because (p \vee q) = \sim p \wedge \sim q]$

(iii) Let $p : x = 2$ is root of quadratic equation $x^2 - 5x + 6 = 0$.
$q : x = 3$ is root of quadratic equation $x^2 - 5x + 6 = 0$.
Then, the negation of conjunction of statement is
$\sim (p \vee q) : x = 2$ is not a root of, quadratic equation $x^2 - 5x + 6 = 0$. or $x = 3$ is not a root of the quadratic equation $x^2 - 5x + 6 = 0$.

(iv) Let p : A triangle has 3-sides.
q : A triangle has 4-sides.
Then, negation of disjunction of the statement is
$\sim (p \vee q)$: A triangle has neither 3-sides nor 4-sides.

(v) Let p : 35 is a prime number.
q : 35 is a composite number.
Then, negation of disjunction of the statement is
$\sim (p \vee q)$: 35 is not a prime number and it is not a composite number,

(vi) Let p : All prime integers are even.
q : All prime integers are odd.
Then negation of disjunction of the statement is
$\sim (p \vee q)$: All prime integers are not even and all prime integers are not odd,

(vii) Let $p : |x|$ is equal to x.
$q : |x|$ is equal to $-x$.
Then negation of disjunction of the statement is
$\sim (p \vee q) : |x|$ is not equal to x and it is not equal to $-x$.

(viii) Let p : 6 is divisible by 2.
q : 6 is divisible by 3.
Then, negation of conjunction of statement is
$\sim (p \vee q)$: 6 is not divisible by 2 or it is not divisible by 3

Q. 2. Check validity of the following statement.
(i) p : 125 is divisible by 5 and 7.
(ii) q : 131 is a multiple of 3 or 11.
[NCERT Exemplar Q. 13, Page 265]

Sol. (i) p : 125 is divisible by 5 and 7.
Let r : 125 is divisible by 5.
s : 125 is divisible by 7.
(ii) q : 131 is a multiple of 3 or 11
Let r : 131 is multiple of 3
s : 131 is multiple of 11
r is not true, s is not true
$\Rightarrow r \vee s$ is not true
Hence, q is not valid.

Q. 3. Prove by direct method that for any real number x, y if $x=y$, then $x^2 = y^2$.
[NCERT Exemplar Q. 15, Page 265]

Sol. Let $p : x = y, x, y \in R$
On squaring both sides,
$$x^2 = y^2 : q \quad \text{[say]}$$
$$p \Rightarrow q$$
Hence, we have the result.

Q. 4. Using centrapositive method prove that, if n^2 is an even integer. then n is also an even integer.
[NCERT Exemplar Q. 16, Page 265]

Sol. Let $p : n^2$ is an even integer.
$q : n$ is also an even integer.
Let $\sim p$ is true *i.e.*, n is not an even integer.
$\Rightarrow$ n^2 is not an even integer.
[since, square of an odd integer is odd]
$\Rightarrow$ $\sim p$ is true.
Therefore, $\sim q$ is true $\Rightarrow \sim p$ is true.
Hence Proved.

Long Answer Type Questions-I

(4 marks each)

Q. 1. Prove by direct method that for any integer 'n', $n^3 - n$ is always even.
[NCERT Exemplar Q. 12, Page 265]

Sol. Case I When n is even,

Let $n = 2k, k \in N$
$$\Rightarrow n^3 - n = (2k)^3 - (2k) = 2k(4k^2 - 1)$$
$$\Rightarrow \quad = 2\lambda, \text{ where } \lambda = k(4k^2 - 1)$$
$(n^3 - n)$ is even when n is even,

Case II When n is odd,

Let $n = 2k + 1, k \in N$
$$\Rightarrow n^3 - n = (2k + 1)^3 - (2k + 1)$$
$$= (2k + 1)[(2k + 1)^2 - 1]$$
$$= (2k + 1)[4k^2 + 1 + 4k - 1]$$
$$= (2k + 1)(4k^2 + 4k)$$
$$= 4k(2k + 1)(k + 1)$$
$$= 2\mu, \text{ when } \mu = 2k(k + 1)(2k + 1)$$
$\therefore$ $(n^3 - n)$ is when n is odd.
So, $n^3 - n$ is always even.

Q. 2. Prove the following statement by contradiction method
p: The sum of an irrational number and a rational number is irrational.
[NCERT Exemplar Q. 14, Page 265]

Sol. Let p is false *i.e.*, sum of an irrational and a rational number is rational.

Let $\sqrt{m}$ is irrational and n is rational number.

$\Rightarrow \quad \sqrt{m} = r$ [rational]

$\Rightarrow \quad \sqrt{m} = r - n$

$\sqrt{m}$ is irrational, where as $(r - n)$ is rational. This is contradiction.

Then, our supposition is wrong.

Hence, p is true.

EXPERT ADVICE

- *This is an easy chapter and does not require calculations.*
- *Understand the meaning of a statement and the role of connectives and quantifiers.*
- *Understand the methods used for checking validity of statements like contrapositive, direct method etc.*

OSWAAL LEARNING TOOLS

***For* Suggested Online Videos**

Visit : *https://youtu.be/c7OWJbyOOjM* Or Scan the Code

Visit : *https://youtu.be/beJjgxCl7Gw* Or Scan the Code

Visit : *https://youtu.be/_uJ8rXDe6hs* Or Scan the Code

CHAPTER

15 STATISTICS

Chapter Objectives

➤ *Data and its types; Measures of Central Tendency : Mean, Median, Mode, Class Interval, Frequency: Measures of Dispersion : Range, Quartile deviation, Mean deviation, Standard deviation of ungrouped and grouped data; Analysis of frequency distributions with equal means but different variances.*

TOPIC-1
Measure of Dispersion

TOPIC - 1
Measure of Dispersion .... P. 207

TOPIC - 2
Variance and Standard Deviation.... P. 213

Quick Review

➤ **Data and its types**

A group of information that represents the qualitative or quantitative attributes of a variable or set of variables is called data.

There are two types of data. These are :

(i) Ungrouped data : In an ungrouped data, data is listed in series *e.g.*, 1, 4, 9, 16, 25, etc.

(ii) Grouped data-It is of two types :

(a) Discrete data : In this type, data is presented in such a way that exact measurements of items are clearly shown.

(b) Continuous data : In this type, data is arranged in groups or classes but they are not exactly measurable, they form a continuous series.

➤ **Measures of Central Tendency**

A certain value that represent the whole data and signifying its characteristics is called measure of central tendency. Mean, median and mode are the measures of central tendency.

● **Mean**

Mean of ungrouped data : The mean of n observations $x_1, x_2, x_3, ..., x_n$ is given by

$$\text{Mean } (\bar{x}) = \frac{x_1 + x_2 + x_3 + ... + x_n}{n} = \frac{\sum_{i=1}^{n} x_i}{n}$$

Mean of grouped data : Let $x_1, x_2, ..., x_n$ be in observations with respective frequencies $f_1, f_2, ..., f_n$.

TIPS...

- *The mean is the amount secured by dividing the sum of values of the items in a series by the number.*
- *Median is an average of position of the numbers.*
- *Mode of a distribution is the value at the point about which the items tend to be most heavily concentrated.*
- *The ratio of SD (σ) and the AM $\bar{x}$ is called the coefficient of standard deviation (σ/x)*
- *The distribution for which the coefficient of variation is less is considered to be more consistent.*

TRICKS...

- *Relation between Mean, Median and Mode*
  (i) Mean – Mode = 3(Mean-Median)
  (ii) Mode = 3 Median – 2 Median
- *Standard deviation of first n natural number can be calculated as*

$$SD = \sqrt{\frac{n^2 - 1}{12}}$$

- *Students should remember that if each observation is multiplied by a constant 'k', the variance of the resulting observations become 'k²' times the original variance.*
- *Always remember that on adding (or subtracting) a positive number to (or from) each observation of a group does not affect the variance.*

Then, Mean

$$\text{Mean } (\bar{x}) = \frac{\sum_{i=1}^{n} f_i x_i}{\Sigma f_i}$$

- **Median**

Median of ungrouped data : Let *N* be the number of observations. First, arrange the data in ascending or descending order.

Then, if *n* is odd,

$$\text{Median} = \text{Value of the} \left(\frac{N+1}{2}\right) \text{observation.}$$

if *n* is even,

$$\text{Median} = \frac{\text{Value of } \frac{N}{2}^{\text{th}} + \text{Value of} \left(\frac{N}{2}+1\right)^{\text{th}} \text{observation}}{2}$$

Median of grouped data

1. For discrete data, first arrange the data in ascending or descending order and find cumulative frequency. Now, find $\frac{N}{2}$, where $N = \Sigma f_i$

   If $\Sigma f_i = N$ is even, then

$$\text{Median} = \frac{\text{Value of} \left(\frac{N}{2}\right)^{\text{th}} + \text{Value of} \left(\frac{N}{2}+1\right)^{\text{th}} \text{observation}}{2}$$

   If $\Sigma f_i = N$ is odd, then

$$\text{Median} = \text{Value of the} \left(\frac{N+1}{2}\right) \text{observation.}$$

2. For continuous data, first arrange the data in ascending or descending order and then find the cumulative frequencies of all classes. Now, find $\frac{N}{2}$, where $N = \Sigma f_i$. Further, find the class interval, whose cumulative frequency is just greater than of equal to $\frac{N}{2}$

Then,

$$\text{Median} = l + \frac{\left(\frac{N}{2} - C_f\right)}{f} \times h$$

l = lower limit of median class

N = Total frequency

C_f = cumulative frequency of class preceding the median class.

f = frequency of the median class

h = Width of the median class

➤ **Limit of the class**

The starting and ending values of each class are called lower and upper limits.

➤ **Class Interval**

The difference between upper and lower boundary of a class is called class interval or size of the class.

➤ **Primary and secondary data**

The data collected by the investigator himself is known as the primary data, while the data collected by a person, other than the investigator, is known as secondary data.

➤ **Frequency**

The number of times an observation occurs in the given data, is called the frequency of the observation.

➤ **Measure of Dispersion**

The measures of central tendency are not sufficient to give complete information about given data. Variability is another factor which is required to be studied under statistics. The single number that describes variability is called measure of dispersion. It is the measure of scattering of the data about some central tendency.

There are following measures of dispersion

1. Range **2.** Quartile deviation **3.** Mean deviation **4.** Standard deviation.

➤ **Range**

Range is the difference of maximum and minimum value of data

Range = maximum value – minimum value.

e.g., Given marks of Sameer and Suresh as follows–

$$\text{Sameer} = 79, 62, 40, 5$$
$$\text{Suresh} = 60, 45, 52, 42$$

For Sameer, Range $= 79 - 5 = 74$

For Suresh, Range $= 60 - 42 = 18$

Thus, range of Sameer > range of Suresh.

So, the scores are scattered or dispersed in case of Sameer while for Suresh, these are close to each other. The range of data gives us a rough idea of variability or scatter but does not tell about the dispersion of the data from the measure of central tendency.

➤ **Mean Deviation**

Mean deviation is an important measure of deviation, which depend upon the deviations of the observations from a central tendency. It is defined as the arithmetic mean of the absolute deviations of all the values taken from a central value or a fixed number *a*. The mean deviation from '*a*' is denoted by MD (*a*) and is defined by–

$$\text{M.D.}(a) = \frac{\text{Sum of absolute values of deviations from '}a\text{'}}{\text{Number of observations}}$$

➤ **Mean deviation for ungrouped data**

Let $x, x_2, ..., x_n$ be n observations. Then, mean deviation about means $(\bar{x})$ or median (M) can be found by the formula

$$\frac{\sum_{i=1}^{n}|x_i - \bar{x}|}{n} \text{ or } \frac{\sum_{i=1}^{n}|x_i - \text{M}|}{n}, \text{ where } n \text{ is the number of observations}$$

➤ **Mean deviation for grouped data**

(i) For discrete frequency distribution : Let the data have 'n' district values $x_1, x_2, ..., x_n$ and their corresponding frequencies are $f_1, f_2 ..., f_n$ respectively. Then, this data can be represented in the tabular form as

x_i	x_1	x_2	x_3	...	x_n
f_i	f_1	f_2	f_3	...	f_n

and is called discrete frequency distribution. Then, mean deviation about mean or median is given by

$$\frac{\sum_{i=1}^{n} f_i|x_i - \text{A}|}{\text{N}}, \text{ where N} = \sum_{i=1}^{n} f_i = \text{total frequency, and A = mean or median.}$$

(ii) For continuous frequency distribution : A continuous frequency distribution is a series in which the data is classified into different class intervals without gaps along with their respective frequencies.

Mean deviation about mean $(\bar{x})$, *i.e.*,

$$\text{MD}(\bar{x}) = \frac{1}{\text{N}}\sum_{i=1}^{n} f_i|x_i - \bar{x}|, \text{ where '}x_i\text{' s' are the mid-point of the intervals and}$$

$$\text{mean}(\bar{x}) = \frac{1}{\text{N}}\sum_{i=1}^{n} f_i x_i$$

Mean deviation about median (M), *i.e.*,

MD (M) = $\frac{1}{N}\sum_{i=1}^{n} f_i |x_i - M|$, where x_i's are the mid-points of the intervals and $\sum_{i=1}^{n} f_i$ = N. Also, median M = $l + \frac{\frac{N}{2} - C_f}{f} \times h$, where l, f, h and C_f are lower limit, the frequency, the width of median class and cumulative frequency of class just preceding the median class.

➤ **Shortcut (Step-deviation) method for calculating the Mean deviation about Mean :** This method is used to manage large data. In this method, we take an assumed mean, which is in the middle or just close to it, in the data. We denote the new variable by u and is defined by

$u_i = \frac{x_i - a}{h}$, where a is the assumed mean and h is the common factor or length of class interval. The mean $\bar{x}$ in step deviation method is given by

$$\bar{x} = a + \frac{\sum_{i=1}^{n} f_i u_i}{N} \times h$$

➤ **Limitations of Mean Deviation**

(i) If the data is more scattered or the degree of variability is very high, then the median is not a valid representative. Thus, the mean deviation about the median is not fully relied.

(ii) The sum of the deviations from the mean is more than the sum of the deviations from the median. Therefore, the mean deviation about mean is not very scientific.

(iii) The mean deviation is calculated on the basis of absolute values of the deviations and so cannot be subjected to further algebraic treatment. Sometimes, it gives unsatisfactory results.

- The cumulative frequency of a class is the frequency obtained by adding the frequencies of all the classes preceding the given class and the frequency of given class.
- Mean deviation may be obtained from any measure of central tendency. However, we study deviations from mean and median in this chapter.

Multiple Choice Questions

(1 mark each)

[A] Objective Type Questions

Q. 1. The mean deviation of the data 3, 10, 10, 4, 7, 10, 5 from the mean is

(A) 2 (B) 2.57

(C) 3 (D) 3.75

[NCERT Exemplar Q. 24, Page 281]

Ans. Correct option : (B)

Observations given by 3, 10, 10, 4, 7, 10 and 5

$$\therefore \quad \bar{x} = \frac{3+10+10+4+7+10+5}{7} = \frac{49}{7} = 7$$

$$\text{M.D.} = \Sigma\frac{d_i}{n} = \frac{18}{7} = 2.57 \quad (\Sigma di = \Sigma|x_i - \bar{x}|)$$

Q. 2. Mean deviation of n observations $x_1, x_2, \ldots\ldots x_n$ from their mean $\bar{x}$ is

(A) $\sum_{i=1}^{n}(x_i - \bar{x})$ (B) $\frac{1}{n}\sum_{i=1}^{n}|x_i - \bar{x}|$

(C) $\sum_{i=1}^{n}(x_i - \bar{x})^2$ (D) $\frac{1}{n}\sum_{i=1}^{n}(x_i - \bar{x})^2$

[NCERT Exemplar Q. 25, Page 281]

Ans. Correct option : (B)

$$\text{M.D.} = \frac{1}{n}\sum_{i=1}^{n}|x_i - \bar{x}|$$

Q. 3. When tested, the lives (in hours) of 5 bulbs were noted as follows 1357, 1090, 1666, 1494, 1623 The mean deviation (in hours) from their mean is

(A) 178 **(B) 179**

(C) 220 **(D) 356**

[NCERT Exemplar Q. 26, Page 281]

Ans. Correct option : (A)

The lives of 5 bulbs are given by

$$\therefore \text{Mean} = \frac{1357 + 1090 + 1666 + 1494 + 1623}{5}$$

$$\bar{x} = \frac{7230}{5} = 1446$$

$$\therefore \text{M.D.} = \frac{\Sigma di}{n} = \frac{890}{x} \qquad (\Sigma di = \Sigma|x_i - \bar{x}|)$$

$$= \frac{89 + 356 + 220 + 48 + 177}{5} = 178$$

Q. 4. Following are the marks obtained by 9 students in a mathematics test 50, 69, 20, 33, 53, 39, 40, 65, 59 The mean deviation from the median is

(A) 9 **(B) 10.5**

(C) 12.67 **(D) 14.76**

[NCERT Exemplar Q. 27, Page 281]

Ans. Correct option : (C)

Marks obtained the 50, 69, 20, 33, 53, 39, 40, 65

Let us write in ascending order

20, 33, 39, 40, 50, 53, 59, 65, 69

Here, $n = 9$

$$\therefore \text{Median} = \frac{9+1}{2} \text{th term} = 5^{\text{th}} \text{ term i.e. } 50$$

$\therefore$ Median = 50

$$\therefore \quad \text{MD} = \frac{\Sigma d_i}{n} = \frac{114}{9} \qquad (\Sigma d_i = \Sigma|x_i - \text{Median}|)$$

$$= \frac{30 + 17 + 11 + 10 + 0 + 3 + 9 + 15 + 19}{9}$$

$$= 12.67$$

[B] Fill in the blanks

Q. 1. If $\bar{x}$ is the mean of n values of x, then $\sum_{i=1}^{n}(x_i - \bar{x})$ is always equal to .... If a has any value other then $\sum_{i=1}^{n}(x_i - \bar{x})^2$, then is ...... than $\sum(x_i - a)^2$

[NCERT Exemplar Q. 41, Page 283]

Q. 2. The sum of squares of the deviations of the values of variables is .... when taken about their arithmetic mean.

[NCERT Exemplar Q. 44, Page 283]

Q. 3. The mean deviation of data is .... when measured from the median.

[NCERT Exemplar Q. 45, Page 283]

Answer

1. 0 and less
2. minimum
3. least

Long Answer Type Questions-I

(4 marks each)

Q. 1. Find the mean deviation about the mean of the distribution.

Size	20	21	22	23	24
Frequency	6	4	5	1	4

[NCERT Exemplar Q. 1, Page 278]

Sol.

x_i (size)	(Frequency) f_i	f_ix_i	$d_i = \|x_1 - x\|$	f_id_i
20	6	120	1.65	9.90
21	4	84	0.65	2.60
22	5	110	0.35	1.75
23	1	23	1.35	1.35
24	4	96	2.35	9.40
Total	20	433		25

$$\bar{x} = \frac{\sum f_ix_i}{\sum f_i} = \frac{433}{20} = 21.65$$

$$\therefore \qquad \text{MD} = \frac{\sum f_i|x_i - \bar{x}_i|}{\sum f_i} = \frac{25}{20} = 1.25$$

Q. 2. Calculate the mean deviation about the mean of the set of first n natural numbers when n is an even number.

[NCERT Exemplar Q. 4, Page 278]

Sol. Consider first n natural number, when n is even i.e., 1, 2, 3, 4,.....n.

$$\therefore \quad M\bar{x} = \frac{1+2+3+...+n}{n} = \frac{n(n+1)}{2n} = \frac{n(n+1)}{2n}$$

$$MD = \frac{1}{n}\left[\left|1-\frac{n+1}{2}\right|+\left|2-\frac{n+1}{2}\right|+\left|3-\frac{n+1}{2}\right|\right]+\left|\frac{n-2}{2}-\frac{n+1}{2}\right|+\left|\frac{n}{2}-\frac{n+1}{2}\right|+\left|\frac{n+2}{2}-\frac{n+1}{2}\right|+...+\left|n-\frac{n+1}{2}\right|$$

$$= \frac{1}{n}\left[\left|\frac{n-1}{2}\right|+\left|\frac{3-n}{2}\right|+\left|\frac{5-n}{2}\right|+...+\left|\frac{-3}{2}\right|+\left|\frac{1}{2}\right|+...+\left|\frac{n-1}{2}\right|\right]$$

$$= \frac{1}{n}\left[\frac{1}{2}+\frac{3}{2}+...+\frac{n-1}{2}\right]\left(\frac{n}{2}\right)\text{terms}$$

$$= \frac{1}{n}\cdot\left(\frac{n}{2}\right)^2$$

[$\because$ sum of first n natural numbers $= n^2$]

$$= \frac{1}{n}\cdot\frac{n^2}{4} = \frac{n}{4}$$

Q. 3. Calculate the mean deviation about the mean for the following frequency distribution.

Class Interval	0-4	4-8	8-12	12-16	16-20
Frequency	4	6	8	5	2

[NCERT Exemplar Q. 16, Page 280]

Sol.

Class Interval	f_i	x_i	f_ix_i	$d_i = \|d_i - x\|$	f_id_i
0-4	4	2	8	7.2	28.8
4-8	6	6	36	3.2	19.2
8-12	8	10	80	0.8	6.4
12-16	5	14	70	4.8	24.0
16-20	2	18	36	8.8	17.6
Total	$\sum f_i = 25$		$\sum f_ix_i = 230$		$\sum f_id_i = 96$

$$\therefore \quad \text{Mean} = \frac{\sum f_ix_i}{\sum f_i} = \frac{230}{25} = 9.2$$

and

$$\text{Mean deviation} = \frac{\sum f_id_i}{\sum f_i} = \frac{96}{25} = 3.84$$

Long Answer Type Question-II (6 marks each)

Q. 1. Calculate the mean deviation from the median of the following data.

Class Interval	0-6	6-12	12-18	18-24	24-30
Frequency	4	5	3	6	2

[NCERT Exemplar Q. 17, Page 280]

Sol.

Class Interval	f_i	x_i	cf	$d_i = \|x_i - m_d\|$	f_id_i
0-6	4	3	4	11	44
6-12	5	9	9	5	25
12-18	3	15	12	1	3
18-24	6	21	18	7	42
24-30	2	27	20	13	26
Total	N=20				$\sum f_ix_i = 140$

$$\because \quad \frac{N}{2} = \frac{20}{2} = 10$$

So, the median class 12-18.

$$\text{Median} = l + \frac{\frac{N}{2} - c_f}{f} \times h$$

$$= 12 + \frac{6}{3}(10-9)$$

$$= 12 + 2 = 14$$

$$\text{MD} = \frac{\sum f_i d_i}{\sum f_i} = \frac{140}{20} = 7$$

TOPIC-2
Variance and Standard Deviation

Quick Review

- **Variance**

The mean of squares of deviations from mean is called the variance and it is denoted by the symbol 'σ^2'. The variance of 'n' observations $x_1, x_2, ..., x_n$ is given by :

$$\sigma^2 = \frac{\sum_{i=1}^{n}(x_i - \bar{x})^2}{n}$$

- **Significance of deviation**

(i) If the deviation is zero, it means there is no deviation at all and all observations are equal to mean.

(ii) If deviation is small, this indicates that the observations are close to the mean.

(iii) If the deviation is large, there is a high degree of dispersion of the observation from the mean.

- **Standard Deviation**

Standard deviation is the square root of the arithmetic mean of the squares of deviations from mean and it is denoted by the symbol σ.

or

The square root of variance, is called standard deviation *i.e.*, $\sqrt{\sigma^2} = \sigma$. It is also known as root mean square deviation.

- **Variance and Standard deviation of ungrouped data**

Variance of n observations $x_1, x_2, ..., x_n$ is given by

$$\sigma^2 = \frac{\sum_{i=1}^{n}(x_i - \bar{x})^2}{n} = \frac{\sum_{i=1}^{n} x_i^2}{n} - \left(\frac{\sum_{i=1}^{n} x_i}{n}\right)^2$$

and, $$\text{Standard Deviation, } \sigma = \sqrt{\text{Variance}} = \sqrt{\sigma^2}$$

$$\therefore \quad \sigma = \sqrt{\frac{\sum_{i=1}^{n}(x_i - \bar{x})^2}{n}} \text{ or } \sqrt{\frac{\sum_{i=1}^{n} x_i^2}{n} - \left(\frac{\sum_{i=1}^{n} x_i}{n}\right)^2}$$

$$= \sqrt{\frac{\sum_{i=1}^{n} x_i^2}{n} - \left(\frac{\sum_{i=1}^{n} x_i}{n}\right)^2}$$

➤ **Variance and Standard deviation of grouped data**

(i) For discrete frequency distribution

Let the discrete frequency distribution be $x_1, x_2, x_3, ..., x_n$ and $f_1, f_2, f_3, ..., f_n$. Then by direct method :

$$\text{Variance } (\sigma^2) = \frac{1}{N}\sum_{i=1}^{n} f_i(x_i - \bar{x})^2$$

$$= \frac{1}{N}\sum f_i x_i^2 - \left(\frac{\sum f_i x_i}{N}\right)^2$$

and $$\text{Standard deviation } (\sigma) = \sqrt{\frac{1}{N}\sum_{i=1}^{n} f_i(x_i - \bar{x})^2}$$

$$= \frac{1}{N}\sqrt{N\sum f_i x_i^2 - \left(\sum f_i x_i\right)^2}$$

where $$N = \sum_{i=1}^{n} f_i$$

$$\text{By short cut method, variance } (\sigma^2) = \frac{1}{N}\sum_{i=1}^{n} f_i d_i^2 - \left(\frac{\sum f_i d_i}{N}\right)^2$$

and $$\text{standard deviation } (\sigma) = \sqrt{\frac{1}{N}\sum_{i=1}^{n} f_i d_i^2 - \left(\frac{\sum f_i d_i}{N}\right)^2}$$

where $d_i = x_i - a$, deviation from assumed mean and a = assumed mean.

(ii) For Continuous frequency distribution

Direct Method : If there is a frequency distribution of n classes and each class defined by its mid-point x_i with corresponding frequency f_i, then the variance and standard deviation are :

$$\text{Variance } (\sigma^2) = \frac{1}{N}\sum_{i=1}^{n} f_i(x_i - \bar{x})^2$$

and $$\text{Standard deviation } (\sigma) = \sqrt{\frac{1}{N}\sum_{i=1}^{n} f_i(x_i - \bar{x})^2}$$

or, $$\sigma^2 = \frac{1}{N^2}\left[N\sum f_i x_i^2 - \left(\sum f_i x_i\right)^2\right]$$

and $$\sigma = \frac{1}{N^2}\sqrt{N\sum f_i x_i^2 - \left(\sum f_i x_i\right)^2}$$

Step-Deviation Method (short-cut method) : Sometimes the values of mid points x_i of different classes in a continuous distribution are large and so the calculation of mean and variance becomes tedious and time consuming. For this, we use the step-deviation method. Here,

$$\text{Variance } (\sigma^2) = h^2\left[\frac{1}{N}\sum_{i=1}^{n} f_i u_i^2 - \left(\frac{\sum_{i=1}^{n} f_i u_i}{N}\right)^2\right]$$

and $$\text{Standard deviation } (\sigma) = h\sqrt{\frac{1}{N}\sum_{i=1}^{n} f_i u_i^2 - \left(\frac{\sum_{i=1}^{n} f_i u_i}{N}\right)^2}$$

where $u_i = \dfrac{x_i - a}{h}$, a = assumed mean and h = width of class interval.

➤ **Analysis of frequency distribution**

The mean deviation and standard deviation have the same units in which the data is given. The measures of dispersion are unable to compare the variability of two or more series which are measured in different units. So, we require those measures which are independent of units.

The measures of variability which is independent of units, is called coefficient of variation denoted as C.V. and it is given by

$$\text{C.V.} = \frac{\sigma}{\bar{x}}\times 100,$$

where $\bar{x}$ and σ are respectively the mean and standard deviation of the data. For comparing the variability of two series, we calculates the coefficient of variations for each series.

➤ **Comparison of Two frequency Distributions with same Mean**

Let us consider two frequency distributions with standard deviations σ_1 and σ_2 and having same mean $\bar{x}$, then

$$\text{C.V. (1st distribution)} = \frac{\sigma_1}{\bar{x}}\times 100$$

and

$$\text{C.V. (2nd distribution)} = \frac{\sigma_2}{\bar{x}}\times 100$$

$$\frac{\text{C.V. (1st distribution)}}{\text{C.V. (2st distribution)}} = \frac{\frac{\sigma_1}{\bar{x}}\times 100}{\frac{\sigma_2}{\bar{x}}\times 100} = \frac{\sigma_1}{\sigma_2}$$

Thus, two C.V.'s can be compared on the basis of values of σ_1 and σ_2. Thus, if two series have equal means, then the series with greater standard deviation (or variance) is said to be more variable than the other. The other series with lesser value of the standard deviation is said to be more consistent than the other.

➤ **Note :**

- A characteristics that varies in magnitude from observation to observation e.g., weight, height, income, age, etc. are variables.
- Due to the limitations of mean deviation, some other method is required for measure of dispersion. Standard deviation is such a measure of dispersion.
- The percentage form of coefficient of S.D. *i.e.*, $\left(\frac{\sigma}{\bar{x}}\right)\times 100$ is called coefficient of variation.
- Standard deviation is independent of change of origin, but it depends of change of scale.

Multiple Choice Questions

(1 mark each)

[A] Objective Type Questions

Q. 1. The standard deviation of data 6, 5, 9, 13, 12, 8 and 10 is

(A) $\sqrt{\frac{52}{7}}$ **(B)** $\frac{52}{7}$

(C) $\sqrt{6}$ **(D)** 6

[NCERT Exemplar Q. 28, Page 282]

Ans. Correct option : (A)

Given data are 6, 5, 9, 13, 12, 8 and 10

$\therefore$ $n = 7$

$$\therefore \quad SD = \sqrt{\frac{\Sigma x_i^2}{n} - \left(\frac{\Sigma x_i}{n}\right)^2}$$

Here, $\Sigma x_i^2 = 619$ and $\Sigma x_i = 63$

$$\therefore \quad SD = \sqrt{\frac{619}{7} - \left(\frac{67}{7}\right)^2}$$

$$= \sqrt{\frac{619}{7} - (9)^2}$$

$$= \sqrt{\frac{619}{7} - 81}$$

$$= \sqrt{\frac{52}{7}}$$

Q. 2. If $x_1, x_2, \ldots, x_n$ be n observation and $\bar{x}$ be their arithmetic mean. Then, formula for the standard deviation is given by

(A) $\sum(x_i - \bar{x})^2$ (B) $\frac{\sum(x_i - \bar{x})^2}{n}$

(C) $\sqrt{\frac{\sum(x_i - \bar{x})^2}{n}}$ (D) $\sqrt{\frac{\sum x_i^2}{n} + (\bar{x})^{-2}}$

[NCERT Exemplar Q. 29, Page 282]

Ans. Correct option : (C)

Formula of S.D. = $\sqrt{\frac{\Sigma(x_i - \bar{x})^2}{n}}$

Q. 3. If the mean of 100 observation is 50 and their standard deviation is 5, than the sum of all squares of all the observation is

(A) 50000 (B) 250000

(C) 252500 (D) 255000

[NCERT Exemplar Q. 30, Page 282]

Ans. Correct option : (C)

Here, $\bar{x} = \frac{\Sigma x_i}{n}$

$\Rightarrow$ $50 = \frac{\Sigma x_i}{100}$

$\Rightarrow$ $\Sigma x_i = 5000$

$\therefore$ S.D. $= \sqrt{\frac{\Sigma x_i^2}{n} - \left(\frac{\Sigma x_i}{n}\right)^2}$

$5 = \sqrt{\frac{\Sigma x_i^2}{100} - \left(\frac{5000}{100}\right)^2}$

$\Rightarrow$ $25 = \frac{\Sigma x_i^2}{100} - 2500$

$\Rightarrow$ $25 = \frac{\Sigma x_i^2}{100} - 2500$

$\Rightarrow$ $\Sigma x_i^2 = 2525 \times 100 = 252500$

Q. 4. If *a*, *b*, *c*, *d* and *e* be the observation the mean *m* and standard deviation *s*, then find the standard deviation of the observations *a* + *k*, *b* + *k*, *c* + *k*, *d* + *k* and *e* + *k* is

(A) *s* (B) *ks*

(C) *s* + *k* (D) $\frac{s}{k}$

[NCERT Exemplar Q. 31, Page 282]

Ans. Correct option : (A)

Observations are a, b, c, d and e

$\therefore$ Mean $= m = \frac{a+b+c+d+e}{5}$

$\therefore$ $\Sigma x_i^2 = 5\text{ m}$

Now mean of *a* + *k*, *b* + *k*, *c* + *k*, *d* + *k* and *e* + *k* is

$= \frac{a+k+b+k+c+k+d+k+e+k}{5}$

$= \frac{(a+b+c+d+e)+5k}{5}$

$= \frac{5m+5k}{5} = m+k$

$\therefore SD = \sqrt{\frac{\Sigma(x_i+k)^2}{N} - \left(\frac{\Sigma(x_i+k)}{M}\right)^2}$

$= \sqrt{\frac{(\Sigma x_i^2 + k^2 + 2x_i k)}{N} - (m+k)^2}$

$= \sqrt{\frac{\Sigma x_i^2}{N} + \frac{\Sigma k^2}{N} - \frac{2k\Sigma x_i}{N} - m^2 - k^2 - 2mk}$

$= \sqrt{\frac{\Sigma x_i^2}{N} + k^2 + 2km - m^2 - k^2 - 2mk}$

$= \sqrt{\frac{\Sigma x_i^2}{N} - m^2}$ $\left[\because \frac{\Sigma x_i}{N} = m\right]$

$= s$

Q. 5. If x_1, x_2, x_3, x_4 and x_5 be the observations with mean *m* and standard deviation s then, the standard deviation of the observations kx_1, kx_2, kx_3, kx_4 and kx_5 is

(A) *k* + 5 (B) $\frac{s}{k}$

(C) *ks* (D) *s*

[NCERT Exemplar Q. 32, Page 282]

Ans. Correct option : (C)

Here, $m = \frac{\Sigma x_i}{N}$, $s = \sqrt{\frac{\Sigma x_i^2}{5} - \left(\frac{\Sigma x_i}{5}\right)^2}$

$\therefore$ S.D. $= \sqrt{\frac{k^2\Sigma x_i^2}{5} - k^2\left(\frac{\Sigma x_i}{5}\right)^2}$

$= k\sqrt{\frac{\Sigma x_i^2}{5} - \left(\frac{\Sigma x_i}{5}\right)^2}$

$=$ ks

Q. 6. Let $x_1, x_2, \ldots x_n$ be n observations. Let w_i – [x_i + *k* for *i* = 1, 2, ..., *n*, where *l* and *k* are constants. If the mean of x_i's is 48 and their standard deviation is 12, the mean of x_i's is 55 and standard deviation of w_i's is 15, then the value of *l* and *k* should be

(A) *l* = 1.25, *k* = – 5 (B) *l* = – 1.25, *k* = 5

(C) *l* = 2.5, *k* = 5 (D) *l* = 2.5, *k* = 5

[NCERT Exemplar Q. 33, Page 282]

Ans. Correct option : (A)

Given that, $w_i = x_i + k$, $\bar{x_i} = 48$, SD(x_i) = 12

$\bar{w_i} = 55$ and SD (w_i) = 15

then, $\bar{w_i} = \bar{x_i} + k$

($\bar{w_i}$ = mean of w_i's and $\bar{x_i}$ is the mean of x_is)

$\Rightarrow$ $55 = 48 + k$ ...(i)

SD of w_i = SD of x_i

$\Rightarrow$ $55 = l \times 12$

$\Rightarrow \quad l = \frac{15}{12} = 1.25$ ...(ii)

From eq. (i) and (ii), we have

$k = \overline{w_i} - \overline{x_i} = 55 - 1.25 \times 48 = 55 - 60 = -5$

Q. 7. The standard deviations for first ten natural numbers is

(A) 5.5 **(B) 3.87**

(C) 2.97 **(D) 2.87**

[NCERT Exemplar Q. 34, Page 282]

Ans. Correct option : (D)

We know that, SD of first n natural numbers $\frac{\sqrt{n^2-1}}{12}$

Here, $n = 10$

$\therefore \quad SD = \sqrt{\frac{(10)^2-1}{12}} = \sqrt{\frac{99}{12}}$

$= \sqrt{8.25} = 2.87$

Q. 8. Consider the number 1, 2, 3, 4, 5, 6, 7, 8, 9, and 10. If 1 is added to each number the variance of the numbers, so obtained is

(A) 6.5 **(B) 2.87**

(C) 3.87 **(D) 8.25**

[NCERT Exemplar Q. 35, Page 282].

Ans. Correct option : (D)

Given numbers are 1, 2, 3, 4, ... 9, 10.

Numbers obtained where 1 is added to the above numbers is 2, 3, 4, 5, ...10, 11.

$\therefore \quad \Sigma x_i = 2 + 3 + 4 + ... + 10 + 11$

$= \frac{10}{2}[2\times 2+(10-1).1]$

$= 5[4 + 9] = 65$

Now, $\quad \Sigma x_i^2 = 2^2 + 3^2 + ... + 10^2 + 11^2$

$= (11^2 + 2 + 3^2 + ... + 11^2) - 1^2$

$= \frac{11\times 12\times 13}{6} - 1$

$\left[\because 1^2+2^2+...+n^2 = \frac{n(n+1)(n+2)}{6}\right]$

$= \frac{11\times 12\times 13}{6} - 1$

$= 506 - 1 = 505$

$\therefore \quad$ Variance $(\sigma^2) = \frac{\Sigma x_i^2}{N} - \left(\frac{\Sigma x_i}{N}\right)^2$

$= \frac{505}{10} - \left(\frac{65}{10}\right)^2$

$= 50.5 - (6.5)^2$

$= 50.5 - 42.25$

$= 8.25$

Q. 9. Consider the first 10 positive integers. If we multiply each number by – 1 and, then add 1 to each number, the variance of the numbers, so obtain is

(A) 8.25 **(B) 6.5**

(C) 3.87 **(D) 2.87**

[NCERT Exemplar Q. 36, Page 283]

Ans. Correct option : (A)

First 10 positive integers are 1, 2, 3, ..., 9, 10

On multiplying each number by – 1, we get

– 1, – 2, – 3, ... , – 9, – 10

on adding 1 to each of the number, we get

0, – 1, – 2, ..., – 8, – 9

and $\quad \Sigma x_i^2 = 0^2 + (-1)^2 + (-2)^2 + ... + (-8)^2 + (-9)^2$

$= \frac{9\times 10\times 19}{6} = 285$

$\left[\because \Sigma n^2 - \frac{n(n+1)(n+2)}{6}\right]$

$\therefore \quad SD = \sqrt{\frac{\Sigma x_i^2}{N} - \left(\frac{\Sigma x_i}{N}\right)^2}$

$= \sqrt{\frac{285}{10} - \left(\frac{-45}{10}\right)^2}$

$= \sqrt{\frac{285}{10} - \frac{2025}{100}} = \sqrt{8.25}$

$\therefore$ Variance $(\sigma^2) = (S.D.)^2 = \left(\sqrt{8.25}\right)^2 = 8.25$

Q. 10. The following information relates to a sample of size 60, $\Sigma x^2 = 18000$, and $\Sigma x = 960$. Then, the variance is

(A) 6.63 **(B) 16**

(C) 22 **(D) 44**

[NCERT Exemplar Q. 37, Page 283]

Ans. Correct option : (D)

We know that variance $(\sigma^2) = \frac{\Sigma x_i^2}{N} - \left(\frac{\Sigma x_i}{N}\right)^2$

$= \frac{18000}{60} - \left(\frac{960}{60}\right)^2$

$= 300 - 256$

$= 44$

Q. 11. If the coefficient of variation of two distributions are 50, 60 and their arithmetic means are 30 and 25 respectively, then the difference of their standard deviation is

(A) 0 **(B) 1**

(C) 1.5 **(D) 2.5**

[NCERT Exemplar Q. 38, Page 283]

Ans. Correct option : (A)

Here, we have $CV_1 = 50$ $CV_2 = 60$

$\overline{x_1} = 30$ and $\overline{x_2} = 25$

$\therefore \quad CV_1 = \frac{\sigma_1}{\bar{x}_1} \times 100$

$\Rightarrow \quad 50 = \frac{\sigma_1}{30} \times 100$

$\Rightarrow \quad \sigma = \frac{50 \times 30}{100} = 15$

and $\quad CV_2 = \frac{\sigma_2}{\bar{x}_2} \times 100$

$\Rightarrow \quad 60 = \frac{\sigma_2}{25} \times 100$

$\Rightarrow \quad \sigma_2 = \frac{60 \times 25}{100} = 15$

$\therefore$ Difference $\sigma_2 - \sigma_2 = 15 - 15 = 0$

Q. 12. The standard deviation of some temperature data in ºC is 5. If the data were converted into ºF, then the variance would be

(A) 81 (B) 57

(C) 36 (D) 25

[NCERT Exemplar Q. 39, Page 283]

Ans. Correct option : (A)

Given that $\quad \sigma_c = 5$

We know that $\quad C = \frac{5}{9}(F - 32)$

$\Rightarrow \quad F = \frac{9C}{5} + 32$

$\therefore \quad \sigma_F = \frac{9}{5}\sigma_C = \frac{9}{5} \times 5 = 9$

$\therefore \quad \sigma_F^2 = (9)^2 = 81$

[B] Fill in the blanks

Q. 1. Coefficient of variation = $\frac{\text{.....}}{\text{Mean}} \times 100$

[NCERT Exemplar Q. 40, Page 283]

Q. 2. If the variance of a data is 121, then the standard deviations of the data is ....

[NCERT Exemplar Q. 42, Page 283]

Q. 3. The standard deviation of data is .... of any change in origin but is .... of change of scale.

[NCERT Exemplar Q. 43, Page 283]

Q. 4. The standard deviations is .... to the mean deviations taken from the arithmetic mean.

[NCERT Exemplar Q. 46, Page 283]

Answer

1. Standard deviation
2. 11
3. Independent; dependent
4. Greater than or equal

Long Answer Type Questions-I (4 marks each)

Q. 1. Two sets of 20 observations, the same standard deviation 5. The first set has a mean 17 and the second mean 22. Determine the standard deviation of the x sets obtained by combing the given two sets.

[NCERT Exemplar, Q. 8, Page 279]

Sol. $n_1 = 20, \sigma_1 = 5, \bar{x}1 = 17$ and $n_2 = 20, \sigma_2 = 5,$

$\bar{x}2 = 22$

$$\sigma^2 = \left[\frac{n_1\sigma_1^2 + n_2\sigma_2^2}{n_1 + n_2} + \frac{n_1 n_2(\bar{x}_1 - \bar{x}_2)}{(n_1 + n_2)^2}\right]$$

$$\sigma = \sqrt{\frac{20 \times (5)^2 + 20 \times (5)^2}{20 + 20} + \frac{20 \times 20(17 - 22)^2}{(20 + 20)^2}}$$

$$\sigma = \sqrt{\frac{1,000}{40} + \frac{400 \times 25}{1,600}} = \sqrt{25 + \frac{25}{4}} = \sqrt{\frac{125}{4}}$$

$$= \sqrt{31.25}$$

Q. 2. The frequency distribution

x	A	2A	3A	4A	5A	6A
f	2	1	1	1	1	1

where, A is a positive integer, has a variance of 160. Determine the value of A.

[NCERT Exemplar, Q. 9, Page 279]

Sol.

x_i	f_i	$f_i x_i$	$f_i x_i^2$
A	2	2A	$2A^2$
2A	1	2A	$4A^2$
3A	1	3A	$9A^2$
4A	1	4A	$16A_2$
5A	1	5A	$25A_2$
6A	1	6A	$36A_2$
Total	$n=7$	$\Sigma f_i n_i = 22A$	$\Sigma f_i n_i^2 = 92A^2$

$\therefore$ Variance $= \frac{\sum f_i x_i^2}{n} - \left(\frac{\sum f_i x_i}{n}\right)^2$

$\Rightarrow$ $160 = \frac{92A^2}{7} - \left(\frac{22A}{7}\right)^2$

$\Rightarrow$ $160 = \frac{92A^2}{7} - \frac{484A^2}{49} = A^2\left(\frac{92\times7-484}{49}\right)$

$\Rightarrow$ $160 = (644-484)\frac{A^2}{49}$

$\Rightarrow$ $160 = \frac{160A^2}{49} \Rightarrow A^2 = 49$

$\therefore$ $A = 7$

Q. 3. For the frequency distribution

x	2	3	4	5	6	7
f	4	9	16	14	11	6

Find the standard distribution. **[NCERT Exemplar, Q. 10, Page 279]**

Sol.

x_i	f_i	$d_i = x_i - 4$	$f_i d_i$	$f_i d_i^2$
2	4	–2	–8	16
3	9	–1	–9	9
4	16	0	0	0
5	14	1	14	14
6	11	2	22	44
7	6	3	18	54
Total	60		$\Sigma f_i d_i = 37$	$\Sigma f_i d_i^2 = 137$

$\therefore$ $SD = \sqrt{\frac{\sum f_i d_i^2}{N} - \left(\frac{\sum f_i d_i}{N}\right)^2}$

$= \sqrt{\frac{137}{60} - \left(\frac{37}{60}\right)^2}$

$= \sqrt{2.2833-(0.616)^2}$

$= \sqrt{2.2833-0.3794}$

$= \sqrt{1.9037} = 1.38$

Q. 4. The mean life of a sample of 60 bulbs was 650 h and the standard deviation was 8 h. If a second sample of 80 bulbs has a mean life of 660 h and standard deviation 7 h, then find the over all standard deviation.

[NCERT Exemplar, Q. 12, Page 279]

Sol. Here, $n_1 = 60$, $\bar{x}_1 = 650$, $\sigma_1 = 8$ and $n_2 = 80$, $\bar{x}_2 = 660$, $\sigma_2 = 7$

$\therefore \sigma = \sqrt{\frac{n_1\sigma_1^2 + n_2\sigma_2^2}{(n_1+n_2)} + \frac{n_1 n_2(\bar{x}_1 - \bar{x}_2)^2}{(n_1+n_2)^2}}$

$\sigma = \sqrt{\frac{60\times(8)^2 + 80\times(7)^2}{60+80} + \frac{60\times80(650-660)^2}{(60+80)^2}}$

$= \sqrt{\frac{6\times64+8\times49}{14} + \frac{60\times80\times100}{140\times140}}$

$= \sqrt{\frac{192+196}{7} + \frac{1200}{49}} = \sqrt{\frac{388}{7} + \frac{1200}{49}}$

$= \sqrt{\frac{2716+1200}{49}} = \sqrt{\frac{3916}{49}} = \frac{62.58}{7} = 8.9$

Q. 5. If mean and standard deviation of 100 items are 50 and 4 respectively, then find the sum of all the item and the sum of the squares of items.

[NCERT Exemplar, Q. 13, Page 279]

Sol. Here, $\bar{x} = 50, n = 100$ and $\sigma = 4$

$$\therefore \quad \frac{\sum x_i}{100} = 50$$

$$\Rightarrow \quad \Sigma x_i = 5000$$

$$\text{and} \quad \sigma^2 = \frac{\sum fix_i^2}{\sum f_i} - \left(\frac{\sum f_i x_i}{\sum f_i}\right)$$

$$\Rightarrow \quad (4)^2 = \frac{\sum f_i x_i^2}{100} - (50)^2$$

$$\Rightarrow \quad 16 = \frac{\sum f_i x_i^2}{100} - 2{,}500$$

$$\Rightarrow \quad \frac{\sum f_i x_i^2}{100} = 16 + 2500 = 2516$$

$$\therefore \quad \sum f_i x_i^2 = 251600$$

Q. 6. If for distribution $\Sigma(x - 5) = 3$, $\Sigma(x - 5)^2 = 43$ and total number of item is 18. Find the mean and standard deviation.

[NCERT Exemplar, Q. 14, Page 279]

Sol. Given,

$n = 18, \Sigma(x - 5) = 3$ and $\Sigma(x - 5)^2 = 43$

$$\therefore \quad \text{Mean} = A + \frac{\sum(x-5)}{18}$$

$$= 5 + \frac{3}{18} + 0.1666 = 5.1666 = 5.17$$

$$\text{and} \quad \text{SD} = \sqrt{\frac{\sum(x-5)^2}{n} - \left(\frac{\sum(x-5)}{n}\right)^2}$$

$$= \sqrt{\frac{43}{18} - \left(\frac{3}{18}\right)^2}$$

$$= \sqrt{2.3944 - (0.166)^2} = 1.59$$

Q. 7. Find the mean and variance of the frequency distribution given below.

x	$1 \le x < 3$	$3 \le x < 5$	$5 \le x < 7$	$7 \le x < 10$
f	6	4	5	1

[NCERT Exemplar, Q. 15, Page 279]

Sol.

C1	f_i	x_i	$f_i x_i$	$f_i x_i^2$
1-3	6	2	12	
3-5	4	4	16	64
5-7	5	6	30	180
7-10	1	8.5	8.5	72.25
Total	n=16		$\sum f_i x_i = 66.5$	$\sum f_i x_i^2 = 340.25$

$$\therefore \quad \text{Mean} = \frac{\sum f_i x_i}{\sum f_i} = \frac{66.5}{16} = 4.15$$

$$\text{and} \quad \text{variance} = \sigma^2 = \frac{\sum f_i x_i^2}{\sum f_i} - \left(\frac{\sum f_i x_i}{\sum f_i}\right)^2$$

$$= \frac{340.25}{16} - (4.15)^2$$

$$= 21.2656 - 17.2225 = 4.043$$

Long Answer Type Questions-II

(6 marks each)

Q. 1. The mean and standard deviation of some data for the time taken to complete a test are calculated with the following results Number of observation = 25, mean = 18.2, standard deviation = 3.25 Further, another set of 15 observation $x_1\, x_2\, ... x_{15}$, also in second, is now available and we have $\sum_{i=1}^{15} x_i = 279$ and $\sum_{i=1}^{15} x_i^2 = 5524$. Calculate the standard derivation based on all 40 observations.

[NCERT Exemplar, Q. 6, Page 278]

Sol. $n_i = 25$, $\bar{x} = 18.2$, $\sigma_1 = 3.25$,

$n_2 = 15$, $\sum_{i=1}^{15} x_i = 279$ and $\sum_{i=1}^{15} x_i^2 = 5524$

$$\sum x_i = 25 \times 18.2 = 455$$

$$\therefore \quad \sigma_1{}^2 = \frac{\sum x_i^2}{25} - (18.2)^2 = \left(\frac{\sum x_i^2}{N} - \bar{x}\right)$$

$$\Rightarrow (3.25)^2 = \frac{\sum x_i^2}{25} - 331.24$$

$$\Rightarrow 10.5625 + 331.24 = \frac{\sum x_i^2}{25}$$

$$\Rightarrow \quad \sum x_i^2 = 25 \times (10.5625 + 331.24)$$

$$= 25 \times 341.8025$$

$$= 8545.0625$$

Combined Standard deviation of the 40 observations

$$\sum x_i^2 = 5524 + 5845.0625 = 14069.0625$$

and $\sum x_i = 455 + 279 = 734$

$$\therefore \quad SD = \sqrt{\frac{14069.0625}{40} - \left(\frac{734}{40}\right)^2}$$

$$= \sqrt{351.726 - (18.34)^2}$$

$$= \sqrt{351.726 - 336.7225}$$

$$= \sqrt{15.0035} = 3.87$$

Q. 2. The mean and standard deviation of a set of n_1 observation are $\bar{x}_i$ and s_1, respectively while the mean and standard deviation of another set of n_2 observation are and s_2, respectively. Show that the standard deviation of the combined set of $(n_1 + n_2)$ observation is given by $\bar{x}_2$ **[NCERT Exemplar, Q. 7, Page 278]**

$$SD = \sqrt{\frac{n_1(s_1)^2 + n_2(s_2)^2}{n_1 + n_2} + \frac{n_1 n_2(\bar{x}_1 - \bar{x}_2)^2}{(n_1 + n_2)^2}}$$

Sol. Let x_i, $i = 1, 2, 3, ... n_i$ and $y_j = j = 1, 2, 3, ... n_2$

$$\bar{x}_1 = \frac{1}{n_1}\sum_{i=1}^{n_1} x_i \, , \; \bar{x}2 = \frac{1}{n_2}\frac{1}{n_2}\sum_{i=1}^{n_1} y_j$$

$$\Rightarrow \quad \sigma_1{}^2 = \frac{1}{n_1}\sum_{i=1}^{n}(x_i - \bar{x}_1)^2$$

and
$$\sigma_2{}^2 = \frac{1}{n_2}\sum_{j=1}^{n}(y_i - \bar{x}_2)^2$$

$$\text{combined mean } \bar{x} = \frac{n_1\bar{x}1 + n_2\bar{x}_2}{n_1 + n_2}$$

$$\text{Combined } \sigma^2 = \frac{1}{n_1 + n_2}\left[\sum_{i=1}^{n_1}(x_i - \bar{x})^2 + \sum_{i=1}^{n_2}(y_i - \bar{x})^2\right]$$

Now,
$$\sum_{i=1}^{n_1}(x_i - \bar{x})^2 = \sum_{i=1}^{n_1}(x_i - \bar{x}_j + \bar{x}_j - x)^2$$

$$= \sum_{i=1}^{n_1}(x_i - \bar{x}_i)^2 + n_1(\bar{x}_j - \bar{x})^2 + 2(\bar{x}_j - \bar{x})\sum_{i=1}^{n_1}(x_i - \bar{x}_i)^2$$

But
$$\sum_{i=1}^{n_1}(x_i - \bar{x}) = 0$$

[$\because$ Algebraic sum of the deviation of value of first series from their mean is zero]

Also,
$$\sum_{i=1}^{n}(x_i - \bar{x})^2 = n_1 s_1^2 + n_1(\bar{x}_1 - \bar{x})^2, \text{ where } d_1 = (\bar{x}_1 - \bar{x})$$

Similarly, we have
$$\sum_{i=1}^{n_2}(y_i - \bar{x})^2 = \sum_{i-1}^{n_2}(y_i - \bar{x}i + \bar{x}i - \bar{x})^2 = n_2 s_2{}^2 + n_2 d_2{}^2$$

Where,
$$d_2 = (\bar{x}_2 - \bar{x})$$

Combined Standard deviation, $\sigma = \sqrt{\dfrac{\left[n_1(s_1^2 + d_1^2) + n_2(s_2^2 + d_2^2)\right]}{n_1 + n_2}}$

Where $d_1 = \bar{x}_1 - \bar{x} = \bar{x}_1 - \left(\dfrac{n_1\bar{x}_1 + n_2\bar{x}_2}{n_1 + n_2}\right) = \dfrac{n_2(\bar{x}_1 - \bar{x}_2)}{n_1 + n_2}$

and $d_2 = \bar{x}_2 - \bar{x} = \bar{x}2\left(\dfrac{n_1\bar{x}_1 + n_2\bar{x}_2}{n_1 + n_2}\right) = \dfrac{n_1(\bar{x}_2 - \bar{x}_1)}{n_1 + n_2}$

$\therefore \quad \sigma_2 = \dfrac{1}{n_1 + n_2}\left[n_1 s_1^2 + n_2 s_2^2 + \dfrac{n_1 n_2^2(\bar{x}1 - \bar{x}2)^2}{(n_2 + n_2)^2} + \dfrac{n_2 n_1^2(\bar{x}2 - \bar{x}1)^2}{(n_2 + n_2)^2}\right]$

So, $\sigma = \sqrt{\dfrac{n_1 s_1^2 + n_2 s_2^2}{n_1 + n_2} + \dfrac{n_1 n_2(\bar{x}_1 - \bar{x}_2)^2}{(n_1 + n_2)^2}}$ **Hence, Proved.**

Q. 3. There are 60 students in a class. The following is the frequency distribution of the marks obtained by the students in a test.

Marks	0	1	2	3	4	5
Frequency	$x-2$	x	x^2	$(x+1)^2$	$2x$	$x+1$

where, x is positive integer, Determine the mean and standard deviation of the marks.

[NCERT Exemplar, Q. 11, Page 279]

Sol. $\therefore$ Sum of frequencies,

$$\Sigma f_i = x - 2 + x + x^2 + (x+1)^2 + 2x + x + 1 \quad (\Sigma f_i = 60 \text{ Given})$$

$$60 = 2x - 2 + x^2 + x^2 + 1 + 2x + 2x + x + 1$$

$$60 = 2x^2 + 7x = 0$$

$$\Rightarrow \quad 2x^2 + 7x - (= 0$$

$$\Rightarrow \quad 2x^2 + 15x - 8x - 60 = 0$$

$$\Rightarrow \quad x(2x + 15) - 4(2x + 15) = 0$$

$$\Rightarrow \quad (2x + 15)(x - 4) = 0$$

$$\Rightarrow \quad x = \frac{-15}{2}, 4 \qquad \left[\frac{-15}{2} \text{ is not natural no.}\right]$$

$$\Rightarrow \quad x = 4 \qquad \because x \neq \frac{-15}{2}$$

x_i	f_i	$d_i = x_i - 3$	$f_i d_i$	$f_i d_i^2$
0	2	–3	–6	18
1	4	–2	–8	16
2	16	–1	–16	16
3	25	0	0	0
4	8	1	8	8
5	5	2	10	20
Total	$\Sigma f_i = 60$		$\Sigma f_i d_i = -12$	$\Sigma f_i d_i^2 = 78$

$$\text{Mean} = A + \frac{\sum f_i d_i}{\sum f_i} = 3 + \left(\frac{-12}{60}\right) = 2.8$$

$$\sigma = \sqrt{\frac{\sum f_i d_i^2}{\sum f_i} - \left(\frac{\sum f_i d_i}{\sum f_i}\right)^2} = \sqrt{\frac{78}{60} - \left(\frac{-12}{60}\right)^2}$$

$$= \sqrt{1.3 - 0.04} = \sqrt{1.26} = 1.12$$

Q. 4. Determine the mean and standards deviation for the following distribution.

Marks	2	3	4	5	6	7	8	9	10	11	12	13	14	15	16
Frequency	1	6	6	8	8	2	2	3	0	2	1	0	0	0	1

[NCERT Exemplar, Q. 18, Page 280]

Sol.

Marks	f_i	$f_i x_i$	$d_i = x_i - \bar{x}$	$f_i d_i$	$f_i d_i^2$
2	1	2	–4	–4	16
3	6	18	–3	–18	54
4	6	24	–2	–12	24
5	8	40	–1	–8	8
6	8	48	0	0	0
7	2	14	1	2	2
8	2	16	2	4	8
9	3	27	3	9	27
10	0	0	4	0	0
11	2	22	5	10	50
12	1	12	6	6	36
13	0	0	7	0	0
14	0	0	8	0	0
15	0	0	9	0	0
16	1	16	10	10	100
Total	$\sum f_i = 40$	$\sum f_i d_i = 239$		$\sum f_i d_i = -1$	$\sum f_i d_i^2 = 325$

$\therefore$ Mean $\bar{x} = \dfrac{\sum f_i x_i}{\sum f_i} = \dfrac{239}{40} = 5.975 = 6$ (approx)

and $\sigma = \sqrt{\dfrac{\sum f_i d_i^2}{\sum f_i} - \left(\dfrac{\sum f_i d_i}{\sum f_i}\right)^2} = \sqrt{\dfrac{325}{40} - \left(\dfrac{-1}{40}\right)^2}$

$= \sqrt{8.124375} = \sqrt{8.125 - 0.000625} = 2.85$

Q. 5. The weights of coffee in 70 jars is shown in the following table

Weight (in g)	Frequency
200-201	13
201-202	27
202-203	18
203-204	10
204-205	1
205-206	1

Determine variance and standard deviation of the above distribution. [NCERT Exemplar, Q. 19, Page 279]

Sol.

CI	f_i	x_i	$d_i = d_i - \bar{x}$	$f_i d_i$	$f_i d_i^2$
200-201	13	200.5	–2	–26	52
201-202	27	201.5	–1	–27	27
202-203	18	202.5	0	0	0
203-204	10	203.5	1	10	10
204-205	1	204.5	2	2	4
205-206	1	205-5	3	3	9
	$\sum f_i = 70$			$\sum f_i d_i = -38$	$\sum f_i d_i^2 = 102$

$\therefore$ Variance $\sigma^2 = \dfrac{\sum f_i d_i^2}{\sum f_i} - \left(\dfrac{\sum f_i d_i}{\sum f_i}\right)^2 = \dfrac{102}{70} - \left(\dfrac{-38}{70}\right)^2$

$= 1.4571 - 0.2916 = 1.1655$

Now, SD $= \sqrt{1.1655} = 1.08$

Q. 6. Determine mean and standard deviation of first n terms of an AP whose first term is a and common difference is *d*.

[NCERT Exemplar, Q. 20, Page 280]

Sol.

x_i	$x_i - a$	$(x_i - a)^2$
a	0	0
$a+d$	d	d^2
$a + 2d$	$2d$	$4d^2$
$a + 3d$	....	$9d^2$
....	....	....
....	....	....
$a + (n-1)d$	$(n-1)d$	$(n-1)^2d^2$

$\because$ Mean $= \dfrac{\sum fx_i}{n} = \dfrac{1}{n}\left[\dfrac{n}{2}(2a+(n-1)d\right]$

$= a + \dfrac{(n-1)}{2}d$

$$\text{SD} = \sqrt{\frac{(x_i-a)^2}{n} - \left(\frac{(x_i-a)}{n}\right)^2}$$

$$= \sqrt{\frac{d^2(n-1)(n)(2n-1)}{6n} - \left[\frac{d(n-1)n}{2n}\right]^2}$$

$$= \sqrt{\frac{d^2(n-1)(2n-1)}{6} - \frac{d^2(n-1)^2}{4}}$$

$$= d\sqrt{\frac{(n-1)(2n-1)}{6} - \frac{(n-1)^2}{4}}$$

$$= d\sqrt{\frac{(n-1)}{2}\left(\frac{2n-1}{3} - \frac{n-1}{2}\right)}$$

$$= d\sqrt{\frac{(n-1)}{2}\left[\frac{4n-2-3n+3}{6}\right]}$$

$$= d\sqrt{\frac{(n-1)(n+1)}{12}} = d\sqrt{\frac{(n^2-1)}{12}}$$

Q. 7. Following are the marks obtained, out of 100, by two students Ravi and Hashina in 10 tests

Ravi	Hashina
25	10
50	70
45	50
30	20
70	95
42	55
36	42
48	60
35	48
60	80

Who is more intelligent and who is more consistent ? [NCERT Exemplar, Q. 21, Page 281]

Sol. For Ravi,

x_i	$d_i = x_i - 45$	d_i^2
25	–20	400
50	5	25
45	0	0
30	–15	225
70	25	625
42	–3	9
36	–9	81
48	3	9
35	–10	100
60	15	225
Total	$\sum d_i = -14$	$\sum d_i^2 = 1699$

$$\sigma = \sqrt{\frac{\sum d_i^2}{n} - \left(\frac{\sum d_i}{n}\right)^2}$$

$$= \sqrt{\frac{1699}{10} - \left(\frac{-9}{10}\right)^2}$$

$= \sqrt{169.9 - 0.81}$

$= \sqrt{169.09} = 13.003$

Now, $\bar{x} = A + \dfrac{\sum d_i}{\sum f_i}$

$= 45 - \dfrac{9}{10} = 44.1$

For Hashina,

x_i	$d_i = x_i - 55$	d_i^2
10	–45	2025
70	15	225
50	–5	25
20	–35	1225
95	40	1600

55	0	0
42	–13	169
60	5	25
48	–7	49
80	25	625
Total	$\sum d_i = -20$	$\sum d_i^2 = 5968$

Let Mean $= 55-\frac{20}{10}=53$

$$= \sqrt{\frac{\sum di^2}{n}-\left(\frac{\sum d_i}{n}\right)}$$

$$= \sqrt{\frac{5968}{10}\left(\frac{-20}{10}\right)^2}$$

$\sqrt{5968-4} = 24{\cdot}348$

For Ravi, $CV = \frac{\sigma}{x}\times 100 = \frac{13.003}{44.1}\times 100$

$= 29.485$

For Hashina, $CV = \frac{\sigma}{x}\times 100 = \frac{24{\cdot}378}{53}\times 100$

$= 45.94$

Hashina is more consistent and intelligent.

Q. 8. Mean and standard deviation of 100 observation were found to be 40 and 10, respectively. If at the time of calculation two observation were wrongly taken as 30 and 70 in place of 3 and 27 respectively, then find the correct standard deviation. [NCERT Exemplar, Q. 22, Page 281]

Sol. Given,

$n = 100, \bar{x} = 40, \sigma = 10$ and $\bar{x} = 40$

$\therefore \quad \frac{\sum x_i}{n} = 40$

$\Rightarrow \quad \frac{\sum x_i}{100} = 40$

$\Rightarrow \quad \sum x_i = 4000$

Now, Corrected

$\sum x_i = 4000 - 30 - 70 + 3 + 27$

$= 4030 - 100 = 3930$

Corrected mean $= \frac{3930}{100} = 39.3$

Now, $\sigma^2 = \frac{\sum x_i^2}{n} - (40)^2$

$\Rightarrow \quad 100 = \frac{\sum x_i^2}{100} - 1600$

$\Rightarrow$ Incorrect $\sum x_i{}^2 = 170000$

Now, Corrected

$\sum x_i{}^2 = 170000 - (30)^2 - (70)^2 + 3^2 + (27)^2$

$= 17000 - 900 - 4900 + 9 + 729 = 164938$

$\therefore$ Corrected $\sigma = \sqrt{\frac{164938}{100} - (39.3)^2}$

$= \sqrt{1649.38 - 39.3\times 39.3}$

$= \sqrt{1649.38 - 1544.49}$

$= \sqrt{104.89}$ **= 10.241**

Q. 9. While calculating the mean and variance of 10 readings, a student wrongly used the reading 52 for the correct reading 25. He obtained the mean and variance as 45 and 16, respectively. Find the correct mean and the variance. [NCERT Exemplar, Q. 23, Page 281]

Sol. Given, $n = 10, \bar{x} = 45$ and $\sigma^2 = 16$

$\therefore \quad \bar{x} = 45 \Rightarrow \frac{\sum x_i}{n} = 45$

$\Rightarrow \quad \frac{\sum x_i}{10} = 45 \Rightarrow \sum x_i = 450$

Correct $\sum x_i = 450 - 52 + 25 = 423$

$\therefore \quad \bar{x} = \frac{423}{10} = 42.3$

$\Rightarrow \quad \sigma^2 = \frac{\sum x_i^2}{n} - \left(\frac{\sum x_i}{n}\right)^2$

$\Rightarrow \quad 16 = \frac{\sum x_i^2}{10} - (45)^2 = \frac{\sum x_i{}^2 - 20250}{10}$

$\Rightarrow \quad \sum x_i^2 = 160 + 20250$

$\Rightarrow \quad \sum x_i^2 = 20410$

$\Rightarrow$ Correct $\sum x_i^2 = 20410 - (52)^2 + (25)^2$

$= 18331$

and Correct $\sigma^2 = \frac{18331}{10} - (42.3)^2$

$= 1833{\cdot}1 - 1789.29 = 438$

EXPERT ADVICE

- *This chapter involves lots of calculations. It is a time consuming but simple chapter based on simple formula. So, must not leave this chapter.*
- *You should know the technique to find variance or standard deviation for different types of data sets.*
- *Do the calculations carefully and recheck you answer at the end.*
- *Make proper tables for this chapter.*

OSWAAL LEARNING TOOLS

For **Suggested Online Videos**

Visit : *https://youtu.be/SFPGVTThJNk*

Or Scan the Code

Visit : *https://youtu.be/LMSyiAJm99g*

Or Scan the Code

Visit : *https://youtu.be/-Zc3A0q9VzI*

Or Scan the Code

Visit : *https://youtu.be/wO1zZAKRSkE*

Or Scan the Code

Visit : *https://youtu.be/T7KYO76DoOE*

Or Scan the Code

Visit : *https://youtu.be/Rtzg_oXPGrI*

Or Scan the Code

CHAPTER

16 PROBABILITY

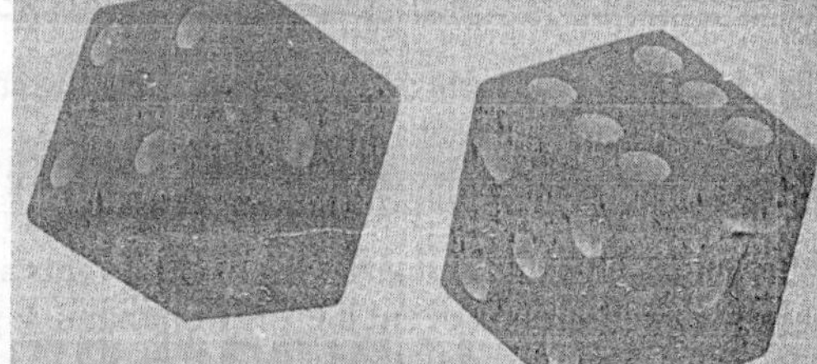

Chapter Objectives

> *Random experiment; Outcomes; Sample spaces (set representation); Events: Types of events; Algebra of events, Occurrence of events; 'not', 'and' and 'or' events; Exhaustive events; Mutually exclusive events; Axiomatic (set theoretic probability; Connections with theories studied earlier classes; Probability of an event; Probability of 'not', 'and' and 'or' events.*

TOPIC-1 Experiments, Events and Sample space

TOPIC - 1
Experiments, Events and Sample space P. 227

TOPIC - 2
Axiomatic Approach to Probability. P. 229

Quick Review

➢ **Experiment**

An operation which can produce some well defined outcomes, is known as experiment. There are two types of experiments. These are.

(i) Deterministic experiment and

(ii) Random experiment.

➢ **Random experiment**

An experiment conducted repeatedly under the identical conditions does not give necessarily the same result every time, then the experiment is called random experiment. *eg* : rolling an unbiased die, drawing a card from a well shuffled pack of cards, etc.

➢ **Outcomes and sample space**

A possible result of a random experiment is called its outcome. The set of all possible outcomes in a random experiment is called sample space and is denoted by S *i.e.,* sample space = {All possible outcomes}.

Each element of a sample space is called a sample point or an event point.

eg: when we throw a die, then possible outcomes of this experiment are 1, 2, 3, 4, 5 or 6.

∴ The sample space, S = {1, 2, 3, 4, 5, 6}

➢ **Event**

A subset of the sample space associated with a random experiment is called an event, generally denoted by 'E'.

An event associated with a random experiment is said to occur, if any one of the elementary events associated to it is an outcome of the experiment.

TIPS...

- *The probability of an event can only be between 0 and 1 i.e., it can't be negative and can also be written as a percentage.*
- *Carefully understand the difference between 'with replacement' and "without replacement".*
- *It has been observed that the experimental probability of an event approaches to its theoretical probability, if the no. of trials of an experiment is very large.*
- *If A and B are any two events, then*
  - $P(A \cap B) \leq P(A)$
  - $P(B) \leq P(A \cup B) \leq P(A) + P(B)$.

TRICKS...

- *The complementary events A and $\bar{A}$ are always mutually exclusive.*
- *If P(A) > P(B), then event A has a higher chance of occurring that event B.*
- *If P(A) = P(B), the events A and B are equally likely to occur.*
- *Probability of occurrence of an event = 1-(probability that it doesn't occur)*

eg : Suppose a die is thrown, then we have the sample space S = {1, 2, 3, 4, 5, 6}. Then, E = {2, 3, 4} is an event.
Also, if the outcome of experiment is 4. Then we say that event E has occurred.

➤ **Type of events**

On the basis of the element in an event, events are classified into the following types—

(i) Simple event—If an event has only one sample point of the sample space, it is called a simple (element) event.
e.g., Let a die is thrown, then sample space,
S = {1, 2, 3, 4, 5, 6}
Then, A = {4} and B = {6} are simple events.

(ii) Compound event—If an event has more than one sample point of the sample space, then it is called compound event.
e.g., On rolling a die, we have the sample space,
S = {1, 2, 3, 4, 5, 6}
Then, E = {2, 4, 6}, F = {1, 3, 5} are compound events.

(iii) Sure event—The event which is certain to occur is said to be the sure event. The whole sample space 'S' is a sure or certain event, since it is a subset of itself.
e.g., On throwing a die, we have sample space,
S = {1, 2, 3, 4, 5, 6}
Then, E = Event of getting a natural number less than 7 is a sure event, since E = {1, 2. 3, 4, 5, 6) = S.

(iv) Impossible event—The event which has no element is called an impossible event or null event. The empty set 'ϕ' is an impossible event.
e.g., on throwing a die, we have the sample space,
S = {1, 2, 3, 4, 5, 6}
Then E = event of getting a number less than 1, is an impossible event, since E = ϕ.

(v) Equally likely events—Events are called equally likely when we do expect the happening of one event in preference to the other.

(vi) Mutually exclusive events—Two events are said to be mutually exclusive, if the occurrence of any one of them excludes the occurrence of the other event *i.e.*, they cannot occur simultaneously.
Thus, two events E_1 and E_2 are said to be mutually exclusive, if $E_1 \cap E_2 = \phi$.
e.g., In throwing a die, we have the sample space
S = {1, 2, 3, 4, 5, 6}
Let, E_1 = Event of getting even numbers = {2, 4, 6}
and E_2 = Event of getting odd number = {1, 3, 5}
then, $E_1 \cap E_2 = \phi$
So, E_1 and E_2 are mutually exclusive events.
In general, events $E_1, E_2, ..., E_n$ are said to be mutually exclusive, if they are pair wise disjoint, *i.e.*, if $E_1 \cap E_2 = \phi \forall i \neq j$.

(vii) Exhaustive events—A set of events is said to be exhaustive if the performance of the experiment always results in the occurrence of at least one of them.
Let $E_1, E_2, ...E_n$ be n subsets of a sample space. Then, events $E_1, E_2, ..., E_n$ are exhaustive events, if $E_1 \cup E_2 \cup E_3 \cup ... \cup E_n = S$.
eg., Consider the experiment of throwing a die. Then,
S = {1, 2, 3, 4, 5, 6}
Let E_1 = event of getting a number less than 3.
E_2 = event of getting an odd number.
E_3 = event of getting a number greater than 3.
Then, $E_1 = \{1, 2\}, E_2 = \{1, 3, 5\}, E_3 = \{4, 5, 6\}$
Thus, $E_1 \cup E_2 \cup E_3 = S$. Hence, E_1, E_2, E_3 are exhaustive events.

➤ **Algebra of events**

Let A and B be two events associated with a sample space S, then—

(i) Complementary event—For every E, there corresponds another event E' called the complementary event of E, which consists of those outcomes that do not correspond to the occurrence of E. E' is also called the event 'event E'.
e.g., In tossing three coins, the sample space is
S = {HHH, HHT, HTH, HTT, THH, THT, TTH, TTT}
Let E = {THT, TTH, HTT} = the event of getting only one head.
Then, E' = {HHT, HTH, THH, TTT, HHH}.

(ii) The event A OR B—The even 'A or B' is same as the event $A \cup B$ and it contains all those element which are either in event A or in B or in both. Thus,

$A \text{ or } B = A \cup B = \{x : x \in A \text{ or } x \in B\}$

(iii) The event A and B—The event A' and B' is same as the event $A' \cap B'$ and it contains all those elements which are both in A and B. Thus,

$A \text{ and } B = A \cup B = \{x : x \in A \text{ and } x \in B\}$

(iv) The event A but not B—The event A but not B is same as the event $A - B = (A \cap B')$ and it contains all those elements which are in A but not in B.

Thus, A but not in B $= A - B = \{x : x \in A \text{ or } x \notin B\}$.

➤ **The following are some events and their corresponding equivalent sets.**

Events	Equivalent sets
(i) Neither A nor B	$\bar{A} \cap \bar{B}$ or $U - (A \cap B)$ [$U \rightarrow$ universal set]
(ii) Exactly one of A and B	$(A \cap \bar{B}) \cup (\bar{A} \cap B)$ or $(A \cup B) - (A \cap B)$
(iii) At least one of A, B or C	$A \cup B \cup C$.
(iv) All three of A, B and C	$A \cap B \cap C$.
(v) Exactly two of A, B and C	$(A \cap B \cap \bar{C}) \cup (A \cap \bar{B} \cap C) \cup (\bar{A} \cap B \cap C)$

Note :

- A sample space is called a discrete sample space, if S is a finite set.
- We can define as many events as there are subsets of a sample space. Thus, number of events of a sample space S is 2^n, where 'n' is the number of elements in S.
- Elementary events associated with a random experiments are also known as in decomposable events.
- All events other than elementary events and impossible events associated with a random experiment are called compound events.
- For any event E, associated with a sample space S, $E' = \text{not } E = S - E = \{\omega : \omega \in S \text{ and } \omega \notin E\}$.
- Simple events of a sample space are always mutually exclusive.
- If $E_i \cap E_j =$ for $i \neq j$ *i.e.*, events E_i and E_j are pairwise disjoint and $E_1 \cup E_2 \cup ... \cup E_n = S$, then events $E_1, E_2, ..., E_n$ are called mutually exclusive and exhaustive events.

Multiple Choice Questions **(1 mark each)**

[A] Fill in the blanks

Q. 1. If S = {1, 2, 3, 4, 5, 6) and E = {1, 3, 5), then $\bar{E}$ is..... **[NCERT Exemplar Q. 39, Page 301]**

Answer

1. {2, 4, 6}

TOPIC-2
Axiomatic Approach to Probability

Quick Review

➤ **Probability of occurrence of an event.**

A numerical value that conveys the chance of occurrence of an event, when we perform an experiment, is called the probability of that event. The different approaches of probability are—

(i) Statistical Approach to Probability—In statistical approach, probability of an event 'A' is the ratio of observed frequency to the total frequency.

i.e.,
$$P(A) = \frac{\text{Number of observed frequencies}}{\text{Total frequency}}$$

(ii) Classical approach to probability—To obtain the probability of an event, we find the ratio of the number of outcomes favourable to the event to the total number of equally likely outcomes. This theory is known as classical theory of probability or theoretical probability.

i.e.,
$$P(A) = \frac{\text{Number of favourable outcomes}}{\text{Total number of possible outcomes}}$$

(iii) Axiomatic Approach to Probability—Let 'S' be the sample space of a random experiment. The probability P is a real valued function whose domain is the power set of S and range is the interval [0, 1] satisfying the following axioms

(a) For any event E, $P(E) \geq 0$.

(b) $P(S) = 1$.

(c) If E and F are mutually exclusive, then

$P(E \cup F) = P(E) + P(F)$

Let 'S' be a sample space containing outcomes.

$$E_1, E_2, \ldots E_n \text{ i.e., } S = \{E_1, E_2, \ldots\ldots, E_n\}$$

Then, from the axiomatic approach to probability, we have—

(i) $O \leq P(E_i) \leq 1, \forall E_i \in S$.

(ii) $P(E_1) + P(E_2) + \ldots + P(E_n) = 1$.

(iii) For any event A, $P(A) = \sum_{i=1}^{n} P(E_i), E_i \in A$.

➤ **Probability of equally likely outcomes**

The outcomes of a random experiment are said to be equally likely, if the chance of occurrence of each outcome is same.

Let the sample space of an experiment is—

$S = \{s_1, s_2, \ldots\ldots, s_n\}$. Also, let all the outcomes are equally likely. *i.e.*, $P(s_i) = p \ \forall\ s_i \in S, 0 \leq p \leq 1$.

By axiomatic approach to probability, $\sum_{i=1}^{n} P(S_i) = 1$.

$$\Rightarrow \quad \underbrace{p+p+\ldots+p}_{n \text{ times}} = 1$$

$$\Rightarrow \quad np = 1$$

$$\Rightarrow \quad p = \frac{1}{n}$$

$$\therefore \quad P(S_i) = \frac{1}{n} = 1, 2, \ldots\ldots, n.$$

➤ **Addition rule of probability**

If A and B are two events associated with a random experiment, then—

$$P(A \cup B) = P(A) + P(B) - P(A \cap B)$$

or
$$P(A \text{ or } B) = P(A) + P(B) - P(A \text{ and } B)$$

It is known as addition law of probability for two events A and B.

When A and B are mutually exclusive events, then

$$P(A \cup B) = P(A) + P(B)$$

When A and B are mutually exclusive and exhaustive events, then $P(A \cup B) = P(A) + P(B) = 1$.

➢ **Probability of the event A or B or C**

If A, B and C are three events associated with a random experiment, then—

$P(A \cup B \cup C) = P(A) + P(B) + P(C) - P(A \cap B) - P(B \cap C) - P(A \cap C) + P(A \cap B \cap C)$.

➢ **Probability of complementary event**

Let E be an event and $(\bar{E})$ be its complementary event. Then, $P(\bar{E}) = 1 - P(E)$.

➢ **Some result on probability of events**

(i) For any two events A and B, $A \leq B \Rightarrow P(A) \leq P(B)$.

(ii) For an event A, $0 \leq P(A) \leq 1$.

(iii) For any two events A and B

$$P(A - B) = P(A) - P(A \cap B)$$

or

$$P(A \cap B') = P(A) - P(A \cap B)$$

Note :

➢ Probability of an impossible or null event is zero *i.e.*, $P(\phi) = 0$.

➢ In case of equally likely outcomes, axiomatic approach coincide with the classical approach of probability.

➢ If A, B and C are mutually exclusive events, *i.e.*, $A \cap B = \phi, B \cap C = \phi, C \cap A = \phi, A \cap B \cap C = \phi$, then $p(A \cup B \cup C) = P(A) + P(B) + P(C)$.

➢ For any two events A and B,

$$P(\bar{A} \cap \bar{B}) = P(\overline{A \cup B})$$

and,

$$P(A \cap B) \leq P(A), P(A \cap B) \leq P(B).$$

Multiple Choice Questions **(1 mark each)**

[A] Objective Type Questions

Q. 1. In a non-leap year, the probability of having 53 Tuesday or 53 Wednesday is

(A) $\frac{1}{7}$ **(B)** $\frac{2}{7}$

(C) $\frac{3}{7}$ **(D) None of these**

[NCERT Exemplar Q. 18, Page 298]

Ans. Correct option : (A)

There are 365 days in non-leap year and there are 7 days in a weak.

$\therefore 365 \div 7 = 52$ weeks + 1 day

So, this day maybe Tuesday or Wednesday.

Required probability $= \frac{1}{7}$

Q. 2. Three numbers are chosen from 1 to 20. Find the probability that they are not consecutive.

(A) $\frac{186}{190}$ **(B)** $\frac{187}{190}$

(C) $\frac{188}{190}$ **(D)** $\frac{18}{^{20}C_3}$

[NCERT Exemplar Q. 19, Page 299]

Ans. Correct option : (B)

Set of there consecutive no.s from 1 to 20 are 1, 2, 3; 2, 3, 4; 3, 4, 5, ... 18, 19, 20.

So, the probability that the no.s are consecutive.

$$= \frac{18}{^{20}C_3} = \frac{18}{\frac{20!}{3!\,17!}} = \frac{3}{190}$$

$$\therefore \text{P (three no.s are not consecutive)} = 1 - \frac{3}{190} = \frac{187}{190}$$

Q. 3. While shuffling a pack of 52 playing cards, 2 are accidentally dropped. Find the probability that the missing cards to be of different colours.

(A) $\frac{29}{52}$ **(B)** $\frac{1}{2}$

(C) $\frac{26}{51}$ **(D)** $\frac{27}{51}$

[NCERT Exemplar Q. 20, Page 299]

Ans. Correct option : (C)

We know that out of 52 playing cards 26 are of red and 26 are of black colour

$\therefore$ P(both cards of different colour)

$$= \frac{26}{52} \times \frac{26}{51} + \frac{26}{52} \times \frac{26}{51} = 2 \times \frac{26}{52} \times \frac{26}{51} = \frac{26}{51}$$

Q. 4. If seven persons are to be seated in a row. Then, the probability that two particular persons sit next to each other is

(A) $\frac{1}{3}$ **(B)** $\frac{1}{6}$

(C) $\frac{2}{7}$ **(D)** $\frac{1}{2}$

[NCERT Exemplar Q. 21, Page 300]

Ans. Correct option : (C)

The two particular persons to be seated next to each other then, they form one group.

How, the permutation of 6 persons = 6! × 2!

and total no. of permutations of 7 persons = 7!

$\therefore$ Required probability $= \frac{6! \times 2!}{7!} = \frac{2}{7}$

Q. 5. If without repetition of the numbers, four-digit numbers are formed with the numbers 0, 2, 3 and 5, then the probability of such a number divisible by 5 is

(A) $\frac{1}{5}$ **(B)** $\frac{4}{5}$

(C) $\frac{1}{30}$ **(D)** $\frac{5}{9}$

[NCERT Exemplar Q. 22, Page 300]

Ans. Correct option : (D)

Four digit number using the digits 0, 2, 3, 5 without repetition and divisible by 5 with given condition is

If unit place be filled with 0

3	2	1	1

Then the no. of ways = 3 × 2 × 1 × 1 × = 6

If unit place be filled with 5

2	2	1	1

Then the no. of ways = 2 × 2× 1 × 2 = 4

$\therefore$ Total no. of ways = 6 + 4 = 10

The total no. of ways of arranging the digits 0, 2, 3, 5 to form – 4 digit number without repetition is 3 × 3 × 2 × 1 = 18

Required probability $= \frac{10}{18} = \frac{5}{9}$

Q. 6. If A and B are mutually exclusive events, then

(A) $P(A) \leq P(\overline{B})$ **(B)** $P(A) \geq P(\overline{B})$

(C) $P(A) < P(\overline{B})$ **(D) None of these**

[NCERT Exemplar Q. 23, Page 300]

Ans. Correct option : (A)

For mutually exclusive events, $P(A \cap B) = 0$

$\therefore P(A \cup B) = P(A) + P(B)$ $[\because P(A \cap B) = 0]$

$\Rightarrow P(A) + P(B) \leq 1$

$\Rightarrow P(A) + 1 - P(\overline{B}) \leq 1$ $[P(B) = 1 - P(\overline{B})]$

$\Rightarrow P(A) - P(\overline{B}) \leq 0$

$\Rightarrow P(A) \leq P(\overline{B})$

Q. 7. If $P(A \cup B) = P(A \cap B)$ for any two events A and B, then

(A) $P(A) = P(B)$ **(B)** $P(A) > P(B)$

(C) $P(A) < P(B)$ **(D) None of these**

[NCERT Exemplar Q. 24, Page 300]

Ans. Correct option : (A)

Given, $P(A \cup B) = P(A \cap B)$

$\Rightarrow P(A) + P(B) - P(A \cap B) = P(A \cap B)$

$\Rightarrow [P(A) - P(A \cap B)] + [P(B) - P(A \cap B)] = 0$

But $P(A) - P(A \cap B) \geq 0$ ...(i)

$[P(A \cap B) \leq P(A)$ or $P(B)]$

and $P(B) - P(A \cap B) \geq 0$ ...(ii)

From eqs (i) & (ii), we get

$P(A) = P(B)$

Q. 8. If 6 boys and 6 girls sit in a row at random, then the probability that all the girls sit together is

(A) $\frac{1}{432}$ **(B)** $\frac{12}{431}$

(C) $\frac{1}{132}$ **(D) None of these**

[NCERT Exemplar Q. 25, Page 300]

Ans. Correct option : (C)

$\therefore$ Total no. of arrangement of 6 + 1 = 7 persons in a row = 7! and girls also interchange then places with 6! ways.

$\therefore$ Required probability $= \frac{6!\,7!}{12!} = \frac{1}{132}$

Q. 9. If a single letter is selected at random from the word 'PROBABILITY'. The probability that it is a vowel.

(A) $\frac{1}{3}$ **(B)** $\frac{4}{11}$

(C) $\frac{2}{11}$ **(D)** $\frac{3}{11}$

[NCERT Exemplar Q. 26, Page 300]

Ans. Correct option : (B)

Total no. of alphabets in the word probability = 11

No. of vowels = 4

$\therefore$ Required probability $= \frac{4}{11}$

Q. 10. If the probabilities for A to fail in an examination is 0.2 and that for B is 0.3, then the probability that either A or B fails is

(A) > 0.5 **(B)** 0.5

(C) ≤ 0.5 **(D)** 0

[NCERT Exemplar Q. 27, Page 300]

Ans. Correct option : (C)

Given, $P(A \text{ fails}) = 0.2$

$P(B \text{ fails}) = 0.3$

$\therefore P(\text{either } A \text{ or } B \text{ fails}) \leq P(A \text{ fail}) + P(B \text{ fails})$

$\leq 0.2 + 0.3 \leq 0.5$

Q. 11. The probability that atleast one of the events A and B occurs is 0.6. If A and B occur simultaneously with probability 0.2, then $P(\overline{A}) + P(\overline{B})$ is equal to

(A) 0.4 (B) 0.8

(C) 1.2 (D) 1.6

[NCERT Exemplar Q. 28, Page 300]

Ans. Correct option : (C)

Given, $P(A \cup B) = 0.6$, $P(A \cap B) = 0.2$

$\therefore P(A \cup B) = P(A) + P(B) - P(A \cap B)$

$\Rightarrow 0.6 = P(A) + P(B) - 0.2$

$\Rightarrow P(A) + P(B) = 0.6 + 0.2 = 0.8$

and $1 - P(\bar{A}) + 1 - P(\bar{B}) = 0.8$

$\Rightarrow P(\bar{A}) + P(\bar{B}) = 2 - 0.8 = 1.2$

Q. 12. If M and N are any two events, the probability that atleast one of them occurs is

(A) P(M) + P(N) – 2P (M ∩ N)

(B) P(M) + P(N) – P (M ∩ N)

(C) P(M) + P(N) + P (M ∩ N)

(D) P(M) + P(N) + 2P (M ∩ N)

[NCERT Exemplar Q. 29, Page 301]

Ans. Correct option : (B)

If M and N are any two events, then $P(M \cup N) = P(M) + P(N) - P(M \cap N)$

[B] True/False

Q. 1. The probability that a person visiting a zoo will see the giraffe is 0.72, the probability that he will see the bears is 0.84 and the probability that he will see both is 0.52.

[NCERT Exemplar Q. 30, Page 301]

Q. 2. The probability that a student will pass his examination is 0.73, the probability of the students getting a compartment is 0.13 and the probability that the student will either pass or get compartment is 0.96.

[NCERT Exemplar Q. 31, Page 301]

Q. 3. The probabilities that a typist will make 0, 1, 2, 3, 4 and 5 or more mistake in typing are respectively, 0.12, 0.25, 0.36, 0.14, 0.08 and 0.11.

[NCERT Exemplar Q. 32, Page 301]

Q. 4. If A and B are two candidates seeking admission in an engineering college. The probability that A is selected is 0.5 and the probability that both A and B are selected is at most 0.3. Is it possible that the probability of B getting selected is 0.7 ?

[NCERT Exemplar Q. 33, Page 301]

Q. 5. The probability of intersection of two events A and B is always less than or equal to those favourable to the event A.

[NCERT Exemplar Q. 34, Page 301]

Q. 6. The probability of an occurrence of event A is 0.7 and that of the occurrence of event B is 0.3 and the probability of occurrence of both is 0.4.

[NCERT Exemplar Q. 35, Page 301]

Q. 7. The sum of probabilities of two students getting distinction in their final examination is 1.2.

[NCERT Exemplar Q. 36, Page 301]

Answer :

1. False 2. False 3. False 4. False 5. True 6. False 7. True.

[C] Fill in the Blanks

Q. 1. The probability that the home team will win an upcoming football game is 0.77, the probability that it will tie the game is 0.08 and the probability that it will lose the game is ......

[NCERT Exemplar Q. 37, Page 301]

Q. 2. If e_1, e_2, e_3 and e_4 and the four elementary outcomes in a sample space and $P(e_1) = 0.1$, $P(e_2) = 0.5$ and $P(e_3) = 0.1$, then the probability of e_4 is .....

[NCERT Exemplar Q. 38, Page 301]

Q. 3. If A and B are two events associated with a random experiment such that P(A) = 0.3, P(B) = 0.2 and P(A ∩ B) = 0.1, then the value of $P(A \cap \bar{B})$ is.....

[NCERT Exemplar Q. 40, Page 301]

Q. 4. The probability of happening of an events A is 0.5 and that of B is 0.3. If A and B are mutually exclusive events, then the probability of neither A nor B is..... [NCERT Exemplar Q. 41, Page 301]

Answer :

1. 0.15 2. 0.3 3. 0.2 4. 0.2.

[D] Match the following question

Q. 1. Match the following.

	Column I		Column II
(i)	0.95	(a)	An incorrect assignment
(ii)	0.02	(b)	No chance of happening
(iii)	–0.3	(c)	As much chance of happening as not
(iv)	0.5	(d)	Very likely to happen
(v)	0	(e)	Very little chance of happening

[NCERT Exemplar Q. 42, Page 302]

Q. 2. Match the following.

	Column I		Column II
(i)	If E_1 and E_2 are the two mutually exclusive events	(a)	$E_1 \cap E_2 = E_1$
(ii)	If E_1 and E_2 are the mutually exclusive and exhaustive events	(b)	$(E_1 - E_2) \cup (E_1 \cap E_2) = E_1$
(iii)	If E_1 and E_2 have common outcomes, then If E_1 and E_2 are two events such that	(c)	$E_1 \cap E_2 = \phi$, $E_1 \cup E_2 = S$
(iv)	$E_1 \subset E_2$	(d)	$E_1 \cap E_2 = \phi$

[NCERT Exemplar Q. 43, Page 302]

Answer :

1. (i) → (d)   (ii) → (e)

2. (i) → (d)   (ii) → (c)

(iii) → (a)   (iv) → (c)   (v) → (b)

(iii) → (b)   (iv) → (a)

Very Short Answer Type Questions (1 mark each)

Q. 1. The accompanying venn diagram shows three events, A, B and C and also the probabilities of the various intersections [for instance, P(A Ç B) = 0.7]. Determine

(i) P(A)   **(ii) $P(B \cap \bar{C})$**

(iii) $P(A \cup B)$ **(iv) $P(A \cap \bar{B})$**

(v) $P(B \cap C)$ **(vi) Probability of exactly one of the three occurs.**

[NCERT Exemplar Q. 11, Page 298]

Sol. From the Venn diagram,

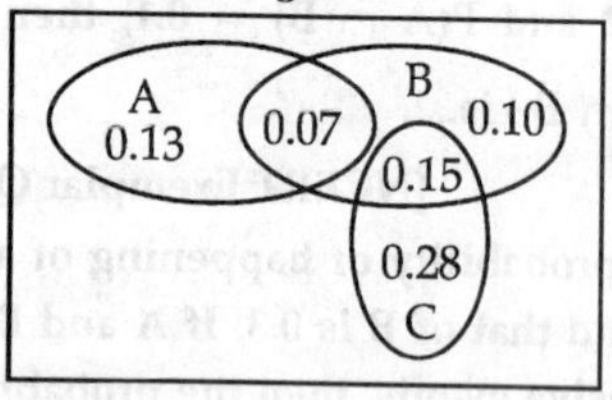

(i) $P(A) = 0.13 + 0.07 = 0.20$

(ii) $P(B \cap \bar{C}) = P(B) - P(B \cap C)$

$= 0.07 + 0.10 + 0.15 - 0.15$

$= 0.07 + 0.10 = 0.17$

(iii) $P(A \cup B) = P(A) + P(B) - P(A \cap B)$

$= 0.13 + 0.7 + 0.07 + 0.10 + 0.15 - 0.07$

$= 0.13 + 0.07 + 0.10 + 0.15 = 0.45$

(iv) $P(A \cap \bar{B}) = P(A) - P(A \cap B) = 0.13 + 0.07 - 0.07$

$= 0.13$

(v) $P(B \cap C) = 0.15$

(vi) P(exactly one of the three occurs)

$= 0.13 + 0.10 + 0.28 = 0.51$

Short Answer Type Question (2 marks each)

Q. 1. Three coins are tossed once. Find the probability of getting (i) 3 heads (ii) 2 heads, (iii) at least 2 heads, (iv) atmost 3 heads, (v) no head, (vi) 3 tails, (vii) exactly two tails, (viii) no tail, (ix) atmost two tails.

[NCERT Exemplar Q. 8, Page 404]

Sol. When three coins are tossed, then the sample spaces—

S = {HHH, HHT, HTH, HTT, THH, THT, TTH, TTT}.

$\Rightarrow \quad n(S) = 8.$

(i) Let A be the event of getting 3 heads.

i.e.,   A = {HHH} $\Rightarrow n(A) = 1$

$\therefore \quad P(A) = \frac{n(A)}{n(S)} = \frac{1}{8}$

(ii) 'B' be the event of getting 2 heads.

i.e.,   B = {HHT, HTH, THH}

$\Rightarrow \quad n(B) = 3$

$\therefore \quad p(B) = \frac{n(B)}{n(S)} = \frac{3}{8}$

(iii) Let 'C' be the event of getting at least two words.

i.e.,   C = {HHT, HTH, THH, HHH}

$\Rightarrow \quad n(C) = 4$

$\therefore \quad P(C) = \frac{n(C)}{n(S)} = \frac{4}{8} = \frac{1}{2}$

(iv) Let 'D' be the event of getting atmost 2 heads.

i.e.,   D = {HHT, HTH, HTT, THH, THT, TTH, TTT}

$\Rightarrow \quad n(D) = 7$

$\therefore \quad P(D) = \frac{n(D)}{n(S)} = \frac{7}{8}$

(v) Let 'E' be the event of getting no head.

i.e.,   E = {TTT} $\Rightarrow n(E) = 1$

$\therefore \quad P(E) = \frac{n(E)}{n(S)} = \frac{1}{8}$

(vi) Let 'F' be the event that 3 tails occurs.

i.e.,   F = {TTT} $\Rightarrow n(F) = 1$

$\therefore \quad P(S) = \frac{n(F)}{n(S)} = \frac{1}{8}$

(vii) Let 'G' be the event that exactly two tails occur

i.e.,   G = {HTT, THT, TTH} $\Rightarrow n(G) = 3$

$\therefore \quad P(G) = \frac{n(G)}{n(S)} = \frac{3}{8}$

(viii) Let H be the event of getting no tail.

i.e., $H = \{HHH\} \Rightarrow n(H) = 1$

$\therefore \quad P(H) = \frac{n(H)}{n(S)} = \frac{1}{8}$

(ix) Let I be the event of getting atmost two tails.

i.e., I = {HHH, HHT, HTH, HTT, THH, THT, TTH}

$\Rightarrow \quad n(I) = 7$

$\therefore \quad P(I) = \frac{n(I)}{n(S)} = \frac{7}{8}$

Q. 2. If a card is drawn from a deck of 52 cards, then find the probability of getting a king or a heart or a red card. [NCERT Exemplar Q. 15, Page 299]

Sol. ∵ Number of possible event = 52

and favourable events = 4 king + 13 heart + 26 red – 13 – 2 = 28

$\therefore$ Required probability $= \frac{28}{52} = \frac{7}{13}$

Q. 3. A sample space consists of 9 elementary outcomes $E_1, E_2, \ldots\ldots E_9$ whose probabilities are

$P(E_1) = P(E_2) = 0.08$, $P(E_3) = P(E_4) = P(E_5) = 0.1$

$P(E_6) = P(E_7) = 0.2$, $P(E_8) = P(E_9) = 0.07$

Suppose $A = \{E_1, E_5, E_8\}$, $B = \{E_2, E_5, E_8, E_9\}$

(i) Calculate P(A), P(B) and $P(A \cap B)$.

(ii) Using the addition law of probability, calculate $P(A \cup B)$.

(iii) List the composition of the event $A \cup B$ and calculate $P(A \cup B)$ by adding the probabilities of the elementary outcomes.

(iv) Calculate $P(\overline{B})$ from P(B), also calculate $P(\overline{B})$ directly from the elementary outcomes of $\overline{B}$.

[NCERT Exemplar Q. 16, Page 299]

Sol. Given, $S = \{E_1, E_2, E_3, E_4, E_5, E_6, E_7, E_8, E_9\}$

$A = \{E_1, E_5, E_8\}$, $B = \{E_2, E_5, E_8, E_9\}$

$P(E_1) = P(E_2) = 0.08$

$P(E_3) = P(E_4) = P(E_5) = 0.1$

$P(E_6) = P(E_7) = 0.2$, $P(E_8) = P(E_9) = 0.07$

(i) $P(A) = P(E_1) + P(E_5) + P(E_8)$

$= 0.08 + 0.1 + 0.07 = 0.25$

Now, $P(B) = P(E_2) + P(E_5) + P(E_8) + (E_9)$

$= 0.08 + 0.1 + 0.07 + 0.07 = 0.32$

$A \cap B = \{E_5, E_8\}$

$P(A \cap B) = P(E_5) + P(E_8) = 0.1 + 0.7 = 0.17$

(ii) $P(A \cup B) = P(A) + P(B) - P(A \cap B)$ ...(i)

On substituting these values in Eq. (i), we get

$P(A \cup B) = 0.25 + 0.32 - 0.17 = 0.40$

(iii) $A \cup B = \{E_1, E_2, E_5, E_8, E_9\}$

$P(A \cup B) = P(E_1) + P(E_2) + P(E_5) + P(E_8) + P(E_9)$

$= 0.08 + 0.08 + 0.1 + 0.07 + 0.07 = 0.40$

(iv) ∵ $P(\overline{B}) = 1 - P(B) = 1 - 0.32 = 0.68$

and $\overline{B} = \{E_1, E_3, E_4, E_6, E_7\}$

$\therefore \quad P(\overline{B}) = P(E_1) + P(E_3) + P(E_4) + P(E_6) + P(E_1)$

$= 0.08 + 0.1 + 0.1 + 0.2 + 0.2 = 0.68$

Q. 4. Determine the probability p, for each of the following events.

(i) An odd number appears in a single toss of a fair die.

(ii) At least one head appears in two tosses of a fair coin.

(iii) A king or 9 of hearts of 3 of spades appears in drawing a single card from a well shuffled ordinary deck of 52 cards.

(iv) The sum of 6 appears in a single toss of a pair of fair dice.

[NCERT Exemplar Q. 17, Page 299]

Sol. (i) When a die is throw the possible outcomes are S = {1, 2, 3, 4, 5, 6} out of which 1, 3, 5, are odd,

$\therefore$ Required probability $= \frac{3}{6} = \frac{1}{2}$

(ii) When a fair coin is tossed two times the sample space is

S = (HH, HT, TH, TT)

In at least one head favourable events are HH, HT, TH

$\therefore$ Required probability $= \frac{3}{4}$

(iii) Total cards = 52

Favourable = 4 king + 9 of heart + 3 of spade = 4 + 1 + 1 = 6

$\therefore$ Required probability $= \frac{6}{52} = \frac{3}{26}$

(iv) When a pair of dice is rolled total sample events are 36. Out of which (1, 5), (5, 1), (2, 4), (4, 2) and (3, 3).

$\therefore$ Required probability $= \frac{5}{36}$

Long Answer Type Question-I

(4 marks each)

Q. 1. If the letters of the word 'ALGORITHM' are arranged at random in a row what is the probability the letter 'GOR' must remain together as a unit ?

[NCERT Exemplar Q. 1, Page 296]

Sol. Number of letters in the word 'ALGORITHM' are 9. If 'GOR' remain together, then considered it as 1 number.

$\therefore$ Number of letters = 6 + 1 = 7

Number of word, if 'GOR' remain together = 7!

Total number of words from the letters of the word 'ALGORITHM' = 9!

$\therefore$ Required probability $= \dfrac{7!}{9!} = \dfrac{7!}{9\times8\times7!} = \dfrac{1}{9\times8} = \dfrac{1}{72}$

Q. 2. Six new employees, two to whom are married to each other, are to be assigned six desks that are lined up in a row. If the assignment of employees to desks is made randomly, what is the probability that the married couple will have non-adjacent desks ?

[NCERT Exemplar Q. 2, Page 296]

Sol. Let the couple occupied adjacent desks consider those two as 1.

There are (4 + 1) *i.e.*, 5 persons to be assigned.

$\therefore$ Number of ways of assigning these five persons $= 5! \times 2!$

Total number of ways of assigning 6 persons = 6!

$\therefore$ Probability that the couple has adjacent desk

$= \dfrac{5!\times2!}{6!} = \dfrac{1}{3}$

Probability that the married couple will have non-adjacent desks $= 1 - \dfrac{1}{3} = \dfrac{2}{3}$

Q. 3. In a large metropolitan area, the probabilities are 0.87, 0.36, 0.30 that a family (randomly chosen for a sample survey) owns a colour television set, a black and white television set or both kinds of sets. What is the probability that a family owns either anyone or both kinds of sets ?

[NCERT Exemplar Q. 6, Page 297]

Sol. Let E_1 be the event that family own colour television set and E_2 be the event that family own Black and white Television.

It is given that

$P(E_1) = 0.87$

$P(E_2) = 0.36$

and $P(E_1 \cap E_2) = 0.30$

We have to find probability that a family owns either anyone or both kind of sets *i.e.*, $P(E_1 \cup E_2)$.

Now, $P(E_1 \cup E_2) = P(E_1) + P(E_2) - P(E_1 \cap E_2)$ [by addition theorem]

$= 0.87 + 0.36 - 0.30$

$= 0.93$

Q. 4. If the letters of the word 'ASSASSINATION' are arranged at random. Find the probability that

(i) four S's come consecutively in the word.

(ii) two I's and two N's come together.

(iii) all A's are not coming together.

(iv) no two A's are coming together.

[NCERT Exemplar Q. 14, Page 298]

Sol. Total number of letters in the word 'ASSASSINATION' are 13.

Out of which 3A'S, 4S's, 2 I's, 1 T's 2n's, 1.0's *i.e.* = B

(i) If four S's come consecutively in the word, then we considered these 4 S's as 1 group Now, the number of letters is 10.

S	S	S	S	A	A	A	I	I	N	N	T	O
1				9								

Number of words all S's are together $= \dfrac{10!}{3!2!2!}$

Total number of word using letters of the word 'ASSASSINATION'

$= \dfrac{13!}{3!4!2!2!}$

$\therefore$ Required probability $= \dfrac{10!}{3!2!2!} \times \dfrac{3!4!2!}{13!}$

$= \dfrac{10!\times4!}{13!} = \dfrac{4!}{13\times12\times11}$

$= \dfrac{24}{1716} = \dfrac{2}{143}$

(ii) If 2 I's and 2 N's come together, then there as 10 alphabets.

Number of word when 2 I's and 2 N's are come together

$= \dfrac{10!}{3!4!} \times \dfrac{4!}{2!2!}$

$\therefore$ Required probability $= \dfrac{\dfrac{10!4!}{3!4!2!2!}}{\dfrac{13!}{3!4!2!2!}}$

$= \dfrac{4!10!}{2!2!3!4!} \times \dfrac{3!4!2!2!}{13!}$

$= \dfrac{4!10!}{13!} = \dfrac{4!}{13\times12\times11}$

$= \dfrac{24}{13\times12\times11} = \dfrac{2}{143}$

(iii) If all A's are coming together, then there are 11 alphabets. Number of words when all A's come together $= \dfrac{11!}{4!2!2!}$

Probability when all A's come together

$= \dfrac{\dfrac{11!}{4!2!2!}}{\dfrac{13!}{4!3!2!2!}} = \dfrac{11!}{4!2!2!} \times \dfrac{4!3!2!2!}{13!}$

$= \dfrac{11!\times3!}{13!} = \dfrac{6}{13\times12} = \dfrac{1}{26}$

Required probability when all A's does not come together

$= 1 - \dfrac{1}{26} = \dfrac{25}{26}$

(iv) If no two A's are together, then first we arrange the alphabets except A's.

S	S	S	S	I	N	T	I	O	N

All the alphabets except A's are arranged in $\frac{10!}{4!2!2!}$

There are 11 vacant places between these alphabets.

So, 3 A's can be place in 11 places in $^{11}C_3$ ways = $\frac{11!}{3!8!}$

$\therefore$ Total number of words when no two A's together

$$= \frac{11!}{3!8!} \times \frac{10!}{4!2!2!}$$

$$\text{Required probability} = \frac{11! \times 10!}{3!8!4!2!2!} \times \frac{4!3!2!2!}{13!}$$

$$= \frac{10!}{8! \times 13 \times 12}$$

$$= \frac{10 \times 9}{13 \times 12} = \frac{90}{156} = \frac{15}{26}$$

Long Answer Type Question-II (6 marks each)

Q. 1. If an integer from 1 through 1000 is chosen at random, then find the probability that the integer is a multiple of 2 or a multiple of 9.

[NCERT Exemplar Q. 3, Page 296]

Sol. Multiple of 2 from 1 to 1000 are 2, 4, 6, 8,......, 1000

Let n be the number of terms of above series *i.e.*, 1 to 1000

$\therefore \quad l = 1000$

$\Rightarrow \quad 2 + (n-1)2 = 1000$

$\{l = a + (n-1)d \; a = 2, d = 2\}$

$\Rightarrow \quad 2(n-1) = 998$

$\Rightarrow \quad n - 1 = 499$

$\Rightarrow \quad n = 500$

$$P(A) = \frac{500}{1000}$$

$l = 999$

$a = 9, d = 9$

These are m numbers.

Since, the number of multiple of 2 are 500.

So, the multiple of 9 are 9, 18, 27, ..., 999

$\therefore \quad = 99$

$\Rightarrow \quad 9\text{m} - 1 = 990$

$\Rightarrow \quad \text{m} - 1 = 110$

$\therefore \quad \text{m} = 111$

$$P(B) = \frac{111}{1000}$$

Since, the number of multiple of 9 are 111, now the multiple of 2 and 9 both are 18, 36,...., 990

Let p be the number of terms in above series.

$\therefore \quad p\text{th term} = 990$

$\Rightarrow \quad 18 + (p-1)18 = 990$

$\Rightarrow \quad (p-1)\,18 = 972$

$\Rightarrow \quad p - 1 = 54$

$\therefore \quad p = 55$

& $\quad p(A \cap B) = \frac{55}{1000}$

Required probability = $P(A) + P(B) - P(A \cap B)$

$$\frac{500 + 111 - 55}{1000} = \frac{556}{1000} = 0.556$$

Q. 2. An experiment consists of rolling a die until a 2 appears.

(i) How many elements of the sample space correspond to the event that the 2 appears on the *k*th roll of the die ?

(ii) How many elements of the sample space correspond to the event that the 2 appears not later than the *k*th roll of the die ?

[NCERT Exemplar Q. 4, Page 296]

Sol. In a through of a die there is 6 sample points.

(i) If 2 appears on the *k*th roll of the die.

So, first $(k-1)$ roll have 5 outcomes each and *k*th roll results 2 *i.e.*, 1 outcomes.

$\therefore$ Number of element of sample space correspond to the die. Then 2 appears on the *k*th roll of the die $= 5^{k-1}$

(ii) If we consider that 2 appears not later than *k*th roll of the die, then it is possible that 2 comes in first throw *i.e.*, 1 outcome.

It 2 does not appear in first throw, then outcomes will be 5 and 2 comes in second throw *i.e.*, 1 outcome, possible outcome = 5 × 1 = 5

Similarly, if 2 does not appear in second throw and appears in third throw.

$\therefore$ Possible outcomes = 5 × 5 × 1

Given, series $= 1 + 5 + 5 \times 5 + 5 \times 5 + \times 5 + ... + 5^{k-1}$

$$= 1 + 5 + 5^2 + 5^3 + ... + 5^{k-1}$$

$$= \frac{1(5^k - 1)}{5 - 1} = \frac{5^k - 1}{4}$$

$$\left\{ a, ar, ar^2 .... \quad S_n = a\left(\frac{r^n - 1}{r - 1}\right) \right\}$$

Q. 3. A die is loaded in such a way that each odd number is twice as likely to occur as each even number. Find P(G), where G is the event that a number greater than 3 occurs on a single roll of the die. [NCERT Exemplar Q. 5, Page 297]

Sol. It is given that, 2 × Probability of even number = Probability of odd number

$\Rightarrow \quad P = 2P$

Let (A add number, B even number)

$\Rightarrow \quad P(A) : P(B) = 2 : 1$

∴ Probability of occurring odd number,

$$P(A) = \frac{2}{2+1} = \frac{2}{3}$$

and probability of occurring even number.

$$P(B) = \frac{1}{2+1} = \frac{1}{3}$$

Now, G be the even that a number greater than 3 occur in a single roll of die.

So, the possible outcomes are 4, 5 and 6 out of which two are even and one odd.

∴ Required probability $= P(G)$

$= 2 \times P(A) \times P(B)$

$= 2 \times \frac{1}{3} \times \frac{2}{3} = \frac{4}{9}$

Q. 4. A team of medical students doing their internship have to assist during surgeries at a city hospital. The probabilities of surgeries rated as very complex, complex routine, simple or very simple are respectively, 0.15, 0.20, 0.31, 0.26 and 0.80. Find the probabilities that a particular surgery will be rated

(i) complex or very complex.

(ii) neither very complex nor very simple.

(iii) routine or complex.

(iv) routine or simple.

[NCERT Exemplar Q. 8, Page 297]

Sol. Let E_1, E_2, E_3, E_4 and E_5 be the event that surgeries are rated as very complex, complex, routine, simple or very simple, respectively.

$P(E_1) = 0.15$, $P(E_2) = 0.20$, $P(E_3) = 0.31$, $P(E_4) = 0.26$, $P(E_5) = 0.08$

(i) P (complex or very complex) = $P(E_1 \text{ or } E_2)$

$= P(E_1 \cup E_2) = P(E_1) + P(E_2) - P(E_1 \cap E_2)$

$= 0.15 + 0.25 - 0 = [P(E_1 \cap E_2) = 0]$

$= 0.35$

(ii) P (neither very complex nor very simple)

$= (P\,E'_1 \cup E'_5) = P(E_1 \cup E_5)'$

$= 1 - P(E_1 \cup E_5)$

$= 1 - [P(E_1) + P(E_5)]$

$= 1 - (0.15 + 0.08)$

$= 1 - 0.23$

$= 0.77$

(iii) P (routine or complex) = $P(E_3 \cup E_2)$

$= P(E_3) + P(E_2)$

$= 0.31 + 0.20 = 0.51$

(iv) P(routine or simple) = $P(E_3 \cup E_4) = P(E_3) + P(E_4)$

$= 0.31 + 0.26 = 0.57$

Q. 5. Four candidates A, B, C and D have applied for the assignment to coach a school cricket team. If A is twice as likely to be selected as B and B and C are given about the same chance of being selected, while C is twice as likely to be selected as D, then what are the probabilities that

(i) C will be selected ?

(ii) A will not be selected ?

[NCERT Exemplar Q. 9, Page 297]

Sol. A is twice as likely to be selected as B.

$$P(A) = 2P(B)$$

$$\Rightarrow \quad \frac{P(A)}{2} = P(B)$$

C it twice as likely to be selected as D.

$$P(C) = 2P(D) \Rightarrow P(B) = 2P(D)$$

$$\Rightarrow \quad \frac{P(A)}{2} = 2P(D) \Rightarrow P(D) = \frac{P(A)}{4}$$

B and C are given about the same chance of being selected.

$$P(A) + P(B) + P(C) + P(D) = 1$$

$$P(A) + P(B) + P(C) + P(D) = 1$$

$$\Rightarrow \quad \frac{4P(A)+2P(A)+2P(A)+P(A)}{4} = 1$$

$$\Rightarrow \quad 9P(A) = 4 \Rightarrow P(A) = \frac{4}{9}$$

(i) $P(C \text{ will be selected}) = P(C) = P(B) = \frac{P(A)}{2}$

$$= \frac{4}{9 \times 2} \qquad \left[\because P(A) = \frac{9}{4}\right]$$

$$= \frac{2}{9}$$

(ii) $P(A \text{ will not be selected}) = P(A') = 1 - P(A)$

$$= 1 - \frac{4}{9} = \frac{5}{9}$$

Q. 6. One of the four persons John, Rita, Aslam or Gurpreet will be promoted next month. Consequently the sample space consists of four elementary outcomes S = {John promoted, Rita promoted, Aslam promoted, Gurpreet promoted}. You are told that the chances of John's promotion is same as that of Gurpreet Rita's chances of promotion are twice as likely

as Johns. Aslam's chances are four times that of John.

(i) Determine

P (John promoted), P (Rita promoted),

P (Aslam promoted), P (Gurpreet promoted),

(ii) If A = {John promoted or Gurpreet promoted}, Find P(A).

[NCERT Exemplar Q. 10, Page 297]

Sol. Let E_1 = John promoted, E_2 = Rita promoted, E_3 = Aslam promoted, E_4 = Gurpreet promoted

According to problem $P(E_1) = P(E_4)$ & $P(E_2) = 2P(E_1)$, $P(E_3) = 4P(E_1)$

property of probability : $P(E_1) + P(E_2) + P(E_3) + P(E_4) = 1$

(i) $P(E_1) + 2P(E_1) + 4P(E_1) + P(E_1) = 1$

$$8P(E_1) = 1 \Rightarrow P(E_1) = \frac{1}{8}$$

$$P(E_2) = 2\times\frac{1}{8} = \frac{1}{4}$$

$$P(E_3) = 4P(E_1) = 4\times\frac{1}{8} = \frac{1}{2}$$

$$P(E_4) = P(E_1) = \frac{1}{8}$$

(ii) John or Gurpreet promoted

$$P(E_1 \cup E_4) = P(E_1) + P(E_4) - P(E_1 \cap E_4)$$

$$= \frac{1}{8}+\frac{1}{8}-0 = \frac{2}{8} = \frac{1}{4}$$

Q. 7. One urn contains two black balls (labelled B_1 and B_2) and one white ball. A second urn contains one black ball and two white balls (labelled W_1 and W_2). Suppose the following experiment is performed. One of the two urns is chosen at random. Next a ball is randomly chosen from the urn. Then, a second ball is chosen at random from the same urn without replacing the first ball.

(i) Write the sample space showing all possible outcomes.

(ii) What is the probability that two black balls are chosen ?

(iii) What is the probability that two balls of opposite colours are chosen ?

[NCERT Exemplar Q. 12, Page 298]

Sol. It is given that one of the two urn is chosen, then a ball is randomly chosen from the urn, then a second ball is chosen at random from the same urn without replacing the first ball.

(i) ∴ Sample space S = {B_1B_2, B_1W, B_2B_1, B_2W, WB_1, WB_1, BW_2, B_1W, W_1B, W_1W_2, W_2B, W_2W_1}

∴ Total sample point = 12

(ii) If two black ball are chosen.

So, the favourable events are B_1B_2, B_2B_1, *i.e.*, 2

$$\therefore \text{Required probability} = \frac{2}{12} = \frac{1}{6}$$

(iii) If two balls of opposite colour are chosen

So, the favourable events are (B_1, W), (B_2W), (WB_1), (WB_2), (BW_1), (BW_2), (W_1B_1), (W_2B) *i.e.*, 8.

$$\therefore \text{Required probability} = \frac{8}{12} = \frac{2}{3}$$

Q. 8. A bag contains 8 red and 5 white balls. Three balls are drawn at random. Find the probability that

(i) all the three balls are white

(ii) all the three balls are red.

(iii) One ball is red and two balls are white.

[NCERT Exemplar Q. 13, Page 298]

Sol. ∵ Number of red balls = 8

and number of white balls = 5

(i) P (all the three balls are white)

$$= \frac{^5C_3}{^{13}C_3} = \left(\frac{\frac{5\times4}{2}}{\frac{13\times12\times11}{3\times2}}\right) = \frac{5\times4\times3}{13\times12\times11} = \frac{5}{143}$$

(ii) P (all the three balls are red)

$$= \frac{^8C_3}{^{13}C_3} = \frac{\left(\frac{8\times7\times6}{3\times2\times1}\right)}{\left(\frac{13\times12\times11}{3\times2\times1}\right)} = \frac{8\times7\times6}{13\times12\times11} = \frac{28}{143}$$

(iii) P (one ball is red and two balls are white)

$$= \frac{^8C_1\times{}^5C_2}{^{13}C_3} = \frac{8\times10}{13\times2\times11} = \frac{40}{143}$$

EXPERT ADVICE

- *This is very important chapter. Go through all the examples and questions given in NCERT text book and practice questions from reference books.*
- *Make sure that your fundamentals are clear in this chapter as it is only based on your understanding of the topic.*
- *Take your time to read and understand the questions before answering them.*

OSWAAL LEARNING TOOLS

***For* Suggested Online Videos**

Visit : *https://goo.gl/c1J28a*

Or Scan the Code

Visit : *https://goo.gl/isW9R5*

Or Scan the Code

Visit : *https://goo.gl/fzDJdM*

Or Scan the Code

Visit : *https://goo.gl/yMwvyW*

Or Scan the Code